CLASSIC

HOLLYWOOD,

CLASSIC

WHITENESS

CLASSIC

HOLLYWOOD,

CLASSIC

WHITENESS

Daniel Bernardi, Editor

University of
Minnesota Press

Minneapolis · London

Published by the University of Minnesota Press
111 Third Avenue South, Suite 290
Minneapolis, MN 55401–2520
http://www.upress.umn.edu

Library of Congress Cataloging-in-Publication Data
Classic Hollywood, classic whiteness / Daniel Bernardi, editor.
    p. cm.
    Includes bibliographical references and index.
    ISBN 0-8166-3238-3 (alk. paper)—
    ISBN 0-8166-3239-1 (pbk. : alk. paper.)
    1. Minorities in motion pictures. 2. Exoticism in
  motion pictures. I. Bernardi, Daniel, 1964– .
    PN1995.9.M56 C59 2001
    791.43′6520693—dc21   2001000522

Printed in the United States of America on acid-free paper

The University of Minnesota is an equal-opportunity
educator and employer.

12 11 10 09 08 07   10 9 8 7 6 5 4 3

I dedicate this book to four friends and mentors who, while I was a doctoral student at UCLA, had a lasting impact on my research and life:

BOB ROSEN, for his generosity and insight
NICK BROWNE, for his openness and support
VIVIAN SOBCHACK, for her rigor and humor
PAULA STEPHENS, for her trust and friendship

Thank you.

CONTENTS

PART IV. INDUSTRY

ACKNOWLEDGMENTS

The first acknowledgment I would like to make is that this was a very difficult book to edit. The fact that I changed jobs and moved to a different city while working on the project complicated my work. Nonetheless, my editor at the University of Minnesota Press, Jennifer Moore, stood by the book. She is excellent at what she does, not simply for her ability to blend patience with gentle prodding, but also for her insights into organization and structure.

Toward this end, this book owes everything to the contributors (including those who, often for reasons out of their control, did not make it into the book). I appreciate all of their hard work, revisions, support, and persistence. What is good about this book comes from them. I take responsibility for everything else.

A few of my students at the University of Arizona provided important work to get this project into final shape. Leigh Baltzer came in at the last minute and helped me pull it all together. Berto Trinidad read each chapter, pushing me to rethink the book's structure. He also helped organize the stills and prepare the manuscript (no easy task for a project this size). Anne Thwaits also was of great assistance—and all after graduating and getting a "real" job.

RACE
AND THE
HOLLYWOOD
STYLE

Daniel Bernardi

"The White race is a club, which enrolls certain people at birth, without their consent, and brings them up according to its rules. For the most part the members go through life accepting the benefits of membership without thinking about the costs." —*Race Traitor*

Classic Hollywood, Classic Whiteness builds upon the questions and arguments developed in my first anthology on film history, *The Birth of Whiteness: Race and the Emergence of U.S. Cinema.*[1] In that volume, contributors from such diverse fields as critical race studies, cultural studies, film history, literary studies, and social history address the relationship between race and film from around the turn of the century to the 1920s, or the early and silent periods. In arguing that early cinema constructed whiteness as the "norm by which all 'Others' fail by comparison," the volume sets forth to reveal the distinct ways in which race informed the inception and development of fictional narrative cinema—crossing audiences, authors, genres, studios, and styles. Contributors investigate such subjects as exhibition, genre, intertextuality, narrative, reception, stardom, and stereotyping.

In this collection of essays, a larger group of scholars addresses the relationship between race and the U.S. cinema from around the advent of sound to 1960, or the Classical Hollywood period. Like *The Birth of Whiteness*, this volume reveals the distinct ways in which race worked its way into movie magic: the extent to which it informed our classics, directed aesthetic choices, collaborated in the moral voice of popular narratives, enhanced the star system, promoted and sometimes bypassed censorship, and drew upon national and international events. Although the focus here is the Classical period, this volume also argues that whiteness remained the "norm by which all 'Others' fail by comparison." While the meaning of race shifted into and within this period—i.e., it was distinct in important ways from early cinema and remained mobile in this period—whiteness nonetheless reigned supreme. This anthology details the various ways in which the pale formation maintained its hegemony in Hollywood from the birth of sound to the contemporary era.

This period is anything but cut off from other moments of cinema. Nevertheless, it warrants special attention for several reasons. First, films made between 1927 and the contemporary period coincided with significant social and international events that affected the shifting yet ubiquitous U.S. racial formation.[2] These include the Great Depression, World War II, the Korean "conflict," segregation, and the emergence of the contemporary civil rights movement. *Classic Hollywood, Classic Whiteness* addresses class conflict during the depression; the politics of segregation, particularly around the rhetoric of miscegenation; and the relationship between race and war. Indeed, an entire section of this volume is devoted to the subject of war inasmuch as films of this genre show how race simultaneously threatens and unifies in times of national combat.

The second reason Classical Hollywood merits bracketed attention has to do with continuity filmmaking, which became nothing less than a paradigm of commercial cinema in the period. In what Noel Burch calls "the zero degree style of filming," Classical Hollywood consistently subordinates mise-en-scène, cinematography, and editing, among other aesthetic choices, to a coherent, character-driven system of storytelling.[3] Style works to ensure and highlight the intelligibility of the story. Of course, the continuity style had been in use since at least 1917, as David Bordwell, Janet Staiger, and Kristin Thompson point out in *The Classical Hollywood Cinema*.[4] Its birth can even be traced to D. W. Griffith's American Biograph work, among other early filmmakers and production houses.[5] Nonetheless, the advent of sound in 1927 completed the dominance of the continuity style, as this aesthetic choice was also subordinated to the coherence of storytelling. Moreover, while numerous films can be seen as deviating from the Hollywood style—Orson Welles's *Citi-*

zen *Kane* (1941) comes to mind—these works are exceptions considering the degree to which the paradigm dominates the stylistic possibilities of Classical Hollywood narration. Even those works that offer an aesthetic flair outside of the story also offer plot, characters, and tidy endings—*Citizen Kane* included. Several of the articles in this collection address the relationship between Hollywood narration and race. A few focus on sound.

The Classical period is also marked by the dominance of a Ford-like studio system, what I have been calling Hollywood, over almost every aspect of film-making: from production to the star system to distribution and exhibition. Studios like Warner Bros. and Paramount Pictures literally ran show business, and a number of the racial representations and stories found in their products can be traced to institutional policies and practices. Stretching from the enforcement of blackface into the Production Code Administration and beyond, the studios systematized the popularization of American whiteness. And, the dominance of the system is a force that cannot be equally attributed to either moments before the studios forged an alliance or after the government and television, among other forces, competed for the studios' power and control. Most of the articles in this volume address the machinations of the studio system. Several focus on the industry's racial policies and practices.

One of the overriding goals of this anthology, then, is to show *how* a color line defined by whiteness directed the trajectory of the Hollywood style. What role did the Hollywood studio system play in the articulation of race in films of the period? What was the impact of the sociopolitical context, from war and peace to segregation and civil rights? What do color and whiteness look like and what stories do they tell in cinema of the period? In what ways did whiteness enhance or make meaningful Hollywood aesthetics? In what ways did the practice of racism in the industry and in its movies shift and change?

That Classical Hollywood was racist is, of course, no major discovery. This book and its contributors are not satisfied with merely pointing out the obvious. Instead, they historicize and analyze the particular ways in which the meaning of race extended its power over cinema during the reign of the Classical Hollywood style. Whiteness, it will be shown, was everywhere a fact in the heyday of the studio system, crossing audiences, authors, genres, studios, and styles.

WHY WHITE?

While it is perhaps clear that race and racism were factors in the dominance of the Hollywood style, it might not be clear why whiteness is the critical bull's-eye of this project. True, studies of whiteness are an important aspect of critical race studies, but the representation of color is the overarching factor during the period, as will be shown. Yet, it is also the case that everywhere there is color in Hollywood, there is whiteness. The pale formation is ubiquitous, but the point here is that whiteness cannot be extrapolated from race or racist practices. Indeed, the function of whiteness in the racial formation gives the meaning of race and the power of racism sociocultural and historical currency. Thus, if we are to critically interrogate the forms and functions of color during this period, we must look at the pervasiveness of whiteness. Conversely, if we are to critically interrogate whiteness, we must look at the qualities of color.

Sometimes the institutional activities and collective policies of the studio system manipulate whiteness like a puppet. The Classical mode of production is not only managed by the "children" of European forefathers and recent immigrants who benefit from the color line, but also by the conscious and unconscious practices of white decision making and procedures. In other words, representations of whiteness can be traced to economic, institutional, and individual practices and procedures. Not unlike George Lipsitz's details about local and federal laws and economic policies in *The Possessive Investment in Whiteness: How White People Profit from Identity Politics,* there is extant evidence in Hollywood of a possessive investment in the pale formation.[6] A number of the contributors to this volume disclose and contextualize this paper trail, finding numerous indications of a perception that whiteness was in the best interests of those who could pass as white.

Sometimes whiteness lurks outside the shadows of mise-en-scène, engulfing color, as if to represent what it is not. In these instances, whiteness aspires to be what Richard Dyer recognizes as "invisible," showing that it is there, in force, a natural and divine norm to be pursued but not to be questioned.[7] This form of whiteness is nonetheless visible as white, replete with its own body of visual and narratological evidence. Ranging from white characters to white lighting techniques to stories of white superiority, this evidence is the stuff of texts and tales. Hence, the look and story of whiteness is a specifiable something, involving a body of images, aesthetics, and stories that is everywhere a fact. We merely need to open our critical eyes to its refraction.

On some occasions, whiteness is there only in fact—as a way in which redness, blackness, brownness, and yellowness represent what it is not. In these instances, color is both resistant to the hegemony of racism and proud of its uniqueness. Which is to say that, when we see color, we are not always seeing white puppets (even though that color is likely being pulled and twisted by whiteness). In the performances of such stars as Hattie McDaniel, Sessue Hayakawa, Iron Eyes Cody, Lupe Vélez, among others, race reveals itself to be more than just a system of stereotypes. The movements and expressions of these stars reveal instances of magnificence that are anything but deficient, deviant, controlled, or out-of-control. Past, future, spirituality, freedom, perseverance, community, insight, and passion are present in the colors of Hollywood, though for some, seeing this refraction of race is as difficult as seeing whiteness itself.

Contributors to this volume engage all of these forms of race, but mostly they concentrate on the divisive aspects of the pale formation. There is a need for future projects to present a fuller critique of the beauty and resistance of color. The rationale for this collection goes to both the past and to academic politics, as I feel strongly that the racist power of whiteness in U.S. film history necessitates interventionist investigations. The lack of such investigations in the film studies canon suggests why.

While fairly recent to film scholarship, whiteness studies has actually been around for years. W. E. B. Du Bois and Richard Wright offered critiques of whiteness long before any contemporary scholar.[8] Chicanos and Nuyoricans (Puerto Ricans living in New York) have always talked about their relationship to whiteness, for it partly defines who we are and what we are not. Native Americans have never stopped talking about paleface, the savagery of Manifest Destiny, or the peculiar institutions of treaties and reservations. Admittedly, in the struggle against racism, the subject of whiteness slipped from the forefront in favor of the history of individual colors. This has been the case since at least the late 1960s when the civil rights movement focused on securing legal and political equality for minority groups. Today, however, studies of whiteness have (re)emerged as an important, critical scholarly subject. This is partly in response to the neoconservative movement of the 1980s and early 1990s, particularly the politics of "reverse" discrimination and, more fundamentally, the critique of and resistance to that movement by many contemporary activists and scholars. While focusing on whiteness is no easy task, given the politics of race today, doing so is a necessary step in the pursuit of a multicultural project.

For many scholars, whiteness is an identity, a social formation, a form of representation, a political-legal infrastructure, and/or a pathology. At the heart of much of this work is the argument that whiteness is synonymous with racism. In this view, the pale order drives the racial formation bus. At the core of the racial formation is the pursuit and maintenance of an economic and political-legal hierarchy of cranium sizes, blood percentages, intelligence, phenotypes, vernacular, culture, and behaviors. In this way, whiteness becomes the opposite of equality, divinity, or beauty, all that it purports to embody. Indeed, the critique that whiteness *is* racism led the Cambridge-based journal, *Race Traitor,* to proclaim, "Treason to whiteness is loyalty to humanity."[9] However extreme this call to arms might seem, the point is well taken: to reject racism, one must reject white identity and all that it offers in privilege and in pain.

The goal of scholarship that views whiteness as synonymous with racism is to eject the formation from the driver's seat so that the meaning of race is no longer a determining factor in our history. Implicit in work on whiteness is the hope that one day racism will no longer shape our identities and social interactions, economic and political structures, representation and stories—at least not to the despairing extent that it does today. However idealistic, this hope is nonetheless the interventionist project at the heart of this volume.

Scholarship on whiteness has many angles and nuances. Literary studies, for example, is often less interested in discussing white identity per se than in locating the roots of white culture in the novelizing of African and African-American traditions and stereotypes. This approach was initiated by Toni Morrison's *Playing in the Dark,* which investigates the impact of an Africanist presence in America's literary consciousness, or the canon of literary studies. In this poetic book of criticism, Morrison defines whiteness as an imagined response to figures of blackness. The construction of the Other, she argues, serves to define the Subject. With poignant insight and graceful prose, Morrison shows us how whiteness is "blackness."[10]

In sociopolitical history, whiteness studies often centers on the relationship among identity, culture, and social history. Alexander Saxton's *The Rise and Fall of the White Republic* traces the history of whiteness during the infancy of the nation, uncovering the pale formation in the class politics and mass culture of nineteenth-century America.[11] Also, in his book *The Wages of Whiteness,* David Roediger broadly argues that "whiteness was a way in which white workers responded to a fear of dependency on wage labor and to the necessities of capitalist work discipline."[12] Noel Ignatiev's *How the Irish Became White* takes on the workings of ethnic assimilation, and Ruth Frankenberg's *White Women, Race Matters* looks at the function of race within a focus group of predominantly "white" women. Ignatiev and Frankenberg show how European-American ethnic and gender identities are racialized as white.[13] Collectively, these scholars detail the ways in which whiteness is infused with national interests, class consciousness, ethnic assimilation, patriarchy, and gender formations.

In film studies, Michael Rogin and Richard Dyer investigate everything from the ways in which whiteness represents color to the representation of whiteness itself. Rogin's *Blackface, White Noise* looks at how Jewish Americans performed blackness in order to become white. Al Jolson's *The Jazz Singer,* he argues, appropriated a blackened-up image of blackness to "Americanize the immigrant son." [14] Dyer, on the other hand, "considers the implications of a particular group of people being categorized by means of the colour white . . . in a culture so bound up with the visual and visible." [15] His book, *White*, analyzes Christian intertextuality and Hollywood lighting techniques, among other discourses and mechanisms. Rogin's and Dyer's works, and the work on race in media studies in general, show us how popular culture is a full partner in the hegemonic activities of the U.S. racial formation.

While these scholars address the history and rhetorical permutations of the pale formation, becoming the pavement supporting much of the thinking and writing that went into this anthology, whiteness studies is finding itself faced with some potential potholes. As an area of interest in a scholarly industry with its share of falsities and fads, whiteness studies is heading down a road that already shows a number of stress cracks. These cracks amount to binary arguments, essentializing assumptions, and reductive explanations: the stuff of bad theory and politics. Which is to say that whiteness studies, due in part to the structural and poststructural methods brought to bear on the subject, has its own contradictions and moments of hypocrisy. Nonetheless, studies of whiteness must try to see and work to avoid these cracks and potholes, forging ahead so that we can continue, with self-reflection and a wider field of vision, the process of our projects.

Some studies implicitly maintain racial binaries. Revealing the "wigger" in all of us, [16] whiteness is defined against or through blackness, with some scholars seeing blackness as the "root" of American culture. While poignant, this trend tends to ignore the histories of redness, brownness, and yellowness, among other colors. Race becomes white and black. In so doing, it implicitly recreates the binary—white versus black—upon which the racial formation often relies for fuel. For example, Morrison's work, for all its insight, all but ignores the redness in the white imagination, despite the fact that many of her literary sources seem as obsessed with natives as they are with slaves. White versus black is too simple an answer, leaving too many people out of history. If we are all black, we are also all noble savages (and Latin lovers, model minorities, etc.). The racial formation is more complex and multifaceted than it is clear-cut or binary, and scholars working on whiteness must address this historical complexity.

A second potential and related crack in the path of whiteness studies is the tendency of some works to essentialize real people. Whiteness means white human beings, who are taken or uncritically assumed to be the same thing as European-Americans or even anybody with "light" phenotypes. White becomes a biological "essence" of sorts, making this trend reductive and fatalistic. This is because an essence is not only built on a singular causal factor—blood, genetics, God—and is thus a reduction of the highest order, but is also something that is impossible to change outside of utter abstraction or utopian platitudes. In this way, it is depressingly fatalistic. The effort to link whiteness to European-Americans is intended to show how all "Americans" are assigned race. Nevertheless, doing so outside of history (nurture rather than nature) makes white European-American sound a bit too much like Caucasoid, and if there are Caucasoids, there are Negroids and Mongoloids. I do not think we want to go there.

A third crack in our path is the tendency to label all discourses and forms of authority as white. Individualism, the frontier, liberty, and patriarchy are all white. Indeed, all that is America is white. While the pale formation certainly informs other discourses and power formations, some significantly so, labeling everything and anything white ultimately collapses the specificity—and thus the significance—of this enduring formation. Which is to say that, as opposed to a universalized everything, whiteness is a specifiable something. It is not the grand total of American experience, and thus our historical methodologies must reveal the distinctions as much as the connections. Not any old history will do. Whiteness might be everywhere a fact, but it is surely not everything. It shifts and changes and is replete with contradiction, therefore its practices and tactics also shift, change, and contradict with time and space. What are needed, it seems to me, are more grounded, detailed analyses of particular instances of whiteness, which are then linked to each other and other myths and forms of power.

The final stress crack in the path of whiteness studies is one that I find particularly problematic. It is the tendency to sidestep the facets and facts of racism and engage in the fetishism of "white" culture. Whiteness is a culture and a people, and that culture and those people possess unique histories outside of racism. Here, whiteness studies tries to reveal the unique aspects of the pale formation, often showing how "whites" can be as oppressed as "coloreds." My response to this work goes to both historiography and the politics of an interventionist study. First, while there are communities of people who pass as white that have certainly suffered oppression, their histories have been told and retold under the banner of Western Civilizations. The canon of scholarship on America, from history to literature, rarely sees the study of immigration, ethnicity, class, and gender as social and discursive processes informed by racism. Studies of whiteness of this kind replicate existing work. Second and related, this type of whiteness studies tends to ignore the one thing that makes the pale formation an otherwise necessary subject of analysis: its possessive investment in racism. After all, whiteness is not the result of a race per se, but a historical process that is about a priori definitions of "race." As Roediger, Ignatiev, Frankenberg, Rogin, and others have shown, whiteness only binds otherwise diverse peoples together when color comes into the picture, making their whiteness equivalent to their racism. Such studies of whiteness end up reifying racism. Whiteness might be more than just racism to many, but it is fundamentally about racism when seen from the perspective of sociocultural history.

In my view, whiteness studies can never be far from the kind of loyalty to humanity called for by *Race Traitor*. Whiteness is racism. Nevertheless, just as not all people of color are colorful, not all who pass as white are racist. We must recognize that the myth of a white people, however powerful and long-lived, is not transhistorical or even transcultural. Not all European-Americans are white, just as not all people of color are colored. Again, the evidence for this is history: those who count as white and those who count as colored have changed over the course of the Republic's journey. Indeed, the designators or markers of white and color are a result of seeing and hearing white and non-white phenotypes and traditions, and this too has changed over space and time. The Irish have not always been white, neither have the Jews, the Italians, or, for that matter, the Aryans and Jesus Christ. The ranks of whiteness have changed with history thanks to mutations in culture, dialects, cosmetics, and "miscegenation." What is also needed is analysis of how different groups of people become or do not become white and colored and, in particular, how whiteness works to privilege those in—or aspiring to be in—its pack. These particular instances of whiteness can and should be linked to other formations and myths in an effort to reveal the specificity and multiplicity of power formations in the United States. What we are seeking are the highways that enable whiteness to flow, as well as the intersections that allow it to spread, integrate, and separate.

How can we deal with the specificity yet multiplicity of whiteness in such a way that the cracks in our field of study do not consume our project? This, of course, is a difficult question to answer, and I assume that many roads lead to that Mecca. In terms of the logic that went into organizing this volume, I see whiteness, and thus race, as a performance: a performance about passing. As I have suggested, there are no white people per se, only those who pass as white. And passing as white, at least in the United States, has almost always had something to do with "acting" and "looking"—making—white. To stretch the Shakespearean metaphor: if all the world's a stage, then the people in this country perform race, often without knowing they are doing so. Whiteness, clinging as it does to common sense notions of genetic or divine difference, is the perfect performance: the actors' method is accepted as natural and the audience often forgets that they are in a theater and, as bell hooks advises, can "talk back." [17] Of course, as a consequence, this depressingly brilliant play extends beyond the wings and the pit of the theater and out into the world of materiality and meaning.

The performance of whiteness attempts to trick us into believing—experiencing and expressing—that there are those who count as white and those who do not, and thus the story the performance tells is the story of passing. There are no white people, only people who pass as white. Although historically accurate to say that many European-Americans now pass, many do not. In fact, some people of color pass not only for white but for other colors as well. At this moment, for example, I often pass as white despite my being "Latino." Traveling in Italy, I passed as native until I spoke English. Likewise in Israel, I passed as Israeli—Christian, Jew, and Arab—until I spoke up. When I am in Puerto Rico or around Puerto Ricans in the United States, nobody questions that I am Latino, even though I do not speak Spanish nearly as well as I would like, and that I am "half" Italian. Who passes at what moment and in what place are historical and discursive questions, and the performance is not necessarily conscious and is almost never conscientious, inasmuch as those who count as white emerge, transform, and reemerge with space, time, and method.

Studies of whiteness require more in-depth analysis of the particularity and permutations of whiteness. In literary and media studies, this involves deconstructing, or defamiliarizing, the textual and narratological properties of whiteness and plotting how those qualities change with modes, styles, genre, and periods. To perform such an analysis also entails taking on the industry (Hollywood) for its diligent efforts to appease the thin white line. In cultural studies and social history, it requires shedding a colored light on the policies, practices, laws, and macroformations of racial "ins and outs," showing how these became, remain, and, in some cases, lose their profitability and privilege. By mixing the two approaches, whiteness studies can better resist the tendency toward reductionism. This tendency essentializes people and universalizes the subject, thus burdening our project with the same contradictions and a-historicism(s) that we are trying to unravel and avoid. It also allows us to see the sociocultural power—the racism—of whiteness in all of its outright ugliness and repressed beauty.

STUDYING WHITENESS

Scholars contributing to this collection come from diverse disciplines. Their interests are varied, ranging from genres such as science fiction to stars like Dorothy Dandridge. They address films as unique as *December 7th* (1943) to processes as complicated as the relationship between self-censorship and U.S. foreign policy. Together, these contributors offer a book that reveals the extent to which whiteness was everywhere a fact in the production, distribution, and exhibition of the Classical Hollywood style.

The first part, "Class," investigates the relationship between race and socioeconomic conditions. Focusing on *A Night at the Opera* (1935) and *To Be Or Not To Be* (1942), Nicholas Sammond and Chandra Mukerji show how the Marx Brothers and Ernst Lubitsch treated ethnicity as a performance of whiteness in order to placate nativist, patriotic anxieties about Jewish assimilation. Aaron Baker considers the role of sports films in the Classical period, in particular the ways in which the genre emphasized race in order to distract attention from other social and economic conditions. In the process, black athletes in these films function to affirm and support white male self-definition. Eric Avila examines the ways in which science fiction films of the 1950s emphasize the "darker side" of the big city, capitulating to the practice of white flight. Finally, Gina Marchetti continues her work on the "yellow peril" with a close reading of *Sons of the Gods* (1930).[18] She shows how the narratological elements of this film "work together to displace the issue of class onto issues of racial, ethnic, and sexual identity."

Extending many of the lines of analysis used in the section on class, the second part focuses on the relationship between race and gender. In her close reading of *The Three Faces of Eve* (1957), Allison Graham interrogates the representation of the well-to-do Southern white woman and her iconographic role in the segregationist fervor of the 1950s. In particular, Graham shows us how the fears harbored by integrationists in the 1950s worked their way into the film in the form of a medical drama about the battle for "mastery" between "Eve White" and "Eve Black." Next, Karen Wallace addresses the sign of the "Indian" and the efficacy of comedy. Concentrating on *The Paleface* (1948), Wallace considers the relationship between masculinity and frontier femininity (in the characters of Bob Hope and Jane Russell), and how these configurations of gender solidify "Indianism" and, in the process, American "subjectification." The third essay in this section is by Joanne Hershfield, who examines the economics of race during Hollywood's Latin American musical craze. Focusing on Mexican actress Dolores del Río, Hershfield interrogates the relationship between cinematic representations of racialized sexuality and Hollywood's dependence on foreign markets.

The section on gender also deals explicitly with sex. Thomas E. Wartenberg explores the ways in which *King Kong* (1933), via the monstrous but loving figure of Kong himself, criticizes Hollywood films for employing stereotypical representations of black male sexuality. Marguerite H. Rippy provides an exceptional analysis of the stardom of Dorothy Dandridge, showing us how

Dandridge was "destroyed" by a media obsessed "with reproducing the commodification of white femininity on a black body, and second by the cultural desire to sample black exoticism without having to confront the national history of exploitation and violence that accompanied that body." In the final essay in this section, Gary W. McDonogh and Cindy Hing-Yuk Wong investigate Hong Kong readings of *The World of Suzie Wong* (1960), uncovering the international dynamics of racialized gender formations at the end of the Classical period.

The third part situates race within the context of war. At issue is patriotism and the ways in which racial Others can meet the standards of "true" Americans despite not being "full" Americans. Roberta E. Pearson continues her analysis of films that feature General George Armstrong Custer, Sitting Bull, Crazy Horse, and the battle of the Little Bighorn/Greasy Grass.[19] Using journalistic sources and marshalling Edward Said's concept of Orientalism, Pearson places her case studies "within their historical context with regard to contemporary attitudes toward both Custer and native Americans." Hernan Vera and Andrew Gordon look at "sincere fictions" of whiteness in Civil War films, showing how the Civil War was deployed as a means to dramatize the "split in the white self." Moving into considerations of World War II, Karla Rae Fuller investigates Orientalist figures in *Dragon Seed* (1944) and *Bugs Bunny Nips the Nips* (1944). Fuller shows us how Hollywood tried to differentiate between Asian nations for "the purpose of creating sharp divisions between our Chinese ally and Japanese enemy." Geoffrey M. White and Jane Yi focus on the representation of the Japanese and multicultural Hawaii after the attack on Pearl Harbor in John Ford's wartime documentary, *December 7th*. White and Yi reveal the ways in which the documentary works toward isolating Japanese-Americans from patriotism. Closing out this section, Martin F. Norden explores the relationship between racism and ableism in veteran "problem" films *Home of the Brave* (1949) and *Bright Victory* (1951). Norden shows how the changes in the vision of racism and ableism from the earlier film to the later one relate to the "shifting contours of the American socio-political landscape."

The final part considers the machinations of the studio system. Complementing Hershfield's analysis of Dolores del Río, Brian O'Neil provides an in-depth study of Addison Durland's efforts on the part of the Production Code Administration to construct an authentic image of Latin America during World War II. Arthur Knight focuses on black stardom, revealing the ways in which Hollywood saw African-Americans and African-Americans saw stars. Sarah Madsen Hardy and Kelly Thomas analyze John M. Stahl's *Imitation of Life* (1934) and Oscar Micheaux's *Ten Minutes to Live* (1932) in order to "address how technology and ideology work together to negotiate tensions surrounding the shifting meaning of race in the popular American imagination during the early sound period." In the final essay, Peter Stanfield investigates the shifting meaning of the ballad of "Frankie and Johnnie." Stanfield argues that this song is quintessentially American due to its "ambiguity toward the character's racial status."

While this anthology is quite large, the project of addressing whiteness in Classical Hollywood cinema remains far from complete. As with *The Birth of Whiteness*, this collection contains gaps. Not adequately addressed is the function of race in several genres, including film noir and black films. Nor is there a complete analysis of race as portrayed in either *Gone with the Wind* (1939) or *The Searchers* (1956), two films canonized in both popular and academic circles. There is also a need for more focused attention on the films of John Ford. Although the work of Ford is addressed in this book, his filmography, particularly the westerns, requires sustained attention. Ideally, these subjects will be explored in subsequent projects.

Even with these gaps, *Classic Hollywood, Classic Whiteness* shows that when we are talking about race and the Classical Hollywood style, we are in some measure talking about whiteness and its relation to other forms of power, including color, class, gender, sexuality, nation, and the industry. Thus, while some of the articles focus on the representation of color or the representation of whiteness, each implicitly or explicitly informs our understanding of the marked and remarkable durability of the pale formation.

NOTES

Special thanks to Donald Kirihara for providing valuable comments on this introduction.

1. Daniel Bernardi, ed., *The Birth of Whiteness: Race and the Emergence of U.S. Cinema* (New Brunswick, NJ: Rutgers University Press, 1996).

2. By racial formation, I am referring to the theory that sees race as a sociopolitical and cultural network of meanings. Michael Omi and Howard Winant, *Racial Formation in the United States: From the 1960s to the 1990s*, 2d ed. (New York: Routledge, 1994). For an extension of this work to the context of contemporary film and TV, the period in which Omi and Winant are most interested, see Daniel Bernardi, *Star Trek and History: Race-ing Toward a White Future* (New Brunswick, NJ: Rutgers University Press, 1998).

3. Noel Burch, *Theory of Film Practice* (New York: Praeger, 1973), 110–113.

4. David Bordwell, Janet Staiger, and Kristin Thompson, *The Classical Hollywood*

Cinema: Film Style and Mode of Production to 1960 (New York: Columbia University Press, 1985), 9.

5. See Tom Gunning, *D. W. Griffith and the Origins of American Narrative Film: The Early Years at Biograph* (Urbana and Chicago: University of Illinois Press, 1994).

6. George Lipsitz, *The Possessive Investment in Whiteness: How White People Profit from Identity Politics* (Philadelphia: Temple University Press, 1998).

7. See Richard Dyer, "White," *Screen*, 29, no. 4 (autumn 1988).

8. For a useful analysis of whiteness studies in academia, see Shelly Fisher Fishkin, "Interrogating 'Whiteness,' Complicating 'Blackness': Remapping American Culture," in *Criticism and the Color Line: Desegregating American Literary Studies*, ed. Henry B. Wonham (New Brunswick, NJ: Rutgers University Press, 1996). My critique of whiteness in this introduction owes much to Fishkin's work in this article.

9. For a compilation of this journal's first five editions, see Noel Ignatiev and John Garvey, eds., *Race Traitor* (New York: Routledge, 1996).

10. Toni Morrison, *Playing in the Dark: Whiteness and the Literary Imagination* (Cambridge: Harvard University Press, 1992).

11. Alexander Saxton, *The Rise and Fall of the White Republic: Class Politics and Mass Culture in Nineteenth-Century America* (New York and London: Verso, 1990).

12. David Roediger, *The Wages of Whiteness: Race and the Making of the American Working Class* (New York and London: Verso, 1991), 13.

13. Noel Ignatiev, *How the Irish Became White* (New York: Routledge, 1995). Ruth Frankenberg, *White Women, Race Matters: The Social Construction of Whiteness* (Minneapolis: University of Minnesota Press, 1993).

14. Michael Rogin, *Blackface, White Noise: Jewish Immigrants in the Hollywood Melting Pot* (Berkeley: University of California Press, 1996).

15. Richard Dyer, *White* (London: Routledge, 1997), 42.

16. "Wigger" is a colloquial expression meaning "white nigger" or "whites acting black."

17. bell hooks, *Talking Back* (Boston: South End Press, 1989).

18. See Gina Marchetti, "Tragic and Transient Love in *The Forbidden City*," in Bernardi, *The Birth of Whiteness*, as well as in Gina Marchetti, *Romance and the "Yellow Peril": Race, Sex, and Discursive Strategies in Hollywood Fiction* (Berkeley: University of California Press, 1994).

19. See Roberta E. Pearson, "The Revenge of Rain-in-the-Face? Or, Custer and Indians on the Silent Screen," in Bernardi, *The Birth of Whiteness*.

PART I

CLASS

"WHAT YOU ARE ... I WOULDN'T EAT"

Ethnicity, Whiteness, and Performing "the Jew" in Hollywood's Golden Age

Nicholas Sammond and Chandra Mukerji

In Ernst Lubitsch's *To Be Or Not To Be* (1942), a Nazi officer is asked if he knows the lead character, a ham actor. He replies, "Oh yes . . . what he did to Shakespeare, we are now doing to Poland." When the film premiered, during wartime, the line was considered grossly inappropriate—how tasteless to compare the depredations of the Nazis to a bad rendition of *Hamlet*. Still, the line had an undeniable resonance: what was Hitler but a tin-pot dictator, a second-rate caricature of a leader, laying to waste not only Europe, but an idea of Europe as the seat of civilization? Lubitsch's equation of Shakespeare with oft-conquered Poland speaks volumes about 1930s Hollywood's uneasy negotiation of race and ethnicity in and for America. Poland was considered a source of many poor immigrants to America, providing ethnic diversity but little that could be celebrated as an addition to American culture. Shakespeare was the marker of the finest of European high culture, thought to represent an Anglo superiority of character, a thinly veiled, racialized ideal of whiteness.

Those in Hollywood, many of whom were Jewish and some of whom were Poles as well, told stories in their films about America and Europe, the popular and the classy respectively. Simultaneously, they faced the need both to create a profitable industry and to make film seem a reputable part of American culture. The use of high-art themes in Hollywood films represented an industry working to extract from an elite white culture a nod toward American film as an acceptable art form and toward Hollywood as a source of cultured Americanness. This project of cultural elevation was often undermined by the popular appeal of most Hollywood products, which were geared to an audience ambivalent about elite culture and dubious about the possibility of upward mobility and assimilation. This ambivalence often manifested itself in Hollywood films of the 1930s and 1940s as a complex of anxieties about race and ethnicity in American culture, revealing how Hollywood tried to manage its own identity while proposing an American one through its negotiation of racial and ethnic markers. Race in this case was not based solely on a simple dichotomy between black and white. Whiteness also operated as an unpolluted ideal that relied upon the production and ongoing definition of ethnicity as an alternative means for establishing and maintaining difference.

In an incisive analysis of how ethnic (particularly Jewish) performers used blackface minstrelsy to establish their whiteness, Michael Rogin asserts that "[h]istory, not biology, distinguishes ethnicity from race, making the former groups (in the American usage) distinctive but assimilable, walling off the latter, legally, socially, and ideologically." [1] While Rogin focuses his analysis on the complex operations of racial masquerade, we are interested in extending the problem to include masquerades of class and ethnicity and in following the operations of pretense, performance, and natural hierarchy in film. Why and how was ethnicity associated with immigrants and the working class and whiteness with the middle and upper classes? How were these meanings produced, opposed, and regulated in Hollywood movies? What were the necessary relations between upward mobility and assimilation, and how did these relations operate? Finally, if assimilation involved a discernable (and, in the case of its representation, almost ritual) movement from the performance of ethnicity into the enactment of Americanism, what can the mechanism of passing—which denied the possibility of this movement and replaced playful performance with anxious pretense—tell us about the meanings of ethnicity and whiteness in the 1930s and 1940s?

In this essay we compare Lubitsch's *To Be Or Not To Be* to the Marx Brothers film *A Night at the Opera* (Sam Wood, dir., 1935) in order to unravel a few strands in Hollywood's complex negotiation of race and ethnicity prior to and during World War II. These films both share an uneasiness around certain categories of race and class and a seemingly willful ambiguity in the face of virulent racial discourses at home and abroad. Yet, they diverge in their responses to these conditions. *A Night at the Opera* apparently champions ethnicity and mocks the pretenses of upper-class whiteness. At the same time, though, it celebrates the assimilation and upward mobility of its protagonists and reduces to a generic ethnicity the very explicit racial and national stereotyping common to the vaudeville stage from which much of its humor derives.

To Be Or Not To Be, on the other hand, offers the strange spectacle of a high farce set in occupied Warsaw. If *A Night at the Opera* presents a comic vision of European sophistication and civilization under assault by its rebellious poor ethnic relations, *To Be Or Not To Be* shows European whiteness collapsing from within. Lubitsch's Europe is besieged by evil and demented buffoons who have violated the border between comedy and tragedy. The film is an elegy for an idea of Europe in which whiteness was inflected through class—meaning both socioeconomic standing and style. Just as the Marx Brothers represented a broadly performed generic ethnicity, Ernst Lubitsch, in his public persona and in his work, represented a high modernity that minimized the distance between the performer and the performed, in which the affect behind the character's emotions derived directly from the performer's history. The comedy of the Marx Brothers favored the medium shot to demonstrate the broad performativity of the body. The verisimilitude of high-modern drama was best exemplified in the close-up that could capture the tear in the eye or the quiver of the lip that revealed real emotion.[2]

Yet, both films struggle with whiteness. This essay moves between registers—between the object and the conditions of its making—in an attempt to contain the contradictions they offer in that struggle. Irving Thalberg's insistence that *A Night at the Opera* be more narrative than previous Marx Brothers movies did more than add a rather obligatory love story to the plot. It created a situation in which two narrative modes—one more clearly associated with the performative ethnic body and the other with the abstract white individual—had to find a common ground on the screen. Likewise, the Europe of *To Be Or Not To Be* was the European theater of operations and an imaginary of taste and civilization, providing significant cultural capital both to directors such as Lubitsch and to the men who hired them.

The structuring absence in this particular interplay between ethnicity and whiteness is Jewishness. Lubitsch's recourse to an elevated European status had much to do with Hollywood's negotiation of American anti-Semitism. Likewise, the Marx Brothers' vaguely ethnic personae simultaneously invoked longstanding vaudeville traditions and the industry's uneasiness with openly Jewish actors; a generic ethnicity served better than a specific one. In the 1930s, the dominant discourse around the inclusion of European immigrants in American society and culture was that of assimilation. If not Black, Latino, or Asian, an immigrant could leave behind the culture of his or her origins and join American culture by espousing and assuming white middle-class values and by abandoning the dress, manners, and language of his or her ethnic origins.[3] For American Jews, assimilation was a little more complicated. A Polish Jew, for instance, was both Polish and Jewish.[4] While Poles might have been considered potentially white, the case was not so clear for Jews—whether being Jewish was a matter of race, culture, or religion remained an open question, as did whether Jews could be assimilated.[5] National identities and cultures were redeemable, but the ambiguous status of diaspora Judaism, and centuries of antipathy toward Jews, positioned an explicitly Jewish identity as a disturbingly transnational entity.

World War II did little to change that. At the outset of the war, American Jews were generally divided on how best to aid Jews in Europe. Most more-assimilated German-American Jews argued for a generalized patriotic call to defeat the Nazis; Jews more recently arrived from Eastern Europe, for an explicit plea for rescue addressed to their fellow Americans.[6] In Hollywood, Jewish producers had faced years of anti-Semitic attacks from nativist groups, who accused them of subverting American morals; as war approached, isolationist anti-Semites added the charge of conspiring to draw the United States into the conflict.[7] Although different groups of Jews in Hollywood disagreed as to tactics, Jewish producers generally chose a path of least resistance, publicly presenting themselves and their products as American and patriotic while downplaying their specific concerns as Jews.

For some time, Hollywood had deployed various strategies of passing: anglicizing names, reinventing immigrant stars as European exotics, and importing European stars and directors who might otherwise have been considered immigrants. Since the advent of sound, Hollywood had also increasingly avoided the sympathetic portrayal of Jews on the screen.[8] The implicit strategy had been to create convenient fictions and silences—to pass—and the rise of Nazi racial regimes in Europe and their supporters in this country seemed to confirm the wisdom of that choice. Prior to the war, many of the claims made by the Nazis were also made quite publicly in the United States by persons as famous as Henry Ford and Charles Lindbergh. The safest course of action suggested deflecting anti-Semitism obliquely, not confronting it directly.[9]

Films such as *A Night at the Opera* and *To Be Or Not To Be* stepped carefully around issues of race and ethnicity. As the 1930s progressed, Jewish producers in Hollywood increasingly avoided ethnically explicit tales of assimilation that might fuel nativist depictions of them as resistant to assimilation or more a threat than an asset to America. Better to pass (pretend not to be Jewish) or to naturalize assimilation (treat ethnicity as a performative choice that could be, with varying degrees of difficulty—and perhaps some small loss—discarded). Some movies, like *A Night at the Opera*, deployed the broadly performative versions of ethnicity popularized in vaudeville (within which one could read Jewishness if one so chose), but did not define major characters as Jews (particularly when the actors were, in fact, Jewish). Foregrounding the movement of immigrants to America, these films presented assimilation as a kind of generic social possibility that would supersede or eliminate the limitations caused by particular cultural origins or class location.[10] Other films, like those directed by Lubitsch, engaged middle-class white American yearnings for Europe as a source of cultural authenticity and authority, as well as nostalgic desires for a culture that never existed and a mythic heritage on which to build. These films were to elevate the medium by incorporating European theatrical conventions and literary forms, taking Americans back to Europe to find not immigrants, but high-art aesthetics.[11]

The Europe we meet in *To Be Or Not To Be* is a collision of that imaginary with an historical reality grown too large to avoid. The Europe that delivers high modernism also creates the Nazis and too clearly links cultural superiority to domination. The Polski Theater is replaced with the European theater of operations, and the actors are left without a script, forced to improvise. Cast adrift in a new social order even crueler than the bitter imaginary of Hamlet, they stumble through a burlesque of subterfuge in which the Nazis are both audience and costars, the success of which depends upon their ability to pass as those who would kill them.

In *A Night at the Opera*, ethnicity is performative, a play of surfaces like that of vaudeville, typified by oversized costumes, overdone accents, and dogged crassness, offering entertainment rather than edification, amusement rather than advancement, virtuosity rather than internal development.[12] The film reappropriates and celebrates stereotypes, making the narrative thread of perfunctory assimilation appear a backdrop, simultaneously inverting and affirming racial hierarchy.[13] In contrast, the constitution of an identity based on European superiority, of passing directly into whiteness, requires a different kind of work more like that of high-modern theater. This kind of performance is centered around believability—the harmony of one's inward character with one's outward appearance—in a world assumed to be grounded in a fundamental and stable reality. Words and deeds are meant to reinforce each other, naturalizing pretense and making it seem the basis for recognizing true difference. In this world, a person's character is substantial only if it develops within the flow of the narrative. If the terms of the narrative shift, however—

as when the fantasy of Europe became untenable in World War II—then character is revealed as pretense, substance merely a conceit, and whiteness an act of collaboration, and we return to *A Night at the Opera*.[14]

A NIGHT AT THE OPERA

> A Jew can't play a Jew. It wouldn't look right on the screen.
>
> —Sam Goldwyn, as quoted in Michael Rogin, *Blackface, White Noise*

A Night at the Opera opens in the putative home of opera, Milan. An American widow, Mrs. Claypool (Margaret Dumont), has hired Otis B. Driftwood (Groucho), a faux impresario, to win her a place in American high society through the sponsorship of a new Italian opera star, Rodolpho Lassparri (Walter Wolf King). A contending impresario, Herr Gottlieb (Sigfried Rumann), signs Lassparri and an unknown soprano, Rosa (Kitty Carlisle), to premiere at the New York Opera. Driftwood accidentally signs Rosa's lover, an unknown tenor named Ricardo Baroni (Alan Jones), who is managed by Fiorello (Chico). Claypool, Gottlieb, Lassparri, and Rosa board a boat for America (the SS *Americus*), and Driftwood follows, determined to lay claim to Claypool's millions.

While the elites above deck enjoy a smooth passage, the poor (read "real" immigrants)—including the Marx Brothers, except sometimes Groucho—make the best of cramped quarters and simple fare below deck as they approach their transformation from Italians into American ethnics. Ricardo, Fiorello, and Lassparri's much-abused valet, Tomasso (Harpo), stow away in Driftwood's baggage. The stowaways wander into steerage (which is packed with immigrants) in search of food, are discovered and imprisoned, escape, and eventually take the place of three vaguely "European" aviators bound for a dignitary's welcome in New York. The three are unmasked at the welcoming ceremonies and chased by a police detective. Eventually, they end up at the premiere of *Il Trovatore*, along with Driftwood, who has subdued Gottlieb and taken his place in Mrs. Claypool's box. When the dust from the final chase has settled, Ricardo has replaced Lassparri as tenor, and the audience demands that he and Rosa become the new stars of the opera. As a condition of his newfound fame, Ricardo demands amnesty for the Marx Brothers, which is granted.

On the whole, and like many Marx Brothers movies, *A Night at the Opera* reads as an immigrant assault on the standards and mores of high society.[15] In the first scene, Driftwood offers to help Mrs. Claypool into high society by

Figure 1.1. *A Night at the Opera* (1935).

facilitating a donation of $200,000 to the New York Opera, but he stands her up at a restaurant only to dine there with another woman. Mrs. Claypool discovers him at the adjoining table:

MRS. CLAYPOOL: Mr. Driftwood, three months ago you promised to put me into society. In all that time, you've done nothing but draw a handsome salary.

OTIS P. DRIFTWOOD: You think that's nothing, huh? How many men do you know drawing a handsome salary nowadays? Why, you can count them on the fingers of one hand . . . my good woman!

CLAYPOOL: I'm not your good woman!

DRIFTWOOD: Don't say that, Mrs. Claypool. I don't care what your past has been. To me you'll always be my good woman. Because I love you. There. I didn't mean to tell you, but you . . . you dragged it out of me. I love you.

CLAYPOOL: It's rather difficult to believe that when I find you dining with another woman.

DRIFTWOOD: That woman? Do you know why I sat with her?

CLAYPOOL: No.

DRIFTWOOD: Because she reminded me of you.

CLAYPOOL: Really?

DRIFTWOOD: Of course. That's why I'm sitting here with you. Because you remind me of you. Your eyes, your throat, your lips! Everything about you reminds me of you. Except you. How do you account for that?

She, of course, cannot account for it. But perhaps we can. She is attempting to buy her way into "society," using Driftwood as her cat's-paw. Although she has money, she lacks the culture and refinement necessary to gain entrée. Once she has (through Driftwood) purchased a tenor for the opera, she will have demonstrated her discernment. As Mrs. Claypool approaches her goal, the insecure woman who first hired Driftwood disappears behind a pretentious veneer of sophistication that renders her unrecognizable to him.

Here, two systems of valuation collide. In the working-class world of vaudeville, performance was very much located in the body and judged by mastery of one's particular shtick, were it comedy, dancing, singing, or juggling.[16] The performer never disappeared within the character; rather, the character remained the trademark of the performer's craft, his or her signature. The Marx Brothers' characters were, of course, straight from vaudeville. From one movie to the next, their names changed, but costume, gesture, accent (or silence), and shtick remained constant. Their costumes fit them poorly, as if they found them backstage and threw them on. Groucho was always the con man; Chico, the street hustler; Harpo, the hobo. They invariably provided the same basic ingredients: a piano solo, a harp solo, and rapid verbal patter. As American ethnics, the Marx Brothers had neither the authentic culture of new immigrants nor the naturally superior character of true elites; unlike Rosa and Ricardo, they performed their roots rather than grew from them. In contrast to many in Hollywood, the Marx Brothers demonstrated no interest in trying to escape this liminal location; rather, they embraced it. (With one small exception, of course: their roots were, in part, Jewish, and this they did not perform.)[17]

In the theater of the elite culture to which Mrs. Claypool wished to gain access, however, character continuity and sustained psychological development determined the value of a performance, and an actor was considered successful if she could convince the audience that she had become the role she was playing. Driftwood's appraisal of Claypool at this moment suggests that she has failed in both performative modes. Her character is purchased—neither mastered from without nor derived from within—and lacks clarity in either register.

This opening sequence sets up a tension between pretense and natural character that animates the entire story. Pretense and performance are omnipresent—not only in the construction of ethnic identity or in Driftwood's efforts to con everyone, but also in the constitution of an elite status that claims to be grounded in natural virtue and economic advantage alone, but that requires social manipulation and personal impression-management. The assimilating characters, Rosa and Ricardo, are the exceptions: their unremitting sincerity demonstrates a harmony between inner desires and outward show. Their inevitable assimilation into whiteness is a consequence of their natural virtue. From the beginning, we know that the young couple will obtain their happy ending because they relate honestly to others and are always neatly dressed and well spoken. From their Italian roots, they bring to America neither a huckster's desire for fame and fortune nor an immigrant's longing for native culture, but rather a distinctly European civility and good taste.

Overall, the movie operates through sets of symmetrical reversals and layered identities. Almost every action occurring at the beginning in the mythical "Italy" will produce repercussions in America, and every identity—save that of Ricardo and Rosa—is merely a surface not yet stripped away. In the second scene, the camera views Harpo in a dressing room mirror. Dressed in Lassparri's Puncinello costume, Harpo empties his atomizer into his throat and unsuccessfully attempts to sing an aria to himself. When Lassparri finds him, he beats Harpo mercilessly, demanding that he remove the costume. Harpo does, revealing a sailor's uniform, which foreshadows the shipboard portion of the film. Then he peels away the uniform to reveal a gypsy wench's costume, which refers to the operatic climax of the film when Harpo takes his revenge on Lassparri for the beatings, humiliating the tenor in his debut at the New York Opera. In this chaotic finale, Harpo lowers a succession of backdrops behind Lassparri as he attempts to sing, including a woodland scene, a New York fruit peddler's cart, and the bridge of a battleship. Not only does Harpo rob Lassparri of his voice (the singer is booed off the stage), he also effectively decontextualizes Lassparri's character, reminding both audiences that opera has as much to do with popular performativity as it does with high-art theater.

These symmetries continue like signposts throughout the film. When Rosa departs on the SS *Americus* to become a diva, she and Ricardo perform a farewell duet in which she sings down to him from the deck and he up from the pier. At the end of the film, when the two sing the climactic duet from *Il Trovatore* in their triumphant New York Opera debut, their positions are reversed:

Ricardo sings down from tower and Rosa sings up to him from the stage. The mirroring suggests a reversal of fortune—they are now stars—and a re-ordering of gender hierarchies that had threatened Ricardo's masculinity when he was classed an immigrant interloper while Rosa remained a star.

Likewise, the peasant dances in the steerage of the SS *Americus* are re-capitulated, down to the outlandishly formal "folk" costumes, in the gypsy dances of *Il Trovatore*. In almost every case, the narrative mirroring points to the increasing instability of believable character, the performed nature of so-cial and cultural norms, and the constructed quality of the divide between high and low, ethnic and white. Ultimately, though, the narrative seems to recuperate those terms through the successful assimilation of Rosa and Ri-cardo—an action that depends upon the willingness of the high and low characters to perform their proper functions, acting as a hyperactive back-drop against which unfolds a wooden ritual of assimilation.

The ritual is stiff because no one in the movie audience paid to see Rosa and Ricardo assimilate. They came to see the Marx Brothers, and the narrative ca-pitulates to that reality in two moments in the film. These are important, not simply because they indicate the pressure of the movie's reception on its nar-rative, but also because the exposed seams of the story reveal an instability in the notion of ethnicity. The first moment occurs aboard the SS *Americus*. Driftwood goes to the captain's table for dinner, while Tomasso, Fiorello, and Ricardo find their way to the lower decks. In first class, Groucho cracks wise, which only Rosa seems to appreciate. Below deck, the others find a peasant feast in progress, with singing and dancing and huge plates of pasta being dished up for all. Warmly welcomed by the Italian immigrants, the three re-turn the favor by performing for the crowd. Ricardo sings the film's big pro-duction number ("Cosi-Cosa," a song about the easygoing nature of Italian peasants), Fiorello performs piano tricks for the children, and Tomasso clowns and plays the harp. The whole sequence presents an abbreviated vaudeville revue—from song, to dance, to comedy.

At the height of this shipboard chorus number, the camera pulls back and up into a Busby Berkeley-style overhead shot, revealing a perfectly synchro-nized folk spectacle in which wheels of dancers turn within each other. Unlike the Berkeley spectacles, which celebrate the presence of the stage, this scene interrupts the narrative to offer up the peasant body as naturally performa-tive, part of a larger organism ordering itself for the viewer's pleasure. This number prefigures the gypsy chorus in *Il Trovatore*, in which Harpo and Chico hide and which they use to humiliate Lassparri and Gottlieb. The shipboard number is a celebration of an ethnicity at ease with its natural performativity and that welcomes unquestioningly those willing to perform themselves honestly. At the same time, though, both choruses act as colorful backdrops to a narrative of assimilation: the necessary rustics against which the protagonists can stand out. Which reading obtains? Is one chorus "real" and one not? The assimilationist narrative requires an ethnicity happy to be abandoned. "Opera" is entertaining not for its verisimilitude, but for its performativity, and the whiteness that claims a franchise on understanding its finer points is a bit of a yawn.

During this number, Chico, Harpo, and Ricardo are discovered when Lassparri recognizes them in the crowd. Although they are thrown into the brig, the stowaways soon escape their prison and steal the uniforms and beards of the three European aviators traveling to America as heroes. With Driftwood acting as their representative, the imposters are greeted by the mayor of New York and whisked off to a parade in their honor. Upon arriving at the reviewing stand, they are asked to speak about their exploits as aviators. Fiorello addresses the crowd first:

FIORELLO: What'll I say?

DRIFTWOOD: Tell 'em you're not here.

FIORELLO: What if they don't believe me?

DRIFTWOOD: They'll believe you when you start talking.

FIORELLO: Friends . . .

DRIFTWOOD: Talk fast. I see a man in the crowd with a rope . . .

FIORELLO: How we came to America is a great story, but I don't tell that . . .

He, of course, cannot tell that story. In a scene that recalls the opening dialogue between Groucho and Dumont, Driftwood questions Fiorello's existence, and, in a sense, the nature of passing. He suggests that Fiorello tell the truth: the European aviator never arrived, but the immigrant did. They came on the same boat, but only one got off, carrying both identities. As before, the surface and the interior do not match. Behind valued European figures (such as Ernst Lubitsch or Erich Von Stroheim) lurk immigrants. One misspoken word (in this case, "Friends") can give the game away and turn the crowd against him. Fiorello cannot tell the story of how he came to America because he would have to admit that he slapped on his persona—no more than a costume and a fake beard—just before he stepped off the boat. He would reveal that being a classy European in America is a performative act, a pretense like Claypool's that renders him recognizable to some and unrecognizable to others. Neither can the Marx Brothers tell their story, the story of Jews coming to Hollywood, but they can happily perform the role of working-class ethnics, rendering themselves visible and hidden at the same time. As Harpo's beard disintegrates, so does their performance of European civility. They flee the reviewing stand with the police in hot pursuit.

The narrative seams split again following Groucho and Chico's colloquy on visibility and being. A detective traces the fugitives to Driftwood's hotel suite, two adjoining rooms that share a balcony. In the chase that ensues, Chico and Harpo move the furniture from one room into the other without being seen. The camera pulls back to reveal the edge of the wall between the rooms, exposing the realistic hotel suite as a stage set. By revealing the stage, the narrative seems to be patiently acknowledging the interruption. That the detective does not see or hear the brothers is, of course, unbelievable: toward the end of the chase, Harpo imitates a door by placing a cot in front of his body and offering his fist as a doorknob. Then Chico becomes a rocking chair and Harpo an old woman in that chair. Groucho pulls a fake beard from nowhere and reads a newspaper. The detective bursts in and, finding an old immigrant couple at home, says, "Oh I beg your pardon. I must be in the wrong room." In a parody of assimilation, the illegal aliens have instantly naturalized (to the point of becoming furnishings). The scene goes to black, and the story continues.

Henry Jenkins has suggested that the depiction of the Marx Brothers as mounting a coherent ideological opposition to the social norms of their time is overly optimistic and ignores both the history of film convention and production "and the performance tradition(s) from which they emerged."[18] It may also be a mistake to assume, as have many critics and biographers of the brothers, that Irving Thalberg's imposition of a coherent narrative structure on the Marx Brothers in *A Night at the Opera* and subsequent films constrained the social critique inherent in their comedy.[19] Rather, the decision of Thalberg and MGM to impose a conventional Hollywood narrative structure on the Marx Brothers' performances may be read as the intersection of contradictory discourses of race, ethnicity, and class at which imperfect, yet important, resolutions were produced. *A Night at the Opera* may ostensibly celebrate ethnicity and disrupt racializing discourses, but it also presents a narrative fantasy of assimilation that both elides the ethnicization of immigrants and reaffirms the notion that whiteness can be imported directly from Europe as high culture. That culture is embodied in Rosa and Ricardo, whose natural virtues erase their origins. The seeming contradiction between this narrative and the slapstick racial and class antagonisms of the other characters reveals the uneasiness of a Hollywood that (profitably) celebrated its ethnic and working-class roots, but still conformed to a social order that viewed those roots as inferior and threatening.[20]

TO BE OR NOT TO BE

> "I think Europeans do it better."
>
> —Mrs. Claypool to Otis B. Driftwood, *A Night at the Opera*

In *To Be Or Not To Be*, a Polish theater troupe takes on the role of the Gestapo, first in jest and later in earnest, performing a stage comedy and a historical tragedy to "prick the conscience" of an American audience willing to watch some Shakespeare, but not so sure about defending Europeans from Nazism. Just as Hamlet had some second-rate players enact a drama of unspeakable horror to make manifest what could not be spoken, so Ernst Lubitsch has his bumbling Polish repertory group bring Americans face-to-face with the Nazi invasion of Poland and *some* of its devastating consequences. In this convulsed world, tragedy and comedy cannot be disentangled because the historical drama will not stay within the confines of civilized forms. For the operation of racism in European politics and the relative unspeakability of this fact in early 1940s Hollywood, demonstrated by the tension between its presence and absence in *To Be Or Not To Be*, reveal as much about American racial politics as they do about Europe under the Nazis.[21]

While silent films offered both sympathetic and stereotypical representations of Jews well into the 1920s, as film more firmly established itself as a national medium, its producers came under increasing pressure to conform to and reproduce prevailing norms of Americanness, particularly in terms of race, ethnicity, class, and gender. By the 1920s and 1930s, calls to regulate, reform, and censor the industry often came laced with anti-Semitic sentiments. Reform groups of various stripes complained that the predominance of Jews in the industry threatened the integrity of American culture.[22] In terms that ranged from the implicit to the quite explicit, nativist reformers argued that Jews in Hollywood were unassimilated (if not unassimilable), hence unable or unwilling to invest their products with the morals and values that would impart to their viewers the qualities necessary for becoming a good American. Ironically, in one type of response to this pressure, Hollywood studio heads imported directors and producers from Europe, both to improve the industry's image by lending it a touch of class and to reinvest that image with more "artistic" European high-art traditions that would appeal more to middle-class sensibilities.[23] This process of erasing ethnicity and creating whiteness (either American or European) was recapitulated in dramatic and comedic narratives of assimilation. By the 1930s, the focus of these narratives had shifted from the conflict between the unassimilated and the assimilating generations to the barriers to assimilation caused by the protagonists' limited ability to erase their pasts.[24]

With passing, however, came the anxiety of potential unmasking, either by white peers or by members of one's abandoned past. While being "European" offered a certain measure of greater security against unmasking than did being American, by the end of the 1930s (and the coming of World War II), even that category had become unreliable. The racial politics of the Nazis and their collaborators made the concept of European whiteness increasingly unstable and fraught and complicated an American whiteness allied to it through cultural markers. By the late 1930s, the symbolic "Europe" imported by Hollywood for an infusion of "class" and "culture"—for example, Ernst Lubitsch, Erich Von Stroheim, Alexander Korda, Maurice Chevalier, Marlene Dietrich and Laurence Olivier—was on a collision course with a real Europe in which fascism was on the march. The Europe that Hollywood had imported and produced was the locus of a poetic ontogenesis that had created and developed literary traditions. Clearly distinguishing between comedy and tragedy, these traditions marked the proper relationship between the development of a plot and the development of characters in response to the pressures of the narrative.

In this imaginary Europe, classical forms fused with social class to create a dividing line between art and mere entertainment, to provide the sort of edification that middle-class reformers demanded of a national cinema. In the real Europe, however, the Nazis were redrawing the geographic and demographic landscape and suppressing as "degenerate" the modernist art movements that had produced many of the great European imports. The destabilization of this imaginary reached the United States, as Charles Lindbergh stumped for isolationism, decrying the influence of Jews in the motion picture industry, and a U.S. senator, Gerald P. Nye, accused Hollywood of trying to draw the country into war. "In each of these [film] companies there are a number of production directors, many of whom have come from Russia, Hungary, Germany, and the Balkan countries," stated Nye, who contended that these directors were "naturally susceptible" to "racial emotions."[25] Once the United States entered the war on the side of England, many of the overt anti-Semitic attacks on Hollywood and its European imports subsided. The nation chose Shakespeare's people over Germany's master race, making the category

"European" problematic as a resource for the culturally ambitious but giving Anglo whiteness a new cachet. In light of this, we may reasonably ask, which Europe is the setting for *To Be Or Not To Be,* and what can that film tell us about the state of being "European" as a vehicle for passing into whiteness?

The film opens in 1939. A theater troupe in Warsaw is rehearsing *Gestapo,* a play critical of the Nazis. Shortly before the play is due to open, the Polish censors shut it down for fear of offending Hitler, and the troupe has to fall back on its old standby, *Hamlet.* The company's lead actors, Jozef and Maria Tura (Jack Benny and Carole Lombard), play Hamlet and Ophelia. Maria becomes involved in a romantic dalliance with a Polish flier (Robert Stack), who repeatedly walks out on Hamlet's soliloquy to visit her backstage. As a result of this liaison, the Turas, and the company, become embroiled in a plot to assassinate a Polish collaborator, Professor Siletsky (Stanley Ridges), in order to keep him from exposing the Polish underground to the Nazis. Siletsky is eventually killed, but in order to pull this off and cover their tracks, the troupe is forced to impersonate both the professor and members of the Gestapo. When their ruse is discovered, they are forced to stage a new drama to escape from Poland, faking an assassination attempt on Hitler while he attends a command performance at the Polski Theater in order to steal his personal plane, which they fly to England. In England, they are awarded for their bravery by being permitted to perform *Hamlet* in Shakespeare's homeland. During Hamlet's soliloquy, a British flier walks out of the performance. . . .

The film's first scene is a montage. The camera frames the names of Polish proprietorships—each eponymous with its owner—one by one in a series of medium shots from the perspective of a passerby on the street. As each sign appears, the narrator intones the name, linking a place (Warsaw) with a people (Poles) through a litany. The narration continues, in word and image, with a reverie on a normal day in Warsaw—until Hitler appears on a street corner, stopping traffic and frightening the public. The narrator offers to explain his presence by taking us to Gestapo headquarters. There, two officers (one, Benny) are coercing a little boy to inform on his father when they are interrupted by the arrival of the führer. They cry, "*Heil* Hitler!" to which Hitler replies, "*Heil* myself." A voice yells, "That's not in the script!" The camera pulls back, and we discover that the whole thing is a play. The director, Dobosh (Charles Halton) upbraids Bronski (Tom Dugan), the actor playing Hitler, for ad-libbing until interrupted by another man, the "Jewish" character, Greenberg (Felix Bressart):

GREENBERG: Do you want my opinion, Mr. Dobosh?

DOBOSH: No, Mr. Greenberg, I do not want your opinion.

GREENBERG: Then let me give you my reaction: a laugh is nothing to be sneezed at.

This enrages the director, who insists that the play is meant to be a serious drama, an indictment of the Nazis. The veneer of high drama has been marred with a vaudevillian sensibility by Greenberg, who, we are soon told, is a Jew. Another bit player, Ravitch (Lionel Atwill), storms onto the set, complaining that Bronski and Greenberg are just "two little actors who want to enlarge their parts." Greenberg replies, "What you are, Mr. Ravitch, I wouldn't eat." The angry Ravitch yells, "How dare you call me a ham!" The set erupts into chaos. If European theater is meant to be a source of truth and cultural order, it is breaking down as the script and the director lose their civilizing grip.

Maria Tura adds to the disorder by walking onto the stage in a full-length satin evening gown, which she intends to wear in a concentration camp scene. She acts the Hollywood star, without a trace of concern for the moral content of the story. Greenberg loves the idea, uttering what will be his signature line: "It'll get a terrific laugh." The director is beside himself, now even accusing Bronski, the actor playing Hitler, of not being believable. At this point, Bronski marches into the street to prove that he can fool an audience, which he does until a young girl calls him "Mr. Bronski" and asks for his autograph.

Ultimately, though, the Polish censors do stop the drama; the play is closed down for fear of insulting Hitler. The company is forced to revert to its old standby, Hamlet, a play in which the social order is subverted and actors are used to reveal the unspoken. The point is reinforced by a shot of a poster of Hamlet being slapped over that of Gestapo and failing to cover it. Reduced once again to mere foot soldiers, Bronski and Greenberg discuss lost opportunities:

BRONSKI: When Dobosh said to me, "Bronski, you're going to play Hitler," I thought it was the real start of my career.

GREENBERG: Don't worry, Bronski. They can't keep real talent down.

BRONSKI: And the day will come when you'll play Shylock.

GREENBERG: The Rialto scene! Shakespeare must've thought of me when he wrote it. It's me! "Have I not eyes . . . . have I not hands . . . organs, senses, dimensions, passions? Fed with the same food, hurt with the same weapons, subject to the same diseases? If you prick us, do we not bleed? If you tickle us, do we not laugh? If you poison us, do we not die?"

BRONSKI: It moved me to tears!

GREENBERG: Instead, I have to carry a spear.

BRONSKI: That's all we do, carry a spear. Carry a spear in the first act. Carry a spear in the second act . . .

GREENBERG: Carry Ravitch off in the last act.

BRONSKI: How I'd like to drop that ham right in the center of the stage.

GREENBERG: It'd get a terrific laugh.

There are several strange things about this scene, not the least of which is that a Jew would think of himself as just like Shylock, that "gentile fantasy" of a Jew.[26] Of course, we know that Greenberg is a Jew . . . but what kind of Jew? He has been given the name of a German (not Polish) Jew. He keeps kosher. He is always looking for the cheap laugh. He is never directly referred to as a Jew (the screenplay rewrites Shakespeare to omit the word), but we are given all the signifiers.[27] When Greenberg cries, "It's me!" the camera shifts from a two-shot to a medium close-up; Greenberg is a "Jew": a sincere and believable gentile stereotype of what a Jew should be.[28]

While one could argue that Lubitsch needed to convey to a white American audience that Greenberg's Jewishness was important, it was not important enough to be referred to directly or to be made a significant component of the plot (as it would in Mel Brooks's 1983 remake of the same title). In wartime America, the distance between being Jewish and being white remained great enough that identification with a Jewish character was not a given. If, in the logic of the film, *Hamlet* (and Shakespeare) represents the old "European" social order, then Greenberg could carry a spear and aspire to be Shylock. In the new social order of *Gestapo,* he can play the "Jew" who is the same as Shylock, offering reactions to Bronski's Hitler. Yet, just as an actual Jew in occupied Poland would simply not have been present in the Polski Theater, the existence of a believable (i.e., nonperformative) Jew in *To Be Or Not To Be* seems equally impossible.

Like Bronski, the actual Hitler does not stick to Dobosh's script. The spear carriers upset the social and moral order, dumping the king in the middle of the stage: the Nazis invade Poland without a declaration of war. They bomb Warsaw during a performance of *Hamlet,* and the cast finds itself huddled in the basement of the theater:

TURA: Well, anyway, we don't have to worry about the Nazi play anymore.

RAVITCH: No. The Nazis themselves are putting on a show now, and a much bigger one.

MARIA: There was no censor to stop them.

Following the bombing and subsequent invasion, the opening montage repeats. This time, however, the narrator is initially silent and the signs are broken and buried in the rubble. This rupture between the spoken and the visually signified is one of the central metaphors of the film. In a dishonored world in which Nazis impersonate patriots and patriots impersonate Nazis, the only thing that threatens to reveal the truth is the voice. Through slips of the tongue, characters reveal the discontinuities between their performances and their identities. The voice of the omniscient narrator is silent as the broken names pass. The landscape is littered with shattered meanings; a tragic vaudevillian farce has replaced a nobler, unified drama. As the troops arrive, the narrator delivers an elegy for Poland. The passing of seasons is marked by a second montage of Nazi edicts pasted on Polish walls. Bronski and Greenberg reappear, shoveling snow outside the Polski Theater. Greenberg sadly repeats his abridged Shylock speech while staring out at the rubble, the "we" in his monologue referring now to all Poles.

A comedy about the Nazi invasion of Poland—even one with an implicitly Jewish character—disconcertingly contains no overt reference to Nazi racism, the sealing of the Warsaw ghetto, or the deportation of Jews to concentration camps. The Gestapo notices contain no explicit references to Jews and a voice-over decries the Nazi victimization of a generic "Polish people." False notes, however, sound in this voice-over, which ignores Polish collaboration and Nazi atrocities, and form a question around the erasure of race in the film. That a Jewish director, working in an industry founded largely by Jewish immigrants, would make a film about the German invasion of Poland with no references to the plight of European Jews speaks to the delicate position of Jews in the United States and Hollywood during this period.[29] Lubitsch's silence seems sadly profound—at least in retrospect—as evidence of an American political culture in which many Jews in Hollywood hesitated to admit to Jewishness, be it secular, religious, ethnic, or cultural.

A sympathetic reading of this section of the film suggests that the Nazi invasion and its new regime of whiteness had created a condition in which all Poles were subject to the same prejudice and hatred that historically had been directed toward Jews. This, of course, was not the historical reality: some Poles had persecuted Jews prior to the Nazi invasion, and many continued the persecution by aiding the Germans in shipping Jews to concentration camps. Yet this sort of historical accuracy neither fit the trope of wartime propaganda, which To Be Or Not To Be very much was, nor accorded with Hollywood's symbolic Europe, in which social distinction was supposed to be natural, not prejudicial.

Lubitsch did not simply subscribe to these conventions, however. He used comedy to undermine the racialized social hierarchy advocated by the Nazis. Unlike the usual movie Nazis, who are portrayed as cold, ruthless automatons, Lubitsch's Nazis are buffoons. They do gags straight out of the play *Gestapo* and engage in the kind of repetitive shtick that was more at home on the vaudeville stage than in the "cultured" comedies for which Lubitsch was known. The head of the Gestapo, Colonel Erhard (Sigfried Rumann) and his assistant, Schultz, whom the colonel blames for his own mistakes, are clowns pretending to be conquerors.[30] No wonder their ruse is easily punctured by this troupe's better (though by no means good) actors.

If the Gestapo are clowns, then who is the villain in the film? Ironically, it is the Polish professor, Siletsky. Perhaps Polish collaboration with the Nazis could not be mentioned—just as the fate of Jews in Poland could not be discussed directly—but the film could present it through this one character, just as it used Greenberg to point to Polish Jews. It is not hard to read in Siletsky a condemnation not only of Polish collaboration, but also of American so-called patriots such as Charles Lindbergh, Henry Ford, and Father Coughlin. Under the guise of patriotism, they did more to foster anti-Semitism in the United States than any of the short-lived and undersubscribed overtly fascist movements that came and went in this country in the 1930s.[31] Nor is it difficult to read in the film an uneasiness with participating in a system of passing that existed to accommodate American anti-Semitism and that, by 1942, was becoming increasingly untenable. Choosing an identity for self-interested purposes was becoming harder to justify as the line between a polite fiction and an unpleasant reality was breaking down:

SILETSKY: Mrs. Tura. You're an actress, aren't you? And naturally in the theater it's important that you choose the right part . . . but in real life it's even more important that you choose the right side . . . .

MARIA: The right side? What is the right side?

SILETSKY: The winning side.

Siletsky asks Mrs. Tura to spy for the Nazis. In payment, he will return to the Turas their fashionable apartment and supply them with the luxuries necessary to entertain in style. All she must do is inform on her fellow Poles.

MARIA: Oh, naturally, it's all very attractive and tempting. But what are we going to do about my conscience?

SILETSKY: Well, we've simply got to convince you that you're going to serve the right cause. I wonder if you really know what Nazism stands for?

MARIA: I have a slight idea.

SILETSKY: In the final analysis, all we're trying to do is create a happy world.

MARIA: And people who don't want to be happy have no place in this happy world. Well, that makes sense.

SILETSKY: We're not brutal. We're not monsters. Now tell me, do I look like a monster?

MARIA: Of course not, professor.

SILETSKY: We're just like other people. We like to sing. We like to dance. We admire beautiful women. We're human . . . and sometimes very human.

Siletsky suggests to Maria Tura that becoming a collaborator is really just a matter of acting the part, of entertaining: all the props will be provided. All she must do is become a Nazi and then pass as a good Pole. She need only employ her skills from the theater: learning lines, using sets, getting into another character's mind. She suggests this would be hard for her because she cannot so easily abandon her conscience. She is an actress from the European art world, trained to embrace the soul of the theater, not just its techniques. She expects the theater, and life, to distinguish clearly between humans—like herself—and monsters like Siletsky.

This is Siletsky's fantasy of her: an actress so in touch with her emotions that they overwhelm her intellectual faculties. With one kiss, she seems converted. The situation is ironic: wearing the evening dress that was so inappropriate for the concentration camp scene, Maria feigns the loss of a virtue she actually retains in order to convince Siletsky that her conversion is sincere. In grotesque parody, Siletsky mouths Shylock's sentiments to convince Maria that to be a Nazi is to be as human as the next person, perhaps more so. He is so enamored with the apparent authenticity of his own performance that he manages only to deceive himself: he fails to notice that he has been wooing a character, not the actress. It is appropriate, then, that Siletsky soon meets his end in the Polski Theater, hiding from his pursuers onstage behind the curtain. Shots are heard and the curtain rises. He falls bleeding on the set of *Hamlet*, recapitulating the death of the play's most prominent collaborator, Polonius, whose hollow, ironic motto is, "To thine own self be true."

From this point on, taking on another persona (passing) and facing the deadly potential of exposure become the central themes in the film. Members of the company pretend to be the professor and Gestapo officers in an attempt to subvert their enemies and win their freedom. Believable acting leaves the stage and is practiced (with varying degrees of success) on the street. Importantly, no matter how awkwardly the actors seem to us to play their parts, their ruses finally succeed in disorganizing the enemy. Is it that the buffoonish Nazis mistake performativity for a harmony between interior and exterior? Or, does the players' shabby masquerade of class pass in a Europe descending into a grotesque parody of civilization?

This representation of the theater troubles Hollywood's treatment of European culture as a generic form of "classiness." In Lubitsch's world, some culture is indeed classy because it contains a moral purpose, but other culture simply deploys markers of status to justify prejudice and racial hierarchy. In the final sequence of the film, he tries to reverse this by using prejudice and racial hierarchy to bring down self-interested power and to save the company of the Polski Theater. The actors learn that Hitler is scheduled to come to Warsaw and attend a play in his honor. They need a diversion: the Gestapo is closing in on them. Dressed as Nazis, they plan to sneak Bronski-as-Hitler into the theater. Greenberg-as-Jew will attempt to assassinate him. They will rush the "führer" to safety, taking the assassin with them and borrowing Hitler's personal car and plane in the process: [32]

DOBOSH: If we can arrange that Greenberg suddenly pops up among all those Nazis . . .

GREENBERG: It'll get a terrific laugh.

DOBOSH: No it won't. Greenberg, you've always wanted to play an important part.

GREENBERG: What do you want me to do, Mr. Dobosh?

DOBOSH: If you don't play it right, we're all lost. If you do play it right, I still can't guarantee anything.

For their finale, Greenberg is to be allowed, at long last, to play the "Jew" openly. Even though he has passed as white, as a generic Pole, for most of the film, now he must stage a specifically Jewish assault on Bronski's Hitler. Dobosh fears, though, that Greenberg's irresistible impulse to play for the cheap laugh will undermine the authenticity of their performance. If Greenberg is to be recognizable to the Nazis as a Jew, he must play Shylock; if he is believable in the role, he will make the other players convincing as Nazis. If he plays it wrong and lapses into the other register of "Jewishness," that of the comic, he will surely give them away as impostors. Yet even if Greenberg plays it right, there is no guarantee: the Nazis must suspend their disbelief. Witnessing Greenberg's mastery of the "Jew," and the faux Nazis' mastery over that Jew, the Nazis accept the performance, and, after a couple more instances of Gestapo shtick, the company arrives safely in England.

Felix Bressart's Greenberg-as-Shylock offers the most sincerely dramatic moment in the film. The scene seems to disprove Goldwyn's dictum that Jews could not play Jews in Hollywood. Or does it? The Jew that Greenberg plays to pass his friends into absolute whiteness is a fiction, a part written by a gentile for gentile actors. The camera holds Greenberg in a medium shot, the edges filled with Nazi soldiers. As he proclaims his humanity, it cuts to a close-up. Bressart's tightly framed face expresses deep passion and conviction, the camera eliminates his body (the comedian's tool), and Greenberg's compulsive need to play for the laugh is gone. Greenberg, it seems, has conquered the performative stereotype of the ethnic comic, only to replace it with a more aesthetically acceptable one. Now he is the Jew playing the gentile playing the Jew, and at last he is recognizable. The film is neither a clear condemnation of anti-Semitism nor a critique of passing. If anything, it expresses a profound discomfort with the destabilization of a symbolic Europe and a system of aesthetics that were supposed to stand for the noblest expression of the human condition.[33] If Greenberg was a leading character forced into the role of Shylock for the sake of furthering the system of passing, the film might be read as a critique. Hollywood, however, was not in a position to allow that possibility. As Rogin points out, Hollywood's limited palette of Jewish characters in the 1930s and 1940s virtually erased the Jew as a sympathetic, realistic character and left little room for anything but the stereotype, usually the comic.[34] The decision of the majority of Jewish producers in Hollywood to assume a mantle of generic American patriotism over an overt appeal for rescue further limited the discursive confines in which the film was made.[35]

What remains is ambivalence. The film met with mixed reviews, the most common complaint being that it was wrong to make a comedy about war-torn Poland. One reviewer went so far as to insinuate collaboration, linking Lubitsch's German birth with his comic treatment of the bombing of Warsaw.[36] Comments such as this led Robert Stack to point out that Lubitsch was in fact Jewish and from "the Old Country."[37] Many of the reviews went further, complaining that Lubitsch had inappropriately mixed reality and fantasy.[38] Defending himself in March 1942, Lubitsch wrote, "I was tired of the two established, recognized recipes. . . . Drama with comic relief and comedy with dramatic relief. I had made up my mind to make a picture with no attempt to relieve anybody from anything at any time."[39] While it is understandable that critics would have been disturbed by a comic presentation of a war still being waged, it also seems clear that Lubitsch was being disciplined for violating the classical conventions for which he had been imported and for

Figure 1.2. *To Be Or Not to Be* (1942).

calling attention to their subversion at the moment when their purported point of origin was collapsing. By 1942, being "European" no longer meant passing into a whiteness marked by class and culture. Rather, it meant association with a world in which whiteness had become racialized, visible, and not altogether classy.

CONCLUSION

It would be a mistake to argue that *A Night at the Opera* and *To Be Or Not To Be* exist on the same continuum of changes in the meaning of race and ethnicity in the 1930s and 1940s. Rather, the films represent two distinct operations, both important to the production of whiteness. *A Night at the Opera* represents the fading of a celebratory, performative ethnicity that operated, at least in part, outside of the narrative of assimilation. It had its roots in a dying vaudeville tradition dedicated to entertainment that, at best, paid lip service to progressive notions of moral and social edification and advancement.[40] *To Be Or Not To Be* points to the collapse of the category of "European" as a vehicle for a sort of instant assimilation into whiteness that bypassed the intermediary steps of immigration, ethnicization, and Americanization. Arising from an

American fantasy of Europe as the fountainhead of polite society and high culture, the association of "European" with "class" proved, for a time, a means of legitimation, both for imported artists and for the industry that imported them. When World War II made the contradictions inherent in that model apparent, it began to lose its intended effect.

What the two films do share, however, is the increasing difficulty, during the early years of sound film, of representing Jews on screen. While *The Jazz Singer* (1927) may seem a glaring exception to Goldwyn's rule, it negotiates Jewishness by an appeal to whiteness through blackface and by a plot that foregrounds the main character's eventual (if painful) assimilation.[41] Even though off screen Groucho could crack wise about being Jewish, and the intellectual press could make much of the Jewish roots of the brothers' humor, on screen they were not overtly Jews.[42] If *A Night at the Opera* offers the spectacle of an uneasy accommodation between an unrecuperated ethnicity and an assimilationist love story, it does so from a safe distance. World War II would seem to settle the question of whether Jews were a different race from whites, or merely ethnic, and would pave the way for overtly Jewish filmmakers such as Woody Allen and Mel Brooks. In 1935, however, the safest course of action was simply to avoid the issue altogether—or at least to approach it obliquely via acceptable expressions of ethnicity.

Given the anti-Semitism Hollywood faced in the 1930s and early 1940s—both covert and overt, and often virulent—the inclusion of a "Jew" in the cast of *To Be Or Not To Be* may seem bold. Yet Lubitsch carefully avoided any explicit mention of Greenberg's Jewishness (even to the point of rewriting Shakespeare), and the character conformed to the standard stereotype of the Jewish male as effeminate and ineffectual.[43] The movie's title, *To Be Or Not To Be*, sums up the dilemma faced by Hollywood producers in general and by Lubitsch in particular. It is a question that the inquirer does not necessarily get to answer, one that is echoed in Fiorello's dilemma on the reviewing stand. If he tells his audience that he doesn't exist, will they believe him? If they don't believe him, will they lynch him? His survival depends upon his (mis)recognition by others. In spite of their enormous economic and representational power, the position of many Jews in Hollywood depended upon a tacit agreement under which they could pass as white as long as they regulated the boundary between Jewishness and whiteness. The exposure of Nazi atrocities would play a part in beginning to change that, but not for several years. In the meantime, they participated in and helped reproduce a racial system in which whiteness and ethnicity were separated into two systems joined by assimilation and regulated by markers of class. Ironically, by excluding Jews from this representational system, they provided grist for anti-Semitic demagogues who claimed that it was the "unassimilated" in Hollywood who were undermining America.[44] Perhaps Groucho put the problem most succinctly in his paraphrase of Hamlet's soliloquy: "I don't want to belong to any club that will accept me as a member."[45]

NOTES

1. Michael Rogin, *Blackface, White Noise: Jewish Immigrants in the Hollywood Melting Pot* (Berkeley: University of California Press, 1996), 12.

2. American film and theater share a common ancestor in melodrama, which also favored a focus on emotion. The difference, however, between melodrama and psychorealism was in their discursive production. Briefly put, melodrama (and silent film) was meant to express and inspire strong, unambiguous emotions, while psychorealism was meant to demonstrate the emotional and psychological reality of the character's experience.

3. Cf. Michael Omi and Howard Winant, *Racial Formation in the United States: From the 1960s to the 1990s,* 2d ed. (New York: Routledge, 1994).

4. Cf. Karen B. Sacks, "How Did Jews Become White Folks?" in *Race,* ed. Steven Gregory and Roger Sanjek (New Brunswick: Rutgers University Press, 1994), 80.

5. "Public opinion data from 1938 . . . reveal that 31 percent of a national sample answered 'less' to the question, 'Do you think Jews in the United States are as patriotic, more patriotic or less patriotic than other citizens'; 41 percent believed that 'the Jews have too much power in the United States.' In 1940, another survey found 17 percent of a sample naming Jews as that 'nationality, religion, or racial group' which is a 'menace to America'; to the same question, 6 percent named Catholics; 2 percent, blacks; 14 percent, Germans; 6 percent, Japanese." From David H. Bennett, *The Party of Fear* (Chapel Hill: University of North Carolina Press, 1988), 265.

6. Henry L. Feingold, *The Politics of Rescue: The Roosevelt Administration and the Holocaust, 1938–1945* (New Brunswick: Rutgers University Press, 1970).

7. Rogin, *Blackface, White Noise,* 88–89; Bennett, *The Party of Fear,* 245–60.

8. Rogin, *Blackface, White Noise.* See, for instance, *Time Magazine,* 1938.

9. Bennett, *The Party of Fear;* J. Hoberman, *Bridge of Light: Yiddish Film Between Two Worlds* (New York: Schocken Books, 1991), 322.

10. Comedies and dramas of the late 1920s and early 1930s were more likely to have explicitly Jewish characters, particularly those featuring Al Jolson and Eddie Cantor or assimilation tales such as Frank Capra's *The Younger Generation* (1929). By the mid-1930s, these strongly Jewish characterizations, along with other strong ethnic portrayals, were disappearing. Drawing on records of the Motion Picture Producers and Distributors of America (MPPDA), Ruth Vasey has argued convincingly that the evacuation of strong ethnic characters from Hollywood fare had to do with fears of undermining sales in new foreign markets. (See "Foreign Parts," in *Movie*

Censorship and American Culture, ed. Francis Couvares (Washington, DC: Smithsonian, 1996). In terms of explicitly Jewish characters, however, such an explanation does not obtain.

11. These films represented an effort on the part of Hollywood producers to fend off criticisms of the industry as undermining middle-class values. See Richard Maltby, "The Production Code and the Hays Office," in *Grand Design: Hollywood as a Modern Business Enterprise,* ed. Tino Balio (Berkeley: University of California Press, 1995). Examples of films in this category are *Anna Karenina* (Clarence Brown, dir., 1935), *Romeo and Juliet* (George Cukor, dir., 1936), and *The Charge of the Light Brigade* (Michael Curtiz, dir., 1936).

12. Cf. Henry Jenkins, *What Made Pistachio Nuts? Early Sound Comedy and the Vaudeville Aesthetic* (New York: Columbia University Press, 1992).

13. It should be noted, however, that in general the Marx Brothers did little to invert the hierarchy when it came to black stereotypes. The portrayals of blacks in the brothers' movies seem to do little more than confirm the most offensive generalizations about blacks of the time. These racial stereotypes foreclose the possibility of assimilation for blacks.

14. By necessity, we will focus on the particulars of each film and the circumstances surrounding its production and reception. In doing so, we are neither trying to produce definitive readings nor ignoring the possibility of the production of alternative meanings in their reception. Rather, we hope to provide one template for considering audience reception of the films. See, for example, note 26.

15. Cf. Jenkins, *What Made Pistachio Nuts?*

16. Robert W. Snyder, *The Voice of the City: Vaudeville and Popular Culture in New York* (New York: Oxford University Press, 1989); Jenkins, *What Made Pistachio Nuts?* 59–72.

17. Rogin, *Blackface, White Noise,* and Eric Lott, *Love and Theft: Blackface Minstrelsy and the American Working Class* (New York: Oxford University Press, 1993). Rogin and Lott have written in detail about the use of blackface as a means of producing and negotiating racial and class difference. Less has been written about the performance of ethnicity and its role in negotiating inclusion in whiteness. See, for instance, Harley Erdman, *Staging the Jew: The Performance of an American Ethnicity* (New Brunswick: Rutgers University Press, 1997).

18. Jenkins, *What Made Pistachio Nuts?* 10.

19. Ibid.; see, for instance, Paul D. Zimmerman and Burt Goldblatt, *The Marx Brothers at the Movies* (New York: Putnam's, 1968), or Allen Eyles, *The Marx Brothers: Their World of Comedy* (London: A Zwemmer Ltd., 1966).

20. Importantly, the vaudeville traditions from which the Marx Brothers emerged engaged ethnic stereotypes that were often imposed from without and associated with quasi-racial conceptions of natural hierarchy. The immigrant communities that attended vaudeville, lived in, through, and around these stereotypes and the assumptions of difference they both carried and masked. Even "white" immigrants such as the Irish were seen as racial Others to WASP elites, so race was an unspoken partner of ethnicity for many immigrant groups, not just Jews. No won-

der, then, in vaudeville and in the early metropolitan film production that coexisted with it, assimilation was presented and received as a complex matter, involving both the celebration of class advancement and the mourning of cultural loss and personal identity (Rogin, *Blackface, White Noise*; Hoberman, *Bridge of Light*). In this world of ethnicity, no wonder then that conceptions of race were close enough to the surface to be a continual worry to immigrant Jews in Hollywood (and elsewhere), who were seeking acceptance and a way to make a living in the United States.

21. The most obvious exception to this silence was Charlie Chaplin's *The Great Dictator* (1940), which opened to very mixed reviews (some quite hostile) and was poorly received by the American public. It is worth noting that while Chaplin claimed not to be Jewish, the Nazis vilified him as such.

22. Bennett, *The Party of Fear*; Maltby, "The Production Code."

23. Robert Sklar, *Movie-Made America: A Cultural History of American Movies* (New York: Random House, 1975).

24. Rogin, *Blackface, White Noise*; Hoberman, *Bridge of Light*.

25. Quoted in Neal Gabler, *An Empire of Their Own: How the Jews Invented Hollywood* (New York: Crown Publishers, 1988), 345.

26. Erdman, *Staging the Jew*, 20.

27. The Shakespeare reads, "I am a Jew. Hath a Jew not eyes? Hath not a Jew hands, organs, dimensions, senses, affections, passions?" (Shakespeare 1976).

28. Greenberg is the one character clearly meant to signify "Jew." This is not to say that audience members could not read other characters or actors as Jewish. There is, of course, a long-standing tradition among different audience groups of identifying Jewish actors who are passing as other than Jewish—such as Jack Benny in this film. This distinction, while important and worthy of further consideration, is outside the scope of this paper.

29. Gabler, *An Empire*, 2.

30. These two characters were later to reappear in the bizarre television sitcom, *Hogan's Heroes*.

31. Cf. Bennett, *The Party of Fear.*

32. Since Nazis are only male, Maria Tura is required to sit out this final performance and gets picked up at her home afterward.

33. "There's a revolution on in the world. Is laughter to depart? Is gracious and graceful living, wit and the jocund interplay, the amusing warfare of man and woman all to vanish? Must I weep for the world that was and not be permitted to re-create it? Devoutly I hope not. For then I should not desire to make more films. I should be content to die." Ernst Lubitsch, 1943. Quoted in Scott Eyman, *Ernst Lubitsch: Laughter in Paradise* (New York: Simon & Schuster, 1993), 289.

34. Rogin, *Blackface, White Noise*, 154–55.

35. Gabler, *An Empire*.

36. Herman G. Weinberg, *The Lubitsch Touch: A Critical Study* (New York: Dover, 1968), 246.

37. Eyman, *Ernst Lubitsch*, 301.

38. Ibid., 301.

39. Quoted in ibid., 291–92.

40. Robert W. Snyder, *The Voice of the City: Vaudeville and Popular Culture in New York* (New York: Oxford University Press, 1989).

41. Cf. Rogin, *Blackface, White Noise.*

42. Cf. Anthony Lewis, "The Jew in Standup Comedy," in *From Hester Street to Hollywood: The Jewish-American Stage and Screen,* ed. Sarah Blacher Cohen (Bloomington: University of Indiana Press, 1983), 61; Joe Adamson, *Groucho, Harpo, Chico, and Sometimes Zeppo: A History of the Marx Brothers and a Satire on the Rest of the World* (New York: Simon and Schuster, 1973, 76; "As Others See Us: The Marx Brothers Abroad," *The Living Age* 343 (December 1932): 371–72; Louis Chavance, "The Four Marx Brothers: As Seen by a Frenchman," *The Canadian Forum* 13 (February 1933): 149.

43. Cf. Erdman, *Staging the Jew.* Note, for instance, that when Greenberg begins his assault on Hitler, he does so by emerging from the ladies' room.

44. Cf. Gabler, *An Empire*; Bennett, *The Party of Fear*; Maltby, "The Production Code."

45. Groucho Marx, *Groucho and Me* (New York: Random House, 1959).

2

FROM SECOND STRING TO SOLO STAR

Classic Hollywood and the Black Athlete

Aaron Baker

With the exception of a few race films, African Americans appear only as minor characters (if at all) in feature-length movies about sports from the coming of sound through the beginning of the civil rights movement. A cycle of Hollywood films in the early 1950s that featured Black athletes followed closely on the opening of previously all-White professional sports to African-Americans just after World War II. These, however, were stories of self-reliance and White paternalism that attempted to de-emphasize social determinants of racial identity. In the almost half century since that time, Blacks' participation in Hollywood movies has increased slowly and unevenly and, like their involvement in professional sports, has been restricted to a limited range of performative and behind-the-scenes roles.

During the Classical period, most of the infrequent appearances by Black characters were in films about prize fighting, the least exclusionary professional sport for reasons of race.[1] Similar to the representation of women in Classic Hollywood films, Blacks function in these narratives of White, male self-definition through athletic competition as supportive, but self-negating, helpers. Occasionally, Blacks (along with Mexican or Chicano characters) act as opponents, obstacles that the protagonists must overcome in order to realize their heroic identities. The primary focus on individual White protagonists in most Classic sports films fits with what Robert Ray calls Hollywood's tendency to affirm "American beliefs in individualism, ad hoc solutions, and the impermanence of all political problems."[2] In the 1940s and 1950s, this individualist emphasis manifested itself in the large number of biography films about athletes or coaches: Hollywood released almost thirty sports biopics in those two decades. George Custen points out that the inclination of biopics toward the stories of a few, mostly White, men is an important part of a Hollywood version of history "limited in historical setting"—through its overvaluation of the actions of individuals—and therefore "ideologically self-serving" for those who run the movie business.[3] Biopics serve the promotion of self-reliance in Classic Hollywood narrative structured around the desires and actions of one or a few main characters, as well as demonstrate the symbiosis between professional sports and movies. Regardless of any gestures made to teamwork, fair play, and fan communities throughout their history in the United States, commercial sports have given the greatest recognition to individual star performance.

To better illustrate how Black characters in Classic sports films support the construction of self-reliant White masculinity, let me briefly describe the importance of individual performance in media representations of American professional sports.[4] In doing so, I will make certain generalizations about professional sports and the media (including the film industry) that may seem dehistoricized. I would argue, however, that since their inception in the last half of the nineteenth century, professional sports have frequently been portrayed as disproving the idea of a socially constructed identity, whether defined by race, ethnicity, class, sexuality, gender, or any other category. Borrowing from the work of the Annales historians, Stephen Hardy has referred to such diachronic meanings as the "long residuals" of sports culture that have "crossed time and context."[5] Like Hollywood movies, professional sports fit squarely within the traditional American mythology that champions the promise of unified identity through individual achievement. The extensive discourse on star athletes in various media (including the Hollywood biopic) has been the principle voice of this mythology in American professional sports. Such belief in agency supports the utopian promise of sports: once the contest begins, success depends primarily on preparation, determination, and effort.

Movies and other media texts about sports at times digress with endorsements of teamwork and fair play to allay audience fears about the potential for athletic competition to devolve into social Darwinism. Yet, ultimately, the individualist mythology has a stronger appeal as utopian narrative, and it certainly best represents the interests of those who own teams, newspapers, networks, movie studios, and the other corporations that use sports to do business. Even when teamwork figures prominently in narratives about athletics, it does not reduce the value placed on individual performance. Rather, like the bourgeois nuclear family, the team operates as a social structure to foster the development of self-reliant individuals; self-effacing play therefore subordinates itself to the more recognized actions of the star.

Borrowing from Richard Dyer's analysis of entertainment and utopia, I would claim that the idealized identity of professional athletes responds to the real needs of fans for greater economic means, for a sense of personal accomplishment, and for recognition from others.[6] What films about sports stars lack are specific strategies for how to achieve success in these areas. Instead, they offer spectacular celebrations of the achievements of stars, offset by a realist aesthetic of reportage disavowing that the whole performance is staged for our consumption and reassurance. This realist style figures most prominently in action scenes involving footage of actual contests or set in stadia filled with crowds of extras and employing authentic uniforms, equipment, and often real athletes. Frequently narrated by announcers in the style of television or radio coverage, these cinematic contests feature a continuity editing style that makes the sequence of shots seem motivated by the logic of the events rather than by choices made by the filmmakers. Heightened realism in scenes in which the star competes is especially important in validating an ideology of agency that assumes that individual performance counts most in making the athlete what he is.

As Dyer points out, the conservatism of utopian entertainment comes from how it offers promises of a better life if we just follow the rules and try harder. In other words, not only does such entertainment avoid specific suggestions for changing the current social reality, it also links the achievement of happiness to adherence to the status quo. Yet, Dyer adds that this utopian response only works if one ignores—as entertainment usually does—how social identities such as race, class, gender, and sexuality complicate self-definition. On the contrary, the acknowledgment of social forces in the constitution of identity makes evident that the opportunity, abundance, and happiness in utopian narratives are not there for everyone to the same degree. Even when they acknowledge the disadvantage of racism, sexism, or class difference (homophobia is still widely ignored), sports movies generally hold up individual performance as the best way to deny the influence of these obstacles.

However, the more one regards sports movies as not just utopian but also historical—texts about the multiple determinants of the past and/or the contexts in which they are made and seen—the more these films illustrate what

Mikhail Bakhtin called "dialogism," or the combination of different discursive positions within one text. In applying Bakhtin's ideas about literature to ethnic and racial representation in film, Robert Stam describes as his goal to "call attention to the voices at play in a text, not only those heard in aural 'close-up,' but also those voices distorted or drowned out by the text."[7] Using this idea of textuality to approach sports films, one can see how the protagonists overcome external obstacles to succeed. One can also see, however, how the protagonists are formed in part by social forces—whether they work to define race or other types of identity—and by the choices those forces offer.

Two biopics, *Knute Rockne-All American* (1940) and *Gentleman Jim* (1942), offer good examples of how Classic Hollywood sports narratives position Blacks to help define ostensibly self-reliant, White male protagonists, yet are in fact dialogical on the issue of race. With World War II already underway in Europe, *Knute Rockne-All American* endorsed U.S. involvement through its emphasis on the democratic freedoms and opportunities in American society that made a war worth fighting. As the film opens, we are told that Lars Rockne brought his son, Knute, and the rest of his family from Norway "following the new road of equality and opportunity which led to America." The film unintentionally shows, however, that such opportunity did not extend to African Americans. Despite only very brief appearances, the two Black characters in *Knute Rockne-All American* qualify its affirmation of the American Dream. In an early scene when young Knute plays football for the first time in a sandlot game, an African-American boy, running the ball for the other team, knocks him flat. The only other African-American character shows up much later in the film when Rockne, now the famous football coach at Notre Dame, returns to South Bend on the train after a tough loss. A Black porter stops at the door of his compartment and asks Rockne if he would like his suit brushed off before they arrive. The presence of the porter ironically recalls the boy who had run over little Rock in the football legend's first experience with the game that was to make him famous. The difference in social position between Rockne and the porter suggests why the experience of the African-American boy appears nowhere but in the one early scene. The promise of equal opportunity, which both Blacks and Whites were called upon to defend in the war, extended to some parts of American society and not to others.

Gentleman Jim is also dialogic in how it shows 1890s boxer Jim Corbett fighting his way to the heavyweight title, yet at the same time negotiating between different conceptions of masculinity, social class, and race. Through his "scientific" boxing, mannered charm, and stylish appearance, Corbett renounces the working-class masculinity of his Irish-American family to define a more "respectable" type of prizefighter. His development of this "gentlemanly" style at an elite men's club necessitates his acceptance of a bourgeois notion of masculinity that invalidates the ethnic, working-class identities of his father and two brothers as well as that of the man from whom Corbett takes the heavyweight belt, John Sullivan. Corbett's opportunity for self-advancement also requires that he avoid endangering the dominant discourse of White supremacy that, as Gail Bederman shows, intersected in the arena of prizefighting with constructions of masculinity in turn-of-the-century American society.[8] *Gentleman Jim* therefore refers indirectly to, but never mentions by name, the Black fighter Peter Jackson, a top heavyweight of the period whom Sullivan, and Corbett once he became champion, refused to meet in the ring.[9]

In fact, Corbett's separation from his immigrant family and his Black colleagues were both gestures typical of the historical transformation that Noel Ignatiev describes in his book, *How the Irish Became White*:

> The Irish who emigrated to America in the eighteenth and nineteenth centuries . . . commonly found themselves thrown together with free Negroes. Irish- and Afro-Americans fought each other and the police, socialized and occasionally inter-married, and developed a common culture of the lowly. . . . In antebellum America it was speculated that if racial amalgamation was ever to take place, it would begin between those two groups. As we know, things turned out otherwise . . . the result of choices made, by the Irish and others, from among available alternatives. To enter the white race was a strategy to secure an advantage in a competitive society.[10]

Gentleman Jim, through its rejection of Irish origins and erasure of Blacks from the fight game, and *Knute Rockne*, by its use of African Americans in traditional supportive roles, both demonstrate a primary concern with White masculinity.

Thomas Cripps explains the restriction of Blacks in Classic Hollywood films to roles as subordinate helpers, obstacles to be overcome, or their complete exclusion, as a consequence of the studio system's practice (monitored by the Production Code Administration) of avoiding controversy on issues of race. This evasion fit into Hollywood's tendency to avoid choice on matters of ideological debate so as not to risk offending its desired audience.[11] According to Cripps, the result was that "antebellum Hollywood's aversion to the racial contradictions in American life reduced African Americans to absent, alibied for, dependent victims of marketing strategies aimed at a profitable universality"; this conception of a mass audience was based on the assumption that the vast majority of viewers wanted reaffirmation of the racial status quo—or avoidance of racial difference entirely.[12] In the case of Hollywood sports films, such sidestepping of the contradiction between Black disadvantage and the promise of American opportunity translated into narratives about the achievements of White, male athletes, occasionally aided by, or at the expense of, African-American characters. Until the message movies of the early 1950s, these sports films entirely avoided any portrayal of the denial of competitive opportunities to African Americans, even if such a story was as firmly grounded in historical events as those about the success of White athletes.

Though generally utopian, Classic Hollywood sports films at times emphasize race, but they do so in order to distract attention from other issues of social identity. In two boxing films, *The Champ* (1931) and *Winner Take All* (1932), racial difference (here involving Latinos as well as Blacks) is used to de-emphasize the class antagonism of Depression America. During the 1930s, unemployment rates of 25 percent and higher for young people in the United States prompted an especially large number of working-class young men to try prizefighting.[13] Around eight thousand boxers entered the ring as professionals during that decade, although only a small percentage achieved title contender status.[14] The popularity of boxing as one of the few avenues to the American Dream in those lean years may explain the large number of Hollywood films about prizefighting made during the 1930s. Such Depression-era films depict boxing as a means of advancement for disenfranchised urban youth and, at the same time, use the sport as a metaphor for the economic hard times.

Warner Bros. dominated the Depression cycle of boxing films, presenting them as aesthetically spare, "socially conscious" melodramas (*Winner Take All*, 1932), the hallmark genre of the studio in the 1930s. *The Champ* (1931), however, was made at Warner Bros.'s political and stylistic opposite, MGM. Unlike most Depression-era boxing films, it gives unqualified endorsement to individual self reliance, essentially discounting any notion that social or economic forces might put limits on the rise to success.

The Champ stars Wallace Beery as Andy, a punch-drunk ex-heavyweight champion who lives a roller-coaster life in Tijuana with his young son, Dink. The ex-champ enjoys occasional hot streaks at the craps table, but much of the time he is drunk and broke. Dink's mother, Linda, and her wealthy second husband, Tony, offer to take custody of the boy so as to give him a more stable home life and a chance to go to school. Dink, though, prefers to stay with his father, who loves the boy intensely. Anxious to provide better for Dink, Andy steers clear of the casinos and bars long enough to get a fight with the heavyweight champ of Mexico. For most of the bout, the Mexican fighter punishes the out-of-shape American, but Andy somehow knocks out his opponent with a desperation punch. Despite his victory, the strain and punishment of the fight prove too much for Andy, and he dies of a heart attack in his dressing room. The film ends with Dink crying uncontrollably at the loss of his father and running into his mother's arms.

As I mentioned earlier, Hollywood films have often avoided taking sides in ideological debates, preferring instead to assert that an unlimited potential for new achievement and wealth in America can overcome contradictions or conflict. *The Champ* avoids the need for choice by displacing the class conflict between Andy and Tony into frontier imagery of conquest, as presented in the defeat of the Mexican champion.[15] Richard Slotkin describes how, as early as the 1870s, the newly developed mass-circulation press sought to effect a similar displacement of the class warfare that had erupted between workers and the corporate order. Even if the cause of the workers represented the "values of self-government and freedom of opportunity" on which the country was founded (and for which the Civil War had ostensibly been fought), demands for political and economic self-determination threatened to undermine the profits of big business.[16] To avoid this obvious contradiction between corporate interests and egalitarian ideals, the press used the imagery of race war, taken from the mythology of the frontier, to describe the class conflict between workers and management. Working-class people were often likened to "redskin savages" as a way of undermining their ability to use democratic institutions in battles against landlords and employers. Such a comparison recast class conflict in terms of "a choice . . . between 'savagism' and civilization."[17]

More than fifty years later, *The Champ* still employs this displacement strategy by shifting its focus from the class difference between Andy and Tony to the fight between the White American boxer and the Mexican champ. In making this shift, the film also counts on leftover antagonism toward Mexico from a recent conflict with the United States. In 1927, after the Mexican Congress passed legislation claiming a bigger share of the profits from oil that American companies were pumping in Mexico, Washington threatened military intervention.[18] The defeat of Mexico's heavyweight champion provides a convenient means by which domestic class anger, fueled in American society by the Depression, could be projected outward onto the racial Other. As the two fighters represent their respective countries, the United States can also symbolically reassert its claim to new frontiers and natural resources that make class warfare unnecessary at home. *The Champ* succeeds in performing this displacement and knocks out two of the inconvenient "lower" characters with one punch, defeating the Mexican and at the same time enabling Andy to die heroically. The film's last image of Dink in his mother's arms becomes a social Darwinist affirmation of "progress and right order" achieved through the removal of "inferior" peoples in favor of those better fit to survive the Depression.[19]

Winner Take All also uses national/racial difference to avoid class conflict. It tells the story of an Irish-American fighter from New York, Jimmy Kane (played by Jimmy Cagney), who, his health ruined by fighting too often, goes to a dude ranch in New Mexico for a rest cure. At the desert resort, he meets a young widow named Peggy, whose little boy Dickie is also ill. Soon after meeting Jimmy, Peggy receives a letter from her insurance company stating that it will not honor her late husband's life insurance policy because he had missed several premium payments just before his death. To cover Peggy and Dickie's expenses at the spa, Jimmy decides to go to Tijuana and win the money in a prizefight. Jimmy's victory over a Mexican boxer, like the climactic fight in *The Champ*, displaces any stand the film might take against the insurance company with race war imagery of European-American conquest of the West.

The Champ and *Winner Take All* employ Mexican fighters as the racial Other but place Blacks in minor roles within the White protagonist's circle of supporters. In *The Champ*, Dink has a Black companion who helps keep Andy sober and away from the gaming tables. In *Winner Take All*, a Black trainer named Rosebud warns Jimmy about relationships with other women who will lead him away from his boxing career and new family. After Jimmy realizes that his fast-lane friends have deceived him, he decides to return to fighting and family, and he finds Rosebud and Peggy still in his corner. Writing a century before these pugilistic melodramas, Alexis de Tocqueville described how "the circle of family and friends" that apparently qualified self-sufficient masculinity in fact fits well into the American mythology of individualism: "with this little society formed to his taste, [the individual] gladly leaves the greater society to look after itself."[20] Such familial, multiracial support groups would become a convention of the sports film, turning up in movies from *Body and Soul* (1947) and *The Harder They Fall* (1956) to *Rocky III* (1982), *Field of Dreams* (1989), and *White Men Can't Jump* (1989). Most of the time, these groups allowed female and Black characters to contribute to the success of the White protagonist without challenging traditional gender roles or the racial status quo.

While *The Champ* and *Winner Take All* employ racial difference to distract from class antagonism in American society, another 1930s boxing film, *Golden Boy* (1939), reverses that displacement and portrays class solidarity between Black and White fighters resulting from their common experience of exploitation in the fight game. After killing a Black fighter in the ring and then seeing the strength and unity of the dead boxer's family despite their loss, *Golden Boy's* protagonist, Joe Bonaparte, realizes that he has become as destructively ambitious and isolated as the gangster who manages him. Bonaparte therefore decides to give up prizefighting and return to the support and responsibility of his own family and neighborhood. Although it represents the costs of American individualism through the scene with the Black family, *Golden Boy* still follows Classic Hollywood's practice of using African-American characters to define White protagonists.

The moral and material motivations for change in how Hollywood movies showed Blacks came about because of the Second World War. The U.S. government's desire to "enunciate a strong position on democracy" in contrast to fascism, coupled with its inability to wage total war without the inclusion of Black Americans, prompted concessions in a number of areas, including Hollywood. In 1942, studio heads promised Walter White, executive secretary of the National Association for the Advancement of Colored People, that they would "improve the quality and quantity of black roles." [21] One example of such improvement was the 1947 boxing film, *Body and Soul*.

Like *Golden Boy*, *Body and Soul* uses the corruption and exploitation of professional boxing to indict capitalism. Its writer, Abraham Polonsky, and its star, John Garfield, both knew the Clifford Odets play from which *Golden Boy* was adapted.[22] In fact, Odets had written the Joe Bonaparte role for Garfield, but the director of the original Group Theater production, Harold Clurman, turned the actor down as too inexperienced for the part.[23] Within its anti-capitalist critique, *Body and Soul* also includes *Golden Boy*'s assumption of proletarian brotherhood between the working-class ethnic and Black boxers in the face of a corrupt fight business that cares little for the welfare of its participants.

Unlike the Black boxer in *Golden Boy*, who has no lines, appears only briefly during a fight, and is clearly a device of White characterization, Ben Chaplin (Canada Lee) in *Body and Soul* is a major figure in the story. During the time in which the Garfield character, Charley Davis, fights his way up to a title shot, Ben is the champ, and clearly at the top through work and ability rather than crooked deals with gamblers. The relationship between the Black champion and his White manager is one of genuine respect and concern, and a similar relationship develops between Ben and Charley. Although he has a head injury, Ben is forced to defend his title against Charley by a powerful promoter and gambler named Roberts, who controls the New York fight scene. Charley takes the title and the bout significantly worsens the Black fighter's physical condition; nonetheless, Ben's courage moves him to the "moral and dramatic center" of the film as he teaches the Garfield character the importance of integrity in withstanding the exploitation of the fight game.[24] While Ben therefore contributes to the moral formation of the White lead, the size and importance of Lee's role in *Body and Soul* was a step forward for Black representation in Hollywood. "Obviously it was Garfield's movie," states Thomas Cripps, but "Canada Lee as Ben. . . . provided the ethical bridge between the complaisant Charley and the resolute Charley."[25] Writing in the *New York Times,* Bosley Crowther pointed out the importance of this character in *Body and Soul,* noting: "It is Canada Lee who brings to focus the horrible pathos of the cruelly exploited prize fighter."[26]

The anti-Communist pressure that would soon create problems for leftwingers like Polonsky and Garfield also strongly influenced the first Hollywood sports films with Black leads. *The Jackie Robinson Story* (1950), *The Harlem Globetrotters* (1951), and *The Joe Louis Story* (1953) are films about how hard work and self reliance, guided by paternalistic Whites, enabled young Black athletes to gain access to the highest level of professional sports. Like other message films in the decade after the war, these three films employ location settings, some nonprofessional actors, and generally modest production values in a manner indebted to Italian neorealism. Although that representational style fits the assumptions about integrationist strategies that made these films acceptable in the conservative political climate of that time, it also allowed the three films to represent less monochromatic views about race.

The Joe Louis Story covers the events of the champion's career up through his last fight, a loss to Rocky Marciano in 1951. Like the 1938 race film about Louis, *The Spirit of Youth,* the 1953 biopic maintains the carefully controlled public image that had been constructed for Louis in order to avoid memories of the last African-American heavyweight titleholder, the controversial Jack Johnson, and therefore overcome White resistance to a Black champion. In both films, the Louis character is soft-spoken, polite, modest, and obedient to authority, whether it be his mother, his handlers, or, most importantly, the White sportswriters and boxing promoters with whom he must interact once he becomes champ. Both films show a scene in which he asks his mother for her permission to become a prizefighter. Both films also regard Louis's first big loss (to German heavyweight Max Schmeling in 1936) as a youthful mistake that only reinforces his work ethic and desire to succeed.

When *The Joe Louis Story* opened in November 1953, the *Chicago Defender* reported that "before a line of the script was written, Joe was closeted for over a month with producer [Stirling] Silliphant and script-writer [Robert] Sylvester," and that Louis had "plenty to do with making the film" in his capacity as "chief technical advisor."[27] Yet, consistent with the modest, unassuming image that Louis maintained his entire career to appeal to a White audience, the film bears no marks of his control. A White sportswriter character narrates in flashback much of the film's representation of Louis's life, and the credits list Mannie Seamon, the champion's White trainer, as the film's technical advisor.

The Harlem Globetrotters also depicts the need for an African-American protagonist to advance his interests and those of his race as both are defined by White owners. Nelson George points out that, from the time of the team's origins in the 1920s, the African-American artistry of the Globetrotters' style of basketball laid the groundwork for the spectacular athletic aesthetic that dominates the NBA today. George also notes, however, that the management of the Globetrotters' owner, Abe Saperstein, offers "a definitive example of white paternalism and Black male submission."[28] Saperstein, of course, was also a member of an oppressed ethnic minority, and his involvement with the Globetrotters was not unlike that of the moguls in Hollywood, where, as Neal Gabler remarks, "There were none of the impediments imposed by loftier professions and more firmly entrenched businesses to keep Jews . . . out."[29] The lack of interest that WASP businessmen showed in African-American sports opened up possibilities for Saperstein and basketball and baseball promoter Eddie Gottlieb, both of whom could get better bookings and financial deals than those available to Black management.

The Harlem Globetrotters tells the story of a former All-American player named Billy Townsend. After joining the Trotters, Townsend makes it clear that he is more concerned with his own stardom than with the success of the team. He helps the Trotters win the opening matchup of an important three-game series against the New York Celtics, but before the second contest, Townsend sneaks out of the hotel to get married and aggravates an old knee injury when he runs into a garbage can on the sidewalk. Gamblers see Townsend hurt himself and pass the information on to the Celtics, who exploit his reduced mobility in the second game by pressuring him whenever he gets the ball. When Saperstein finds out about the injury after the game, he releases the young star, telling him that he neither understands how to be a team player nor appreciates the importance of the Trotters winning to the pride of his race. His own pride hurt by his release, Townsend signs a lucrative contract with another team, contingent upon his resting the injured knee until the following season. In the interim, Townsend (an honor student in college as well as an All-American) takes a job teaching chemistry at a small African-American college. There he sees the racial pride that the students and faculty take in the Trotters, and he begins to feel guilty about losing the opportunity to set a successful example for other young Blacks. Just before the decisive third game with the Celtics, Townsend gives up his lucrative contract and returns to help the Trotters win.

The Harlem Globetrotters represents Abe Saperstein as concerned above all with the welfare of his players and with the symbolic importance of the team as a source of pride and inspiration for African Americans. The year before the film was released, however, the real-life Saperstein's handling of a Trotters player named Nat "Sweetwater" Clifton demonstrated a more self-serving management style. Joining the team in 1947, Clifton, like Billy Townsend, was a stylish and talented former college star, who made a strong addition to the Trotters' lineup alongside Goose Tatum and Marques Haynes. During a barnstorming tour in the summer of 1950, Clifton confronted Saperstein after he discovered that the White players, their opposition during the series, were paid more money. Knowing that the New York Knicks were interested in adding an African-American player to their roster, Saperstein soon sold Clifton's contract to the NBA club.[30]

Clifton's experience with Saperstein demonstrated that the Trotters's owner, unlike his character in the 1951 film, was not always most concerned about the welfare of the Trotters or their importance as a symbol of racial pride. In fact, in the case of Nat Clifton, Saperstein seemed willing to sacrifice some of the team's ability to win when it conflicted with his desire to keep labor costs down. The deferred gratification and gradualism that the Saperstein character in the film asks the young star to accept therefore appears less a strategy for Black advancement than for maximizing owner profit.

> I had to get a man . . . who would carry the burden on the field. I needed a man to carry the badge of martyrdom. The press had to accept him. He had to stimulate a good reaction of the Negro race itself, for an unfortunate one might have solidified the antagonism of other colors. And, I had to consider the attitude of the man's teammates.
>
> —Branch Rickey, as quoted in Murray Polner, *Branch Rickey*

Like *The Joe Louis Story* and *The Harlem Globetrotters*, *The Jackie Robinson Story* portrays a self-reliant African-American athlete, who sacrifices in order to prove himself. While it forcefully presents a message of utopian individualism, this biopic of the first Black man in the twentieth century to play "Organized Baseball" also dialogically offers evidence of a more complex racial identity.

The Jackie Robinson Story portrays the title character's reluctant acceptance of Dodger owner Branch Rickey's strategy for Robinson's behavior once he breaks the color barrier in organized baseball. Rickey's plan of passive resistance—Robinson was to turn the other cheek to the racist abuse directed at him—is important in avoiding the interracial violence that would have created pressure to stop the owner's "great experiment." The strategy also represents the Black player's acceptance of self-denial and deferral of gratification, qualities that many White Americans valued and thought African Americans lacked. Randy Roberts and James S. Olson describe the widespread belief among White fans at the time of Robinson's debut that the Black male was

> incapable of organized team sports, where raw talent and brute strength were secondary to mental acuity, careful planning, and coordinated execution. . . . Imagine Sambo trying to master Knute Rockne's singlewing shift. . . . Nor could whites imagine blacks playing with the intensity of Ty Cobb, the dedication of Lou Gehrig. . . . Nature had designed them to laugh, sing, dance, and play but not to sacrifice, train, work, compete, and win.[31]

By going it alone in pursuing the difficult task of proving himself, by shouldering the pressure, and by accepting the emotional and physical pain from all the racist abuse hurled at him, Robinson demonstrated that he was just as willing as any White person to rely on hard work, self-reliance, and deferred gratification to ensure a better future.[32]

Perhaps because Rickey's assistant, Arthur Mann, cowrote the script and oversaw the project according to his boss's specifications, *The Jackie Robinson Story* presents its title character in terms of the same integrationist strategy.[33] When they first meet, Rickey tells Robinson (who played himself in the film): "I want a player with guts enough not to fight back." After a graphic description of the racist abuse he will face, Robinson assures Rickey that he can turn the other cheek.

The biopic's representation of Robinson, aimed at acceptance by White viewers, does not start, however, with his career playing for the Dodgers. The use of a White, male voice-over makes clear who is telling the story. From the very first image of Jackie as a boy, through radio commentary during games in his first two seasons with Montreal and Brooklyn, through a summary of the larger meaning of his success as the movie ends, this voice-over narration reminds the viewer of Rickey's paternalistic guidance and states clearly the film's ideology of cold war patriotism and self-reliance.

Soon after the opening shot of Jackie as a boy and the statement by the voice-over that "this is the story of a boy and his dream," a montage sequence establishes Robinson's early adoption of a strong work ethic. The viewer watches the young Robinson shine shoes and deliver newspapers on his bicycle. This brief montage segment sets up an entrepreneurial affinity between Robinson and Rickey, which the film will later develop. Just as Robinson is judged exceptional for his willingness to work, plan, and take chances, and is therefore the right Black to enter a previously all-White business, so Rickey stands above other Whites, whose fear of racial difference prevents them from seeing the commercial potential in integration. Even the brief reference to Robinson's time in the military reinforces his characterization as a man unafraid of hard work and risk taking. No mention is made of Robinson's battle with Jim Crow laws in the Army or his narrow escape from receiving a dishonorable discharge. Instead, we see a scene of girlfriend Rae Isum showing a picture of Jackie in his lieutenant's uniform to a friend, telling her that he has been given a position "as some kind of athletic director" by the Army.

Along with its emphasis on self-reliance, *The Jackie Robinson Story* also individualizes Robinson's experience of racism to imply the appropriateness of his unique opportunity and self-sufficient responses to its roadblocks. The film does not specify that Robinson was one of several African-American players considered by Rickey. This glaring omission works to separate Robinson from the "pressures that were mounting to end America's apartheid" by the conclusion of World War II.[34] As historians such as John Hope Franklin and Manning Marable have shown, the civil rights movement had already begun to challenge racial restrictions on employment and housing in American society by the time Robinson joined the Dodgers. In fact, Marable makes the case that the anti-Communist hysteria represented by Robinson's testimony before the House Un-American Activities Committee shown at the end of *The Jackie Robinson Story* was a factor in slowing down the start of the civil rights movement.[35]

Breaking the color barrier in baseball was not just about Rickey's desire to help the Dodgers win pennants and Robinson's ability to compare favorably on and especially off the field with White players. As Ben Rader explains, it was also prompted by Rickey's desires both to draw on a rapidly growing population of African Americans in Brooklyn as potential paying customers and to appeal politically to the city's increasingly important Black voters. New York mayor Fiorello La Guardia had already begun to court African Americans when in 1945 he established a special committee "to consider race relations, including the apparent discrimination against Blacks by the local Dodgers, Giants, and Yankees."[36] The nearly 4.5 million Blacks who had migrated to northern cities since World War I "represented both potentially new baseball customers as well as a new political bloc."[37] Between 1940 and 1950, the Black population of Brooklyn alone nearly doubled.[38]

In his analysis of how the idea of enterprise has contributed to the historical construction of White identity as the standard of human normalcy,

Figure 2.1. Robinson reenacts his testimony before the House Un-American Activities Committee for *The Jackie Robinson Story* (1950).

Richard Dyer makes the following statement that could be used to describe Rickey in *The Jackie Robinson Story*:

> The idea of leadership suggests both a narrative of human progress and the peculiar quality required to effect it. Thus white people lead humanity forward because of their temperamental qualities of leadership: will power, far-sightedness, energy.[39]

Throughout *The Jackie Robinson Story*, Rickey's business acumen—specifically his vision and his determination to break the color barrier in baseball—is contrasted with the fear of racist Whites, who dislike his controversial and risky plans to improve his team and to access the untapped fan market of 15 million Black Americans. Rickey's "organized" entrepreneurial talents are also contrasted with the "disorganized" and inefficient practices of Black baseball. While Rickey directs his system of scouting "Mexico, Cuba, [and] all the Latin American countries" from his sun-lit office filled with leather furniture and big game trophies, the Negro Leagues are shown through several scenes of small fields, dirty locker rooms, beat-up buses, greasy roadside restaurants, and various references to a lack of formal player contracts. Discrediting the business practices of the Negro Leagues in this way validates Rickey's appropriation of its players and fan base.

Disregarding how such ideas of racial identity affect Rickey's great experiment, *The Jackie Robinson Story* represents instead the discrimination directed at Robinson as occurring through individual actions, implying therefore the appropriateness of his self-reliant responses. The representation of a more institutionalized pattern of racism—when none of the schools to which Robinson applies after leaving UCLA offer him a coaching job—is soon followed by a scene featuring a corresponding unbiased institution (in its patriotic fervor, the film has the audacity to portray the Army as this counterweight of opportunity). Like the individualizing of racism and Robinson's response, this depiction of an equal-opportunity institution suggests the absence of structural racism.

The Joe Louis Story, The Harlem Globetrotters, and *The Jackie Robinson Story* each employ a formal style resembling that of Italian neorealism, using real locations and nonprofessional actors and exhibiting a commitment to representing important social issues. Of course, the first two of these formal variations from Classic Hollywood style were not new to movies about sports. Actual stadia and athletes playing themselves had long been a rhetorical strategy of such films, a way of presenting their viewpoint as grounded in real people and places. Yet the realist style also aligned these films with the cycle of message films produced in Hollywood in the late 1940s, movies like *Gentleman's Agreement* (1947), *Pinky* (1949), and *Home of the Brave* (1949), which, like neorealism, conveyed a "social commitment and humanistic point of view," and an interest in trying to "rehabilitate the national reputation." [40] Through this formal similarity to other socially engaged movies, the self-reliant ethos in these three sports films gains validity by offering a similar, apparently well-intentioned, response to social problems—here the conflict between racism and the democratic values of opportunity for all—seen within a "realistic" view of the world.

Writing about *The Jackie Robinson Story* in the *Chicago Defender*, A. S. "Doc" Young called it "not a fantastically lavish production, nothing like Cecil B. De-Mille. It's just a straight forward, uncolored story about Jackie's trials, tribulations and successes." [41] The stylistic modesty to which Young refers— the lack of color and the absence of lavish sets and sweeping camera work, the general avoidance of visual spectacle like that found in a DeMille epic or an opulent musical like *Singin' in the Rain* (1952)—also characterizes *The Harlem*

Figure 2.2. Robinson's aggressive, improvisational style of play in *The Jackie Robinson Story.*

Globetrotters and *The Joe Louis Story.* This formal reserve underlined an integration strategy of gradualism and self-denial as the most effective for Black advancement.

Yet, at the same time, the realist aesthetic in *The Jackie Robinson Story* and *The Harlem Globetrotters* is also used to document examples of a Black cultural style at odds with such promises of future return for continued sacrifice. In the latter film, real game footage shows the basketball skills that made the Trotters famous, especially center Goose Tatum's accurate low-post shooting and guard Marques Haynes's ball handling. Haynes's speed, dribbling, and passing skills inspired "the modern black athletic aesthetic" displayed by more recent NBA stars such as Earvin "Magic" Johnson, who has cited the Globetrotter guard as the inspiration for his "Showtime" style of improvisational play.[42] With its emphasis on combining the pleasure of creative flair with competitive efficacy, this improvisational style qualifies the deferred gratification proscribed for African Americans in a White-controlled economy.

In the Jackie Robinson biopic as well, his performance at several points counters the film's dehistoricizing tendency, despite the ways in which his abilities are made to seem unique. One prominent instance occurs in the action scenes in which Robinson uses an aggressive, improvisational style of play perfected during his time in the Negro Leagues. Rader describes the Black baseball of the Negro Leagues as

> more opportunistic, improvisational, and daring than white ball. . . . Nothing summed up the uniqueness of black baseball more than its sheer speed[,] . . . combined with the bunt [Robinson had an astounding 47 bunt hits his first year with the Dodgers], the hit-and-run play, the stolen base, and taking the extra base.[43]

In *The Jackie Robinson Story*, at least three scenes of Robinson feature this assertive, improvisational style. In the first, he doubles and then steals third and home while playing, appropriately enough, in the Negro Leagues. The lack of any voice-over narration of these feats suggests a bush-league status for Black baseball as indicated by its lack of radio coverage. Yet, even in two later scenes of Robinson playing for Montreal and Brooklyn, the radio announcers who explain beforehand the significance of Robinson's play—"in baseball, it's not who or what you are, but can you play the game"—become oddly silent as we see him in action.

In the second scene, a Montreal radio announcer sets the scene but then says nothing as Robinson reaches first on a bunt, steals second, goes to third on the wild throw, and then—by faking a dash for the plate—forces the pitcher to balk him home. The third scene shows the game with Brooklyn that clinched the pennant. Here, Robinson doubles, steals third, and comes home on a wild throw to win the game. Again, the narration so important in describing the significance of Robinson's experience elsewhere in the film goes silent, as if it is incapable of explaining the meaning of this style of play.

In their time, these three sports movies were very liberal films, clear departures from the tradition of Black representation in Hollywood. In fact, the screenwriter for *The Jackie Robinson Story*, Lawrence Taylor, found that no studio in Hollywood would back the project because of its Black protagonist. Two major studios did express interest, but they wanted the story changed to focus on a White male character who teaches Robinson about baseball. Although Arnold Rampersad states that Taylor regarded such a change as "out of the question," to a degree, that is what the picture wound up to be.[44] On a practical level, such White patronage may have been necessary to get these films on the screen, just as Louis's Uncle Tom image was the price of a heavyweight title and Robinson's restraint was required to avoid the interracial violence that would have been used to justify shutting down the great experiment. Like Robinson's breaking of the color line, these films represented a step forward: they gave Blacks an unprecedented opportunity to demonstrate their abilities in a major cultural venue, and they made evident the moral incongruity between American exceptionalism and the racist resistance to such opportunity. Where the liberal thinking in these films hinders historical honesty is in the dogged insistence on showing racism as a problem best understood and responded to in individual terms. Yet, within the cold war climate in early 1950s America, this emphasis on individualism was probably a necessary qualification of the complex racial identity these films portray.

NOTES

1. Sports historian Steven Riess reports that 1,800 Blacks fought professionally in the 1930s; by 1948, nearly half of all contenders were Black. See *City Games: The Evolution of American Urban Society and the Rise of Sport* (Urbana: University of Illinois Press, 1989), 116.

2. Robert Ray, *A Certain Tendency in the Hollywood Cinema 1930–1980* (Princeton: Princeton University Press, 1985), 31.

3. George Custen, *Bio/Pics: How Hollywood Constructed Public History* (New Brunswick: Rutgers University Press, 1992), 8.

4. I use the term "sports" rather than "sport" because the former is better understood by more readers as referring to the rule-governed, physical contests that are my concern here. Sports films have been made about amateur athletes, from the college films of the 1920s (for example, Harold Lloyd's 1925 *The Freshman*) to the slew of recent Disney productions about children and extraordinary animals. Yet, because of the box office potential for films about performers who already have proven commercial viability, most sports movies concern professional athletes. Moreover, because they claim to represent the highest standard of skill and organization, professional contests offer themselves as a model for how sports should be played at all levels.

5. Quoted in S. W. Pope, *The New American Sport History: Recent Approaches and Perspectives* (Urbana: University of Illinois Press, 1997), 6.

6. Richard Dyer, "Entertainment and Utopia," in *The Cultural Studies Reader,* ed. Simon During (London: Blackwell, 1993), 271–83.

7. Robert Stam, "Bakhtin, Polyphony, and Ethnic/Racial Representation," in *Unspeakable Images: Ethnicity and the American Cinema,* ed. Lester D. Friedman (Urbana: University of Illinois Press, 1991), 256.

8. See Gail Bederman, *Manliness and Civilization: A Cultural History of Gender and Race in the United States, 1880–1917* (Chicago: University of Chicago Press, 1995).

9. Jeffrey Sammons and Michael T. Isenberg describe Jackson's career and his exclusion from heavyweight contention. See Sammons, *Beyond the Ring: The Role of Boxing in American Society* (Urbana: University of Illinois Press, 1988), and Isenberg, *John L. Sullivan and His America* (Urbana: University of Illinois Press, 1988).

10. Noel Ignatiev, *How the Irish Became White* (New York: Routledge, 1995), 2.

11. Ray, *A Certain Tendency*, 55–69.

12. Thomas Cripps, *Making Movies Black* (New York: Oxford University Press, 1993), 4–5.

13. Otto L. Graham, Jr., "Years of Crisis: America in Depression and War, 1933–1945," in *The Unfinished Century*, ed. William E. Leuchtenburg (Boston: Little, Brown, 1973), 381.

14. Riess, *City Games*, 112.

15. I am using here Charles Eckert's idea of displacement as he describes it occurring in "proletarian" or "socially conscious" films of the 1930s and 1940s. Using both Freudian psychoanalysis and Lévi-Strauss's study of myth, Eckert sums up this process as a combination of displacement "as Freud defines this term (the substitution of an acceptable object of love, hate, etc., for a forbidden one)" and the transformation of unsolvable dilemmas like that in myths in order to "resolve the dilemma at another level, or to somehow attenuate its force." See Charles Eckert, "The Anatomy of a Proletarian Film: Warner's Marked Woman," in *Movies and Methods*, vol. 2, ed. Bill Nichols (Berkeley: University of California Press, 1985), 420.

16. Richard Slotkin, *Gunfighter Nation: The Myth of the Frontier in Twentieth-Century America* (New York: Atheneum, 1992), 19.

17. Ibid., 20.

18. Josefina Zoraida Vazquez and Lorenzo Meyer, *The United States and Mexico* (Chicago: University of Chicago Press, 1987), 134–38.

19. Slotkin, *Gunfighter Nation*, 21.

20. Quoted in Ray, *A Certain Tendency*, 61.

21. John Hope Franklin, *From Slavery to Freedom: A History of Negro Americans*, 6th ed. (New York: Knopf, 1988), 389. Thomas Cripps, *Black Film as Genre* (Bloomington: Indiana University Press, 1979), 42.

22. Cripps, *Making Movies Black*, 211.

23. Robert Sklar, *City Boys: Cagney, Bogart, Garfield* (Princeton: Princeton University Press, 1992), 82.

24. Cripps, *Making Movies Black*, 212.

25. Ibid.

26. Quoted in ibid.

27. These quotes appeared in the 7 November 1953 and 14 November 1953 issues of the *Defender*.

28. Nelson George, *Elevating the Game: Black Men and Basketball* (New York: Harper Collins, 1992), 42.

29. Neal Gabler, *An Empire of Their Own: How the Jews Invented Hollywood* (New York: Anchor Books, 1988), 5.

30. George, *Elevating the Game*, 100.

31. Randy Roberts and James S. Olson, *Winning is the Only Thing: Sports in America Since 1945* (Baltimore: Johns Hopkins University Press, 1989), 27.

32. Ben Rader notes that "at the personal cost of persistent headaches, bouts of

depression, and smoldering resentments, Robinson eased the way for his acceptance by publicly ignoring the racial slurs of the players on the other teams." See Rader's *Baseball: A History of America's Game* (Urbana: University of Illinois Press, 1992), 152.

33. Arnold Rampersad, *Jackie Robinson* (New York: Knopf, 1997), 224.

34. Rader, *Baseball*, 149.

35. Manning Marable, *Race, Reform and Rebellion: The Second Reconstruction in Black America, 1945–1990* (Jackson: University of Mississippi Press, 1991), 31–32. Robinson's achievement is best seen as part of a larger movement attempting to change the status of African Americans after World War II. His disillusionment about race relations at the time of his death in 1972 parallels the trajectory of the civil rights movement from hopefulness and belief in integration in the latter half of the 1950s and early 1960s to despair about the willingness of White America to offer African Americans as a group the same rights and opportunities. The pessimism expressed in his 1972 autobiography, *I Never Had It Made*, echoes the disillusionment that fueled a move toward a more militant nationalistic strategy in the Black community during the same period.

36. Rader, *Baseball*, 149.

37. Ibid.

38. Based on United States Census figures reported in Jerome Krase and Charles LaCerra, *Ethnicity and Machine Politics* (Lanham, MD: University Press of America, 1991), 248.

39. Richard Dyer, *White* (New York: Routledge, 1997), 31.

40. David Cook, *A History of Narrative Film* 3d ed. (New York: W. W. Norton, 1996), 421.

41. *Chicago Defender*, May 20, 1950.

42. George, *Elevating the Game*, 52–53.

43. Rader, *Baseball*, 145–146. A colleague of mine at Arizona State University, Keith Miller, wrote a very interesting essay about Robinson's use of this style, which Miller says was called "trickeration" in the Negro Leagues. "Jazz on the Basepaths: Trickeration Baseball and Jackie Robinson's Narrative Denial," unpublished manuscript.

44. Rampersad, *Jackie Robinson*, 223.

3

DARK CITY

White Flight and the Urban Science Fiction Film in Postwar America

Eric Avila

I am an invisible man. No, I am not a spook like those who haunted Edgar Allan Poe; nor am I one of your Hollywood movie ectoplasms. I am a man of substance, of flesh and bone, fiber and liquids—and I might even be said to possess a mind.   —Ralph Ellison, *Invisible Man*

At the outset of *Invisible Man*, Ralph Ellison seeks to dispel white perceptions of black people. Such perceptions, he realized, often drew upon the vast array of images that saturated the cultural life of mid-twentieth century white America. Writing in the early 1950s, a time when American movie audiences reveled in the spectacular images of alien invasions, Ellison took strides to deny his similarity to "Hollywood movie ectoplasms." Although he painfully recognized his invisibility as a black man in cold war America, he also protested his visibility in cultural productions like the urban science fiction film of the 1950s. Ellison, like other black intellectuals discouraged by the misrepresentation of black Americans in popular culture, recognized the ominous affinity between the alien Other of science fiction film and the racialized Other of American history. *Invisible Man* draws upon the painful awareness that racialized minorities in the United States are usually invisible as human beings and often visible only through the disfiguring lens of American popular culture.[1]

Ellison's commentary upon the cultural milieu of cold war America resonated within a material context in which the racial divide between black America and white America widened. Such disparities were most visible in the cities, where the force of suburbanization furthered the distance between white and black. "White flight" names the process by which American cities of the postwar period saw increasing racial segregation and socioeconomic fragmentation. As racialized minorities concentrated in American inner cities during the late 1940s and throughout the 1950s, millions of "white" Americans took to new suburban communities to preserve their whiteness. Through the postwar collusion of federal policy, local land development strategies, and the popular desire to live in racially exclusive and homogenous neighborhoods, "chocolate cities" and "vanilla suburbs" became the spatial and racial paradigm of American life during the 1950s.[2]

Typically, white flight refers to political practices and economic processes that enforce the racial divide between the suburbs and the city.[3] However, there is a cultural dimension to this process that has been overlooked. As an ideology rooted both in a historical preference for private rather than public life and in contemporary anxieties about subversion and deviance, white flight penetrated the sphere of American popular culture and affirmed whiteness often at the expense of racialized minorities. The rise of Hollywood science fiction paralleled the acceleration of white flight in postwar America and not only recorded popular anxieties about political and sexual deviants, but also captured white preoccupations with the increasing visibility of the alien Other.

Historically, science fiction film and literature have posited the city as the object of both utopian and dystopian fantasies about modernity. The urban science fiction film of the 1950s, figuratively and literally, emphasized the darker side of urban life. Films such as *Them!* (1954) and *War of the Worlds* (1953) emerged at the height of postwar suburbanization, a time when millions of white Americans reaped the privileges of affordable housing in the suburbs and rejected the city as a viable way of life. The perceived threat to the American city underlies both cultural constructions like the urban science fiction film and material processes such as white flight. Indeed, such films confirmed the suburban suspicion of city life through spectacular representations of the alien Other and its violent onslaught upon the city. Within the changing racial geography of the postwar, postindustrial metropolis, the urban science fiction film provided a cultural arena where suburban America could measure its whiteness against the image of the alien Other. In their

Figure 3.1. Promotional poster for *War of the Worlds* (1953).

representational emphasis, visual style, and promotion, films such as *Them!* and *War of the Worlds* recorded popular perceptions of racialized minorities in the age of white flight.

RACE AND SPACE IN POSTWAR AMERICA

Conventional understandings of 1950s science fiction film have looked to the political climate of the cold war to explore the deeper meanings of science fiction cinema. Martians, monsters, giant insects, crawling eyes, fifty-foot women, blobs, pods, various "its" and other "things" were all commonly understood as cinematic apparitions of Communists and the "Red Menace." And rightly so. Science fiction film offers a window onto the political culture of postwar America, a time when Americans built bomb shelters in their backyards, practiced disaster drills with a religious devotion, and gazed fixedly upon the televised witch-hunts of the House Un-American Activities Committee (HUAC). Through films such as *Invasion of the Body Snatchers* (1956), *It Came From Outer Space* (1953), and *Invasion of the Saucer Men* (1957), Americans could work out their obsession with Communist subversion and catch a glimpse into the nexus between politics and culture in postwar America.[4]

Figure 3.2. Promotional poster for *Them!* (1954).

Communists, however, were not the only subversives in postwar America. As it had throughout American history, the presence of racialized minorities continued to trouble white Americans. The "race question," however, seemed all the more poignant in the age of *Brown v Board of Education.* Before, white Americans could confront their racial anxieties in a separate but equal world. During the 1950s, however, the lines between black space and white space increasingly blurred, particularly in the cities, where racialized minorities, blacks in particular, concentrated in unprecedented numbers. Although cities have historically functioned as points of contact between diverse social groups, the nature of sociodemographic upheaval and economic change proved so pronounced that it forced white Americans to confront the darker face of the city in postwar America.

The urban science fiction film emerged within this racial climate. Because this brand of cinematic science fiction took as its subject the plight of the city, its meaning is further illuminated by an understanding of the spatial transition from the industrial city of the nineteenth century to the post-industrial metropolis of the twentieth century. Implicit in this transition is the concentration of racialized minorities in the inner city and the subsequent racial polarization of the city between its dark core and white suburbs. As black Americans secured housing and employment in the older, industrialized cores of such cities as Detroit, Philadelphia, and Los Angeles during the postwar era, white Americans secured housing and employment in newly developed suburban communities. Within this context, the popularity of films about alien invasions suggests that mainstream white audiences may have viewed the movement of blacks and other racialized minorities into the cities as not so much a migration, but rather an invasion of what had previously been white space. "Invasion" became a key metaphor, central to understanding larger social processes in postwar America, including the urbanization of African-Americans.

The urban science fiction film coincided with the rise of the black ghetto as the dominant feature of urban life in postwar America. U.S. mobilization for World War II and the postwar economic boom initiated a dramatic spatial shift in the nation's black population. The urbanization of African-Americans entailed the migration of blacks from the South to the Northeast and West. The largest decennial black migration occurred between 1940 and 1950. Overall, between 1940 and 1970, more than 4 million blacks left the South for Northern and Western cities. On the eve of World War II, 70 percent of American blacks lived in the South, whereas only 53 percent lived there thirty years later.[5] The number of black urbanites, moreover, increased dramatically in the United States between 1945 and 1960. During that period, New York's black population increased two and one-half times, and the number of blacks tripled in Detroit. The West, however, experienced the greatest growth in its African-American population. Los Angeles, a city with a relatively small black population until 1940, saw an 800 percent increase in its black population, from 75,000 to 600,000.[6]

Given the white response to black urbanization, the ghetto became the dominant experience of African-American life in postwar America. Many whites deployed violence against the encroachment of African-Americans upon white space. Throughout the postwar era, white aggression toward blacks and other non-whites increased, particularly in such public spaces as buses, schools, restaurants, and, to a larger extent, in private spaces such as the residential neighborhood. For example, in Levittown, Pennsylvania, a planned community of 60,000, a Confederate flag–waving crowd threw stones at the one house that belonged to a black family in 1957.[7] In 1945, the Ku Klux Klan firebombed the Fontana, California, home of a black family that refused to move from a white neighborhood, killing the wife and only child of civil rights activist O'Day Short.[8] The Cicero Riots of 1951, similarly, demonstrated the extent to which white Chicagoans would go to protect the whiteness of their neighborhoods. There, a crowd of six thousand invaded and wrecked the home of a black war veteran, hauling his furniture into the street and setting his apartment on fire.[9] As blacks became more visible in postwar American cities, many white Americans fought, by any means necessary, to uphold the barriers between black space and white space.

Most whites, however, found a less violent yet more thorough means of enforcing the color line. Although the suburbanization of the United States began in the 1920s, it was not until the postwar era that the process gave way to white flight through the collusion of public policy and private practices.[10] Federal legislation during the Roosevelt administration established the means for postwar suburbanization, particularly through the creation of the Homeowner's Loan Corporation (HOLC), the Federal Housing Authority (FHA), and the Veterans Administration (VA). The FHA and the VA adopted the underwriting practices of the HOLC, which devised a racially discriminatory system of financing home loans. The FHA and VA, in turn, influenced the lending policies of private financial institutions, which avoided investment in "affected" areas. By severely limiting the flow of capital into the inner city, the FHA and VA significantly enhanced the impoverishment of those areas and encouraged the selective exodus of working-class and middle-class whites to the suburban periphery.[11]

Policy making at the local level bolstered these federal attempts to facilitate suburbanization. The innovation of municipal incorporation strategies influenced the course of suburbanization throughout the American Sun Belt and ensured the reproduction of white space. The infamous "Lakewood Plan" shaped the socioeconomic geography of southern California and the American Sun Belt during the 1950s and 1960s. In 1950, developer Ben Weingart, along with two partners, purchased 3,375 acres of farmland in the southwestern portion of Los Angeles County. There they built Lakewood, a community of seventeen thousand homes, including the nation's largest shopping center. Rather than incorporating into the county, the residents of Lakewood contracted county services for minimal costs, while remaining an independent municipality. Following Lakewood's example, twenty-five municipalities in southern California adopted the Lakewood Plan between 1945 and 1960.[12]

The invention of the "contract city" ensured tighter control over the social composition of southern California suburban communities. Lakewood Plan cities could effectively direct the makeup of a local population to exclude service-demanding, low-income, or renting populations, usually blacks and quite often Latinos as well. Judged by the sociospatial character of suburban southern California during the postwar period, the Lakewood Plan was an overwhelming success. In 1950, there were thirty-eight cities in southern California with less than one percent black populations; these cities contained 24 percent of the metropolitan area's population. In 1970, by contrast, there were 58 cities with less than one percent black populations, containing 33 percent of the regional population. Both the number of segregated cities and the population living within those cities increased. Essentially a white political movement, the Lakewood Plan defined white resistance to black urbanization during the postwar era. By enacting more privatized methods of city government, Lakewood Plan cities ensured the reproduction of white space in the suburban Sun Belt of postwar America.[13]

THE REAL OTHER

The racial character of the postwar suburban boom emerged from wartime anxieties about the "alien invasion" of American cities. In Los Angeles, for example, the local media generated mass hysteria with its wartime rhetoric directed against the Japanese and Japanese-Americans. The "Great Los Angeles Air Raid" demonstrated the level of anxiety in Los Angeles regarding such an invasion. At 2:25 A.M. on February 26, 1942, the U.S. Army announced the approach of hostile aircraft, activating the city's air raid warning system for the first time. The February 27 issue of the *Los Angeles Times* reported:

Roaring out of a brilliant moonlit western sky, foreign aircraft flying both in large formation and singly flew over Southern California early today and drew heavy barrages of anti-aircraft fire—the first ever to sound over United States continental soil against an enemy invader.

Despite the fleeting moment of panic, no one reported the dropping of bombs or the sighting of enemy aircraft. In fact, the "air raid" never occurred, but the incident revealed the extent to which the people of Los Angeles psychologically anticipated the kind of "alien" invasion dramatized in films such as *Them!* and *War of the Worlds.*[14]

Popular anxieties about invasion did not subside with the end of the war, but rather increased as the influx of other racialized groups displaced the Japanese as the alien invaders. *U.S. News and World Report,* for example, alarmed its readers in 1956 with a report of a black invasion of Los Angeles. An article, entitled "West Coast, Too, Has its Race Problem," labeled the influx of Southern blacks to Los Angeles as a "race problem" to its white readership. As the mere presence of blacks in post-emancipation America constituted a "race problem," their increasing visibility in postwar American cities illustrated the heightened poignancy of that "problem." This was especially the case in Los Angeles, which absorbed a greater number of African-Americans than any other city of the postwar era. "At every hand," reported the magazine, "in the factories, offices and schools of Los Angeles, you find growing numbers of the 'new negro' in America—ambitious and aggressive in his demands."[15]

Certainly, *U.S. News and World Report* did not possess any special expertise about the changing racial demography of a city like Los Angeles. The magazine, however, recorded popular perceptions of urban life during the 1950s. Millions of Americans who identified as white looked upon the "darkening" of the city as nothing less than a crisis. That crisis took shape in the national culture not only in such alarming reports of the growing numbers of "ambitious and aggressive Negros," but also in science fiction thrillers about the alien invasion of American cities. At a time when blacks concentrated in inner cities in unprecedented numbers and when "whites" fled older portions of the city for the suburban periphery, urban science fiction thrillers such as *Them!* and *War of the Worlds* confirmed popular suspicions of American urban life.

THE REEL OTHER

Hollywood faced its own crisis in the age of white flight. Suburbanization shifted the locus of American popular culture during the postwar era and emptied downtown movie theaters in cities across the nation. Still reeling from the turmoil of the HUAC witch-hunt, Hollywood suffered another blow when movie attendance sharply declined during the late 1940s and continued to fall in the early years of the following decade. Among other factors, the postwar retreat from the public arena and the concurrent emphasis upon private life played no small part in that decline. One astute critic observed in 1950 that "tall grass will be shortly growing amidst the ruins of Rialtos, Criterions, Granadas and other abandoned landmarks from coast to coast."[16]

As the cultural component of suburbanization, television also challenged the hegemony of Hollywood in the cultural landscape of postwar America. While white suburbanites retreated from the real world of increasing complexity and diversity, television offered a glimpse into an alternative world that reflected and reinforced a white suburban worldview. That world had little place for minorities, save the few stereotypical references to the jungle natives of Tarzan films and the manufactured Indians of TV westerns. Television, moreover, afforded the opportunity to "go out," without compromising the privacy of the single-family home. The advent of this medium radically changed the spatial context of popular culture, underscoring the postwar retreat from public life. Manufacturers marketed television as a way of "bringing the world to people's doorsteps," emphasizing the security and convenience of home entertainment. As a privatized cultural experience, television pulled suburbanites away from older sites of public amusement and accelerated the fragmentation of what had once been the diverse multitudes of urban audiences.[17]

Unable to compete with the convenience and availability of television, Hollywood struggled to maintain its sovereignty in the cultural terrain of postwar America. Innovations in special effects became a strategy for luring spectators back to the movies, and science fiction film became a major venue for marketing these special effects technologies. Thus, a film like *War of the Worlds* could draw huge audiences without the names of major motion picture stars. "What starring honors there are," wrote one film critic for *Variety* in a review of *War of the Worlds*, "go strictly to special effects, which create an atmosphere of soul chilling apprehension so effectively audiences will take alarm at the danger posed in that picture."[18]

Special effects alone, however, do not explain the immense popularity of science fiction thrillers like *Them!* and *War of the Worlds*. To spark an audience "comeback" to the movies, Hollywood needed more than just technical innovations such as rear projection and miniature sets—it needed to connect, almost psychically, with its audience, recording its hopes and aspirations, as well as its despair and anxiety. Given the social, political, and cultural climate of postwar America, Hollywood emphasized the dark side of the collective conscious, projecting the concerns that dominated public discourse. Thus, anxieties about Communism surfaced in films such as *Double Indemnity* (1944), which exposed the "evil within," and *Invasion of the Body Snatchers* (1956), which stressed the external threat from abroad. Similarly, films like *Mildred Pierce* (1945) and *Rebel Without a Cause* (1955) revealed American anxieties about powerful women and the sexual threat to domestic stability in postwar America. Such films articulated the concerns that preoccupied postwar Americans.

While sexual and class anxieties inform the meaning of these films, race was a dominant factor. Science fiction films like *Them!* and *War of the Worlds* named racial anxieties about "alien" invasions that troubled suburban Americans of the 1950s. Of course, these films are open to multiple interpretations and clearly allude to other anxieties of the day, but it is their urban settings that complicate any facile interpretations of the Martians of *War of the Worlds* or the giant ants of *Them!* as exclusively Communists. Cold war anxieties, after all, were neither urban nor rural. Racial anxieties, however, emerged from a prevalent perception that American cities were really under "attack" during the postwar period. In their narratives of alien invasion and their emphasis upon the difference between "us" and "them," the urban science fiction film effectively reached the suburban audiences that had largely forsaken the city as a satisfying way of life.

Both *War of the Worlds* and *Them!* are narratives about alien invaders and the destruction they wrought upon American cities. Central to these narratives is a visual distinction between "us," a homogenous citizenry, and "them," the alien Other. *Them!* depicted the invasion of Los Angeles by giant ants, enlarged by overexposure to radiation from atom bomb testing sites in the desert. Although an allegory for the dangers of atomic energy, the film presents creatures as ordinary as ants transformed into hideous aliens who invade vulnerable cities and attack their innocent citizenry. The giant ants, with bulging eyes and deadly mandibles, recall historic stereotypes of racialized groups as animalistic and especially alien. Such stereotypes ran rampant in times of international or domestic crisis. Japanese-Americans, for example, became rats in the political cartoons of the early 1940s. In the late nineteenth century, similarly, when California suffered from economic depression and high unemployment, Chinese-Americans bore the brunt of racist stereotypes, depicted in visual and literary media as bats with sharp claws and gnarled fangs. African-Americans have suffered such vicious kinds of representation throughout their history, stereotyped in the national culture most often as simian creatures. At various points in American history, racialized groups have been likened to monkeys, bats, rats, ants, and other creatures, reinforcing the perceptual affinity between nonhuman and nonwhite.[19]

Figure 3.3. Recalling historical stereotypes in *Them!* (1954).

War of the Worlds takes such representation a step further, as Martians replace ants as the alien Other. The Martians of *War of the Worlds* land upon Earth in search of a more hospitable climate for procreation. Though we know the Martians only by their sleek metal saucers that hover above the ground, a few scenes reveal a grotesquely inhuman Other. In one sequence of images, the noted scientists, Dr. Clayton Forrester, and his companion, Sylvia Van Buren, take refuge inside an abandoned home. Although Sylvia is rarely seen apart from the company of men, she is momentarily separated from Forrester, distracted by a hunch that the invaders are nearby. As Van Buren searches the quarters alone, audience suspicion is heightened: the encounter with the Martians seems dreadfully imminent. With the camera behind her, Sylvia is unaware that an alien is watching her every move. The camera mimics the alien's predatory gaze, targeting the white woman as the object of the alien's (and by visual implication, the audience's) desire. As the bright, slimy green arm of the Martian reaches toward her, the whiteness of her skin contrasts sharply with the alien physiognomy. The *Los Angeles Herald Express* noted this graphic scene, remarking upon the "skinny tentacles" of the Martians, with "vacuum cups at the end of each finger" and "flesh which looks like a piece of pulsating raw liver." [20]

War of the Worlds draws upon a common trope of the urban science fiction film. The alien lust for the white woman is evident not only in the narrative content of the urban science fiction film, but also in its publicity materials. For example, the garish advertisement poster for *Invasion of the Saucer Men* captures some of white America's deepest anxieties about the alien Other. In the central image of the advertisement, a scantily clad white woman with heaving breasts flails in the clutches of a hideous green alien monster. In the background is the metropolis, under attack by flying saucers. Again, the alien bears a familiar resemblance to cultural stereotypes of racialized minorities, blacks in particular. With their bulging round eyes, enormous heads, and dark, almost black skin, the saucer men seem more familiar than alien, recalling lurid representations of "coons," "sambos," and "pickaninnies" in American popular culture. The blackness of the aliens contrasts sharply with the milky whiteness of the woman's skin. She is helpless in the grips of an alien predatory sexuality, naming historical anxieties about black male lust for white women. Such anxieties, of course, are not unique to the urban science fiction genre, but draw upon the racist practices of early filmmaking.

The films of D. W. Griffith, for example, often emphasize nonwhite male lust for white women, a lust almost always motivated by an attempt to rape. The character of Gus in *Birth of a Nation* (1915) epitomizes then-prevalent white perceptions of a ferocious black male sexuality and its threat to white women. His lust for Elsie Stoneman culminates in a famous chase scene in which she leaps to her death to avoid sacrificing her virtue to the mulatto sexual predator. Prior to the release of *Birth of a Nation, The Girls and Daddy* foreshadowed Gus's behavior. The film narrates the story of two thieves, one white and one in blackface, who, unlike the white burglar, lustfully chases after two white women. Although Griffith did not invent the cinematic stereotype of black or mulatto men as lustful monsters preying upon the virtue of white women, he popularized those stereotypes, which, in turn, informed the work of subsequent generations of filmmakers.[21]

During the postwar period, a time when the national culture reemphasized the sanctity of the nuclear family, the urban science fiction film echoed the work of former generations of filmmakers like Griffith and reiterated the alien threat to white women. Some historians have illuminated the ways in which suburbanization reasserted the nuclear family as the most fundamental unit of American society. The many threats that preoccupied postwar Americans—Communists, homosexuals, racialized minorities—were viewed as dangers not so much to the individual or to the society at large, but rather to the stability and coherence of the American family. The national culture, moreover, almost always coded the family as white. In the racialized climate of postwar America, white flight could be viewed therefore as a collective attempt to maintain the hegemony of the white nuclear family.

In their representations of the alien threat to white womanhood, urban science fiction films such as *Them!* and *War of the Worlds* also implied the vulnerability of the white family. As their narratives dramatized alien invasions of the city and their occupation of urban space, the films emphasized the direct threat to the dominance of the white American family. In *Them!*, that threat is realized as the ants kill the white father of a family and take his two sons hostage, leaving their mother in despair. The whiteness of the two boys is visually enhanced when the ants hold their young captives in the darkness of the city's sewer system. The threat to the nuclear family in *Them!* again recalls an earlier discourse of the white family in the films of Griffith, where stories of the family usually involve a racial component that casts nonwhite males as a threat to the dominance of white patriarchy. The aim of such stories, of course, is to segregate the races and uphold the unity of the family, the purity of the white woman, and the power and divinity of the white family. *Them!* extends that message into the postwar era of U.S. history, emphasizing once again the nonwhite/nonhuman threat to the stability of the American family.

War of the Worlds, similarly, asserts the divinity of the white family while exposing the potential threat to that institution. In the climactic scene of the film, as masses of Los Angelenos take refuge inside a church shortly before the imminent holocaust, a white family—mother, father, son, and daughter—huddles together in prayer, gazing up toward the image of Christ at the altar. As the camera hones in upon their faces, the audience is reminded exactly who the victim is in this narrative of alien aggression. Lighting, thrown upon their faces at a $45°$ angle, highlights the fair skin, blonde hair, and blue eyes of the family members. The sanctity of this image is reinforced through editing, which cuts from images of the white family to the image of a white Christ at the altar, the supreme embodiment of Western humanity. Such editing supports a visual association between Christ and the family within a racialized context of whiteness.[22]

Yet, while these films exalt the white woman and the white family, they simultaneously emphasize the deadly potential of alien motherhood. *Them!*, for example, is a film about alien motherhood run amok, depicting the nightmare of uncontrolled, mindless reproduction of the Other. The film's climax is loaded with sexual tension, as the "queen" ant takes shelter in the "egg chamber" deep within the sewers of Los Angeles. The queen ant represents the nativist's worst nightmare: alien procreation gone mad, uncontrollable and unstoppable. Such representations of endless reproduction do not simply res-

Figure 3.4. Representing a threat to whiteness (*Them!* 1954).

onate with postwar anxieties about maternal domination. Rather, they underscore popular fears about alien motherhood in particular. The antagonist, after all, is an insect. Ultimately, climactic tension is resolved as the phallic bazookas of the army incinerate the queen and her eggs, thereby securing the city for white supremacy and against the reproduction of the alien Other.[23]

Another way in which these films lend themselves to the construction of whiteness is through racial censorship. James Snead argues that "omission," or exclusion, is the most common form of racial stereotyping, but also the most difficult to identify because its manifestation is absence itself. In other words, the absence of black characters in film is a form of stereotyping, one that reinforces the idea that blacks and other non-white groups are obscure, marginal, and dependent. Both *Them!* and *War of the Worlds* feature white scientists, white generals, white presidents, white policemen, white pilots, white ministers, white nurses, white doctors, and other racialized figures of authority. Blacks, however, play neither major nor minor roles in either film, positing a polarized landscape in which the only Other is the alien Other.[24]

Racial images are coupled with urban images in such science fiction films, dramatizing the political and cultural conditions of the United States in the age of white flight. Just as the term "white flight" implies the movement of white masses away from the city, films such as *Them!* and *War of the Worlds* depict the flight of a homogenous white citizenry from the violent onslaught of the Other. In *Them!*, for example, "UFO reports" confirm that "flying saucers shaped like ants" are heading west toward Los Angeles. Subsequent images cut to urban crowds in frenzied preparation for the imminent arrival of "them." A state of emergency is declared and the National Guard is called upon to protect the white citizenry from the "savage and ruthless" invaders. Panic ensues prior to their arrival as, with what must have been a startling similarity to the actual tests of the Emergency Broadcasting System, radio and television broadcasters announce:

> By direction of the President of the United States, in full agreement with the Governor of the State of California, and the Mayor of Los Angeles, the city of Los Angeles is, in the interests of public safety, hereby claimed to be under martial law . . . curfew is at 1800 hours. Any persons on the street or outside their quarters after 6:00 P.M. tonight will be subject to arrest.

Similarly, in *War of the Worlds*, the prospect as well as the reality of doomsday maintains the air of suspense. Though the aliens initially descend upon a small California town, it is their slow, yet steady approach toward the metropolis that constitutes the suspense of the narrative. The path of the Other from the small town to the metropolis recalls the great migration of blacks during the 1940s and 1950s, in which masses of black rural Southerners migrated to cities like Los Angeles. Migration becomes invasion in *War of the Worlds* as the Martians draw nearer to the city. The skies darken upon their arrival and panic descends upon the hoards of Angelenos, who flee in desperation. Police cars patrol the streets of downtown to maintain what little social order remains, their loudspeakers blaring, "Everybody listen carefully! We must evacuate the city! All major highways have been marked to lead you to shelter and welfare centers in the hills." The very anticipation of doomsday in the urban science film corresponded to the sense in the postwar American city that someone or something was about to bring crisis and destruction.

As panic ensues, the masses flee the city. The exodus is a significant part of *War of the Worlds*. As people jam the freeways with their possessions bundled atop their cars, others take flight on foot, seeking refuge in the hills above the city. A voice-over narrates the spectacle of catastrophe, implying the historical process of white flight itself:

> As the Martians burned fields and forests, and great cities fell before them, huge populations were driven from their homes. The stream of

flight rose swiftly to a torrent. It became a giant stampede—without order and without goal. It was the beginning of the route of civilization—of the massacre of humanity.

Finally, the aliens arrive, and it is doomsday for the city. Special effects recreate the holocaust. "See Los Angeles Crumble Before Your Very Eyes!" runs the headline of the *Los Angeles Herald Express* on November 11, 1953. The realism of such images of destruction are enhanced not only through innovations in special effects, but also through the use of real and recognizable buildings and landscapes, which promote audience identification with the crisis upon the screen. In *War of the Worlds*, for example, a spectacular scene depicts the obliteration of the Los Angeles City Hall, a symbol of municipal authority and civic order exploding in a brilliant burst of flames. In other science fiction films, the use of the Empire State Building, Times Square, the Washington Monument, or the Golden Gate Bridge serves to name the urban scene and to deepen our familiarity with the events taking place in the film. In each instance, the result is the same: total eradication of the most poignant symbols of Western progress and American civilization.

Susan Sontag identifies a certain kind of poetry in such images, which she describes as the "aesthetics of destruction." Images of aliens and their onslaught upon the city held an ambiguous fascination for postwar white suburban audiences, who not only recoiled in horror from such a vision of their own destruction, but also took a certain delight in that vision. Urban, industrial audiences have historically held mixed feelings toward the macabre, the alien, and the exotic, drawing upon ambivalent feelings of shock, terror, curiosity, and even delight. The urban science fiction film, with its emphasis upon disaster, disorder, and the grotesque, inherits its appeal from carnival sideshows and dime museums, which drew thousands who paid admission fees to ogle at such curiosities as "the Fee Jee Mermaid" and "What is it?"[25]

The postwar popularity of films like *War of the Worlds* and *Them!* revealed the extent to which this fascination persisted, even among suburban, postindustrial audiences of the 1950s. Although suburban audiences found themselves increasingly regimented into racial, sexual, and economic hierarchies, they maintained a lurid attraction to the baser elements of the culture. Through terrifying spectacles of disaster and horrific representations of the alien Other, the urban science fiction film may have offered an arena where American audiences could sublimate the attraction to, or even love of, the Other. Recalling the intense popularity of Orson Welles's 1939 radio broadcast of *War of the Worlds*, one film critic anticipated a similar reception of the film adaptation in 1953, "just as listeners willingly mesmerized themselves into being scared half to death by the Welles broadcast, so will viewers take vicarious pleasure in the terror loosened in the film."[26]

CONCLUSION: THE POST-WHITE FLIGHT CITY

While films such as *War of the Worlds* and *Them!* represent the city in the age of white flight, other urban science fiction films portray the city after the exodus. In her study of the urban science fiction film, Vivian Sobchack identifies images of a "dead" city, devoid of people, as another common trope of the genre. New York, for example, is an empty concrete canyon in *Five* (1951), where nothing moves save a slowly moving car in which the two main characters ride. In *On the Beach* (1954), San Francisco is equally lifeless, as submarine crewmen search for the source of a mysterious radio signal. Similarly, in *The World, The Flesh and the Devil* (1959), a single character roams through the vacant cityscapes of Times Square and Wall Street. This is the post-white flight city: "cars eternally stalled on a bridge, newspaper blowing down a city street caught up in some ill-begotten draft, street lights and neon often blinking on and off in a mockery of animate existence," writes Vivian Sobchack, "this is the iconography of the post-holocaust city in the 1950s to the mid-1970s."[27] As white suburbanites turned their backs upon the old downtowns and retreated to the suburbs, images of empty cities reflected and reinforced the symbolic "death" of the city in postwar America.

The ultimate post-white flight city, however, emerged after the heyday of the urban science fiction film. Ridley Scott's *Blade Runner* returns the science fiction audience to Los Angeles in the year 2019, after the flight of ex-suburbanites to the "off-world" colonies in outer space. Electronic advertisements hover above the noxious hypersprawl of twenty-first century Los Angeles, promising the good life in the depths of outer space: "a golden land of opportunity awaits you in the off-world colony!" Such campaigns recall the turn-of-the-century booster promotions of Los Angeles, in which people of adequate means fled the over-industrialized, immigrant-ridden cities of the eastern seaboard. Scott's Los Angeles is not far from that history. His city represents a negative melting pot, where nonwhite immigrant groups are left to scavenge over the scraps of a deindustrialized landscape. An ugly street language, a hybrid dialect of Spanish, Japanese, and German, has replaced English. This is Los Angeles after alien colonization (most likely Japanese investors), where whiteness is a historical figment of an ancient civilization.

Images of the post-white flight city projected the racial anxieties that surfaced in such postwar blockbusters as *Them!* and *War of the Worlds*. While these films are not exclusively about white anxieties, the spatial emphasis of *Them!* and *War of the Worlds*, that is, their use of the city as setting and subject, suggests that it is essential to understand the spatial transformation of postwar America in order to grasp the multiple meanings of these films. Americans suburbanized in unprecedented numbers during the post–World War II era, abandoning older portions of the inner city. By and large, that process was a privilege afforded to those who could identify themselves as white, while nonwhite, racialized minorities "filled in" the decrepit spaces left behind, moving us toward Ridley Scott's ominous vision of the twenty-first century city. As white flight and suburbanization promoted the racial polarization of postwar America between "chocolate cities" and "vanilla suburbs," cultural productions such as the urban science fiction film represented that polarization in graphic images of alien invaders and the spectacular disintegration of American cities.

The racial politics of suburbanization in postwar America drew not only upon material processes, such as the Lakewood Plan and the racially-biased lending policies of the FHA and VA, but also upon the production of cinematic spectacles such as the urban science fiction film. Although such films did not create white flight, they dramatized the anxieties that undergirded the racial politics of suburbanization. The urban science fiction film created a space in which white Americans could imagine themselves and their predicament in the years following the conclusion of the Second World War. The invasion and ultimate obliteration of the city so graphically represented through the advanced technology of special effects corresponded to the very real rejection of urban life by white America. The urban science fiction film conjured a realm of dreadful possibilities that heightened the sense of urgency with which white Americans abandoned the older portions of cities like Detroit and Los Angeles and sought refuge in homogenous communities like Lakewood. Just as it was not difficult for white suburban Americans to sympathize with the terrified masses of films such as *Them!* and *War of the Worlds,* so it was not difficult for black inner-city writers such as Ralph Ellison to suspect that they might have been the "Hollywood movie ectoplasms" of 1950s science fiction.

NOTES

1. My thanks to James Cook for pointing out this citation from *Invisible Man* to me.
2. These terms were introduced by Reynolds Farley, Howard Schuman, Diane Colasanto, and Shirley Hatchet, "Chocolate City, Vanilla Suburbs: Will the Trend

Towards Racially Separate Communities Continue?" *Social Science Research* 7 (1978): 330. George Clinton, with Parliament-Funkadelic, also recorded a song entitled "Chocolate Cities, Vanilla Suburbs" in 1978.

3. The literature on the spatial and racial organization of the postindustrial metropolis is extensive. See Thomas Sugrue, *The Origins of the Urban Crisis: Race and Inequality in Postwar Detroit* (Princeton, NJ: Princeton University Press, 1998), and Arnold Hirsch, *Making the Second Ghetto: Race and Housing in Chicago, 1940–1960* (Chicago: University of Chicago, 1998). See also Douglas S. Massey and Nancy A. Denton, *American Apartheid: Segregation and the Making of the Urban Underclass* (Cambridge, MA: Harvard University Press, 1993), and Reynolds Farley and Walter Allen, *The Color Line and the Quality of Life in America* (New York: Russell Sage, 1987).

4. Peter Biskind, *Seeing is Believing: How America Learned to Stop Worrying and Love the Fifties* (New York: Pantheon Books, 1983), and Michael Rogin, *Ronald Reagan, The Movie* (Berkeley: University of California, 1987).

5. Arnold Hirsch, "Black Ghettos," in *The Reader's Companion to American History*, ed. Eric Foner and John A. Garrity (New York: Houghton Mifflin Company, 1991), 112.

6. Gordon de Marco, *A Short History of Los Angeles* (San Francisco: Lexikos, 1988), 164.

7. Richard Polenberg, *One Nation Divisible: Class, Race and Ethnicity in the United States Since 1938* (New York: Penguin, 1980), 162.

8. Mike Davis, *City of Quartz: Excavating the Future in Los Angeles* (London: Verso, 1990), 400.

9. Paul Gilje, *Rioting in America* (Bloomington: Indiana University Press, 1996), 165.

10. George Lipsitz, *The Possessive Investment in Whiteness: How White People Profit from Identity Politics* (Philadelphia: Temple University Press, 1998).

11. Kenneth T. Jackson, *Crabgrass Frontier: The Suburbanization of the United States* (New York: Oxford, 1985), 195–203.

12. Gary Miller, *Cities by Contract: The Politics of Municipal Incorporation* (Cambridge, MA: MIT Press, 1981).

13. Ibid., 22.

14. Jack Smith, "The Great Los Angeles Air Raid," in *Los Angeles: Biography of a Metropolis*, ed. John and LaRee Caughey (Berkeley: University of California, 1976), 364.

15. "West Coast, Too, Has its Race Problem," *U.S. News and World Report*, July 14, 1956, 36.

16. John Houseman, "Hollywood Faces the Fifties," *Harper's*, December 2, 1950, 50.

17. Lynn Spiegel, "Installing the Television Set: Popular Discourses on Television and Domestic Space, 1948–1950," *Camera Obscura* 16 (1988): 14–20.

18. *Variety*, November 3, 1953, 6.

19. Marlon Riggs, *Ethnic Notions* (San Francisco: California Newsreel, 1986), videocassette.

20. *Los Angeles Herald Express*, November 26, 1953.

21. Daniel Bernardi, "The Voice of Whiteness: D. W. Griffith's Biograph Films," in *The Birth of Whiteness: Race and the Emergence of U.S. Cinema*, ed. Daniel Bernardi (New Brunswick, NJ: Rutgers University, 1996), 122.

22. For a discussion of cinematic lighting and whiteness, see Richard Dyer, *White* (London: Routledge, 1997), 116–42.

23. Charles Ramirez Berg, "Immigrants, Aliens and Extraterrestrials: Science Fiction's Alien 'Other' as (Among Other Things) New Hispanic Imagery," *CineAction!* 18 (fall 1989).

24. James Snead; Colin MacCabe, ed.; and Cornel West, ed., *White Screens, Black Images: Hollywood From the Dark Side* (London: Routledge, 1994), 6–7.

25. James Cook, "Of Men, Missing Links and Nondescripts: The Strange Career of P. T. Barnum's 'What is it?' Exhibition," in *Freakery: Cultural Spectacles of Extraordinary Body*, ed. Rosemarie Garland Thompson (New York: New York University, 1996), 139–57.

26. *Variety*, March 3, 1953.

27. Vivian Sobchack, "Cities on the Edge of Time: The Urban Science Fiction Film," *East-West Film Journal* 1, no. 3 (December 1988): 11.

4

"THEY WORSHIP MONEY AND PREJUDICE"

The Certainties of Class and the Uncertainties of Race in *Son of the Gods*

Gina Marchetti

Made in 1929 and released in January 1930, *Son of the Gods* (directed by Frank Lloyd and based on a story by Rex Beach), a Vitaphone sound feature from Warners/First National, is marked by several different cataclysmic changes in both the movie industry and American society. The film tells the story of Sam Lee (Richard Barthelmess), the son of a wealthy Chinese merchant, who becomes the victim of racism when he falls in love with a European-American socialite, Allana Wagner (Constance Bennett). After both nearly self-destruct because of their taboo relationship, Sam learns he is actually white. While he continues to embrace his Chinese upbringing at the end of the film, Sam's true identity frees him from the stigma of an interracial marriage.

Made in the early days (quite literally) of the Depression, the film retains a Jazz Age sensibility and ambiance. Ukuleles, roadster sports cars, dance halls, casinos on the Riviera, tuxedoes, and champagne figure prominently in the mise-en-scène. Wild flappers, college boys, indulgent millionaires, and playboy playwrights dominate the cast of characters. However, *Son of the Gods* marks the end of an era. Although no direct reference is made to this fact in the film, everything in it seems disturbingly out of step. Nothing is certain; everything appears to be on the verge of collapse. Individual identity is so confused that changing race is presented as easier than moving up or down on the social ladder of class. In fact, as the supposedly physically self-evident fact of race becomes problematic, class divisions, prerogatives, and identities go unchallenged.

Although, in many ways, *Son of the Gods* is a social problem film, explicitly calling for racial tolerance, it is, in other significant ways, a film about the solidity of class at a time when bankrupt former millionaires were plunging from the windows of their penthouse offices. Because individual social standing could change dramatically and quite suddenly, *Son of the Gods* cannot deny completely the mercurial nature of human identity. Rather, it ambivalently recognizes fundamental changes of identity while also denying the possibility of any type of upward or downward class mobility.

The film's static, enclosed early sound style adds to this ambivalent presentation of stasis and change. The generally motionless compositions, lack of camera movement, restrained editing, and standard studio sets underscore the film's presentation of its class milieu as incorruptibly solid, comfortably artificial, and self-contained. Still a new component of the motion picture, synchronized sound is presented in a slow, measured way. The dialogue is clearly articulated and carefully coached, for example. In fact, *Son of the Gods* relies primarily on words, accents, tones, and inflections to convey the preponderance of its plot information. When occasional street scenes appear or when action replaces the spoken word in the drama, a rupture can be felt, and these moments seem to be privileged dramatically as turning points in the narrative.

This analysis of *Son of the Gods* focuses on the ways in which the narrative, visual, and aural elements of the film work together to displace the issue of class onto issues of racial, ethnic, and sexual identity. In this case, the possibility of class mobility functions as a latent presence not directly addressed by the film. However, class issues can be detected in every twist of what might, at first, appear to be a highly unlikely plot about the surprisingly malleable nature of racial and ethnic identity.

THE VISIBILITY AND INVISIBILITY OF CLASS

From the critical perspective of the 1990s, *Son of the Gods* may appear ideologically confusing. The film is certainly contradictory. Antiracist dialogue competes with plot twists that ensure segregation. Liberated women end up in bondage because of romance. An ethnic identity floats free of racial stigma to ossify, pointing to the roots of the myth of the Asian American "model minority."[1] All of this confusion hovers around the issue of class and class privilege.

Like the Exclusion Laws still in force when *Son of the Gods* was produced, the film divides the Chinese community based on money and occupation. These laws ended the entry of Chinese laborers, who had done so much to build up the mining, transportation, and agricultural industries in America. It must be remembered that the discriminatory laws of the nineteenth century coincided with the rise of the labor movement in the United States. Class consciousness was too often founded on racist fears, and Chinese laborers became easy targets. As an appeasement to the white union movement, these laws softened class conflict by appealing to a common racism between white employer and employee.

Even though legal immigration was restricted into virtual nonexistence, cracks appeared in the system. Rich merchants, students, scholars, and diplomats came and went as sojourners during the early part of the twentieth century. Before immigration loopholes were closed, Chinese women came into the United States in small, but significant numbers. Many Chinese took advantage of the chaos created by the San Francisco earthquake to become "paper sons"[2] and make a go at life in America. Ronald Takaki calls the Chinatowns of this period "gilded ghettoes."[3]

Excluded from the main labor force, the Chinese worked in laundries or ethnic restaurants. They also worked as grocers or curio merchants. During this period, the Chinese in the United States became increasingly urbanized, and American Chinatowns became tourist attractions. A polarized vision of the Chinese grew even more firmly entrenched. The poor, struggling, ignorant, illiterate, love-starved "coolie"[4] rubbed elbows in Chinatown with the wealthy mandarin, the beneficiary of a romanticized, ancient, and mysterious Chinese civilization.

In *Son of the Gods*, this polarized, class understanding of Chinese racial and ethnic difference forms the foundation for the rationalization of a racism modified by an embattled tolerance. While both the coolie and the mandarin threatened mainstream America's sense of a homogenous, white, Anglo-Saxon identity, wealth seemed to make the threat less urgent. Indeed, in the construction of the myth of the "model minority," old, racial stereotypes of superior, but lifeless, intelligence; self-deprivation to the point of near insanity; and ethnic clannishness endure as a legacy of the popular figuration of the mandarin. Fu Manchu and Charlie Chan have metamorphosed into the Chinese American technician, mid-level bureaucrat, and computer "nerd" of the late twentieth century.

In *Son of the Gods*, an argument surfaces that Sam Lee should not be excluded from the international fellowship of the bourgeoisie. However, this urbane, old-world culture finds itself at odds with a more conservative, racist, and puritanical American identity. To find its way out of this conundrum, *Son of the Gods* relies on more than a plot twist. The film, in many confusing turns of logic played out in the dialogue, carefully strips away ethnicity from race. Although Sam Lee is eventually revealed to be a white foundling, he can remain a mandarin. At some obscure level, Chinese ethnicity is separated from Asian race. Still mysteriously and magically wealthy and Chinese, Sam embraces both the white race in the form of Allana and his own reclaimed racial identity. Through Sam's romance with Allana, the film ties racial identity to the myth of "true love." Allana and Sam can fall in love "naturally," only if miscegenation disappears from the plot. Class makes this magic happen in *Son of the Gods*.

As Stuart Hall points out, "central issues of race always appear historically in articulation, in a formation, with other categories and divisions and are constantly crossed and recrossed by the categories of class, of gender and ethnicity." [5] In the case of *Son of the Gods*, this crossing and recrossing can create a certain amount of confusion, which eventually leads to narrative, if not ideological, resolution. While race has historically been used to rationalize slavery, colonialism, and imperialism based on supposedly self-evident physical and biological attributes, ethnicity tends to be linked to affiliations based on language, culture, and national origin. When Allana, for example, calls Sam a "Chinaman," it cannot be determined whether her prejudice is racially motivated or based on a feeling of ethnic superiority or nationalism. The two concepts are so closely intertwined at that point in the film that the question becomes moot. However, as the "white" Sam Lee bows to the portraits of his adoptive parents at the end of the film, race and ethnicity separate. In spite of his race, Sam wishes to remain Chinese, and, in response to racial taboos and a strong undercurrent of biological determinism in the film, being ethnically Chinese becomes separated from the Asian race. At this point, the film links ethnicity with culture and civilization rather than with race. The film and American thinking generally remain slippery, then, about the differentiation of ethnicity and race. [6] Sometimes the two terms appear synonymous, while, at other times, race and ethnicity function in very distinct ways. This slipperiness, in the case of this film, makes tolerance and racism compatible.

Class, however, is a different issue in *Son of the Gods*. While ethnicity is removed from biology, class becomes linked to "natural selection." Sam is described as "clean" and a "thoroughbred," making his place within the bourgeoisie appear to be a question of nature and biology. Although his biological parents never appear, the dialogue intimates that Sam was born to rule. Even when he tries to escape his class position, something fundamental and inborn seems to pull him up into the ranks of the bourgeois elect.[7]

Sam's world may be exotic because it is "Oriental" or because it is haute bourgeois. One eye sees race and the other class, but both blend into a three-dimensional vision of wealth, which is beyond the reach of the vast majority of the film's viewers.[8] In the silent era, the trappings of the Orient found their way into the mise-en-scène of many commercially successful films. As Sumiko Higashi notes in her extensive work on the films of Cecil B. DeMille, Orientalia became inextricably linked to the pleasures and potential dangers of consumerism and the construction of a new middle class in America.[9] Edward Said points out that the Orient functions as "a sort of surrogate or even underground self"[10] in European (and, by implication, Euro-American) discourses about Asia and Asians. Desires for upward mobility and the ambivalence created by those desires find their expression in Orientalist discourses and in Orientalist imagery.

In *Son of the Gods*, the trappings of Orientalism connote both wealth and racial difference. Sam Lee blends into the world of upper-class Europeans as well as that of the chinoiserie that surrounds him in Chinatown. It is only within the American middle classes that he finds himself alienated and a stranger. At one point, he bitterly remarks, "I hoped to be an American. I tried to become one. But there are forces too great opposing this." Although the forces opposing his assimilation appear to be based on race, class, too, plays its part in making Sam a stranger. At home on the Riviera, why should Sam be out of place on the streets of New York? The ideological job of the narrative becomes one of recuperating Sam's money for America, of tearing it out of the hands of a foreign bourgeoisie. Orientalia promises wealth and refinement, tainted by the foreign, implicitly corrupt, and decadent civilization of China. The taint must somehow be removed so that class privilege can be rationalized.

In addition to its association with wealth and the emerging leisure class of early twentieth century America, Orientalia has always had a sexual dimension, associated with luxury, sensuousness, eroticism, perversity, and decadence. Both Miriam Hansen[11] and Gaylyn Studlar[12] have discussed extensively the relationship among the white female viewer, depictions of sexuality, and Orientalism in the silent era.

There is an established link between Orientalism and sexuality in the cinema. In addition, Hollywood has a commitment to heterosexual romance as an overarching narrative strategy. Therefore, it should come as no surprise that the racial, ethnic, and class tensions in *Son of the Gods* should be dramatized through the love affair between Sam and Allana. Racism becomes an impediment to true love. Class ranks are solidified through marriage. Potentially wayward women are domesticated. Class identity becomes part of bourgeois domesticity.

RACISM AND RACIAL CHAMELEONS—THE APPEAL OF A FANTASY

Son of the Gods opens with Sam Lee away at college. Although his Chinese ethnicity is known by most of his acquaintances, he becomes a victim of racism, which involves a misunderstanding occasioned by his "European features." During a coed outing, Sam's female companions become uncomfortable when they discover that Sam is Chinese. They refuse further association with Sam. Sam returns to New York to see his father, Lee Ying (E. Alyn Warren), who reluctantly gives his blessing to his son's desire to see the world as a cabin boy on a steamer. His cabin boy days are short-lived, however. A playwright, Bathurst (Claude King), befriends Sam and whisks him off to the French Riviera. There, he meets and falls in love with a California heiress, Allana Wagner. When Allana finds out that Sam is Chinese, she shuns him and publicly shames him by striking him in the face with her riding crop.

After his father's death, Sam takes over the family business in New York. Embittered, he refuses to continue extending credit to white customers and shuns Allana's attempts to reconcile. Eventually, Sam discovers he is really a white foundling, adopted by Lee Ying and his wife. Although Allana returns to Sam still believing he is Chinese and although Sam himself continues to treasure his Chinese upbringing, their kiss at the conclusion of *Son of the Gods* is untroubled by any hint of miscegenation. They are of the same "race."

This remarkable change in racial identity may appear to be contrived or even bizarre. However, it actually figured as a favorite film device for resolving the apparently irreconcilable conflict between Hollywood's desire to titillate with tales of miscegenation and its need to provide the audience with a "happy ending" undisturbed by racial difference. In *From Scarface to Scarlett: American Films in the 1930's,* Roger Dooley observes the following about interracial couples in Hollywood films of that era:

> The only possibility of happiness for such star-crossed lovers was if by some unlikely plot device it turned out that they were, after all, of the same race. Either the apparently darker one was actually white, orphaned and reared by kindly natives as their own, or less commonly, the apparent white learned that one of his/her parents, usually the mother, was actually Indian, Malay or whatever. This dodge was used three times in 1930 alone.[13]

The appeal of these narratives about mistaken racial identity at first may seem baffling. After all, a fundamental stratification within American society bases itself on the certainty of racial differences. A narrative that questions the apparently self-evident classification of individuals according to race would seem to threaten this social structure.

However, part of the American mythos also involves the promise of assimilation; i.e., that ethnic and other differences can disappear into the American "melting pot." A narrative in which ethnic differences can magically disappear and acceptance into the American mainstream be granted would likely strike a cord of recognition among new immigrants, minorities, and working-class members of the audience. These viewers might relish a fantasy of sudden transformation that would make their lives materially better. Therefore, this plot device fulfills wishes and maintains taboos all at the same time.

In the case of *Son of the Gods,* specifically, this device allows tensions relating to changes in class standing to be displaced onto the far less likely prospect of a change in racial classification. Further, this device becomes even more conventional through its manifestation in the form of the Hollywood romance. This film, then, inextricably links the question of class and racial identity to sex and romance. In the realm of bourgeois ideology, both race and class standing can be solidified or disturbed by romantic entanglements.

With the decay of the aristocracy, the rise to power of the bourgeoisie also coincided with closer contact with peoples from Africa, the New World, and Asia through the processes of imperialism, colonization, and diaspora. Therefore, this obsession with "blood" and "racial purity" can be interpreted as a bourgeois "rule by blood" replacement for the fallen aristocracy's claim to hereditary power. American history has been replete with threats to white bourgeois rule coming from Native Americans, African slaves, Chinese laborers, and Caribbean and Mexican neighbors. Therefore, in the American popular imagination, this insistence on racial divisions to rationalize class rule traditionally has been quite strong.

Although in most narratives dealing with race and American identity female characters more usually and easily change their racial/class identity, it is not uncommon for this type of identity crisis to be linked to a question of male gender identity and sexual potency. For example, in *Son of the Gods,* Sam Lee both finds his "true" race and "gets the girl" at the same time. His class standing remains unchanged; his economic dynasty is assured by marriage within the bourgeoisie; and his masculinity blossoms without the taint of any Chinese "perversity" or "effemininity" within his sexual make-up. By the film's conclusion, Sam Lee has been established as rich, white, and in love with a rich, white woman. He has fulfilled the American promise of assimilation, wealth, and romantic fulfillment for those new immigrants in the audience who may have come to America looking for all three. At the same time, the fantasy solidifies class and racial hierarchies under a veneer of liberalism for viewers who have already established themselves, but who now face the uncertain consequences of the stock market crash.

CONSTRUCTING AN IDENTITY

In order for this unlikely narrative to work at all, *Son of the Gods* must very carefully construct its protagonist's identity as solidly bourgeois, but questionably Chinese. A crucial part of this construction of the character of Sam Lee comes from Richard Barthelmess's earlier association with a Chinese role in D. W. Griffith's *Broken Blossoms* (1919).[14] Barthelmess does not appear to wear any special make-up to mask his features in *Son of the Gods*, so his racial identity emerges exclusively from the dialogue and his past association with Asian roles. The contradiction between his visible race and the illusion constructed through the dialogue resolves itself in the eventual discovery of Lee's racial identity. However, throughout most of the film, the characters (and, presumably through the "suspension of disbelief," the audience) never question either their initial acceptance of Lee as white or their eventual discovery that he is, in fact, Chinese. Lee himself never questions his constantly mistaken racial identity. When he discovers his true background, he appears to be surprised.

Son of the Gods never takes up the narrative theme of "passing for white," which appeared in literature and films around the same time—e.g., *Scar of Shame* (1927), *Imitation of Life* (1934). Although mistaken for white, Lee never actively or consciously tries to "pass" or hide his Chinese identity. On the contrary, everyone in the film knows he is Chinese and simply accepts that he has European features by happenstance. The exceptions to this are, of course, Lee's love interests and their immediate family and friends. The film presents Lee as naïve, sensitive, guileless, and perhaps more than a little stupid; he comes across therefore as too honest and forthright to even think about the possibility of passing for white. Thus, the question of passing remains at the edge of the text as an unvoiced narrative possibility. In fact, it only emerges at all when Lee hesitates to tell Allana that he is Chinese. At one point in the film, the conversation turns to questions of race and romance. Allana reveals that she was engaged at one time to an East Indian. This pronouncement seems to absolve Sam of any real deception. He assumes that Allana is not prejudiced. Allana ends the discussion with a kiss.

By avoiding the question of passing, *Son of the Gods* also sidesteps the ideological issue of whether or not race *should* matter. Although the film seems to call for tolerance, it clings to several racist assumptions: miscegenation leads to tragedy, racial confusion can throw both personal and socioeconomic relations into chaos, and even the most benevolent assimilation into an alien race can result in excruciating unhappiness. The film, therefore, remains contradictory. It condemns and maintains racial divisions through the working out of its narrative developments.

Moreover, the film's apparent call for racial tolerance is further put in doubt by its firm insistence on the solidity of class hierarchies. Although Sam Lee's race cannot be visibly discerned, his class position can very easily be seen. He first appears in the film competing in a polo match. He wears elegant clothes, attends college, owns a roadster, and agrees to treat an entire party of his friends and their dates to an evening of dining and dancing. When the issue of Sam's Chinese background comes up, one of his parasitic college pals counters a racist remark by pointing to Sam's inheritance: "Sam's father is the richest Chinese man in New York. Why, he's the Chinese Marshall Field. . . . Working your way through college and turning your nose up at a swell fellow like that." In fact, throughout the film, racism is never attacked as senseless prejudice, but as a misrecognition of the importance of class standing over skin color. At one point, Allana (hypocritically, as it turns out) tells Sam, "There are no taboos among people of our class." She seems to be stating a truism that the power of money erases any ill consequences of skin color or ethnic background. Wealth elevates and equalizes.

Allana is also trying to affect a sophistication that is somewhat alien to her. In fact, her racism marks her as "nouveau riche" in the eyes of "old money." Only those newly admitted to the ranks of the bourgeoisie, like Allana, or those on the edges of wealth, like the girls working their way through college, dare to voice any racial prejudice in the face of the power of class standing. Sam's mentor, Bathurst, points to Allana's own ill breeding and ignorance when she seeks him out after Sam has left the Riviera. Allana blurts out, "I'm a Californian. I was raised among Chinamen," wrinkling up her nose and spitting out the word "Chinamen." Without blinking, Bathurst counters that she was raised among "coolies," while "Sam Lee is a gentleman."

The film, in fact, carefully sets up this opposition between coolies and gentlemen. An argument is put forward that the former can rightly be looked down upon, while the latter should be accepted supposedly because of their "civility," "breeding," and "culture" (but, more likely, because of their money). Ideologically, the Chinese in Son of the Gods function less as markers of racial and cultural difference and more as emblems of class variation.

The other ethnic groups in the film are very clearly linked with specific class positions. Through their jobs, dress, accents, and comportment, the principal Irish characters, Lee Ying's secretary Eileen (Mildred Van Dorn) and the policeman Dugan (Robert Homans), are depicted as unquestionably working class. The Anglo-Americans (as well as all the Europeans with speaking roles) are bourgeois, either "old money" like Bathurst, nouveau riche like Allana and her family, or aspiring and upwardly mobile like Sam's college friends.

The Chinese characters, on the other hand, fall into two distinct classes. Sam's father Lee Ying affects long fingernails and a scholar's gown, Hollywood's standard attire for the Chinatown mandarin merchant. However, he displays his class position not only through his clothes, but also through an elaborate office set, complete with circular doorways, hidden temple chambers, and the usual Hollywood chinoiserie. Sam's personal servant Moy (King Hoo Chang)—the only Chinese character in the film played by a Chinese actor—makes his class position clear in equally stereotypical ways: through his job as a domestic servant, his heavily accented English, and his "vulgar" hobby of frequenting dance halls where white taxi dancers take Asian customers.

Sam's identity crisis not only rests on his precarious balance between two races, but also, perhaps more importantly, on his unsteady positioning between these two troubling visions of Chinese men as either effete, effeminate, (literally) impotent mandarins, or ignorant, sexually unbalanced or immature workers.[15] On the two occasions when white women romantically spurn Sam, he looks to his "roots" by returning home to his father, the Confucian classics, and the family business. However, both times this return to his mandarin heritage quickly segues into a search for his identity through contact with the great masses of the "unwashed."

Certainly, the fantasy of the poor, confused, rich boy trying to find his true destiny by turning to manual labor and contact with working people has always had an important place within American popular culture. The "self-made man" forms part of an ideological ploy to assuage fears that the bourgeois acquisition of wealth may not rest entirely on "merit" and hard work. The wealthy hero in Hollywood seems more valued after he has proven his ability to accumulate money on his own. In terms of Hollywood economics, an occasionally working-class hero, like Sam Lee, might be a more reasonable point of identification for a predominantly working-class movie audience, even if that audience dreams of upward mobility and covets fame and fortune.

Within Hollywood narratives, then, Sam's desire to put his father's money aside and make his own way would fall within a popular formula. In this case, however, race and ethnicity complicate the plot. Sam voices his desire to lower himself into the working classes because he wants to understand both his own ethnicity and American racism. He wants to comprehend his election to the ranks of the rich, but he also wants to understand the relationship between class and race. Both the privileges of class and the venom of racism confuse him. Speaking of white American society, Sam complains, with a note of bewilderment in his voice, "They worship money and prejudice."

A great deal of the narrative revolves around proving to Sam and to the audience that he is a member of the elect, destined to be rich, and inherently unable to fall from his elevated class standing. Lee Ying sends his son off to see the world as a cabin boy on a steamer with the reminder, "You are a son of the gods, for they sent you in answer to a prayer." Although this line can be interpreted simply as an elderly father's doting remark to an only son or as a portent of the eventual discovery of Sam's adoption, it can also be viewed, more subtly, as a reminder that Sam is a member of the elect, unalterably part of the bourgeoisie.[16]

This interpretation proves correct. Without ever showing Sam as a cabin boy, the film provides the information, through the device of a letter shown on the screen, that Sam has been given a job as "consultant" by the wealthy playwright Bathurst. While lounging on the Riviera, Bathurst just happens to be writing a play with a Chinese theme. Never appearing in a cabin boy's uniform, Sam continues to wear his Ivy League attire. Moreover, he proves his "divine right" to the ranks of the wealthy by turning his salary into a small fortune in the casinos. Bathurst, the staff and guests at the hotel, as well as Allana, never question Sam's class standing.[17]

When Allana violently breaks off her relationship with Sam, he returns to New York's Chinatown, only to discover that his father has died. Agonized, Sam tells his confidante Eileen: "I hoped to be an American. I tried to become one. But there are forces too great opposing this. . . . I am Chinese . . . and, from now on, I shall live as one." Sam begins to wear padded Chinese jackets and silk skullcaps. He refuses to lend money to white-owned businesses. Part of Sam's expression of his Chinese identity takes the form of "slumming." In fact, the film links Sam's search for racial/ethnic/national identity with a desire to descend into the working classes. All of this, moreover, is bound up with Sam's masculinity and frustrated sexual expression.

One night, Sam's servant Moy invites him to go to a favorite dance hall. Moy inquires, "You like white arms?" Sam, at first, refuses. The next scene, however, opens with Moy buying tickets at the dance hall. The place is furnished like a German beer garden with Chinese lanterns incongruously hanging from the ceiling. The camera tracks around the establishment, revealing that the preponderance of the clientele is Asian while the taxi dancers are all white.

When Allana's father comes to look for Sam, the bargirls point him out as one of the regulars. However, *Son of the Gods* again shows that Sam's class standing makes him somehow "different." Seated above the dance floor, at a table alone, Sam refuses the taxi dancers' requests for a spin around the dance floor. Despondent, Sam remains a voyeur, passively watching what Allana's father judges to be a "vulgar" (read: perverted, unnatural) display of interracial contact. That Sam's voyeurism, passivity, and implied sexual impotence may be more "perverse" than the fairly innocent, lively dancing going on among the working-class dancers below remains beyond the parameters of the discourse.

However, even Mr. Wagner's condemnation of Sam's visits to the dance hall does little to shatter what is presented as "natural" in the film: namely, class standing and "true" (heterosexual, racially segregated) love. Allana has been punished for both her racism and self-assertion by her descent into alcoholism and illness. Sam has also been punished for his interracial romantic desires by the loss of his love object and its attendant bitter depression. The film is now free to find a way to reunite the couple and prove their love is "natural." The fact that Sam can save Allana from her illness, just as her unwavering commitment to their romance can save Sam from sliding into the ranks of the working-class Chinese community, underscores the film's insistence that romance can and should solidify class ranks.

Two significant narrative absences help to confirm this interpretation of the presentation of class and race in *Son of the Gods*. First, no Asian women appear as possible romantic partners for Sam Lee. Celibacy is also not taken seriously. Since Lee Ying's relationship with his wife is held up as a model for personal fulfillment and happiness, Sam's desire for female companionship is not only presented as self-evident, but also is made more emotionally urgent by his fond looks at the portrait of his deceased mother. The narrative does not allow for the very different twist of Sam not being accepted by a Chinatown family because he looks too white.

Second, although Eileen appears in the film as a young, attractive, single woman, her relationship with Sam remains platonic. This may seem odd inasmuch as Sam so desperately looks for love and the vocally anti-racist Eileen seems to be available. Her relationship with Sam appears to be warm. For example, she grabs his hand when she greets him on his return from college, gives him a Catholic religious charm when he goes off to see the world, and mourns with him when his father dies. Moreover, the dialogue continuously confirms her regard for Sam: she describes him as "clean" and a "thoroughbred." Out of pity for his failed relationship with Allana, Eileen even arranges for Sam to find out the truth about his racial identity for "Miss Wagner's" sake. Despite all this consideration, however, Eileen is never shown as carrying a torch for Sam, nor does he seem to have any romantic interest in her. As threatening as the possibility of miscegenation may be, the film still presents interracial romance as a more viable option than cross-class alliances. *Son of the Gods* does not even hint at the possibility of romance between different classes. Buried far beneath its liberal surface, *Son of the Gods* clings to a Puritan notion of wealth as a sign of God's grace and sexuality as an expression of a "natural" class order.

DISMANTLING AN IDENTITY: DRAMATIC EXCESSES AND NARRATIVE FISSURES

For the most part, *Son of the Gods* appears to be a staid, linear, early sound film, relying on dialogue, rather than editing, camera movement, or figure movement, for its dramatic and narrative progression. However, there are some key exceptions to this general rule of style. The dance hall scene, for example, includes comparatively more figure and camera movement, and it serves to mark the film's most blatant flirtation with the taboo topic of downward class mobility. However, the film soon shies away from this possibility by depicting Sam as a stationary figure, perched immobile above the teeming "masses" below him.

Two other scenes also stand out in *Son of the Gods* because of their comparatively excessive movement—on temporal, dramatic, as well as visual levels. In the first, Allana confronts Sam about his ethnic background, and in the second, a flashback explains the circumstances surrounding Sam's adoption. In most respects, these two scenes function in opposite ways. The first represents a violent break in the continuation of the bourgeois family and patriarchal social order. The second, on the other hand, marks the continuation of the male-headed family and its completion through the adopted son. The first displays a woman's violent self-assertion, which is presented as dangerously inappropriate. The second begins with Sam's adoptive mother's funeral, i.e., a still, silent, "appropriate" public female presence. In fact, it is not surprising that Mrs. Lee should only appear in the film as a lifeless object inasmuch as her inability to have children sets the entire plot in motion. If she had not been barren, Sam would not have been adopted. He therefore would not have suffered racial discrimination because of the adoption.

Son of the Gods, therefore, links both race and class to gender relationships. These two scenes bring this aspect of the film to the surface. In the first, Allana's confrontation with Sam is relatively brief. After being told by her father that Sam is Chinese, Allana goes to meet Sam for tea at the hotel café. She has just come from riding, and she still wears her riding habit and carries her riding crop. Sam, in contrast, arrived earlier, impeccably dressed, speaking French to some acquaintances and the waiter. He is presented as a model bourgeois gentleman. Sam sits alone at a table when Allana storms in. In medium close-up, whip in hand, she shouts, "You cur, you liar, you cheat, you

Figure 4.1. Sam Lee confronted by Allana Wagner in *Son of the Gods* (1930). (Image courtesy of the Museum of Modern Art Film Stills Archive.)

dirty, rotten Chinaman." She begins to beat Sam's face with her riding crop. A reverse shot shows blood on Sam's face, and another close shot of Allana shows her continuing to beat him. In a medium shot, she finally walks away. A reverse close-up shows Sam touching the blood on his face, then leaving the table, and the screen fades to black. The violent action that accompanies Allana's curses marks this scene as different from the more static scenes that make up most of the rest of the film. The use of close-ups also distinguishes this scene inasmuch as such shots are used sparingly throughout the film. In this scene, the style changes to underscore the disruptive qualities of the scene and its underlying dramatic force and narrative import.

In addition to the threat of miscegenation and the possibility of class mobility, the violent assertion of a woman's will fundamentally threatens the uncertain social structure represented in *Son of the Gods*. Up to this point, Allana seems a typical Jazz Age "modern woman." [18] She appears to be sexually experienced, unsettled, sophisticated, wealthy, independent, strong-willed, directionless, fickle, self-indulgent, self-destructive, and unself-consciously dangerous to hapless males who may strike her fancy. By beating Sam, Allana concretizes her dangerous potential. Although the threat she poses to him may be negatively coded as racist, it certainly, too, stems from her ability to express violently a volition independent of male control. If Sam had nearly succeeded in taming her through their engagement, then this scene reveals her refusal to be brought into the fold.

Because Allana's expression of her individual will is so strong, her degradation and humiliation must be equally forceful so that she can be recuperated into the patriarchal family at the end of the film. To this end, Sam's mistaken racial identity comes in quite handy. In fact, this film fits in a long tradition of Hollywood narratives that use the Asian male as an instrument of punishment for the wayward, independent, and/or sexually adventurous white American female.[19] Sam manages to bring Allana into line by embodying both of the usually mutually exclusive attributes that Hollywood ascribed to Asian males: sadistic perversion or total impotence and emasculation.

In this case, Sam expresses his sadism through his passivity. When Allana beats him, Sam remains motionless. He does not try to protect himself and he certainly does not strike back. As Allana gradually self-destructs because of her desire for him, Sam remains passive, refusing to see her (except when she is delirious) and thereby avoiding any further confrontation. Thus, *Son of the Gods* both fulfills social expectations of a sadistic Asian masculine sexuality, while also allowing the hero to remain free of any hint of physical abuse, and affirms the notion that Asian men are passive, effeminate, impotent eunuchs. Sam remains Asian just long enough for Allana to realize that "true love" is the answer to all her problems. She finally decides that she must devote herself completely to Sam and give up her own independent desires. Through her desire for her Asian lover, her "natural" masochism surfaces. Her love for Sam is not presented as a search for a freer sexuality outside of white, male control, but as part of her masochistic, "essential," feminine desire to be dominated by a sadistic male. Ideologically, *Son of the Gods* naturalizes what might otherwise be a threat to the perception that white, male rule is natural, eternal, just, and divinely sanctioned. If the American patriarchy (represented by Allana's father) can no longer control the violent excesses of the "new woman," it remains to the supposedly more rigid Chinese patriarchy to help keep white American women under male dominance.

Another scene in *Son of the Gods* also breaks with the static style of the rest of the film. In this case, that break is with the linear temporal order. What the film marks as a dysfunctional female sexuality also lies at the core of the narrative and ideological importance of this scene. Here, however, the threat comes not from a violent expression of will, but from a physical dysfunction, i.e., the inability to conceive children, a failing typically blamed on females.

Lee Ying's barren wife functions as Allana's polar opposite. Whereas Allana

Figure 4.2. The funeral procession for Sam's mother. (Image courtesy of the Museum of Modern Art Film Stills Archive.)

is an active presence in the film, Sam's adoptive mother is an absence. The film refers to her only through the dialogue and shows only her funeral procession and portrait. However, this absent maternal figure provides the film with an idealized femininity, supposedly lost to the independent, assertive Allana.

The flashback places the continuation of the patriarchal order above all else. The policeman reveals that Sam's adoption was illegal and that Lee Ying lived in fear of the discovery. In suggesting that even a policeman sees that the law is unjust and so becomes a willing accomplice in this misdeed, the film seems to toy with the idea that American law is racist and fundamentally unjust. However, the film does this under the guise of the necessity for patrilineal descent and inheritance for the maintenance of the existing social order.

At this point, the specter of class mobility briefly appears again. As a foundling, likely abandoned because of poverty or illegitimacy, Sam represents the possibility of a change in class standing. However, this possibility only briefly surfaces and quickly vanishes. Sam immediately and without question accepts his role as the son of Lee Ying. Any thought that he is unworthy to be a member of the bourgeois elect can be dispelled because he has suffered for this change in class position through his problems with racism. He also seems to

Figure 4.3. Sam honors his mother's portrait. (Image courtesy of the Museum of Modern Art Film Stills Archive.)

be a "natural" member of the privileged classes, recognized as such by the working-class Eileen, who recognizes him as a "thoroughbred," implicitly different from herself. Although Sam's acceptance of his adoptive parents might be praised as the film's liberal call for the toleration of racial difference, it really functions to place the continuation of bourgeois, patriarchal relations above all other considerations. In fact, the revelation of Sam's origins also has a more sinister racist undertone. It magically "whitewashes" Lee Ying's capital so that the bourgeois elect can be "Caucasian." [20]

At the film's conclusion, Sam's acceptance of Allana's love (signified in the final shot of their kiss) serves to bring the wayward white woman back into the fold, to solidify class lines, and to continue strict patriarchal rule through white America's acceptance of the "truth" of the Asian sexual hierarchy. Under the cloak of an antiracist message, *Son of the Gods* manages to perpetuate racist notions of Asian sexuality, while shoring up white, male, bourgeois rule. If the film's representation of sexual contact between the races shocked in any way, that shock completely disappears at the conclusion of the film.

Son of the Gods deals with high society, a world on the brink of collapse. The Depression threatens class hierarchies and the myth that the rich rule by divine right. Immigration (primarily from Southern and Eastern Europe, since, as noted, Asian immigration during the 1920s was controlled to the point of near nonexistence) [21] questions American identity as Anglo-Saxon/Northern European and Protestant. The legacy of the suffragette movement opens up the possibility for a female identity outside of patriarchal definitions of femininity. *Son of the Gods* takes up all of these challenges to the status quo, acknowledges their existence, and, by subsuming them into an apparently "just" argument for tolerance, actually works to affirm the established social order.

However, like most Hollywood films, *Son of the Gods* remains ideologically slippery. Even the critic for *Motion Picture News*, Walter R. Green, noted: "Its plea for racial and religious tolerance will rate with the classes, while the dramatic and sentimental love story will get [sic] over with the masses." [22] Hollywood films always have something for everyone. A preferred reading might call for a strictly white, male, bourgeois ruling order under the veil of a liberal, fair, and color-blind America. However, negotiated readings can be teased out that show a morally bankrupt, white upper class; a new, independent, sexually courageous American woman; an inventive and clear-headed, ethnic working class; and an Asian ethnic community that has made a positive contribution to American society. [23] Although the film plays any potentially feminist, antiracist, and/or working-class readings against each other, these potential interpretations exist and may have provided part of the film's narrative pleasure for its diverse, early Depression audience.

NOTES

A version of this paper was originally presented at the 1992 Society for Cinema Studies Conference held in Pittsburgh, Pennsylvania, on a panel entitled "Film and the Question of Class," cochaired by Rick Berg and David James.

1. Ronald Takaki, *Strangers from a Different Shore: A History of Asian Americans* (New York: Penguin, 1989), 474–83.

2. False papers were used at Angel Island to show a blood relationship between unrelated people in order to facilitate entry into the United States. These fictive relations were commonly known as "paper sons," since a Chinese father could bring children (but not wives) into the United States. See ibid. for more information.

3. Ibid., 239.

4. Based on the Chinese "ku" and "li," meaning "bitter labor."

5. Stuart Hall, "New Ethnicities," in *"Race," Culture and Difference,* ed. James Donald and Ali Rattansi (London: Sage, 1992), 255.

6. The U.S. census, for example, seems to be constantly redefining racial and ethnic categories. "Hispanics" can be from a number of races. South Asians sometimes fit in one racial category, sometimes another. Politics and power masquerading as biology and demographics make these determinations subject to constant historical change. For more on defining race and ethnicity within the American cinema, refer to Lester D. Friedman, ed., *Unspeakable Images: Ethnicity and the American Cinema* (Urbana: University of Illinois Press, 1991).

7. It must be remembered that theories of eugenics and social Darwinism were quite common at the time. While most scientists now agree that "race" does not make much sense as a biological fact (i.e., there is as much variation within the so-called "races" as between them), pseudoscience continues to be used to shore up racial categories and maintain social dominance. The political and economic implications of racism also continue to endure.

8. While class may be an area of struggle, it has not been a high priority for film theory or criticism recently. Class has become another element in a laundry list of difference that includes race, ethnicity, gender, sexuality, and age. In fact, class has been absorbed by many of these other categories. However, to echo Stuart Hall, race cannot be understood without a concomitant analysis of other types of difference based on power and social hierarchies. Class has figured prominently in every aspect of the history of American film, from exhibition locations, marketing strategies, and labor relations within the industry to the depiction of class hierarchies within film narratives. To look at a film like *Son of the Gods* and see race without class is pointless. The film deliberately interweaves issues of race, ethnicity, gender, sexuality, and class, not to clarify its ostensible message, but to obfuscate it.

9. Sumiko Higashi, *Cecil B. DeMille and American Culture: The Silent Era* (Berkeley: University of California Press, 1994) and "Ethnicity, Class and Gender in Film: DeMille's *The Cheat*," in Friedman, *Unspeakable Images,* 112–39.

10. Edward Said, *Orientalism* (New York: Vintage, 1979), 3.

11. Miriam Hansen, "Pleasure, Ambivalence, Identification: Valentino and Female Spectatorship," *Cinema Journal* 25, no. 4 (summer 1986), 6–32.

12. Gaylyn Studlar, "'Out-Salomeing Salome': Dance, the New Woman, and Fan Magazine Orientalism," in *Visions of the East: Orientalism in Film,* ed. Matthew Bernstein and Gaylyn Studlar (New Brunswick, NJ: Rutgers University Press, 1997), 99–129.

13. Roger Dooley, *From Scarface to Scarlett: American Films in the 1930s* (San Diego: Harcourt Brace Jovanovich, 1979), 205.

14. Noted in Nick Roddick, *A New Deal in Entertainment: Warner Brothers in the 1930s* (London: British Film Institute, 1983), 145.

15. Eugene Franklin Wong discusses a similar split in representations of Asian males in Hollywood in *On Visual Media Racism: Asians in the American Motion Pictures* (New York: Arno, 1978). Generally speaking, there seems to be no necessary connection between the extreme representations of Asian male sexuality in Hollywood and the depiction of any given character's social class. In other words, wealth does not always go along with impotence and working-class identities do not necessarily correspond to an active, potentially predatory sexuality. In fact, it seems that *Son of the Gods* may go against the general trend of "yellow peril" fantasies in which wealth is more commonly associated with sexual potency and domestic servants play "eunuch" roles.

16. This equation of divine right and wealth is analyzed most thoroughly in the classic study by Max Weber, *The Protestant Ethic and the Spirit of Capitalism*, trans. Talcott Parsons (New York: Scribner's Sons, 1930).

17. In fact, only Allana's father suspects that anything might be wrong with his daughter's romance, and he thinks that Sam may be a gigolo, not that he is Chinese.

18. Analyzed by Sumiko Higashi in *Virgins, Vamps, and Flappers: The American Silent Movie Heroine* (Montreal: Eden Press, 1978).

19. See Gina Marchetti, *Romance and the "Yellow Peril": Race, Sex and Discursive Strategies in Hollywood Fiction* (Los Angeles: University of California Press, 1993). Also see the discussion of rape narratives in Ella Shohat and Robert Stam, *Unthinking Eurocentrism: Multiculturalism and the Media* (New York: Routledge, 1994).

20. It is, therefore, not surprising that another possibility does not surface in the film, i.e., that Sam may be the result of an interracial love affair. Although that may explain why he could "look" white and Asian under different circumstances, it would not serve the ideological purposes of the narrative.

21. See Takaki, *Strangers from a Different Shore*, and Lynn Pan, *Sons of the Yellow Emperor: A History of the Chinese Diaspora* (New York: Kodansha, 1994).

22. From *Motion Picture News*, February 8, 1930. Quoted in Roddick, *A New Deal*, 147.

23. For more on ideology and textual interpretation, see Stuart Hall, "Encoding, Decoding," in *The Cultural Studies Reader*, ed. Simon During (London: Routledge, 1993), 90–103.

PART II

GENDER

5

"THE LOVELIEST AND PUREST OF GOD'S CREATURES"

The Three Faces of Eve and the Crisis of Southern Womanhood

Allison Graham

The southern white woman has long been a conventional figure in our cultural iconography. Soft-spoken and flirtatious, the belle (or "peach") has functioned as a rebuke to the masculinized women of American industrialism and as an emblem of the femininity that blooms unbidden in agrarian simplicity. To the defenders of racial segregation in the 1950s, she symbolized a threatened and embattled way of life that, ironically, had existed primarily as legend for more than one hundred years. Invoking a fantasy to defend a fantasy, segregationists rallied around their favorite icon when the Supreme Court issued its May 1954 school desegregation decision in *Brown v Board of Education.* Judge Tom Brady of Greenwood, Mississippi, sounded the clarion two months later in *Black Monday,* a tract that became the manifesto of the emerging White Citizens' Councils. The "peaceful and harmonious relationship" between blacks and whites in the South, he claimed, "has been possible because of the inviolability of Southern womanhood." [1] And who, exactly, was a southern woman? "The loveliest and the purest of God's creatures, the nearest thing to an angelic being that treads this terrestrial ball is a well-bred, cultured Southern white woman or her blue-eyed, golden-haired little girl."[2] "The Southerner," wrote African-American sociologist Calvin Hernton in 1965, "had to find or create a symbol, an idea of grace and purity, that would loom large in a civilization shot through with shame, bigotry, and the inhuman treatment of . . . six million black people. Sacred white womanhood emerged in the South as an immaculate mythology to glorify an otherwise indecent society."[3]

For all her fragility, the golden-haired girl of plantation mythology proved to be a durable symbol of segregationist fervor. In the midst of the deliberations on the *Brown* case, President Dwight D. Eisenhower told Chief Justice Earl Warren that the opponents of integration "are not bad people. All they are concerned about is to see that their sweet little girls are not required to sit in schools alongside some big black bucks."[4] One might wonder, though, if all white women in the region would have recognized themselves among those included in the magic circle of protected womanhood. "I was born trash in a land where the people all believe themselves natural aristocrats," writes South Carolina novelist Dorothy Allison. "The women of my family? We are the ones in all those photos taken at mining disasters, floods, fires. We are the ones in the background . . . ugly and old and exhausted."[5] Peering out from the Depression-era photographs of Walker Evans, Margaret Bourke-White, and Dorothea Lange, such faces became the stuff of alternative legend: the sunken, tattered residents of Dogpatch. Ridiculed by decades of cartoonists and filmmakers and pitied by liberal-minded defenders of the New Deal and the War on Poverty, the stereotypical hillbilly or redneck woman reminded Americans that another South existed adjacent to the crumbling mansions.

Despite their uncontested whiteness, the women of the Other South failed to make an appearance in postwar segregationist rhetoric, even though their male relatives insisted on their inclusion. After Roy Bryant and J. W. Milam murdered Emmett Till in 1955, they claimed they were merely defending the honor of Bryant's wife. A twelve-year-old northern black boy's whistle or wink at a working-class white woman provided a convenient excuse for white Mississippians to assert their "sovereignty" to the nation, but as soon as Milam and Bryant were acquitted by an all-white jury, their former supporters turned their backs on the men, refusing to rent land to the embarrassing "peckerwoods."[6] For most segregationists, the iconic southern white woman bore little resemblance to the actual women who were apparently so threatened by the specter of miscegenation. The belle, not the peasant, emblazoned the banner of southern victimization at the hands of federal "race-mixers." Achieving her allure through juxtaposition to her "trailer trash" sister, she embodied the ennobled—and endangered—racial purity of an entire region.

By the mid-1950s, white Americans' love affair with the plantation myth had undergone several revisions, but the infatuation was as strong as ever. Under the spell of Tennessee Williams, Hollywood modernized its antebellum sets and treated filmgoers to the new spectacle of southern decay. The mansions, juleps, and magnolias remained, but the residents of the screen South now began to enact the psychological crises of a dwindling subculture. Repression, hysteria, and sexual dysfunction were the new southern stories, as hothouse whites raged against the dying of a caste. Imagining themselves the last specimens of unadulterated whiteness, southern neurotics boasted of bloodlines while showing all the signs of pathological inbreeding. Although the popular image of the incestuous hillbilly never extended to the regionally-inbred members of Delta society, by the 1950s a significant number of movies began to point in that direction. Countering that implication, however, was a palpable national nostalgia for antebellum plantation days, a recognition in itself that the dream of racial purity, while doomed, exerted a powerful pull on the American imagination.

In Hollywood's formulations of the 1950s and 1960s, decadent whiteness was gaudily made up, its death throes enacted in near-camp performances that would earn Oscars for many actors. Throughout the critical years of the civil rights movement, in fact, "southern decay" movies proved immensely popular. In their studied aversion to contemporary social reality, however, they seemed to display an unspeakable racial hysteria. At the center of the scenario, of course, was the southern white woman. Privileged (or once privileged), desirable (or once desirable), and impossibly frustrated, she testified again and again to the need for racial rejuvenation. The Tennessee Williams adaptations of the 1950s undoubtedly provided the most flamboyant showcases for her sexual torment. Like Carol Cutrere (played by Joanne Woodward) in his *The Fugitive Kind* (1959), characters like Blanche DuBois (*A Streetcar Named Desire*, 1951), Baby Doll (*Baby Doll*, 1956), and Maggie the Cat (*Cat on a Hot Tin Roof*, 1958) demanded "to be noticed, and seen, and heard, and felt." Other characters added their voices to the chorus of the decadent screen South: sultry Ruby Gentry ("sashaying in from the swamps" to meet her ruin in the 1952 film of the same name), nymphomaniacal Marylee Hadley (feverishly mamboing during her father's death in *Written on the Wind*, 1956), and demented plantation belle Susanna Drake (feigning pregnancy to snare her abolitionist husband in *Raintree County*, 1957).

Ironically, Hollywood was telling the most virulent segregationist what he wanted to hear: it was the white woman who was most "at risk" in an integrated society. It was also suggesting something unthinkable to the racist: the white woman herself was the aggressor. Clearly, setting Freudian fables of repression in the South had its price. If Hollywood continued to displace its racial concerns onto narratives of sexual neurosis, its most desirable archetype, the southern belle, could not withstand the pressure. The "immaculate mythology" would shatter, revealing the nakedly "indecent society" of Tara, Belle Reve, and every other backlot plantation. If the daughters of Scarlett were to survive, they must be reconstructed for a filmgoing audience increasingly aware of the tensions between the South of the screen and the South of the front pages.

Seeming to meet the challenge head-on, Twentieth Century-Fox released *The Three Faces of Eve* in 1957 to nearly unanimous critical and popular acclaim. Based on the 1957 book of the same name by psychiatrists Corbett Thigpen and Hervey Cleckley (which, in turn, was based on their 1954 article in the *Journal of Abnormal and Social Psychology* entitled, "A Case of Multiple Personality"), the movie tells the story of the medical treatment of one "Eve White." This working-class Georgia housewife, according to the narration, "had one personality more than Dr. Jekyll" (a personality named—what else—Eve Black). Praised for her "tour de force" performance, "newcomer" Joanne Woodward won the Oscar for her portrayal of the tortured Eve. The "clean documentary clarity" [7] of Nunnally Johnson's screenwriting and direction so hailed by critics like Bosley Crowther marked the film's obsession with its own truthfulness. Johnson claimed, in fact, that his main difficulty in writing the script was "trying to get some form that would convince somebody that this wasn't simply fiction." [8] Black and white photography and ominous music announce the film's "serious" intent in the opening credit sequence, but the introduction and voice-over narration by "noted journalist and commentator" Alistair Cooke push the conventions of fifties realism into the service of nonfiction documentation. Citing names, dates, and places, Cooke informs the viewer that the story to unfold is "true" and "needed no help from the imagination of a fiction writer." Through this framing narrative, Cooke establishes himself as the psychiatrists' surrogate voice, a voice that introduces each sequence in Eve's story and subsequently relinquishes narrative control to Lee J. Cobb's "Dr. Luther" (the character based on Dr. Thigpen).

Impossibly distanced from the original material, then, the character of Eve enacts her traumas before the "tripled" scrutiny and mediation of male professionals: physicians, journalist, actor. Not until 1977 did the "real" Eve, Chris Costner Sizemore, tell her own story, and it bore little resemblance to the film. (Sizemore, for example, provides details of the twenty-two personalities she had manifested, quite a difference from the "three faces" so neatly delineated

Figure 5.1. Promotional poster for *The Three Faces of Eve* (1957).

in the film.) Nevertheless, the patina of "public service"[9] clung to *The Three Faces of Eve*, polished not only by studio publicists but also by many in the medical profession. Twentieth Century-Fox presented plaques to Drs. Thigpen and Cleckley "in recognition and appreciation of your service to the movie industry and the whole world," and the president of the Georgia Medical Association declared upon the film's release, "This movie is a milestone in the progress of medicine."[10]

Interestingly, a similar film released by MGM that year attracted little critical attention and showed disappointing box office returns. Like *The Three Faces of Eve*, *Lizzie* tells the story of a contemporary white woman (played by Eleanor Parker) tormented by a "dark" second self. Both films were shot in black and white, both locate psychological dysfunction in childhood trauma, and both focus on successful psychiatric intervention. The failure of *Lizzie* to strike responsive chords among filmgoers, however, makes the success of *The Three Faces of Eve* all the more intriguing. Set in an anonymous, generically American town, *Lizzie* seems suspended in geographic limbo, much like a television show of the era. (Its flat lighting, in fact, lends it a "teledrama" look, in contrast to the more conventionally cinematic high-contrast lighting of *The Three Faces of Eve*.) Although other differences exist between the films, the painstakingly detailed realism of Nunnally Johnson's film cannot be overlooked as a factor in its popularity. Ostensibly serving as documentation of the story's accuracy, such specificity grounded *The Three Faces of Eve* in a highly charged field of connotation and provided a powerful cultural subtext for the narrative.

Premiering in much-ballyhooed galas in Augusta, Georgia, in September 1957, with a newly-minted South Carolina star in the title role, the "true" story of a southern woman ravaged by her "black" and "white" selves could not have been more ironically timed. That month, Governor Orval Faubus of Arkansas, making political capital from the growing regional outcry against the *Brown* decision, refused to support the desegregation of Central High School in Little Rock. This action forced President Eisenhower to send in the U.S. Army to protect the nine black children who had enrolled in the school.[11] Although a number of southern school districts had voluntarily integrated their schools following the Supreme Court's 1955 implementation decree and had even repelled segregationist attempts to rescind integration orders, Little Rock marked a dramatic turn in southern politics: the rise of Massive Resistance to integration. In 1956, 101 southern senators and congressmen had issued the "Southern Manifesto," in which they pledged to fight the *Brown* decision by "any lawful means." In this emerging resistance movement, "states' rights" became the mantra of politicians, White Citizens' Council leaders, and everyday segregationists.

Documented extensively by network news, the Little Rock crisis quickly developed into an international story. CBS reporter Robert Schakne asked white students to restage their protest chant ("Two—four—six—eight—we don't wanna integrate") for his cameras, a move he regretted when Governor Faubus publicized the tactics of New York journalists. National audiences saw mobs of white men and women jeer, push, and kick black students and black reporters. Meanwhile, the governor, depicted in news magazines like *Time* as a backwoods yokel straight from the *Li'l Abner* comic strip, sat in his mansion, a "victim" of northern incursion into a sovereign southern state. The "Second Reconstruction" had begun, and the new carpetbaggers—federal lawyers, officials of the NAACP, and the news media—were marauding across the region, defaming an entire way of life.

To segregationists, the federal interest in public schools was no accident. Where better to begin the indoctrination of a nation into the "creed" of race mixing? Desegregation of schools could lead to only one thing: intermarriage. Clearly a Communist plot to weaken the country, miscegenation would spawn a "race of mongrels." In tract after tract, speech after speech, bitter-end segregationists preached the horrors of "mongrelization" and urged resistance to the federally ordered outrage. The ravaging of southern womanhood appeared imminent. Soon, the South would be shrouded in black—"Black," Judge Brady wrote, "denoting darkness and terror. Black signifying the absence of light and wisdom. Black embodying grief, destruction and death." [12]

According to segregationists, the propaganda of integration was not the province of federal employees alone. The rest of the nation was conspiring as well to push the message of racial mingling. For example, the Mississippi State Sovereignty Commission, the state-funded agency charged with aiding segregationist projects, claimed in its newsletters throughout the 1950s and 1960s that a "Paper Curtain," an impenetrable wall of media lies, extended along the northern side of the Mason-Dixon line. Like the Iron Curtain in Eastern Europe, the Paper Curtain was the creation of Communist-inspired ideologues. Hollywood, not surprisingly, was a member of the Paper Curtain conspiracy, filling its movies with subversive images of southern white degeneracy and black superiority.

For its part, however, Hollywood had long capitulated to southern white tastes. For decades, movies had "segregated" African-American performers in scenes that could easily be excised by southern censors (Lloyd Binford of Memphis being the most powerful, controlling the content of films distributed within a large area of the mid-South). A number of films were still banned or severely reedited in portions of the South, but, in general, the Production Code Administration fretted over the representation of black Americans and did remarkably little to rock conservative white southern attitudes. Interestingly, outlandish plantation stereotypes met with general approval from white southerners and non-southerners alike, an indication that the romanticized South served more than southern political and social interests. By constantly invoking a mythical, harmonious past—or a modernized version of the same setting—white Americans could no doubt feel insulated from the racial realities of the nation at large. If the South was so charmingly eccentric, could relations be as tense as the escalating news reports suggested? Was it not, perhaps, as white southerners often claimed: race was a "complex" issue, best understood by those who had "grown up with" and "taken care of" black Americans?

By September 1957, though, the dissonance between nonfiction and fiction was unavoidable to even a casual viewer of American media. How could a Hollywood film purport to paint a documentary-like portrait of a contemporary southerner without at least recognizing the social and psychological crises of the region? In light of the film's historical context, the story of the battle between Eve White and Eve Black for the "mastery" (in Alistair Cooke's words) of one woman's "character" seems an almost blatant indicator of the era's racial hysteria. The displacement of race onto the realm of gender, however, suggests that Hollywood practices and southern politics may have been closer in spirit than defenders of either would consciously acknowledge.

As directed by Nunnally Johnson and played by Joanne Woodward, Eve White is, according to one of her doctors, a "dreary little woman from across the river," a put-upon, dutiful wife to her television repairman husband, whose ungrammatical commands and threats to "slap" or "kill" her meet with her own ungrammatical acquiescence. Eve White is, simply, a hick. Described by Corbett Thigpen in his professional manuscripts as "a colorless woman," she belongs to a social class that is all but eradicated by the end of the book *and* the film. An embarrassment to fifties progress, she seems mired in an agricultural past, a farm girl obedient to a working-class man who cannot begin to comprehend the words of her doctor. ("Nothin' wrong with you but this multiplied thing," Ralph White says to Eve). After being confronted by the emergence of a new personality, Ralph asks his uncomprehending wife, "What kind of dope do you think I am?" His question is answered before long by his wife's "shadow self," Eve Black: "a jughead," "a creep," "a jerk," "a peapicker."

The transformation of dreary Eve White into playgirl Eve Black in Dr. Luther's office is accompanied by the well-worn conventions of gender shorthand: jazzy clarinet music complemented by a bluesy guitar, cigarettes, unpinned hair, bare legs on display. Situated within the heavily shadowed office of Dr. Luther, however, these conventions signal the film's indebtedness to film noir, a visual style rarely, if ever, seen in "southern" narratives. Veering abruptly from the realist codes of its opening, the mise-en-scène—like Eve herself—is transformed within the confines of the psychiatrist's office. Like a repressed urge, the new style emerges as a complement to Eve Black's desires, her aspirations to membership in a forbidden, noir world. From the moment Eve begins her psychological excavation, low-key lighting, along with noir's signature venetian blind shadows, dominate the mise-en-scène, usually to the accompaniment of a languid clarinet. The style may seem appropriate in Eve Black's scenes (bars, motels, attempted seductions in the sanitarium), but when Eve White's respectable lodgings appear as draped in shadows as a haunted house, the subtextual implications of the woman's crisis become harder to ignore. As an historically specific character, Eve is hardly the only troubled soul in the film; her environment itself is shadowed by an unnameable fear.

Augusta, Georgia, may have seemed an unlikely setting for noir malaise, but the expressionist tropes so favored by German-influenced stylists had become charged vehicles for conveying a myriad of postwar anxieties—not the least of which was race. Dark alleys, basement nightclubs, dim hotel rooms: most of the conventional locations of film noir evolved within a fundamentally racialized milieu, namely, urban jazz. Although Hollywood for decades had appropriated black music as a marker of white illicitness, by the 1940s it found a complementary iconography in an underlit fantasy world of downtown dives. (In a film like Fritz Lang's 1953 *The Blue Gardenia*, for example, the connection is made obvious when Nat "King" Cole performs for unscrupulous white customers in the club of the same name.) In *The Three Faces of Eve*, however, jazz and blues compete with romanticism for "mastery" of the soundtrack. Just as noir lighting encroaches upon the initially established realist look of the film, so do Eve Black's clarinet and guitar continually upstage Eve White's mournful violins.

Eve Black's materialization within the overdetermined mise-en-scène and soundtrack of film noir places her squarely in the tradition of cinematic bad women. Yet, ironically, it is in her "black" incarnation that Eve is most visibly white. As drab Eve White, she hides her hair beneath an unobtrusive hat. Later, as Jane, the "third face" of Eve, she pulls her hair into a stylish French twist, her propriety further enhanced by tasteful pearl earrings. Eve Black's hair, however, hangs loose. Bleached a gleaming blond, Joanne Woodward's naturally brown hair catches light like nothing else in the frame and graphically emphasizes the inappropriateness of Eve's "black" persona. Although the film may appear to reverse the traditional white/pure, black/impure gender dichotomy, it ultimately reinforces it because Eve Black's impersonation of a fallen woman is doomed from the start. The "badness" of the shining white woman is a facade, an incorrect personality that will be corrected by a recovered memory of her real identity. Her exaggerated whiteness, then, serves two rhetorical purposes. On the one hand, it displays the "scandal" of the sexualized white woman, a metaphorically blackened image that hints at miscegenation. On the other hand, it redeems whiteness by suggesting that gross sexuality is merely imitative, not essential.[13]

The biblical and archetypal overtones of Corbett Thigpen's names for his patient are, of course, obvious. (Eve Black, in reality, was Chris Costner, Chris Sizemore's maiden name.) However, the film dialogue of Eve Black articulates a distinctly nonbiblical awareness of gender politics. "The thing is," she says, analyzing Eve White's relationship with Ralph, "she don't even really care anything about him. She just tells herself she does 'cause she thinks she ought to." Intervening in the unhappy marriage of the Whites, Eve Black tells the downtrodden housewife, "Leave the so-and-so. Take the kid . . . and beat it. What can he do about it?" She even threatens to "fix Ralph's wagon." How? "I'm gonna come out and stay out." After all, Eve White is in no position to fight back; according to Eve Black, "She's gettin' weaker and I'm gettin' stronger."

Eve Black's escalating threats to "stay out" indicate that, rather than a study of psychic "integration" (as several critics have claimed), the film is, in fact, a study of disintegration. The Black and White Eves do not "cohabit" peaceably, not even with mutual independence. In Thigpen's 1954 article on his patient, he noted, "Perhaps we must assume in the multiple personalities at least a primordial functional unity." If such a unity once existed, though, it was most likely "in the stage of mere potentialities" and hence a purely theoretical construct. In the face of such a scenario, Thigpen asked, "what chance is there that an adequate integration might occur?"[14] Four years later in his book, the psychiatrist stated the case more graphically: if Eve Black was indeed "a hidden, unconscious, or subconscious side of the whole person," how could a compromise be struck? "Would appeasement lessen the rebellious drive or would it serve chiefly to incite it? Would Eve Black, encouraged and emboldened, merrily cry havoc and loose at once the dogs of total and relentless war?"[15]

In the film, the dogs are loosed, but the war between Eve's White and Black "selves" is essentially a rout: Eve White simply gives up in the face of Eve Black's relentless aggression. Lacking the energy, intelligence, and will to fight, the "dreary little woman" suffers the taunts and pranks of her "black" self until she declares herself ready to die. Interestingly, though, her only sense of what's "wrong" with her comes about through medical intervention. It is

Dr. Luther who tells her about her other self and makes her aware of her nightly masquerade in seedy bars as "Miss Black." This aspect of the film is consistent with Thigpen's account. "Though Mrs. White has learned that there is a Miss Black during the course of therapy," he wrote, "she does not have access to the latter's awareness. When Eve Black is 'out,' Eve White remains functionally in abeyance, quite oblivious of what the coinhabitant of her body does, and apparently unconscious." [16] Eve Black, however, "preserves awareness while absent. Invisibly alert at some unmapped post of observation, she is able to follow the actions and the thoughts of her spiritually antithetical twin." [17] So acute is Eve Black's knowledge of her twin that "[w]hen it suits her, she deliberately and skillfully acts so as to pass herself off as Eve White, imitating her habitual tone of voice, her gestures, and attitudes." [18]

The ability of the Black twin to "pass" as the White one pitches the film precariously close to the edge of Hollywood's gender and racial representational boundaries. In one scene, Eve Black attempts to seduce the hopelessly confused Ralph White. To the familiar clarinet whine on the soundtrack (by now her "theme"), she drinks straight bourbon and prances about a motel room in a revealing dress. "Honey, there's a lot of things you ain't seen me do. That don't mean I don't do 'em," she tells him. Wanting assurance that the temptress is really his wife, Ralph lunges at her. Were it not for the screen conventions of 1957, perhaps the scene would end with Ralph's "infidelity" to his wife—and evidence of Eve Black's promiscuity. As it is, Eve Black remains a tease, jumping from the bed and scampering across the room.

Although Chris Costner (the "real" Eve Black) was a tease, too, she nevertheless engaged in sex with Ralph and had even, at some point before her "twin" married, lived with a violently abusive man (who, according to Sizemore's autobiography, was already married). The film erases this episode, but the script makes no secret of the Black twin's association with illegitimacy. Eve Black's open hostility to marriage and childbearing, as well as her preference for play over work, mark her, in Thigpen's words, as "a travesty of woman," who would, "if unrestrained, forever carry disaster lightly in each hand." [19]

Two-thirds of the way into the film, then, we reach an untenable impasse. Dr. Luther's "search for one stable and complete woman," Alistair Cooke tells us, is stalled. Clearly, the rebellion of Eve Black is nearing victory; she has become the center of the narrative, the illicit and "appealing" visual focus. Just as clearly, though, the rebellion of the shadow self is doomed. The overdetermined cultural connotations of the dark twin, the merging of racial and gender oppression into one persona, virtually assure her timely demise. The dogs of war loosed by Eve Black may be raging offscreen, but onscreen they are humanely euthanized. Appealing to Universal Law to solve the narrative tangle, Alistair Cooke asks rhetorically, "What, in short, had nature in the first place intended this woman to be?"

The answer emerges in Dr. Luther's office: the "third face" of Eve. As the twins were battling to the death, a new woman, it seems, was forming in the recesses of their psyches—a tactful, poised woman whose memory bank is a tabula rasa. Who is she? "I don't know," she tells the doctors. What is her name? "I'm afraid I don't know that either," she replies and promptly names herself Jane. Compared to this new woman, Eve White appears "colorless and limited"; [20] compared to Eve Black, she is mature and sexually discreet. Jane has another advantage over her fading sisters: she is decidedly middle-class. Miraculously "cured" of her boondocks accent and its attendant bad grammar, Jane speaks the same "language" as Dr. Luther. "I hope she'll be the one to live," Eve Black tells the doctor, realizing her end is near. It is Jane, Eve White agrees, who can be a proper mother for her child.

The class connotations of Jane's mid-American accent were surely not lost on the film cast. Like many actors before her (Ava Gardner being the most outspoken on this issue), Joanne Woodward spent years getting rid of her southern accent only to imitate it later on screen. The recapitulation of her own career in the story of Eve did not escape her. "It was the easiest role I ever did," she told an interviewer in 1959. "Like me, Eve had the most unintegrated personality in the world." [21] Calling forth a lower-class version of her former voice, Woodward would once again watch its erasure at the hands of "professionals" (in this case, the fictional Dr. Luther) and its replacement by an upscale "norm." A native of Columbus, Georgia, director and screenwriter Nunnally Johnson initially refused Woodward's offer to use a southern accent: "I had heard some of the phony Southern accents in *Baby Doll* and I didn't want any part of that kind of acting." [22] Woodward's "pot-likker talk," however, convinced him that she could do "the real thing." [23] It was, he noted in a 1957 letter, "a great asset both to the character and to the picture." [24]

Although Johnson consulted constantly with Drs. Thigpen and Cleckley during the scripting and directing of the film and wanted the pivotal office scenes to be "exactly like I'd seen in the films that the doctors made," [25] he apparently did not consider authenticity of accent a great asset to the doctors' character portrayals. Corbett Thigpen's decidedly upper-class Low Country accent (which can be heard in his audiotaped readings from *The Three Faces of Eve*) was remarkably like that of Johnson (which can be heard in trailers for the film). Yet Lee J. Cobb, like Edwin Jerome (who played "Dr. Day," the psychiatrist based on Hervey Cleckley), played Dr. Luther as non-southern, leaving

Ralph White, Eve White, and Eve Black as the only indicated southern characters in a film set in Augusta, Georgia!

Not surprisingly, none of these characters survives the narrative. Eve White divorces Ralph halfway through the film, and both Eves "die" in Dr. Luther's office after Jane's emergence. Ironically, however, this new character, who meets Dr. Luther's approval as a "complete" woman, was actually Chris Sizemore's imitation of her college-educated cousin Elen. "During Elen's visits to her cousin," Sizemore wrote in 1977, "when she had rambled on about her college life and the opening vistas of her own mind, she had been filling unborn Jane's storehouse of memories." [26] Elen was the first to realize that Jane "was faintly similar to roles Chris had played in their pretend games as teenagers, such as the famous actress, or the most beautiful woman in the world. Suddenly, the hair tweaked on Elen's scalp. It was like looking in a psychic mirror. It was her own self she was feeling, was hearing. That was her own voice, her own speech, her exact phrases, terminology!" [27] Jane, "the dignified southern lady," [28] the "complete" woman, was, in fact, a complete construction.

The psychic mirroring that forms the story of "Eve," complicated as it is, extends beyond the discourses of medicine and the "recuperative" autobiography into the complementary practices of Hollywood representation. Drs. Thigpen and Cleckley ended their 1954 analysis of Eve by charging that "[s]ome, no doubt, will conclude that we have been thoroughly hoodwinked by a skillful actress . . . taken in by what is no more than superficial hysterical tomfoolery." "It seems possible," they continued, "that such an actress after assiduous study and long training might indeed master three such roles and play them in a way that would defy detection." However, they warned, "in plays the actors are given their lines, and their roles are limited to representations of various characters only in circumscribed and familiar episodes of the portrayed person's life." [29] When we remember that Joanne Woodward's much-lauded Method acting throughout the 1950s was aided by her own psychoanalysis, the notion of "true" and "false" selves exposed by careful probing—whether in therapy or in acting—evaporates. "I'm a sponge and can be anything anybody wants me to be," Woodward said at the time. [30]

The erasure and reconstruction of personality central to Hollywood star making are often recapitulated onscreen in stories of makeovers, blossomings, and transformations. In *The Three Faces of Eve*, however, the torturous birth of a "complete" woman is also the birth of a star. "A year ago all but unknown," [31] as described in *Life* in 1958, Joanne Woodward metamorphosed onscreen into, as *Time* put it, "easily the twinklingest star that Hollywood has constellated this year." [32] Just as the struggling actor became established star, so too did the real Eve, a troubled assortment of fragile personalities, become a "stable" feminine role model. Jane, the college girl constructed from Chris Sizemore's dim perceptions of the ideal 1950s coed, became Jane, the key-lit New Woman of fifties progress. The coaxing (and coaching) of a middle-class persona from the morass of white trash alternatives occurred both on-screen and off, as Woodward rediscovered and discarded her "innate southern charm." [33]

Although many early psychic traumas accounted for the fracturing of Size-more's personality, only one is shown in the film, and its recollection by Jane not only "kills" the Black and White Eves but also jumpstarts Jane's memory. Interestingly, the event (young Eve being forced to kiss the face of her dead grandmother) is itself a marker of class. They "didn't mean any wrong by it," Jane tells Dr. Luther, explaining the backward superstitions of her family. "It's just the way people thought in those days." With this farewell to rural folk-ways, Jane experiences a rush of school memories. Her education erupts, as lines from Shakespeare and teachers' names spill from her mouth and she tearfully exclaims, "I can remember! I can remember!" Possessed of the edu-cation Eve White and Eve Black lacked, miraculously "cured" of her southern accent, Jane can finally be launched into contemporary American life. Her farewell letter to the doctors, introduced by Cooke and read by her in voice-over, and the film's brief final scene testify to her recovery. Long buried is the blues-in-the-night world of Eve Black; permanently installed is the brightly lit world of fifties domesticity. Reunited with her daughter and newly married to an understanding, middle-class man (who, unlike the ill-educated Ralph White, has no southern accent), Jane has taken her place in a reconstituted, modernized southern white family. In the final shot, as lush orchestration swells (no clarinets or guitars lurking here), the threesome drive off along a Spanish moss-lined highway. "Here we all are—Bonnie, Earl, and me—going home together," Jane says.

As southern education became the locus of postwar racial strife, national audiences responded sympathetically to the "true story" of a reeducated American Eve. Rejecting any notion of successful integration of white and black, *The Three Faces of Eve* reconstructed a new and improved whiteness from the ashes of the southern wasteland. By not only failing to interrogate whiteness, but also insisting on its recuperation during a time of immense racial dislocation, it adhered to a formula that would be followed by many subsequent films (the 1988 *Mississippi Burning* being the most egregious ex-ample). When all is said and done, it seems that social class is the real en-emy—not just of mental health and racial harmony, but of white supremacy itself. "Peasants," Dorothy Allison writes, are always a problem in southern narratives. "Call us the lower orders, the great unwashed, the working class, the poor, proletariat, trash, lowlife and scum. . . . Make it pretty or sad, laughable or haunting. Dress it up with legend and aura and romance." [34]

Eve White and Eve Black, the hillbilly and the social mulatto, are local "color," humorous, pathetic, ultimately—and necessarily—disposable. Obstacles to progressive representations of the South, they offer proof—by their inevitable demise—that the times are indeed changing. Poverty, ignorance, and ill breeding, the film tells us, are relics of an Erskine Caldwell past. By exoticizing the southern white woman and marking her as distinctly anachronistic and self-destructive, *The Three Faces of Eve* could walk the tightrope between national sympathies. Displacing racism onto the conflicted body of the working-class white woman, the film appears to examine and condemn an inherently class-bound social pathology. Yet, by consistently marking southernness as Other, it provides reassurance that whiteness itself is not an issue. Through its insistence on its own realism and documentary truth, *The Three Faces of Eve* plays midwife to the birth of an icon of the New South: the educated, accentless, supremely genuine everywoman of the fifties. Racial boundaries may be wavering offscreen, but onscreen we are reassured that American whiteness is not just progressive. It is entirely natural.

NOTES

1. Tom Brady, *Black Monday* (Jackson, MS: Citizens' Councils of America, 1955), 46.

2. Ibid.

3. Calvin Hernton, *Sex and Racism in America* (New York: Anchor, 1965), 14.

4. David Halberstam, *The Fifties* (New York: Fawcett Columbine, 1993), 421.

5. Dorothy Allison, *Two or Three Things I Know For Sure* (New York: Plume, 1996), 33.

6. William Bradford Huie, *Wolf Whistle and Other Stories* (New York: New American Library, 1959), 50.

7. Bosley Crowther, review of *The Three Faces of Eve*, *New York Times*, 27 September 1957, 16.

8. Dorris Johnson and Ellen Leventhal, *The Letters of Nunnally Johnson* (New York: Knopf, 1981), 149–50.

9. "Good Acting," *The Saturday Review* 40, no. 26, 28 September 1957, 26.

10. Chris Costner Sizemore, *I'm Eve* (New York: Doubleday, 1977), 392.

11. Ironically, Joanne Woodward would win critical praise in 1981 for her performance in the television drama *Crisis at Central High*, in which she portrayed the racially moderate teacher, Elizabeth Huckaby. The role was based on Huckaby's diary of the 1957 integration standoff in Little Rock.

12. Brady, *Black Monday*, 1.

13. Interestingly, *Lizzie* employs a similar pattern of racialized color coding. The light-haired heroine's psychic disintegration is revealed to have occurred in childhood when her mother's dark lover molested her. Before that, she had overheard the man and her bleached-blonde mother conspiring to desert "the brat" and head for Mexico. "Blondes are popular in Mexico," he tells the mother. As "Lizzie the slut," the heroine impersonates her false-blonde mother by cruising a rundown bar for "Latin" men. Underscoring the racial subtext is the appearance in several scenes of Johnny Mathis as a singer in the bar—the only African-American performer in the film.

14. Corbett H. Thigpen and Hervey Cleckley, "A Case of Multiple Personality," *Journal of Abnormal and Social Psychology* 49, no. 1 (1954): 148.

15. Corbett H. Thigpen and Hervey Cleckley, *The Three Faces of Eve* (New York: McGraw-Hill, 1957), 105–6.

16. Thigpen and Cleckley, "A Case of Multiple Personality," 138.

17. Ibid.

18. Ibid., 140.

19. Thigpen and Cleckley, *The Three Faces of Eve*, 144.

20. Thigpen and Cleckley, "A Case of Multiple Personality," 145.

21. "Joanne Woodward: The Fugitive Kid," *Look*, 23 December 1959, 123.

22. Johnson and Leventhal, *The Letters of Nunnally Johnson*, 157.

23. Ibid.

24. Ibid.

25. Ibid., 150.

26. Sizemore, *I'm Eve*, 342.

27. Ibid., 334.

28. Ibid., 341.

29. Thigpen and Cleckley, "A Case of Multiple Personality," 147.

30. "Joanne Woodward," 122.

31. "Tension and Triumph for a Young Actress," *Life* 44, 7 April 1958, 81.

32. "The New Pictures," *Time* 70, 23 September 1957, 48.

33. "Good Acting," 26.

34. Allison, *Two or Three Things*, 1.

6

THE REDSKIN AND

THE PALEFACE

Comedy on
the Frontier

Karen Wallace

The American Indian is a stock character in American film and literature. He is little more than a cliché, serving more often than not as a narrative device rather than as a fully developed and significant character. In his essay "The Other Question: Difference, Discrimination and the Discourse of Colonialism," Homi K. Bhabha writes, "It is the force of ambivalence that gives the colonial stereotype its currency [and] ensures its repeatability in changing historical and discursive conjunctures." [1] Bhabha challenges the meta-narrative of colonial discourse that reifies signs and argues whether or not they are adequate representations. He suggests as an alternative "that the point of intervention should shift from the *identification* of images as positive or negative, to an understanding of the *process of subjectification* made possible (and plausible) through stereotypical discourse." [2] This paper seeks to address the misrepresentations of the Indian in Hollywood film. As per Bhabha's discussion, it will look at the ways in which the sign of the Indian has itself become the object of study. Rather than focus on the traditional Western that demonizes Indians as a matter of course, we examine comedy and the ways in which stereotyping goes unchallenged by virtue of the genre. In this discussion of Norman Z. McLeod's film *The Paleface* (1948), we will examine the pervasive process of "subjectifying" the sign "Indian" and the particular efficacy of comedy.

The Paleface opens on a frame filled by an Indian feather headdress over which the title is superimposed. Music plays; the drumbeat is vaguely militaristic. The names of the stars fade in as the tone of the music becomes more playful. The headdress tilts backward, showing Bob Hope, the star of the film, beneath it. He leans forward again as the credits dissolve to the names of the minor players. The opening frame thus establishes the paradox upon which McLeod bases his film: Hope's character is both Paleface and Redskin. As such, he reifies the myth of the Noble Savage. As Robert Berkhofer, Jr., explains "[it is] the very contrast presumed between Red and White society that gave rise to the idea of the Indian in the first place. Since Whites primarily understood the Indian as an antithesis to themselves, then civilization and Indianness as they defined them would forever be opposites." [3] The opposition between White and Red, right and wrong, pervades *The Paleface*. Red comes to represent all the evils of the time and the Redskin is the perfect vehicle for their articulation. The tension in the close shot of the headdress and Hope's face—a result not only of the full frame but also the contradictions in signification—is relieved by the change in music, only to be reestablished a moment later in the first scene.

The story begins with a sequence on a rainy, gloomy night, setting an ominous and dark tone. Two horsemen, leading a third riderless horse, gallop to the local sheriff's station. They dismount and, before entering the building, cover their faces with handkerchiefs and draw their guns. Once inside, their purpose is clear: to "liberate" the one prisoner, a woman who is dressed conspicuously in a leather hat and suit. She is Jane Russell. The music is suspenseful and emphasizes the tension of the scene until the climax, when the robber opens the door of the cell and thunder crashes as Russell rises and walks toward the camera. The three ride off, soaking wet, Russell coerced at gunpoint.

The references to "reality" throughout the film are essential to understanding and accepting the conflict that will ensnare Hope's character, not the least of which is the intent to make the audience aware of Jane Russell as herself. Fade to the interior of a well-lit and stylish room. Two men wait for Russell's arrival. One of the villains delivers the prisoner, announcing her as "Calamity Jane." The audience has already accepted the character as Jane Russell by default. Thus, as in vaudeville, the narrative becomes a parody of itself; the audience is fully aware that they are watching a farce in which Bob Hope and Jane Russell play cowboys and Indians.

In his study of representations of Indians, Raymond Stedman explains:

Examiners of cinema should always remember that . . . battle dramas have never declined appreciably. They have simply changed locales and enemies. When it has not been a proper time to hate the beasts of Berlin, some other adversary—some other recent, if more confined, threat to civilization—has always been found; the native tribesmen of the Khyber Pass . . . and, to be sure, the American Indians. With an eye more to the box office than to historical truth, producers have selected the enemy of convenience. . . . The various subspecies of war films have been almost identical in substance and format. Only the costumes, locales, and pseudodialects need to be changed in order to identify the guilty.[4]

Familiar with the Western, the audience knows to expect a conflict with the local tribe. Pan to another man, obviously the one in charge. Governor Johnson introduces himself, then the Commissioner of Indian Affairs, Mr. Emerson, and his secretary, Mr. Martin. The subtext on which the narrative is based privileges the savage Indian and the threat he embodies. More a projection of Western fears than anything, the Indian of American rhetoric is *the* symbol of the wilderness, personifying evil. In Christian/colonial discourse, the American metanarrative specifically, the devil, fallen or exiled from Heaven, resides in the wilderness. The wilderness is thus the source of the demonic, and the hero's journey is a quest for redemption within the demonic: to recover the wilderness is to restore Man's relation to God, confirming the ideology of Manifest Destiny.

The Indian in the popular imagination remains little more than a device with which to articulate the apprehensions inherent in hegemonic discourse. Thus, the Governor announces to Calamity Jane Russell that they have a job for her, one that requires the utmost secrecy: "A group of white renegades is smuggling guns to the Indians. We've got to find out who they are before we have an Indian war on our hands." Commissioner Emerson clarifies the problem: "Six months ago we sent out two of our best agents. Their bodies were found horribly mutilated." The Indian is succinctly and effectively defined with this brief statement.

In *The Paleface*, we only see a "real" Indian after he has been demonized in this initial sequence. Ready to massacre an entire territory of presumably innocent white settlers at a moment's notice, the Indian personifies that side of man's nature that is so frightening: emotion, irrationality, disorder, and violence. The initial frame of McLeod's film that makes the Indian synonymous with the headdress imbues the sign with meaning, indicating the subtext of imperialism. The close shot of Hope as an Indian is the subjectification of the

Figure 6.1. "Real" Indians in *The Paleface* (1948).

Indian in process: the sign (headdress) is endowed with subjectivity by its proximity to the actor. The identification of each is made ambiguous as the headdress, representing savagery, is resemanticized on the head of the famous comedian, transforming the fearful into the ridiculous. By the end of the film, however, the headdress is remade as the heroic because it indicates civilization's dominance over the wilderness.

The Indian headdress represents the fetishization of the Indian stereotype. Bhabha contends that the stereotype and the fetish are synonymous. He explains that

> without the attribution of ambivalence to relations of power/knowledge [it would be impossible] to calculate the traumatic impact of the return of the oppressed—those terrifying stereotypes of savagery, cannibalism, lust and anarchy which are the signal points of identification and alienation, scenes of fear and desire, in colonial texts. It is precisely this function of the stereotype as phobia and fetish that, according to [Frantz] Fanon, threatens the closure of the racial/epidermal schema for the colonial subject and opens the royal road to colonial fantasy.[5]

Figure 6.2. Bob Hope dressed as an Indian in *The Paleface* (1948).

Colonial discourse creates the Indian as an ambiguous sign: both frightening and powerless, the notion of the Dying Savage is fetishized on the basis of his subordination, reflecting the American's search for a discrete identity. The Indian in American narrative symbolizes the righteousness of American imperialism, allowing cinema to maintain the precarious balance of the mythic frontier. There must always be one more savage doomed to die or the American idea of itself will collapse. "The frontier is the outer edge of the wave—the meeting point between savagery and civilization," [6] writes Frederick Jackson Turner, emphasizing the ambiguity of the West. The establishment of what Turner refers to as each new frontier always results from an Indian war.[7] We feel nostalgic for a lost past, lamenting the passing of a simpler time and its last relic. *The Paleface* relies on the dying yet stoic Indian to subvert other contemporary stereotypes; yet, the film perpetuates his erasure from America.

Defined by conflict with the Indian, the Frontier is essential to understanding American filmmaking in general. The reductive nature of American history results in the visual misrepresentation of Indians in popular culture. As Ward Churchill explains, "The essential idea of Native America instilled cinematically is that of a quite uniform aggregation of peoples . . . which flourished with the arrival of whites upon their land [which] then vanished somewhat mysteriously."[8] Stedman attributes the establishment of the Indian as a device to David Belasco, particularly to his play *The Girl I Left Behind Me* (1893 with Franklin Fyles). "Offering a marvelous lesson for the Hollywood inheritors of his melodramatic tradition," writes Stedman, "Belasco created one of the great sustained suspense sequences of all time—without showing a single Indian on the attack. He did it through suggestion, pacing, and an attention to detail. . . . Ironically, it was two film directors—D. W. Griffith and John Ford—who best grasped the Belasco inheritance."[9] *The Paleface* moves in the fairly straightforward narrative of the conventional Ford Western: the wilderness is the source of the demonic, and the Indian is demonic because of his familiarity with wilderness. In the film's second sequence, Jane, guns drawn, prepares to escape from the Governor via the window. Commissioner Emerson pleads with her: "Unless you help us, the west will be drenched with the blood of white settlers. Thousands of lives, women and children . . . ." Jane listens, but also notices that the secretary, Mr. Martin, has moved to the opposite end of the room. He holds a gun, aimed at her, so she shoots him in the hand. Several factors in this single moment contribute significantly to the nuances of the story: not only is Jane a dead shot, but also there is an Indian headdress behind Mr. Martin, the traitor. Here McLeod reveals the ambiguity in the American's position, juxtaposing the treacherous traitor and the bloodthirsty savage, the threat of both neutralized by the already established associations of the headdress with Bob Hope.

Indians are used as foil for the characteristics of the hero in the American paradigm, thus the Governor represents civilization in its institutions, while Martin represents the shadow side of civilized Man and is consequently juxtaposed with the symbol for wilderness. The sequence is unsettling; complicated by the centrality of a female character, Calamity Jane, in a clearly male-dominated genre, this scene is immediately ambiguous, recalling the initial conflation of Redskin and Paleface. The narrative with which the film begins seems to be a standard issue Western, yet the close-up of Hope as an Indian establishes *The Paleface* as a comedy. The audience is held in suspense as the Governor tells Jane, "We thought we'd send a woman, a woman who can take care of herself. . . . We need your help desperately." Another loud clap of thunder follows, the exaggerated emphasis calling attention to the film's satire and self-reflection, while Jane pours herself some whiskey and asks for more details.

Conveying power and masculinity, Jane seems like the "man" for the job. Her forceful swallow of whiskey underscores her masculinity while intensifying her "Indianness." Despite her beauty and desirability, Russell's portrayal of Calamity Jane as a bandit is effective. Much of the tension in this sequence, and those following, is due to our anticipation of Hope and his brand of comedy, complicated by a context that seems so inappropriate to our expectations. Russell participates in the mixed messages, playing a hard-edged, powerful frontierswoman, while remaining quintessentially Jane Russell, starlet.

The film's subtext validates its hyperbole and self-reflexive representations. The story of Calamity Jane and her exploits were popular in the form of the serialized dime novel. In the saga of *Deadwood Dick,* Jane was the hero: "Calamity repeatedly saved Dick from being hanged or hacked to pieces while she herself managed to stay alive without any such assistance from him." [10] A historical figure, infamous during her life for her alcoholism and tall tales, Calamity Jane became a noble and attractive fictional character in the pages of Ned Wheeler's novels.[11] "Dressed in buckskin trousers adorned with fancifully beaded leggings . . . ," writes Doris Faber, "she looked 'regally beautiful. . . .' Then, 'piercing the gloom of the night with her dark, lovely eyes, searchingly, lest she should be surprised, she lit a cigar at full motion—dashing on, on, this strange girl of the Hills went, on her flying steed.'" [12] In casting Jane Russell, sultry and voluptuous, the filmmakers replicate the melodrama of the fictional Calamity Jane and her cohort, Deadwood Dick. They draw attention to the fanciful nature of the legendary bandit, using the ambiguity between the legend and the real woman to destabilize our sense of "truth."

Moving pictures offered a text that seemed both simpler and more complex than that of the dime novel. Lewis Jacobs writes that, following the introduction of Technicolor in 1932, "all progress in movies has been toward achieving a more effective reality. The film's two new allies, sound and color, have freed it from certain mechanical restrictions and brought it closer to the world of fact." [13] Color enables the inclusion of cultural coding with all its nuances. Like language, any effective text is binary, oscillating between poles, or terms of ambivalence, and in the end undoes itself, whatever way it is read. Meaning vanishes upon close contact, like the Indians in the film. The headdress in the opening sequence is made of black and white feathers tipped at both top and bottom with red. As the movie progresses, the heroine goes through a stage of "development" in which she wears red. Juxtaposed with the red Indians, red connotes not only blood and death, specifically, but also danger generally whether the threat is gendered or political, e.g., "the Reds." Everything in the film is hyperbolic, asserting the vaudevillian nature of Hope's performance as well as its ambivalence. Jane's costumes are overdone; wearing buckskin or a red dress, she is the Indian and the whore. The Indians' costumes are also exaggerated; they are dressed to perform in a Wild West show,

Figure 6.3. Jane Russell as powerful frontierswoman in *The Paleface* (1948).

not to overrun the continent. The film's humor depends upon the acceptance of the Indian as an ambivalent sign, its ambivalence enabled, in fact, by its fixity. His tragedy confirmed by his fixed place in history, the Indian, and Jane to a lesser extent, becomes Hope's straight man. Deprived of an actual space for confrontation and progress, cinematic representation becomes the site of both for American imperialism.[14]

"Colonial power produces the colonized as a fixed reality which is at once an 'other' and yet entirely knowable and visible," writes Bhabha. "It employs a system of representation, a regime of truth, that is structurally similar to realism."[15] In *The Paleface*, the frontier signifies the reality of American history, despite its essentially nebulous nature and dependence upon the Indian, yet the frontier deconstructs itself in the process of being created. This allows the film to explore duality and the ambiguity of stereotypes, especially those embodied by the savage yet noble Indian. The figure retains its potency, at least in part, because of its inherent paradox. The Indian represents prelapsarian Adam, for whom the world has become too hard, and the foil for Hope's character, the Adamic figure who *does* survive the "fall." Thus, though he cannot survive, the Indian represents a stage through which the American *must* pass.

The essence of the frontier does not change, though it is eventually more theoretical than concrete.

As Frederick Turner wrote in 1920:

> The wilderness masters the colonist. It finds him a European in dress, industries, tools, modes of travel, and thought. It strips off the garments of civilization and arrays him in the hunting shirt and the moccasin. It puts him in the log cabin of the Cherokee and Iroquois and runs an Indian palisade around him. Before long he has gone to planting Indian corn and plowing with a sharp stick; he shouts the war cry and takes the scalp in orthodox Indian fashion. . . . Little by little he transforms the wilderness . . . here is a new product that is American.[16]

The closing of the frontier in 1890, signified by the end of the Indian Wars, is particularly important in making the representations of Indians seem credible; we know the Indians are not a *real* threat. In Turner's influential Frontier Theory, we have a synopsis for *The Paleface*. The film follows a conventional narrative strategy, crisis-conflict-resolution, that delineates the regression that must occur before the Frontiersman can be born. The Government, in the form of the Governor and the Indian agent, offers Jane a pardon in exchange for helping them; if she refuses, she faces a long prison term. Reflecting the film's nature, the scene is ambiguous. No one is truly trustworthy or heroic, despite the menace of the Indian. The men coerce Jane into helping them, and she agrees out of self-interest. Thus, McLeod introduces Jane Russell as his ersatz hero. The men's deviousness shows through in both their clothes and behavior: they dress respectably in suits and are formal in both language and affect, despite their actual intentions. Jane is almost worse, dressed like an Indian man in a buckskin coat and pants, her figure carefully emphasized with a cinched waist to recall that of the naked savage. The politicians are making the Frontier safe for settlers, yet they do so in an unethical way. Jane is a beautiful woman, yet she manifests the qualities of the Indian. Her costume and demeanor reflect the uncertainty of the period. There is a clear tension between them, as there is between Jane and government agents, one with which the audience must grapple as well. It is not easy to decide who the villain is here: the men are presented as manipulative and crafty, while Jane embodies chaos and unreliability.

Unlike the conventional Western, this film does not portray the Indian as a threat to women. Instead, women also signify "Indianness": irrationality, chaos, and corruption. Stedman explains the ways in which both writers and filmmakers use the figure of the Indian to imply sexuality and licentiousness.

"In the Cecil B. DeMille epic of 1947, *Unconquered*," he writes, ". . . a well-traveled insinuation was inserted more than once, just to make certain that even a dozing movie-goer could anticipate what was in store for a torn-bodiced Paulette Goddard in the hands of Boris Karloff's Senecas. The frontier saga, cinema-style, seldom put forth sheiks in breechclouts. Its captor Indians offered mainly shame and terror." [17] As a reproduction of the Indian, Woman is not a logical target for the Indian's aggression because they are essentially the same.

Hope plays the main character, "Painless" Peter Potter, the "Paleface" of the film. He is the focal point of the plot, though the story emphasizes the frontier and Indian/white relations. The connotations of "Paleface" indicate the premise upon which the film is based. Potter is described in opposition to the Indian, who represents both his adversary and the obstacle to Progress. Certainly a most convenient scapegoat in the emerging cold war era, the Indian, with his red skin, symbolizes a complex range of threats to American Civilization and its progress. Yet, Potter is also synonymous with the Indian; the Indian cannot manifest any sexual potency because Potter is impotent. The Indian represents a metaphysical power, not a sexual one. Potter is intended as Jane's lover, thus, in contrast to the tragic love story, she must remain inviolate. Their characters are alike and parallel each other; consequently, they are never in direct conflict. Calamity Jane, with whom the Indian barely interacts, represents the Other in that she too poses a threat to white men. With no proper sense of her place, i.e., in relation to men, Jane threatens the social order as much as the Indians do. Potter makes this explicit later in the film. The song "Buttons and Bows," his love song to his bride, emphasizes this point: "You'll be mine in buttons and bows . . . in a city where women are women in peek-a-boo clothes . . . where your friends don't tote a gun."

As the story progresses, Jane agrees to the deception. The Governor and the Commissioner set up a meeting for her with a lawyer, Jim Hunter, who will give her more information and pose as her husband. In order to ambush the white men selling guns, the couple will join a wagon train "going out West" from Fort Deerfield. "As man and wife," the Governor and Commissioner explain, "you'll be lost in the crowd." The scene dissolves to the secretary's bandaged hand holding a shot glass of whiskey. The camera pulls back to show Martin flanked by three men sitting at a bar, to whom he reveals Jane's plans. He warns, "She'll be traveling as a lady. But she's a killer, a dead shot." [18] He looks at his bandaged hand as he finishes his sentence.

With Martin thus revealed as the traitor, the story can begin in earnest. Dissolve to the coach arriving at Fort Deerfield. Wearing a scarlet dress and hat, Jane is the epitome of the fallen woman, seductive and deceitful. However, we know she is attempting to protect the settlers, thus McLeod confirms her ambiguity as a symbol. She walks to the office of attorney Jim Hunter, where she finds him slumped over his desk. Assuming he is asleep, she discovers that he has been shot. Under his hand she finds a note that he had been writing: "notify HANK BILLINGS Buffalo Flat." She leaves the office, but is soon aware of men following her. She evades them by entering the dentist's office. This is our first glimpse of Bob Hope. Dressed in a suit with his hair slicked back, he stands over a man, tapping the man's teeth to find the rotten one. The sign behind Hope says "Painless Peter Potter."

We now leave the familiar and dramatic world of the Western to enter that of farce, the latest trend in popular film of that time. Explaining this new vogue in cinema, Lewis Jacobs writes, "Hardly less rich in information about everyday life in the [pre-World War II] period than the dramas were the hundreds of comedies. These not only 'clowned' human foibles but pointedly satirized them." [19] A self-conscious parody of the Western, *The Paleface* subverts the genre's conventions by establishing first a masculine woman, then an effeminate man, as the protagonist. [20] Transgressing traditional gender constructs, Painless Potter is the fool—inept, naïve, and innocent. Playing at dentistry, Potter moves step by step through a manual as he attempts to pull the right tooth. In contrast, Jane is a crack shot, hired by the government on the basis of her renowned skill. Potter's foolishness is emphasized when a rough-and-tumble "real" cowboy pulls the gentleman with the rotten tooth from the chair and demands immediate treatment. Potter has no recourse, being both weak and cowardly, and so goes to work. Meanwhile, the camera cuts to Jane, sitting in a corner, watching the silhouette of her pursuer outside the window; this shot serves to highlight both her danger and Potter's naiveté.

Potter catches sight of Jane, remarking under his breath, "You've got just the kind of mouth I'd like to work on." Losing all concentration and focus, he proceeds with his work. His special trick as a dentist is the magic laughing gas—hence the nickname "Painless." This device becomes a trope throughout the film because it allows for the possibility of change, which thus enables Jane to be recovered finally as a respectable woman and part of the community. There seems to be a leak in the gas tank and both Potter and his patient start to giggle, while Potter continues mooning over Jane. Jane joins other women upstairs in the women's bath. When Potter pulls the wrong tooth, the man, still laughing, gives him fifteen minutes to get out of town, then punches him in the face. Knocked backward over a counter by the blow, Potter passes out. Meanwhile, the three men prepare to ambush Jane, recalling for the audience Martin's treachery and the gravity of the Indian problem.

The men, guns drawn, throw the women into a state of confusion. Seeing

Jane's red dress hanging outside one of the stalls, the men shoot. Jane, dressed only in her underwear and holster, emerges from another stall and shoots all three men. At the sound of gunfire, other men pour into the room and try to revive one of the villains, while the proprietress revives Potter, asking him to do something. Completely unaware of what has happened, he prepares to leave, telling her, "I'm going back East, where men may not be men, but they're not corpses either." As Potter gets into his wagon, the camera cuts to the dying man, who reveals to an accomplice that the federal agent is traveling to Buffalo Flats. Jane escapes to the balcony and jumps into Potter's wagon. The men see the wagon leave and assume that Potter is the agent. The tension builds as Potter enters the liminal space between two evils: the Indians in front of him, the mercenaries behind.

Dissolve to the wooded trail going out of town, where Jane has joined Potter. She offers no explanation for her sudden presence. Potter merely jokes with her about being chased. It is an awkward moment in the plot development, one that requires a total suspension of disbelief. Given Potter's fears and incompetence, it is odd that he would accept Jane's presence without question. The sudden jump in logic does confirm, however, the significance of the subtext: the need to keep the Frontier safe from marauding Indians subsumes all incongruities in plot.

The Paleface is truly a frontier movie in that the film, like the frontier, is changing, ambiguous, and its boundaries are always moving. The film is replete with boundaries and transgressions, literal or metaphoric. The mise-en-scène throughout the film emphasizes thresholds, for example. Marking the liminal status of both the circumstances and the characters, many scenes feature windows through which the audience either views the action or is viewed. John Cawelti suggests that the American Western of the 1960s and 1970s undergoes a radical change in structure as critical perspectives on American history change: "In effect, this amounts to an almost complete reversal of some of the symbolic meanings ascribed to major groups in the Western. The pioneers become a symbol of fanaticism, avarice and aggressive violence, while the Indians represent a good group with a way of life in harmony with nature and truly fulfilling to the individual. It is through his involvement with the Indians and their way of life that the hero is regenerated." [21] *The Paleface*, seldom critiqued, is anomalous for its era. It represents a transitional phase between the conventional perspectives of Ford and Griffith and that which Stedman describes. The repetition of literal boundaries reinforces the film's transitional nature.

Jane tells Potter that they will be joining the wagon train. He acquiesces, though reluctantly: "that's Indian country out there." Jane challenges him,

"You're not afraid of a few Indians, are you?" Potter jokes in response: "It's not the Indians I'm afraid of, it's their attitude. They're hatchet happy." The Indian is confirmed as narrative device, revealed as the force that will bring Potter and Jane together. She depends on him as ostensible protector, though the roles are clearly reversed. In order to get her way, Jane kisses him, distracting him so that she can knock him out with the butt of her gun. As Jacobs explains, "'Daffy' comedies became the fashion [post-war]." He goes on to say that:

> Here the genteel tradition is "knocked for a loop": heroes and heroines are neither ladylike nor gentlemanly. . . . These films were all sophisticated, mature, full of violence—hitting, falling, throwing, acrobatics, bright dialogue, slapstick action—all imbued with terrific energy. In these films the rebel, the individualist, is once more respected. The artist, the eccentric, the unaccountable is now the sane person in a chaotic world.[22]

"Boy, can you kiss," Potter says before passing out. After he regains consciousness, Jane convinces him that she loves him and that they have agreed to marry. In a brief scene, a minister marries them. Nothing more than a close shot of their hands, the marriage is funny and meant to be taken lightly. At the end of the wedding, Potter kisses the minister instead of Jane, who is out of frame, reasserting his feminized role as well as the slapstick that characterizes the action of the film.

Dissolve to the wagon train as they prepare to head West. Potter is credulous and gullible, clearly unprepared for the journey. "Going west in a covered wagon, that's my kind of life," he tells her. "Blazing new frontiers, facing danger, privation and death. Is that my kind of life?" Jane, ever unflappable, gathers information about the renegades, leaving Potter to worry about his own safety. The film subverts gender roles in order to highlight Bob Hope's vaudevillian talents as well as the satiric nature of the plot. Cawelti writes of the new Western that "[in] its reversal of traditional valuations of the symbolic figures and groups of the Western story, this new formula has a great deal in common with another recent form which I have labeled, rather facetiously, the legend of the Jewish cowboy." He explains that the heroes of these films "win our interest and sympathy not by courage and heroic deeds, but by bemused incompetence, genial cowardice, and the ability to face the worst with buoyancy and wit. They are six-gun schlemiels and existentialists in cowboy boots."[23]

Jane discovers a wagon full of dynamite and Potter remains oblivious to the danger he faces. As part of her treachery and those qualities associated with the Indian and with the fallen woman, Jane takes advantage of Potter's innocence. Through innuendo, she has just convinced the men following them that Potter is the federal agent, when the wagon train's leader warns them, "The sooner we get past that Indian country the better." Potter responds nervously as they prepare to set out. "Indian country. Do we have to go that way?" He looks to Jane, who replies, "Now, Painless, I'll be with you. You're not afraid, are you?" He jokes again, telling her, "No, I can always get another scalp." This brief exchange reemphasizes not only Potter's cowardice, but also his misplaced suspicions: he is afraid of Indians when he should fear Jane. Finally, forgetting to rehitch his team, Potter is dragged from his wagon by the horses as Jane watches; this presents a hyperbolic image to reinforce his role as fool.

Fade to the wagon train moving through open country, with the visual splendor of snow-covered peaks in the background. Though they start toward the left fork, the lead men decide, "We'll take this trail to the right. Yeah, we better. That one leads deep into Indian country." At this point, Hope sings the major musical number, "Buttons and Bows." The song reflects the plot of the movie: he wants to return to the city where a woman is really a woman, not a gun-toting fiend like Jane. Marking a clear distinction between East and West, he sings of his desire to recover Civilization and, instead, takes the wrong fork, leading straight to Indian Country. Fade to Jane, driving the wagon. The text "Then Night Fell" appears on the screen, the letters falling down and off the frame. This serves to refocus our attention on the film's contrivances and our relation to Bob Hope: only we are aware of the joke. Jane takes control of the situation, deciding they and those in the wagons following them should stay the night in the cabin they find. The scene is transitional: it is here that they first encounter Indians and that the director changes the coding. McLeod reclaims Jane by demonizing the Indian.

Potter's first encounter with an Indian occurs as he prepares to consummate his marriage (he and Jane taking the bedroom, and the bed, because they are newlyweds). The sequence establishes the Indian as a threat, yet simultaneously emasculates him by making him the butt of the jokes. Potter carries Jane over the threshold of the bedroom. He closes the one window, saying "We don't want any dust to blow in." Meanwhile, an Indian creeps around the corner of the house and goes inside the wagon to look at Potter's supplies. Inside the cabin, Jane sends Potter out for a glass of water. While he is gone, she escapes out the window. In the wagon, the Indian accidentally turns on the laughing gas and inhales. He giggles, surprised at himself. Dressed absurdly, like a combination of Roman soldier and wooden Indian, the man has two braids with white feathers attached at the crown of his head. He carries a tomahawk and wears beaded moccasins. His cloth "breastplate" seems made to resemble metal and has red ribbons adorning each side, just at the point where his nipples are. Forming a triangle, his face paint begins at his widow's peak, descends his forehead to marks around his eyes, then frames his cheeks. Again, red is the predominant symbol for danger in the forms of socialism, sex, Indians, devious women, the Other. The Indian, in an odd pairing with Calamity Jane, is naïve and silly. This twinning reflects Jane's ultimate weakness, her femininity. Using color to its best advantage, the film mocks the melodrama of the traditional John Ford Western and feminizes Indians and Jane to neutralize the danger they represent.

Jane walks around the wagon while the camera angle switches to the front, allowing us to see the Indian inside as through a window. Jane climbs in the front of the wagon, preparing to sleep inside. At the same time, the Indian escapes out the back and goes into the bedroom through the open window, reemphasizing the liminal quality of the frontier, of women, and of the Indian. Meanwhile, returning with a bucket of water, Potter knocks on the door, expecting, of course, to find Jane. The scene is hilarious because we know that Jane and the Indian have switched places. The Indian hides behind a skin hung on a wooden rack to serve as a dressing curtain, where Jane had been standing when Potter left the room. He is wary, poised with his tomahawk in the air. Potter bends down to fill the ladle and, seeing the "red" legs, says, "My, you're blushing right down to your little tootsies, aren't ya? Here you are, Cuddles." Standing opposite the Indian behind the curtain, Potter holds out the ladle. When the man takes it, Potter touches his hand. The Indian throws the water out, followed by the ladle. "My but you're an odd girl," remarks Potter, as both giggle. "Gee, I'm glad I picked a girl with a sense of humor." The Indian is feminized, thus disempowered and neutralized as a threat: he does not laugh at the irony of the situation, but rather does so involuntarily because of Potter's laughing gas.

Asking if everything is all right, Potter reaches over the curtain to touch his bride. He touches the man's shoulder and squeezes his arm. "My but you're a muscular little thing, aren't you? Those dresses are awfully deceiving." Moving his hand down the man's arm, he comments, "Smooth, smooth." The Indian giggles again and Potter says, "Oh, I didn't mean to tickle you." "Isn't that sweet," he continues, "you put your hair up in braids." Potter grabs a braid and pulls the Indian into the room. Despite all the clues, Potter is blind to what is in front of him. His eyes closed, ostensibly to protect Jane's modesty, Potter kisses the man, who hits him in the head with his tomahawk just as Jane, in an earlier scene, had hit him with the butt of her gun. "Boy, can you kiss," Potter mutters, eyes still closed, before falling unconscious onto the bed. The Indian walks to the window, but before he exits, turns proudly to look at Potter, the moment ruined as he giggles again, then creeps away. The frame fades to morning, marked with the text "Then Dawn Broke," which blows up in a cloud of smoke. The film now returns to the traditional plot structure and we see our first hostile Indians, creeping behind the well.

Cut to Jane, walking back into the bedroom. Replaced by the Indian, she wears blue gingham, as the Indian now represents those qualities that had stigmatized her and required her to wear red. She finds Potter still lying across the bed. "Boy, I can't get over your kisses," he tells her. Cut to the exterior of the cabin exterior, where the waiting Indians disperse as Potter walks outside. He takes his razor, a towel, and a mirror to the well to shave. He hangs his mirror on the tree nearby and spreads lather on his face. From the corner of his eye, he glimpses what seems to be a tree moving. In the background, an Indian disguised by tree branches moves across the frame. He stops moving each time Potter looks around. Finally, he walks out of the frame, even though Potter is looking right at him. "Must be a Virginia creeper," he says. The mirror falls then and, as he bends to retrieve it, an arrow hits the tree, just above where his head would have been. Oblivious, Potter stands up and hangs the mirror on the shaft of the arrow. Another arrow hits the tree, cutting the side of his face turned away from us. "I'm shaving too close," he remarks. "Boy, I must be a nervous wreck." He notices the arrows then and turns, showing the blood on his face. "It's an arrow. Someone had to shoot. Who shoots arrows? Cupid? No. It couldn't be Cupid. William Tell? No, that's silly. Couldn't be William Tell, no apple. Indians. Yeah, In . . . could be. Indians!" The reality of his situation finally apparent, he runs toward the cabin yelling "Indians! Indians!" The previous scene having shown the Indian's buffoonery, the ensuing fight is no longer significant. Instead, we focus on the interaction between Jane and Potter.

The settlers, all of whom presumably slept through the preceding drama, lock the cabin door as Potter approaches. Jane throws a holster with two guns out the window and closes the shutter. "Pick up those guns and take care of yourself," she says. "Take care of myself? There's a million Indians out here against one coward!" he yells. He hides in an empty barrel just below the window as the Indians emerge from the forest, one at a time. Jane, using a rifle through an opening in the window shutter, shoots and kills each as they approach the house. Potter, shooting simultaneously, with his eyes closed, assumes that he is killing them. The end of the film depends upon the reversal of roles depicted in this scene. Jane is the hero and Potter the hapless victim, yet there is some confusion between the two. The Indians fall dead in a tidy heap. Potter ventures out to look at the last, wounded Indian lurching about as he dies tragically. The other Indians run back into the forest, apparently afraid of Potter. He hits the man on the head with the butt of his gun, as Jane had hit him while they kissed, and the man falls dead onto the heap.

The rest of the wagon train arrives at that moment, having found the wayward wagons. "They started it," Potter says childishly, pointing to the pile of bodies. One of the old men with Potter rushes to explain that Potter saved the whole train by luring the Indians away. "I did? Yeah. Oh, he's right. I did. That's what I did." As thanks, the man gives Potter his rifle. Holding it over his shoulder, Potter remarks, "I'll knock off a couple of Indians for you." The gun goes off, killing an Indian who had been hiding in a tree and now falls to the ground. As they congratulate him, Potter remakes himself as the fool: "At this time, I'd like to say a few words." Another voice interrupts, saying, "Let's get out of here before those redskins come back." "Those were the words," Potter agrees, as he runs toward his wagon and Jane. "You've got the courage of a lion, Doctor," says the old man who had given him the rifle. "Oh that's nothing," replies Potter. "Brave men run in my family." The scene ends on this pun, as Potter's horses drag him from the wagon again.

Cut to Buffalo Flats and the Dirty Shame Saloon. A short sequence of events establishes the conflict in the town. The men guilty of running guns have been watching Potter from the saloon. They walk past the dancing showgirls to an office in the back. A half-finished mural on the wall opposite the door features white settlers standing on shore among some trees and a few naked Indians emerging from a body of water. The saloon owner, Preston, stands on a stepladder as he paints color onto the skin of one of the Indians. The scene is patently absurd: again, the filmmaker gives us the subtle reassurance that we are in on the joke. Irritated that the men have interrupted him, Preston listens to their explanation about the agent. Meanwhile, a man dances in the saloon with the star showgirl, Pepper. Her boyfriend, Joe, enters and shoots him. Joe threatens the other men, establishing his menace, then leaves. At that moment, the wagon train arrives. People gather around the wagon, cheering Potter. Watching the spectacle from the saloon's window, Preston suggests that Pepper seduce Potter, assuming that Joe will then kill him.

Following Jane into the local hotel, Potter is surrounded by adoring women. "I'm tired. I've been fighting Indians all day," he tells them, lowering his voice a few tones. While he registers, Jane spots her next contact, the blacksmith Hank Billings, across the street. Suddenly, she announces to Potter that she is divorcing him. With mock admiration, Jane explains Potter's new place in American history: "You're a legend now, a hero." She beckons him to the window, saying, "Look outside. Once that was a forest. Then it became a trail. Then a town, and soon it'll become a city. . . . There'll be a statue of a great man . . . and under the statue it'll read, Painless Peter Potter, successor to Wild Bill Hickok and Buffalo Bill Cody. The intrepid hero who saved an entire wagon train by killing eleven Indians." "Twelve," he replies, his new hubris evident.

Jane tries another approach. "You're a hero now. I'm just a little nobody. You belong to the people. This is the end of the road." Though he fails to recognize all the implications of Jane's speech, Potter finally realizes that she has not been entirely honest with him. In anger he mutters under his breath, "I'll show her," and walks toward the Dirty Shame Saloon. On his way, he passes a man dressed conspicuously as cowboy. The man presents a caricature of the figure, emphasizing Hope's performance. "How'd you like a little conversation?" Potter asks. "Why I'd be tickled to death," the man answers. "Follow me," orders Potter, and they walk off together.

Cut to Jane and Hank Billing at the smithy. We now arrive at the crisis point in the narrative. Jane reveals her identity to the blacksmith, who explains the gravity of the situation to her. "You've landed smack dab, right in the middle of the lowest down skunk of a scheme they ever smeared across the west . . . somebody is running guns in to the Indians. Enough rifles to massacre every white man in the territory. Can't understand why they ain't attacked already." She explains in turn that the Indians are waiting for the dynamite coming in on the wagon train. Jane explains Potter's presence and tells Billings that they must see who retrieves the dynamite in order to expose the renegades. He worries that the villains are sure to kill Potter, to which she replies, "They'll think the federal agent's dead. Then I can operate." The film continues oscillating between poles: the horror of the "Indian Problem" and the humor of Bob Hope. Cut to Potter, standing again with the cowboy. They have switched clothes and the man is chuckling to himself. Clearly, Potter has used his laughing gas to get his way. Potter goes to the saloon to show off his new persona. Preston greets Potter. "Gentlemen," Preston announces to the men assembled. "We have a celebrity in our midst. It's a rare privilege to shake the hand of the greatest Indian fighter west of the Mississippi."

The references to Indian agents and to a general Indian threat suggest that the film is set in the pre-1850s West, a period known for the violence against Indians and the valorization of the "Indian Fighter." [24] Preston invites Potter, the hero, to join him for a drink. Surrounded by showgirls competing for his attention, Potter stands awkwardly with his foot in a spittoon; he is clearly not heroic. The second musical number starts and Pepper walks up to him, scattering the other women and singing about a woman's efforts at seduction. The song and Pepper's seduction of Potter complete the caricature of the Cowboy. The lyrics are ironic, suggesting the forthcoming showdown between Potter and Joe, rather than a romantic tryst. Pepper, dressed in green with green plumes in her red hair, echoes the images that characterize Indians and Calamity Jane: feathers, licentiousness, and the color red. She dances seductively in front of Potter, singing "I'll kiss you in my own sweet way." Her plumes tickle his nose, reprising the by-now infamous kiss that knocks him unconscious. Pepper and Potter dance, his spurs jangle, a parody of his new identity. Joe comes in and Potter, caught up in his new look and charisma, threatens the gunfighter. They arrange to duel at sundown. Joe leaves, and Potter drinks a shot of whiskey. He tells the bartender that he wants "four fingers of Red Eye. . . . I always feel like a drink before a killin'." This quip references both the pervasive part alcohol played in Indian/white relations and the demonic relationship between alcohol and war. Dissolve to the sun setting. Joe waits outside, target shooting. The scene is clearly satiric. Joe shoots small balls from the top of a sign. Rather than filming the scene in a continuous shot, the filmmaker cut each gunshot with the next to highlight the contrivances of the plot.

In a set-up to one of the funniest sequences in the movie, men give Potter advice as he walks toward the door. "He draws from the left so lean to the right." "There's a wind from the east so better aim to the west." "He crouches when he shoots so stand on your toes." Unlike the typical standoff—two men approach each other from opposite ends of the main street—Potter walks alone, repeating the men's instructions. The pithy words of wisdom become a litany of nonsense as Potter searches for Joe: "He draws to the left, so stand on your toes; there's a wind from the east, better lean to the right; crouches when he shoots, better aim to the west; he draws from his toes so better lean to the wind. Ha, ha. I got it."

Past shadows and around blind corners, Potter and Joe hunt each other. The two finally appear in the same frame, and it seems that they might actually meet. They walk toward the camera, each on one side of the tobacco store, in front of which stands a wooden Indian. Potter is muttering, "draws to the wind, so lean when you stand. No. Stands on his crouch with his toes in the wind. No."

Joe walks into the shop as Potter rounds the corner, touching the wooden Indian and signaling him to keep quiet. Potter's muttering and this final plea to the wooden Indian are part of the slapstick Hope brings to the film. Potter walks through the store behind Joe as Joe passes the wooden Indian behind Potter. The Indian remains silent. Potter walks into the road as a woman drives by in a horse and carriage. She separates him first from the Indian, then from Joe. Joe and the Indian are now juxtaposed in contrast to Potter, the image reifying the plot. In a final nod to the satire, the camera cuts to the undertaker, standing in his doorway and smiling at the men. The carriage pulls ahead and the men turn finally to face each other. Joe draws his gun as Jane, in a room above the smithy, draws hers. She shoots Joe before Potter even frees his gun from its holster. When Billings questions her sudden support of Potter, Jane explains that in order to catch the men selling dynamite, she must rely on Potter as her decoy for a while longer.

The contrast between Jane's meeting with Billings and Potter's absurd gun-fight highlights the inherent incongruity of the film. In those moments when Hope talks to the audience—referring, for example, to Horace Greeley with his "Go West, young man!"—his buffoonery is undermined. Thus, this scene allows for his assumption of power: shedding his urban persona, Hope disguises himself as a cowboy, participating actively in the narrative as Potter. In like manner, Joe's death symbolizes the end of the old order, the Old West, and its lawlessness. The American Adam triumphs.

Seeing Potter win the duel, Preston tells his men, "Get a hold of Yellow Feather." The significance here lies in the cooperation between the lone Indian and the "bad guys": the Indian is further condemned by association with those who beleaguer the innocent dentist. Gretchen Bataille and Charles Silet offer a succinct explanation for the Indian's role in Hollywood film. This explanation is clearly at play in *The Paleface*:

> The appeal of the traditional Western is that it provided clear, simple solutions to complex problems and solidified the triumph of the forces of white civilization. . . . The American Indian became the ultimate Hollywood stereotype—easily understood and emotionally necessary—one which provided a universal theme by satisfying the universal fears and uncertainty of the audience.[25]

The plot turns yet again on itself as the Indian is reestablished as the villain, and Potter as the ritual victim and the sacred fool. In her apparent disregard for Potter's humanity, Jane is complicit in the Indian's inhumanity. She tells Billings, "I'll round up our goat," identifying Potter positively as the ritual scapegoat. Pepper comes to congratulate Potter, but Jane sees she must reclaim her husband. She punches Pepper in the jaw to make her point, sending the woman crashing through a wooden banister. Potter feigns pride, but of course takes Jane back. He enjoys being the hero, telling her "You may kiss my cheek" as they walk into the hotel.

Fade to hall outside their hotel room. The amorous Potter nails a sign to the door, "Beware Mad Dog." He goes in to see Jane, prepared to challenge any suggestion of his ineptitude or passivity. Again, they kiss and she knocks him out with the butt of her gun. McLeod reverses the roles again, however, when Jane suddenly apologizes to the unconscious Potter, then chastises herself for getting "soft." This is the first indication that she is recoverable, tamable. Just then, Hank Billings staggers into the room. He tells Jane that the dynamite is in the undertaker's parlor; then he falls forward, revealing an arrow in his back. The arrow signifies the Indian and recalls the need for an Indian fighter, be it Jane or Potter. She wakes Potter, pleading with him to help her. "Any other girl'd be tickled pink to be alone with a guy who's killed fourteen Indians for her," Potter tells her petulantly. He agrees to go, but says in parting, "And you know that statue you told me about, tell them to carve on it, Painless Potter, schmo." Potter's self-consciousness throughout the film stands in direct contrast to that of his enemies: the white renegades; the government agents who are ultimately responsible for putting him in danger; Jane and Pepper; the "real" cowboys; and, most importantly, the Indians. Hope playing Potter is the film's one stable element. Following the showdown with Joe, Potter and Hope are one, the actor giving the character substance. Walking toward the door, Potter notices the corpse on the floor. Unnerved, he nevertheless continues on to the funeral parlor.

"Get out of here," Potter whispers to a black cat in front of the parlor. "Do you want me to sic a mouse on you?" The reference is clear: Potter is the mouse. He is the David who defeats the Goliath threatening Progress, which is represented by the alliance of the Indians and the white mercenaries. Potter climbs in the window above the front door and looks around the room. A crucial point in the narrative, this scene is the enactment of Potter's death as an incompetent and subsequent rebirth as a hero. He has abandoned elements of his cowboy costume so that he no longer looks ridiculous; now the ambiguous connotations associated with the black cat serve to redefine his character. The cat walks through the door, which Potter had assumed was closed. This emphasizes both his foolishness, even while he is being brave, and the cat's innate intelligence, or implicitly supernatural qualities. Potter finds the dynamite hidden under two tables, on one of which lies Joe's corpse. When Preston and his men come in, Potter lies on the other table, pretending to be dead. "We're using the dentist's wagon in case there's a slip up," the men say. While they load the dynamite, the cat crawls under the sheet covering Potter, making him giggle and tickling his nose with its tail, recalling both the laughing gas and Pepper's plumes.

Often associated with women and with power, the cat symbolizes the demonic. As Barbara Walker explains, "ideas of connection between human and animal were more or less diabolized under the Christian system, which regarded animals as soulless or demonica. . . . Black animals were especially suspected of harboring demons, since black was the color of underworld beings in general." [26] There is a transference of this supernatural power when Potter bites the cat's tail and reveals himself. He gets up and threatens the men, standing with his back to yet another window. An Indian in a buffalo headdress opens the pane, grabs Potter, and easily pulls him through the window. In this scene, which is crucial to the plot, evil shifts from the white mercenaries to the Indian, who actually overpowers Potter, and confirms the Indian as the "real" threat to America. In the transitional space of the film, roles are ambiguous, the bad guys are hard to define, and the essential silliness of the entire situation (war for dominance) is made clear. Jane, wearing buckskin again, leaves their hotel room through the window. Climbing from the balcony down a tree, she is captured, too. (Having exited the civilized world by unconventional means—through windows—she and Potter have returned to the liminal space of the wilderness.) Both she and Potter are taken to the campground of the local tribe.

The climax of the film occurs in the liminal space that belongs to the Indian. Transitory and surreal, the Indian camp is the space of transformation, where Potter is remade into the Hero and Jane is recovered as the Woman. They are reclaimed as the archetypes we value. Fade to a clearing surrounded by teepees and Indians, many of whom sit with drums, beating in rhythm. Inside a teepee, Jane reveals her treachery to Potter. "Hearing those drums, I figured this was my last chance," she tells him, regretting her manipulation and betrayal. "I bet I handed you a lot of laughs," he says ruefully, recognizing and thereby neutralizing his naiveté. Suddenly Jane exposes herself as a vulnerable woman, a contrast to the heartless criminal the government men believe her to be: "Painless, there's one more thing I gotta tell you. I gotta tell you that I love you." The shot/reverse shot—a close-up of Potter, then Jane—shows her sincerity and restored humanity.

They kiss and he marvels at not being knocked out. The tribal medicine man enters the teepee, chanting, and dances a circle around them. He throws powder at Potter, recalling Potter's fear of dust blowing into the cabin and signifying the Indian who does "blow" in. The medicine man wears a headdress that obscures his face, making him anonymous and, like Hope, synonymous with the headdress. He leaves and Chief Yellow Feather enters with two other men, one of whom is easily recognizable as Iron Eyes Cody. The chief is played by an actor identified as Chief Yowlatchie who, along with Cody, confirms the Indians' authenticity. We know that they are real Indians, just as Jane Russell and Bob Hope are real celebrities. Chief Yellow Feather speaks to Potter in Hollywood pidgin, "How." "Not so good," replies Potter. Yellow Feather talks privately to his men in their own language. The Indians come across as secretive and devious, notwithstanding their innate stupidity. "How," he says again before leaving with his men. "I'll let you know," retorts Potter.

Jane, having understood the conversation, reveals that the Indians are planning to kill Potter. He asks how. "Well, with Indians," she says hesitantly, "the bigger hero you are, the bigger the torture." The savagery of the Indian is thus reinstated, despite his buffoonery, as it confirms Hope/Potter's heroism. Jane explains that they will bend two trees toward each other and tie one to each of Potter's legs. Then they will cut the ropes and he will be ripped in half. As Potter tries to assimilate the information, the medicine man returns, shrieking and throwing more powder in Potter's face. Several men drag Potter and Jane outside where Iron Eyes Cody speaks a language unintelligible to Potter and to us. "Yeah, that's your story," Potter replies sarcastically. Chief Iron Eyes is the Indian who motivates the others' actions. Thus, a "real" Indian, playing himself, is responsible for the violence against the innocent dentist/Bob Hope. His humor intact, Potter remains calm as the Indians tie his feet to the trees. "Just think," he jokes, "I'll be traveling east and west at the same time." The overt doubling is important here as Potter metamorphoses, shedding his incompetence completely. The medicine man cuts the ropes and, instead of being killed, Potter is catapulted away. Iron Eyes points to the empty boot left hanging in one of trees. Shamed before the "white squaw," Chief Yellow Feather proclaims "Bad medicine," and they exile the medicine man. "Go. Do not come back," Iron Eyes commands.

Potter, meanwhile, lands in an enormous tree. His shouts for help echo in white text next to him, high above the ground: "Help!" The text strongly suggests an unreal, cartoonish element reminiscent of the dime novel, connecting this scene to the earlier ones framed by "Then Night Fell" and "Then Dawn Broke." Potter climbs down and, after some indecision, returns to the camp for Jane. He argues with himself, pretending to be two people in imitation of the splitting Jane had graphically described earlier. Suddenly, however, his alter ego is real, heard as a voice-over, and we recognize that it is his conscience talking. His character restored, he doubles back to save Jane, but he runs into the exiled medicine man. They confront each other, both growling and pawing at the ground in a parody of a fight. As he had with the cowboy, Potter tells the Indian he wants to trade clothes, but the medicine man responds by throwing powder in Potter's face. Unfazed, Potter grabs some dirt and casts it back on his adversary. Then he reaches for a fallen branch and the now discredited medicine man flees. Painless Peter Potter erases the Indian from the narrative when he bests the tribal medicine man. Historian Roy Harvey Pearce writes that

[by the 1770s] Americans were coming to understand the Indian as one radically different from their proper selves; they knew he was bound inextricably in a primitive past, a primitive society, and a primitive environment, to be destroyed by God, Nature and Progress to make way for

Civilized Man. Americans after the 1770's worked out a theory of the savage which depended on an idea of a new order in which the Indian could have no part.[27]

Thus when Potter throws a stone and hits the fleeing man on the head from an impossibly long distance, demonstrating his new heroic powers, he destroys the primitive. The sound effects that emphasize the action are drawn from cartoons, as they were earlier when Potter was shot from the bent saplings. Potter's heroism derives from the power of the conqueror as well as that of the conquered; as we discover, Potter steals the medicine man's clothes and becomes *both* cowboy *and* Indian.

Meanwhile, the traitorous white men, including the secretary Martin, deliver rifles and dynamite to the Indians, who have decided to burn Jane, like a witch at the stake. Drumming begins, with angry whoops from the assembled Indians. Potter shows up disguised in the medicine man's regalia, performing the part as he had that of the cowboy. The Indians, in "traditional" dress, are dancing and waiting for the ritual burning. Potter throws powder in one man's face in order to steal his drum. The powder symbolizes Potter's newly acquired magic and his transformation from the hapless dentist to the potent and effective Hero. He identifies himself to Jane, who is tied to a stake. "Burn him, burn him with white squaw," says Yellow Feather when Iron Eyes reports that the medicine man has come back.

The Indians dance with spears and tomahawks, after erecting another stake to burn Potter. "Who're they gonna burn over there?" he asks Jane. "The medicine man," she tells him. "Serves him right for practicing without a license." "Yeah," says Jane," they think you're the medicine man." Finally aware of his danger, Potter cuts the cords around Jane's wrists to free her. He then leads the dancing Indians away, past other Indians whose savagery is emphasized by the rifles and dynamite around them. He grabs a gourd of gunpowder and wanders away. Holding the gourd upside down, Potter inadvertently leaves a trail of powder, the explosive reifying the medicine man's magic powder. The Indians, believing he is their medicine man, threaten Potter, and he retreats, the trail of gunpowder growing. They take him to the stake and light fires beneath him and Jane, igniting the trail of explosive. The flames throw everyone into a panic. The trail of fire leads back to the pile of munitions, which explodes. As the Indians scatter, Potter and Jane escape. Potter leaves the raven/buffalo headdress on the stake, abandoning Indianness inasmuch as the power to dominate has been effectively transferred. In conquering the wilderness, the hero uses its demonic qualities, but must subsequently discard them to prepare the way for decent folk. Potter has the "good

Figure 6.4. Ritual burning scene in *The Paleface* (1948).

medicine" and leaves the Indians' "bad medicine," in the form of the familiar headdress, to burn. He and Jane drive the wagon out of the camp, the Indians and the mercenaries, including Martin and Preston, in pursuit. "Grab a rifle and start shootin'," yells Jane. "Give me one of those guns." "Yes ma'am," Potter replies and starts shooting.

Bataille and Silet argue that

> [the view of Indians as subhuman or inspired by the devil] remained a powerful theme and . . . ultimately civilization demanded that the confrontation between Indian and white result in Indian capitulation to white domination. Individual Indians could be "good," but the group had to be depicted as "bad" to justify the existing exploitation by government and religious authorities.[28]

Similarly, Potter shoots at two Indians from an anonymous group, who seem to fall from their horses only to sit back up in their saddles. "Pretty tricky, those foreigners," is his wry comment. Shooting in earnest now, he runs out of ammunition. He tries throwing dynamite at the men, dropping the first lit stick on the floor of the wagon. The horses are separated from the wagon as the linchpin works its way free. Jane jumps on the horses and rides one way; Potter and the wagon roll another. He realizes finally that Jane has come around behind him in a now literal reversal. "Jump, Painless!" She saves him, and the wagon blows up, taking the lives of the three traitors. He comments sarcastically, "Darnit. There goes my dental diploma."

Cut to a sign "Happy Honeymoon" on the back of a carriage. Potter and Jane walk out of the city hall, both dressed in white. In a final twist, Jane decides to drive. Their roles, however, are now reversed: the horse, unhitched, takes off, dragging Jane behind. No longer in control as she was with the runaway wagon, Jane now wears buttons and bows and is the kind of woman for whom Potter had wished. Says Potter, facing the camera, "What do you want, a happy ending?" and so the film ends. Things are finally restored. Buffalo Flats is recovered as a respectable town; Jane, now Mrs. Potter, is a respectable married woman, having abandoned her gun and buckskin; and Potter is the capable, competent hero, Hope. The narrative of the opening sequence, which established the historical background and realism, culminates in this last scene. The Indians have been "disappeared," and the demonic white men are dead. Jane has fulfilled her double mission and may now take on her true identity as a docile and honest woman.

McLeod recovers Bob Hope and Jane Russell in the roles with which we are familiar. Hope speaks finally to the audience, letting us off the hook by ending the joke: "What do you want?" he asks. Notoriously racist and superficial, representations of Indians are both essential to the articulation of the American self and the rule in Hollywood filmmaking. This is demonstrated clearly in *The Paleface*. Rather than providing a critique of these images in terms of their authenticity and negative connotations, we may heed Bhabha's advice and analyze instead the process of subjectification, the establishment of a sign as its own referent. As *The Paleface* illustrates, comedy and humor are particularly effective ways in which to misrepresent the Other. Like the minstrel in blackface, the Indian provides a solid basis for the comedians' humor. The manipulation of signs reifies the vanishing Savage in a palatable way. This is, after all, just a comedy.

NOTES

1. Homi K. Bhabha, "The Other Question: Difference, Discrimination and the Discourse of Colonialism," in *Out There: Marginalization and Contemporary Cultures*, ed. Russell Ferguson, et al. (New York: New Museum of Contemporary Art, 1990), 71–88.

2. Ibid., 78.

3. Robert F. Berkhofer, Jr., *The White Man's Indian: Images of the American Indian from Columbus to the Present* (New York: Vintage Books, 1978), 29.

4. Raymond William Stedman, *Shadows of the Indian: Stereotypes in American Culture* (Norman: University of Oklahoma Press, 1982), 161.

5. Bhabha, "The Other Question," 78.

6. Frederick Jackson Turner, "The Significance of the Frontier in American History," in *The Frontier in American History* (New York: Holt, Rinehart & Winston, 1962), 9.

7. Ibid., 3.

8. Ward Churchill, *Fantasies of the Master Race: Literature, Cinema and the Colonization of American Indians*, ed. M. Annette Jaimes (Monroe, ME: Common Courage Press, 1992), 232.

9. Stedman, *Shadows of the Indian*, 141.

10. Doris Faber, *Calamity Jane: Her Life and Legend* (Boston: Houghton Mifflin Co., 1992), 38.

11. Ibid., 37.

12. Ibid., 40.

13. Lewis Jacobs, *The Rise of the American Film: A Critical History* (New York: Teacher's College Press, 1969), 448. He writes also that "the year 1929 has been generally regarded as the most important epoch in the movies' technical history. Tools, materials and every phase of production were rapidly developed and altered to meet the new critical demands of the talkies and to free the director from mechanical restrictions. Films improved steadily as the dependence of the camera upon the microphone was relieved and as the microphone was given the mobility of the cameras. The creative possibilities of sound were gradually disclosed." (439)

14. Gretchen Bataille and Charles Silet, *Images of American Indians on Film: An Annotated Bibliography* (New York: Garland Publishing, Inc., 1985), xvii.

15. Bhabha, "The Other Question," 76.

16. Turner, "The Significance of the Frontier," 8.

17. Stedman, *Shadows of the Indian*, 106. Stedman offers a full discussion of the Indian and, in particular, his virility. (74–117).

18. Jacobs, *The Rise of the American Film*, 27. Jacobs notes that "a few players in these pictures [sensational action thrillers] won tremendous popular followings, and it is interesting to note that they were all women: Kathlyn Williams, Helen Holmes, Pearl White, Ruth Roland. All were renowned for their stunts, physical prowess, and daring. Their exploits paralleled, in a sense, the real rise of women to a new status in society—a rise that became especially marked on America's entrance into the war, when women were offered participation in nearly every phase of industrial activity."

19. Ibid., 154.

20. Ibid. Jacobs writes, "Dozens of movies portrayed the American ideal of stalwart virtue. Most vigorous were the new 'Westerns.' In 1908 the cowboy, a fresh and

colorful character, was introduced in the Bronco Billy series, which set a fashion and continued for years. The sweep and action of the frontier produced much more physical exhilaration than other types of film." (143)

21. John G. Cawelti, "Reflections on the New Western Films: The Jewish Cowboy, The Black Avenger, and The Return of the Vanishing American," in *The Pretend Indians*, ed. Gretchen Bataille and Charles Silet (Ames: Iowa State University Press, 1980), 113.

22. Jacobs, *The Rise of the American Film*, 535–56.

23. Cawelti, "Reflections on the New Western Films," 113.

24. Andrew Jackson, for example, was a renowned Indian fighter. As president, he ordered the removal of the Cherokee nation from Georgia against the ruling of the Supreme Court in 1832.

25. Bataille and Silet, *Images of American Indians on Film*, xxi–xxii.

26. Barbara G. Walker, *The Woman's Dictionary of Symbols and Sacred Objects* (New York: HarperCollins, 1988), 247.

27. Roy Harvey Pearce, *Savagism and Civilization: A Study of the Indian and the American Mind* (Berkeley: University of California Press, 1988), 4.

28. Bataille and Silet, *Images of American Indians on Film*, xix.

7

DOLORES DEL RÍO, UNCOMFORTABLY REAL

The Economics of Race in Hollywood's Latin American Musicals

Joanne Hershfield

When *Photoplay* conducted a search in 1933 for the "most perfect feminine figure in Hollywood," using "medical men, artists, designers" as judges, the "unanimous choice" of these selective arbiters of female beauty in the United States was the Mexican actress, Dolores del Río.[1] The question posed by the fan magazine search and the methodology employed to find this "most perfect" figure reveal a number of discursive parameters that defined femininity and beauty during that particular moment in U.S. history. At the same time, the selection of Dolores del Río betrays an enigma unique to Hollywood: given the particular environment of social attitudes and beliefs in the 1930s around questions of racialized sexuality, how is it that a foreign star like del Río was elevated above popular white stars such as Irene Dunne, Fay Wray, and Norma Shearer?

While del Río was an Other in terms of her place in U.S. culture, Hollywood was able to fold her into the fabric of North American conceptions of femininity and female beauty. In the very visible arena of American cinema, del Río was an "acceptable" Other, even while Mexicans in general were relegated to a lower status in the U.S. racial hierarchy. Richard Dyer finds a similar complication in the production and reception of African-American singer and actor, Paul Robeson, during that era. Despite the dominance of racist beliefs and practices, Robeson was able to cross the color line in American popular culture and move beyond the "accepted" limits of black stardom.[2] Faced with the dilemma of a black man who attended both Rutgers and Columbia University and starred in both football and film, one critic "could only conclude that Negroes seemed to be 'natural born actors.'"[3] For Dyer, the confusion about Robeson's place in the public's imagination lies in "the problem of the body," a problem that is a function of both the "biologism of race" and the "justification of the capitalist system itself."[4] Robeson's accomplishments and successes in the American marketplace challenged scientific and popular discourses about race and racial characteristics of blacks in general.

Within a capitalist system that was blind to everything but the pursuit of profit, the problem of race, so visibly present on the body of del Río the movie star, could be surmounted if necessary. More specifically, these problems were effaced through del Río's placement in Hollywood's discourse of stardom, a discourse mediated by the demands of the marketplace.

A number of recent studies examine the processes by which an actor's race or ethnicity worked to construct, reinforce, or challenge discourses of racism in the classical Hollywood cinema. This essay, however, will use the case of del Río to interrogate how cinematic representations of racialized sexuality were negotiated in response to Hollywood's dependence on its foreign markets.[5] I look at three Latin American musicals of the 1930s that featured del Río: *Girl of the Rio* (1932); *Flying Down to Rio* (1933), a film that marked the debut of Fred Astaire and Ginger Rogers; and *In Caliente* (1935). I examine the promotion and reception of del Río's star text within the economic context of the United States and Hollywood in the 1930s, specifically in regard to political and economic relations with Latin American nations.

Del Río's star text was distinguished by a historically situated image of an exotic foreign woman who is attracted to (and attractive to) white men. This image was transmitted through a range of symbolic and economic practices, which included fan and trade magazines and the popular press. Like other celebrities, however, del Río was more than an image: she was a vessel that circulated cultural conceptions and values between producers and consumers of popular culture about beauty, feminine sexuality, national identity, and race. While female stars are primarily defined along a scale of sexual desirability, the color of del Río's skin and her facial characteristics marked her above all as not white.

Hollywood producer and director Edwin Carewe "discovered" the twenty-year-old del Río in Mexico. At the urging of Carewe, Dolores came to Hollywood in 1925 with her husband and was immediately cast as a vamp named Carlotta de Silva in one of Carewe's films, *Joanna* (1925). After a few bit parts, she landed her first leading role in First National's *Pals First* (1926) opposite Lloyd Hughes. That same year she was selected as one of the "WAMPAS Baby Stars," a yearly beauty pageant of young actresses headed for stardom, sponsored by the Western Association of Motion Picture Advertisers. The 1926 line-up included future stars Mary Astor, Fay Wray, Joan Crawford, and Janet Gaynor, among others. A subsequent starring role in Raoul Walsh's *What Price Glory* (1926), as Charmaine, a French barmaid, solidified del Río's status as a movie star.[6] In demand after Walsh's picture, she starred in an adaptation of Leo Tolstoy's *Resurrection*, directed by Carewe in 1927; *The Loves of Carmen* (1927, R. Walsh); *The Trail of '98* (1928, Clarence Brown); and *Ramona* (1928, Carewe), the third film version of Helen Hunt Jackson's popular nineteenth-century novel. Despite her accent, del Río survived the industry's shift to sound. Her first "talkies" were *Evangeline* (1929, Carewe) and *The Bad One* (1930, George Fitzmaurice).

Del Río was one of a number of Hispanic actors, along with Lupita Tovar, Lupe Vélez, Delia Magana, Gilbert Roland, and Ramon Novarro, who managed to find work in Hollywood during the silent era and the rise of the studio system.[7] Most Hispanics, however, were restricted to roles as "foils to or sex objects of Anglos" within an arena of considerable interracial, heterosexual behavior.[8] At the same time, the equation between color of skin and ethnicity affected the way in which certain actors were "labeled," and these labels in turn influenced the kinds of roles available to these actors. Due to Anglo-American racism, which specified racial types according to narrowly defined characteristics such as skin color and facial characteristics, light-skinned Hispanics moved in and out of ethnic roles more easily.[9] The label "Spanish" removed these actors somewhat from the more negative connotation of "Mexican." Others, especially mestizos or mulattos, were stuck with stereotypical "greaser, bandido, and 'Native'" roles.[10]

In her analysis of Hollywood's representation of Mexicans and Mexico in early silent cinema, Margarita de Orellana argues that Hollywood was not "trying to suggest that all Mexicans were like those represented on the Screen. Their object rather was to present the Mexican as a representative foreigner, to give the 'other' a shape and form."[11] The "shape and form" of this "other," however, was predicated on dominant ideologies of the race and perceived racial characteristics of "the Mexican" and was represented in Hollywood films in terms of racialized sexuality. Mexican male characters in the silent Hollywood cinema were dark-skinned, swarthy mestizo (mixed blood) "greasers"; the women, in contrast, were generally docile, sensual, and light-skinned with Spanish (European) rather than Indian or mestizo features. De Orellana remarks that while this Other woman may "belong to a higher social class [than the men], she remains culturally and racially inferior to the North American." [12]

Del Río's film characters embodied many of these cinematic stereotypes but also exceeded them. In addition to portraying Mexican women, she was often cast as an Other kind of exotic foreigner, portraying, for example, a French barmaid, a Brazilian heiress, and a Polynesian princess. Hollywood thus used del Río to exploit the public's fascination with foreign locales and peoples. In fact, much of the promotion and popular criticism of del Río in the 1930s focused on her high-class "exotic" appeal, an appeal made acceptable by situating the star as "almost" white. A *Photoplay* feature, "Four Most Beautiful Women," emphasizes the so-called lightness of del Río's skin color and her class status as "European" rather than Indian: "the exotic Latin . . . reminiscent of a Velasquez portrait, is typified in the mellowed ivory beauty of this convent-bred Mexican . . . but behind her glowing black eyes lies the restless spirit of her Spanish ancestry." [13]

Del Río was also incorporated into the discourse of "naturalness" that defined female beauty in the 1930s: she was described as a "natural beauty: . . . her raven hair has never known curling-iron or finger wave." She wears her hair "in the straight, severe lines typical of the high-class Spanish Senorita. It has never been cut. Her eyebrows are natural too. She plucks only a few stray ones near the eyelid." [14]

After the wild excesses of the 1920s flapper (the name given to young, middle-class women fond of fashion, music, and parties and immortalized in the novels of F. Scott Fitzgerald),[15] America moved to reclaim more traditional ideals of femininity and women's roles. In 1933, *Photoplay* informed its readers that Hollywood now wanted natural "girls who radiated vitality, stamina, sincerity, the clean-cut, clear-eyed girls of this new era who typify the backbone of our nation and who emulate the sturdiness of our pioneer women." The article gives as examples Jean Parker and June Vlasek, who was defined as "an American girl despite her foreign name." Playing off President Roosevelt's New Deal and his National Relief Administration (NRA) and making references to the Production Code Administration (PCA), *Photoplay* notes that "there's to be a new deal now in the way of girls, along with other codes which have come to mean so much in industry. The 'NRA' functioning to pull America out of the rut has swung its force in the direction of femininity. . . . We've had enough of sirens and flappers and we're ready now for the sedative qualities of sobriety." [16]

By the 1920s, Hollywood was setting the fashion for style and beauty in the

United States, featuring the flapper as emblematic of America's "new woman." Skirts moved up above the knee, women bobbed their hair, society girls and sales clerks traded in their woolen tights for silk stockings, and respectable young women smoke and drank in public. Clara Bow, Hollywood's "It Girl," was America's sweetheart, and "a cult of youthfulness, sensuality, and beauty" defined femininity in the 1920s and "made millionaires out of Coco Chanel, Charles Revson, Helena Rubinstein, and Elizabeth Arden."[17] Then, in the 1930s, as the U.S. public experienced not only an economic crisis, but also a crisis of social and cultural values as jobs, families, and social institutions were destroyed, gender roles were again challenged and revised.

The 1929 stock market crash exacerbated fears and concerns that had been building since the end of the nineteenth century when the U.S. population was predominantly white, rural, and Protestant. The twentieth century was marked by expanded industrialization and urbanization; increased immigration and resulting ethnic friction; the migration of many African-Americans from the South to Eastern cities in search of jobs; and the rise of a society consumed by commercial mass culture. By the time Franklin D. Roosevelt assumed the presidency in March 1933, many feared the "impending collapse of the American economic and political system."[18]

Hollywood had to respond to and contest this mood in order to reclaim audiences and recover from the disastrous effects of the Depression. At the time of the crash, the large, vertically integrated motion picture studios, funded primarily by money from Wall Street, were in strong shape. Jack Alicoate, publisher of the *Film Daily Yearbook (FDY)*, noted in his introduction to the 1930 edition that "the motion picture industry enters 1930 in the most prosperous condition in its comparatively short but eventful history."[19] A year later, gross receipts began to fall, but it was not until 1933 that the industry felt the full effects of the crash. Alicoate's introduction to the 1933 *FDY* warned, "unless the general economic situation takes a decided change for the better, the industry can hope for little in the way of progress and genuine prosperity."[20] In March 1933, box office receipts "were forty percent of what they had been in January of 1931."[21]

In the 1930s, foreign markets became even more critical for Hollywood's profit margins.[22] At the same time, Hollywood had to contend with the growth of a number of Latin American film industries, primarily those of Mexico and Argentina. In 1930, the introduction of sound technology advanced these national industries and threatened Hollywood's dominance. In response, a number of U.S. producers fostered the development of film projects that employed Latin American themes, places, and stars. Moreover, studio distributors stationed in Latin America suggested that Hollywood studios could do "a tremendous business if we could get them to insert some Spanish dialogue in their pictures." [23]

Despite the studios' best attempts, Latin American audiences rejected Hollywood's Spanish-language films. They wanted to hear their own Spanish accents, not those of Spain or Los Angeles. Little changed in regard to Hollywood's command of Latin American screens. By 1937, Latin America listed third, after the United States and Europe, among Hollywood's most important film markets. [24] Ninety percent of all films exhibited throughout Latin America were produced in the United States. [25] Hollywood thus operated the most influential system of representations worldwide. It dominated the film markets of most nations, and subjects of those nations continually saw themselves stereotyped on their neighborhood screens. Gangster films, foreign adventure narratives, and even comedies and musicals were replete with racist portrayals of Asians, Mexicans, Italians, and other non-Anglo-Saxon groups.

Foreign markets had always been important, not only for the revenue those markets generated for the film industry, but also for the ways in which Hollywood films enlarged the market for other mass-produced products. [26] U.S. film companies did not operate in isolation from other economic and political institutions. The industry, represented by their trade association, the Motion Picture Producers and Distributors of America, Inc. (MPPDA), enjoyed tacit cooperation, as well as oversight, from the federal government. The establishment of the Motion Picture Section in the Bureau of Foreign and Domestic Commerce in 1925–1926 secured support for Hollywood's expansion into international markets. Then, in 1933, the newly elected president, Franklin D. Roosevelt, announced his intention to broaden the Bureau's scope south of the border.

The MPPDA's Production Code of 1930, which limited film representations of sex, crime, and violence, constrained Hollywood to a certain degree. [27] However, larger political and economic pressures also influenced what audiences around the world could view at their neighborhood movie theater. For example, the United States was facing increasing diplomatic pressure from European, Asian, and Latin American governments to monitor the content of Hollywood films.

Given the importance of the Latin American region to U.S. political goals, the Department of Commerce compelled studios to make their stories about and representations of Latin American nations and people "acceptable." Moreover, as argued above, Hollywood did not want to jeopardize foreign box office profits by antagonizing those audiences.

Despite these restraints, exotic stereotypes "continued to prove irresistibly attractive to producers." [28] Ella Shohat and Robert Stam define exotic stereotypes as "tropes of empire" and remark on how these stereotypes tend to focus on stars' bodies, most often the bodies of women. Latin American women were associated "with verbal epithets evoking tropical heat, violence, passion, and spices. Thus Lupe Vélez becomes 'the Mexican Spitfire,' Acquanetta the 'Venezuelan volcano,' Olga San Juan the 'Puerto Rican pepperpot,' Marie-Antoinette Pons the 'Cuban hurricane.'"[29] Besides the "verbal epithets," Latin American women were defined by stereotypical behaviors that clearly mark them as Other (not white).

One look at publicity materials from del Río's musicals reveals how studios relied on these "tropes of empire" to market their Latin American stars and films. For example, the headline of a 1934 *Photoplay* article tells us that "Dolores Extols Passive Love." The article goes on to describe how "her golden skin, smooth as mellowed ivory and her dark, flashing eyes bespoke the lure of those maidenly 'senoritas' who peep at life from behind cloistered shutters. . . . When the young man comes to call on a senorita in Mexico . . . he brings his guitar."

A promotion still from *Wonder Bar* (1934, Lloyd Bacon), in which del Río plays an undifferentiated gypsy-like Latina dancer, features her in an embrace with costar, Ricardo Cortez, also of Latin American heritage. Describing the embrace, the photo caption reads: "The passive manner—Dolores is touched by the Latin technique Ricardo Cortez uses in this amorous scene." Another promotion for the same film states that "Old Mexico, with its star-strewn skies and brooding mountains, its age-touched haciendas and orchid-grown jungles, is a perfect setting for such a languorous romance."

Another *Photoplay* story features a picture of del Río wearing a low-cut dress and lots of eye makeup: "Meet the Duchess, otherwise the exotic Dolores del Río. . . . Contrast her dark loveliness to the blond Jean Harlow across the page and you'll know why Hollywood wins the world's beauty sweepstakes without any trouble." While, as noted, the "lightness" of del Río's skin color was emphasized in articles about her beauty, much of Hollywood's promotional material in the 1930s focused on her "dark loveliness," darkness being a synonym for Other women who were set in opposition to American blondes like Harlow.[30] It was her films, however, that most forcefully presented the young star to audiences at home and abroad as "other."

The Latin American musical found success both abroad and at home by exploiting exotic locales such as Mexico, Brazil, Cuba, and Argentina, as well as exotic stars like del Río, Lupe Vélez, and Ramon Novarro.[31] Gary D. Keller notes that, with the arrival of sound, "the stereotype of the Latin world as lively and musical, characterized by fiestas (when not siestas)" immediately became commonplace.[32] These musicals provided U.S. audiences with pictures of foreign countries and other cultures, relying on the appeal of spectacle, exotic costumes and settings, and dark-skinned performers. Stars like del Río were employed to authenticate those representations and attract fans on both sides of the border.[33]

Ruth Vasey suggests that, after the introduction of sound, "'foreignness' became less clearly associated with particular ethnic and national groups and became abstracted into an amorphous category of the alien. . . . Even geography became less distinct."[34] Films like *Girl of the Rio, Flying Down to Rio,* and *In Caliente* foregrounded Latin America in their titles and promotional materials and clearly situated their narratives south of the border. At the same time, the films blurred national and cultural distinctions between various Latin American nations so that Brazilians wore Mexican sombreros and spoke with Cuban accents while Mexicans danced Brazilian sambas and rumbas and spoke with Castilian accents.

While these musicals primarily addressed a North American audience's desire for pure entertainment and exotic spectacle, they strove at the same time to attract Latin American audiences. Hollywood therefore had to consider the political and social ideologies of its domestic audience and take into account the cultural values and desires of its foreign audiences.[35] In trying to do both, the narratives of these films had to maneuver through the land mines of U.S. racist attitudes and practices, land mines that were very often invisible to Hollywood filmmakers.

Del Río's first Latin American musical, RKO's *Girl of the Rio,* was a 1932 talkie version of the silent film, *The Dove* (1927), starring Norma Talmadge. In a rare role as a Mexican woman, Del Río plays Dolores, "the Dove," a singer in the Purple Pigeon, a questionable nightclub in the fictitious town of Mexicana, Mexico, on the Mexico-Texas border. Norman Foster stars as Johnny, who works across the street in a small gambling house, the Club International, and is in love with the Dove. Leo Carrillo as Don Jose Maria Lopez y Tostado constantly informs everyone that he is "the bes' damn *caballero* in all Mexico."

The original silent version of *The Dove* was one of a number of films banned in Mexico in the 1920s. The Mexican government objected to the "greaser" stereotypes that pervaded Hollywood westerns from 1906 through the 1920s and finally resorted to prohibiting all the films of offending production companies.[36] While Hollywood understood that negative stereotypes could affect their foreign box office income, U.S. racist ideology continued to pervade cinematic representations of ethnic, racial, and national characteristics.

In *Girl of the Rio,* Mexico is depicted as a barely civilized frontier that exists just over the U.S. border, a landscape of small towns filled with nightclubs that function as thinly disguised brothels, disreputable gambling establishments,

Figure 7.1. *Girl of the Rio* (1932).

and vast expanses of huge haciendas owned by ignorant, wealthy, Mexican stereotypes who speak with fake greaser accents and are only interested in women, alcohol, and money. Mexico objected vehemently to this second version of *The Dove*. Mexican officials considered *Girl of the Rio* to be "offensive" and permitted it to be "exhibited only in a censored version." [37]

Del Río, making a comeback after a mysterious illness that many in Hollywood described as a "nervous breakdown," plays the Mexican senorita opposite a number of white women from the U.S. side of the border who work at the Purple Pigeon as "hostesses." While the film goes out of its way to paint del Río's character as feminine and virtuous, it also plays into the conventional stereotypes about Mexican women. Although del Río was in her thirties by this time, her Dove comes across as a sweet and naive young girl, who speaks broken English with a "cute" foreign accent that immediately connects her with the greaser *caballero*, Don Jose, who speaks with the same funny accent. [38]

While the film was not a box office success, RKO did not blame it on del Río and immediately cast her in King Vidor's *Bird of Paradise* (1932) as "the savage princess, Luana." [39] Studio promotional materials describe the film as "a flaming pageant of forbidden love! . . . white man . . . native girl . . . caught in the torrid drama of life on a moon-drenched isle . . . as the raging god in the Mountain sunders the earth, splits the skies and hurls the seas to a bottomless pit because they broke the savage taboo!" Vidor's big-budget film reaped large profits for RKO and restored del Río's star status. RKO immediately cast her in *Flying Down to Rio*, with Fred Astaire and Ginger Rogers. The 1933 film was Astaire and Rogers's first hit and the first of a series of RKO musicals that featured the dancing duo.

Del Río stars in the role of Belinha, a South American heiress who meets and falls in love with a wealthy U.S. playboy, bandleader, and amateur stunt pilot named Roger (Gene Raymond) at a nightclub in Miami. By sheer coincidence, Roger's band is invited down to Rio de Janeiro to inaugurate the opening of a new hotel owned by Belinha's wealthy father, Señor de Resende. When the hotel's grand opening (and its future) is threatened by greedy capitalists from an unnamed European nation, the band functions as the cultural arm of the U.S. government and steps in to save Sr. de Resende from certain ruin by staging a spectacular performance in the air with Ginger and a chorus of showgirls mounted on the wings of stunt planes.

The film was typical of the Hollywood backstage musical, which interwove a romantic plot with the trials and tribulations of mounting a theatrical musical. According to Thomas Schatz, the musical genre's "gradual narrative progression toward a successful show and the principal performers' embrace project a utopian resolution" of the conflict between "object and illusion, between social reality and utopia." Specifically, Schatz proposes that these films offer audiences "utopian visions of a potentially well-ordered community." [40] The well-ordered community of *Flying Down to Rio* happens to be an "imagined community" of nations committed to transnational capitalism, engendered by a history of economic and cultural imperialism. Despite the fact that by the 1930s Brazil's population was primarily Afro-Brazilian and poor, this film presents the Brazilian community as white and wealthy.

At the conclusion of *Flying Down to Rio*, Belinha rejects her dark-haired South American boyfriend (Raul Roulien) for the blond, white hero. Like a number of films of that period, *Flying Down to Rio* promotes interracial romance. However, unlike those films, it also seems to condone miscegenation in the face of U.S. racist attitudes: the pair intends to marry and, given the function of marriage in the 1930s, most probably to propagate. *Flying Down to Rio* thus allows the romance to come to the conventional Hollywood narrative closure, unlike films such as *Bird of Paradise*, which had to kill del Río's character. The difference in the narrative resolution of these two films may be attributed to the fact that in *Bird of Paradise*, del Río plays a dark-skinned "savage princess" from a non-Christian South Seas tribe, while in *Flying Down to Rio*, she is a light-skinned, upper-class woman, the daughter of a wealthy,

Figure 7.2. Dolores del Río in *Flying Down to Rio* (1933).

Europeanized Brazilian capitalist. The discrepancy in the film endings, however, could also be ascribed to the importance of the Brazilian market to RKO's distribution networks and the relative unimportance of the Pacific markets in the 1930s. Consider that the narrative of *Flying Down to Rio* tells the story of a North American cultural envoy (the band) rescuing a failing Brazilian commercial enterprise from shadowy fascist figures. The film thus unabashedly promotes Roosevelt's policy of Pan-Americanism and free trade. In choosing her American boyfriend over her Brazilian fiancé, Del Río's character reinforces this narrative and political project.

Sérgio Augusto points to a number of political and economic "coincidences" surrounding the production of *Flying Down to Rio* that can be linked to the film's narrative structure and to the kinds of national representations the film projected. For one, producer Lou Brock proposed the film to the head of RKO, Merian C. Cooper (director of *King Kong*), who was also on the Board of Directors of Pan Am Airlines, which was expanding its routes in South America. Second, the release of the film coincided with Franklin D. Roosevelt's introduction of his Good Neighbor Policy in 1933. Finally, is it merely coincidence that Belinha and Roger send wires to Rio de Janeiro via RCA Communications, an RKO business partner? [41]

The Good Neighbor Policy embraced economic, political, and cultural strategies in an effort to assuage anti-American sentiments in place since the Spanish-American War in 1898. The policy was also intended to temper growing isolationist sentiments in the United States that were threatening business interests in Latin America. Roosevelt, motivated by pressures to expand U.S. markets in Latin America during the Depression, was convinced by businessmen that Hollywood films sold U.S. products. Finally, as World War II geared up in Europe, the Good Neighbor Policy aimed to sell "Americanism" in order to counter the growing Axis commercial and ideological influence in the Latin American region. [42]

Producers therefore took care with how Hollywood represented Latin Americans. An August 26, 1933, letter from Dr. James Wingate of the MPPDA to the executive producer of *Flying Down to Rio*, Merian C. Cooper, notes that "we also feel that the dialogue on page 30 by Belinha, 'That's how nice girls are brought up in my country. Complete supervision from . . . how do you say it? . . . infancy to adultery,' will be resented by the South American people." The Production Code Administration approved the film on July 21, 1935, only after RKO complied with a request to "tone down" the Carioca dance "and to remove the offensive sex suggestiveness." [43] At the same time, the dominant discourse around questions of race also influenced the PCA's concern with the film. In a letter to Sidney Kramer of the RKO Distributing Corporation, the PCA suggests that "the entire colored troop, with the exception of the finale, might well be dispensed with."

Despite the success of *Flying Down to Rio*, RKO did not renew del Río's contract, and she moved over to Warner Bros. for a starring role in *Wonder Bar* (1934) with Al Jolson, Dick Powell, Ricardo Cortez, and Kay Francis. Warner Bros., a pioneer in the development of sound technology with their Vitaphone, brought the first sound film, *The Jazz Singer*, to the screen in 1927 and produced *Lights of New York* (1928), the first "100 percent all talkie."

Warner Bros. picked del Río up, hoping "she would bloom into another Garbo," the Swedish star under contract with Metro-Goldwyn-Mayer.[44] However, neither *Wonder Bar* nor del Río's next picture, *Madame Du Barry* (1934), did as well as the RKO films. Warner Bros. returned her to the Latin American musical genre with *In Caliente* (1935), a musical set in Caliente, Mexico, starring Pat O'Brian, Edward Everett Horton, Glenda Farrell, and Leo Carrillo. The film was part of a musical series—including *42nd Street, Gold Diggers of 1933*, and *Footlight Parade*—produced by the studio with the choreographer, Busby Berkeley. *In Caliente* showed reasonable profits, but, unfortunately, the film did not advance del Río's career, despite aggressive publicity on the part of Warner Bros.

The studio relied on stereotypes about Mexico and Mexicans to promote the film. Confusing Mexico with Spain, promotional material advertised the dancing in *In Caliente* as "a new spanish custom . . . it's torrid! It's Tropical! . . . Seething with senoritas" (actually blondes with black wigs). The promos touted "Warner Bros.' Flaming Filming of Mexico's Million Dollar Paradise of Girls, Song and Laughter."

The *Motion Picture Herald* reported that a number of theaters sponsored a "Caliente Night Ball or Party, Lets Debs Go Hotcha For Charity. . . . Notables go in Mex costumes." The writer suggests "tieups with Mex, Styles, Foods. . . . Restaurants might advertise mex dishes, like Chili Con Carne and the like." Warner Bros. offered three "life-sized, hand colored figures" for lobby displays and a new service, "Rent-a-Costume. . . . The woman's costume consists of a laced mantilla and beautiful gown. Men receive a sombrero, trousers, bolero jacket and shirt."

A script for a radio spot was published that has del Río and Pat O'Brian driving down to Mexico:

O'BRIAN: "Look, what is that down there blocking the road?"

DEL RÍO: "It is a cart, such as our peons use."

O'Brian yells at Pedro Gillermo Teresa San Isidoro y Pinares del Monte to move his cart while del Río reminds O'Brian, "Perhaps he do not understand English." Pedro, who happens to be armed like all Hollywood Mexicans, replies: "I unnerstan the Eenglish. Steeck 'em up! Queeck."

Photoplay called *In Caliente* one of the "Best Pictures of the Month," along with *Public Hero No. 1* and Shirley Temple's *Our Little Girl. Variety* noted that "for the Latin territory, Miss Del Río alone insures it a strong box office draft."[45] In addition to the film's promotion, five *Photoplay* feature articles on del Río coincided with the opening of *In Caliente*. All of the articles focused on her "dark beauty." "Pick Makeup 'to fit' face, is Del Rio Tip." Dolores del Río suggests "that every woman should select very carefully the shades best suited to her inherent type of beauty. . . ." She further explains that "the dark, dry skin needs a cream foundation." Another *Photoplay* foregrounds del Río's upperclass foreignness: "Luncheon at Dolores Del Rio's. . . . Flower Bowl—handmade antique Mexican. Service Plates and Bread and Butter Plates—Sterling hand-made by Sojihe in Mexico with crystal from Bullocks and China from England."

Despite the film's success, del Río could not come to an agreement with Warner Bros. on her next contract. She moved to Columbia Pictures and made one film, *Devil's Playground* (1937), playing a Mexican dancer named Carmen, who weds one man and seduces his best friend. The role of the femme fatale realigned her with the negative stereotypes of Mexican women: *The Hollywood Reporter* described del Río's Carmen as the "predatory Mexican. . . . She has a part that exactly fits her talents and her looks. She is uncomfortably real."

The film failed, del Río broke her contract with Columbia, and she moved again, this time to Twentieth Century-Fox. There she starred in three films: *Ali Baba Goes to Town* (1937), *Lancer Spy* (1937), and *International Settlement* (1938). She returned to Warner Bros. for *I Live for Love* (1938), another musical directed by Busby Berkeley. In this film, she played a temperamental South American stage star. According to *The Hollywood Reporter*, the film was "put together for the display of Dolores del Rio's exotic charms and the pleasing baritone of Everett Marshall." [46] These last few films effectively marked the end of del Río's Hollywood career. She returned to Mexico in the early 1940s to become one of the foremost Mexican stars of the Golden Age of Mexican cinema. Occasionally, she returned to Hollywood to portray ethnic women: a Mexican in John Ford's *The Fugitive* (1947); an Indian woman opposite Elvis Presley in *Flaming Star* (1960, Don Siegel); and an Indian in Ford's *Cheyenne Autumn* (1964).

The Latin American market continued to be crucial to Hollywood's profit margin. By 1938, Hollywood's European audience was dwindling in response to the effects of the Spanish Civil War, Hitler's rise to power, stricter censorship regulations in Europe, and higher import tariffs. Nathan Golden, director of the U.S. Commerce Department's Film Division, advised the industry to continue to pursue the Latin American market, which still accounted for 10.6 percent of Hollywood's foreign revenue. [47] Hollywood relied on the Latin American musical into the 1940s with films like *Down Argentine Way* (1940) with Betty Grable, Don Ameche, and the Brazilian star Carmen Miranda, *Weekend in Havana* (1941) starring Betty Grable, and *Road to Rio* (1947), starring Bing Crosby, Bob Hope, and Dorothy Lamour. As Brian O'Neil's analysis in chapter 16 of this anthology shows, under the guidance of the Production Code Administration's Latin American specialist, Addison Durland, the industry continued to reproduce cinematic stereotypes of Latin American nations and subjects.

I have argued that representations of race and gender in Hollywood cinema need to be examined not only within the context of public discourse but also in relation to pressures of the market during particular historic moments. The argument brings to light some problems with existing studies of the evolution of stereotypes that are concerned primarily with the relation between ideology and representation. The case of del Río evidences the ways in which economic and political concerns often compete with ideological ones. The casting of del Río in starring roles in Latin American musicals also illustrates how Hollywood tried to resolve these tensions: the Mexican-born star appealed to Latin American audiences while her light skin, European features, upper-class roles, and a star text that recognized her as beautiful by U.S. standards, appeased the American public.

Ultimately, behind the facade of Berkeleyesque musical numbers and international romance lay a complex discourse about U.S. national identity, an identity that was partially predicated on notions of racialized sexuality. In representing this discourse, Hollywood studios walked a fine line between concern for profits in foreign markets and the good will of its domestic audiences at home.

NOTES

1. *Photoplay*, February 1933, 74.
2. Richard Dyer, "Paul Robeson: Crossing Over" in *Heavenly Bodies: Film Stars and Society* (New York: St. Martin's Press, 1986), 102–3.
3. Quoted in Michael E. Parrish, *Anxious Decades: America in Prosperity and Depression, 1920–1941* (New York: W.W. Norton & Co., 1992), 135.
4. Dyer, "Paul Robeson," 103.
5. For an analysis of how international markets and politics shaped Hollywood's national, racial, and ethnic representations see Ruth Vasey, *The World According to Hollywood, 1918–1939* (Madison: University of Wisconsin Press, 1997).
6. Contrast del Río's career with that of the Brazilian actress, Carmen Miranda, who, according to Ana M. López, "travels and is inserted into different landscapes, but she remains the same from film to film, purely Latin American." See López's "Are All Latins from Manhattan? Hollywood, Ethnography, and Cultural Colonialism," in *Unspeakable Images: Ethnicity and the American Cinema*, ed. Lester D. Friedman (Urbana: University of Illinois Press, 1991), 75.
7. António Ríos-Bustamante attributes this to the large Spanish-speaking population in Southern California. By the 1920s, Los Angeles, already the center of U.S.

film production, was a "major market for Mexican and Latin American popular culture." See his "Latino Participation in the Hollywood Film Industry, 1911–45," in *Chicanos and Film: Representation and Resistance*, ed. Chon Noriega (Minneapolis: University of Minnesota Press, 1992), 20–21. See also Gary D. Keller, *Hispanics and United States Film: An Overview and Handbook* (Tempe: Bilingual Press, 1994).

8. Keller, *Hispanics and United States Film*, 39. Although a number of Latino actresses did find access into Hollywood through their theater or musical stage successes, they rarely played the female roles outlined by Keller.

9. Ríos-Bustamante, "Latino Participation," 7.

10. Ibid., 20.

11. Margarita de Orellana, "The Circular Look: The Incursion of North American Fictional Cinema 1911–1917 into the Mexican Cinema" in *Mediating Two Worlds: Cinematic Encounters in the Americas*, ed. John King, Ana M. López, and Manuel Alvarado (London: BFI, 1993), 10.

12. Ibid., 13.

13. "Four Most Beautiful Women," *Photoplay*, September 1937.

14. *Photoplay*, September 1932, 57.

15. Janet Staiger notes that the emergence of the American flapper was recognized as early as 1915 by H. L. Mencken, who described this new woman as "educated . . . trim and confident . . . graceful, rosy, healthy, appetizing." Quoted in Staiger's *Bad Women: Regulating Sexuality in Early American Cinema* (Minneapolis: University of Minnesota Press, 1995), 2–3.

16. *Photoplay*, September 1933.

17. Parrish, *Anxious Decades*, 152. Parrish writes that "the number [of women] who patronized beauty parlors for manicures, permanent waves, and hair-dying grew at an astonishing pace. . . . By 1930 the cosmetics industry had grown from $17 million a year to over $200 million" (151–52).

18. Gerald D. Nash, *The Great Depression and World War II: Organizing America, 1933–1945* (New York: St. Martin's Press, 1979), 19.

19. *Film Daily Yearbook*, 1930, 3.

20. *Film Daily Yearbook*, 1933, 3.

21. Andrew W. Bergman, *We're in the Money: Depression America and Its Films* (New York: New York University Press, 1971), xxii.

22. Ruth Vasey notes that "between the world wars the industry consistently derived about 35 percent of its gross revenue from export earnings." See her "Foreign Parts: Hollywood's Global Distribution and the Representation of Ethnicity," in *Movie Censorship and American Culture*, ed. Francis G. Couvares (Washington, D.C.: Smithsonian Institution Press, 1996), 213.

23. Letter from B. A. Morgan to Kelly (April 16, 1930). Quoted in Gaizka S. de Usabel, *The High Noon of American Films in Latin America* (Ann Arbor: UMI Research Press, 1982), 103.

24. Ibid., 126. By this time, Paramount, MGM, Twentieth Century-Fox, Warner Bros., and RKO had established distribution branches in the larger urban centers

of Latin America. See Suzanne Mary Donahue, *American Film Distribution: The Changing Marketplace* (Ann Arbor: UMI Research Press, 1987), 143–53.

25. Jorge Schnitman, *Film Industries in Latin America: Dependency and Development* (Norwood, NJ: Ablex Pub. Corp., 1984), 16–17.

26. In the 1930s, the value of U.S. direct investments in Latin America "was much more than twice the value of its investments in any other geographical area of the world." United States Department of Commerce, *American Direct Investments in Foreign Countries* (Washington, D.C., 1930), 18. Quoted in Donald M. Dozer, *Are We Good Neighbors? Three Decades of American Relations, 1930–1960* (Gainesville: University of Florida Press, 1959), 9.

27. As Ruth Vasey, among others, has noted, the Production Code Administration "had a profound effect on the construction and realization of Hollywood's narratives." *The World According to Hollywood*, 6.

28. Vasey, "Foreign Parts," 227–28.

29. Ella Shohat and Robert Stam, *Unthinking Eurocentrism: Multiculturalism and the Media* (London: Routledge, 1994), 138–39.

30. *Photoplay*, January 1936, 18. RKO's promotional material for *Flying Down to Rio* focused on the foreign elements of the film: Del Río, the Carioca, and the tango. The same *Photoplay* column notes that "in the patio scene where she [del Río] sat with a number of American society girls and flirted so dexterously with Gene Raymond . . . the American girls were very frank in their gestures of admiration . . . but del Rio was fascinating. She coquetted (sic) with lowered eyes, then she peeped at him through the lattice of her fingers."

31. In 1930, Hollywood released thirty "Hispanic" films, more than forty in 1931, and fifteen in 1932. See John King, *Magical Reels: A History of Cinema in Latin America* (London: Verso, 1991), 32.

32. Keller, *Hispanics and United States Film*, 121.

33. Shohat and Stam write that, in general, Hollywood's Latin American musical "allotted its narrative 'spaces' in ethnic and national terms, homologizing segregationist attitudes in the larger society." While racist discourse did shape representations to a certain extent, other, competing forces mediated those pressures. *Unthinking Eurocentrism*, 231.

34. Vasey, *The World According to Hollywood*, 101.

35. Vasey notes that "by 1934 consultations [between Mexican officials and representatives of the Production Code Administration] took place as a matter of course." "Foreign Parts," 227.

36. Vasey argues that the Mexican problem "helped in several ways to bring home to the American producers the implications of their participation in global distribution." Ibid., 19.

37. Carlos Monsiváis, "Dolores del Río: The Face as Institution," in *Mexican Postcards* (London: Verso, 1996), 77. Del Río apologized to her country for her role in the film. Apparently, she had insisted that the action take place somewhere in the Mediterranean, but was overruled by RKO. Mexican officials ultimately prohibited

the distribution of the film in Mexico on the basis of the negative portrayal of Leo Carrillo's Don Jose.

38. This fake accent was a major mark of the stereotype.

39. As I discuss elsewhere, films like *Bird of Paradise*, despite fears of miscegenation, focused on Americans' repressed fascination with interracial romance. Joanne Hershfield, "Race and Romance in *Bird of Paradise*," *Cinema Journal* 37, no. 3 (spring 1998): 3–15.

40. Thomas Schatz, *Hollywood Genres: Formulas, Filmmaking, and the Studio System* (New York: Random House, 1981), 188.

41. Sérgio Augusto, "Hollywood Looks at Brazil: From Carmen Miranda to *Moonraker*," in *Brazilian Cinema*, ed. Randal Johnson and Robert Stam (New York: Columbia University Press, 1996), 356.

42. See chapter 16 in this volume for Brian O'Neil's analysis of the economic, political, and institutional parameters of the Good Neighbor policy as it developed in the 1940s.

43. Letter from the PCA to Sidney Kramer of RKO Distributing Corporation. The PCA also suggested that "the entire colored troop, with the exception of the finale, might well be dispensed with."

44. Parrish, *Anxious Decades*, 30.

45. The reviewer also commented that "as a story it's one of those things. As a plug for the Agua Caliente development, Wirt Bowman, Joe Schenck, et al. should underwrite the production cost. It's almost a commercial plug for the Mexican resort across the border from San Diego." *Variety*, July 3, 1933, 14.

46. *The Hollywood Reporter*, October 7, 1938, 3.

47. de Usabel, *The High Noon*, 136.

8

HUMANIZING
THE BEAST

King Kong and the
Representation of
Black Male Sexuality

Thomas E. Wartenberg

King Kong (1933, dirs. Merian C. Cooper and Ernest B. Schoedsack), the classic horror-adventure film, has had a varied reception by film scholars. Although Kong has been recognized to function as a stand-in for Black males—by James Snead, for example, in his insightful if somewhat incomplete interpretation of the film[1]—there has been disagreement about the significance of this fact. Snead emphasizes the presence of multiple plots in the film and, hence, the possibility of divergent reactions to it. Nevertheless, he generally sees the racial message of the film as residing in the narrative sequence in which Kong is shot to death for his rampage in New York City. Snead views the film as deeply racist in that it suggests that Black transgression of the dominant order should be met with violent retribution. Although *King Kong*, unlike *Birth of a Nation* (1915), stops short of sanctioning Klan vigilantism, on this reading the film's racial politics are no less racist than those of the silent classic.

Thomas Cripps is somewhat less critical of the film's racial politics in his classic study of Blacks in American film, *Slow Fade to Black: The Negro in American Film, 1900–1942*. However, Cripps dismisses *King Kong* as "a freak horror movie about a giant ape [that] came to stand as an allegory for Black experience" only because of the "maze of barriers" that prohibited Hollywood films from employing a more direct representation of the experience of Blacks in "tropical locales."[2] Although Cripps here betrays his awareness that the film embodies a criticism of the colonial mistreatment of Blacks, he denies that the film's critique has any real significance because it does not directly address this issue.

On the other hand, Rhona J. Berenstein argues for the progressive nature of *King Kong*'s racial politics. Stressing the similarities between Kong and his captive, Ann Darrow (Fay Wray), Berenstein claims that the film "suggests that dominant culture's investment in a racial hierarchy, in asserting the primacy of Whiteness and the mastery of White masculinity, is . . . tenuous at best."[3] Like Snead, Berenstein focuses upon the sequence culminating in Kong's death. However, Berenstein maintains that viewers' identification with Kong makes his death less an occasion for the celebration of White civilization's victory over the forces of darkness than a reason to question the society that demands such violence. On her reading, *King Kong*'s politics are less racist than previous critics thought.

The divergence in film scholars' assessment of the political implications of *King Kong* is troubling. In this chapter, I argue that an important source of the difference in scholars' interpretations is attributable to their failure to pay sufficient attention to the complex, self-referential structure of the film's narrative. In my view, *King Kong* criticizes Hollywood films for employing a stereotypical racist representation of Black males as sexual monsters who crave White women. In order to do so, the film first replicates the very representational structure it later criticizes. That is, *King Kong* initially presents its monstrous ape in terms that fit the racist stereotype dominant in Hollywood representations of Black males. Then, rather than maintain this view of Kong, the film employs a romantic narrative in which Kong figures as a tragic hero. Because Kong can feel romantic love for Ann Darrow, he becomes an object of viewers' admiration and empathy, not their fear and hatred. This allows the film to criticize the stereotype of the Black male as a savage beast. *King Kong* demonstrates the problems with Hollywood's attribution of a monstrous sexuality to Blacks by presenting Kong as a chivalrous hero, capable of love rather than mere lust. Through its identification of Kong with the stereotypical view of Black male sexuality, the film is able to criticize the racism of this stereotype in a way that has escaped the attention of the film's critics. Rather than simply a document in the history of racist portrayals of Blacks in Hollywood cinema, *King Kong*'s representation of Kong stands as an early, self-conscious attempt to counter such racist depictions.

PLOT SYNOPSIS

King Kong tells the story of a film crew that brings an enormous ape to New York from a mysterious island in the Pacific with disastrous consequences. The film begins in Manhattan, where Carl Denham (Robert Armstrong), a theatrical producer, has chartered a boat for a secret voyage. Denham plans to sail the boat, filled with explosives and gas bombs, to an undisclosed location. At the start of the film, all that remains is to find a young woman to take part in the adventure as the star of the film Denham intends to make. He finds his star in Ann Darrow, a starving actress who agrees to come along. Early the following morning, the ship slips out of port, bound for the mysterious island located west of Sumatra in uncharted waters.

During the voyage, the mystery only heightens. Denham informs his first mate, Jack Driscoll (Bruce Cabot), of their destination and explains that their object is to capture on film a deadly monster. The creature lives on the island behind a huge wall that protects the natives from him. After first telling Darrow that the sea is no place for a woman, Driscoll eventually falls in love with her. When Denham coaches her on how to scream when she sees a large beast, it is clear that he intends to film her with the monster on the island.

The next sequence of the film takes place on Skull Island. As the crew lands, they witness the natives performing a ritual sacrifice of a virgin to Kong, the huge ape that lives behind the ancient wall separating the islanders from a jungle populated with prehistoric beasts. Once the natives see the film crew, they stop the ceremony, saying it has been ruined by the Whites' presence. That night, the islanders kidnap Darrow from the ship in order to give her to Kong in place of the native virgin.

When Kong takes Darrow with him into his prehistoric world, Denham, Driscoll, and other members of the crew set off to rescue her. The film then presents a series of violent encounters in which Kong fights both with the crew as well as with a variety of prehistoric beasts. Eventually, Driscoll manages to rescue Darrow, but Kong pursues them back to the shore, killing many natives as he breaks down the wall in pursuit of Darrow. Denham fires the gas bombs stored onboard. He wants only to knock Kong unconscious, not to harm him, because he intends to bring the ape back to Manhattan to exhibit on stage as the Eighth Wonder of the World.

The Manhattan sequence begins with Denham's exhibition of Kong to a New York theater audience. Kong is revealed in chains, to the excitement and titillation of the audience. When Kong thinks Darrow is being attacked by flashbulb-wielding photographers, he breaks his chains, escaping from

Figure 8.1. King Kong on the rampage in Manhattan (*King Kong,* 1955).

Denham's—and society's—control. Leaving destruction in his path, Kong searches for Darrow and finally finds her, though not without first killing many people in some of the film's most memorable and terrifying sequences.

Kong makes his way with Darrow to the Empire State Building, where he finds himself under attack by fighter planes. Placing Darrow safely on a ledge, Kong bravely faces his attackers, who have been holding their fire so as not to harm Darrow. They resume their attack, however, after Kong deposits Darrow on the ledge, unleashing all their force against him. His body riddled with bullets, Kong falls dead to the pavement below, to the horror and fascination of the gathered audience.

THE DEMONIZATION OF BLACK MALE SEXUALITY

Before turning to my analysis of *King Kong,* we need to understand how Hollywood films demonized Black male sexuality. In *Toms, Coons, Mullatoes, Mammies, and Bucks,* his classic study of the limited stereotypes available for Blacks within American film, Donald Bogle claims that traditionally only three roles were available for Black males in Hollywood films. Two of these—the "tom,"

or "socially acceptable Good Negro," and the "coon," or "Black buffoon"—
soothed White fears of Black males by portraying them as harmless and ineffectual.[4] In particular, neither of these two stereotypical representations involved a portrayal of Black males as sexual beings. By desexualizing the Black
male, these depictions quelled White fears of Black male sexuality.

The third role available to Black males—that of the "brutal Black buck"—
objectified White fears of Black males. Bogle traces the origin of this stereotype
to D. W. Griffith's 1915 classic film, *Birth of a Nation* and describes it as follows:

> Bucks are always big, baaddd [*sic*] niggers, oversexed and savage, vio-
> lent and frenzied as they lust for White flesh. . . . Griffith played on the
> myth of the Negro's high-powered sexuality, then articulated the great
> White fear that every Black man longs for a White woman. Underly-
> ing the fear was the assumption that the White woman was the ulti-
> mate in female desirability, herself a symbol of White pride, power, and
> beauty. . . . Thus the Black bucks of the film [*Birth of a Nation*] are psycho-
> paths, one [Gus] always panting and salivating, the other [Silas Lynch]
> forever stiffening his body as if the mere presence of a White woman
> in the same room could bring him to a sexual climax. Griffith played
> hard on the bestiality of his Black villainous bucks and used it to arouse
> hatred.[5]

The representation of Black males as bucks, as described by Bogle, involves a
number of factors. First, as Bogle's animal metaphor implies, the sexual desire
attributed to Black males by this representation is more appropriate to savage
beasts than to civilized human beings. The Black male who is represented as
a buck is seen as dominated by an uncivilized or savage sexuality, one that
rules him and is incapable of civilized restraint. This representation thus associates the Black male with an animalistic desire, untouched and uncontrolled
by civilization.

A second attribute of the Black buck is a transgressive sexual desire that
targets White women. Mesmerized by the mere presence of White, usually
blond, women, the Black buck fixates on one as the object of his desire and then
stops at nothing to satisfy that desire. For this reason, the Black buck is easily
assimilated to a rapist: the buck is overpowered by his desire to have sex with
the White woman, who is the object of his lust. As Bogle points out, both of the
central Black male characters in *Birth of a Nation*—Gus and Silas Lynch—
are represented as having this transgressive desire for a White woman.

Rather than using Bogle's terminology, I shall refer to this stereotype as one
that represents Black male sexuality as *monstrous* because this term more precisely captures the nature of the stereotype. According to *Merriam Webster's*

Figure 8.2. Gus, one of the Black Bucks in *Birth of a Nation* (1915).

Collegiate Dictionary, a monster is "an animal or plant of abnormal form of structure." The sexuality attributed to Black males through this stereotype is monstrous, then, because this sexuality is represented as abnormal. Black males are represented as possessing a sex drive that is animalistic—and, thus, not appropriate to human beings—and that drive is represented as focused upon White women, thus breaking the norm against miscegenation. Unlike civilized White males, Black men are depicted as monsters rather than persons because their sexual impulses are savage and transgressive.

This stereotype's positing of an uncontrollable desire on the part of Black men to have sex with White women calls for additional analysis. As Bogle points out, for this representation to be convincing, the appeal of White women has to be universalized, so that they function as suitable objects of desire for males of all races. This representation of White women as instantiating the norm of human (hetero)sexual desire is deeply problematic. As well as enshrining a norm of heterosexuality for all races, it makes an ideal of beauty established within White culture normative for the species as a whole—and, in the case of *King Kong*, across species. In addition, it limits women's sexuality to the role of being the object of male desire, negating their ability to function as desiring subjects by displaying a sexual desire of their own.

What is the narrative function of this stereotypical representation of Black males as sexually monstrous? Within a racist setting—such as that assumed by the makers of *Birth of a Nation*—the presentation of Black males as sexual monsters functions to legitimate White aggression against Blacks. In the case of *Birth of a Nation,* this allows the film to justify a politics of Ku Klux Klan vigilantism by portraying it as necessary to preserve the purity of White women—and, hence, of the White race—from the sexual predation of Black males. Through this narrative strategy, the film not only attempts to rekindle a perceived need for Klan vigilantism to enforce racial segregation in the twentieth century, it also sexualizes the politics of race in an explicit and insidious manner.

Bogle attributes many important tendencies in Hollywood's representation of Black males to concerns that resulted from the conflicts that developed around *Birth of a Nation* after its release. The film was the subject of such serious confrontation and protest that, according to Bogle, Hollywood filmmakers simply eschewed the representation of Black males as sexual monsters.[6] Rather than risk making films that might evoke similar controversy, they assigned Black males to the stereotypical roles of the tom and the coon, thereby rendering them desexualized and nonthreatening. As Bogle summarizes his view, "many of Hollywood's hang-ups and hesitations in presenting sensual Black men on screen resulted, in part, from the reactions to the Griffith spectacle."[7]

By emphasizing Hollywood's fears of controversy, Bogle draws attention to the progressive reaction on the part of Blacks and antiracist Whites to the appallingly racist representation of Black males in *Birth of a Nation.* In focusing on that reaction, however, he fails to acknowledge the ongoing appeal of the image of the monstrous Black male for racist White viewers. As a result, Bogle ignores how the racist stereotype of Black males affected even filmmakers who wanted to reject it by presenting Black males through nonstereotypical representations. Indeed, one can trace a pattern of desexualization of Black males in American cinema that shows the continuing worry on the part of even progressive filmmakers that what Bogle calls "sensual Black men on screen" will be perceived by (racist) White viewers as sexually monstrous.[8] Their concern that White viewers would react to Black male sensuality as a form of monstrous sexuality made it difficult for American filmmakers to present Black males as having any form of sexual being at all.

More important in the present context, however, is Bogle's claim that Hollywood filmmakers simply steered clear of the representation of Black males as sexual monsters for fear of provoking political controversy. This implies, first of all, the complete acceptance within Hollywood of this stereotype, as if no Hollywood director or producer was repelled by the racism of this view of Black males. In addition, the claim suggests that no Hollywood films attempted to criticize this stereotype of the Black male. While it may be true that no Hollywood film attempted a direct critique of this stereotype, at least one successful and popular Hollywood film did make this stereotype of Black male sexuality an object of criticism. *King Kong* attempted to refute the stereotype of Black males as sexual monsters through its sympathetic portrait of a huge ape. I turn now to an investigation of the complex representational and narrative strategies that enabled the film to develop its critique of this racist mode of representation.

KONG, THE LITERAL SEXUAL MONSTER

As we have seen, Hollywood filmmakers were wary of the stereotype of the sexually monstrous Black male. Not only did they worry that employing this stereotype would provoke hostility on the part of audience members who objected to its racism, but they also were concerned that the susceptibility of other audience members to the stereotype would cause them to see any sensual Black man on the screen as a sexual monster. Only the desexualized stereotypes of the tom and the coon seemed viable ways of representing Black men on film. This limitation placed Hollywood filmmakers in a difficult bind. There seemed no way to present a Black male as a sensual being that would not activate the very stereotype such a presentation would attempt to circumvent.

King Kong represents an innovative solution to this problem. The film uses its huge black ape as a stand-in for Black males so that it can criticize Hollywood's demonization of this group. Because Kong is not in point of fact a Black man, the film is able to articulate its social criticism in a veiled form that can escape both the anxious eyes of the censor and the conscious racist attitudes of (some members of) its audience. This representational strategy enables *King Kong* to endorse a progressive political perspective that might have been foreclosed to it had the film attempted to tackle more directly the issue of the racism of Hollywood films and of White Americans. Rather than simply being, as some critics have charged, a racist film, *King Kong* breaks new ground in its criticism of Hollywood's racist representations of Black men.

The representational strategy employed by the film amounts to a literalization of the stereotype of the Black male as a sexual monster. That is, instead of using the representational metaphor of the Black man being a monster, the film substitutes an actual monster in place of the Black man, while retaining all the sexual characteristics that the racist stereotype attributes to Black men.[9] The monster Kong's sexuality precisely matches that attributed to Black men by the stereotype: his sexual desire is quite literally monstrous and possesses both the savage and transgressive elements posited by the stereotype. Kong's sexual desire is for human beings, thereby transgressing the natural boundary between the species. It is also savage insofar as he seems to kill his sexual partners, the sacrificial Black virgins offered by the natives on Skull Island. By using Kong to literalize the stereotype of the sexually monstrous Black male, the film makes the stereotype an object of criticism without directly triggering the racist attitudes that make it impossible for the audience that supports the stereotype to inspect their response critically.

The film's critique relies on a narrative strategy that uses the stereotypical representation of the Black male as a sexual monster in the Skull Island sequence of the film and then shows the inadequacy of that understanding of Kong's motivation in the Manhattan sequence. In this way, the film implicates the viewers in a racist way of seeing. At the same time, the use of a stand-in veils the criticism, so the audience is not as likely to resist the film's critique.[10] On the jungle island, Ann Darrow is saved from the violent transgression of Kong's abduction, and the audience experiences the ape's defeat by Carl Denham and his troupe as a victory for the ideals of American society. The defeat of the monster is seen as saving society from the threat of Kong's sexual desire, a clear reference to the politics inherent in the stereotype of the Black male as a sexual monster. On the other hand, the audience perceives Kong's death at the end of the Manhattan sequence as a tragedy because it now empathizes with Kong and believes that, despite his monstrous shape, he is no longer motivated by savage lust. The audience therefore sees his death as a demonstration of the violence inherent in the stereotypical representation of Black men as sexual monsters, a violence that is attributable to White American society's need to subjugate its "others." This second defeat of the Kong-Darrow couple emerges as a critique of a society that unfeelingly exploits Kong for its amusement and profit.

The film initiates its representational strategy before the audience even sees Kong in a sequence in which his characteristics as a monster are emphasized. On the sea voyage, Carl Denham, Kong's eventual captor, describes the mythical Kong: "Neither beast nor man, something monstrous, still living, still holding that island in the grip of fear."[11] Such a description makes it clear that Kong is the cause of deep-seated social anxiety. One reason Denham gives for fearing Kong is that he is a monster, something that stands outside of the categories of human thought. Kong's size and physical power make him a freak of nature, an ape existing beyond all natural categories. He is to be feared because his strength and violent nature exceed the capacities of any other creature, even those of the dinosaurs with which he exists in the wild.

Once Kong is actually seen by the film troupe, however, we discover the real threat to society: Kong is the literal embodiment of the stereotype of the Black male as a sexual monster. Before the troupe's arrival, Kong is not focused on having sex with a White woman for the simple reason that he has never seen one. However, Kong's sexual desire still makes him an object of terror because that desire seems satisfied only by a human partner, the consequence for whom is death. For this reason, the natives on the island must periodically sacrifice a virgin to him to keep him at bay. Only through this provision is Kong made to honor the barrier that separates his space on the island from that of the natives.

Kong's lust for a human sexual partner marks his desire as transgressive because it violates the categorical distinction between the human and the animal. Even before he fixates on Darrow, Kong thus represents a threat to humanity because of his sexual desire. In this way, the film both literalizes the image of the Black male as a sexual monster and distances it through the substitution of a real monster for the metaphoric monstrosity of the Black male. The film uses this representational strategy to make that stereotype an object of its critical reflection.

Earlier, we saw that *Birth of a Nation* represented Black males as sexual monsters in order to justify a narrative in which Black males were subdued by White males. The Skull Island sequence of *King Kong* replicates this narrative structure, although it does so within the context of a standard 1930s jungle film. As I have explained, Kong lives on an island and the natives fear him. These natives are the only Black human beings present in the film and they are represented in very standard racist ways for the film's time period. Clearly primitive people, they are virtually identical to the "savages" who populate the film *Tarzan, the Ape Man*, made the year before *King Kong*. They live in fear of Kong and, as primitive savages with limited intelligence and culture, they can only accommodate themselves to his wrath by sacrificing virgins to him.

The film presents Western capitalist society, in the person of Carl Denham, as capable of a different arrangement with Kong's transgressive desire. Instead of simply fearing Kong, Denham believes himself capable of controlling the ape. Although he initially seems only interested in capturing Kong's image on film, Denham thinks that he can use Kong for his own self-aggrandizement by making the ape into an object for the fascinated gaze of the New York theater-going public.[12]

Figure 8.3. Kong's monstrous nature.

It is worth noting that the very characteristics that make Kong something to be feared, and even killed, also make him an object of fascination for Denham and the other members of his expedition. Indeed, their reaction to him mixes fear with attraction. The plan that Denham hatches involves an explicit recognition of this. We see here an anticipation of Michel Foucault's claim that interdiction is one of the central means for the incitement of desire.[13]

If we consider only the Skull Island sequence of the film, *King Kong* implicates its audience in the stereotypical response to a sensual Black male. Kong is quite literally a monster whose sexuality is a threat to women. Not only does he seem to kill the native virgins sacrificed to him, but his possession of Darrow threatens her with a similar fate. The film actually shows Kong undressing her, although a variety of other prehistoric beasts interrupt his attempt at foreplay. In this way, Kong occupies the same representational space as Black males in the stereotype.

This association of Kong with the stereotype of the sexually threatening Black male established by *Birth of a Nation* is effected not merely by the film's representation of Kong, but also by the way that it represents the White beauty's response to him. Darrow reacts to Kong in exactly the same way that

Figure 8.4. Film troupe fascinated by the fallen Kong.

Little Sister and Elsie Stoneman respond to Gus and Silas Lynch, respectively: each greets her sexually aggressive "monster" with screams of fear and an attempt to flee her tormentor. *King Kong* relies on the parallelism of these reactions to further emphasize Kong's literal embodiment of this stereotype.

The film's presentation of Kong as a sexual monster allows it then to present his capture as a victory for the forces of (White) Western civilization. Because the audience perceives Kong to be a threat to Darrow, it welcomes Denham's and Jack Driscoll's attempts to subdue him. Here, the film treads on the familiar territory of representing a being's sexuality as monstrous in order to justify its subordination. Only instead of presenting the subordination of Blacks as the justified outcome of the efforts to subdue their transgressive sexuality, the film now presents Kong's capture according to a similar narrative logic. The audience sees Driscoll and Denham as heroically subduing Kong and thereby saving Darrow from his grasp.

At the end of the Skull Island sequence, then, the audience has experienced a satisfactory resolution to the threat posed by Kong. Reacting to Kong along the lines of the stereotype of the Black male, the audience wants his defeat in order to assure Darrow's rescue. Denham's plan to transport Kong back to civilization may give some audience members pause. Nevertheless, the ability of

Figure 8.5. Kong with his captive, Ann Darrow (Fay Wray).

Denham and his troupe to subdue a savage monster satisfies the racist White audience's desire to see White civilization as capable of subjugating that which threatens it.

In this way, *King Kong* not only reproduces the basic narrative structure of *Birth of a Nation*, it also presents Kong's capture and display as an allegory for the appeal of such a film. Denham's attempt to titillate his theater audiences with the spectacle of a terrifying ape under his control allegorizes the situation of film audiences. They are as thrilled by the display of Denham's capture of Kong and rescue of Darrow as they were by the Klan's rescue of Whites from the clutches of "savage Blacks" in the earlier classic.

UNDOING THE STEREOTYPE

A remarkable feature of *King Kong* is that in its Manhattan sequence, the film shows the inadequacy of its previous understanding of Kong, an understanding that justified society's attempt to subdue him in order to keep him from possessing Darrow by subduing him. By the end of the film, the audience, who no longer sees Kong's desire as monstrous, is critical of society's attempt to eradicate the threat posed by him.[14] Instead, White society is seen as using violence against "others" to subdue its own imagined fears, embodied in its stereotypical reaction to those others.

Although the Manhattan sequence of the film continues to show that Kong's enormous strength enables him to wreak serious destruction, it no longer presents him as simply a monstrous Black beast seeking to possess a White woman. Indeed, it subjects its earlier representation of Kong to criticism by showing that Kong is not the lustful beast Denham's troupe took him to be. Instead, Kong appears motivated by genuine love for Darrow, a love that enables him to treat her with concern and gentleness. Until this point, the audience had not suspected the beast capable of manifesting such tender feelings.

Throughout the Manhattan sequence, *King Kong* emphasizes that Kong really loves Darrow and does not simply lust after her. This becomes apparent at the beginning of the sequence. When Kong first sees Darrow on the stage, he does not strain at his chains as a sexually crazed monster might. He attempts to break the chains only when he perceives her to be in danger, and he does so in order to protect her, not ravish her. At this point, Kong plays a new role: the romantic hero who overcomes obstacles and difficulties to save the life of his beloved. The inadequacy of an understanding of Kong as a monster motivated by a transgressive desire for a White beauty is clear, for he has become a romantic hero concerned about the safety of the woman he loves.

Kong's metamorphosis from savage beast to romantic lover is an important narrative element of the film. Although Kong has been transformed by the love he feels for Darrow, the audience's understanding of him is still determined by the monstrous sexual desire he seems to exhibit in relation to the native women who are sacrificed to him. What emerges, however, is that Kong did not pose the threat to Darrow that Denham and his troupe—and then the audience—imagined because Kong actually loves her. In the New York sequence, this love becomes apparent: Kong treats Darrow with a tenderness and concern that seem incompatible with his violent nature. The film thus presents romantic love as having the power to subdue nature. Kong's love of Darrow transforms him from a monster with a savage sexual desire into a creature capable of experiencing the tender emotion of romantic love for another. In this sense, Kong has become socialized and is no longer a creature whose sexuality can adequately be represented by the stereotype of the monstrous Black male.

King Kong adopts a variety of different strategies to prepare its audience for perceiving Kong's transformation. One such strategy involves the development of a parallel between Kong and Jack Driscoll, the first mate who becomes Darrow's fiancé. When Driscoll first encounters Darrow on the boat en route

Figure 8.6. The captive Kong.

to Skull Island, he sees her as a woman who should not be onboard and whose presence will only create problems. Indeed, in their first encounter, Driscoll actually hits Darrow, albeit accidentally. Darrow's beauty, however, subdues Driscoll's misogynist aggression. He falls in love with her and becomes her protector against Denham's reckless use of her to further his project of capturing Kong on film. Love transforms Driscoll by subduing the "beast" in him and turning him into a protective lover. This narrative element prepares the audience for seeing a similar transformation in Kong. Because the film has already shown how White female beauty can turn male violence into emotional tenderness, this change in Kong makes him seem almost human.

Following the same narrative logic, the film presents Darrow's beauty as having a transformative power. It can transform Kong from the Skull Island creature exhibiting a monstrous sexual desire for Black women into the chivalrous lover, whose existence the audience becomes aware of, in the New York sequence. Her beauty socializes his uncivilized desire into the socially manageable form of romantic, even courtly, love. This is an important aspect of *King Kong*'s narrative: Kong's susceptibility to Darrow's beauty provides the grounds for his transformation and thus an audience's empathy with him.

Figure 8.7. Kong and Ann Darrow (Fay Wray) on the Empire State Building.

During the film's penultimate and most famous sequence, Kong and Darrow high on the Empire State Building, the audience is allowed a full and unambiguous recognition that Kong's sexual nature has been transformed by the power of Darrow's beauty. In a series of remarkable shots in which the camera assumes the place of both Kong and the gunners, the audience sees Kong tenderly protect Darrow as he faces the death the gunners are all too eager to give him. Kong seems aware that Darrow is his only hope for safety, for the gunners hold their fire when they realize that Kong is carrying her. However, rather than rely on Darrow to protect him from the bullets, Kong gently places her out of range of the gunners and faces their onslaught alone. When he is seriously wounded, he tenderly reaches down to stroke Darrow before turning to face his own death. Such behavior establishes Kong as a romantic hero, rather than the savage beast he had seemed to be. Socialized into the role by the beauty of a White woman, Kong accepts his death as the sacrifice necessary to protect the life of his beloved.[15]

We can see *King Kong* as providing an alternative to G. W. F. Hegel's claim that risking one's life in a life-and-death struggle is automatically a step in the development of freedom. In his *Phenomenology of Spirit,* Hegel asserts that human beings encounter each other most fundamentally as threats to their own certainty and existence. In order to confirm their own existence, then, they must seek each other's death. In the process, each also risks his own life. Hegel champions the importance of this struggle by claiming that "it is only through staking one's life that freedom is won." [16]

In its portrayal of a variety of prehistoric beasts engaged in just such life-and-death struggles with Kong, the narrative of the film can be seen as an attempt to refute Hegel's claim that staking one's life is an essentially humanizing act. So long as these beasts are simply fighting for their own survival, there is nothing elevating about their struggles. According to the film, the crucial difference occurs in a battle that arises not out of self-interest, but for the sake of another—a development that love for another makes possible. Then, the significance of a willingness to lose one's life is transformed: the creature that risks its life for the sake of another does achieve freedom in the Hegelian sense. Thus, when Kong fights not merely to keep possession of Darrow but also to keep her safe because he loves her, he has become a different being, one whose love for another humanizes him.

Many critics have emphasized the parallelism between the episodes in the Skull Island sequence and those in the New York sequence. [17] What has not received sufficient attention is the difference in how the audience responds to Kong's violent rampage in New York City and his rampage at the end of the Skull Island sequence. Despite the fact that both rampages include similar narrative episodes, the audience reacts differently to the New York sequence. The reason for the difference is that the audience realizes that Kong is not searching for Darrow simply in order to gratify his sexual desire, but because he feels a lover's genuine concern for the welfare of his beloved. Although Kong's rampage results in tremendous destruction, the devastation is only a by-product of his partial (mis)understanding of the situation in which he finds himself. Kong wreaks havoc because he approaches a threatening environment in the only way he knows as a creature from a violent jungle in which only the strongest survive. He is not simply a savage beast, however; his desire has been socialized through his recognition of White beauty.

By the end of the film, the audience has come to empathize with Kong and his love for Darrow. Rather than seeing Kong's love for Darrow as a violent transgression of a creature with a monstrous sexuality whose threat needs to be contained, the audience views society critically for its failure to understand the love that motivates Kong. He remains a monster with enormous physical powers, but after his removal from his native context, Kong becomes an innocent victim of a society that seeks to exploit him for profit. The audience comes to see society's need to kill that which it feels threatened by as misguided and tragic. As he gazes at his fallen captive Denham says, "Oh no. It wasn't the airplanes. It was beauty killed the beast." This, the last line of the film, can be read as emphasizing that Kong's death was due to his susceptibility to Darrow's beauty; it is this susceptibility that makes him take on the planes without the protection afforded by Darrow's presence. Because Kong is capable of sacrificing himself for his beloved, his death shows romantic love to be incompatible with a regimented social existence. The film suggests that more is lost through the socialization of desire than simply an individual's ability to gratify their desires; romantic love itself is destroyed. Despite the victorious presence of the Darrow–Driscoll couple at the end of the film, we are left with a sense that grand passion has been annihilated. Kong's love for Darrow towers high above that of Driscoll. For this reason, I do not see the presence of the Darrow-Driscoll couple at the end of the film as vindicating White heterosexual love from the threat posed by Kong's transgressive desire. Its victory is Pyrrhic because it represents a diminished form of romantic love.

In its Manhattan sequence, *King Kong* employs the view of romantic love that Denis de Rougemont described as typically Western.[18] Romantic love is a great, ennobling passion that is incompatible, in this view, with everyday marriage. Kong becomes a tragic hero because he embodies this type of love, a love that exceeds the emotions of our normal lives as greatly as his physical presence surpasses our own. In Kong's tragic fate we can also read our own, for by living in society, we accept a set of rules that exclude grand passions such as those he exhibits.

The Manhattan sequence of the film thus leaves its audience in a state very different from that experienced at the end of the jungle island sequence. After the Skull Island scenes, the audience was glad that Darrow had been rescued from the grasp of the monstrous Kong with his monstrous sexual desire.[19] At that point, Kong's transgressive desire was seen simply as a threat that needed to be defeated so as to maintain the social order. However, the end of the Manhattan sequence presents Kong as something other than a monstrous beast. Because he has been moved by Darrow's beauty, Kong has become humanized. The film no longer presents Kong's actions as motivated simply by a violent, transgressive desire that requires repression, but now depicts them as the result of the more complex emotion of romantic love. The display of this emotion shows this creature to be not so different from any of us, to be, in fact, capable of a love grander than that which many of us actually experience in our lives. As a result, the audience views his death as tragic, the result of a social reliance on violence that denies other, less destructive solutions to problems. The film endeavors to make its audience critical of American society's need for spectacle and its use of violence.

At this point, we need to recall that the film uses Kong as the literalization of the stereotype of the sexually monstrous Black male. How does the change in the film's representation of Kong affect its audience's view of the stereotype? I have just asserted that the film wants its audience to come to see Kong not as a monster guided by lust for a White woman, but as a creature whose physical differences from human beings conceals the similarity in the feelings he shares with human beings. Most notably, the film develops this strategy of humanizing Kong by showing him capable of romantic love. Despite his monstrous physical shape, Kong's main difference from most of us is simply the grandeur of his passion.

In the context of the representation of Black males as sexual monsters, the film's implications are clear: it is a mistake to see Black men as sexual monsters because they are human beings like all of us. Seeing them as sexual monsters involves the very same misinterpretation of their motivations that implicates the audience when it judges Kong to be motivated solely by a transgressive sexual desire for a White woman. Through its complex representational and narrative strategies, the film has shown the problems with the typical Hollywood representation of Black men as sexual monsters and the concomitant narrative justification for their subjugation. By showing Kong to be motivated by desires different from those posited by the stereotype, *King Kong* criticizes the political perspective of a film like *Birth of a Nation* for its failure to represent Black men in an appropriate manner.

However, even as it criticizes the racist representation of Black men as sexual monsters, *King Kong* retains an important element of this stereotype—namely, the universalization of White women's beauty as the norm for female beauty across both races and species. When discussing Bogle's claim about Black bucks, I noted that an important element of the representation of Black men as sexual monsters was the presentation of their desires as transgressive, i.e., targeting White women. While *King Kong* intends to criticize the viability of this stereotype by presenting Kong as a romantic lover, it retains a highly problematic element of the stereotype: the White woman as the norm of sexual attractiveness. The film's presentation of Darrow's beauty as capable of subduing the savage Kong by inspiring love in him is particularly troubling. Kong is not similarly affected by the appearance of the Black virgins sacrificed to him, despite the fact that these are, presumably, the most beautiful of the native women. As a result, the film retains the stereotypical depiction of White European norms of beauty as universal and superior to the norms of other cultures and peoples. Even as it strives to criticize the stereotype of Black men's monstrous sexuality, *King Kong* endorses a racist and Eurocentric system of aesthetic valuation, one that specifically denigrates Black women.

Despite this residual presence of the stereotype, it is important to acknowledge how *King Kong* uses the transgressive love experienced by its huge ape as a vehicle for criticizing Hollywood's stereotypical view of Black males as sexual monsters. Whereas Cripps sees the film's indirect strategy for criticizing the racism of American society and its film industry as a defect, I see it as an elegant and imaginative way to circumvent the difficulties facing a film that seeks to criticize this stereotype. Because it focuses on an ape, rather than a Black man, the film's humanization of the ape—the grounds for its criticism of the stereotype—does not run up against a racist reaction that would deny that possibility. Instead, the film enables (White) viewers to see that their own reactions to difference are structured by assumptions about the significance of that difference that are, in fact, unfounded. In the context of the racism of America in the 1930s, *King Kong* could articulate its criticism of that racism because it veiled it in the tragic story of an ape who loved not wisely but too well.[20]

NOTES

Throughout this paper, I capitalize Black and White in order to keep attention focused on the fact that racial categories are socially constructed.

1. James Snead, *White Screens/Black Images: Hollywood from the Dark Side* (New York and London: Routledge, 1994), 1–36.

2. Thomas Cripps, *Slow Fade to Black: The Negro in American Film, 1900–1942* (Oxford and New York: Oxford University Press, 1977), 278.

3. Rhona J. Berenstein, *Attack of the Leading Ladies: Gender, Sexuality, and Spectatorship in Classic Horror Cinema* (New York: Columbia University Press, 1996), 197.

4. Donald Bogle, *Toms, Coons, Mulattoes, Mammies, and Bucks: An Interpretive History of Blacks in American Films* (New York: Viking, 1973), 4, 7.

5. Ibid., 13–14.

6. For a good description of the struggle over *Birth of a Nation*, see Cripps, *Slow Fade to Black*, 41–69.

7. Bogle, *Toms, Coons*, 16. Bogle does not make clear what he means by qualifying the claim with "in part."

8. I discuss some examples of this tendency in chapters 6–9 of *Unlikely Couples: Movie Romances as Social Criticism* (Boulder, CO: Westview Press, 1999).

9. Snead points out that the film depends on a long history of the identification of Blacks with "ape-like creatures." See *White Screens/Black Images*, 20.

10. Throughout my discussion of *King Kong*, I refer to "the audience" and its response to the film. In so doing, I am not referring to any actual theater audience, but rather to a normative conception of how the film intends its audience to respond to it.

11. For interesting claims about the anxiety that anomalies present as well as individuals' need for order, see Mary Douglas, *Purity and Danger* (New York and Washington: Praeger, 1966).

12. *King Kong* thus self-reflexively posits film as itself a tool of social violence, a feature of the film emphasized by Snead in *White Screens/Black Images*.

13. For this claim, see Michel Foucault, *The History of Sexuality, Part One*, trans. Robert Hurley (New York: Pantheon, 1978). *Jungle Fever* (1991) is another film that employs this Foucauldian idea.

14. It would be possible for a viewer to ignore this element of the narrative and to see Kong's punishment as justified by his transgressions. In fact, both Darrow and Driscoll seem to share this view. However, there are narrative elements that this view fails to integrate.

15. Here, too, Kong's actions parallel those of Driscoll. On Skull Island, Driscoll faced danger in order to rescue the woman he loved, as Kong does in New York. Their love for a White beauty channels both males' aggression in an appropriate direction.

16. Hegel makes this claim in the passage on Self-Consciousness in his *Phenomenology of Spirit*, trans. A. V. Miller (Oxford: Oxford University Press, 1977), 114.

17. See, for example, Noël Carroll, "*King Kong*: Ape and Essence" in *Planks of Reason: Essays on the Horror Film*, ed. Barry Keith Grant (Metuchen, NJ and London: Scarecrow Press, 1984), 215–44. Carroll's larger point is that the film is "a popular illustration of Social Darwinist metaphors" (216).

18. See Denis de Rougemont, *Love in the Western World* (New York: Pantheon, 1956).

19. This response to the film requires that the audience members not yet identify with Kong.

20. I want to thank Angela Curran and Daniel Bernardi for their helpful comments and suggestions on earlier versions of this paper.

9

COMMODITY, TRAGEDY, DESIRE

Female Sexuality and Blackness in the Iconography of Dorothy Dandridge

Marguerite H. Rippy

She did not wish to give the photographers power over her—to be merely their (our) Object. In escaping from the pursuing lenses, she was asserting her determination, perhaps her right, to be something altogether more dignified: that is, to be a Subject. Fleeing from Object to Subject, from commodity toward humanity, she met her death.

—from "Crash" by Salman Rushdie

The above observation by Salman Rushdie on the death of our latest icon of femininity, Princess Diana, is striking in that it could so aptly describe the death of Dorothy Dandridge more than a generation earlier. Rushdie captures both the psychological complexity of mass identification and desire and the corporeal burden it places on women who embody cultural desire. There lies in objectification a fundamental inhumanity that derives pleasure from the flight of the object toward subjectivity (the act of pulling away from the grasp, the hand thrust toward the camera in an attempt to block the lens); there is a sadism in our desire to return the woman-as-object to her photographic frame that feminist film theory has thoroughly interrogated.[1]

We seem less willing, however, to explore the relationship of the sadistic voyeur to the black female body. The relationship of the female body to the construct of racial difference remains obscure, despite the fact that race as a category of difference is as essential to national identity in twentieth-century American culture as gender is to the formation of individual identity. Female bodies marked as black signify both sexual and racial difference and therefore risk becoming caught between the very different demands of black nationalism and intellectual feminism. Black nationalism frequently attempts to recover an authentic black voice in American history by embracing discrete biographical narratives as a means of establishing an African-American historical and political subjectivity. Feminist theory, on the other hand, traditionally has been interested in disrupting the discourse that makes it possible to think of the body as a discrete entity. Revealing the divergent theoretical agendas of these movements, the critical reaction to Dorothy Dandridge (1922–1965) either treats her with adulation, through biographical recovery that frequently recapitulates the patriarchal structures in which she was enmeshed during her lifetime, or subordinates Dandridge's blackness to her femininity. A stubborn critical silence remains regarding Dandridge as a cultural icon who bore simultaneous burdens of blackness and femininity. Dandridge was destroyed first by a media obsession with reproducing the commodification of white femininity on a black body and second by the cultural desire to sample black exoticism without having to confront the national history of exploitation and violence that accompanied that body.

Her cinematic performances challenge normative expectations by replacing the common image of the victimized white female body with the image of a black female body victimized by masculine violence—both black and white. Dandridge portrayed the victimization of the black woman when it was politically inexpedient for both black and white mainstream political establishments to dwell on the image of black female suffering. As a result, she fell into institutional disfavor even as she fed a public desire for controversy. Dandridge's body was always a tool of dominant discourse, but one that forced that discourse into self-examination. She moved the boundaries of what could be said, spoken, and represented in relation to racial difference, even if she never signified outside a system of patriarchal representation.

The victimization of the black female body appears in several of Dandridge's films, including *Tarzan's Peril* (1951), *Tamango* (1957),[2] *Island in the Sun* (1957), *The Decks Ran Red* (1958), and her well-known *Carmen Jones* (1954). All these films portray Dandridge's interracial appeal as both inescapable and taboo, and the films specifically label these desires as tragically self-destructive to both desirer and desired. Ultimately, however, these performances fall into the category of masquerade rather than mimicry because the traditional paradigm of woman-as-object reinscribes Dandridge's exposure of racial exploitation. Her on-screen objectification increasingly moved off-screen as well, and media discourse continually confused her personal and public performance. This conflation encouraged several "sex goddess" figures, including Dandridge's contemporary Marilyn Monroe (1926–62), to obliterate their self-destructive images through self-destructive acts.[3] In these cases, following Rushdie's paradigm, biography merged with representation, and the act of flight from objectification became a flight from the body itself. The media refused to address Dandridge and Monroe as subjects who suffered the consequences of the contradictory roles women in this era were forced to play in order to negotiate among economic success, national anxieties, and individual desires. Instead, the media framed these women as victims of "tragic" circumstance.[4] Posthumously, the dangerous ambiguity of Dandridge's image intensified inasmuch as the narrative of self-destruction and tragedy befits the white suffering female icon whose presence enables traditional models of heterosexual desire.[5] When mapped onto the black female body, however, this paradigm of self-destructive sexuality recalls a national history of rape, torture, murder, and exploitation that unmasks the true "deviant" history of whiteness within black/white relations.[6]

DANDRIDGE AND MONROE: MEDIA CONSTRUCTIONS OF DELECTABLE TRAGEDY

> Even as a kid, I understood that Dorothy Dandridge called a lie
> to the assumption that the movie goddess could only be some
> fair-haired white beauty. She had proved that Black women
> could be cast as something other than giggling maids or hefty
> nurturers without lives of their own.
>
> —from *Dorothy Dandridge: A Biography* by Donald Bogle

In the era of Classic Hollywood cinema, Dorothy Dandridge was an omnipresent icon of femininity, a star of the first degree. From her death until quite recently, however, her image and career appeared to have been buried with her body. Dandridge's posthumous oblivion is all the more striking when compared with the posthumous reputation of the Classic Hollywood sex goddess, Marilyn Monroe. Monroe's career shared many of the vicissitudes that plagued Dandridge, but, unlike Dandridge, her iconographic status has heightened posthumously. The celebration of the white sex goddess and the erasure of

Dandridge illustrate the contradictory roles of race and gender in the American iconography of miscegenation—defined here as the body of cultural associations that prompted the social and legal discouragement of racial intermarriage, which, in turn, were based upon a fear of tainting the *white* race rather than a more general fear of racial mixing.[7] These cultural demands to represent both race and gender mark the careers and posthumous images of both Dandridge and Monroe.

Both women were trapped within contradictory and destructive demands of the masquerade of femininity that shaped them to fit male desire. Expected to be highly sexual, childlike, and physically available, they were also expected to serve as figures of idealized domesticity, conventionally concerned with the care and maintenance of a dominant husband.[8] Dandridge's particular performance of these demands, however, mimed the traditional sex goddess model because she both embodied and challenged national anxieties circulating around racial difference and sexual desire. At the same time, she expanded the restrictive repertoire of stereotypes available to black actresses of this era—which, as Dandridge's biographer Bogle notes above, altered the image of black femininity.

Both of the models of female sexuality described in the paradox above— the sexual siren and the domesticated wife—contextualize Monroe and Dandridge as prosthetic counterparts to heterosexual male desire and aid in the construction of their images as passive objects of this desire. This, despite the fact that each woman played a visible role in the creative and economic shaping of her image. Indeed, several of Dandridge's films—including two central to this essay, *Tamango* and *Island in the Sun*—explicitly represent a fear of male inadequacy provoked by racially marked female bodies. The controversy surrounding her performances resulted in government surveillance of her as a possible threat to American political values, the boycott of her films by conservative Southern community organizations, and public debate over her interracial relationships—controversies that remain hallmarks of her career more than a generation after her death.

The economic success of both Dandridge and Monroe depended upon their ability to produce an image of victimization that evoked sexual desire tinged with anxiety. The sex goddess role was an image produced by the female body, but elicited by a particular model of heterosexual male desire. As such, its performance represents a partnership between actress and culture in which economic reward results from satisfying a cultural desire for images of sexual victimization. Thus, my point in discussing the relationship between the biographical tales of abuse surrounding Dandridge and Monroe is to regard the correlation of violence and sex as a culturally revealing image, rather than as a biographical fact. My purpose is not to conjecture about the characters of Dandridge and Monroe, but rather to speculate on what aspects of American cultural identity demand the eroticism of female victims.

The sex goddess seems to embody a sadomasochistic patriarchal ideal of beauty that reached its pinnacle of popularity in the 1950s.[9] Donald Bogle describes this particular era as reflecting a transition between an earlier feminine ideal, in which "beauties were not supposed to be troubled or isolated. . . . Their drop-dead looks were usually symbols of their power and their destructiveness,"[10] and a new "beauty-as-loner" image, which he correlates with a modern version of the tragic mulatto.[11]

Another defining characteristic of cinema in this era was a tension between the cult of stardom and the emerging auteur ideology. In this equation, the star bore the burden of audience desires—through her media biography as well as her cinematic performance—while the auteur reaped the critical acclaim surrounding individual performances. Although Dandridge did serve as a cultural role model, the image of her body is not easily confined within a singular narrative. She simultaneously represented desires of the film industry and the nation, and her performances were elicited by white male directors and regulated by production codes. As such, her body marked a point of contention between social and individual fantasy that embodies the political nature of desire, a focal point that begs interpretation through the multiple fields of psychoanalysis, black feminism, and cultural analysis.

Biography heavily informs the interpretation of both Dandridge and Monroe, and they—like many other performers of the "sex goddess" image[12]— are associated with early and repeated violent subjugation: Monroe was raped in early foster care; Dandridge was abused by her female childhood caretaker. Later, as adults, both experienced a chain of disastrous and high profile heterosexual relationships that enhanced the popularity of their images but destroyed them personally. The images of both Monroe and Dandridge depended upon their identification as tragic figures, and their reviews are filled with phrases evoking tragedy alongside any triumph. This sense of mystery and tragedy supported their portrayal as desirable enigmas who were symbols of passive female suffering, created by the lack of adequate male dominance.

The 1997 biography of Dandridge by Donald Bogle provides an excellent example of the resilience of this myth of female suffering as caused by the lack of sufficient male guidance. Bogle repeatedly blames Dandridge's failures on the absence of her father during childhood, as well as the nefarious influence of her mother's lesbianism. Bogle regards Dandridge's mother, Ruby, as an unhealthy influence, despite the fact that throughout her life, Dorothy treated her as a close friend. He remains nostalgic, however, toward Dandridge's father Cyril, although she appears to have met him no more than four times in her life. Repeatedly absolving the father of responsibilities that he regards as central to motherhood, Bogle adheres to the traditional notion that the absence of the father is an inevitably psychological devastating phenomenon. Bogle is equally uneasy with the sexuality of Ruby and Dorothy as associated with whiteness. While Ruby's lesbianism brands her as the "bad" mother, and the absent father marks Dorothy's tragic destiny, Bogle's anxieties also focus upon the Dandridge women's choice of white sexual partners. He positions both Dandridge women within the confines of traditional cultural expectations: compulsory heterosexuality and stable racial identity categories.[13] Bogle biographically recovers Ruby and Dorothy only to reinterpret them through 1950s ideology.

Dandridge's tragic nature is often described in gustatorial terms, which focus on her body as "forbidden fruit," on her success as "bittersweet," and on her complexion as "café au lait."[14] This tasty suffering is so completely associated with her image that it becomes hard to separate Dandridge's name from the word "tragedy" in media sources, even those that predate her death.[15] The root of this tragedy lies in Dandridge's failure to maintain her autonomy from her media image; the *performance* of cultural associations between femininity and sex, blackness and primitivism—associations with which she was never comfortable—ultimately subsumed the performative body. In her ability to perform the masquerade of feminine sexuality, she became the figure of tragedy itself.

In one of Dandridge's early soundies, *Paper Doll*, she dances to life from a photograph, evidently wished into being by the longing of the man gazing at her picture.[16] Although Bogle refers to *Paper Doll* as "an innocently romantic number that . . . touched on the Black media's desire for its own glamour girls,"[17] this desire to imitate white "glamour girls" fundamentally opposed attempts of female artists like Dandridge to exhibit themselves as subjects rather than objects. The sex goddess role encouraged actresses to focus almost exclusively on their bodies as visual stimulus for the male, and this focus implied a lack of subjectivity—or humanity, in Rushdie's terms—on the part of the performer. This debilitating aspect of the sex goddess performance applies across color lines, as Gloria Steinem and Richard Dyer note in their discussions of Marilyn Monroe.[18] For example, the promotional image that the studio circulated for Dandridge's most widely publicized film, *Carmen Jones*, depicts her posed as Carmen, standing with hands on hips, legs spread, head tossed back in an atmosphere of assertive availability. Although references to Dandridge additionally contain a racial component (as demonstrated by

Figure 9.1. Dorothy Dandridge became widely associated with this publicity pose for
Carmen Jones (1954).

the media quotations printed later within this study), the generic sex goddess
image already confused the sexual availability of the character with that of
the actress, a confusion that Dandridge unsuccessfully attempted to resist.
Dandridge's discomfort with her marketing as a sexual object reflected her
awareness of the traditional association of the black woman with the sexual

wanton, a concern shared by the political movements for black advancement and feminism.[19] Her role in *Carmen Jones* further fueled these anxieties because it developed a mainstream variation on the sexually available role she had already established in her nightclub act, a role she abhorred, according to her sister.[20]

Nevertheless, Dandridge was far from a victim of circumstance when it came to portraying the sex goddess image. Despite her association with sexual victimization, she emphasized the visual physicality of her performances, and her early nightclub act foregrounded her body through a wardrobe of tight dresses and sensual lyrics. In environments such as the club Mocambo, which was decorated as combination aviary and jungle, Dandridge repositioned herself as a "visual, rather than a vocal performer," according to Bogle.[21] As industry standards allowed greater display of her body, she sought increased literal exposure. In 1962, she performed a topless scene in *The Murder Men*, a film version of her television performance in the episode, "Blues for a Junkman," on the series, *Cain's Hundred*.[22]

Dandridge's race figured prominently in her sexualization. Unlike Monroe, who actively sought to increase her sexual connotations by widely publicizing her nude body outside cinematic roles and sexually punning in media sound bites,[23] Dandridge was consistently sexualized in the media discussion of her offstage life, despite her attempts to frame this sexualization as "performance." Her song lyrics, composed by men, powerfully accentuated the sexuality and victimization of her body and were well received by her audience, as evidenced by the reprinting of suggestive lyrics in several of her reviews.[24]

Primarily, however, her sexuality was associated with the color of her skin and the movement of her body within her performances. The media treated Dandridge as if she had integrated sexuality into her image beyond her act, although she worked diligently to contradict this image in her interviews. Many of the reviews acknowledged her discomfort with her highly sexual image, even as they reinforced it. For example, Louie Robinson notes, "Miss Dandridge did not want the identification of the passionate woman of easy virtue."[25] A 1952 *Time* article printed her suggestive song lyrics, then paradoxically described her as "a rather earnest and demure woman offstage."[26] A 1955 *Time* review condescendingly noted that she "hanker[s] after some intellectual life. Dorothy Dandridge slips into a pink shirt and tight slacks and thinks seriously about her private personality."[27]

Although Dandridge was associated with bestial desire and sensuality through her skin tone, her depiction in the media largely attributes her success to a male director or agent. This reaction might be labeled the Trilby syndrome, in that male reviewers and critics always eagerly sought a Svengali behind her performances. The credit often went to Phil Moore, who was presented not only as the author of her lyrics, but also as the artist of her image. Moore is an interesting choice because he worked with several "sex goddess" actresses on their performances of feminine sexuality. In fact, he worked with Ava Gardner, Marilyn Monroe, and Dorothy Dandridge simultaneously at an early, formative point in all three of their careers.[28] *Time* attributed Dandridge's nightclub success to "the practiced eyes of Pianist-Arranger Phil Moore,"[29] ignoring the fact that she had been performing since she was a young girl and had already received regular nightclub bookings. Similarly, *Life* suggested that Phil Moore "brought out Dorothy's suppressed sultriness,"[30] and *Ebony* reported in a 1986 article that Phil Moore "taught her to mask her shyness" so that she could be a nightclub success.[31]

Indeed, Moore's involvement with Dandridge reveals the calculated strategy needed to shape female performance to fit masculine desire. Moore did write the lyrics to many of the sexually subservient songs that garnered media attention for Dandridge, and he may have helped Dandridge craft her nightclub routine's appeal to patriarchal notions of sexuality. Dandridge, however, saw her relationship to Moore as one of artistic equality, and she has been quoted as saying to him before seeking another lyricist, "You are playing Svengali. I am nobody's Trilby. I'm an artist in my own right."[32] This denial of female agency can be explained partly, as Dyer has noted, by a mainstream 1950s ideology of sexuality, which was based on a theory that "women are to *be* sexuality, yet this really means as a vehicle *for* male sexuality."[33] Dandridge was denied credit for her physical performances, and the media attributed her movements, and those of Monroe, either to nature or to male mentorship.[34] However, both Dandridge and Monroe studied with the Hollywood Actors Laboratory, a West Coast version of the Group Theatre. The Actors Lab focused on acting as a craft that rejects typecasting, and both women evidently took this concept seriously. The Actors Lab was an interesting influence on both women as well because of its inclusion on the private *Red Channels* 1952 blacklist. This choice of craft over conformity to mainstream cultural values indicates that both women were willing to damage their marketability for the sake of their craft. Monroe emerged from the Actors Lab association unscathed, but Dandridge found herself in the midst of a controversy over racial boundary-crossing as a nationally threatening act. The incident foreshadowed the trajectory of her career.

At an informal Actors Laboratory gathering in 1948, Dandridge danced with actor Anthony Quinn, unwittingly sparking a media controversy. Columnists Hedda Hopper and Jim Henaghan censured Dandridge's dance as an interracial dancing scandal, and the black press and Hollywood Democratic Committee responded in defense of the Lab's activities. The Actors Lab had been labeled a Communist front by State Senator Jack Tenney's California Joint Fact-finding Committee on Un-American Activities in 1948; therefore, many of their activities seemed suspect to the public. Quinn poses an interesting choice for Dandridge's racial transgression in that he apparently signified whiteness only in contrast to Dandridge's blackness; other media passages highlight his Mexican origins in contrast to Americanness. Later controversies surrounding Dandridge would focus more explicitly on her contrast to whiteness in transracial relationships.[35]

Although the 1948 incident was presumably controversial in its threat to antimiscegenation statutes of the time, a 1952 MGM inquiry cited this event as indicative of Dandridge's "Un-American" political affiliations with organizations such as the NAACP, the Progressive Citizens of America, and the Hollywood Arts, Sciences and Professions Council. This example is one of many that demonstrate that Dandridge's portrayal of black female sexuality, unlike Monroe's portrayal of whiteness, carried with it an anti-American connotation for primarily white institutions of the time, including the government and the film industry. Whereas the sexual association with femininity is common to both black and white media sources, hegemonic discourse contains an association between blackness and national otherness as well.

Increasingly over the course of Dandridge's career, the media targeted at black audiences adapted a mainstream vision of women as pleasure objects. *Jet* magazine provides an excellent example of the black media mimicry of increasingly successful American girlie magazines. In the section "The Week's Best Photos," it depicted black women in the Betty Grable-style "bathing beauty" tradition.[36] In this context, Dandridge appears in the first of "The Week's Best Photos" on September 23, 1965.[37] The one photograph shows her reclining on a bed, twisted among silk sheets. The caption describes her as "a sultry, sex symbol, widely pursued by men," and adds an anecdote attributed to her in which a prince offers her $100,000 to sleep with him. This photo and anecdote were used to sell her "autobiography," with which, most sources agree, she had little creative involvement. The visual impact of Dandridge's body was often used to sell consumer products. Although she endorsed products ranging from Rice-A-Roni to Old Gold Cigarettes, these endorsements never brought her the economic success of her white counterparts. Largely restricted to the black press, her advertisements appeared mainly in *Ebony* and *Jet*, and her commodification, unlike Monroe's, lost its potency after her death.

Yet if her economic value diminished following her death, the interpretation of her performances as physical/visual events changed little over the following twenty years, as evidenced by Walter Leavy's retrospective article on

Dandridge in *Ebony* in 1986. Leavy comments, "[Nightclub audiences] really liked what they saw—the flawless figure, the dreamy eyes, the smooth *café au lait* complexion, the sensuous mouth and smooth elegance." [38] In fact, the success of her career increased proportionally in relation to her association with "native" sexuality. The club Mocambo in Los Angeles elicited this association through both its jungle decor and overt advertising. Club ads described Dandridge's act as "a volume of sex with the living impact of the Kinsey report." At the club, copies of Alfred Kinsey's sexual behavior study were sold for $15.[39] The review of this act in *Variety* again associated her success with contrived female sexuality, praising the "sly suggestion" of her lyrics, as well as "gestures that tease the senses." In addition, the reviewer enthusiastically asserts that "sexual innuendoes were rarely absent." [40]

The dehumanization of her media image increased as she won greater fame. In 1955, following Dandridge's Academy Award nomination for her performance in *Carmen Jones, Time* published a review that described her body in detail and emphasized its availability. The reviewer praised her "bee-stung lips," "white-sheathed hips," "warm brown eyes [which] singled out two or three lucky males for what appeared to be special invitations," and "long, discreetly undulating body." [41]

Unlike her contemporary Monroe, Dandridge consistently resisted such objectification, working from the earliest stages of her career to contextualize her sexuality as "performance" rather than naturalized reality.[42] In a precedent-setting trial in 1957, Dandridge sued *Confidential* magazine and won a $10,000 settlement for a slanderous article that linked her to illicit affairs. Rebutting the very notion of sex appeal, Dandridge said, "I don't believe in sex appeal. What people call sex appeal is the tremendous vitality generated by a good actress. It has nothing to do with tight sweaters and low-cut dresses." [43] Dandridge made several public statements on this subject in 1957 in an attempt to refute articles in *Hep* and *Sepia*, as well as the *Confidential* article, all of which ran stories about Dandridge's sex life as a string of interracial affairs. She tried to counter these stories with her own article in *Sepia*, in which she suggested that she stayed unmarried "for the sake of members of my race." [44] She may have chosen to sue *Confidential* in particular because it was known for titillating its readers with interracial tales of desire. Despite her public and open resistance to this sexualization of her image beyond her act, the industry and the media continued to define her in physical terms.

VIOLENCE AND SEXUALITY: THE TIES THAT BIND

Nowhere is the divergence of Dandridge's professional credibility and personal humiliation clearer than in her 1954 Academy Award nomination for her leading role in *Carmen Jones*. She received critical acclaim for her performance in a sensationalistic role. The film graphically depicted her being beaten, chased, tied up, and finally murdered. The role of Carmen demanded a physical enactment of the patriarchal punishment of aggressive female sexuality, and several media sources began to refer to Dandridge simply as "Carmen." [45] Partially, this association grew out of the marketing campaign for *Carmen Jones*, which used Dandridge's body as a powerful visual lure. Although Harry Belafonte received top billing, Dandridge's body dominated the promotional imagery. In a three-page advertisement that ran in *Variety* on November 17, 1954, a full-page silhouette of Dandridge as Carmen dominates the text printed over her body: "the whole nation is flipping for CARMEN." [46] As the reader turns the page, a picture of a miniature Dorothy Dandridge in front of an overwhelming shadow of her figure provides the centerpiece for a series of favorable movie review quotations that reinforce the focus on Dandridge's "sultry," "blazing" performance. Hedda Hopper exclaims, "I got so excited I burned a big hole in the front of my dress. Yep, the film is that hot." [47]

This "heat," however, seems to be generated from the energy of violence. *Carmen Jones* was controversial in its challenge to the standards of middle-class morality, as represented by the Breen Production Code comment that the film was problematic in its lack of condemnation of Carmen's immorality and its "overemphasis on lustfulness." [48] The scenes of violence against Carmen's body, however, were less controversial than her kissing scenes. One scene in particular exhibited a level of violence against Dandridge's black body that would never have been demonstrated against a white icon such as Monroe. When Carmen breaks free from Joe (Harry Belafonte), she attempts to escape by running down a line of moving train cars. Following a harrowing leap from the train, Belafonte throws a struggling, biting Dandridge to the ground and binds her arms and legs together before hauling her back to his jeep. Apparently, both actors performed their own stunts, and it seems likely that this level of graphic violence against the female body was permitted only because Dandridge was marked as black. [49] At the same time, however, the depiction of violence against the black female body, even when rendered by a black man, made visible a cultural reality theretofore obscured. By making visible the violence visited upon the black female body, Dandridge selected a career path that both invoked and challenged the traditional taboo image of the white female body victimized by the black male. Many of her later films placed Dandridge opposite a white male counterpart, openly challenging traditional taboos.

Throughout Otto Preminger's Technicolor production of *Carmen Jones*, he courted controversy by positioning Dandridge's body as the focal point of the action and the dialogue. Her conscientiously crafted wardrobe accentuates her breasts, hips, and legs, as her loud bawdy language and lipstick highlight her mouth. In fact, as Joe strangles Carmen in the final scene, her open mouth becomes the symbol of her death. Trembling, a bit open, highly stylized and sensual, her mouth remains the final image of the tragic Carmen, and it seems to be the source of much of the anxiety surrounding this image, as well as the desire. The mouth of the black woman was already a powerful symbol of cultural anxiety, as demonstrated by the ban on interracial kissing in the cinema, a ban that several of Dandridge's later roles would challenge. Indeed, the visibility of Carmen's mouth and body became a source of anxiety for Dandridge herself, as she resisted her increased association with the role of the sexually promiscuous and physically abused woman.

The popularity and controversy of *Carmen Jones* drew from a variety of cultural sources. Archetypally, as Bogle assesses, *Carmen* invoked "a long-held male concept of the alluring, sexually potent woman who has the power to enslave and destroy men and who therefore must be destroyed." [50] Politically, *Carmen* was released in 1954 amid a flurry of cultural controversy from both black and white political sectors. Its release coincided with the emergence of the civil rights movement, and it could have been interpreted as reifying the image of the black woman as a sexual wanton. [51] In order to alleviate this controversy, the proceeds from the premiere were donated to the NAACP.

Carmen was not the first role to bestialize and subjugate Dandridge, [52] but it was largely responsible for trapping her within the "sex goddess" image. In an effort to separate her nightclub act from the role, she remarked to an Associated Press photographer, "I don't want people who come to see me to think that they're going to see me as I was in the picture. There's no relation to the two. In night clubs, my material is highly sophisticated, I wear beautiful gowns that completely cover me. I'm not earthy and I'm not fiery." [53] Many of her defenders joined her effort to distance herself from Carmen's "low-class" promiscuity, repeatedly using the adjective "ladylike" to describe Dandridge. Director John Peyser captures this paradoxical sexuality in his description of Dandridge as "somebody you'd like to climb into bed with. . . . She had the same kind of feeling or air that Grace Kelly used when she was here. . . . Dorothy gave you the 'queen' feeling. She was a lady." [54] This paradox of wanton and "lady" is linked to whiteness through comparisons to white icons like Monroe and Kelly, and through Dandridge's widely regarded crossover appeal to white male audiences. Even recently, Bogle has suggested that the media perceived Dandridge as a lady because she was "worthy of White male adoration." [55] Her successful imitation of the ideal of white female sexuality led her to be identified as much with Marilyn Monroe and Grace Kelly as it did with Eartha Kitt and Josephine Baker. The pedestal of "ladylike" behavior, however, proved as debilitating to Dandridge as it had to her white counterparts. In contrast to her demure offscreen image, most of her onscreen performances, particularly the post–*Carmen Jones* roles, depict her as a sexually available, ethnically marked woman.

AN AMERICAN EXPATRIATE: *TAMANGO* AND *ISLAND IN THE SUN*

The power of Dandridge's sexual connotations may have caused the demise of her career even as she was reaching her greatest popularity, for she increasingly became associated onscreen and off with interracial affairs, most notably with Otto Preminger, director of *Carmen Jones*. Her screen career after *Carmen Jones* accentuated her vulnerability to violent male desire and heightened this controversial association by depicting transgender violence as transracial as well. She tried to compensate for this increased emphasis on her sexual availability by reframing herself as a domestic icon. Ironically, however, the violence of her screen portrayals moved into her domestic life: her divorce from her second husband, Jack Denison, on the grounds of abuse and the drama of her death conjure up the disturbing images from her films. Denison, a failed businessman, helped to bankrupt Dandridge emotionally and financially as well as alienate her from separatist black and white communities.

Dandridge's interracial associations proved both titillating and controversial. Studios repeatedly placed her opposite leading white male actors, then undercut the project, fearing audience disapproval. As her performances increasingly catered to white male audiences, directors who paired her with white leading men attempted to distance their films from the racial controversy raging in American culture by recontextualizing Dandridge as anything but African-American. As Michael Omi remarks, she "presented a quandary for studio executives who weren't sure what race and nationality to make her. . . . what they refused to entertain as a possibility was to present her as what she really was, a black American woman." [56] She appeared as an African "tribeswoman" in *Tarzan's Peril* (1951) and *The Decks Ran Red* (1958), a Cuban slave of African descent in *Tamango* (1957), a West Indian woman in *Island in the Sun* (1957), and a woman of undetermined European origins in *Malaga* (1960). In fact, following *Carmen Jones*, she was contextualized almost exclusively as non-American. [57]

From the earliest stages of her career, Dandridge's performance style integrated elements that reflected a "non-American" exoticism. Some of her first soundies were titled *Jungle Jig* and *Congo Clambake*. Her nightclub act at the Waldorf featured an "island-style" dance number that reportedly drove the crowd wild. [58] It was popular enough to be depicted in a triptych of photos showing her performing the erotic removal of her shoes in a 1955 *Ebony* article with the caption "Barefoot at the Waldorf." [59] Her exoticism marked a cultural boundary that was subject to constant renegotiation in the 1950s— a boundary between unacceptable interracial sex and acceptable interracial violence. For example, the positioning of Dandridge's legs when she played Melmendi, the African queen in *Tarzan's Peril*, seems to have caused considerable concern. The Breen Code officials were unconcerned with the act of physically tying up her body, but they warned that she must not be "staked out in such wise that her legs are spread-eagled. Such a position . . . would be offensively sex suggestive." [60] This develops as the cultural code for depicting Dandridge's sexuality—biting, wrestling, and touching are permissible as long as the violence of the contact is emphasized over its sexual nature. Frequently, her body is most accessible to male counterparts during moments of violence. She is rarely allowed an embrace motivated by affection, but is frequently clutched, clinched, and bound during moments of violent desire inflamed by her resistance or rebellion.

Island in the Sun and *Tamango* are of particular interest because of Dandridge's appearance in both films as a woman who crosses racial boundaries and challenges traditional miscegenation taboos and because of the marketing of these films through images of sexual violence surrounding her body. In both these films, she elicits potentially "tragic" male desire across racial boundaries. The films were promoted through images depicting the threat of white male hands and lips to the black female body. One video version of *Tamango* captions the cover with a quotation, issuing from the lips of Dandridge's character, Aiche, to Curt Jurgens's character, "I've always hated your hands on my body!" [61] Captioned "love as bold and daring as the casting!" advertisements portrayed a bare-chested Jurgens restraining both Dandridge's hands in his own as she tries to pull away from him. This caption could also have applied to *Island in the Sun*, which provoked heated media debate over its interracial love theme. A story in *Jet* subtitled "Torrid New Love Story Stars Interracial Love Code Debate" wrapped the political motive for miscegenated imagery within an aesthetic motive, a call for greater "realism." [62] In the article, Dandridge attempted to bracket the film outside American social controversy, commenting, "Margot, whom I play, is not an American Negro girl but a West Indian, and she would not be self-conscious about or sensitive to an interracial love affair. It happens all the time in the West Indies." [63] The plot of the film, however, is driven precisely by the controversy three interracial West Indian relationships generate. Although it may happen "all the time in the West Indies," the film nonetheless depicts all the characters as being highly sensitive to this race-crossing.

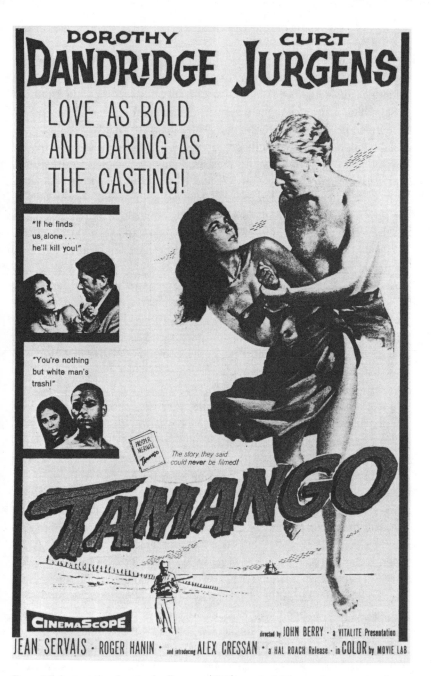

Figure 9.2. A promotional poster for *Tamango* (1957) as entertaining controversy, visually emphasizing the violence of the interracial relationship between white male master and black female slave. (Image courtesy of Photographs and Prints Division, Schomburg Center for Research in Black Culture, New York Public Library, Astor, Lenox, and Tilden Foundations.)

Both Dandridge and *Jet* avoided discussing interracial relationships as a facet of "reality" that had long gone underrepresented in American society. Dandridge must have been keenly aware of the controversy provoked by interracial relationships, following the media discussions of her relationship with Preminger, her later marriage to Jack Denison, and the many rumored interracial relationships between these two events. The transgressive potential of Dandridge's post–*Carmen Jones* roles is also evident in the number of her films that were scripted or directed by blacklisted artists: Robert Rossen directed *Island in the Sun,* John Berry directed *Tamango,* and Donald Ogden Stewart wrote the screenplay for *Malaga.* All three films could have shared the promotional caption given *Tamango,* "The story they said could never be filmed."

Island in the Sun presented a slightly different inflection on the interracial dilemma for Dandridge. The film represented Darryl Zanuck's desire to contrast Dandridge's racial connotations with the racial ambiguity he had elicited in previous mixed-race roles by using "white" actresses, such as Joan Fontaine in *Pinky* (1949) and Ava Gardner in *Showboat* (1951).[64] In *Island in the Sun,* Joan Collins fulfills the role of the woman who appears alternately black or white, depending upon context. Zanuck contrasts Collins's ability to simulate blackness while remaining ultimately "white" with Dandridge's blackness. The discourse surrounding Dandridge's character, Margot Seaton, correlates Dandridge's body with authentic exoticism in contrast to Collins's mimicry of exoticism.

However, like the later *Tamango,* this film sanitized sex by invoking racial (and racist) ideologies. In order to avoid the interracial kiss formerly forbidden by the Breen code, Zanuck decided to emphasize the black male lover's political convictions in one relationship (Harry Belafonte/Joan Fontaine) and the black woman's career ambitions in the other (Dorothy Dandridge/John Justin). This method of dealing with the taboo on interracial kissing stirred considerable controversy, as evidenced in the subtitle to *Jet*'s cover story, "John Justin & Dorothy Dandridge: They make love, but can't kiss in new movie." Dandridge regarded the inability to kiss her leading man as "unnatural," but she also recognized the interracial kiss as a matter of national definition and suggested that they shoot two versions, a sanitized version for American audiences and an interracially explicit version for European audiences.[65]

Island in the Sun depicts three interracial relationships within a context of both familial and national redefinition. Each interracial relationship signifies a personal or national tension, followed by a transformation. One plot line follows a post-colonial Oedipal trajectory, in which Maxwell Fleury (James Mason) violently projects anxieties over his failure as a son and husband onto native bodies, and then, as his racial identity shifts toward "blackness," onto a single white male figure, Hilary Carson. At first, Fleury embodies Frantz Fanon's analysis of the white colonizer's psychology and provides a resounding affirmative answer to Fanon's question, "When a white man hates black men, is he not yielding to a feeling of impotence or of sexual inferiority?" [66] Fleury doubts his masculinity in relationship to his wife, his father, his older brother, and British colonial rule. *Island* provides a critique of white male colonization through the figure of this fatally flawed son whose inadequacy is racially marked.[67] Fleury is contrasted to David Boyer (Harry Belafonte), a "natural" leader of men consistently referred to as both "dangerous" and "powerful."

Interwoven with this narrative of crisis in white colonial masculinity is Dandridge's role as the provocateur of another wandering son of the British colonial structure. The relationship between Dandridge's character and John Justin's character is revolutionary in that she inspires him to choose life with her instead of service to the governor. Perhaps this depiction is most surprising for the lack of violence directly attending the affair between Justin and Dandridge. Their scenes together are remarkably peaceful treatments of Dandridge's allure: she dances a little, brushes his cheek to avoid the taboo kiss, and reads his manuscript criticizing British colonization. Her "sexiness" is still associated with exotic rhythm and tradition (she performs a limbo number for a carnival crowd that includes Justin), but in her case, unlike in any of the other interracial storylines in *Island,* carnival rebellion is not tragic but fun, and revolution comes without trauma.

Although the promotional materials for *Island* sensationalize Dandridge's performance through exotic associations with the primitive, they avoid the graphic depictions of violence to her body that mark many of her other films. In one promotional photograph, for example, she poses before a woven mat, an African mask over her right shoulder. In another, she peeks out from underneath a large palm frond. One review referred to *Island in the Sun* as "the sexiest West Indian travelogue ever made." [68] Certainly, the film depicts Dandridge as a typical exotic, available for the pleasure of the British military; even Belafonte's character remarks that her relationship with a white husband will succeed because "the other wives look sort of dull when she walks into the room." However, Dandridge's Margot Seaton is also a woman who successfully navigates the colonial system by realigning herself with a colonizer, who then criticizes the system from within. Margot's body serves as a tool for negotiating personal advancement rather than self-destruction, and the lack of violence surrounding her role as interracial partner makes this one of Dandridge's less objectified depictions of the exotic and primitive.

The restrained treatment of Dandridge in *Island in the Sun* proves all the

Figure 9.3. Dandridge in a publicity photograph for *Island in the Sun* (1957).

more striking when contrasted with her role in *The Decks Ran Red* (1958). This film situates Dandridge as a wanton woman onboard a ship threatened by mutiny (a plot shared with *Tamango*). In a carefully posed promotional photo for *Decks*, Dandridge's shirt is literally being torn from her body. She pulls away from her attacker, looking up in terror at his lustful gaze. This suggestion of fear became a titillating aspect of her later performances, which increasingly focused on the destruction of her body through bondage or rape.

Figure 9.4. Shades of film noir lend tragic edge to the exotic paradise of *Island in the Sun* (1957).

Tamango provides an excellent example of American culture's "kill me, don't kiss me" production code regarding interracial desire. The plot revolves around Curt Jurgens's portrayal of a white slave trader, Captain Reinker, who faces a slave ship mutiny led by a black lion hunter, Tamango. Dandridge plays Jurgens's slave/lover Aiche, who feeds his desire for sadistic control of both blackness and femininity. The dilemma in this production is which male discourse will ultimately define Aiche: Tamango's doctrine of violent black

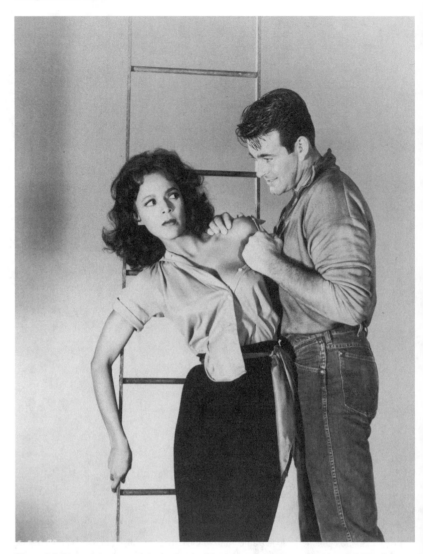

Figure 9.5. Male violence and desire for the black female body revealed in publicity photo for *The Decks Ran Red* (1958). (Image courtesy of Photographs and Prints Division, Schomburg Center for Research in Black Culture, New York Public Library, Astor, Lenox, and Tilden Foundations.)

separatism or Captain Reinker's doctrine of white capitalistic exploitation. Both men attempt to seduce Aiche into complicity with their philosophies for survival. Reinker tells her that she, like him, is interested only in her own economic advancement. He offers as an example the first instance of his sexual domination, when she "sold" herself to him for a few trinkets.

In *Tamango*, men literally battle for possession of Dandridge's body. Tamango ends his rebellion by dragging Aiche down into the slave hold with him as a hostage, hoping to barter her body for his own survival. When Reinker shows himself willing to sacrifice Aiche's body in order to preserve his own masculine dominance, Tamango decides to "free" her. Interestingly, Reinker offers her freedom as well in a previous scene. Both men, however, offer Aiche a false choice. She is trapped, literally, between two spaces of masculine violence; there is no space for her freedom on the slave ship. In the end, she chooses liberation through death and solidarity with Tamango and his men. Because of her "mixed-race" status, frequently alluded to in the film, Aiche is forced to choose between two tragic alternatives of blackness and whiteness, neither of which provides a source of freedom or independence for her.

Tamango is additionally interesting in that it is one of the few films that depicts Dandridge in final solidarity with, rather than in deviation from, her race. In several of her films (*Carmen Jones* included), she plays an outsider to her fellow blacks. *Tamango* goes to great lengths to demonstrate Aiche's solidarity with her captive counterparts, a task made difficult by her comparatively privileged status as mistress to the white slave trader. In several early scenes, she recounts the childhood horrors imposed by slavery that drove her to buy into the vernacular of her oppressor, rejecting any notions of freedom or resistance. *Tamango* ultimately depicts Aiche as choosing black unity over self-advancement. This assertion coincided with Dandridge's own attempts to alleviate the interracial controversies that haunted her extra-filmic career by reasserting her interest in the advancement of her race over her own personal desire.[69]

Aiche's dilemma echoes Dandridge's own subject position in another way as well. Dandridge had rejected the role of Tuptim in *The King and I* a few years earlier because, according to Bogle, she was reluctant to play a slave.[70] However, following the success of *The King and I* and her own three-year drought between *Carmen Jones* and *Island in the Sun*, Dandridge seems to have reconsidered this decision. Offscreen, she appears to have made a choice similar to that of Margot Seaton in *Island in the Sun*: economic independence and survival supersede previous notions of racial advancement.

ALL-AMERICAN OR AFRICAN-AMERICAN? COMMODIFICATION AND DESIRE

From her appearance in *Tarzan's Peril*, Dandridge was positioned as an object of white male desire that provoked destructive violence. The very act of portraying this violence illuminated a cultural paradox that challenged mainstream notions of morality for both black and white cultural entities of the era. Too frequently, however, her crossover appeal to audiences manifested itself through the violence of male hands, both black and white. She was literally manhandled throughout her cinematic career, and her divorce due to physical and emotional abuse implies that ultimately her onscreen performance merged dangerously with her offscreen existence. Ironically, despite Dandridge's continued efforts to separate herself from her portrayals, the pattern of racial and gender choices that marked her cinematic roles came to mark her own life as well. Like Aiche, caught between black and white male worlds of violence, Dandridge ultimately chose self-destruction as her form of authorship.

The destructive nature of female objectification was intensified for Dandridge because the 1950s vision of female sexuality in which she was caught was also racist. According to her autobiography, Dandridge recognized her distance from the white sex goddesses of her era: "America was not geared to make me into a Liz Taylor, a Monroe, a Gardner. My sex symbolism was as a wanton, a prostitute, not as a woman seeking love and a husband." [71] This quotation acknowledged the dichotomy that white female sex goddesses were expected to embody, physically evoking sexuality while remaining subservient models of domesticity. In an era when female stars were used to sell products ranging from lingerie to refrigerators, an image that integrated the trappings of middle-class morality with glamorous sexuality was highly prized. [72] Dandridge accepted domesticity as an integral part of stardom, necessary to enhance her marketability.

Although Dandridge lamented that she was not allowed to portray the domestic aspect of her image onscreen, she was repeatedly recontextualized as "domestic" in the media, particularly by the media written for an African-American demographic. The domestication of the black woman was a political goal of the black organizations in the 1950s, as they attempted to combat the sexualized image of the black woman with images of her domestic subservience. A problematic figure, Dandridge alternately embodied each of these popularized forms of femininity. Although *Ebony* frequently referred to Dandridge as "Hollywood's first authentic love goddess of color," [73] the writers also repeatedly described her in domestic terms. [74] Seeking to emulate the media treatment of white "sex goddesses," *Ebony* depicted Dandridge as a domesticated sex goddess, one who desires love and a husband. The magazine openly expressed regrets that the white film industry did not exploit her more, complaining that her films "did not reflect the continuity of exploitation that would normally have been lavished upon a feminine star who burst upon the world scene with the impact Miss Dandridge had evidenced." [75] The very notion that exploitation is something that can be "lavished" is ironic coming from a media source that sought to increase respect for African-Americans. However, magazines such as *Ebony* chose to advance a patriarchal African-American paradigm of female sexuality that, like the mainstream media, reinscribed female sexuality within domesticity.[76]

Up to this point, we have examined primarily the living career of Dandridge and her relationship to the 1950s ideal of femininity that elevated the image of woman as sexual victim to the status of a sublime object. This sublimation does not apply equally to black and white images, however. The nature of racism does not desexualize black femininity; rather it elevates *white* female sexuality *in relationship to* black female sexuality. Whereas the white woman (Monroe) becomes an idealized, inaccessible, sublime object of desire, the body of the black woman is perceived as the accessible, material means of attaining carnal satisfaction.[77] This image plays out on the screen through the more violent images of subjugation that surrounded Dandridge in contrast to the glamour of the white sex goddess appeal.

Dandridge's image, until recently buried and forgotten by mainstream American media, reveals a basic contradiction within American misogyny when juxtaposed with Monroe's image, which has been reconstituted and recirculated with increasing value. While images of violently subjugated women are widely circulated, the reality of the systematic social violence practiced against the black woman has been historically obscured. Cultural desires were regulated (and reflected) by cinema codes that demanded that either Dandridge be placed opposite black leading men who do violence to her body or that her onscreen interaction with white actors be carefully policed to conform to mainstream moral and political expectations. When white actors were scripted to enact the popular trope of romantic rape with Dandridge, their physical contact with her either emphasized violence, rather than sex, or was edited from the text entirely. In order to distance her image from contemporary American cultural and political tensions, Dandridge was explicitly marked as non-American. The icon of the suffering woman, so central to Monroe's posthumous popularity, necessitates the figurative burial of Dandridge because of the cultural implications of her skin tone.

Dandridge and Monroe were both transformative and transformed, and as their bodies traveled through our culture, their images accumulated a variety of meanings. Marked by our anxieties and desires, their bodies became cultural fetish objects made accessible by the lenses that captured them. Fleeing from their own bodily representation, both resisted objectification by eliminating the body-as-object, a sheer act of subjective self-destruction. For Monroe and Dandridge, however, anatomy became reality, and subjectivity became an elusive fiction.[78] For Monroe, the course of commodification seems complete. Her image has proliferated and become absorbed into the national

Figure 9.6. Dandridge as "African" in *Tarzan's Peril* (1951).

body, her mouth waiting for us on every postage stamp, her beauty mark transforming, in one recent advertisement, into a Mercedes-Benz emblem.

For Dandridge, however, the full exploitation afforded by commodification has yet to occur. The irony is that in attempts to recover Dandridge's image, we may also participate in her commodification and cultural absorption as yet another pop culture icon. The question has become who will play her in

Figure 9.7. Dandridge branded as male property, metaphorically linked to caged birds, in *Tamango* (1957).

the film version of her life, Whitney Houston or Janet Jackson or Halle Berry? [79] This simplification propagates the process of female commodification without attempting to trace its origins, resuscitating the image only to bring in the box office cash once more. A resilient cycle of fantasy, performance, and commodification surround the sex goddess. Unearthing Dandridge from cultural oblivion illuminates the awkward paradox that exhumation remains an act of violence, and recent attempts to confine her within a singular biographical narrative (to establish the *definitive* Dandridge) fail to convey the complexity underlying her cultural meaning. By playing the various parts of the sex goddess—Jezebel, racial activist, wife, and mother—her body left a wake of disarray: changed cinema codes, altered social taboos, and provoked legal sanctions against media speech. She collided with discourse even as she disappeared into silence, and she remains in our culture as a collective work, an indelible image of anxiety and desire.

NOTES

1. Although studies exploring the sadistic gaze within cinema are too numerous to be listed here, some examples include Teresa De Lauretis, *Alice Doesn't: Feminism, Semiotics, Cinema* (Bloomington: Indiana University Press, 1984); Mary Ann Doane, *Femmes Fatales: Feminism, Film Theory, Psychoanalysis* (New York: Routledge, 1991); Laura Mulvey, *Visual and Other Pleasures* (Bloomington: Indiana University Press, 1989); Kaja Silverman, *The Acoustic Mirror: The Female Voice in Psychoanalysis and Cinema* (Bloomington: Indiana University Press, 1988); Diane Waldman, "Film Theory and the Gendered Spectator: The Female of the Feminist Reader," *Camera Obscura* 18 (1988): 80–94; Linda Williams, "Film Bodies: Gender, Genre and Excess," *Film Quarterly* 44 (summer 1991): 2–13.

2. The initial French-language version of *Tamango* was copyrighted in 1957.

3. The cycle of cultural success and personal devastation appears through many acts of suicide and self-destruction by female "stars" (several of them professional acquaintances of Dandridge), including Nina Mae McKinney, Carole Landis, and Billie Holiday.

4. As Mary Ann Doane notes, "the gap between body and psyche is not absolute," and the body always acts as a prop for psychic desire. For example, in her re-interpretation of Jean Laplanche, Doane argues that the "presexual instinct of self-preservation" informs the oral drive of hunger which feeds the desire for the metonymic breast. "Woman's Stake: Filming the Female Body" in *Psychoanalytic Criticism: A Reader,* ed. Sue Vice (Cambridge, MA: Polity Press, 1996), 197, 193–210. The cases of Monroe and Dandridge, however, symbolize an inversion of this formulation: for them, the flight of the psyche away from the body results in a rejection of the presexual instinct for self-preservation.

5. Slavoj Žižek refers to the elusive object as the "sublime object of desire," ever-unattainable, but ever-desirable and lethal in its attraction. See his *Looking Awry: An Introduction to Jacques Lacan through Popular Culture* (Cambridge, MA: MIT Press, 1991), 83.

6. This is not to ignore the literary tradition of black female suffering in the character of the tragic mulatta, but rather to suggest that the *visual* image of black female suffering was much more controversial than its well established literary counterpart.

7. In 1924, the Virginia Assembly passed the *Act to Preserve Racial Integrity*. This act provides an excellent example of the codification of this approach to racism in the twentieth century. Virginia Acts of Assembly 1924, ch. 371, 1924.

8. Richard Dyer's analysis of Monroe provides one case in point of an actress evoking both sides of this sexual/domestic paradigm. Other critics of this approach include Christine Gledhill, Molly Haskell, Teresa De Lauretis and Laura Mulvey. Richard Dyer, "Monroe and Sexuality," *Heavenly Bodies: Film Stars and Society* (London: Macmillan, 1986), 19–66.

9. Ibid., 24. Dyer notes as evidence for the 1950s interest in sexual relations the publication of the Kinsey reports, as well as the first publication of *Confidential* in 1951 and *Playboy* in 1953. Dyer refers to the 1950s as an era when "sex was seen as perhaps the most important thing in life."

10. Donald Bogle, *Dorothy Dandridge: A Biography* (New York: Amistad, 1997), 235.

11. Ibid., 294.

12. For a discussion of the pattern of abuse in relation to other actresses, see Gloria Steinem's article, "Women in the Dark: Of Sex, Goddesses, Abuse, and Dreams," *Ms. Magazine*, January–February 1991, 37. She discusses other "sex goddess" actresses who suffered abuse in childhood that continued into their adult careers. These include Rita Hayworth, Lana Turner, Hedy Lamarr, and Kim Novak.

13. Bogle, *Dorothy Dandridge*. Several times in this biography, Bogle associates both homosexuality and whiteness with deceit, manipulation, and the breakdown of the traditional patriarchal family. For example, Dorothy's friendship with the gay actor Joel Fluellan is attributed to his "clever manipulation" of her vulnerability from a "fatherless upbringing" (160). Descriptions of Ruby's white female partner, Dorothy Foster, and of Dorothy Dandridge's husband, Jack Denison, emphasize their skin tone in conjunction with their culpability for familial problems (257, 307). Bogle's anxieties reflect a fetishistic fascination with skin color, and, as interviewer, he often voices these anxieties through others. For example, Bogle's passage describing Otto Preminger-on-Denison blends the perspective of the interviewer with that of the interviewed: "Otto . . . observed that Denison was the Whitest looking man he had ever seen. 'He had long white hands and fingers. . . . He had *white* hair and *white, white* skin.' Preminger's comments about the very White-looking Mr. Denison were not meant as a compliment" (342). The emphasis Bogle adds to the whiteness, and his clarification, lest the reader misunderstand, that whiteness is not an asset in a sexual partner, reflect a fascination with the politics of skin that limits the insight of Bogle's thoroughly researched biography.

14. Walter Leavy, "The Real Life Tragedy of Dorothy Dandridge," *Ebony*, September 1986, 136–37; Louie Robinson, "Dorothy Dandridge: Hollywood's Tragic Enigma," *Ebony*, March 1966, 71; Bogle, *Dorothy Dandridge*, 123.

15. *Jet* extended the aura of pathos to her daughter by publishing a story by Charles Sanders entitled, "Tragic Story of Dandridge's Retarded Daughter," August 22, 1963, 22–27. See also Walter Leavy, "The Mystery and Real Life Tragedy of Dorothy Dandridge," *Ebony*, December 1993, 36–42, and Leavy, "Real Life Tragedy";

Robinson, "Dorothy Dandridge"; and Dandridge's promotional, posthumous auto-biography, Dorothy Dandridge and Earl Conrad, *Everything and Nothing: The Dorothy Dandridge Tragedy* (New York: Abelard-Schuman, 1970), which served as the basis for the HBO film, *Introducing Dorothy Dandridge*, first airing on August 21, 1999.

16. This number was accompanied by the Mills Brothers song, "Paper Doll."

17. Bogle, *Dorothy Dandridge*, 92.

18. Steinem, "Women in the Dark," 37. Dyer, "Monroe and Sexuality," 21, similarly comments that Monroe was frequently photographed from the side to accentuate the physical features of her figure and was "set up as an object of male sexual gaze."

19. Agent Earl Mills told Bogle that Dandridge was "concerned about the myth a lot of people had about black women and their sexual activities." Bogle, *Dorothy Dandridge*, 259.

20. Ibid., 256.

21. Ibid., 201.

22. Ibid., 477–79.

23. Dyer argues that Monroe associated herself with a new "naturalized" mode of sexuality by unapologetically becoming the first *Playboy* centerfold in 1953, posing for the nude calendar shot of *Golden Dreams*, and doing a nude bathing scene in the unfinished *Something's Got to Give*. In addition, Monroe's sexual quips were so associated with her that they became known as "Monroeisms." One famous example was the line delivered to the American troops in Korea: "I don't know why you boys are always getting excited about sweater girls. Take away their sweaters and what have they got?" Dyer, "Monroe and Sexuality," 26, 36.

24. *Time* reprinted two full paragraphs of lyrics. First, in 1952 the magazine reprinted lyrics from "Love Isn't Born, It's Made," in "Eye and Ear Specialist," *Time*, February 4, 1952, 50; then the following stanza in 1955: "Never mind the noise in the market / Only mind the price of the fish / Remove your nose from the grindstone / And do the things you wish," in "Two for the Show," *Time*, May 2, 1955, 42. In 1955, *Ebony* pictured her with a caged canary in "Dorothy Dandridge's Greatest Triumph," July 1955, 37–41. This figure alludes to the lyrics reproduced in a *Life* article about her act, "Put me in a cage and I'll be your canary," as well as her performance at the birdcage-decorated club Mocambo. "Shy No More," *Life*, November 5, 1951, 68. Later, in *Tamango*, she is introduced in a scene with caged birds (see Figure 9.7).

25. Robinson, "Dorothy Dandridge," 76.

26. "Eye and Ear," 50.

27. "Two for the Show," 42.

28. Gardner was working on her role as the tragic mulatto Julie in *Showboat* at the time, suggesting that Moore was a master not only of feminine wiles, but also of racialized female sexuality.

29. "Eye and Ear," 50.

30. "Shy No More," 67.

31. Leavy, "Real Life Tragedy," 137. This article appears to be a rewrite of Rob-

inson, "Dorothy Dandridge," and was edited and republished by *Ebony*, December 1993, 36–42.

32. Dandridge and Conrad, *Everything and Nothing*, 86. In this somewhat suspect posthumous "autobiography," Dandridge confesses the rehearsed nature of the sexuality of her nightclub act, saying, "By this time I had learned how to present myself. . . . I swayed in a sinuous way as I sang . . . the numbers Phil Moore wrote for me" (84). Quotations from Dandridge's autobiography should not necessarily be taken as authentic because the manuscript was unfinished at the time of her suicide and was not published until five years later by coauthor Earl Conrad. In addition, it contains contradictory passages that recapitulate many misogynist notions of her passivity.

33. Dyer, "Monroe and Sexuality," 41.

34. Dyer provides a thorough discussion of Monroe's naturalized image in *Heavenly Bodies*, and for a discussion of Billy Wilder as Monroe's Svengali, see "Walk Like This, Marilyn," *Life*, 20 April 1959), 101–4.

35. Bogle provides a thorough discussion of this incident in *Dorothy Dandridge*, 54–57.

36. Like Grable's famous pin-up shot, many of these photos use the awkward over-the-shoulder pose to focus on the woman's rear end while including the obligatory face. In the weeks surrounding Dandridge's death, *Jet* featured numerous such shots, including "Yummy Yvonne," September 11, 1965, 34, and "Bottoms Up," September 16, 1965, 37. "On and Off," September 11, 1965, 33, featured the "Stars 'n' Stripes panty girdle," and was pulled from the market following a protest by the Daughters of the American Revolution. Again, the confrontation of "Americanness" vs. feminine sexuality and race caused political controversy and economic crisis.

37. "This Week's Best Photos: A Sultry Sex Symbol," *Jet*, September 1965, 31.

38. Leavy, "Real Life Tragedy," 137.

39. "Mocambo," *Variety*, September 16, 1953, 55.

40. Ibid., 55.

41. "Two for the Show," 42.

42. The ambivalence of Monroe's resistance to objectification can be noted in her last print interview with *Life* in which she said, "That's the trouble, a sex symbol becomes a thing—I just hate to be a thing. But if I'm going to be a symbol of something, I'd rather have it be sex" (quoted in Dyer, "Monroe and Sexuality," 61).

43. "Is Dandridge Too Sexy for Television?" *Hue*, May 1957, 55.

44. Quoted in Bogle, *Dorothy Dandridge*, 374.

45. "On the 'Bright Road' of 'Carmen' and 'Joe,'" *New York Times*, October 24, 1954, 5–6 (X); Nancy Seely, "The Road Ahead for *Carmen*," *New York Post*, November 7, 1954.

46. "The Whole Nation is Flipping for Carmen," *Variety*, November 17, 1954, 10–12.

47. Ibid., 10.

48. Bogle, *Dorothy Dandridge*, 266.

49. The physicality of this scene also suggests that black actors and actresses

were seen as more "expendable" commodities than their white counterparts. It is remarkable that Dandridge was able to run on a moving train in high-heeled pumps, much less that she was directed to jump from the train and be thrown to the ground by her costar.

50. Bogle, *Dorothy Dandridge*, 293.

51. *Brown v Board of Education* was tried in 1954; Rosa Parks's initiation of the bus boycott occurred in 1955. Explicitly, race and interracial marriage were undergoing redefinition; the *Perez v Lippold* California decision in 1948 declared state miscegenation law unconstitutional, but the Virginia *Loving v Commonwealth* miscegenation case challenged the *Perez* decision between 1958 and 1967.

52. *Tarzan's Peril* also elicited visual pleasure through physical bondage. According to a 1951 *Life* magazine caption of Dandridge bound and gagged in this role, "Her part so impressed producer that role was enlarged." "Shy No More," 67.

53. Quoted in Bogle, *Dorothy Dandridge*, 322.

54. Quoted in ibid., 478.

55. Ibid., 375.

56. Michael Omi. "In Living Color: Race and American Culture," in *Signs of Life in the USA*, ed. Sonia Maasik and Mark Solomon (Boston: St. Martin's Press, 1994), 458.

57. After *Carmen Jones*, the only film in which she played an African-American woman, was *Porgy and Bess* (1959), another Preminger-directed remake of a successful American musical.

58. Bogle, *Dorothy Dandridge*, 327.

59. "Dorothy Dandridge's Greatest Triumph," 38.

60. Quoted in Bogle, *Dorothy Dandridge*, 183.

61. *Tamango*, dir. John Berry (Charlotte, NC: Ivy Classics Video), 1992.

62. Louie Robinson, "Why Dandridge Can't Kiss Her White Film Lover: Torrid New Love Story Stars Interracial Love Code Debate," *Jet*, December 13, 1956, 56–61.

63. Ibid., 58.

64. Bogle refers to these roles as "the gypsies, the 'half-breeds,' the Asians, the pretty Native American squaws . . . the tragic mulattoes." *Dorothy Dandridge*, 317.

65. Robinson, "Why Dandridge Can't Kiss," 58.

66. Frantz Fanon, *Black Skin, White Masks* (New York: Grove Press, 1967), 159.

67. Fleury initially provides a fascinating rebuttal to Fanon's assertion that "a white man in a colony has never felt inferior in any respect . . . ." (Ibid., 92). Maxwell embodies the disintegration of the colonial structure of family and nation, illuminating the complexity of Fanon's assertion that "there are close connections between the structure of the family and the structure of the nation" (141).

68. Quoted in Bogle, *Dorothy Dandridge*, 384.

69. Dandridge invoked racial solidarity when attacked either by dominant white discourse for her "un-American" associations or by black organizations like the NAACP for her controversial portrayals of a sexually objectified black woman, which did not fit contemporary notions for the "advancement of colored people."

70. Bogle, *Dorothy Dandridge*, 332–33.

71. Dandridge and Conrad, *Everything and Nothing*, 183.

72. Many recent critics have written on the commodification of the female star to sell domestic products during this era. See, for example, Charles Eckert, "The Carole Lombard in Macy's Window," or Charlotte Cornelia Herzog and Jane Marie Gaines, "Puffed Sleeves Before Tea-Time" in *Stardom: Industry of Desire*, ed. Christine Gledhill (London: Routledge, 1991). In addition, Dyer discusses the contradictory demands placed on female stars in his essay, "Four Films of Lana Turner" in *Star Texts: Image and Performance in Film and Television*, ed. Jeremy Butler (Detroit: Wayne State University Press, 1991), 214–39.

73. This phrase was popularized by *Ebony* in 1962 ("The Private World," 117). *Ebony* also declared Dandridge "Hollywood's first and only authentic Negro love goddess" in 1966 (Robinson, "Dorothy Dandridge," 71); and "Hollywood's first authentic Black sex symbol" in 1986 (Leavy, "Real Life Tragedy," 136) and in 1993 (Leavy, "The Mystery and Real Life Tragedy," 36).

74. In 1962, *Ebony* published an article featuring Dandridge's idyllic Hollywood home and husband, Jack Denison—a short time before she would file for both bankruptcy and divorce. She is described as a "sex symbol . . . the world over," but pictures feature Dandridge lounging in various rooms of her house, the text explaining that "next to her career, interior decorating rates as her principal interest." She is shown spending a quiet evening with her husband after dinner, which Dorothy, "a homebody, likes to prepare . . . at home herself." (Louie Robinson, "The Private World of Dorothy Dandridge," *Ebony*, June 1962, 116–17, 121.) Earlier in the 1955 article, "Dorothy Dandridge's Greatest Triumph," *Ebony* had already begun depicting Dandridge as an erotic homemaker, referring to her as the "curvaceous Miss Dandridge" (37), but quoting her as saying, "If I have a hobby, I guess it's fancy cooking" (40). *Jet* also endorsed Dandridge's domestic image, with an article titled "Will Marriage Hurt Dandridge's Career? Career Always Secondary to Husband Says Screen Star," (April 9, 1959), 14–16.

75. Robinson, "Dorothy Dandridge," 75.

76. Karen Alexander expresses her frustration as a black female reader with *Ebony*'s sexist format and discusses Dandridge's relationship to misogyny in "Fatal Beauties: Black Women in Hollywood," Gledhill, *Stardom*, 45–54.

77. Again, words attributed to Dandridge in her dubious autobiography: "So many white men think there is nothing sweeter than having a brown boff on the side, under wraps, taken in the dark or kept behind the scenes" (Dandridge and Conrad, *Everything and Nothing*, 104).

78. In part, I am recalling Mary Ann Doane's warning to feminist readers that "anatomy is destiny only if the concept of destiny is recognized for what it really is: a concept proper to fiction."

79. Berry won the question, at least temporarily: she played the title role in the 1999 HBO production, *Introducing Dorothy Dandridge*.

10

ORIENTALISM
ABROAD

Hong Kong
Readings of
The World of
Suzie Wong

Gary W. McDonogh and
Cindy Hing-Yuk Wong

A few days after Hong Kong's July 1, 1997, transition from British sovereignty to reunion with China, the *South China Morning Post* reviewed a new book about local prostitution under the feature headline "Sex after Suzie Wong." The article thus highlighted a novelistic/film narrative as a symbolic landmark in local "history":

> The fictional Cinderella *World of Suzie Wong* . . . caught the colour of 1950s Wan Chai when swaggering matelots roamed the bars looking for rest and recreation (known as R & R), love and laughter.
>
> But it failed to capture the harsh realities of a life serving sex. . . .
>
> Wan Chai's neon-lit streets were home to hundreds of brothels, dance halls and massage-parlours in Suzie's days. . . .
>
> Whereas Suzie and her sisters were usually mainlanders, the modern day Suzie Wong is a Filipina or Thai girl who came after hearing of the relative riches that can be earned. . . .[1]

This juxtaposition of an English author's 1950s fantasy-turned-Hollywood-romance to the 1997 political events marking the fate of 6.5 million people seems incongruous. Yet, it nonetheless reflects relations of nation, race, power, and representation that have shaped Hong Kong's existence and the gazes that interpret and challenge these power relations.

Given the global presence of Hollywood, the reference to Suzie Wong was not unfamiliar to many readers, including British colonials, American expatriates, Chinese, and others. A key symbol for those whose dream or experience of Hong Kong had been shaped by mass media, the figure of Suzie Wong, in fact, recurred in handover commemorative issues produced by *Time, Newsweek*, and the *Far Eastern Economic Review*. Even a sober *Reuter's* report on economic development began "Suzie Wong has straightened out her life and is studying for a business degree." [2] For Chinese, however, who constitute the primary population of Hong Kong, such a pervasive symbol seemed mystifying, erroneous, irrelevant, or insulting. Apart from the reductionism that the Suzie Wong story represents, this myth is also perceived to be a historical artifact of colonialism, drawn from texts that few really know. Hence, divided readings of the movie provide powerful illuminations of the impacts of Hollywood film across time and space, especially when race, class, and gender are projected and read across cultures.

Cinema, as a communicative medium, long has cut across boundaries of race and nation even as it transformed accounts of both. This transnationalism took on unique dimensions in the case of Classical Hollywood Cinema. Despite the competition and resistance in other nations, Hollywood's stars, images, and ideology filled screens from Berlin to Buenos Aires, Hong Kong to London. Alternative flows emerged, of course, in the migration of stars, directors, and themes to Hollywood as well as in the more limited American reception of foreign art, documentary, and ethnic films. Yet, this unbalanced globalism, which transcends cinema to characterize the strengths and blindnesses of the American century itself, poses special problems when cultural constructions like race and gender were exposed to audiences distant from the norms that Hollywood took for granted. Sometimes a Hollywood portrayal evoked empathy: African-American scholars have shared with us the improbable popularity of *Imitation of Life* (1959) in Caribbean communities negotiating their intricacies of family and color. Other visions proved problematic: China banned Harold Lloyd's *Welcome Danger* (1929) when riots broke out in Shanghai. In another example, Hong Kong's British censors at that time forbade depictions of either white women in indecorous clothing or armed conflict between Chinese and whites in order to protect "a small settlement of white men on the fringe of an Empire of Asiatics." [3] Still, Western traditions of representation of the East, embodied in opera, travel literature, and early films constituted a discourse of Orientalism on which Hollywood frequently drew.[4]

The World of Suzie Wong (1960) long has been taken as emblematic of Holly-wood's Orientalization of both Asians and women.[5] Yet, as a South Asian stu-dent from Hong Kong, trained in an American university, recalled to us, this perception is also learned within American cultural discourses:

> I saw the movie *The World of Suzie Wong*, in a class at _____ entitled "The Portrayal of Asian Women in Hollywood." The movie definitely con-veyed the idea that Chinese women were desperate to find the means to escape their circumstance—and in order to do so—it had to be a "white Male" who would be able to take care of her and her debts and problems. One needs to keep in mind—the time period in which this film was made, after World War II when things were bad in Asia and the main aim was to find a way to survive—and in this case, if it meant prostitu-tion, it had to be done.

Here, her reading has absorbed both film criticism and historical sources in order to interpret the film as a document about her homeland. Still, it would have been unlikely that she would have seen the film at all in Hong Kong.

This doubly transnational reading suggests why *The World of Suzie Wong* presents such a compelling case in understanding Classical Hollywood's con-struction of race. From its origins as a novel by a British colonial wanderer in Asia, through its years on the London and New York stage, to its movie pro-duction in Hong Kong and British studios, to its reading as a movie in the-aters, on television, and in classrooms, the implications of the film's depic-tion of race, gender, and power have spilled beyond Hollywood or America. In Hong Kong, its ostensible location, both plot and images were refracted by the divisions between colonized Chinese subjects and white expatriates and colo-nizers in that society, in the 1960s and through the territory's subsequent eco-nomic expansion. Our ethnography of these readings—based on interviews and archival resources (newspapers, fan magazines, and government reports) as well as later intertexts in film, criticism, and everyday life—also underscore issues of power, control of representation, and memory that have taken on special importance within a changing Hong Kong. These include the diverse meanings of imperial America vis-à-vis the global status of Hong Kong and the quest for authentic, hybrid Hong Kong identities.

We begin with the plot and images of the film (and to a lesser extent, its re-lation to the novel and play), recognizing issues covered cogently by Gina Mar-chetti in *Romance and the "Yellow Peril"* (1992) and clarifying the film's impli-cations outside the prism of Classical Hollywood expectations. We then move to Hong Kong interpretations of *The World of Suzie Wong* that emerged be-tween late 1959 and 1961, from the film's location shooting through its premiere there. Readings from Chinese and English press, as well as memories of those who saw it in its early screenings, underscore fundamental ruptures of colonial Hong Kong. These, in turn, foreshadow two streams of subsequent interpretation that embody and reproduce divisions of race, culture, class, and participation in Hong Kong life. The first, dominated by an expatriate (Anglo-American) imagination, has taken *The World of Suzie Wong* as a key symbol of the "authentic" Hong Kong, expressing a reality (now lost) of race, space, and relations. The second, which we found to dominate memory and interpretation within the Chinese population of Hong Kong, is based on *non-viewing*, coupled with artifactual knowledge. That is, although people almost invariably reported that they had never seen the film, they had clear images of "what it was about" and how it represented Western racism toward Chinese. Yet, we also encountered intellectual reflections on the movie, including Peter Chan's film, *Tiim Mat Mat* (*Comrades, Almost a Love Story*, 1996), which raise different and significant questions about the reconstitution of Hong Kong as a hybrid society.

SUZIE'S WORLDS: THE FORMATION OF TRANSNATIONAL TEXTS

The mythic framework of *The World of Suzie Wong* scarcely originated with Richard Mason's popular novel, which drew successfully on older Anglo-American stereotypes of Asian women, the seductiveness of forbidden love, and beautiful prostitutes in exotic locations waiting to be saved by white men. Mason, a novelist and screenwriter, specialized in works dealing with interracial relations in tropical climes of the British Empire. After finishing a novel in Jamaica, he claimed that he chose Hong Kong on impulse. Here, his encounter with his new "plot" became a creation myth in its right, reconstructed as a scene in the novel and movie:

> I went down the first night to have my *chow fan* [fried rice], and saw all these women in the bar and I realized that it was virtually a brothel. I was thrilled. . . . At the time I had no idea at all and thought it was just an ordinary hotel. But I thought "This is fabulous, I've found it!" From that moment I knew I had my book. I thought that was unbelievable, like a gift from God." [6]

This mythic framework also divorced Mason and his fictional avatars from ongoing transformations of Hong Kong in the 1950s and 1960s. After being decimated under Japanese occupation, Hong Kong's population and economic structure after 1949 faced an influx of capital and people from the newly Communist mainland. Refugees ranged from wealthy Shanghainese entrepreneurs to others trapped in crowded, dangerous squatter settlements. These produced new linguistic, regional, and class divisions in the city alongside other plural elements already shaped by decades of colonialism. Immigration and isolation also spurred growth, and, in time, a new sense of Hong Kong identity.[7] Some in Britain and the colony had spoken of self-determination for Hong Kong after World War II, but regional political development in the post-war period shifted the colonial government to a policy of wariness toward the Communist north and appeasement of local Chinese through social programs and economic development. A coalition of British colonial interests and Hong Kong Chinese elites has underpinned subsequent Hong Kong growth and globalization. Although squatters and refugees in *The World of Suzie Wong* serve as markers of the Communist threat, social divisions beyond a simple biracial colonial society carry little textual weight in this highly individual love story.[8]

Yet in the same interview cited above, which grounded the "reality" of his text, Mason hedged about the individuality of his title character:

> Suzie Wong was a mixture of the different girls in the bar that I observed. She was certainly not based on just one girl. . . . There was, I think a girl called Suzie who, because I used her name in the book, thought it must be her and even consulted a lawyer to sue me, but it didn't work. Because it wasn't her. I just thought Suzie was a good name, rather like naming a pet, you look for a good name. Then the Wong came.[9]

The image of an impoverished Chinese prostitute reading an English book and consulting a barrister to interact with the colonial courts is completely foreign to the realities of post-war Hong Kong. This interview, however, evokes not only the specter of the "real Suzie," which has haunted local/expatriate reading ever since, but also a more characteristic Orientalist distance: "rather like naming a pet" remains a harsh image.

Mason's novel became a best seller, despite critical reservations. The play adaptation reached Broadway in 1958: hence, readings of *The World of Suzie Wong* were established even before the movie took shape. *New York Times* drama critic Brooks Atkinson caustically noted that *The World of Suzie Wong* "omitted nothing that will fascinate the tired businessman and fill his little heart with hope."[10] Not surprisingly, this flashy melodrama, with its melange of "smiling, chatterish, girlish prostitutes, amorous sailors, Chinese peddlers, unctuous hotel keepers, deferential police and other theatrical symbols of the inscrutable East,"[11] was a Broadway hit, complementing the more "respectable" contemporary imagery of decorous Asian-Americans in *Flower Drum Song*.

Figure 10.1. Gender and social roles on display in the Broadway version of *The World of Suzie Wong*. (Image courtesy of Friedman-Abeles.)

On Broadway, Suzie was played by France Nuyen, a Marseilles-born actress of Vietnamese, Chinese, and French descent. Tsai Chin, a Shanghai-born actress, took over the role in London. Again, critics dismissed its thin plot and exotic titillation; in her autobiography, Chin cites a *Daily Mail* column entitled, "Are We Being Corrupted by Suzy Wong?"[12] Despite such reviews, the play ran for two years and again prepared other readings for the film and for Hong Kong. As Chin recalls:

> For a pretty flimsy play it was incredible how much of a stir *Suzie Wong* created. The name Suzie Wong became synonymous with the oriental tart with a heart. Real London tarts adopted the name when advertising their charms in newsagents' windows. In Hong Kong tourists were trekking down to Wan Chai in hopes of catching a glimpse of the real person who, according to the author, never existed.[13]

Chin also decries the fashion craze that led London women to dye their hair black, pencil their eyes into an almond shape, and wear cheong-sams, the tightly-cut dress that became associated with Suzie: "Walking and sitting in a slit skirt requires grace of movement and the high-buttoned collar requires grace of movement." [14] Clothes, in fact, became a recurrent component of myths of race and sexuality.

The novel, play, and movie—and their cumulative readings—constituted over time a "multimedia" complex. The narrative follows Robert Lomax (and his subjectivity) through the twin struggles of becoming an established painter and developing a relationship with the vivacious, suspicious but innocent bargirl, Suzie Wong. Here, we concentrate on the movie, while noting some critical changes from earlier media. In the novel, for example, Lomax is British, escaping the colonial tedium of rubber plantations. In the film, he becomes an American architect (William Holden), escaping business. The novel also provides both background and a later history for the romantic pair after Hong Kong.

Clearly, the film exults in the visual spectacle of Hong Kong as a critical device within its narrative. The movie begins, for example, on the Star Ferry crossing from Kowloon to Hong Kong, providing a panoramic gaze of the center city well known to tourists, readers, and filmmakers today. On this ride, the newly arrived Robert begins to sketch Chinese passengers, establishing his vocation and his observer's relation to the local population. Among those he sketches is a Western-garbed young Chinese girl, who objects vehemently and even calls upon the police to deter his attentions. Nonetheless, he overcomes this initial barrier, and Mei-Ling (Nancy Kwan) eventually regales Robert with stories of her wealthy father and arranged marriage.

In the crowd leaving the ferry, Robert loses sight of the girl, but directs his attention to settling down. Ignoring a Chinese policeman's warning that Wan Chai is "not for him," he heads for this Chinese district, where location shots again immerse him in Chinese crowds and highlight differences in food, customs, and faces. Glimpsing Mei-Ling leaving the Nam Kwok hotel, he enters to inquire about her and decides to stay in the ramshackle but spacious room he finds there, to the bemusement of the proprietor. Robert later descends to the bar and encounters a parade of Chinese women and British sailors, who foreshadow his eventual realization that his newfound residence is actually a brothel. As he chats with girls there, he recognizes Mei-Ling, who is revealed to be the bargirl, Suzie Wong.

Robert engages Suzie as a model, with no sexual services required. She, however, tells the other girls that he is her wealthy boyfriend, so jealous that he beats her, which she portrays as a mark of commitment. As their romance grows, Suzie shows him around the city. Here, she is clearly the guide and dominant figure in most Chinese-language (location) shots, while the ro-

Figure 10.2. France Nuyen in a cheong-sam, on Broadway. (Image courtesy of Photofest.)

mance and other narratives are primarily advanced in the British studio shots. This contrast defines not only diegetic space but also questions of authenticity and historical record that shape later appreciations of the film. Local scenes also established important intertextual relations to other Hollywood Hong Kong films, especially the 1956 *Love is a Many-Splendored Thing,* in which William

Figure 10.3. Suzie (Nancy Kwan) dancing with a sailor in the 1960 film. (Image courtesy of Photofest; Bert Cann, photographer.)

Holden, as an American journalist in Hong Kong, wins a beautiful Eurasian doctor (non-Asian Jennifer Jones).[15]

Robert is almost always portrayed as solid, dedicated and just, although insensitive to Suzie's feelings for him. He becomes, in Gina Marchetti's term, a "White Knight," saving a prostitute and finding his own salvation.[16] Suzie,

Figure 10.4. Suzie (Nancy Kwan) as a guide in Hong Kong. (Image courtesy of Photofest.)

although poor and sexually exploited, is beautiful, intelligent, and resourceful. Her knowledge of the everyday world of Hong Kong Chinese—evoked via
vivid filmic postcards—stands in continual contrast to Robert's knowledge of
an outside world (which dominates Hong Kong). As their relationship grows,
Robert also discovers that Suzie has a child, Winston, whom she leaves with

Figure 10.5. William Holden between two worlds. (Image courtesy of Photofest.)

an amah in a dense hillside squatter settlement and whom Robert carries paternally in their excursions. Through Suzie, Robert experiences a "Chinese" Hong Kong he does not initially understand but appropriates through his art.

On a visual and narrative level, Robert also deals with British society ensconced in bank offices, elegant hotel restaurants, and spacious homes. Through his initial letter of introduction to a local banker, he deals with men and women whose façades reveal scheming duplicity underneath. The daughter of the banker, for example, strives for his affection by sharing and marketing his vision of the Chinese "other," rather than by entering his Chinese world. Her intrusion in the hotel produces a direct visual and narrative confrontation. A married British businessman, moreover, takes Suzie as a mistress until he is forced to seek Robert's help in ridding himself of his Chinese burden.

Race is thus defined asymmetrically throughout *The World of Suzie Wong.* There is almost no discussion of Robert's racial identity; "white" was an unmarked category for Hollywood as well as for Hong Kong colonial domination. Suzie recognizes (and, at times, uses) his English fluency, style, and access to colonial society in Hong Kong and abroad. Nonetheless, British colonial hy-

Figure 10.6. Race, sex, and violence in *The World of Suzie Wong* (1960). (Image courtesy of Photofest.)

pocrisy is underscored through scenes depicting the public horror over liaisons between "white" men and Chinese women, which are nevertheless constant features of Wan Chai (the obverse case is never even brought up). Moreover, emotional and physical brutality mark these relations, as seen in the encounters of white sailors and businessmen with bargirls. Against this, Robert Lomax establishes his superiority by his tolerance and gentleness, even as he paints an Orientalized vision of Suzie's Chineseness.

The Chinese society of Hong Kong, however, is reduced to brothels, squatters, and exotic tourist sites, inhabited by a single stratum and almost a single gender whose Chineseness is embodied in face, language, and clothes. Nor can Suzie enter the British world, as we are reminded when her unease in a posh restaurant (identified with the historic Peninsula Hotel in later readings) undercuts her cleverness and beauty. Here, her illiteracy forces her to point to the menu, ordering a "vinaigrette" as her dinner, which Lomax gallantly shares.

As Marchetti has noted, clothes also represent important signifiers for race and class in this movie as in *Love is a Many-Splendored Thing*.[17] White characters wear generally nondescript Western clothes throughout the movie, although men are clearly divided between suits and uniforms. Suzie shifts from casual "Western" attire in the opening scene (slacks, blouse, and raincoat) to the cheong-sam at work. The contrast of the banker's daughter and Suzie is also one of ball gown and cheong-sam as well as race and class. Robert, however, rejects Western clothes for Suzie in the most brutal scene of the film, where he strips her of a newly bought Western dress provided by the businessman who keeps her. Authenticity, for him, is embodied in the archaic Chinese costumes of his portraits or, more commonly, the cheong-sam. The film visually insists that this costume is emblematic of the prostitute. In fact, it was the common wear of Hong Kong Chinese women of the time, from school uniforms to elegant party dresses, but these women *never appear* in *The World of Suzie Wong*. Prostitutes probably wore cheong-sams, cut tighter or higher, but the dress had many meanings.[18] Nonetheless, this brutality over clothes and correct behavior graphically undermines Robert's superior stance and leads to a critical rupture in his relations with Suzie.

Despite differences, love triumphs over race, class, and sex, glorifying American inclusiveness over colonial prejudice.[19] Suzie turns to Robert at the climax of the film to help her save her child when a monsoon destroys the squatter settlement. Robert at first defies the Chinese police evacuating the camp and then breaks through the line to save Suzie, although her child is lost. In the final scene, Suzie, Robert, and her friends among the bargirls burn incense and gifts for the child, including a "letter of introduction" like that which Robert had used to enter British society, which Suzie sought for her child entering a new world. The lovers walk off, then, to an unspecified future.

While condemning one racism, Hollywood conceals the essentialization inherent in Robert and Suzie's relationship of power and knowledge. Suzie Wong is certainly strong, resilient, and smart, and there are times when any audience might share her subjectivity. But all in all, the audience is textually placed to see her world through the eyes of Robert, white, male, and American, and to be relieved when Suzie is united with his world. What if the audience cannot share that position?

LOCAL READINGS: FROM PRODUCTION
TO SCREENING IN HONG KONG, 1959–1961

By 1959, Hong Kong location shooting began on the movie version of *The World of Suzie Wong*. When stars France Nuyen and William Holden arrived in the city in late December, "the 20-year-old Eurasian beauty" [20] quickly captured press attention. Yet hers was not an uncritical reception: a reporter noted that "Miss Nuyen, daughter of a Chinese father and a French mother, told reporters that she could not speak Chinese but was learning how to" and that she had never traveled to Asia. Another racial/cultural issue emerged when Nuyen was asked whether she preferred "an American or a Chinese as a companion." [21] She tactfully avoided any direct issues, although the press already had mentioned her Hollywood liaison with Marlon Brando.

Paramount publicity threw both stars into local society, including parties and charity events for the New Year lavishly covered by the English and Chinese dailies. As shooting started in January, the English press continued to praise Nuyen's beauty and discipline, sometimes with highly Orientalist imagery, while underscoring her lack of local knowledge. One telling vignette depicted her painfully practicing Chinese writing while asking her tutor "Does this look like anything to you?" [22] Nonetheless, movie critic Alan Castro lauded Nuyen's efforts to explore the city in her free time. Moreover, "Hongkong, incorrigibly blasé . . . about celebrities, has taken quickly to this fascinating young film actress. Everywhere she goes, France attracts attention. And they say 'There's Suzie Wong'—a sure sign that France Nuyen will be remembered here well and long." [23] Or did it, indeed, suggest how much she and the character stood out?

The representation of Hong Kong itself also captured press attention.[24] The novel had already demanded some emblematic location scenes—the Star Ferry, Wan Chai, Aberdeen harbor (Figure 10.4)—and long shots of the port and squatter settlements. These were also tourist "places to see" in Hong Kong (although Robert paints people, rather than places, as S. N. Ko shrewdly notes).[25] The crowded boats and floating restaurants of Aberdeen, for example, also figured in *Love is a Many-Splendored Thing*, as well as in Princess Alexandra's 1960 state visit.[26] Still, the very language of the *Hong Kong Tiger Standard* evokes expatriate distance from everyday Chinese life. References abound to "the *famous* Wanchai *native* market" or "the *incredible* congestion of junks, floating homes and restaurants at Aberdeen's Tai Pak pier."[27] By contrast, a Chinese viewer complained "they only chose the worst parts of Hong Kong—none of the nice Chinese areas." Wan Chai had respectable residential zones, but Suzie's worlds were defined by outsiders looking for Hong Kong rather than multiple levels of Chinese urban/colonial life.

We found little Chinese daily news about production, except for *Sing Tao Daily*'s society page snippets.[28] However, a popular Chinese-language movie magazine, the *Milky Way Pictorial* (*Ngan Ho Wah Pao*) made *The World of Suzie Wong* a centerpiece. Here, Nuyen's race and cultural authenticity dominated coverage. In a section entitled "She is an Oriental flower," for example, author Lau Seung Ngan asserted that Nuyen's "skin is between yellow and dark, nice brows, small cherry mouth; the nose is not as horribly high as with other Europeans."[29] Compared to local actresses, "in terms of beauty, she is not as pretty as Lin Dai and You Man; in terms of figure, she is not as shapely as Yip Fung and Ge Lan. However, she has her own style, that the others cannot match."[30] Questions of identity soon became murky, mingling heritage and commitment:

> Nuyen wore a tight sweater, a tight Western skirt, just like a Chinese Cheong-sam. . . . She looks like a black peony. Her hairstyle is Italian, . . . very European. Nevertheless this French Chinese Eurasian has a great deal of Chinese "blood." She is like an Oriental flower, embodying Chinese seeds. Although she has European mannerisms, that's because she was born and raised in Europe. After coming to the East, given time, she will become more Asian because of the "constitution" of her blood.[31]

Ongoing interests in Nuyen's racial heritage, cultural style, and language skills all appealed to fundamental themes in a continuing Chinese discussion of racial purity/superiority.[32] Nuyen was attractive but ambiguous as a "Chinese" woman, and this issue eclipsed concerns with her role.

Milky Way, like the *Standard*, paid less attention to William Holden, presumably because Hong Kong readers were already familiar with him from *Love is a Many-Splendored Thing* and his international stardom. Moreover, while the earlier film had confirmed him as a White Knight for the "Hollywood" audience, Holden kept an apartment in Hong Kong and invested in local broadcasting. At a party hosted by local hotel and movie tycoon Lok War-Tho of Din Mah Studios, Holden mingled with the Hong Kong elite and local stars like Grace Chan and Dolly Soo (while Nuyen stayed home).[33] While filming *The World of Suzie Wong*, he also worked with CBS News on a documentary about Hong Kong life, as experienced through the lives of three men and their families: a poor Chinese refugee, an English executive, and a member of the new Chinese elite. This bridged the worlds he represented in the two films. As critic S. N. Ko later noted when this documentary was revived for the Hong Kong International Film Festival, this brief TV piece came much closer to expressing the complexities of Hong Kong lives than did Hollywood depictions, although the documentary shared the same "aesthetic" vision.[34] Later, Holden's Hong Kong obituary even quoted him rather curiously as saying that "I think Hong Kong and the name Holden have become synonymous."[35] Both *Milky Way* and the *Standard* treated Holden as a "host" for Nuyen, an inversion of their on-screen identities. Still, the former pointedly questioned Holden as a language teacher, hoping that Nuyen's Chinese would surpass that of Ingrid Bergman in *Inn of the Sixth Happiness* (1958) (and thus reiterating Nuyen's problem of authenticity).[36]

In opposition to Hollywood and its audiences, the *Milky Way* article concluded with a more significant appeal to an imagined Asian community of race, language, and culture:

> When Westerners look at Eastern theater and cinema all they want is novelty. Easterners looking at Eastern theater and cinema are asking for realism. Although movies that used Hong Kong as a backdrop, like *Love is a Many Splendoured Thing* . . . had good box office in the West, Hong Kong people do not find them very real.[37]

Milky Way's primary focus was not Hollywood but Hong Kong moviemaking, which had already begun to enter a golden age. Hence, *The World of Suzie Wong* was not perceived as a "screen opportunity" for Hong Kong, as the English-language press saw it, so much as an alternative representation with biases that could be readily criticized.

The range of Hong Kong cinema at the time may also explain *Milky Way's* lack of concern with the depiction of a Chinese prostitute that has preoccupied other critics, including Anglo-American feminists. Labeled *Fung Chin Lui Ze* (literally "wind, dust girls"), women of dubious reputation, working in bars and dance halls, were already established characters in local films. In 1960, for example, Grace Chan (Ge Lan), a major star, played a seductive bar singer in *The Wild Wild Rose* (*Ye Mui Gwai Tzi Lun*), very loosely adapted from Bizet's *Carmen*. Despite her Westernized costumes and the heady Hong Kong nightclub ambience (including a few Western faces in the audience), the story is very "traditional." It focuses on filial responsibility and the moral decay of a schoolteacher, who abandons his mother and fiancée to pursue the singer, only to kill her at the end. Another movie, *Her Sister's Keeper* (*Tzi Mui Ching*

Sau, 1961), deals with a woman who works as a dance hall girl in order to put her younger sister through college. *Fung Chin Lui Ze* could be selfless, giving up their futures, love, and happiness for their families or helping their loved ones. Such vital framing social relations were absent for Suzie in *The World of Suzie Wong*, emphasizing its myopic view of Chinese life.[38]

Problems emerged in the production, however, which had nothing to do with its Hong Kong settings or racial attitudes. In early February, with location shooting complete, Nuyen suddenly withdrew from the picture. Paramount, offering multiple and contradictory explanations, launched a global search for a replacement.[39] Among the possibilities named in Hong Kong news were Lin Dai, Hong Kong's top female movie star; Japanese actress Nobu McCarthy; Natalie Wood; Hong Kong ingenue Nancy Kwan; and some Filipina stars. The list shows Hollywood's "flexibility" in casting Chinese roles, as Jennifer Jones had already shown in *Love is a Many-Splendored Thing*. Yet it may also reveal a play for Chinese markets. Lin Dai, in particular, treated the news as a publicity stunt inasmuch as she already had signed with Shaw Brothers studios for the next six months.[40]

Certainly, from the moment the Hong Kong press announced Kwan's selection, she was packaged as a "local girl conquering Hollywood." Kwan's father was a Hong Kong Chinese architect and her mother, an English model. The *Standard* elaborated on a Eurasian mystique in its front page story: "Daintily lovely in the Oriental manner, Miss Kwan gets her freckles—it is believed—from a Scottish grandmother."[41] Like Nuyen, Kwan came from an elite background: she lived in a wealthy Kowloon neighborhood and had attended the prestigious Maryknoll school before pursuing dramatic studies abroad. Unlike Nuyen, though, Kwan had a local identity: she handled her initial press conference fluidly in Cantonese and English and said the first thing she wanted to do was to eat "*cheung fan* [rice noodles] and mangos."[42] To Chinese viewers, however, she remained, like Nuyen, *Boon Tang Fan*, literally, "half Chinese, half barbarian."

The myth of her "discovery" nevertheless grew quite complicated in the press. According to most sources, Kwan already was connected with *The World of Suzie Wong* productions, at least in a road show, and had been considered earlier for the movie part. However, an article in *Sing Tao Daily* noted that Ray Stark, the film's producer, discovered Kwan while she was in Hong Kong for summer vacation from her ballet school in England. He auditioned her in Wing Wah Studio, sent her to Hollywood for training, and signed her to a seven-year contract. The article further noted that while other Asian actresses had appeared in Hollywood productions, including Miiko Tana in *Sayonara* (1957) and Lisa Lu in *Mountain Road* (1960), they had received lower screen billings than Marlon Brando and James Stewart. The article saw Kwan as a breakthrough in a way that the film was not:

> Her name appears after William Holden, but the sizes of the characters are the same. On the other hand, Michael Wilding and Sylvia Sims, who are more famous, have their credits following Kwan's. The ordering of credits and the sizes of the characters may not mean much to the audience, but in the eyes of the actress, they are very important.[43]

This article added that *The World of Suzie Wong* was featured as the Thanksgiving film at Radio City Music Hall, where Stark held a lavish party for Kwan before the screening, using Chinese decorations and serving Chinese food. Hence, Kwan not only represented Hong Kong but also brought Chinese culture to Hollywood on terms unlike those of the movie scenario. Racism was situated in Hollywood, not in the picture or the role, and Kwan was the Knight to overcome it. Not all agreed: the pro-Communist paper *Dai Kung Pao* allowed that Kwan acted well, but complained that "even though she went to school in Hong Kong, and was a Chinese with British nationality, when she spoke Cantonese, it was bad." [44]

Like Holden, Kwan would create global intertexts for the film. She followed *The World of Suzie Wong* with her starring role as a Chinese-American nightclub singer in *Flower Drum Song*, contrasting the traditional Chinese mail-order bride, played in the film by Japanese actress Miyoshi Umeki. By the late 1960s, her Hollywood career declined, and she later appeared in low-budget Hollywood and Hong Kong movies. She also did television promotions for "Oriental Pearl Crème" in both Hong Kong and the United States that conveyed a strongly commoditized vision of ageless Asian beauty. Nonetheless, nearly forty years later, Kwan was called upon by the *Far Eastern Economic Review,* a leading Hong-Kong based English-language periodical, for its special handover issue. Once again clad in a cheong-sam (conservative blue), she talked about her background rather than her film career. She recalled the mystifying distance she felt from mainland refugees in the 1950s (ironically, the purported social origins of the Suzie Wong character).[45] This confirmed a social reading of Kwan in Hong Kong that we found among several middle-class Chinese friends who spoke of her family background and connections in terms quite distinct from the role with which outsiders identified her.

Press reports provide tantalizing suggestions that the character of Suzie changed along with the star and director (Richard Quine replaced Jean Negulesco). Nuyen had claimed that she agreed to make the film only because screenwriter John Patrick "gave Suzie new dimensions, new charm and understanding." [46] After the reshuffle, Nuyen's interpretation was referred to as "a voluptuous Suzie, earthy, immoral, with little saving grace."[47] Reports suggested Kwan presented a more amenable image of Asian submissiveness.

"Nancy's advantage is her Oriental mind," said one assistant director. "She has gotten hold of the whole attitude of the mind of Suzie Wong as the girl is portrayed—a woman whose surroundings are immoral but whose heart is clean and even innocent . . . this may appear a paradox, but that is what the picture is all about."[48]

Without access to any footage of Nuyen, it is impossible to verify this change. Yet, it evokes an interesting tension between a headstrong Asian woman and the vulnerability Kwan depicts in the movie.

The World of Suzie Wong opened in November 1960 to generally bland American reviews. For Bosley Crowther, Nancy Kwan and the Hong Kong scenery were the highlights of a film that was "the glowingest commercial for love conquering everything, including the taint of prostitution, that these eyes have ever seen." Hong Kong itself took more space in his review than the plot or other actors: "the image of Hong Kong is brilliantly and sensuously conveyed, all crowds and colors and noises and even allusive smells."[49] Hong Kong reporter Alan Castro also stressed this starring role for the city and the local heroine as he gathered New York reviews for Hong Kong audiences. He quoted the New York *Journal-American,* for example, as saying "the cameras are at their most effective when they range over the Hong Kong [sic]." He cited critic Kate Cameron of the *Daily News* at even greater length: "the best thing about *The World of Suzie Wong* is that the fascinating city of Hong Kong plays an important part in the picture. . . . Nancy Kwan makes a beautiful little Chinese stray. She plays the girl with a naivete and a pertness that endear her to the audience. Bill Holden, it seems to me, is miscast as the artist."[50]

The World of Suzie Wong finally arrived in Hong Kong on August 14, 1961, at the height of the summer holidays. Although its two-week run paled beside the nine-week stay of *Ben Hur,* the film's stretch at the prestigious Queen's and Royal cinemas was respectable in Hong Kong, where movies changed several times per week. Reviews in the English-language press, by this time, had shifted from the euphoria of production to more critical readings. Depicting "the real" Wan Chai as an outwardly respectable tenement community harboring an unostentatious world of vice, Castro labeled the movie "a betrayal of our famous Wan Chai. And it proves once again that they can't ever capture in motion pictures the delicate blend of faked but enchanting 'respectability' and delectable bawdiness that makes up the world in which our Suzie Wongs live."[51] Little attention was paid to the fact that the movie's Wan Chai was actually composed of shots in many districts. While Castro noted that Kwan's portrayal "shows a surprisingly profound understanding of the Wan Chai bar girl," he scorned studio scenes and the accented Chinese and Mayfair English dialogue. In this regard, the critic also claimed control over the authenticity of the story for a local English colonial audience.

Chinese reviews were more complex. *Sing Tao* was pleased with the recognition of the city, but the review in *Dai Kung Pao*, the major pro-Communist Chinese newspaper, excoriated the film in an article entitled, "Not Real, Painful to Watch." The author, Tziu Yuek-Si, asserted that although the film was filmed in Hong Kong, local Chinese would object to it "because it is an American film, and it is a film that deliberately insults Chinese. So when Chinese watch the film, they will find it repulsive." [52] The article blamed this offense on its external political context as well as on racial and cultural attitudes:

> Furthermore, after the liberation of China, Hong Kong has been in the international spotlight. The Americans are using Hong Kong as an intelligence front post, and have built a grand consulate, with an abundance of assistant consuls. Therefore, in the eyes of the Western countries, Hong Kong becomes a legendary place."

Robert's initial encounter with Suzie merits an especially unromantic reading from Tziu:

> The film starts by exhibiting Chinese feudal customs, with Suzie Wong telling Lomax that she is a rich girl who is going to marry someone she has never met, a man who has been to America. Obviously she is lying, but she is boasting, and protesting. The aim of the film is to show that America is a land covered with gold. . . . On the other hand, the film is saying these arranged marriages are the essence of the Chinese culture. The film shows the ignorance, superstition, and rudeness of the Chinese. For example, Suzie Wong is proud of being beaten by her lover and she believes in oracles (which are portrayed wrong). The film also emphasizes the filth and unhygienic conditions of Hong Kong. [53]

Overall, politics evoked an ire that sex and race did not. "The most vicious misrepresentation appears when an English police officer claims that there are six to seven thousand Chinese refugees coming to Hong Kong per day. This is a big lie, and the director is deliberately hurting Hong Kong, to achieve his political ends." [54]

While most Chinese in Hong Kong did not oppose the film so strongly for political reasons, neither did they find it "real." One woman, for example, recalled, "We were curious to see it. But it was very bad. It was insulting to Chinese; they only showed the bad parts of Hong Kong. Hollywood didn't know how to make good pictures about us." Others simply dismissed it: Hong Kong was the place where they lived, not a site of exotic redemption.

If the movie was not especially popular in Hong Kong, its release nevertheless raised the important issue of global attention. As critics have observed, *The World of Suzie Wong* is, in many ways, a story of the cold war era, highlighting both the military presence of American and British sailors in the Nam Kwok and the supply of young women who filled the bars and the dangerous squatter settlements on Hong Kong's slopes.[55] Those in charge of burgeoning industrial production were also preoccupied with American quotas that would recognize Hong Kong's difference from an embargoed China and promote local growth. By 1960, 23 percent of Hong Kong's foreign trade was tied to the United States and trade negotiations were followed closely in the news.[56] Thus, critic Alan Castro linked Hollywood and trade directly when he commented on "the Suzie Wong community in town all but making us forget the smarting humiliation of textile quotas."[57]

Annual government reports valued media exposure as a corollary to economic growth. The colonial information services also produced documentaries about Hong Kong opportunities for both local and global distribution. Before Christmas 1960, for example, the *Standard* noted the release of *A Million Lights Shall Glow,* produced by the Hong Kong Tourist Association, which sought to present the territory as "a little bit of England."[58] Kwan herself was later recruited for such documentaries.[59] Yet, fictional representations also sold the colony. Indeed, the image of the innocent, lovestruck prostitute countered perceptions of business trickery that had led to a front page complaint in the *Standard*: "once upon a time Hong Kong was a name that suggested romance to Americans—including even the most prosaic businessman. Today, 'Hongkong' is just about the dirtiest word many an American can think about."[60]

Nor were *The World of Suzie Wong* and Holden's CBS production the only American visions of Hong Kong discussed in the colony. The premiere of ABC television's *Hong Kong* series also made local news under the headline "Hong Kong Girl Cast as Regular in a TV Series." The series "was built around a supper club called the Golden Dragon, an eclectic place where an American newspaperman (actor Rod Taylor) drifts in and out with endless beautiful women," repeating *The World of Suzie Wong* scenario.[61] Another report on December 18, 1960, mentioned an NBC project, *Our Man in Hong Kong.*[62] Even *The World of Suzie Wong* producer, Ray Stark, discussed a second project, *Kowloon,* to star both Kwan and Jacqueline Chan (the bargirl Gwinny in *The World of Suzie Wong*). This project never materialized, although Hong Kong still would figure in the global intrigue of James Bond films.

This is not to say that simple economic analyses explain either Hollywood's choice of *The World of Suzie Wong* and Hong Kong or the readings of the local English-language elite. Instead, the divisions of race and power in Hong Kong, which separated a colonial government and business elite from a complex Chinese population, reinforced divergent concerns about the film, its message, and its readings abroad as well as at home. Here, those living with colonial race relations outside the United States reinterpreted or set aside the White Knight scenario of American racial relations in order to recast the story as one, true or false, about Hong Kong itself. For the colonized Chinese, in fact, inauthenticity was an old story, one that confirmed Chinese difference even while pieces of the film might be salvaged for a different story. For others in the colony, truth, power, and memory proved more elusive. This divergence, in fact, would continue to grow as Hong Kong changed.

THE FOREIGN GAZE AND THE FORGOTTEN ARTIFACT: DECADES OF SUZIE WONG

As the Hong Kong historian Carl Smith notes in his study of the Wan Chai district, *The World of Suzie Wong* cannot be divorced from the changes in that district and its urban and global contexts. Wan Chai was not identified with bars and prostitution until the turn of the century. After World War II, its growth reflected both Chinese immigration and foreign military concerns. *The World of Suzie Wong* coincided with the dawn of American involvement in Vietnam, which would transform Hong Kong into a site for military "Rest & Recreation" and reinforce the screen myth.[63] As Americans fought Asians who resisted the American dream, Wan Chai became a haven for tired "White Knights." In a history of the American Club in Hong Kong, for example, an army lieutenant turned loose in the city remembers, "If you were really smart you also picked up a solid gold Rolex watch for US $50. Then it was off to Wanchai and a visit to the wonderful world of Suzie."[64]

English-language works on Hong Kong from the late 1960s make this search for Suzie Wong a vital part of learning the city. Gene Gleason's *Tales of Hong Kong* (1967), for example, included extensive notes on the cheongsam as seductive wear and the social geography of prostitution in the city. He identified Suzie Wong as "a whole new mythology for the city. Now there are perhaps a dozen local girls who claim to be the original Suzie Wong. . . . Suzie lives on in all her protean identities as a prime tourist attraction."[65] Others warned of a fall from paradise. Sean O'Callaghan's *The Yellow Slave Trade* (1968) depicted the reality of Suzie along a very different moral and physical trajectory, although his warning still depended on the "reality" of *The World of Suzie Wong*:

To the tourist and the serviceman in Hong Kong, a visit to Wanchai, the waterfront area where Richard Mason set the scene for his *World of Suzie Wong*, is one of the first on his itinerary. Perhaps no other prostitute achieved such lasting fame so quickly—for, strange as it seems, there was a real Suzie Wong. . . . A few years ago a friend of mine, who worked on Hong Kong radio, found the real Suzie Wong. She was a fat, dirty, disease-ridden whore of about thirty-five, living in one of the back alleys of Wanchai. While once she may have looked like Nancy Kwan, drink and disease had so transformed her that she looked like any of the other thousand or so prostitutes who beg or search the garbage tines for a living when their good looks are gone and they are no longer of any use to the masters, the traffickers.[66]

O'Callaghan also incorporated political tensions of the era, claiming many bargirls were Communist agents. He projected cold war hysteria onto older Hollywood myths.

As time passed, nostalgia began to dominate this Hollywood-shaped perception of Hong Kong. A 1981 guide to Hong Kong "by night" alerted bachelors to more changes: "The famous district of Wanchai beckons you today as it has beckoned young men for decades. But be warned: Suzie Wong has cut her long hair, changed into denims, gone into the factories and left her world to a new species of night-bird."[67] Still, the realities of the old world of Suzie Wong and its attractiveness to new males in the city were taken for granted.

Paradoxically, ongoing interpretations of change reinforced *The World of Suzie Wong* as a dominant image of the city for outsiders, especially as global business brought many foreigners for short, profitable stints, constantly reconstituting the resident white population. New generations of Westerners continued to search for an exotic or essential Hong Kong reality, through a white male gaze verified by the movie and novel as historical relics. John Hoskins epitomizes this view in his sketch, "If You Knew Suzie," from a 1994 collection of readings for visitors to the territory. He explains that he first encountered Suzie Wong when he was nine years old, through "a picture on the cover of a London theatre program depicting a lovely Chinese girl provocatively dressed in a skin-hugging cheong-sam."[68] Later, taking a job in Hong Kong, he bemoans his inability to locate this world: "instead of being sheathed in beautiful Chinese silk, the new Suzie Wongs were decked out in weird dresses that seemed as if the maker had run out of material by the time she reached the bodice."[69] Finally, "in time I did meet Suzie Wong (that, naturally was not her real name) with whom I was to share a flat in Wanchai for almost a year."[70] Yet his Wan Chai fades as "his" Suzie moves on to other bars and he withdraws to Bangkok. Nonetheless, a fleeting "real experience" of Hong Kong confirms the mythic orders of race and class glimpsed in the *World of Suzie Wong* literary-filmic complex.

Hong Kong British author George Adams provides a more extended revisionist treatment of Suzie Wong in his 1992 story, "The Return of Suzie Wong." His sequel begins with the elderly widow, Mrs. Robert Lomax, flying first-class from her retirement home in Florida to Hong Kong, wistfully looking at pictures of her successful children and grandchildren. Her return to Hong Kong allows meditation on changes in the city and its vulgarization, including the newly-built cityscape and the world of prostitution, represented by the déclassé attitudes of Filipina bargirls. In this world, "the talk was in the tradition of Nam Kok but there was a cheap cynicism about it that made Mrs. Lomax very sad. In her day, girls had a little more dignity and tact."[71] Adams recognizes a demographic transformation of Hong Kong as women from nearby, poorer Asian countries have sought work there, but he uses this recognition to glorify the mythic past.

Suzie meets her onetime coworker Gwinny, married to a successful businessman in Vancouver and part of a new Hong Kong diaspora. Their tea and conversation at the Peninsula Hotel is not a transgression, as it was in *The World of Suzie Wong*, but a right. Nevertheless, Suzie finds her closest communion with Betty Lam, a character in the novel who had snared the noble Robert and tricked Suzie into jail (subplots not included in the film). With this bedraggled prostitute, Suzie recaptures the memories that have haunted her in flashbacks. She then dies peacefully in her hotel room.

Despite his sympathetic tone, Adams nonetheless conveys a neocolonial nostalgia. By taking Suzie's point of view, he completes the White Knight fantasy, showing her happiness at her escape to America as well as her perceptions of the idyllic world of the Nam Kwok with her artist lover. Her assent transcends the novel and film and affirms relations of class and gender: "suddenly all the buildings disappeared. There were only Robert and herself rolling through Central, looking deep into each other's eyes, smiling radiantly with the realisation of their love."[72]

This tradition of looking for "the real Suzie" and of using *The World of Suzie Wong* as a myth of history and place explains continuing references beyond 1997. An international Web guide to prostitution, for example, still lingers over links between Suzie Wong and Wan Chai. Meanwhile, an article on Western restaurants revitalizing the area in 2000 notes that "Suzie Wong gives it the edge."[73] An Internet search for Suzie Wong adds other sites from Singapore, France, Germany, and Mexico, as well as those offering Thai prostitutes. Suzie Wong, in many Western male eyes, remains a shorthand for the Other as woman, Asian, and subject. Indeed, a similar White Knight scenario (with postmodern decay) underpinned Wayne Wang's 1998 film on the Hong Kong handover, *Chinese Box*.

This reading has diverged sharply from the experience and meaning of *The World of Suzie Wong* for Chinese. While we found Hong Kong Chinese who could tell us about Nancy Kwan as a person, it proved difficult to find those who actually knew *The World of Suzie Wong* in any medium. Over several months in which we researched this paper, we spoke to more than one hundred Chinese about the movie. This included a rather broad cross section in age, from students through retirees, and class, from established working class through relatively wealthy. Only a handful (seven) had seen the movie at all; two were university students who had seen it as assigned work—one, as part of the Hong Kong Film Festival and the other, in the United States as part of a class on Asian-American studies. None of the seven considered the film particularly important or noteworthy. In fact, the largest video chain in Hong Kong lacked a copy of the film for rental during the year (1996–1997) we were there, and an expatriate complained that she had been unable to purchase a copy. Another expatriate film teacher, however, had shown it in class, recalling that her students were struck by the changes in the Hong Kong landscape, but that they thought the text ridiculous. We have subsequently met other Hong Kong Chinese in the United States who have seen the movie on television or video and who share a sense of nostalgia in seeing their city in color rather than in the black-and-white images of Cantonese-language movies. The visual/narrative division of the movie between location and studio thus takes on a completely different meaning. They, too, tend to reject the plot itself as uninteresting.

Despite this limited *readership,* many of these people had knowledge of the film's existence and implications. As a male student in his twenties elaborated:

> It seems that I have heard the name from my classmate in primary school. In my faint memory, I also heard the name from a TV show at least ten years ago, but not sure. In the TV show, a man called a woman "Suzie Wong," and the woman was very angry. . . . I am not sure the mention of Suzie Wong in this TV show is the same as the Suzie Wong in *The World of Suzie Wong,* but from then on I guess that if someone called a woman as "Suzie Wong" it meant that she is a prostitute.

Generally, people based their judgments on fragmentary images of the plot (a prostitute falls in love with a foreigner), which they knew from secondary references—expatriate questions and news references have kept the film alive as a symbol, if not as a cinematic experience. Most Chinese did not find these elements surprising or especially racist. They knew that the film was also inaccurate, because Westerners did not know or understand Hong Kong. Some also expressed frustration because of what the simple presence of *The World of Suzie Wong* as an antiquated melodrama said about Western images of Hong Kong. One lawyer retorted with irritation, "Should I see *Roman Holiday* if I am going to Italy?"

One particular image also recurred in discussion: that of Suzie astride a chair, alone, with the collar of her cheong-sam undone. The association of a visual image with an unseen movie was puzzling until we realized that it was drawn, in part, from the publicity still used on the cover of the book, including the most recent paperback edition available in Hong Kong. The picture clearly shows Kwan as sexy yet vulnerable. It also echoes publicity shots of Nuyen for the Broadway show. Yet, in fact, the cheong-sam is buttoned. The image of the unbuttoned cheong-sam, we hypothesize, was ingrained in Hong Kong consciousness as an indication of a slatternly woman (as it appears in older Cantonese movies) and it had been imposed upon *The World of Suzie Wong*.

The stars also retain meanings. William Holden was known as a Hollywood star more than for his Hong Kong associations. Scarcely a stellar presence among the plethora of stars in Hong Kong cinema, Kwan, as noted above, was known for her television promotions as much as for her films. Still, one could see echoes of the promotion once given her in the build-up following Michelle Yeoh's casting in a new James Bond movie. In the 1990s, however, this was framed in terms of competition and triumph by Hong Kong actors and directors in Hollywood, spearheaded by *men* like John Woo, Ringo Lam, Jackie Chan, and Chow Yun-Fat.

It is difficult to strike a balance between those who are vocal in remembering a movie and those for whom it is unimportant: there seem to be few models in film studies, literature, or ethnography to interpret how a work is *not* seen. Yet, the disparity here seems central to understanding the differences of race, class, and gender that continued to constitute late colonial society in Hong Kong. The film knowledge of middle-class Western expatriates and tourists has become built into the imagination of Hong Kong. Even if race and gender do not function as in *The World of Suzie Wong*, outsiders can believe they did so in the mythic past. While most Chinese in Hong Kong arrived from the mainland or were born after the period depicted in the film, they are not concerned with *The World of Suzie Wong* in their varied imaginations of what their lives and city could be. Hong Kong identity, and its expression in multiple media, proves more complex, assertive, and contentious now than it was in the colonial 1960s.[74] Even the history of film in Hong Kong centers on Hong Kong-made films, rather than on how Hong Kong was viewed from abroad, despite the contemporary popularity of Hollywood. Yet, these Chinese must still face demands from the global networks that have been vital to contemporary Hong Kong development, including banal references to *The World of Suzie Wong.*

This lack of knowledge of the film as visual narrative, as well as its transformation into artifact, has been nuanced by more erudite commentaries. The 1980 Hong Kong television production *Goodbye Suzie Wong,* for example, fictionalizes the story anew through an old bargirl whose life demythologizes the original work. Typical of the vision of a new wave of Hong Kong filmmakers emerging from television, this short piece exemplifies a stronger sense of Hong Kong identity in society and of the representations to which this identity spoke. The 1989 Hong Kong International Film Festival also revived *The World of Suzie Wong* within a retrospective entitled *Changes in Hong Kong Society through Cinema* that includes the insightful essays of Law Kar and S. N. Ko to which we have referred. In the retrospective, *The World of Suzie Wong* is treated as a historical document, incorporated into Hong Kong Chinese history. Ko's essay, in fact, concludes with a comparison between Hollywood's Other and a Hong Kong cinema facing its own dangers of Orientalization:

We find the same form of singularity and ghettoization that Hollywood movies display. Paris, San Francisco or New York—their contacts with the actual city seem spurious and superfluous, and relationships with actual inhabitants either non-existent or aggressive. Moreover, we find in some Hong Kong films, the same sort of muted racism that characterised Hollywood's treatment of the Chinese (cf., the treatment of Filipinas in *Marianna* [1982]). In truth, the Hong Kong Other of the Hollywood cinema is represented by the Hong Kong cinema itself.[75]

In 1996, new reverberations of Suzie Wong appeared in Peter Chan's highly successful *Tiim Mat Mat (Comrades, Almost a Love Story).* Here, the star-crossed transnational lovers, Li Xiao-Jun (Leon Lai Ming) and Li Chiao (Maggie Cheung Man-Yuk), are both Chinese. They leave the mainland to find fortune in Hong Kong and New York, where they must grapple with the failures of both Chinese and American Dreams. Obviously, this alters the geography of an earlier Hollywood gaze through a mature Hong Kong cinema. The film also engages *The World of Suzie Wong* in two interlocking subplots.

First, Xiao-Jun lives in a brothel where he encounters a white foreigner involved with a prostitute. This Australian, Jeremy (Christopher Doyle), is also an English teacher, although his drinking in the classroom belies any pedagogical impulse. Moreover, the prostitute "Cabbage" is Thai, reflecting the changing realities of Hong Kong prostitution. However, Jeremy and Cabbage seem to find a happy ending, leaving for her home in Thailand. As Xiao-Jun tells her that he may come visit them soon, Jeremy adds, "Better hurry, Cabbage has AIDS." The romance of conquest and new life are transfigured by the realities of a profession without happy endings.

The madam, Xiao-Jun's aunt, provides a second subplot with her direct reference to William Holden as a White Knight figure. Throughout the movie, she talks about her date with William Holden, maintaining a shrine to him in her room with an enlarged portrait surrounded by fan magazine clippings. Xiao-Jun and others treat it as the harmless reverie of an old woman; indeed, no reference is made to *The World of Suzie Wong*, nor would a mainlander be expected to know the film. Toward the end of the movie, as the aunt becomes increasingly ill, Xiao-Jun watches *Love is a Many-Splendored Thing* on video and learns more details about how his aunt met Holden during the filming of that movie and had dinner with him at the Peninsula Hotel. This is a complex intertextual reference: it cites one movie while evoking the critical scene from another, *The World of Suzie Wong* as shown in Figure 10.5. Still, the spectator is unsure whether this is a reference to the actualities of filming or an incorporation of movie myth into memory. After his aunt's death, Xiao-Jun finds a Peninsula Hotel menu, napkin, and silverware in her trunk, as well as photos of his aunt and a man who resembles Holden. His aunt had the happy ending of a myth, but it remains an ambivalent one, a past that evaporates with the burning of all her souvenirs.

Chan plays with these elements, drawing on his knowledge of Hollywood, but he changes genres and references. Given that most Chinese in Hong Kong, including film specialists, have not seen *The World of Suzie Wong*, Chan's references are obscure for a Hong Kong audience. Local critic Li Cheuk-To noted that Chan was more trained in film history than many other directors: "Those people who know the intertext can appreciate it on that level; on a dramatic level it still works: that's why he's successful on two levels."[76]

This ambiguity in itself underscores the many features of position—beyond race, class and gender—that may shape readings and the implications that must be teased out of these. Hybridity and confidence have now become hallmarks of a Hong Kong identity that no longer demands an approving gaze from the West, but incorporates, plays with, and subverts that gaze. This is evident in the right both to ignore Hollywood as well as to reread a movie— and above all, in the right to appropriate as part of Hong Kong history what was created by white Westerners for white Western eyes.

CONCLUSIONS: HOLLYWOOD ABROAD AND THE READINGS OF RACE

It seems curious, perhaps, that a book/play/movie complex by a fairly obscure British writer in the 1950s should have generated the decades of elaborations of readership that we have traced here. The worlds depicted for Suzie

Wong were not innovations in the depiction of Asia or Asians; neither did *The World of Suzie Wong* offer new visions of romance. Yet, it was embedded in many changing histories of race and power, both in the United States and in Hong Kong, global and local. In both places, perhaps, it has become a touch-stone—and a divider—even among those who have not seen the film.

Our examination of readings of *The World of Suzie Wong* underscores cultural categories of race and gender, which the movie took for granted, as well as those that have emerged from its presence in divided social milieux. Anglo-and Asian-American critics attack it for its paternalistic interracial romance and stereotypes. While evident to critics at the time, these features have taken on new connotations of "what was wrong" with Hollywood. In general, we agree with these views, but suggest they only represent part of the picture.

Situating the movie within the categories of race, gender, and power within the society it pretended to depict, we see how different experiences have shaped appropriation of the movie. In Hong Kong, whites, who have constituted a politically if not numerically dominant segment of the city, have faced the "decay" of the colonial relations criticized by the movie and the book. *The World of Suzie Wong* now seems to evoke a promise that colonial superiority once was real and romantic. Colonialism has given way to neocolonialism as Americans, Japanese, and mainland Chinese occupy center stage. Prostitutes are global, rather than local. However, these readings highlight continuing claims to own the truth, even if that truth is fictional.

Chinese readings prove more complex. From a Hong Kong standing warily apart from Hollywood to a global city in control of—or at least contending for control of—its own image, we see transformations of identity and culture. *The World of Suzie Wong* is a film and a myth that outsiders impose on Chinese-ness and Hong Kong itself. It is possible to feel nostalgia for the landscapes of the movie, but not for the society of falsehoods it represents. Yet, *The World of Suzie Wong* also is a text that can be recast in building a new, hybrid Hong Kong identity. This does not suggest that Chinese readings of the film are not informed by stereotypes of Western attitudes toward Hong Kong or equally problematic concepts of racial purity. Yet these readings underscore how these elements are transformed in rethinking Hong Kong.

These complex appropriations of a single film suggest not only the transnational impact of Hollywood imagery of race and gender, but also the ways in which imagery and meanings have escaped Hollywood control. The White Knight becomes Arthurian or barbarian, depending on one's vantage; those divided by race and power outside the United States transform text and relationship to Hollywood as well. Film, in its representation and reproduction of race, represents a cultural practice. As such, it invites reading, resistance, and reinterpretation. In practice, in Hong Kong, "Suzie Wong" has created worlds of her own. A reading through Hong Kong eyes, therefore, interrogates both Classical Hollywood's imageries of race and those of the America it reproduced.

NOTES

1. Deborah Herd, "Sex after Suzie Wong," *Sunday Morning Post*, July 6, 1997, Agenda Section, 1–2. She refers to Kate Whitehead and Nury Vittachi, *After Suzie— Sex in South China* (Hong Kong: Chameleon, 1997).

2. Andrew Browne, "Suzie Wong's World Flattened by Highrise Hong Kong," www.techserver.com/newsrooom/nt/624suzsuz.html, 1997.

3. Ruth Vasey, *The World According to Hollywood, 1918–1939* (Madison: University of Wisconsin Press, 1997), 148, 153.

4. Edward N. Said, *Orientalism* (New York: Vintage, 1979); Nick Browne, "The Undoing of the Other Woman: Madame Butterfly in the Discourse of American Orientalism," in *The Birth of Whiteness: Race and the Emergence of U.S. Cinema*, ed. Daniel Bernardi (New Brunswick, NJ: Rutgers University Press, 1996), 227–256; Gina Marchetti, "Tragic and Transcendent Love in *The Forbidden City*," in Bernardi, *The Birth of Whiteness*, 257–270.

5. Mimi Chan, *Through Western Eyes: Images of Chinese Women in Anglo-American Literature* (Hong Kong: Joint Publishing, 1989); Gina Marchetti, *Romance and the "Yellow Peril": Race, Sex, and Discursive Strategies in Hollywood Fiction* (Berkeley: University of California Press, 1992); James S. Moys, *Marginal Sights: Staging the Chinese in America* (Iowa City: University of Iowa Press, 1993); Jimmy Yap, "Bridesmaids Revisited," review of *Mail-Order Brides and Other Oriental Take-Aways* (Singapore: Action Theatre Homepage www.happening.com/sg/performance/picks/mail-order, 1997).

6. Guy Haydon, "About the Author," in *The World of Suzie Wong*, by Richard Mason (Hong Kong: Pegasus Books, 1994). During our research, this was the only edition available for sale in Hong Kong. Mason's novel was first published by William Collins Sons & Co, Ltd. of London in 1957.

7. Henry Lethbridge, *Hong Kong: Stability and Change* (Hong Kong: Oxford University Press, 1978); B. K. Leung, *Perspectives on Hong Kong Society and Culture* (Hong Kong: Oxford University Press, 1994); Matthew Turner, "Hong Kong Sixties/Nineties: Dissolving the People," in *Hong Kong Sixties: Designing Identity*, ed. Matthew Turner and Irene Ngan (Hong Kong: Hong Kong Arts Centre, 1996), 13–36; "Soi Si Wong Dik Sai Gai," *Hong Kong Sixties*, 63–75.

8. The book is somewhat more explicit about Suzie's mainland origins and the ties of other prostitutes with a changing Chinese nation-state, as well as adding other travels and subplots.

9. Haydon, "About the Author."

10. Brooks Atkinson, review of *The World of Suzie Wong*, *New York Times*, October 15, 1958.

11. Ibid.

12. Tsai Chin (Chou Tsai Chin), *Daughter of Shanghai* (London: Chatto & Windus, 1988), 115.

13. Ibid., 117.

14. Ibid. This image of the cheong-sam was also being played with in Macau at this time as is manifest in Deolinda da Conceicao's *Cheong-Sam a Cabaia* (Macau: Instituto Cultural de Macau, 1995), originally published in 1956. The title story in this volume deals with a woman lured from virtue by rich urban life.

15. Chin, *Daughter,* 109–124.

16. Marchetti, *Romance,* 113–15.

17. Ibid., 114–16.

18. *Love is a Many-Splendored Thing* shows the same preoccupation with clothes, although Chinese women of other classes are shown in cheong-sams. Holden, the hero nonetheless, rejects Western clothing for Jones.

19. Marchetti, *Romance.*

20. Thomas Tan, "'I Think I'll be an Old Maid,' Says 'Suzie Wong' Girl France," *Hong Kong Tiger Standard,* December 29, 1959.

21. Ibid.

22. Alan Castro, "The Movie Circle," *Hong Kong Tiger Standard,* January 14, 1960.

23. Alan Castro, "Suzie up at 6 and Does Yoga: Movie Circle," *Hong Kong Tiger Standard,* January 7, 1960.

24. Dennis Norman, "Suzie Wong Starts Go Through Paces in Opening Scenes," *Hong Kong Tiger Standard,* January 3, 1960.

25. S. N. Ko "Under Western Eyes," *Changes in Hong Kong Society Through Cinema* (Hong Kong: Hong Kong International Film Festival, 1989), 65.

26. *Hong Kong Report for the Year 1960* (Hong Kong: Government Press, 1961).

27. *Hong Kong Tiger Standard,* December 29, 1959.

28. The three daily English-language papers could be read by a tiny minority of English-educated Chinese. The orientation of a paper like the *Standard* at this time, however, betrays its primary focus on the life of the expatriate English colony, its business concerns, and home ties. Chinese newspapers, however, to this day are read almost exclusively by Chinese populations, although their number and variety—thirty-nine dailies in 1961, with an estimated circulation of 600,000 (*Hong Kong Report for 1961*: 261)—make readership a daunting area for further investigation. Today, English-language press audiences are more mixed.

29. Lau Seung Ngan, "France Nuyen and William Holden Arrive in Hong Kong" ("Yeun Lan Si Yue Wai Lin Haw Deng Loi Gong"), *The Milky Way Pictorial (Ngan Haw Wah Pao),* February 1960.

30. Ibid.

31. Ibid.

32. Frank Dikotter provides an excellent elaboration of this discussion in *The Discourse of Race in Modern China* (Hong Kong: Hong Kong University Press, 1992). Other relevant issues of gender and sexuality are also found in his *Sex, Culture, and Modernity in China* (Hong Kong: Hong Kong University Press, 1995).

33. Alan Castro, "The Movie Circle," *Hong Kong Tiger Standard,* January 7, 1960.

34. Ko, "Under Western Eyes," 67.

35. *South China Morning Post*, November 18, 1991.

36. Lau, "France Nuyen," 23.

37. Ibid., 24.

38. Sam Ho Si-Wing, "The Songstress, the Farmer's Daughter, the Mambo Girl and the Songstress Again" ("Go Loi, Chun Loi, Yu Man Bah Loi Long"), *Mandarin Films and Popular Songs: 40s to 60s* (Hong Kong: Seventeenth International Hong Kong Film Festival, 1993), 50–68; Turner and Ngan, *Hong Kong Sixties: Designing Identity*, 63–75. See Stephen Teo's *Hong Kong Cinema: The Other Dimension* (London BFI, 1997), 29–39.

39. The studio said that her voice cracked (*Hong Kong Tiger Standard*, February 10, 1960). Other reports, in both the Chinese and English-language press, indicated her unhappiness at being separated from Marlon Brando and cited an eating disorder that resulted from that separation ("France Grows Fat," *Hong Kong Tiger Standard*, February 10, 1960). This may also be a veiled reference to rumors of her pregnancy, with Brando as the father. See Peter Manso, *Brando: The Biography* (New York: Hyperion, 1994), 517, 521.

40. Ibid.

41. "Nancy Selected to Play Role of 'Suzie Wong,'" *Hong Kong Tiger Standard*, February 15, 1960.

42. "Nancy Kwan Gets Big Welcome," *Hong Kong Tiger Standard*, May 7, 1960.

43. *Sing Tao Daily*, August 10, 1961.

44. Tziu Yuek-Si, "Not Real, Painful to Watch" ("But Jun Sat But Song Ngan"), *Dai Kung Pao*, August 21, 1961.

45. Nancy Kwan, "Real Life, Not a Movie," *Far Eastern Economic Review*, 1997, 84.

46. *Hong Kong Tiger Standard*, December 29, 1959.

47. "Nancy Sets Suzie Wong on Course," *Hong Kong Tiger Standard*, May 12, 1960.

48. Ibid.

49. Bosley Crowther, review of *The World of Suzie Wong*, New York Times, November 11, 1960.

50. Quoted in Alan Castro, "The Movie Circle," *Hong Kong Tiger Standard*, November 24, 1960. The disparity between 19-year-old Kwan and 42-year-old Holden also bothered Chinese critics. It also raises questions of gender relations in Hollywood, as well as issues of race and colonialism, that go beyond this essay.

51. Alan Castro, "Well, For Goodness Sake—But Nancy's Tops!" *Hong Kong Tiger Standard*, August 19, 1961.

52. Tziu, "Not Real."

53. Ibid.

54. Ibid.

55. Ko, "Under Western Eyes"; Marchetti, *Romance*.

56. *Hong Kong Report for the Year 1961*.

57. Alan Castro, "The Movie Circle," *Hong Kong Tiger Standard*, January 4, 1960.

58. *Hong Kong Tiger Standard*, December 22, 1960.

59. Government Information Service Film Catalogue, mimeograph, 1980.

60. *Hong Kong Tiger Standard,* April 28, 1960.

61. *Hong Kong Tiger Standard,* December 21, 1960.

62. *Hong Kong Tiger Standard,* December 18, 1960.

63. Carl Smith, *A Sense of History: Essays in Hong Kong Social and Urban History* (Hong Kong: Educational Publishing, 1995); and Arthur Hacker, *Arthur Hacker's Wanchai* (Hong Kong: Odyssey, 1997).

64. Andrew Coe, *Eagles and Dragons: A History of Americans in China and the Origins of the American Club, Hong Kong* (Hong Kong: American Club, 1997), 184.

65. Gene Gleason, *Tales of Hong Kong* (London: Robert Hale, 1967), 22–23. See also Gleason's *Hong Kong* (London: Robert Hale, 1964).

66. Sean O'Callaghan, "The World of Suzie Wong," in *The Yellow Slave Trade: A Survey in the Traffic in Women and Children in the East* (London: Blond, 1968), 29. Whitehead and Vittachi describe a similar contemporary scene, involving an aging prostitute named Josephine, in *After Suzie,* 49.

67. Roger Boschman, *Hong Kong by Night* (Hong Kong: CFW Guidebooks, 1981).

68. John Hoskins, "If You Knew Suzie," in *Traveller's Tales, Hong Kong,* eds. James O'Reilly, Larry Habegger, and Sean O'Reilly (San Francisco: Traveller's Tales, Inc.), 241.

69. Ibid., 242–43.

70. Ibid., 243. Arthur Hacker's tourist-oriented *Wanchai* also devotes pages to the formation and impact of the novel, play, and film as well as to its ramifications in the present.

71. Ibid., 47.

72. Ibid., 52.

73. www.worldsexguide.org/hongkong; Kate Whitehead, "Suzie Wong Gives the Edge," http://www.totallyhk.com/LifeStyle/TotallyEats/Article/FullText_asp _ArticleID-20000719144604532.asp.

74. Turner, "Hong Kong Sixties/Nineties."

75. Ko, "Under Western Eyes," 67. See also Law Kar, "Suzie Wong and her World," in *Changes in Hong Kong Society Through Cinema* (Hong Kong: Urban Council, 1998), 61–63. Reconsideration of this film also figures in Turner and Ngan, *Hong Kong Sixties.*

76. One might also look at other reinterpretations of this icon by Korean filmmaker Helen Lee in her film, *Sally's Beauty Spot* (1992) and her 1997 article, "A Peculiar Sensation," *Cineaste* 23, no. 1 (winter): 36–39. Other Asian-Americans have also reused this icon with titles like "Suzie Wong is Dead."

PART III

WAR

11

INDIANISM?

Classical Hollywood's Representation of Native Americans

Roberta E. Pearson

In the mythical west of Cecil B. DeMille's *The Plainsman* (1936), Wild Bill Hickock and Buffalo Bill, two legends of the frontier, make camp together. An Indian appears, wearing a bullet-holed cavalry officer's coat and leading a horse with a Company E guidon flying from its saddle. The two Western heroes capture the Indian, who speaks to them in Cheyenne as Wild Bill translates for Buffalo Bill (and for the audience). Bill's translation ceases as the film cuts to a flashback, a classic image of Custer's Last Stand. The equally legendary yellow-haired general, clad in buckskins, stands by an American flag, surrounded by circling Indians. Hit by a bullet, Custer grips his chest and slumps to the ground, his arm crooked around the flagstaff. The cessation of the diegetic narration raises an intriguing question: is the view of the Last Stand authorized by the Indian who began the story or the white man who translates?

The image track shows us the representation of the climactic moment of the Battle of the Little Bighorn currently dominant in white culture, yet the narration purported to incorporate an aspect of "authentic" Native American culture. Rather than speaking the standard substandard English of many Hollywood Indians, this Cheyenne actually speaks Cheyenne. Or at least we, the audience, are led to believe that he speaks Cheyenne, which amounts to much the same thing for the Euro-American viewer. The Hollywood film causes the Indian character to speak his native language, thereby perhaps granting his narration a greater authenticity. Yet his perspective authorizes a flashback congruent with white culture's vision of the Last Stand and Custer's heroic death. If it is indeed the Cheyenne whose narration authorizes the flashback to the Last Stand, he gives an account of the battle at odds with that of the historical Cheyenne, who claimed that they did not even know that Custer led the troops they fought.

The tension between soundtrack and image track points to the complexities of Classical Hollywood's representation of Native Americans that I wish to explore in this chapter. Of course, a huge number of classical Hollywood films feature Native American characters, but here I focus on six films that feature General George Armstrong Custer, his Plains Indians opponents, particularly Sitting Bull and Crazy Horse, and the Battle of the Little Bighorn (Euro-American) or of the Greasy Grass (Native American): *The Plainsman*; *Custer's Last Stand*, a fifteen-part serial from 1936; *They Died With Their Boots On* (1941); *Seventh Cavalry* (1956); *Sitting Bull* (1955); and *Chief Crazy Horse* (1956). I use journalistic sources to place these films within their historical context with regard to contemporary attitudes toward both Custer and Native Americans. There are convincing intellectual and scholarly reasons to choose these particular texts to discuss the Classical Hollywood depiction of Native Americans.[1] General George Armstrong Custer, who came to prominence during the Civil War as the boy general with the golden locks, owes his continuing fame primarily to having been killed, together with all the members of his immediate command, by a combined force of Sioux and Cheyenne at the Battle of the Little Bighorn on June 25, 1876. No white survivor remained to relate the tale of Custer's last moments on earth. The country revered Custer as a savvy Indian fighter and his Seventh Cavalry as a crack regiment, and the news of their defeat reached the media centers of the East just as the nation began to celebrate its centenary. For these reasons, Custer, from the moment of his death, was established as a popular hero. His oft-reconfigured representation centrally relates to notions of American national identity and to shifting ideologies concerning westward expansion and Euro-Americans' treatment of Native Americans. His Native American foes, particularly their most high-profile leaders, Sitting Bull and Crazy Horse, have been similarly reconfigured, a reconfiguration particularly marked in 1950s Hollywood. As several commentators have pointed out, the "social-conscience" and "problem" films of the postwar period include several sympathetic to the Native American, among them *Broken Arrow* (1950), *Devil's Doorway* (1950), *Apache* (1954), and

White Feather (1956).[2] Both *Sitting Bull* and *Chief Crazy Horse,* as well as to some extent *Seventh Cavalry,* are part of this cycle, while *The Plainsman* and *They Died With Their Boots On* predate it.

The five films I have chosen relate to their respective ideological climates in complex and contradictory fashions, forming ideal texts to interrogate the applicability of Edward Said's concept of Orientalism to the Euro-American representation of Native Americans: is there an "Indianism"? Many scholars have taken his book, *Orientalism,* to have general applicability to all colonial situations, including those of settler nations such as the United States. In this highly influential work, Said argues that linguists, anthropologists, historians, and others have accumulated massive amounts of information in order first to define and then to dominate the Orient. "To have such knowledge of such a thing is to dominate it, to have authority over it. And authority here means for 'us' to deny autonomy to 'it'—the Oriental country—since we know it and it exists, in a sense, as we know it."[3] Said implies here and elsewhere that academic Orientalism has been an entirely Western construct, owing little if anything to a nondiscursive, non-Western reality, however that vexed term might be conceived. Yet, knowledge derived only from a Western perspective and refusing to incorporate the perspective of the colonized might have little utility. Robert Young claims that Said wants to have it both ways: to argue on the one hand that Orientalism is "a representation that has nothing to do with the Orient" and, on the other, that "its knowledge was put in the service of colonial conquest, occupation, and administration," which means that it had some degree of input from the dominated other.[4]

Said oscillates between these two positions, sometimes granting that the dominant to some degree incorporates the perspective of the dominated. Nevertheless, the general impression conveyed by his massive tome is that Orientalism has been monolithic and unchanging over the several centuries and several countries that his study covers. The scene from *The Plainsman* reveals a tension between dominant representation and the Other's self-representation, Hollywood often incorporating the latter even if merely to serve the instrumental purpose of verisimilitude. However, the 1950s films I wish to discuss exhibit an even greater tension in this regard, precisely because Hollywood's representation of Native Americans did not remain stable but rather changed noticeably from decade to decade with regard to the incorporation of the Other's self-representation in response to the ever-changing ideological climate. Since the moment of first contact, the dominant representation of Native Americans has been vexed and contradictory. This representation has often been characterized by the binary perspective of the "noble savage," whose untutored instincts render him superior in some respects to the white man, and the "savage savage," so low on the evolutionary ladder that he merits only swift and certain extermination.

HISTORICAL CONTEXTUALIZATION

Even at the moment when Native Americans most threatened westward expansion, the Plains Indians Wars of the 1860s and 1870s, white attitudes toward Indians remained contradictory. Those in the East often exhibited sympathy for the original inhabitants of the land, condemning the cruelty and the excessive force exercised by the U.S. military. Those in the West, however, viewed Indians simply as obstacles, scoffing at the softhearted liberalism of the easterners. Custer complained of this contradiction: "How many military men have reaped laurels from their Indian campaigns? Does he strive to win the approving smile of his countrymen? . . . If he survives the campaign he can feel assured of this fact, that one half of his fellow-citizens at home will revile him for his zeal and pronounce his success . . . a massacre of poor, defenseless, harmless Indians; while the other half, if his efforts . . . are not crowned with satisfactory results, will cry, 'Down with him.' " [5] Still, all agreed on one point: whether by physical extermination or cultural assimilation, the Indian would ultimately vanish.

After the end of the wars, government policy hastened the dissolution of tribal structures and the absorption of Indians into the dominant culture, the government officially disclaiming this assimilationist policy only in the 1930s. In 1933, Franklin Roosevelt appointed John Collier Commissioner of Indian Affairs, who quickly pressed for major legislation to enable Native Americans to preserve their traditional culture. The original version of the Indian Reorganization Act (IRA) stated, "It is hereby declared to be the purpose and policy of Congress to promote the study of Indian civilization and preserve and develop the special cultural contributions and achievements of such civilization, including Indian arts, crafts, skills and traditions." Although the 1934 final version eliminated this paragraph, the IRA, dubbed the Indian New Deal, gave Indian tribes an unprecedented amount of self-government. Representation, however, did not necessarily follow official policy. As Mary Weston shows in her useful study of the journalistic depiction of Native Americans, much coverage of the IRA and its intended beneficiaries resorted to well-established stereotypes. [6] In 1934, *Time*, reporting on an occasion on which John Collier spoke to Native Americans, noted with apparent surprise that they "met not crouched around council fires but seated in armchairs in an oak panelled room." *The Literary Digest*, reporting another such meeting that year, characterized the Native Americans in attendance as "young bucks, old men with sculptured faces, a few squaws and a few papooses too young to be left behind."[7]

The complex interrelationships among texts and ideologies revealed by the disjunction between official government policy and journalistic representation holds for the period's Custer texts. In 1934, Frederick Van de Water authored the first sustained attack upon Custer's position as national hero in his biography entitled *Glory Hunter.* The most proximate reason for the book's release may have been the death of Custer's wife the previous year. During her several decades of widowhood, Libbie Custer so ferociously defended her husband's reputation that few critics had been willing to risk her wrath. The reassessment of the famous Indian fighter may also have been partially determined by the government's about-face on Indian policy and the emergent cultural relativism that had prompted it.

Both the Custer films from the 1930s, however, construct a spotlessly heroic general, partly by contrast with his nefarious Indian foes. *The Plainsman*'s refusal to reevaluate history might stem from another component of the ideological climate, the Depression, which was more determinative than the government shift on Indian policy. The film's celebration of the pioneer spirit and the heroic exploits of the titular plainsman suited a moment of crisis that threw into question the national ideology of individual achievement. In the film's conclusion, two dead heroes, Wild Bill Hickock and George Armstrong Custer, ride together at the head of a cavalry column, the Stars and Stripes prominent beside them. A title declares, "It shall be as it was in the past . . . not with dreams, but with strength and courage shall a nation be moulded to last."

Custer's Last Stand features the same historical characters as *The Plainsman* (Wild Bill Hickock, Buffalo Bill Cody, Calamity Jane, and Custer), but it seems totally unmarked by the period's ideological climate. As we shall see below, *Custer's Last Stand* presents the most reduced stereotypes of Native Americans of all the texts examined in this essay. This is in keeping with a phenomenon of cultural lag that I have observed with other Custer texts. Those texts at the bottom of the cultural hierarchy—e.g., boys' adventure novels or comic books or Poverty Row serials—seem to serve as a repository for what Raymond Williams would term the residual components of the hegemonic structure. Texts further up the hierarchy more readily adapt to hegemonic reconfigurations.

They Died With Their Boots On (1941) responded even more directly than *The Plainsman* to its period's ideological demands. In the latter film, Custer had little more than a walk-on role, the character's minor function perhaps further accounting for the failure to reflect the current reevaluation of the general's heroic status. *They Died With Their Boots On,* however, was a biopic, focused exclusively on the general. Warner Bros. engaged in extensive historical research, yet seems deliberately to have ignored the Van de Water biography to produce a story of a mythic hero suitable for a nation on the brink of war. An article appearing in *Scholastic Magazine* in 1944 to some extent confirms this speculation as to the effect of the war upon Custer's image and that of his foes. The piece, entitled "George A. Custer—Hero of Two Wars," asserts that Custer "won a brilliant victory over the Cheyenne Indians in the Battle of the Washita."[8] This "brilliant victory" has been described by others, Van de Water among them, as a senseless massacre of innocents in which Custer's troops slaughtered women and children. *Film Daily,* in its review of *They Died With Their Boots On,* similarly celebrated Custer's defeats of Native Americans. "George Custer . . . the greatest of the Indian fighters has taken on more stature in the hands of his film biographers than almost any of the great Americans who have been immortalised on celluloid."[9]

Neither the cultural relativism and governmental policies of the 1930s nor Van de Water's biography prevented the valorization of Custer as Indian fighter in texts from the early 1940s, World War II being the most salient feature of the ideological climate. By contrast, the three 1950s films examined here, *Seventh Cavalry* (1956), *Sitting Bull* (1955), and *Chief Crazy Horse* (1956), were produced during a period of ideological turmoil. This turmoil was marked on the one hand by the rise of a postwar liberalism that culminated in the civil rights movements of the 1960s and, on the other, by the repression and conformity resulting from cold war pressures. Both liberalism and the cold war shaped government policy toward Native Americans during this period, as those on both ends of the political spectrum espoused social and cultural assimilation, albeit for different motivations. Liberalism, then still in the melting pot rather than the tossed salad multiculturalist phase, believed that equality demanded similarity: in a land with equal opportunity for all, all must be equally alike. No longer should Native Americans dwell on reservations apart from the mainstream of American society. Cold warriors, fiercely opposed to what they saw as the lack of individualism in Communist societies, also wanted to get Native Americans off the reservations in order to break the collective ties of the tribe. In 1953, the U.S. House of Representatives adopted a resolution to "end [Native Americans'] status as wards of the United States," initiating a series of laws, collectively known as "termination," that cut Native Americans' federal benefits and attempted to relocate them from the reservations.[10]

Weston argues that newspapers during this period, in keeping with government policy and liberal assimilationism, portrayed the so-called "good Indian" as one who abandoned his own culture to embrace that of the white man. As the *Christian Science Monitor* reported in 1952, "The picturesque, beaded, feathered, and quaint American Indian has just about vanished from the lands of his ancestors. In his place stands Mr. Indian, modern American citizen. Clad in a business suit, his keen black eyes view the passing scene with growing understanding and appreciation of his rights and obligations." [11] This positive, but assimilationist, representation of Native Americans appears in the period's Custer texts. Horace Sutton, writing about the Battle of the Little Bighorn, asserted that "Custer was at Little Bighorn . . . because some men wanted to be free and other men wanted gold." [12] Just like twentieth-century Americans fighting godless communism, nineteenth-century Native Americans fought godless Mammon—and all in the name of freedom. Another example comes from the 1960s, but its inclusion is warranted because the text was produced by archetypal 1950s liberal Rod Serling. In a fascinating *Twilight Zone* episode from 1964 entitled "The 7th Is Made Up of Phantoms," three National Guardsmen, on maneuvers at the Little Bighorn battlefield, encounter many of the same signs of Indian presence that their predecessors had found in 1876. Their disbelieving commander tells them, "If you meet any Indians, will you take it very slow? Because they're all college graduates and they're probably running tests on the soil." [13]

Postwar liberalism's sympathy for the Native American seems to have justified debunking that famous Indian fighter and, some said, Indian hater, George Armstrong Custer. In 1947, *Time* reported that Custer's supposed psychoneurosis fascinated psychiatrists. Dr. Paul R. Hawley, new medical chief of the Veterans Administration, said, "Custer's attack was one of the worst botched jobs in the annals of Indian warfare," brought about by the general's need to compensate for his earlier court-martial. Psychiatrist Karl Menninger diagnosed Custer as "a psychopath marked by extreme vanity, inhumanity, ruthlessness and a complete lack of loyalty to any friend or cause." Menninger asserted that a symptom of Custer's psychopathology was his "attacks on Indian camps, [in which] he habitually slaughtered the women and children." Menninger found "it hard to understand why the name of Custer still stands in U.S. history as that of a great hero." [14] Two of the 1950s texts discussed here to some extent reflect this debunking of Custer, although the Custer as outright madman thesis did not appear in Hollywood cinema until 1970 with the release of Arthur Penn's *Little Big Man.*

While postwar liberalism may have sanctioned another look at Custer and Native Americans, the cold war mentality ensured that such reevaluation could not go too far. In 1951, *Life* featured an article on the seventy-fifth anniversary of the Little Bighorn Battle. Calling the battle a massacre, the article referred to the Native Americans as "waves of yelping Sioux" and asserted that "the Seventh Cavalry has since continued its record for gallantry in the

Korean War, in which it has been a mainstay."[15] The *New York Times* also commented on the anniversary, its editorial, as one might expect from the traditionally liberal paper, less cold war hard-line than *Time*. The paper noted criticisms of Custer but asserted that he was still "indisputably a standout in American lore." It provided justification for the Native Americans, arguing that the battle resulted from the incursion of prospectors into the Black Hills. However, contemporary events shaped the *Times'* representation of history just as they shaped the magazine. The editorial ended, "So Yellow Hair died with his men of the Seventh Cavalry Regiment, fighting against overwhelming odds. The Seventh Cavalry Regiment knows a little about such things, for it is serving in Korea today."[16] Another article from the *Times* epitomizes the period's ideological tensions and contradictions. In a fashion more typical of 1930s cultural relativism than of 1950s assimilationism, reporter J. Donald Adams asks, "When will we learn to think of [the Indians] not merely as savages (whose savagery Western man has more than matched) but as the possessors, not only of the land from which we uprooted them, but of a way of life whose human dignity, spiritual strength, and awareness of beauty contained elements for which we may envy them." Despite his admiration for Native Americans, Adams, writing in a period that exalted the military's recent bravery in World War II and current bravery in Korea, clung to a heroic vision of Custer's Last Stand. He visited the Little Bighorn battlefield, guided by a "young Crow, veteran of the war in the Pacific," who said that elderly Sioux had told him that Custer's men were "roaring drunk" on the day of the battle. Said Adams, "I prefer not to credit their story, because it diminishes the gallantry which we associate with the "last stand."[17]

The ideological tensions of the 1950s clearly marked the conditions of production and reception for *Seventh Cavalry, Sitting Bull,* and *Chief Crazy Horse.* Although I have found little concerning the production of my three key 1950s films, the producers seem to have incorporated the period's ideological contradictions. In *Seventh Cavalry,* two sympathetic characters espouse diametrically opposed views. The distraught wife of an officer slain at the Little Bighorn keens, "Dead, all dead, all those men who were with Custer, massacred, tortured, Sitting Bull making big medicine with Sioux braves around the fire and the Sioux squaws with knives in their hands amongst the bodies of our dead and wounded. And my Jim one of the dead." This view of the Native Americans as massacring, torturing, mutilating savages was held by many nineteenth-century Westerners, and perhaps some mid-twentieth-century Americans as well, but it is balanced by the cultural relativist position put forward later in the film by a Native American character. Young Hawk tries to persuade the film's hero, Captain Benson, to leave Custer buried where he fell

Figure 11.1. *Sitting Bull* (1954).

because the Sioux believe that "if Yellowhair's body is removed his spirit will go with him and the fruits of our victory will be lost." The Captain dismisses this view as superstition. Young Hawk ripostes, "Is the white man's belief in the miraculous powers of his own saints and the truth within the teachings of his own faith superstition?" Such dialogue indicates that producers were attuned to the ideological climate. Certainly critics saw the connections between postwar liberalism and changes in the cinematic representation of Native Americans. Said *Senior Scholastic* in its review of *Chief Crazy Horse*, "There is a new twist these days to those movies about our American Indians. Once the redskin was presented as the savage killer, with the heroic American troopers always arriving just in time to save the fort. Today our frontier history is being presented through Indian eyes, and the treachery of the whites is replacing the long-familiar Indian skullduggery."[18] The venerable film critic of the *New York Times*, Bosley Crowther, complained that Hollywood's liberal impulses resulted in the distortion of history in *Sitting Bull*. "One could work up a pique at this picture for playing so loosely with facts merely to be on the currently popular side of a racial theme."[19]

STEREOTYPING

The above examination of ideological and representational shifts reveals that no monolithic and unchanging "Indianism" existed during the three decades of the Classical Hollywood sound cinema. Hollywood films, at least those having to do with Custer, responded in complex and contradictory fashion to the already complex and contradictory representations of Native Americans in the larger culture. However, the Classical Hollywood cinema, like much of popular culture, also depended heavily upon stereotypes, a much used but often poorly grounded term. As employed here, stereotyping does not mean simply the reduction to a few key character traits, often done with secondary characters in Classical Hollywood films for the sake of narrative simplicity. Nor does it mean the reduction of well-known historical characters to a few instantly recognizable signs. Classical Hollywood films purporting to represent the past often used this tactic, one well established by the second decade and discussed by my coauthor and me in *Reframing Culture: The Case of the Vitagraph Quality Films*. We argue that historical films deploy a reduced set of visual signifiers that immediately identify famous historical characters such as Napoleon Bonaparte or George Washington; cinematic representations must be iconographically consistent with the prevalent image that circulates elsewhere in the culture.[20] Just so with Custer: long hair, mustache, goatee, and a cavalry uniform of sorts are the few reduced signifiers that guarantee easy recognition. The culturally agreed-upon representation, however, extends only to image, not to character traits. As with the character of Napoleon, radically different interpretations of Custer's character have circulated since the subject's own lifetime: he is portrayed as, among other things, a villain, a hero, a victim of U.S. government policy, a dashing knight, and a cowardly murderer.

It might be said that there is a Custer type, but not a Custer stereotype. For by stereotype, I mean simplistic representations of the subordinate by the dominant. The dominant develops stereotypes that pinpoint visible differences in gender, sexuality, race, or nationality; generalizes and caricatures these traits; and applies them indiscriminately to all members of a social group. Popular culture texts, lacking the complexity or ambiguity of high culture texts, incorporate stereotypes as a simple and efficacious means of conveying information. Stereotyped characters can be sketched with just a few quick details and easily recognized by all members of a mass audience. Stereotypes reflect a shared cultural meaning that draws both upon the audience's knowledge of other cultural texts and upon familiar assumptions about the caricatured group. The character descriptions in the final script for *They Died With Their Boots On* provide a good example of Hollywood's stereotypical thinking. Elizabeth Custer is a "gentle type," Crazy Horse is a "magnificent physical specimen of great dignity," and Jane (renamed Callie in the film) is "the Custers' colored cook." Just a few words convey the essential information about each of these characters in terms of racial or gender stereotypes. Later in the script, when the officers of the Seventh Cavalry introduce themselves to their new commander, Custer, just one word suffices: "Cooper . . . Elliot . . . Keogh (Irish), Myers (Jewish), Macintosh (half breed), Commagere (French)."[21] Cooper and Elliot, presumably white Anglo-Saxon Protestants and thus part of the invisible dominant, require no descriptors, but each of the other officers is defined purely in terms of his ethnicity.

As these examples illustrate, in 1940s America only white males escape stereotyping: the use of stereotypes ensures that all groups outside the dominant are subject to some degree of "Orientalism." One of the six films under consideration, the fifteen-part serial, *Custer's Last Stand,* depends heavily on the repertoire of Indian stereotypes circulating in 1930s popular culture. The first reel quickly establishes the behavior of these stock Hollywood Indians, who play drums, chant, shoot arrows, take scalps, live in tepees, drink firewater, and speak standard substandard English. The film begins with a close-up of an Indian beating a drum, while another Indian chants. The milieu quickly established, the plot begins as Two Eagles, the medicine man, holds up the sacred arrow that unlocks the medicine cage where the Great Spirit dwells. In the next scene, a scout announces the arrival of a wagon train. The chief says, "We'll take their scalps—come with me." During the attack, the medicine arrow falls into the hands of the whites. The serial's villainous Indian, Lone Wolf, rides to town to seek the help of a renegade white man, Blayde, himself a stereotype, or at least a stock character, inherited from the melodrama. Upon arriving at Blayde's saloon headquarters, Lone Wolf is told that they do not sell liquor to Indians, at least through the front door. Blayde promises to help, and Lone Wolf says, "You will help me gettum arrow. Me wait."

The kinds of stereotypes employed in *Custer's Last Stand* provide an example of an almost perfect "Indianism." Yet even these stereotypes depend to some extent upon an external reality outside the dominant group's self-enclosed representation of the Other. The historical record shows that Plains Indians did live in tepees, use arrows, experience problems with the white man's alcohol, and so forth. At times, *Custer's Last Stand* moves beyond utterly reduced stereotyping and tries to incorporate more detailed aspects of the historical record. These misguided attempts at historical accuracy, however, produce a confusing blend of wildly different time periods and tribal customs. In one scene, the Indians, clearly patterned on Plains tribes such as the Lakota and the Cheyenne, capture a white man and subject him to an Aztec-like human sacrifice ritual. Wearing a buffalo headdress, a medicine man stands over the captive staked out beneath a cloth canopy with a hole in the center. "When the sun runs its circle the medicine knife will find your heart. You will meet the Great Spirit whose sacred arrow you helped steal," he says. The sun shines through the canopy onto the captive's chest and the medicine man traces the sun's outline with his knife, as if preparing to cut out the captive's heart. At this point, of course, the white hero rescues the white captive.

Here the serial mixes together (or up) Indian cultures that existed hundreds of miles and several centuries apart, but a later scene features an important element of Plains Indian religious belief, the Ghost Dance. In 1889 a Paiute Indian claimed that a vision had revealed to him that performing the Ghost Dance would rid the land of the white men and bring back the buffalo. The Ghost Dance spread from tribe to tribe and the unease it caused among the white man led both to the death of Sitting Bull and the massacre of Wounded Knee. In the *Custer's Last Stand* version, however, the Indians wish to test the captured hero's veracity. They explain: "Braves make the Ghost Dance. If your words are true then no harm will come to you. If you lie then Great Spirit will take you to him." They blindfold the hero, beat him, and then release him. In the reel's almost literal cliffhanger ending, the hero walks over the edge of a cliff. Rather than offering the hope of cultural resurrection, this Ghost Dance poses the threat of death. It thus becomes one more obstacle for the white hero, one more plot device—a Ghost Dance in name only, taking place more than a decade before its historical occurrence. However distorted or misrepresented, the serial nevertheless has incorporated an element of the dominated Other's culture.

The implication of distortion or misrepresentation raises vexed issues of the epistemological status and cinematic representation of the historical referent that an essay of this length cannot address. Neither does space permit speculation about the Hollywood cinema's impulses toward historical accuracy or the incorporation of the Other's perspective, although clearly the desire for narrative verisimilitude plays a part. The examples of the Aztec human sacrifice and the Ghost Dance reveal, however, that, although cheaply produced, low-end popular culture products, such as *Custer's Last Stand*, rely to a great extent upon the most reduced stereotypes of the dominated Other. One cannot simply dismiss such texts as always and unrelentingly conveying a perfect Indianism. For whatever reasons, even these low-end texts make the rare muddled gesture toward the Other's perspective, while slightly more up-market texts do so more frequently. Although written by Max Rich and rendered by a massed chorus, the opening song in *Sitting Bull* is presumably intended to represent the views of the titular hero. The musical setting combines Hollywood "Indian," marked by a steady, rhythmic beat, and typical "cowboy" songs such as those found in *Bend of the River* (1952) or numerous other 1950s Westerns. Voicing Sitting Bull's anxieties and spiritual beliefs, the chorus sings, "Great Spirit, spirit of the buffalo that roams the plains, are you gone forever, never, never you're to roam again." Toward the song's end, the chorus implores the Great Spirit to "lead us to the happy hunting grounds to dwell forevermore." Sitting Bull did worry about the disappearance of the buffalo, and, as a Lakota religious leader, a spiritual rather than a war chief, he would have borne special responsibility for the people's religious welfare. The producers of the film took these elements of the historical record and "Hollywood-ized" them into the almost mandatory title song of the 1950s Western.

Sometimes Hollywood producers nod toward the Other's perspective by attempting an unusual degree of ethnographic accuracy. Of all Native Americans, the Plains tribes, such as the Lakota, the Cheyenne, the Pawnee, staged the most sustained resistance to westward expansion. They thus became the most prominent Native Americans in popular culture, their appearance, customs, and rituals providing the basis for stereotypical Indians. Western films occasionally refer to the Sioux (Lakota) or Cheyenne, but for the most part, the plots do not distinguish among the numerous tribes and subtribes that roamed the Great Plains. However, several of the films considered here do attempt, albeit unsuccessfully, to make these distinctions. In *Sitting Bull*, the great chief, having finally decided to wage war, declares, "Send runners to the nations of the Sioux, to the Cheyenne, to the Crow who have been our enemies." This Hollywood Sitting Bull was right in stating that the Sioux were enemies of the Crow, the former having displaced the latter from their homelands. In 1876, the two tribes still held to their long-standing enmity, and it was Crow scouts who led Custer's Seventh Cavalry into battle at the Little Bighorn. The scriptwriters of *Custer's Last Stand* identified Crazy Horse, the still-revered war chief of the Oglala Lakota, as a Cheyenne. The opening titles of one reel declare, "The Great Sioux Nation, under Sitting Bull, Formed a Mighty Confederation with the Cheyenne, Whose Spokesman was Crazy Horse." To be fair, this is a common mistake, one that goes back into the Custeriana of the late nineteenth century. As it did with the Ghost Dance episode, the serial adds a rather strange note of verisimilitude. Having identified Crazy Horse as Cheyenne, the scriptwriters have the character say to Sitting Bull, "We must revenge Black Kettle. I will join you." Black Kettle, Cheyenne chief, was killed by Custer's Seventh Cavalry at the Washita in 1868 and a leader of the Cheyenne may well have wished to avenge his death.

The scriptwriters for *They Died With Their Boots On* also suffered a bit of confusion over Indian tribes. At a climactic point in the film, Crazy Horse warns Custer of the consequences of breaking their agreed-upon treaty. "Long Hair's word good word. But the word of the great white father is broken word. Hear me now Long Hair, if this word broken now not only Sioux but the Cheyenne, the Oglala, the Minniconjou, the Blackfeet, the Sans Arcs and every living tribe between mountains and great water will gather in one last battle. It will be the end of themselves, their gods, the spirits of their fathers and of their enemies." Crazy Horse's threat sounds appropriately fierce, and the enumeration of the various tribes lends it greater weight, but historians and anthropologists among the film's viewers may have been rather surprised at the rewriting of tribal connections. The Sioux, or Lakota, was a large confederation of subtribes that included the Oglala, the Minniconjou, and the Sans Arc.

One historian, Alvin M. Josephy, Jr., has protested the film's portrayal of Crazy Horse, particularly the dialogue. Prior to warning Custer of the consequences of failing to keep the treaty, Crazy Horse assures him that his people are desperate for peace.

My people want make peace. They've lost many braves. Are tired of war. They will give up the Plains forever. They will give up their lodges by the running streams. They will give up their hunting grounds where the buffalo graze. They will give all up but one place. They will not give up the Black Hills for there the spirits of our fathers dwell and there the gods have made their treaties. But all else that is my people we give up but Black Hills.

Describing Crazy Horse as "the most revered patriot of the Western Sioux," Josephy resents the depiction of the war chief Crazy Horse, whom he calls as "goofy-looking, goofy talking." Worse, the film Crazy Horse utters sentiments that his historical progenitor would have scorned. The script, asserts Josephy, sets up "a fictitious meeting with Custer (Crazy Horse never parlayed with whites)" and then has the chief announce "that the Indians will give up all their lands to the whites (!) except the Sacred Black Hills, which the united tribes will defend to the death." [22] Josephy clearly believes that *They Died With Their Boots On* distorts history by accepting the dominant's inauthentic representation of the Others' identity and reproducing an inaccurate account of the Others' history.

TOWARD A CONCLUSION

As a Native American, and thus a member of the dominated Other, Josephy implicitly postulates an "Indianism" that can be corrected by recourse to the perspective of the hitherto ignored Other. This perspective would presumably correct the distortions inherent in "Indianism" through an authentic portrayal of the dominated Others' self-identity coupled with an accurate recounting of the historical record, the authenticity and accuracy constituting the binary opposition of the distortions of "Indianism." However, the concepts of authenticity and accuracy presume a knowable, fixed Other or object of study, a baseline against which to measure deviation, a stability denied by postmodernist critical theory on the nature of language and representation. Dominated Others often seek authenticity through markers of identity predating colonization and untouched by the dominant; Native Americans struggle to preserve their tribal languages or religious rituals to maintain a space apart from white culture. Yet the hybridity characteristic of the late twentieth century makes difficult, if not impossible, the attainment of a pure and essentialist identity. Some historians would argue that such hybridity has been the norm almost from the moment of first contact between Europeans and Native Americans. At that moment, the identities of both colonized and colonizer began to derive from a fluid interchange, a mutual bricolage.[23] For this reason, the revisionist, "new Western" historians dislike the word "frontier," implying as it does a fixed boundary between cultures of essential identity. Instead, they prefer to think of a liminal zone of intermixture that shifted westward over the course of the eighteenth and nineteenth centuries.

These arguments render the concept of authenticity, the Holy Grail to many dominated Others, the merest chimera to both literary theorists and historians. Much the same can be said of the concept of historical accuracy. The film industry has always touted accuracy as a selling point for its historical epics, while traditional historians still seem to judge these epics primarily on the basis of their historical correctness.[24]

Film scholars, necessarily aware of the vexed nature of representation, at least with regard to the texts that have traditionally formed the core of the discipline, have employed the tools of poststructuralist literary theory to interrogate the cinematic and televisual representation of history. Abandoning the obsession with historical "accuracy" that has dominated the discussions of traditional historians, film scholars assert that films about the past reveal more about their period of production than about the period they purport to represent. Here, however, film scholars fall back upon conventional historiographic assumptions: the period of production is postulated as the stable historical referent that the text in question mediates; a film's deviations from or conformance to various aspects of the historical record are taken to illuminate the ideological configurations of its historical conditions of production and reception. Of course, such illumination depends upon the claim that there is indeed such a thing as the historical record, not an easy assumption in the face of postmodernist, poststructuralist challenges to the notion of the historical referent. Space constraints preclude a comprehensive discussion of the intense debate between traditional and postmodern historians concerning historiographic assumptions about the nature of reality. Nevertheless, a quotation from one of the latter, Alan Munslow, sums up well the challenge to older ways of doing history. "Because today we doubt ... empiricist notions of certainty, veracity and a socially and morally independent standpoint, there is no more history in the traditional realist sense, there are only possible narrative representations in, and of, the past, and none can claim to know the past as it actually was."[25]

Committed as I am to a cultural constructionist conception of reality, I am hard pressed to contest this claim from a theoretical perspective. However, I remain worried that ceding it entirely reduces us to an impotent silence. In the absence of any historical baseline against which to judge them, any and all cinematic representations of dominated Others become equally valid. Perhaps then we should seek a third way between the Scylla of postmodernist indeterminacy and uncertainty and the Charybdis of a rigidly held belief in an objective reality existing apart from subjective constructions. Let me therefore suggest a continuum stretching from the Others' claims concerning authenticity and accuracy on the left to the most outrageous stereotyping and historical "distortions" on the right, with the historical profession's agreed-upon "facts" somewhere in the middle. As film historians, then, our task is to locate cinematic representations of the Other somewhere along this continuum, without needing to presume that any point on the continuum matches up with an objectively verifiable external reality. Rejecting the concept of a perfect, monolithic, and unchanging Indianism in favor of such a continuum permits us to seek the determinants—ideological, narrative, production, or what have you—of observed shifts and changes in representation of Native Americans both within and across texts.

NOTES

My thanks to Karen Backstein and Daniel Bernardi for their helpful comments and suggestions.

1. The manuscript in preparation is entitled *Custer's Last Scene: History; Memory; Identity.* I have also written several articles on the topic. See "Custer Loses Again: The Contestation Over Commodified Public Memory," in *Cultural Memory and the Construction of Identity,* ed. Dan Ben-Amos and Liliane Weissberg (Detroit: Wayne State University Press, 1999); "The Twelve Custers, or Video History" in *Back in the Saddle Again: New Writings on the Western,* ed. Edward Buscombe and Roberta E. Pearson (London: British Film Institute, 1998), 197–213; "White Network / Red Power: ABC's Custer," in *The Revolution Wasn't Televised: Sixties Television and Social Conflict,* ed. Lynn Spigel and Michael Curtin (New York: Routledge, 1997), 326–46; "'The Revenge of Rain-in-the-Face'? or, Custers and Indians on the Silent Screen," in *The Birth of Whiteness: Race and the Emergence of United States Cinema,* ed. Daniel Bernardi (New Brunswick, NJ: Rutgers University Press, 1996), 273–99; and "'Custer's Still the Hero': Textual Stability and Transformation," *Journal of Film and Video* (spring/fall, 1995), 82–97.

2. For an article providing a new interpretation of these films, see Steve Neale, "Vanishing Americans: Racial and Ethnic Issues in the Interpretation and Context of Post-war 'Pro-Indian' Westerns," in Buscombe and Pearson, *Back in the Saddle Again,* 8–28.

3. Edward W. Said, *Orientalism* (New York: Vintage Books, 1979), 32.

4. Robert Young, *White Mythologies: Writing History and the West* (New York: Routledge, 1990), 129.

5. George A. Custer, *My Life on the Plains* (Lincoln: University of Nebraska Press, 1966), 26–27.

6. Mary Ann Weston, *Native Americans in the News: Images of Indians in the Twentieth Century Press* (Westport, CT: Greenwood Press, 1996).

7. "Pow Wow," *Time*, March 12, 1934, 15, and "A New Deal for the American Indian," *Literary Digest*, April 7, 1934, 21, both quoted in Weston, *Native Americans in the News*, 57.

8. "They Fought For Freedom: George A. Custer—Hero of Two Wars," *Scholastic Magazine*, March 27, 1944, 11.

9. Review of *They Died With Their Boots On*, *Film Daily*, November 22, 1941, 6.

10. Weston, *Native Americans in the News*, 99.

11. *Christian Science Monitor*, April 19, 1952, quoted in ibid., 104.

12. Horace Sutton, "The Battle in the Buffalo Bean," *Saturday Review*, September 7, 1957, 29.

13. For further commentary on the relationship between government policy and the representation of Native Americans in the 1950s, see Steve Neale, in Buscombe and Pearson, *Back in the Saddle Again*.

14. "The General Was Neurotic," *Time*, August 18, 1947, 90.

15. "It Was Only 75 Years Ago," *Life*, July 9, 1951, 41.

16. *New York Times*, June 24, 1951.

17. J. Donald Adams, "Speaking of Books," *New York Times*, September 3, 1950.

18. "Following the Films," *Senior Scholastic*, May 6, 1955, 27.

19. "Sitting Bull Sitting Pretty," *New York Times*, November 26, 1954.

20. William Uricchio and Roberta E. Pearson, *Reframing Culture: The Case of the Vitagraph Quality Films* (Princeton: Princeton University Press, 1993).

21. Willy Kline and Aeneas MacKenzie, script for *They Died With Their Boots On*, June 17, 1941, Billy Rose Theatre Collection, New York Public Library for the Performing Arts, Lincoln Center, 1, 87.

22. Alvin M. Josephy, Jr. "They Died With Their Boots On," in *Past Imperfect: History According to the Movies*, ed. Marc C. Carnes (New York: Henry Holt and Co., 1995), 148.

23. For a discussion of the historical literature on colonial encounters between Euro- and Native Americans, as well as some provocative reflections on authenticity and accuracy, see Jane Tompkins, " 'Indians': Textualism, Morality, and the Problem of History," in "Race," Writing and Difference, ed. Henry Louis Gates, Jr. (Chicago: University of Chicago Press, 1986), 59–77.

24. For information on the film industry's rhetoric about accuracy, see Uricchio and Pearson, *Reframing Culture*. For historians' attitudes, see Carnes, *Past Imperfect*.

25. Alan Munslow, *Deconstructing History* (London: Routledge, 1997), 16.

12

SINCERE FICTIONS OF THE WHITE SELF IN THE AMERICAN CINEMA

The Divided White Self in Civil War Films

Hernan Vera and Andrew Gordon

A good deal of time and intelligence has been invested in the exposure of racism and the horrific results on its objects. But that well-established study should be joined with another, equally important one: the impact of racism on those who perpetuate it . . . to see what racial ideology does to the mind, imagination, and behavior of masters.

—Toni Morrison, *Playing in the Dark: Whiteness and the Literary Imagination*

SINCERE FICTIONS, OR THE UNBEARABLE WHITENESS OF BEING

In this chapter, we investigate aspects of what we call "the sincere fictions of the white self" as they can be seen in the images of five Hollywood movies across the decades of the twentieth century. These films deal with one of the crucial periods of American race relations, the era of the Civil War and the Reconstruction: *Birth of a Nation* (1915), *The Littlest Rebel* (1935), *Gone with the Wind* (1939), *Raintree County* (1957), and *Glory* (1990). What we find in these movies is a persistence across time in representations of the ideal white American self, which is constructed as powerful, brave, cordial, kind, firm, and generous: a natural-born leader.

We also find that the Civil War is used as a means to dramatize a split in the white self. These movies are not about white versus black but, rather, white versus white: narrativized in *Birth, Rebel,* and *Raintree* as North versus South; in *Gone with the Wind* as antebellum South versus post-Civil War South; and in *Glory* as white liberal Northerner versus white bigoted Northerners. All the movies work toward a final reconciliation or reunification of the split white self, effected through marriage or family reunion in the first four films and through sacrificial death in battle in *Glory*. In each case, blacks play secondary characters, coded to enhance certain properties of the white self.

Since Gordon Allport's groundbreaking work, the study of race relations has been dominated by the concept of prejudice.[1] The word denotes judgments and sentiments toward others; prejudices are representations of others. The term, however, makes no reference to the judgments, sentiments, and representations of self that the encounter with the "other" elicits in the perpetrator of racism. As we know from object-relations theory, a self is comprised of representations of self and representations of others that are indissolubly linked. Racist action always involves both a representation of self and a representation of the other. The self-concept that the presence of the other elicits in the perpetrator, as much as prejudice about the other, helps to explain racist oppression and violence. For example, if I see the other as lazy and dirty, then I am thereby enabled to see myself as industrious and clean. Nazi extermination of the Jews helped to confirm the Nazis in their self-identity as the master race.

According to Otto Kernberg, the process of internalizing object relations takes place on three levels: introjection, identification, and ego identity. Introjection is the earliest stage; the infant takes in an interaction with an outside person. Splitting occurs at this stage as the ego splits off undesirable aspects of the self or splits threatening objects. The next stage, identification, is an intermediate level that involves a relation of subject to object and the taking on of social roles. Finally, ego identity is the highest level of internalization, in which the ego organizes a continuous self from introjections and identifications. Kernberg proposes that the selection of aspects of object relations that go into an identity formation must be in harmony—that is, the introjections and identifications must be more or less congruent and coherently organized.[2]

We want to extend this concept of identity formation into the area of race relations with the notion of what we call "sincere fictions of the white self." We borrow the concept of "sincere fiction" from the sociologist Pierre Bourdieu, who is elaborating on an idea of the sociologist Marcel Mauss. In *The Gift,*

Mauss shows how we engage in a gigantic social lie by pretending that gifts are voluntary and gratuitous, when in reality gift giving is obligatory.[3] Bourdieu extends this notion to suggest that almost all social relations depend upon "the sincere fiction of disinterested exchange":

> *the institutionally organized and guaranteed misrecognition* which is the basis of gift exchange and, perhaps, of all the symbolic labor intended to transmute, by the sincere fiction of disinterested exchange, the inevitable, and inevitably interested relations imposed by kinship, neighborhood, or work, into elective relations of reciprocity.... The labor required to conceal the function of the exchanges is as important an element as the labor needed to carry out the function.[4]

We propose that, in the realm of the self-concept, "sincere fictions" externalize an identity formation: they are a collection of selective identifications whose purpose is to occult other, unwelcome aspects of the self. Identity formation is a process of substitution in which one abandons certain introjects and replaces them with selective identifications. A sincere fiction of the white self builds up over time and partakes of all three levels of identity formation as described by Kernberg. On the level of introjection, it involves splitting; on the level of identification, the adoption of social roles; and on the level of ego identity, the creation of an ego ideal and the final exclusion of unwelcome aspects of the self.

"Sincere fictions" assume the world is a narrative and the subject is constantly acting within its precepts. The fictions are sincere because the subject is unaware of the alternative aspects of object relations he or she could have incorporated into his or her identity. Specifically, we assert that the white American self-concept is a sincere fiction that must be maintained at all times with intense symbolic labor in an effort to misrecognize the brutal reality of American race relations.

The white self-concept has been little studied because it has been taken for granted as "the self," the minority self being "the other," the deviation. The power to redefine or to force misrecognition is a significant power. Divisions of race are, after all, largely arbitrary constructions, fictions: for centuries, the Irish were not recognized as "white," and the Jews were seen as a separate race. In America, racial divisions have always been constructed obsessively around a dichotomous model, white or non-white, with the white self seeing racial others as monolithic. The negative images of the other are distortions that originate in the white mind and spread throughout American culture, but the white mind itself is rarely brought into question.

Inasmuch as we are talking about the identity not simply of individuals, but of the majority group in a culture, part of this symbolic labor in propping up the white American self-concept can be clearly seen in the social myths disseminated by Hollywood movies. Movies aim to address a mass audience through narratives, the sounds and images of which will reverberate among the largest possible number of viewers. The movies could be considered sincere fictions of American culture, made by a major American industry, and for American (and, ultimately, worldwide) consumption. Again to quote Toni Morrison: "the subject of the dream is the dreamer." [5]

THE DIVIDED WHITE SELF

Birth of a Nation (1915), *The Littlest Rebel* (1935), *Gone with the Wind* (1939), *Raintree County* (1957), and *Glory* (1990) all represent the ideal white American self as a natural-born leader. The Civil War dramatizes a split in the white self, and blacks are used to prop up the grandiose image of the white self. As the critic James Snead writes, "*Mythification* involves the realization that filmic codes describe an *interrelationship* between images. American films do not merely feature this or that debased black image or this or that glorified white hero in isolation, but rather they correlate these images in a larger scheme of semiotic valuation." [6]

Such stereotyping is to be expected in the notorious *Birth of a Nation*, which is a hymn of praise to the Ku Klux Klan, but it is surprising to encounter the same stereotypes seventy-five years later in *Glory*, a supposedly liberal film about the first black regiment to fight in the Civil War. This persistence suggests that the sincere fictions of the white self have maintained themselves throughout the twentieth century despite decades of struggle and apparent change in American race relations.

D. W. Griffith's silent film, *Birth of a Nation*, based upon Thomas Dixon's 1905 novel *The Clansman*, stands as one of the seminal American films of the twentieth century in terms of codifying the sincere fictions of the white self on the screen. This notorious film had an enormous impact in its day. Reputed to have inspired a new wave of terror by the Ku Klux Klan, it was also denounced by the NAACP. The movie is divided into three parts—the antebellum South, the Civil War, and the Reconstruction—an epic structure repeated in *Gone with the Wind*. In psychological terms, the three parts roughly correspond to the levels of development of the psychic structure: introjection, identification, and the final formation of ego identity.

The movie elaborates a myth about the South, creating scenes of the three periods of nineteenth-century Southern history: the grace and charm of the plantation South (like Camelot before the fall); the war years, when gallant Southerners fought nobly to the end for a lost cause and vicious Northerners looted and destroyed Southern homes; and Reconstruction, when predatory Northern carpetbaggers incited Southern blacks to lawlessness and riot. These three periods reappear in the structures of both *Gone with the Wind* and *The Littlest Rebel.*

The opening, antebellum sequence of *Birth* introduces two families, the Stonemans in the North and the Camerons in the South. Aristocrats and natural leaders, honorable, noble, and gallant, both families represent the best of the white self. The brothers of the two families are good friends, and a romantic attraction exists between one Stoneman brother and one Cameron sister and one Cameron brother and one Stoneman sister. Mirror images, these families seem destined to unite. In other words, we could say that this opening sequence corresponds to the stage of introjection, when self representations and object representations are not yet differentiated from each other.

There is, however, one "bad object" among these idealized representations of the white self: Congressman Austin Stoneman, father of the Northern family, is a fierce abolitionist, represented as a vindictive and power-hungry demagogue. The film implicitly blames Stoneman, the main villain, for the conflict between North and South and the division of the two families. The fact that his sons are blameless is part of the simplistic pattern of binary oppositions in the film: whites are either noble and selfless or base and self-serving; blacks, either faithful servants or vicious upstarts. Both self and other are split into good and evil, and the splitting accounts for the conflict in the film and the need for a reunification of the white self.

The movie takes a Southern point of view of American history. The antebellum South is represented as Edenic. The Camerons, wealthy plantation owners, are introduced as they reunite, greeting each other with hugs and kisses on the front porch of Cameron Hall. The father is the kindly master, everyone dotes on the little sister, and puppies frolic at their feet. We get an idyllic, sentimentalized version of family love.

The idyll continues with a visit by the family to the cotton fields, where blacks pick cotton in the background, and then to the slave quarters, where happy blacks dance in the presence of the white masters. The slaves are presented as suited to their position and contented with their lot, yet, at the same time, they are blamed for the war. An earlier title card tells us, "The bringing of the African to America planted the first seeds of dis-Union."

The war splits the Stonemans from the Camerons inasmuch as they fight on opposite sides. Both families lose sons. Ben Cameron demonstrates his courage and nobility at the battle of Petersburg. The title card reads: "The Little Colonel pauses before the last charge to succor a fallen foe" as he gives water to a wounded Union soldier. The implication is that these whites do not really hate each other; war is just something they must do, an inevitable process that simply happens. Nevertheless, at this stage there is an uneasy alternation between the wish to destroy the object and the desire to nurture it.

Ben Cameron is captured and due to be executed on a false charge, but his mother successfully pleads for clemency to "the Great Heart," President Lincoln. *The Littlest Rebel* contains a similar scene; in both films, noble, good-hearted Northern officers are exempt from Southern animosity. Also in both films, Lincoln is the ultimate good father, the Great White Saint, the epitome of the best of the white self, the man who, if he had survived, would have effected the reconciliation of North and South—or, to put it another way, would have healed the split white self. Lincoln serves as an iconic figure, an embodiment of the ego ideal in the sincere fiction of the white self.

Congressman Stoneman, a rival to Lincoln, argues against Lincoln's postwar policy of clemency for the South, saying, "The leaders must be hanged and their states treated as conquered provinces." Lincoln wants to treat them like errant children who can again be part of the family: "I shall deal with them as if they had never been away." If Stoneman is the father who rules by force, then Lincoln is the father who rules by love.

With the assassination of Lincoln, Stoneman becomes uncrowned king. Proclaiming "we shall crush the white South under the heel of the black South," he sets up in power in the South his protégé, the mulatto Silas Lynch. Stoneman is a caricature of the Northerner as "outside agitator," who wants to exact revenge against the South by inciting blacks to anarchy (a view that persisted in the South throughout the civil rights movement of the 1950s and 1960s). Lynch is a caricature of the Southern view of the "uppity nigger," who desires miscegenation.

A second war commences, in which the Ku Klux Klan, led by white Southern aristocrat Ben Cameron, and their allies, the "faithful blacks," defend the old social order against invading white Northerners and their proxies, crazed Northern blacks who want to seize power and rape white women. Both families are threatened. The black soldier Gus, described as "the renegade, product of vicious doctrines," tries to rape the Camerons' young daughter. She chooses death before dishonor, and the KKK lynches Gus. The ironically named black leader, Silas Lynch, tries to force himself on Elsie Stoneman. The KKK is seen as the defender of Southern rights, property, and honor—especially of the sexual purity of white women. Ironically, the conventions of screen narrative and representation transform the KKK into heroes with whom we are expected to sympathize. In the final battle, "the former enemies of North and South unite to resist the mad results of the carpetbaggers' political folly." D. W. Griffith tacked on a patriotic coda for the sound re-release of *Birth* in 1930: the singing of the national anthem and a color shot of the star-spangled banner waving in the breeze. This addition suggested that the film celebrated the birth of a new, unified nation, rather than the rise of the KKK.

As James Snead writes, despite its "vituperativeness," *Birth of a Nation* "is in fact a conciliatory film, and one of the more puzzling of its missions is both to castigate the behavior of some Northerners after the war, while at the same time offering a symbolic reunification of North and South (at the expense, it should be added, of black claims to justice)." [7] One way to account for this puzzling, contradictory aspect of the film is to see it as a narrative about the need for the reconciliation of the divided white self. Thus, race relations are really secondary in the film; the rebellious blacks, only a device to force the Northern and Southern whites to reunite as they recognize that they are really brothers under the skin—or rather, brothers because of their skin. It also helps explain another puzzling aspect of the film: the fact that all the major black roles are played by whites in blackface; the "blacks" are whites in clown-like disguise. In *Birth of a Nation,* blacks simply do not matter: they are only counters in the struggle of a split white self to reunite.

The Littlest Rebel replays *Birth of a Nation* twenty years later in the form not of an epic but of a children's story and a minstrel show. *Rebel* is the Civil War reenacted as a *Lassie* movie, with Shirley Temple as the brave youngster and Bill "Bojangles" Robinson as the faithful pet who comes to the rescue of his child master. The co-optation of black song and dance in the musical numbers of Temple and Robinson turns the film into a vaudeville or minstrel show; in one scene, Temple actually wears blackface. Like *Birth, Rebel* is a masquerade, featuring imaginary whites and imaginary blacks. Convoluted levels of misrecognition and self-delusion mark this sincere fiction of the white self: the adult white self masquerades as a little girl, and the little girl pretends to be black.

Once again, we see the agony of a split white self, symbolized by the war between North and South. In the 1930s, however, the fear was not of a Civil War but of a class war. Shirley Temple functions as a redeemer child, who can heal the divisions of the Civil War, or, symbolically, of the Depression. The iconic figure of Lincoln, the Great White Father, now takes on overtones of Franklin D. Roosevelt.

Like *Birth, Rebel* is sympathetic to the South but ultimately conciliatory in an effort to reconcile the divided white self. Temple plays Virgie Carey, only child of a perfect Southern family, lords of a plantation and slaveholders, just like the Camerons in *Birth.* Once again, the family is rich, handsome, loving, brave, and chivalrous, and their black slaves are totally devoted to them. (We wonder what it is in the white American self that expects and demands unswerving love and loyalty from those it oppresses.) The use of a child as the protagonist softens the rabid racism of *Birth*. Offensive stereotypes can thereby be presented innocently by focusing on the friendship of the charming little Virgie and the faithful family retainer, the resourceful Uncle Billy (who might better be called "Uncle Tom").

The pairing of Shirley Temple and Bill Robinson is an attempt to bridge opposites—young and old, female and male, white and black—to defuse the actual tensions between these rigid social categories. The historical remove makes the union of the two possible. James Snead writes, "only the strictly defined conditions and prohibitions of Southern plantation life could furnish the sensibilities of the thirties with acceptable insulation for what we get on screen: the warmth, even heat, of an extremely intimate relationship between an older black man and a younger white girl, on the surface at least a violation of strict racial and sexual decorum." [8] Uncle Billy, however, is presented as an unthreatening character: clever but loyal, affectionate, childlike and asexual, and eager both to serve and to entertain his white masters. He is as much family dog as family retainer. Just as Lassie makes her master, Timmy, seem worthwhile and sympathetic, so Bill Robinson proves the perfect foil for Shirley Temple, always at her service. His love and devotion to the family, whom he repeatedly rescues, are simply taken for granted: the white self deserves no less.

The film opens with a party scene; there are also parties early in *Gone with the Wind* and *Glory*. These social gatherings showcase the white self at its best: rich, charming, and gracious. Little Virgie hosts her birthday party, acting as the perfect Southern belle, imitating her mother. As the ideal white self, she is kind, gentle, condescending, and powerful, attentive to all the rules of etiquette as she commands the slaves who are serving the children. This white self, even as a child, plays her role adeptly. Virgie asks, "How would you like to see Uncle Billy dance?" and Billy smilingly complies.

The serenity and grace of the birthday party—the antebellum idyll—is abruptly shattered by the announcement that war has broken out. (Similarly, the declaration of war disrupts the ball at the Wilkes's plantation in *Gone with the Wind*.) The Carey family, like the Camerons in *Birth of a Nation* or the O'Haras in *Gone with the Wind*, are Southern gentry brought low by the war: the father removed to war, serving as a Confederate scout; the mansion invaded by brutal Union troops; the family reduced to living in the slave quarters; the mother taken ill and dying (like Scarlett's mother in *Gone with the Wind*); and, finally, the father arrested and sentenced to hang as a spy. Despite all these melodramatic events, this remains a child's version of the Civil War: we see no battles and nobody dies except the mother.

In the climax, Virgie emerges as the child savior, the mediator who recon-ciles North and South. Both her father and Colonel Morrison, the Northern officer who took pity on him and gave him a pass, await execution in prison. Uncle Billy and Virgie dance in the street to earn train fare to Washington, where Virgie pleads with Lincoln for clemency for her father and the colonel (in yet another scene lifted from *Birth of a Nation*). She of course charms him, as she charms every authority figure in the film, for they all have hearts of gold that melt before the power of this little girl. She sits on Lincoln's lap as he peels an apple, which he shares with her (but not, we note, with Uncle Billy, who is also present).

In the end, Virgie reunites with her two loving fathers—Captain Carey and Colonel Morrison—and she also has a black father figure in Uncle Billy. Through Shirley Temple, the white self is mythically presented to itself as a re-deemer child: Virgie the virginal, innocent yet powerful, able by virtue of her goodness and charm to dissolve all opposites—North and South, black and white—and to reunite the split white self.

One of the favorite movies of all time, *Gone with the Wind* remains one of the central American myths of the twentieth century. This is the great white American melodrama, an epic, picture-book-pretty, operatic fiction of the white self. It has many parallels to the other movies discussed and shares many similar scenes of the Edenic antebellum South (here shown as a world out of Arthurian romance), the War and the suffering of the South (a paradise lost), and Reconstruction, with further suffering of the South. *Gone with the Wind* is *Birth of a Nation* without the bedsheets and hoods of the Klan.

The film presents a divided white self, but here the division is coded not so much as North versus South but rather as Old South versus New. The movie narrates the transformation from the antebellum plantation South to the modern industrial South. We follow the story of Scarlett O'Hara (portrayed by Vivien Leigh), who changes from an empty-headed young Southern belle be-fore the war into a tough capitalist entrepreneur during Reconstruction.

Ideologically, *Gone with the Wind* could be said to be an apology for capital-ism during the revival of capitalism at the end of the Depression. In 1939, the country had been devastated and was struggling to recover, a situation simi-lar to that of the South during Reconstruction. *Gone with the Wind* represents the peak of the "plantation genre," which flourished in such Hollywood films of the 1930s as *Dixiana* (1930), *Mississippi* (1935), and *Jezebel* (1938). As the Depression continued, the antebellum mansions swelled in size and scale, cul-minating in the fantasy palace of Twelve Oaks in *Gone with the Wind*. The op-ulence of the settings serves as an apology not only for capitalism but also for racism. "The mansion and its grounds are used to legitimate the rule, and masked terror, of the plantation system in the cinematic Old South," writes Ed Guerrero.[9]

In the movie, two contrasting couples represent the split in the white self. Melanie (Olivia de Havilland) and Ashley Wilkes (Leslie Howard) are the epitome of the old white Southern self, or rather, of the sincere fiction of the white plantation owner—generous, honorable, courteous, kind, calm, monogamous, sedate in their lovemaking, but also rather passive and sickly. Their opposites in every respect, Scarlett O'Hara and Rhett Butler (Clark Gable) embody the new white Southern self: selfish, dishonorable, rule breakers, ruthless, lively, polygamous, passionate in their lovemaking, and active and healthy. Scarlett and Rhett are profiteers, perfect capitalists, although Scarlett is far more childish and self-centered and less self-aware than Rhett. Thus, the movie presents us with two sincere fictions of the white Southern self: the old cavalier versus the new entrepreneur.

Behind the story is a yearning for an impossible reunification of the fantasy Old South and the New, for a blend of the supposed grace and charm of the vanished plantation society with the spirit and enterprise of the rising industrial South. The keynote of nostalgia for a lost world of fairy tale or Arthurian romance is struck in the opening: "There was a land of Cavaliers and cotton fields called the Old South. . . . Here in this pretty world gallantry took its last bow. . . . Here was the last ever to be seen of Knights and their Ladies Fair, of Master and of Slave. . . . Look for it only in books, for it is no more than a dream remembered. A Civilization gone with the wind." This explains both Scarlett's longing throughout the film for Ashley, the epitome of the Old Southern cavalier, and Rhett's farewell speech to Scarlett: "I'm going to Charleston, back where I belong. . . . I want peace. I want to see if somewhere there isn't something left in life of charm and grace." Rhett too misses the order of the old world; he is tired of the turmoil of this New South, represented by Scarlett. In psychological terms, this longing for a lost, mythical world of unmitigated happiness and wholeness could represent a desire to return to a stage of pre-oedipal bliss before there was any differentiation between self and objects, before the splitting of the white self.

Although Melanie and Ashley represent the best of the Old South, of the white propertied classes, of the idealized white self, they are victims and losers, unsuited to survive in the postwar South. They lose their land and their home and become dependent upon Scarlett, who is tough enough to make it in the New South: she marries a storeowner to save her land, builds a sawmill, runs it with convict labor, and rebuilds Tara, the O'Hara family mansion.

The movie justifies the creation of the modern white self, the capitalist entrepreneur, but it tries to reconcile itself to the contradictions of capitalism by having it both ways. Scarlett, a survivor, uses any means to come out on top: she is manipulative, venal, ruthless, and driven. Yet, it is difficult to hate her because she constantly suffers. She adapts successfully to the new order of capitalism but pays a terrible emotional price. The audience can applaud itself for not being as selfish as Scarlett and, at the same time, sympathize with her sufferings and see her as a lost little orphan girl. The movie is a melodrama about the sufferings of the white race (we never see blacks suffering).

In terms of cinematic genres, *Gone with the Wind* follows the conventions of the woman's romance. In the course of the movie, Scarlet suffers because of her love for Ashley, a married man, and because of the devastating war and its aftermath. As melodrama, this movie throws in everything: war, violence, serious wounds, bloody amputations, explosions, fire, difficult childbirth, starvation, poverty, loss of home, madness, death of a friend, death of parents, death of husbands, death of a child, murder, attempted robbery and attempted rape, prostitution, adulterous longings, and unrequited love. What more could an audience want?

All the characters in *Gone with the Wind* are types rather than three-dimensional characters, but the film allows a much greater range of types and human qualities among the whites than among the blacks. Reduced to background figures, blacks appear primarily as slaves: loyal servants like Mammy (Hattie McDaniel), stupid and cowardly servants like Prissy (Butterfly McQueen), or clownish servants. Whites are seen as worthy of the subservience, loyalty, and love of the faithful servants. The blacks are no more than conveniences, psychic extensions of the whites, intended to prop them up. Mammy serves three generations of O'Haras, identifies totally with them, and seems to have no family of her own and no life outside that white household. She upholds aristocratic white family tradition and honor and often scolds and upbraids Scarlett. She is like an externalized, walking superego, but as a comically obese black slave, she is unthreatening: bossy but powerless, loving, and eternally loyal.

Autonomous blacks—those who are not servants and who mix freely with "white trash"—are represented, as in *Birth of a Nation*, as dangerous and lawless, liable to assault and rape beautiful, wealthy white women like Scarlett. The nighttime revenge raid on a shantytown by the propertied whites resembles a Klan raid in *Birth of a Nation*, minus only the white robes. The dangerous black characters quickly disappear from view, however, and this is only a minor episode in a busy movie, not the central concern it is in *Birth*.

Figure 12.1. Character types in *Gone with the Wind* (1939).

Because the black servants never change, they act as comforting figures in a turbulent world where everything constantly changes. A beacon of stability, Mammy never alters her behavior or her attitude toward the family, whether she serves them as a slave before the war or as a supposedly free housekeeper after it. The blacks are remnants of the Old South. As Ashley expresses it in a nostalgic speech to Scarlett: "Oh, the lazy days! The warm still country twilight. The high, soft negro laughter from the quarters. The warmth and security of those days." In the end of the movie, the blacks remain the same, but the whites change. Scarlett survives and soldiers on, but she has lost both Ashley and Rhett. The reconciliation between the Old South and the New never takes place, and the white self remains irremediably split, symbolized by the isolated figure of Scarlett. All she has left to cling to is Tara, the symbol of the Old South and of family continuity, but it is an empty symbol now that both the old world and the family are lost. Although the longing to return may persist, the "warmth and security" of pre-oedipal bliss is gone with the wind.

Raintree County (1957) is another Civil War epic, based, like Birth of a Nation and Gone with the Wind, on a popular novel. Again, like Gone with the

Figure 12.2. Mammy (Hattie McDaniel) and Scarlett (Vivien Leigh).

Wind, it is a long movie that begins with an orchestral overture and includes an intermission in the middle. However, *Raintree County* could not emulate the box office success of *Gone with the Wind* because it is an uncomfortable blend of 1950s, Tennessee Williams-style psychodrama with *Gone with the Wind* melodrama.

Raintree simply reverses the polarity of *Gone with the Wind*. Here, the antebellum North, instead of the antebellum South, is the idyllic, utopian land of grace, beauty, and charm. The film opens with beautiful scenes of a lush green landscape in Indiana in the summer of 1859, echoing the opening scenes of Georgia in *Gone with the Wind*.

The hero is an impossibly noble young white Indianan, John Shaughnessy (Montgomery Clift), the fastest runner in Raintree County and valedictorian of his class. Groomed for greatness, he is a poet, a seeker after the mythical raintree of the title. John's plans are derailed when a conniving Southern belle, Susannah (Elizabeth Taylor), falsely claims she is pregnant and thus tricks him into marriage. They honeymoon in the South and return to Indiana, where John becomes a teacher. Eventually she bears him a son. During the Civil War, Susannah runs away to the South with their child, and John joins the Union Army to find them, risking his life in battle many times, devoted to his wife despite the fact that she is crazy.

Susannah is tormented because of her family legacy. Her crazy mother killed her husband and the black maid Henrietta when she found them in bed together and then set fire to the house. Only the child Susannah survived, but she feels guilty for having told her mother about the affair, assumes Henrietta was her real mother, and hates herself, mistakenly believing she has black blood. Susannah is like Scarlett as psychotic rather than neurotic, a Scarlett too much in love with her black mammy. She wages her own internal civil war because she is divided against herself on the race issue.

In this narcissistic fantasy, the Northern white self, represented by John, is a noble abolitionist, but the Southern white self, represented by Susannah, is a crazy slaveholder. The two embark on an unstable marriage. The movie moves from North to South several times. The North is idyllic, and the South, like Susannah, has great surface charm and beauty (represented by a riverboat and a cotillion ball), but it is ultimately a gothic horror of ruined mansions that conceal terrible family secrets, whorehouses with mulatto prostitutes, and madhouses. The North must rid itself of the burden of the perverted South, and the movie ends when the Civil War is over and Susannah kills herself, freeing John to marry his long-suffering hometown sweetheart, who has waited for him patiently.

Despite the 1950s liberal pretensions of the film, blacks appear only as minor characters, background figures, docile servants loyal to their white masters. The focus is on the melodrama of the whites, especially on the impossibly good, heroic John.

More than fifty years separate *Gone with the Wind* and *Glory*. In the interim, the plantation genre withered, the civil rights movement occurred, and the New South prospered. Nevertheless, despite the apparent progress, racial divisions were still deep and wide: America moved from the age of Martin Luther King to the age of Rodney King. A new myth took root in the post–civil rights era: that institutionalized racism no longer exists and that the United States is now an egalitarian society. That is the message of *Glory*, a self-congratulatory film meant to reassure whites and blacks about how far America has come in race relations. In 1990, as in 1915, 1935, 1939, or 1957, Hollywood movies about the Civil War still promulgated sincere fictions of the white self.

Glory is one of a spate of 1990s films on the Civil War that includes Ken Burns's massive documentary, *The Civil War* (1990); *Gettysburg* (1993); and *The Oldest Living Confederate Widow Tells All* (1994). On the surface, *Glory* presents a very different take on the War than that of earlier Hollywood films, offering a Northern liberal point of view and telling a story previously untold in the movies, about black soldiers' service to the Union. It can also lay claim to a greater degree of realism and historical veracity because it is a biopic, or docudrama, based on the exploits of a white hero, Colonel Robert Gould Shaw (played by Matthew Broderick), a Boston Brahmin and abolitionist who commanded the first black regiment to fight in the Civil War. Shaw and his regiment are commemorated in a monument in Boston (which inspired Bostonian Robert Lowell's 1964 poem about the civil rights movement, "For the Union Dead"). Of course, the question of "realism" and "historical authenticity" in Hollywood films is always problematic—even D. W. Griffith considered his *Birth of a Nation* the first "realistic" filmic depiction of the Civil War and included historical figures, such as Lincoln, and tableaus recreating historical events with painstaking care.

Glory follows Shaw's military career from his wounding at the battle of Antietam, through his return to Boston, to the formation and training of the regiment and their first skirmish in the South, and ends with the valiant but futile suicide charge on Fort Wagner in South Carolina, in which Shaw dies along with half the regiment.

Aside from its supposed historical authenticity, the film also offers a greater variety of black characters. It deviates from previous Civil War films by showing blacks as heroic combatants and as realistic figures who grow and develop rather than remaining static stereotypes, docile or comic servants. There is Thomas, an educated Bostonian, born free and raised alongside Shaw, who now works for Shaw's father. The first to volunteer to serve in the regiment, the educated but soft Thomas is a poor soldier during training, but he finally shows his mettle under fire, when he demands to be allowed to fight even after he is wounded. Next is Rawlins (Morgan Freeman), known as "Gravedigger," an escaped slave, the oldest and wisest of the recruits, who becomes a leader and is promoted to sergeant. Third is Jupiter, an illiterate field hand who stammers but is a crack shot. Finally, there is Tripp (Denzel Washington), another escaped slave, embittered, alienated from his fellow blacks, and full of hatred for whites. By the end of the film, Tripp has bonded with the regiment and is loyal to the colonel. The screen time devoted to such a variety of realistic black heroes, portrayed by distinguished black dramatic actors, shows an advance in Hollywood's treatment of African-Americans—although it may also be seen as a marketing strategy to draw a large black audience as well as a white one.

Without the racial issue, *Glory* follows the conventions of a standard Hollywood war movie: the training of the eager, raw recruits through harsh methods to make them ready for battle; the sadistic, foul-mouthed Irish top sergeant who bullies the men for their own good; the commanding officer, stern but kindly, who cannot afford to fraternize with the men but really loves and disciplines them. The audience sympathizes with the grave responsibility and loneliness of his command. We follow the men as they grow into real soldiers, bond together, become loyal to the commander, and, in the final combat, prove their heroism even at the cost of their lives. Although *Glory* could be seen as an antiwar film because of the realistic blood and gore, it also glorifies war as a male proving ground. Moreover, it justifies the Civil War as a brutal but necessary conflict fought for the noble cause of black freedom. This ignores the complicated nexus of economic and political reasons for which the war was actually fought.

Despite the obvious differences of *Glory* from *Birth of a Nation, The Littlest Rebel, Gone with the Wind,* and *Raintree County,* it purveys some of the same sincere fictions about the white self as these earlier films. *Glory* centers on the heroism of Shaw, the great white leader who dared to take command of the first black regiment, built them into a strong fighting force, and gave his life on their behalf. The focus throughout stays on Shaw, whose voice-over narration in the form of letters home controls the narrative, and the black characters remain secondary. Shaw grows from the tentative and baffled captain at Antietam to the brave, self-assertive colonel of the final charge. The view of the black man may have changed in this film, but the view of the white man has not: the ideal white American self is still constructed as powerful, brave, cordial, kind, firm, and generous—a leader. There are no autonomous blacks in this film, only blacks who are led by whites. The blacks are forged into an efficient fighting machine because of their loyalty to the white colonel, who deserves their loyalty because he is the noblest character in the film. Their heroism and sacrifice serves then to validate and glorify Shaw.

The existence of blatant racism among the white Union enlisted men and officers, such as the brutal Irish sergeant and the cruel Colonel Montgomery, also serves to confirm Shaw's nobility, just as in *Birth of a Nation, The Littlest Rebel,* and *Gone With the Wind,* the mean Northern carpetbaggers or predatory Union soldiers serve as foils to the virtue of the Southern heroes or heroines. Once again, we could also view this division as aspects of the split white self.

The treatment of the character Tripp demonstrates how the black characters reinforce the sincere fictions of the white self in *Glory.* Tripp starts out hating whites, but he eventually converts from a "bad black" to a good one who loves the colonel, proving that the whites deserve the loyalty of the blacks. In one scene, Shaw orders Tripp flogged for desertion (Shaw later learns that Tripp was off looking for shoes because the men were so poorly equipped). The scene is deliberately filled with painful reminders of slavery: the white master ordering the disobedient black whipped as a lesson to the other blacks. When

Tripp's shirt is stripped, his bare back reveals the scars of previous whippings he endured as a slave. As the flogging proceeds, the shots alternate between extreme close-ups of Tripp's face as he defiantly stares down Shaw and of Shaw's face as he reacts to the flogging. Tripp's expression never changes, even as tears of pain roll down his face, but Shaw flinches. In other words, Tripp's scene of pain turns into the agony of the great white liberal, who is caught in a bind between his abolitionist beliefs and his duty as a commander to maintain discipline for the good of the men.

In a later scene, Shaw congratulates Tripp for fighting well in their first skirmish and asks him to bear the regimental colors into battle. Tripp refuses, saying, "I ain't fighting this war for you, sir." Nevertheless, Shaw is trying to make up for his previous treatment of Tripp and the two at least are talking. During the final charge, after several flag bearers fall, Tripp retrieves the flag before he too is cut down. In the last scene, as the Confederates toss the bodies of the dead Union soldiers into a mass grave, Tripp winds up with his head resting on the bosom of the colonel. This sentimental image seems to suggest that even the surliest black will eventually come to love the kind and noble white master. In *Birth of a Nation,* the threat of the renegade black Gus had to be neutralized by killing him; in *Glory,* the bad black is neutralized by converting him into a loyal follower of the white leader before killing him. This is scarcely progress.

How is one to explain the persistence of such stereotypes across time in the Hollywood cinema, despite the apparently dramatic changes in race relations in American society? One could say that Hollywood cinema is an economically conservative medium that tends to rely on proven formulas for storytelling. We know, however, that such cinematic formulas change over time. A more probable explanation is that, even as fashions in storytelling change, the deep structure of white American identity persists over time, and the apparent changes in American race relations are largely surface phenomena.

Identity is a construct, a fiction, but it is a deeply embedded, remarkably persistent, and necessary fiction. Sometimes people prefer to die rather than to relinquish their identity. Race is another fiction, preserved in this country because the arbitrary division between white and black helps to maintain white privilege. The fictions of race intersect with the constructions of identity to create the sincere fictions of the white self. These sincere fictions, incorporated on the level of object relations and therefore largely unconscious, sustain a white ego ideal and preserve the notion of the black as the "other," preventing us from recognizing the brutal reality of the racial oppression on which American society has always been based and from recognizing our own internalized racist notions. Until we confront the psychological underpinnings of racism and expose the sincere fictions of the white self, any changes in American race relations will continue to be superficial.

NOTES

1. Gordon W. Allport, *The Nature of Prejudice* (Reading, MA: Addison-Wesley, 1954).

2. Otto Kernberg, "Structural Derivatives of Object Relations," *Object Relations Theory and Clinical Psychoanalysis* (New York: Jason Aronson, 1976), 30–38.

3. Marcel Mauss, *The Gift*, trans. Ian Cunnison (London: Cohen and West, 1954).

4. Pierre Bourdieu, *Outline of a Theory of Practice*, trans. Richard Nice (Cambridge, England: Cambridge University Press, 1977), 171.

5. Toni Morrison, *Playing in the Dark: Whiteness and the Literary Imagination* (Cambridge: Harvard University Press, 1992), 17.

6. James Snead, *White Screens/Black Images: Hollywood from the Dark Side*, ed. Colin MacCabe and Cornel West (New York: Routledge, 1994), 4.

7. Ibid., 44.

8. Ibid., 52.

9. Ed Guerrero, *Framing Blackness: The African American Image in Film* (Philadelphia: Temple University Press, 1993), 23.

13

CREATURES OF GOOD AND EVIL

Caucasian Portrayals of the Chinese and Japanese during World War II

Karla Rae Fuller

The most well known Oriental figures on the Hollywood screen were almost always non-Asian actors made up to look Asian. From the film industry's earliest days, African-Americans, Latinos, Native Americans, and Asians have been impersonated by performers of other racial groups. Notably, the Asian depictions have produced well-known iconic figures, such as Fu Manchu and Charlie Chan, who remain familiar. Still, scholars, critics, and viewers frequently collapse distinctions between portrayals of Asian roles by Caucasian actors and those by Asian actors in order to create a generalized Asian typology. Implicit in the practice of Asian impersonation by Caucasian actors in Hollywood is the assumption that the Caucasian face provides the physically normative standard onto which a racial inscription can take place. The "Oriental" performance by the non-Asian actor is particularly useful to film scholars focusing on racial representation because it keenly exposes the artificial foundations in Hollywood's depiction of race. Through the act of physical embodiment, the Caucasian actor displays patently artificial and theatrical features and offers a site for the projection of displaced desires and fears. Like any masquerade, the artificiality of the impersonation is apparent, and yet this performance practice operates with a high degree of complexity, promoting certain qualities while effacing others.

Edward Said contends that the West has created "highly artificial" enactments of an "Orient," but notably, he asserts that a more useful approach in any critique of these fabrications lies in their deconstruction rather than their denunciation. The Orient as a Western construct has meant, among other nations, Asia, the Far East, the Middle East, Arabia, China, Japan, and India, depending on the historical moment or the nation conceiving it.[1] Hollywood's Oriental exists as a specialized classification (loosely based on Asian culture) that supersedes national or racial identity and thus, allows for shifts, transformations, and reconfigurations over time due to its flexible boundaries. It is precisely this versatile capacity to recreate and reformulate that makes Oriental the term of choice for this essay (as opposed to Asian, or Japanese, Chinese, or others) for it reminds us of the fictional origins and status of Hollywood's Asian characterizations.

This examination of wartime Oriental archetypes (as opposed to the concept of inert or static stereotypes) uses a range of Hollywood products, such as cartoon images, a prestige picture, and a B film.[2] However, it primarily focuses on representations by Caucasian actors in the attempt to reveal a systematized approach in the depiction of race working within the "classical" Hollywood studio era.[3] However, rather than propose a strictly formulaic system of representation, this study offers a schema of performance styles by tracing specific cosmetic devices and physical gestures, dramatic cues, and narrative conventions. Baring the device of the Oriental masquerade in this way establishes the concept of racial difference as far more than biologically based. Hence, the use of the phrase "racial types" and the focus on "physical features" in this essay in no way suggest an assumption of "natural" categories. Rather, it considers this device as a complicated textual construct that functions with "classical" consistencies and redundancies.

Collectively, the films selected in this chapter illustrate the mutability of established Oriental archetypes as well as exemplify important shifts in their wartime evolution from more benign prewar types. Both Oriental hero and fiend take on new meaning during this time as positive portrayals are categorically reversed in the animated short *Bugs Bunny Nips the Nips* (1944). In the epic feature film, *Dragon Seed* (1944), we have the appearance of an important wartime strategy to differentiate Asian national identities with the purpose of creating sharp divisions between our Chinese ally and Japanese enemy. The exploration of racial difference through a single human body depicts the concept of racial alteration as both ultimate fantasy and nightmarish threat in *First Yank into Tokyo* (1945).

ME NO MOTO

> There are thousands of Japanese aliens in southern California but Sol
> Wurtzel can't find one of them to play a heavy role in the forthcoming
> *Secret Agent of Japan* at 20th-Fox. American-born actors of Nipponese
> descent are side-stepping the idea and Chinese players won't even dis-
> cuss it.[4]

This brief article appeared on the front page of *Variety* only weeks after the
attack on Pearl Harbor. Sol M. Wurtzel had been the executive producer (and
occasionally credited as assistant director, "Solly Wurtzel") for many of the
Mr. Moto detective pictures produced by Twentieth Century-Fox. Although
the detective series had ended its run in 1939, the producer's name may have
remained linked with the commercially successful films and with its then heroic Japanese protagonist. The headline transposition of an Oriental movie
hero (Moto) to a villain (or "heavy" as the article specifies) not only reflects the
dictates of the wartime shift in societal attitudes, but also perhaps implicitly
exonerates Wurtzel's earlier involvement with the series. Predictably, *Variety*
not so subtly equates Japanese American (note the use of the racial epithet
"Nipponese") and Chinese actors with the so-called "aliens" supposedly infil-
trating southern California. The reference to the Japanese screen detective
Mr. Moto illustrates how the familiarity of an Oriental Hollywood character
can provide a convenient classification for an unseen and unknown enemy.
At once, slanted, manipulated, and altered, a once singular hero suddenly becomes a symbol for the unequivocal enemy—a massive threat targeted for
extinction.

The racial impersonation of Asians by Caucasian actors remained the predominant performance practice during the Second World War. However, after the attack on Pearl Harbor, government authorities perceived the construction of a Japanese enemy in Hollywood films as critical to the war effort.[5]
Yet, the structure of this Oriental adversary was neither entirely simplistic
nor fixed as the figure of "the Japanese enemy" shifted and adjusted over the
course of the Pacific war years (1941–45). Six months after the attack on
Pearl Harbor, in June 1942, the government established the Office of War Information (OWI) as the sole contact with the Hollywood film industry:[6]

> The presidential order instructed OWI to undertake campaigns to en-
> hance public understanding of the war at home and abroad; to coordi-
> nate government information activities; and to handle liaison with the
> press, radio, and motion pictures.[7]

Even though escapist fare was still the order of the day in Hollywood, the
studios also were strongly "encouraged" by government authorities to pro-

duce films explicitly extolling the virtues of democracy and condemning totalitarianism.[8]

A notable feature in Hollywood's attempt to condemn the Japanese attack on Pearl Harbor was the sudden redefinition accorded to heroic cinematic Oriental detective characters like Mr. Moto. This redefinition invoked the familiarity of these characters but not the esteem and affection they enjoyed before the war, as the "Me No Moto" title so clearly illustrates. Mr. Moto, and also to a much lesser degree, Charlie Chan, were negatively invoked as symbols of the villainy and treachery of the suddenly homogenous "yellow peril" wartime enemy. Why would negative invocations of well-known "heroic" Oriental characters, instead of an unequivocally evil Oriental figure like Fu Manchu (a professed advocate of Asian world domination), be used as symbols for the Japanese enemy? Rather than refer to a known Oriental adversary, Hollywood exploited amicable Oriental characters, perhaps reflecting a lingering sense of treachery and betrayal triggered by the nature of the surprise attack on Pearl Harbor.

BUGS BUNNY NIPS THE NIPS

The cover cartoon for *Collier's* magazine dated December 12, 1942, marking the first anniversary of the attack on Pearl Harbor, presents a Japanese military figure about to drop a bomb on the unsuspecting ships. This figure is not rendered in a recognizably human form within an airplane, but rather manifested as a vampire bat. Without a body, this creature possesses a face, wings, and disembodied gloved fingers clutching the bomb. The face has slanted eyes, a broad nose, and prominent teeth, along with huge fangs and ears pointed in a demonic fashion. Significantly, this creature is also clothed and armed with recognizable icons from both the German and Japanese military. The bat wears a Japanese military cap, carries a sword in one hand, and, curiously, displays a swastika on each wing. This image represents a site where caricature and propaganda meet to produce an impossible image: a creature of evil that has almost nothing to do with the reality of a "racial" type (or human type for that matter). Instead, the image involves the distortion of a number of physical features and iconic symbols displayed to induce hatred. Whether inverting the qualities of heroic Oriental film characters or fusing the qualities of both the German and Japanese military, any apparent incongruity of elements appears to be subordinate to the wartime propagandistic task of arousing a visceral reaction in the American people.

When a caricature is rendered in "pen and ink" (i.e., *Collier's* vampire cover art, editorial cartoons, or war posters of the period), one can find its most extreme manifestations since no human body is required to mediate the message. The functions of caricature in World War II film animation produced by Hollywood included both portrayals that sought to identify and vanquish a formidable wartime adversary along with depictions of this same opponent as hopelessly weak and inferior. Cartoon shorts not only provided uniformly antagonistic versions of the Japanese, but also used humor for comic relief—hence, the tendency in this medium to represent the enemy as either buffoon or superman. The Japanese enemy depicted in *Bugs Bunny Nips the Nips* (Warner Bros., 1944) reveals an antagonist played mainly for laughs. However, a series of vigorously exhibited Oriental clichés characterize the wartime threat, despite its less sinister nature. Physically focused elements of the Japanese wartime caricature predominate in this cartoon, not only in terms of facial features but also in the physique.

Bugs Bunny Nips the Nips demonstrates how caricature in an animated cartoon can facilitate a host of well-worn racial clichés and concepts about the Japanese in particular and the Orient in general. Set "somewhere in the Pacific," this eight-minute cartoon begins with Bugs Bunny landing on a supposedly deserted island. Bugs's initial references to the island as a "garden of Eden" and "Shangri-La" clearly recall the otherworldly havens depicted so vividly in the epic feature *Lost Horizon* (1937) and South Sea island films. His intoxicated reverie about the island illustrates not only the centrality of this element in Hollywood's construction of the Orient, but also exposes how this initial perception can be immediately repositioned to create an impression of utter deception and mortal danger—not unlike the widely perceived nature of the attack on Pearl Harbor. The seductive first impression that successfully lures Bugs unawares into the harsh reality of armed aggression and war again characterizes the wartime Japanese threat as initially (and deceptively) harmless, even pleasant, but then, just as suddenly, as assailing and hazardous. Even in this short, where the Japanese soldier is portrayed as a bungling fool, a critical element in the representation of the Japanese/Oriental threat during World War II emerges, one that stresses the peril of being mislead as much as the risk of being militarily overpowered.

The first meeting between the Japanese soldier and Bugs Bunny exhibits a more literal manifestation of a composite image. However, what makes the introduction of the Japanese soldier most interesting is that he literally appears to share the same body with Bugs. The rabbit's head peeks out above a haystack, but the bowed legs, wrapped in military fatigues, and feet (with a large space separating the first toe from the remainder) appearing below the haystack belong to the Japanese soldier. This combined visual image presents two distinctly separate identities in the guise of a bizarre, yet single, body that exploits familiar wartime physical distortions attributed to the Japanese "race."

Immediately following, another disembodied image, this one a hand, emerges from the haystack holding a hand mirror. The mirror is held up to Bugs's face, which transforms suddenly into a caricatured image of a Japanese face, with extremely slanted eyes and a mouthful of buckteeth. Then, finally, the face of the Japanese soldier springs out of the haystack replacing the mirror to face Bugs, nose to nose. The mirror held only by the hand of the soldier provides the catalyst that transforms Bugs's face into a Japanese one. However, the next moment reveals the Japanese soldier's face, which confronts Bugs's caricatured interpretation with its own cartoonish impishness. Here, we are presented with one distortion projected as ostensibly more authentic than another. Only when placed nose to nose with Bugs's Oriental face are the Japanese soldier's features established as more "real" within the context of the film.

The next sequence introduces two well-known Japanese identities, General Tojo and Mr. Moto. Bugs Bunny's masquerade as a Japanese general, wearing a heavily decorated uniform along with black spectacles, clearly imitates period photographs of the commanding general of the Japanese military. This visual reference to a historical figure is quickly followed by a spoken reference to the fictional character of Mr. Moto. The wily rabbit gives the soldier an anvil with the taunt "Here's some scrap iron for Japan, Moto!" Once again, the audience receives a pointed illustration of the inversion of this Oriental hero's status—in this instance, to provide a well-acquainted name for the wartime enemy. Certainly, the conventions of the Bugs Bunny cartoon character allow the protean rabbit to jump in and out of various disguises, including drag. However, in this film, the appearance of Oriental clichés, such as the moronic sumo wrestler and the coquettish geisha girl (as played by Bugs), further elaborates the markedly comedic tone in the depiction of the Japanese threat. Through the inclusion of these two relatively harmless civilian character types, the wartime foe is established as both humorous and easily beaten.

Bugs Bunny's subsequent full-scale assault on the hordes of Japanese soldiers ("Japs! Hundreds of 'em") involves a "Good Rumor" truck (an obvious takeoff on "Good Humor" ice cream trucks) filled with chocolate-covered ice cream bars embedded with grenades. Bugs greets the hungry soldiers with a host of insults as the soldiers (whose faces are partially obscured) clamor in "Oriental" gibberish while anxiously handing over money for the ice cream. Even when the Japanese caricature is not available to us visibly (due to the obscured faces and bodies in the crowd of soldiers), Bugs verbalizes its physical elements with remarkable clarity and detail. The racial epithets—"bowlegs," "monkey face," and "slant eyes"—audibly support the visual clichés rendered in the animation. As Bugs calls out insults, he uses the physically focused elements of the Japanese wartime caricature. Also, the way in which the Japanese soldiers besiege Bugs's ice cream truck imitates a swarm of bodies, suggesting that the Japanese soldiers do not represent a dangerous threat individually, but rather simply in terms of their numbers. A mob overflowing and easily fooled, they are rendered in this scene as less human figures and more a scourge in need of extermination.

Bugs Bunny Nips the Nips uses a disjointed, but not incoherent, series of symbols and physical peculiarities to introduce the Japanese wartime adversary: conspicuous visual and audible references to the formerly heroic Oriental detective character, Mr. Moto; an emphasis on physical difference/peculiarities to propagate a sense of racial inferiority; and finally, a central positioning of deception and treachery (rather than military might) as the preeminent wartime danger. Still, the generic conventions in the comedic animated work dictate a portrayal of the Japanese threat as fundamentally buffoonish, easily destroyed and dispensed with.

WHITE CHINESE AND YELLOW JAPS

The preceding discussion of animated portrayals of the Japanese enemy stresses the fundamentally composite construction of that enemy as well as delineates its graphically dissected mode of introduction. In this section, we will consider how a degree of wholeness is conferred on the Japanese during the war through the creation of a contrasting relationship with the Chinese. Though the term "Jap" did not originate during the war years, its use at this time was indicative of an active drive to isolate the Japanese people from all other national/racial groups in the minds of the American public.[9] The popular press as well as U.S. army literature contrasted the physical differences between the alien Japanese and the suddenly more compatible Chinese. One such article closely scrutinizes the faces of General Tojo and a Chinese man in search of distinguishing features.[10] A wartime pamphlet provides a detailed and telling comparison of the two "Asiatic" groups: among other variances, the eyes of the Chinese "are set like any European's or American's—but have a marked squint," while the Japanese, according to the pamphlet, is afflicted with "eyes slanted toward his nose."[11]

Along with the effort to create physical distinctions that attempted to ally the Chinese countenance with European physiognomy was the overt exploitation of Sino-Euro (particularly British) political alliances by Hollywood. British actress Merle Oberon's appearance with Chinese troops training in the United States in *Stage Door Canteen* (1943) attests to the effort to depict the Chinese as "good" Asian defenders of Western democratic ideals.[12] Notably, this screen appearance does not emphasize the Chinese army's commitment to defend its own borders but rather stresses its able assistance in the British / U.S. war effort. Pitted against the wily Japanese, the Chinese are positioned as Asian surrogates for the hopes and fears of most Americans. Significantly, at this time, the practice of Caucasian actors portraying Chinese roles in particular provides a useful vehicle to consolidate and propagate the wartime political bond between the interests of the United States and the Chinese, our then allies.

Dragon Seed is based on a best-selling novel of the same name by Pearl S. Buck, a former missionary in China and fervent advocate for wartime aid to the Chinese.[13] MGM hoped to draw on the previous commercial and critical success of another Buck adaptation, *The Good Earth* (1937), as well as fulfill the OWI expectations for the film "to make a major contribution to the war effort."[14] Predictably, the casting of Academy Award winner Katharine Hepburn as the unconventional Jade as well as of screen legend Walter Huston as peasant farmer, Ling Tan, added a prestigious element to the project from the outset. Yet, the overall casting of this film has been erroneously summarized as Caucasian stars playing Chinese characters while the Japanese roles were ostensibly portrayed exclusively by Asian actors.[15] In fact, two major supporting Japanese roles are depicted by Caucasian character actors J. Carroll Naish (as "Jap Kitchen Overseer") and Robert Lewis (as "Captain Sato").

The casting practice of this film follows long established industrial norms of Caucasian stars garnering leading as well as substantial supporting roles (both Chinese and Japanese) and Asian actors remaining as bit and extra players. Nevertheless, it is interesting that the casting of *Dragon Seed* was perceived to split along strict racial lines (Caucasian Chinese and Asian Japanese). This misrecognition suggests a narrative explanation as the film's scrupulous bifurcation between the "good" Asian and "bad" Asian is portrayed not on the basis of character, but solely in terms of nationality. Although not completely unique to *Dragon Seed*, the attempt to create wholly distinct intraracial divisions in this film occurs primarily through the Chinese characters' implicit closeness to American or Western values: an approach designed to persuade American audiences that these Chinese were essentially not very different from themselves. Thus, in this film, the only acceptable Chinese becomes a "white" Chinese.

A QUAINT LANGUAGE

The construction of "white" Chinese goes beyond simply casting Caucasian stars who espouse democratic ideals. Both the creation of distinct similarities and the fabrication of particular differences provide essential components in the performance of the Chinese roles in *Dragon Seed*. As the creative foundation for the film, the screenplay and its evolution can reveal how basic conceptions and ideas were initially negotiated before the start of production.

The Chinese consultant to this film, Wei Hsueh, generated a scrupulously detailed correspondence with MGM. One of the hallmarks of Oriental archetypes is an affected or mannered style of English speech—what Hsueh characterizes as "a quaint language." Notably, his remarks challenge the pretenses of cross-cultural accuracy that this production professed to seek. He reveals its basis (the screenplay) to be perpetuating traditional Oriental archetypal traits.

The examples Hsueh cites illustrate the highly constructed nature of the Chinese characters even at the level of dialogue. His translations make quite apparent the lack of sophistication expressed in the script's hackneyed English style of speech:

> "I have formed a thought" "I am thinking about a thing" idiomatically translated would be, "I am thinking of something." . . . "put out your price and put in your tongue" change to "what is your bottom price?" . . . "I hear them but they are only sounds one after the other." The Chinese would say "I hear them but they are just like other rumors I hear now and then." . . . "I greet you honored cousin" suggest change to read "Have you been well uncle?" [16]

The film is well populated with characters who speak the "quaint" dialogue and not the more familiar and nuanced English translations, so one can only assume that Mr. Hsueh's recommendations in this area were completely disregarded. His comments ultimately testify to the sovereignty and dominion of Hollywood-created Orientals and yet disclose one individual's documented attempt to challenge this.

Set in 1937, *Dragon Seed* chronicles the lives of the Ling Tan clan, a peasant family in war-torn China. This simple family of hardworking farmers, the voice-over narration tells us, were "both good and bad, both wise and foolish" and "therefore they were very much like such families in any other land." In the beginning of the story, the most pressing problem for family patriarch Ling Tan (Walter Huston) and his wife (Aline MacMahon) involves Lao Er's (Turhan Bey) half-hearted attempts to tame his rebellious new wife, Jade (Katharine Hepburn).[17] However, their minor familial squabbles soon recede as rumors of war in the north permeate their small village.

Although a multitude of refugees fleeing the Japanese pass through the village, Ling Tan and other local farmers refuse to leave their land. The Japanese army finally arrives, and the villagers are immediately stunned by the brutality and cruelty of the soldiers. While initially resistant and clinging to a pacifist stance, Ling Tan eventually leaves for the "freelands" to settle with his wife and family as they watch their land burn. The narrator tells us that the future of China will be for Jade's child and children like him, "so truly the seed of the dragon."

Most apparent in the performances of the leading characters in *Dragon Seed* is the sheer diversity of physical features, make-up, speech, and mannerisms among the actors. First, the physical features that the actors bring to their roles should not be overlooked. In particular, Katharine Hepburn and Hurd Hatfield possess high cheekbones and very thin bone structures, at times appearing almost skeletal. However, Turhan Bey, the Turkish actor who plays Hepburn's husband, Lao Er, has very full cheeks and lips and a somewhat broader nose than the other actors.

Indeed, not only does the degree of cosmetic application vary from actor to actor, it also tends to split along gender lines. Generally, the faces of the male characters in the film remain less made-up than those of the women. The men's eyebrows do not appear to be arched, only outlined with dark pencil, and the upper eyelids narrowed only slightly. While actresses Aline MacMahon (Ling's Wife) and Agnes Moorehead (as Third Cousin's Wife) have notably altered eyes and arched eyebrows, Katharine Hepburn appears to possess the most radically altered eyes. Not simply thinner, her eyelids often seem to disappear totally in close-up. Interestingly, the star with perhaps the most distinctive visage in the cast exhibits the most extreme manifestation of the common focus for Orientalizing facial make-up: the upper eyelids.

Even more conspicuous than the physicality and make-up of the actors is the range in their styles of speech. Katharine Hepburn's rather patrician enunciation contrasts the Turkish accent of her screen husband, Turhan Bey, and the Russian-accented speech of Akim Tamiroff (Wu Lien). Remarkably, Huston and MacMahon (whose American accents in no way resemble Hepburn's or one another's) and the rest of the cast make no attempt to adopt even pseudo-Chinese accents. In this film, then, the spoken expression of their nationality relies almost entirely on the idiosyncratic speech patterns originating in the written dialogue. This, of course, tends to foreground "the quaint language" so criticized by the Chinese consultant on the project. Nevertheless, it is this "quaint language" that, regardless of the widely varying accents of the cast, provides a utilitarian (albeit fictitious) common tongue that verbally connects all the actors. In this way, the characters can more plausibly portray members of the same family, village, and nation by speaking a "Chinese" language created not through the consistencies of an accent (which an American actor may or may not be able to master) but rather through idiosyncratic phrasing and syntax.

While pragmatic concerns might be considered initially, this unusual allowance of so much variation in the performances perhaps also stemmed in part from the wartime ideological thrust of the project. One of the primary goals of the project was to depict American ideology, goals, and ideals using the characters of this Chinese peasant family as mere vessels. Thus, fidelity to both the Chinese culture and the customary Hollywood renderings of the Chinese/Orientals seems to have been decidedly less significant to the overall project.

In other words, it might have been preferable to have the cast retain their different American ways of speaking inasmuch as one of the aims of this work was to delineate carefully the "good" Chinese from the "bad" Japanese through their likeness to Caucasian Americans. What might be interpreted as inferior acting skills in another context could provide, at this historical moment, a reassuring similarity to wartime audiences. The variation in physicality and speech reveals how certain features are manipulated or omitted altogether to serve the narrative in specific ways. In this case, the Ling Tan clan replicates and embodies the diversity one might find in an extended American family rather than in a Chinese one.

When Ling Tan and the village elders assemble to meet the Japanese invaders, they anxiously observe a seemingly endless convoy of trucks and tanks, with no easily discernible human figures. Individual faces and facial expressions, by extension, remain indistinguishable. This unusual vantage point is pronounced, prompting one frightened Chinese elder to comment, "but they are machines, how can you talk to machines?" While the upper eyelids of the Japanese soldiers reflect the customary cosmetic alteration, their overall uniformity relies primarily on nearly identical costuming, and interestingly, a distinctive delivery of dialogue. Whereas an array of accents is acceptable in the Chinese characters, all the Japanese characters deliver their lines with an identically flat and piercing intonation. Hepburn, in particular, attempts a more monotone and halting delivery, but the speech of the Japanese exhibits a mechanized rapidity. This biting, yet lifeless, speaking style not only adds a robotic element to the soldier figures, but also underscores the perception of the invading army as "machines" by the Chinese village elders. The Japanese, first introduced through the machines of the airplanes and then through the machines of army vehicles, subsequently "perform" in gesture and dialogue as mechanized creatures devoid of humanity. In each of these instances, the film attempts both to render the enemy inhuman through non-human associations and to link the mechanized technology of war with a disposition of a people.

Hailed for vividly capturing the "grim realism" of wartime China and simultaneously derided for the performative inconsistencies of its Chinese characterizations, *Dragon Seed* exemplifies the attempt to exploit a wartime narrative as ideological propaganda and commercial entertainment. Negotiating traditional Oriental stereotypes and wartime democratic idealism through a conventional Hollywood narrative, this film attempts to create sympathetic wartime Chinese characters in contrast to patently evil Japanese depictions. However, the obvious narrative conflict between Chinese and Japanese in the plot accommodates more intricate national divisions and alliances.

The narrative pits the "good" Chinese farmers against the "bad" Japanese invaders. However, the casting of Caucasians in the leading roles of both nationalities separates the leading Caucasian actors (portraying Chinese or Japanese) from the Asian bit players and extras (cast as Chinese or Japanese). At the level of performance, Japanese and Chinese characters coexist as antithetical configurations. Further, these constructions closely associate the Chinese heroes with explicitly Western ideology, diversity, complexity, and humanity while relegating the Japanese enemy to a negative space of subhuman automated brutality.

LOSING FACE

The phrase "losing face" usually refers to an "Oriental" who suffers (or is threatened to suffer) public humiliation upon exposure of a less than heroic act. However, in the film *First Yank into Tokyo* (1945), released after the end of hostilities in the Pacific, the main character, Major Steve Ross, quite literally "loses his face" when he chooses to undergo irreversible plastic surgery that would make him appear Japanese to complete an undercover intelligence mission near Tokyo. The narrative depicts this choice as the ultimate patriotic act of heroism and sacrifice. Nonetheless, his character endures experiences ranging from the valiant to the degrading. Although the premise and plot of the film superficially appear to support the status quo and racial hierarchy of power relations, they also allow certain transgressive fantasies of miscegenation while exploring the emotional terrain of dual racial embodiment.

A wartime allegory that explores the issues and consequences arising out of the transformation of a Caucasian into an Oriental, *First Yank into Tokyo* specifically foregrounds (and posits as possible) the physical alteration of a Caucasian into a Japanese in the narrative. The common performance practice of

Caucasian actors portraying Asian roles effects a specialized (and complex) function in the plot. The racialized performance practice is not intended to be perceived as a disguise or a seamless visual element in an actor's interpretation of a role. The racial impersonation by a Caucasian actor becomes, in this vehicle, the racial impersonation of a Caucasian character. Remarkably, through the vantage point of its leading character, Major Ross, the "Japanese" archenemy begins to show the hint of a human face.

This project began before V-E Day on May 7, 1945, and was released after the atomic blasts on Hiroshima and Nagasaki in early August of the same year. An initial synopsis of the project (then titled *First Man Into Tokyo*) provided by the RKO Radio Pictures publicity department summarizes its unconventional plot:

> Major Steve Ross (Tom Neal), an American ace, is summoned to Washington for a dangerous mission. Somewhere in a Jap prison camp is the American engineer Lewis Jardine (Marc Cramer), inventor of a new tank gun. It is of the utmost importance to our war effort that information about the gun be brought back to Washington. Because he had been brought up in Japan and speaks the language perfectly, Ross is the man for the job. Plastic surgery will give him Oriental features. Intensive training by loyal Japanese Americans will do the rest.
>
> But once his features are changed Ross must retain them for the rest of his life. And because he believes Abby Drake (Barbara Hale)— the nurse he was in love with—has died on Bataan, Ross accepts the assignment.
>
> After the operation and months of nerve-wracking training in looking, thinking, and acting Japanese, he lands in Tokyo through the Korean underground. Posing as Sergeant Tomo Takashima, Nip war hero sent home to recuperate from shock, he succeeds in becoming an orderly in the prison hospital where Jardine is a patient [and Abby a nurse]. . . .
>
> Aware that he dare not test Abby's love with the Japanese face which he must carry forever, he elects to send her and Jardine away on the sub, while he holds off the Jap patrol sent in their pursuit.
>
> Haan Soo, [a Korean operative, played by Keye Luke] chooses to remain with him, and, while Abby and Jardine make good their escape, the picture ends with these two—a brave Korean and the first American to enter Tokyo—laying down their lives.[18]

This plot summary is of particular interest for what it emphasizes, excludes, and changes. While this studio outline highlights Ross's alliance with the Korean underground figure, Haan Soo, the crucial subplot involving the camp commander, Colonel Hideko Okanura (Richard Loo), goes undisclosed. Before the war, Okanura and Ross had been college roommates in the United States. Unusually observant and, at the same time, constantly distracted by the inexplicable familiarity of Takashima, Okanura eventually exposes Ross's ruse through the recognition of a subtle hand gesture. The most important modification in the narrative changes the information about a "new tank gun" to the plans for the atomic bomb. A dramatic shift surely created to capitalize on public interest in the detonations of the new weapon that ended the war with Japan.

"You're as perfect a Jap as we can turn out."

General Stanton, the official who formally requests Ross's participation in the mission, proudly delivers this line after Ross has successfully completed his rigorous training to become a Japanese. This scene announces the U.S. army's achievement of constructing a Japanese countenance in a Caucasian form. The pride in this accomplishment is not wholly unlike Dr. Frankenstein's self-satisfaction at having created life through his monster. Presented as categorically man-made, Ross's appearance and his mastery of Japanese physicality and cultural demeanor initially demonstrate a crowning feat of U.S. ingenuity: a fantasy of racial subjugation through its embodiment. However, this collective accomplishment for the U.S. military, though potent, is only temporary, as Ross comes to regard himself as a freakish monstrosity, better off dead.

The film begins when Ross, on R&R in San Francisco, is summoned to Washington D.C. Although he does not know the reason for his summons, he does not hesitate to answer his country's call. In a meeting with military and government officials in Washington, General Stanton, director of the mission, ominously characterizes the life-altering surgery as requiring a "personal courage so far beyond the call of duty." Stanton's words can also be heard in voice-over as medical personnel prepare Ross for surgery: "once your features are changed, they can never be changed back." Also in voice-over, Ross's voice replies, simply and dutifully, "I understand, sir." Initially, this film positions the operation squarely in political terms, as a heightened expression of patriotism, but then immediately shifts Ross's motivation to a darker, and more desperate, emotional space. Just as Ross lies on a surgical table and a gas mask placed over his face, his words, in voice-over, can be heard, "I shouldn't have cried. Mom and Dad were dead and Abby, the Japs killed her." Indeed, his subsequent thoughts reveal a profound emotional isolation, with neither parents (both deceased) nor romantic love (Abby, presumed dead) providing him with a reason to live.

With his back to the camera, Ross waits as the doctor carefully unwraps his bandages. Notably, the first display of his new face is experienced through the grave reactions of his surgeon, a nurse, and General Stanton. The audience first glimpses his facial features indirectly as Ross looks into a small mirror and quietly remarks "I almost believe I'm somebody else." First mediated through the eyes of others and then framed in a mirror's reflection that incorporates his own gaze, our own response to Ross's physical transformation necessitates an integration of the awestruck reactions of the characters. In this way, the burden of the features to astonish is displaced onto other "normalized" faces (or, in the case of Ross, his eyes, which reflect a face no longer visible). Clearly, an audience familiar with Caucasian actors made-up to appear Asian in varying contexts requires a precise manipulation of elements to create the desired dramatic impact around the central plot device of the film.

Once he is alone in the hospital bed, Ross inexpressively stares straight ahead into the camera, his new features in direct view: thin upper eyelids; protruding upper teeth; slick straight hair (formerly wavy); thin, barely discernible eyebrows (formerly thick); and a smooth chin (previously with a cleft). He processes the irrevocable consequences of his decision as the voice-over of General Stanton again intones, "Once your features are changed, they can never be changed back. You'll carry the face of a Jap all of your life."

Yet, significantly, surgery completes only part of Ross's racial transformation into a Japanese; the remainder must be acquired through study and practice. General Stanton praises Ross for ultimately passing every test "in features, actions, mannerisms, dialects." Ross, dressed in a tailored suit, responds by bowing, clicking his heels together, and stating facetiously, "Thank you, excewancy. It's been a pweasure to study under youw most tawented teachers." To this, the delighted general replies, "You're now a full-fledged son of Nippon." This scene explicitly acknowledges that culturally specific speech and demeanor play a significant role in the construction of the Japanese soldier.

Understanding the so-called "mental processes" of the Japanese also provides an additional challenge to Ross's potential success on this mission. Despite his claim to an intimate familiarity with Japan due to his upbringing there, Ross, rather than offering a more diverse perspective on the Japanese mind as it were, simply ascribes to the Japanese a "completely reversed approach to things." Nonetheless, he immediately declares confidently to understand "every kink in their corkscrew psychology." Ironically, Ross's "tawented teachers" are identified by General Stanton as "our Japanese American examining board." Curiously, this remark attempts to establish a national solidarity with Japanese Americans, and yet raises the question of why the military did not simply recruit a Japanese American for this dangerous assignment rather than surgically altering a Caucasian soldier.[19] Perhaps because the military implicitly considered the allegiance of Japanese Americans too tenuous? Most likely, the explanation lies not in rational logic, but rather in the powerful lure provided by the fantasy of a "Japanized" Caucasian. Here, the Caucasian actor occupies a critical position as figurative conduit to an alternative and socially transgressive racial experience while safely containing the experience within an explicitly Western framework.

Arriving at the Kamuri prison camp near Tokyo, Ross encounters the commandant Colonel Okanura and his former love, Abby, whom he thought killed at Bataan. At once thrilled and sickened, Ross experiences the social barriers his constructed physical form presents. He must endure the bullying of a corrupt Major Nogira (Leonard Strong), the contemptuous suspicion of Okanura, and repeated denigration by Abby. Neal's performance as Sergeant Takashima consists primarily of inexpressive poses, stiff postures, and stilted English, all of which starkly contrast his spirited interpretation of the (fully) American Major Ross. This is most apparent when contrasted with the performance of Asian actor, Keye Luke. In his portrayal of Haan Soo, Ross's Korean ally, Luke exhibits animated facial expressions, broad smiles and grimaces, flashing and expressive eyes, and a voice of varying tones. Of course, the lack of vitality in Neal's face could be attributed to his heavy make-up, but the wartime Japanese guise typically stripped the face and voice of much of its facility and vibrancy.

Ross's encounters with Abby provide a complex interweaving of thwarted love through the forbidden specter of miscegenation. Notably, throughout the narrative, Ross silently protects Abby from the lustful advances of the Japanese officers. However, Abby repeatedly reacts to Ross as Takashima with a mixture of contempt because she "despises all Japs" and distressed confusion because she feels an "undercurrent" of sympathy for him. Having revealed his identity, mission, and relationship to Abby only to Jardine, Ross needs medical care after his superiors whip him (for reversing an unfair charge against the American nurses). He stoically volunteers to clean his own wounds with antiseptic, but Abby offers to tend to his injuries. In a striking display of repressed desire, Abby, trance-like, tenderly dabs at Ross's shirtless frame. Unbeknownst to her, his hand involuntarily moves up to take hers, but he stops himself, thinking better of it. Jardine stands close by, silently and compassionately observing the doomed lovers. After Ross leaves, Abby guiltily confesses to Jardine her unexplained affinity to this soldier, "I don't hate him. What's wrong with me?" Clearly, this expresses the assumption of wartime racial hatred as the norm.

Abby's attraction to Ross as Takashima explicitly, though tenuously, introduces the element of miscegenation into the narrative. Is she attracted to a Japanese soldier? The film broaches the taboo of interracial sexuality, yet it operates strictly within socially acceptable norms. Ross and Abby have had a previous romantic relationship, so the audience can interpret her attraction as rekindled vestiges from that socially sanctioned coupling. However, one of the driving elements in this film addresses the question of how people can be separated by racial appearance that seldom, as Ross observes, "looks beyond your face." However, Abby's desire in this scene can perhaps also be attributed to Ross's white "essence" or "soul" that can be perceived despite his altered appearance. A soul, by definition, exists as a spiritual essence apart from the physical body and, by extension, the manifestations of racial differentiation. Yet, even the realm of the unseen provides a location where racial difference can express itself as a distinguishing characteristic.

In this scene, the intimacy enacted between Abby and Ross—in reality, two Caucasian American characters—still requires the mediation of an undeniably Caucasian male character, Jardine. Jardine's character serves as a convenient, albeit "compassionate," watchdog, observing the lovers who might be tempted to transgress the established social codes of the prison camp (Abby with humanity, Ross with sexuality). Jardine suggests that Ross reveal his true identity to Abby. This supportive nature conceals the larger social function of his presence as tacit preserver of the status quo. The scene between Abby and Ross clearly illustrates how the threat posed by interracial sexuality can apparently be assuaged at the level of narrative and yet persist on a broader social level that requires additional dramatic containment.

In the end, Ross does reveal his true identity to Abby, but only after he has decided on the impossibility of a life together back in the States. She declares her love and willingness to accept him regardless, but Ross remains firm as Jardine leaves with her on a waiting U.S. submarine. Functioning as a plea for a shared humanity while explicitly espousing a call for U.S. patriotic sacrifice, *First Yank into Tokyo* traverses the volatile ground of racial difference, miscegenation, and, ultimately, racial tolerance.

Unlike *Dragon Seed*, *First Yank into Tokyo* did not garner a great deal of critical attention or praise. Reviewers tended to approach the film strictly in the "B" movie industrial context. The performance of Tom Neal (who had previously portrayed wartime Japanese characters) received generally positive notices.[20] His enactment of the so-called "dual role" in this film drew praise despite its fundamental implausibility. As both a means of racial subjugation as well as an expression of its fluidity, *First Yank into Tokyo* creates an unusual, yet acceptable wartime fantasy/nightmare.[21] Even in wartime, both fear and desire of the Oriental enemy coexist and require close negotiation in their depictions in Hollywood films. Clearly, the idea of racial transformation strongly fascinates, just as the potential transcendence of race deeply threatens and thus, must ultimately be resolutely denied.

CONCLUSIONS

The long-standing industrial practice of casting Caucasian actors/stars as Asians continued unabated during the wartime era, albeit under a new rubric—the difficulty of finding willing Asian actors to play Japanese enemy roles. In this historical context, even familiar Oriental detective characters were reformulated and villainized to serve the needs of wartime discourse as well as those of film narratives. Animated shorts such as *Bugs Bunny Nips the Nips* illustrate how the process of fragmentation and reconfiguration of familiar elements created a contemporaneous Japanese enemy.

Dragon Seed exemplifies the effort to individualize Asian identities between Chinese and Japanese, and, yet, the depictions of the sympathetic Chinese in the film also embody a clearly constructed bias. *First Yank into Tokyo* introduces the concept of racial alteration as both fantasy and threat. This representation offers a radical means of comprehending a different race through the destruction of one's own. It is no wonder that during wartime a production of this sort appeared. Physical carnage, injuries, and death predominated in the visual images of this time. Fears of invasion, infiltration, and subjugation fueled many of the wartime narratives. Nevertheless, a continuity exists as pre-war elements and characterizations provided the essential cues with which to identify the enemy.

NOTES

1. Edward W. Said, *Orientalism* (New York, Vintage Books, 1979), 16–17.

2. The choice of the term archetype, rather than the more pejorative stereotype, attempts to avoid either a strictly positive or a rigidly negative connotation. Its use refers only to recurring character types that can be traced across several films, rather than a strict Jungian definition.

3. David Bordwell, Janet Staiger, and Kristin Thompson, *The Classical Hollywood Cinema: Film Style and Mode of Production to 1960* (New York: Columbia University Press, 1985), xiv. This term is based on the argument in this book that "certain fundamental aspects" of Hollywood filmmaking from 1917–1960 achieved a certain level of consistency and standardization that produced "a unified mode of film prac-

tice . . . a coherent system whereby aesthetic norms and the mode of film production reinforced one another."

4. "Me No Moto," *Variety*, December 31, 1941, 1.

5. Joe Morella, Edward Z. Epstein, and John Griggs, *The Films of World War II* (Secaucus, NJ: Citadel Press, 1973), 11.

6. Ibid.

7. Clayton R. Koppes and Gregory D. Black, *Hollywood Goes To War: How Politics, Profits, and Propaganda Shaped World War II Movies* (Berkeley: University of California Press, 1987), 59.

8. Morella, Epstein, and Griggs, *The Films of World War II*, 13. Also, for an intriguing commentary and/or comparison of U.S. government intervention in the Japanese film industry, see Kyoko Hirano, *Mr. Smith Goes To Tokyo: Japanese Cinema under the American Occupation, 1945–1952* (Washington, D.C.: Smithsonian Institution Press, 1992). This book provides a thought-provoking analysis on the dictates of the U.S. Occupation forces on the Japanese cinema during the immediate postwar period.

9. Neil Harris, *Cultural Excursions: Marketing Appetites and Cultural Tastes in Modern America* (Chicago and London: University of Chicago Press, 1990), 34. In the chapter, "All the World a Melting Pot? Japan at American Fairs, 1876–1904," Harris quotes a *New York Times* newspaper story on the Japanese exhibit at the Philadelphia Centennial Exposition of 1876 that refers to the Japanese workmen as "Japs."

10. "How to Tell Japs from the Chinese," *Life*, December 22, 1941), 81.

11. Michael Renov, "Warring Images: Stereotype and American Representations of the Japanese, 1941–1991," in *The Japan/America Film Wars: World War II Propaganda and Its Cultural Contexts*, ed. Abé Mark Nornes and Fukushima Yukio (Langhorne, PA: Harwood Academic Publishers, 1994), 107.

12. Charles Higham and Roy Moseley, *Princess Merle: The Romantic Life of Merle Oberon* (New York: Coward-McCann, Inc., 1983), 10. Ironically, the Anglo-Indian actress born in Bombay hid her own biracial origins by claiming that she was born in Tasmania of British parents.

13. Script Collection, Margaret Herrick Library, Academy of Motion Picture Arts and Sciences, Beverly Hills, CA. A condensed version of the novel *Dragon Seed* appeared in *Ladies Home Journal*, August 1942, 13–73, along with Buck's ads requesting donations to United China Relief, an organization providing clinical care to Chinese refugees, equipment for field clinics, and supplies for the feeding and care of Chinese children.

14. Koppes and Black, *Hollywood Goes To War*, 240. The authors also note the OWI's expectation that *Dragon Seed* reflect a story dramatized in the vein of a "Mrs. Miniver of China." A commercial and critical hit of 1942, MGM's *Mrs. Miniver*, starring Greer Garson, dramatized the hardships of a middle-class family in wartime Britain.

15. Review in *The Nation*, August 5, 1944, 165. James Agee's scathing review of the film includes this misperception.

16. Ibid., 5–7.

17. Bey's Turkish origins, again, demonstrate Hollywood's tendency to cast exotic "foreigner" actors who could deliver a distinctly non-native intonation to American ears rather than necessarily adopt a specifically Asian accent.

18. From *RKO Radio Studio Handbook of Publicity Data-First Man Into Tokyo*, issued March 6, 1945, Hollywood, California, Production Code Administration, Motion Picture Association of America (MPAA) Files, Academy Library.

19. Also pointed out by Thomas Doherty, *Projections of War: Hollywood, American Culture, and World War II* (New York: Columbia University Press, 1993), 138.

20. Neal played a leading role, Taro, a U.S.-educated, but ultimately treasonous, Japanese soldier in another RKO wartime vehicle, *Behind the Rising Sun* (1943).

21. Review of *First Yank into Tokyo, Variety*, September 5, 1945. Remarkably, the rather "implausible" premise of *First Yank into Tokyo* occurs, in reverse, in the Monogram release *Black Dragons* (1942), starring Bela Lugosi. Lugosi portrays a Nazi scientist who surgically alters members of a Japanese spy ring to appear Caucasian, allowing them to infiltrate the United States and impersonate influential American citizens.

14

DECEMBER 7TH

Race and Nation in Wartime Documentary

Geoffrey M. White and Jane Yi

In 1986 an enterprising film distributor released a video version of *December 7th*, the official 1943 film about the bombing of Pearl Harbor that drew the United States into World War II. Liner notes for the video read:

> Hawai'i:
> President Roosevelt called December 7, 1941, "a date which will live in infamy." On that Sunday morning at 7:55 the Japanese began an air attack that devastated the Pacific fleet and took the lives of 2,343 servicemen. This film is a heavily partisaned look at the day's events, designed to sway even the most avowed isolationist. Since few cameras were actually present during the surprise attack, director and Lt. Comdr. John Ford skillfully blended real action with studio shots, creating a heightened realism.[1]

The awkwardness of recirculating a state-sponsored war documentary ("propaganda") is evident in the phrases "heavily partisaned" and "designed to sway the most avowed isolationist." These allusions to the intentions of film production draw attention to the fact that *December 7th* was made to *do* something—unify a nation and stimulate support for a war—and not simply to inform or report.

To accomplish this, the film employs both documentary and fictional modes of representation. If viewers take the documentary format of the film at face value, it works to convey a sense of veracity, of direct reporting. At the same time, the film's dramatized scenes work to enhance its evocative power and, oddly, create a kind of hyperrealism by reproducing well-known images of Hawai'i, Asian enemies, and mainstream America. The plot, such as it is, relates the story of the bombing attack and its unifying effect on America's multiethnic population. Even with this unusual blend of documentary reportage and social drama, the film succeeded well enough to receive an Academy Award for best short documentary in 1943.[2]

Despite its success, production of the film was surrounded by controversy—so much so that government sponsors suppressed an original, long version and only released it after it was edited to less than half the original length (from 83 minutes to 34 minutes). In this paper, we examine these two versions of the film, and the politics of their production, in order to reflect on the formation of official representations of race and nation in the newly powerful medium of film at mid-century.

We are concerned with the poetics of the film as well as its social and political context, which, in this case, involved a unique confluence of military, government, and Hollywood institutions. Our analysis underscores the point that the state, in such an enterprise, was neither a monolithic nor a unified entity. In *December 7th*, official images of the nation were only constituted and finally circulated through a fractured process of (mis)coordination among multiple interests and prerogatives.[3]

As far as the film's producers and filmmakers were concerned, both the long and short versions were documentary representations of the attack. The use of news footage and narrative voice-over signifies the truth value of both films as direct representations of actual events. Lest there be any doubt, each film begins with the narrator announcing, "Your war and navy department present *December 7th.*" This statement is then followed by a display of documents signed by the Secretary of War and the Secretary of the Navy calling for the production of a film that gives a "factual presentation" of the bombing of Pearl Harbor. Each film thus presents itself as produced in the national interest, speaking in a national voice.

At the same time, both films tell the story of Pearl Harbor as an evocative social narrative about a national citizenry and patriotic sentiments provoked by war. The long version of *December 7th* is most striking in this respect. It makes extensive use of scripted scenes and imaginary characters to construct a national allegory. Indeed, the film's government sponsors expressed concern about the use of fiction, arguing that state sponsorship required a more straightforward documentary style of presentation. Most of the footage cut from the long film consisted of its most overtly fictionalized segments. As a result, the short form of *December 7th* took on more of the appearance of conventional documentary. Even this version, however, incorporated numerous fictionalized scenes, including a prolonged episode in which the narrator converses with the spirits of servicemen who died in the attack.

The long version of *December 7th* includes a lengthy commentary about the social history and cultural composition of multiethnic Hawai'i, focusing mainly on its Japanese American population. This segment is presented as a conversation between two imaginary characters, Uncle Sam and his conscience, "Mr. C," in a hilltop house in Hawai'i, where Uncle Sam is on vacation. Uncle Sam and Mr. C talk about the presence of America in the islands and the loyalty of its multiethnic population, mostly brought to the islands to work its plantations. The film then proceeds to depict the bombing (using studio recreations to portray a "heightened realism"), the recovery effort, and the patriotic sentiments that fueled it. It concludes with a fantasy scene in which two deceased veterans (one of World War II, one of the Pearl Harbor attack) converse about America's international responsibilities in maintaining world order. In this way, the long film opens and closes with conversations featuring characters—Uncle Sam and deceased veterans—who embody the nation. Both of these segments, however, were removed in the editing of the film for ultimate release.

For reasons discussed below, release of the long film was stopped until, a year later, the decision was made to reedit it for use in the government's wartime morale program. As already noted, the major change made in reediting was removal of the fictionalized scenes at the beginning and end of the film. The middle section, focusing on the attack itself, remained virtually intact, as did the subsequent section depicting the mobilization of America's citizenry for the war effort.

Despite the fact that shortening the film produced a work that looked and sounded more like a documentary, the short version of *December 7th* adheres closely to the narrative forms of mythic storytelling: an unsuspecting community is thrown into crisis by an attack that causes death and destruction, but then rises from the ashes to overcome adversity through hard work, ingenuity, and social harmony.[4] Subsequent scenes of rebuilding resolve the emotional turmoil and doubt caused by the attack. The same narrative sequence has provided the storyline for mythic histories of Pearl Harbor ever since, including two official documentaries shown at the Pearl Harbor memorial in Honolulu since 1980.[5]

Numerous explanations for the suppression and cutting of the original film have been suggested, including problems in the film's ambiguous mixing of feature film and documentary technique, its extended excursion into the historical particulars of Hawai'i, and worries by naval authorities that the film portrayed the navy as unprepared for the attack.[6] While film historians have mentioned all these issues, few commentators have discussed what is, in retrospect, the film's central problem: its representation of race and national identity.[7] We contend that the most significant problems with the film pertained to difficulties in constructing a coherent national narrative out of the complex intersections of race, place, and nation in 1941 Hawai'i.

The makers of *December 7th* hoped this work, like many war films of this era, would project images of a plural and democratic nation coming together for the purpose of fighting a war.[8] Specifically, the film tells a story about relations between ethnic and national identity by portraying markedly ethnic communities responding to the Pearl Harbor attack with collective purpose. However, constructing this type of narrative in a locale where the most populous ethnic community consisted of descendants of "the enemy" resulted in a disjointed and contradictory storyline. How could a distant colonial territory of the United States where the majority of the population consisted of Asian immigrant labor be imagined as "America"? Both films attempt to answer this question with narratives of Americanization, although the longer film does so with an extended history of frontier capitalism and modernization.

Before the Pearl Harbor attack, military planners in Hawai'i were more concerned about espionage and sabotage among the islands' ethnic Japanese than they were about the possibility of a direct attack by Japanese military forces. Although virtually no incidents of subversive activity were recorded,[9] racist fears and suspicions were rampant following the bombing. The same fears and hostilities that motivated internment on the mainland led filmmakers John Ford and Gregg Toland (see Note 1) to devote the first half of their film to a fictionalized portrayal of Hawai'i's Japanese residents as extensively involved in subversive activities.[10] While in Hawai'i for work on the film in April 1942, Ford wrote a letter to William Donovan, head of the Office of Strategic Services (OSS, predecessor of the CIA), expressing his views about Hawai'i's Japanese residents:

> We are doing the Japanese espionage stuff [in the film] very thoroughly.
> It's fascinating and quite exciting. Personally, I do not trust any of the

Figure 14.1. Cane cutter at Pearl Harbor in *December 7th* (1943).

Japanese. I honestly believe the majority of them are tainted. It's strange since the "Raid" how very Oriental Honolulu appears—thousands upon thousands of Jap faces. We have been photographing scores of Jap signs to show the character of the town. Now you can hardly see one. They have all taken down their signs and have substituted English lettering. Example; "Banzai Cafe"—beers and liquors—is now the "Keep 'Em Flying Cafe." . . .

From the best sources they estimate about six hundred active agents still loose on the island. I figure triple that number. Some amazing stories of spying leak out daily.

The opening scenes of the long film closely reflect the paranoid vision of Ford. The film presents a series of vignettes of spying in which actors playing Japanese residents are shown eavesdropping on casual conversations about military matters or gazing out on ship movements—all accompanied by an eerie, Oriental sound track.[11] At the same time, other segments of the film cast the Americans of Japanese Ancestry (AJA) population in a very different light: eager to integrate into the "melting pot" of American society and lending support for the war effort. In this manner, the same film alternately portrays Japanese Americans as dangerous and unassimilable and as eager to Americanize, desiring closer identification with the nation. Although contradictory within the scope of a single film, these opposed themes of racial subversion and assimilation have long histories in American discourses of race. One is an exclusionary discourse that constructs difference as a threat to be contained at the borders; while the other represents a more inclusionary view in which assimilation continually revalidates mainstream (white) identity.

NARRATIVE (MIS)TAKES ON THE NATIONAL SUBJECT

Images of assimilation and Americanization emerge most forcefully in the film scenes that portray efforts at recovery in the aftermath of the bombing. In those segments, Hawai'i's American Japanese are depicted renouncing Japanese culture and embracing things American. Insofar as removal of the first section eliminated the more ominous vision of subversive Japanese residents, the short film more clearly presents a narrative of Americanization and national unity. In other words, the reduction in scope worked to resolve the most blatant contradictions in the original film. Whereas John Ford could see the transformation of the "Banzai Cafe" into the "Keep 'Em Flying Cafe" as a kind of subterfuge, deletion of the spying scenes increases the likelihood that such an act would be interpreted as an expression of American loyalty—a kind of intensification of the film's theme of unification.

The long film's opening dialogue between Uncle Sam (played by Walter Huston dressed in coattails and a star-studded vest) and Mr. C (his more skeptical and critical conscience played by Harry Davenport) tells a story of manifest destiny in the Pacific, describing colonial history as a saga of settlement and modernization. As the worldly Mr. C proceeds to interrogate the gullible Uncle Sam about his Hawaiian "paradise," however, a more sinister picture emerges, depicting the local Japanese community as strongly loyal to their homeland.

When prodded by Mr. C, Uncle Sam describes the incorporation of Hawai'i into the U.S. economic and political sphere. He calls it a "pioneering story" that "compares favorably with the opening of the west," emphasizing the benefits of Americanization and modernization for the islands. Mr. C, however, is unimpressed. He reminds Uncle Sam that most of the laborers for this economic success story are Japanese: "Let's not overlook the majority of the population here—the Japanese." With an uncanny resonance to John Ford's reference to "thousands upon thousands of Jap faces," the camera at this point cuts to close-up shots of Japanese faces, accompanied by sinister background music. Here the sound of dissonant "Oriental" music accompanying a quick succession of shots at odd angles creates a sense of nervous confusion

Figure 14.2. Cafe owner in Honolulu removes the bilingual sign for Banzai Cafe.

Figure 14.3. The cafe owner puts up a sign in patriotic English for Keep 'Em Flying Cafe.

Figure 14.4. Uncle Sam (Walter Huston) and Mr. C (Harry Davenport).

contrasting with the familiar and orderly world created by Uncle Sam's efforts at modernization.

Uncle Sam, however, remains undaunted by this challenge to his progressive, pioneering story. He retorts, "And about 120,000 [of about 157,000 local Japanese] are full-fledged American citizens. Don't forget that." He then tells C to listen to a patriotic speech by Dr. Shunzo Sakamaki, "Chairman of the Oahu Citizens Committee for Home Defense." [12] After listening to Sakamaki's inspiring speech, Uncle Sam comments, "As American a spirit as exists in any New England community, by god!" Mr. C, however, sees only essentialized Japanese, using the metaphor "hyphenated" to refer to a kind of polluted national identity, tainted by combination with an irreducible Japaneseness:

A hyphenated spirit, yes. They express their loyalty and no doubt are loyal. They send their children to American public schools. . . . But they also send them to their own language schools, one hundred and seventy five of them, where they're taught Japanese culture, loyalties and morals.

As will be discussed below, the implication that "hyphenated" Americans were less fully American conflicted with government efforts to recruit and mobilize minority citizens.

The film's declaration about the dubious loyalties of "hyphenated" Japanese Americans is followed by the film's most vivid Orientalist image: a Shinto priest, played by Korean American actor Philip An.[13] Wearing dark robes and a placid, emotionless expression, the priest appears against the backdrop of a dark, smoky shrine. The film's offscreen narrator intrudes into the film by calling to the priest, "Pardon me, sir." The priest then turns toward the camera and the narrator asks him a series of questions about Shinto religion. The priest gives his answers in a voice without inflection, a parody of distant Oriental otherness.

> NARRATOR: Pardon me, sir, would you please tell us who you recognize as the supreme being, as deity?

> PRIEST: In Shintoism, we worship the first Japanese Emperor whose creation started the world of mankind.

> NARRATOR: Doesn't that imply the worship of his descendants, the present son of heaven, Emperor Hirohito?

> PRIEST: He is the mortal image of our immortal deity.

Following this exchange, Uncle Sam asks Mr. C incredulously, "Are you implying that all these . . . these people are disloyal Americans?" To this, C responds, "Oh no, indeed not. I wouldn't nor would anyone undertake to separate the loyal from the disloyal. I'm only presenting the facts." In "presenting the facts," Mr. C presupposes the existence of significant numbers of disloyal Hawaiians, even if he cannot separate them out. A declaration that one cannot "separate the loyal from the disloyal" also provides a rationale for the internment policy that was being implemented on the U.S. mainland as the film was under production.[14]

The relentless Mr. C then proceeds to "present the facts" about the Japanese, noting the number of families who, prior to the war, continued to register children with the Japanese consulate in Honolulu so as to maintain citizenship rights in Japan: 17,800 of 39,000 children born to Japanese parents in Hawai'i between 1924 and 1938. He concludes by saying, "If that's Americanism, it's very *hyphenated*" (emphasis added). This finally convinces Uncle Sam that he has cause for concern. He responds by saying, "All right, all right. So there are many Japanese here and they have their language schools and Shinto temples and many are *hyphenated and perhaps disloyal. . . .*" (emphasis added).[15]

Having set the stage with ambiguous demographic evidence about the persistence of Japanese loyalties to Japan, the film moves to scenes of actual spying, with informants delivering information from spies all over the island to the Japanese consulate (see Figure 14.1). Despite the fact that there were virtually no instances of spying among Hawai'i's Japanese Americans, the image created in *December 7th,* and perpetuated in numerous Hollywood films such as *Air Force* (1943), turned wartime hysteria into Hollywood-mediated reality.[16]

For those viewing this dialogue in 1943, C's assertions would have been supported by the fact that he was warning about an attack that had *already* occurred. Mr. C is clearly more perceptive than sleepy Uncle Sam. His views of local Japanese are seemingly validated by the fact that he is predicting the future. He gives a blunt warning about an impending attack: "They'll pick their time and their method and they'll come over here to blow that bastion of military might behind which you sleep so easily to smithereens." He then characterizes the (dis)loyalty of the AJAs of Hawai'i:

> By patriotic subscription they support the war in China. . . . In return Tokyo sends over Shinto priests, educators, writers. . . . And when Tokyo speaks, they all listen, rich and poor alike. So it's plainly a two-way proposition. Put them together and its spells Tokyo I love you.

Sam refuses to see the dangers of the AJA population and soliloquizes about the wonders of multicultural Hawai'i. Mr. C responds, "It's amazing how much you can see with your head buried in the sand." C then departs and, as Uncle Sam dozes, the film begins its narrative of the attack on the Sunday morning of December 7.

ETHNICITY, WAR, AND NATIONAL IMAGINATION

Most of the camera shots during the attack sequence feature distant views of exploding and burning ships or fast-action shots of men shooting back at attacking planes, reenacted for the purposes of *December 7th.* In the midst of all the action, one scene carries a clear signature of ethnicity. An African American sailor, shown in close-up profile, fires a .50 caliber machine gun pointed skyward.[17] This image would have been particularly noticeable in 1942−43, when African Americans in the U.S. military remained in largely noncombatant support positions. However, one of the heroic stories of Pearl Harbor is that of Doris Miller, a mess attendant on board the USS *Virginia* who, amidst the chaos of heavy attack, manned a machine gun to fire back. By weaving this scene into the attack sequence, the filmmakers appropriated an image already produced in official efforts to promote the role of Black Americans in the military. After the attack, Miller was awarded the Navy Cross for his actions, and he became a symbol of the military's attempt to expand minority enlist-ments. At the time of film production, Miller was already prominently depicted in naval recruitment posters and public ceremonies.

Following the scenes of bombing, both films shift to efforts at recovery, showing a nation mobilizing to fight the war. However, the narrative of mobilization is also a narrative of national unification in which dominant national interest subsumes ethnic difference. To create his vision of national community, Gregg Toland produced a "memorial sequence" in which servicemen from diverse backgrounds killed in the attack all speak from the grave with common purpose. In this manner, the film embodies patriotic sentiment, creating a national voice inflected with ethnic and regional difference. To do this, Toland carefully selected the names of individuals from distinct backgrounds so as to depict an American "melting pot." He began by constructing a list of Pearl Harbor casualties with ethnically distinct names from different parts of the country, which he could use to contact their families and include *them* in the film as visual testimony to the diversity of Americans who had already sacrificed for the war.

> I want the names of six families whose sons died at Pearl Harbor on December 7th. They should be from various parts of the United States. . . . One colored family, one Jewish family, one Irish family, one German family, one Filipino family, and a Mexican family. . . . I think you get the general idea from the above. I want representative large cities, small towns, all nationalities, and types of names *for a sort of melting pot memorial* (emphasis added).[18]

Toland's superior, Captain Bert Cunningham, responded to his request with a list of six Navy men, three Marines, and five Army men. The film incorporated seven of these names in the memorial sequence. As each of the dead introduces himself by stating his name, branch of service, and place of residence, the film displays a photo of the person along with a film clip of his surviving parents (and, in some cases, spouse). Each then introduces his parents, who remain mute, providing visual testimony to the wide range of families affected by the attack. Toland wanted this list to be emblematic of the ethnic and regional diversity of the United States, as well as to represent the different branches of military service.[19]

> NARRATOR: For on this Sabbath day 2,343 officers and enlisted men of our Army, Navy, and Marine Corps gave their young lives in the service of our country. Who were these young Americans? Let us pause for a few minutes at their hallowed graves and ask a few of them to make themselves known. Who are you boys? Come on, speak up some of you.

—I am Robert R. Kelley, United States Army. I came from Finlay, Ohio. My parents are Mr. and Mrs. James E. Kelley.

—I am Alfred Aaron Rosenthal, United States Navy. I lived in Brooklyn, New York. My parents are Mr. and Mrs. Henry L. Rosenthal.

—I am Theodore Stephen Zabel, United States Marine Corps. My home town is Castelia, Iowa. Those are my parents, Mr. and Mrs. Stephen Zabel.

—I am Moses Anderson Allan, United States Navy. I lived on a farm in Cove, North Carolina. My mother is Mrs. Abby Allan.

—I am James Webster Lake, United States Navy. I'm from Huntington Park, California. My folks are Mr. and Mrs. William J. Lake.

—I'm Antonio S. Pafoya, United States Army. I lived just outside Albuquerque, New Mexico. My father and mother are Mr. and Mrs. Jesus Pafoya.

—I'm William R. Schick, United States Army Medical Corps. My home was Chicago, Illinois. My parents are Mr. and Mrs. William H. Schick. My wife's name is Lois.

NARRATOR: You have a baby now, Lieutenant. He was born three months after Pearl Harbor. He's named after you, Billy. And you may be pleased to know he was born on your birthday.

LT.: That's swell. Thanks.

NARRATOR: But tell me one thing, Lieutenant, how does it happen that all of you sound and talk alike?

LT.: We are all alike. We're all Americans. [scene shifts to cemetery and graves of soldiers]

This scene occupies a pivotal position in the film's narrative structure. Located between the attack scene and the "recovery" scene showing the unifying effects of the attack, the memorial sequence frames the mobilization effort as a process of social and cultural unification. The voices of the deceased are thus marked as both ethnic *and* American, facilitating a multiethnic national imaginary.

The dialogue with the dead is an effective pragmatic tool for imagining this kind of national subjectivity. By embodying national identity in the form of

Figure 14.5. Robert R. Kelley.

Figure 14.6. The family of Robert R. Kelley.

Figure 14.7. Alfred Aaron Rosenthal.

Figure 14.8. The family of Alfred Aaron Rosenthal.

Figure 14.9. Theodore Stephen Zabel.

Figure 14.10. The family of Theodore Stephen Zabel.

Figure 14.11. Moses Anderson Allan.

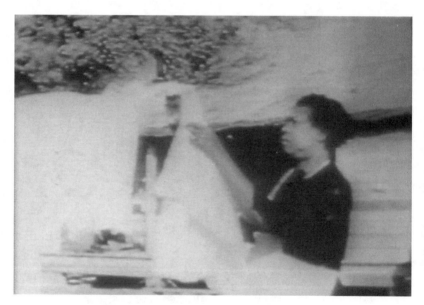

Figure 14.12. The family of Moses Anderson Allan.

Figure 14.13. James Webster Lake.

Figure 14.14. The family of James Webster Lake.

Figure 14.15. Antonio S. Pafoya.

Figure 14.16. The family of Antonio S. Pafoya.

Figure 14.17. William R. Schick.

Figure 14.18. The family of William R. Schick.

individuals speaking in the first person, the film inflects national voice with both individuality and ethnicity. On the one hand, all of the speakers share a number of critical attributes: they are young, male, and military. More importantly, in the words of the film, they all "gave their young lives in the service of our country" (where the collective pronoun "our" indexes the shared national identity of narrator and audience). Yet, each individual speaks within the domestic space of his own family, establishing a degree of oppositional tension between the unifying force of the nation and the visible diversity of America. In case the implicit message of common national identity is not clear enough, this sequence finishes with a rhetorical flourish that says in the collective first person, "We are all alike. We are all Americans."

In this context, Japanese American ethnicity disappears from the scene. In the long film, the force of the opening sequence of Orientalist suspicions renders Japanese American ethnicity invisible. Remarkably, though, Captain Cunningham *did* include a Japanese name in the list of U.S. Army names provided to Toland, who had not requested a Japanese name. Nevertheless, Cunningham listed Private Torao Migita of Weaver Lane, Honolulu, along with four other Army men killed in the December 7th attack.[20] However, Migita's name is one of several that were not included in the list of seven voices speaking from the grave. Looking at the dominant tropes of ethnicity in the short version of *December 7th*, the inclusion of a Japanese American in this hall of Pearl Harbor heroes would not have seriously disrupted the evolving narrative. Still, this sequence was originally scripted for the long version, where the dissonance of a Japanese face appearing after the scenes of spying and the extended interrogation of questionable loyalties might have clashed with the message, "We are all (different but) Americans."

As the films proceed beyond the memorial sequence into a narrative of recovery, they both exhibit more of Uncle Sam's utopian multiculturalism than of wise Mr. C's skeptical essentialism. Here the film shows Japanese Americans in Hawai'i demonstrating their patriotism. Indeed, scriptwriters sought images of loyal citizen-subjects for this section of the film in the earliest stages of writing. For example, in the third draft of the script one writer noted that, "Newsreel shots may be dubbed in here of camouflage being set up, antiaircraft guns being installed. . . . If possible these should include the defense work of loyal Japanese."[21] Ignoring the legal and political pressures brought to bear on Japanese Americans during this period, the film presents Pearl Harbor as the catalyst that prompted local Japanese to break definitively with homeland culture. Addressing "Mr. Tojo," the film states:

> Yes, your bombs, Mr. Tojo, brought many changes and in no small measure served to further complicate the already complex life of the Japanese

in Hawaii. And so to permanently erase their relationship to the home-land, they wiped out or removed every vestige of the written Japanese word. Closed are the language schools, empty and boarded up the Shinto temples, gone the flag of the rising sun. This young American Japanese gave the best illustration that over Hawaii the rising sun had begun to set. [At this point the film shows the scene described by John Ford of a Japanese American man replacing a sign saying "Banzai Cafe" with one reading "Keep 'Em Flying Cafe." See Figures 14.2 and 14.3.]

Here the film's theme of unification is realized in public acts of cultural re-nunciation. By 1943, when the first Japanese American military units were al-ready forming, this vision of the nation as a melting pot was far more consis-tent with official pronouncements than the exclusionary discourse of Mr. C.

In addition to the wholesale removal of the first section, significant smaller changes in the middle section of the short film also worked to diminish the tone of suspicion created in the longer version. The only lines pared from this section come at the end. Editors deleted a few lines about the state of emer-gency in Hawai'i and this passage about the status of Japanese Americans:

Yes all the people pitched in—the Japanese too. They volunteered in great numbers as blood donors. They liberally supported the war bond drive. . . . The younger generation did its share and fully justified Dr. Shunzo Sakamaki's faith and trust in his fellow Japanese. Those that were known to be disloyal or undercover enemy agents were imme-diately taken into custody. Many were forced out of business and in-terned. But despite the wild Tokyo inspired rumors, the scuttlebutt, not one single solitary act of sabotage was committed on the seventh.[22]

Contradictions abound in this section. The narrator asserts that the in-ternment of the Japanese Americans was justified because it targeted only those "known to be disloyal or undercover enemy agents." Yet, almost in the same breath, the narrator declares that "not one single solitary act of sabo-tage was committed on the seventh." The film implies that the anti-Japanese American hysteria resulted from "Tokyo inspired rumors," rather than from domestic racism of the type espoused by Mr. C (and John Ford).

The only other change in this section is as interesting as it is minute. In the original version, we switch to a scene during the day of the bombing in which a reporter is talking to the Japanese consul, who refuses to acknowledge that Japan is responsible for the attack. The reporter insinuates that this man had been burning evidence of spying activities, reinforcing Mr. C's assertion that espionage represents a major threat to American security. This scene re-mained intact in the second version with one small exception: a brief shot was added showing a placard reading "Consulate General of Japan, Honolulu, T.H." Insofar as the speaker is not otherwise identified as the Japanese consul, this change works to draw a more definitive line between the treachery of Japan and the representation of Japanese Americans. Some of the visual imagery from the first version also remains, although alterations in the sound track lend them a quite different tenor. Without the sinister music and Mr. C's relentless voice-over of the long film, scenes of Japanese Americans looking out onto the military bases appear far less ominous.

HAWAI'I AS MULTICULTURAL UTOPIA

The portrayal of Hawai'i as a distinctive kind of place is critical to the mythic story of Pearl Harbor. Then as now, Hawai'i is located on the periphery of the American imaginary. Rather than raise questions about the presence of the U.S. military in Hawai'i, that presence is naturalized by treating the islands as an extension of Manifest Destiny in the Pacific. However, given the central problematic of *race* for *December 7th,* Hawai'i's multiethnic population and colonial history pose a number of complications for national mythmakers. Much of the film(s) can be seen as an attempt to find narrative solutions to these complications. Where the long version tells two contradictory stories— one of essentialized Japanese immigrants who cannot be assimilated and the other of successful Americanization—the short version opts for the latter. In the narrative of assimilation, Hawai'i is portrayed as a place where multicultural mixing is the norm, a veritable tropical "melting pot." Although not consistent, the long film also pursues this vision, beginning with the very first scene when we find Uncle Sam dictating a letter to his secretary, a young Asian-looking woman named Miss Kim. As a vacationing Uncle Sam soliloquizes about Hawai'i, the camera moves in for a tight close-up of Miss Kim.

> *Uncle Sam:* New paragraph: Imagine a transition, Jonathan. You hop a clipper in San Francisco and in less than 24 hours you're in paradise. Silenced is the endless ringing of the telephone. Banished are Mrs. hurry, scurry, worry, and company. Inaudible the hubbub of labor disputes. Gone the nerve wracking feeling that the world in general is a whirling mess and that America in particular can't make up its mind which way it wants to spin, if at all (shot to newspaper front page—date Dec. 6, 1941). Yes sir, Jonathan, when your corns begin to ache and bite there's only one thing to do—take your shoes off. And that's just exactly what I've done. On a flower-covered hilltop in Honolulu, T.H., territory of heaven, Hawai'i. romantic, mystical Hawai'i, where the air is choked with the fragrance of a million flowers.

Figure 14.19. Miss Kim, Uncle Sam's secretary.

Although only a background figure used for stage-setting, Miss Kim's persona and physical appearance are critical to the locating moves of the opening scene. As a young, attractive Asian woman with a flower in her hair, her presence adds to the erotic/exotic image of Hawai'i in Uncle Sam's reverie. Her Korean name, sarong-like Polynesian dress (of the type popularized in film by Dorothy Lamour), and ambiguous, polyglot accent embody Hawai'i as a feminized land of cultural mixing and seductive pleasures. She listens and records what Uncle Sam has to say, repeating his words earnestly but with difficulty. Attractive, passive, and educable, she manifests an ideal colonial subject.

It is significant that Uncle Sam does not live in Hawai'i. He is on vacation there. The vision of Hawai'i as vacation site and escape from the troubles of mainland America sets up a dramatic tension between languid (feminine) pleasure and the (male) responsibilities of the "real world." The latter is rendered in a narrative of progress, industrialization, and international tensions.[23] Like a chastising parent, Mr. C intrudes to remind Uncle Sam of the litany of dangers that await him in the world of international politics. A newspaper dated December 6, 1941, with the headline, "See War! FDR Confers With Knox Crisis Near," rests on a table amidst photos of hula girls, reminding the audience that all this is happening on the eve of disaster, at a moment of loss of "innocence."

When prodded by Mr. C, however, Uncle Sam recounts his history of the incorporation of Hawai'i in the U.S. economic and political sphere, emphasizing the benefits of Americanization and modernization.

> *Uncle Sam:* It's the story of a miracle in an arid sun-smitten desert created by a handful of adroit men with indomitable courage. They and their descendants put into cultivation 244,000 acres. . . . Over 50 million dollars worth a year. Big business. . . . Where once was a village of grass huts, a modern American city arose. Honolulu, the pearl of the Pacific, a modern up-to-the-minute city. . . . Luxurious hotels, Royal Hawaiian and the Moana on legendary Waikiki beach. A bustling port. . . . That, my dear Mr. C, is what was accomplished with a sweet weed and a spiny pineapple in one century. . . .

The line "Where once was a village of grass huts, a modern American city arose" sums up this narrative of progress. "Modern" Hawai'i is presented as living testimony to the power of capitalist expansion to transform the landscape.

For Mr. C, however, this story of economic progress only calls attention to the dangers posed by the large numbers of immigrant Japanese in Hawai'i. To this, Uncle Sam gives a lengthy reply about Hawai'i as a land of beauty and harmony. Although the film frames these remarks as naïve, Uncle Sam's opinions closely resemble the rhetoric of culture that has been used repeatedly in postwar Hawai'i to promote investment and tourism development. As Uncle Sam continues with his narrative, the camera moves from scene to scene, mixing tropical landscape with faces, language, and performances—all signifiers of cultural differences that are at once alluring and benign; these images have fueled a tourist industry ever since.

> *Uncle Sam:* You may see nothing but intrigue and conspiracy lurking behind every closed door and choking the airwaves with military information. I see islands of wondrous beauty (sweeping landscape scenes) sky piercing mountains, deep driven gorges, dashing surf and miles of colorful coastline, tropical skies, the world famous landmarks—Diamond Head, the upside-down falls, the Pali. I see islands inhabited by peoples of many tongues, of many lands, living side by side in neighborliness and friendship (cut to shots of women of various ethnicities, each giving population figures for her ethnic group). A melting pot, yes, but one in which everything literally melts (scenes of multicultural Hawai'i). I see islands to which people from the world over have brought their colorful traditions and customs and adapted them to our American way of life (hula scenes; Korean dance; more hula), islands which say "aloha" to thousands of vacation-bent tourists yearly (women of

various ethnicities saying "aloha"; beach scenes; water sports; tourist scenes), islands once ruled by the great King Kamehameha and over which now in dignified splendor flies the flag of the United States (scene returns to Uncle Sam's hilltop house). It's all down there, Mr. C, if you'll only take time to look.

Beginning with panoramic vistas of an uninhabited, natural landscape of a type often preferred by John Ford, this scene sets up one of the premises of the narrative of progress: that the best lands for colonization and development are those unencumbered by prior settlement of people who have their own cultures and histories. In this narrative, Hawai'i as colonial possession is remade as an extension of America, sited on the "frontier" as undeveloped land awaiting Euro-American occupation and culture, the essential ingredient in transforming raw lands into productive societies.

Even though strong traces of American racialized thinking infiltrate this first cut of *December 7th,* the primary goal was to promote national unity across racial and ethnic lines, to fashion a vision of America as a harmonious multicultural nation. What results is a depiction of the Americanization of multiple immigrant groups, with the identity of the indigenous population rendered invisible or recast as a signifier for the multicultural melting pot as a whole. Hawai'i here becomes a symbol of a fantasized American multiculturalism that *more obviously* could not obtain in the center of mainland America, marked by the black/white racial tensions of the 1930s and 1940s.

CULTURAL PRODUCTION, HOLLYWOOD, AND THE STATE

Pearl Harbor quickly came to signify a critical juncture in national time—a kind of "flashbulb memory" for Americans of the war generation, who still remember where they were when they heard the news.[24] After the immediate radio announcements, the Pearl Harbor story circulated quickly and widely through increasingly powerful technologies of representation. A wide array of representational means—including magazines, radio, newsreels, and feature films—were mobilized to tell the story to the nation.

Beginning with Roosevelt's radio message in which he labeled December 7th, 1941, "a date which will live in infamy," the dominant frame for Pearl Harbor became *remembering*—specifically, collective, *national* remembering. The Associated Press put out a press release a week after the bombing that began "Born last Sunday in Japan's treacherous attack on Hawaii, the phrase 'Remember Pearl Harbor,' has overnight become the battle cry of the nation."[25] By March 1942, Danny Kay's popular song "Let's Remember Pearl Harbor" was playing on radios around the country. Newsreels about the bombing were approved for general release two months after the attack. In line with this trope, *December 7th* also frames its narrative as an act of collective remembering.

The first photos of Pearl Harbor appeared in January 1942 in *Life Magazine*, which then claimed a circulation in the tens of millions, with two out of every three Americans in the military reading the magazine.[26] In February 1942, a Hearst newsreel showed in U.S. theaters under the title: "Lest We Forget! The Truth About Pearl Harbor! First Actual Films Now Released by U.S. Navy—Pearl Harbor Ablaze! First Actual Pictures!"[27] In fact, one of the reasons that Gregg Toland decided to invest in the production of extensive recreations and studio shots was that the general public had already seen all of the actual footage taken of the Pearl Harbor attack in newsreels.[28]

World War II was the first war in which visual representations played a major role in shaping popular understandings of the conflict.[29] Similar to the role of print media in forming a sense of national community in early nation states, the rise of a moviegoing public in America in the 1930s established the technological means and social practices for producing national consciousness through visual narrative. By one estimate, Americans in the 1940s went to the movies an average of three times a month. "Inside the darkened theaters Americans participated in a communal viewing experience unlike any during World War I."[30] Coming just as cinema penetrated the daily habits of Americans of all classes, *December 7th* was intended to engender the very phenomenon it sought to represent: national unification. Even though, in the end, it never played in commercial movie houses, the short version was shown widely in government and military venues.

From the start, the task of making a film about Pearl Harbor was undertaken with the intention of propagating a patriotic sensibility that would create a desire to enlist in the military, to work in wartime factories, and to buy war bonds, among other things.[31] Colonel William B. Donovan, head of the new Office of Strategic Services (OSS, which later became the CIA), commissioned the film. Donovan proposed the idea of a full-length film on Pearl Harbor to his friend, John Ford, who had been appointed as head of a new Field Photographic Unit operating out of Hollywood. Ford supervised the film with little direct government oversight, reporting only to Donovan who in turn reported only to the White House. The Office of War Information (OWI), an amalgamation of various intelligence and information agencies that were having problems coordinating with each other, was not formed until June 1942, four months after Toland began filming in Hawai'i.[32]

As noted earlier, the fact that the film was produced at the instigation of military authorities is enunciated at the beginning of both versions, in the

Figure 14.20. Officers of Navy field photo unit. Lt. Cmdr. John Ford is near the end of the table, wearing glasses.

form of an announcement by the narrator and onscreen memoranda from the Secretary of War and the Secretary of the Navy.[33] Despite their formal sponsorship, military authorities exercised very little oversight over the production of *December 7th*. They decided to stop production of the film only when called upon by officials of the Bureau of Motion Pictures, a newly formed branch of the OWI charged with coordinating relations between the government and Hollywood. Nelson Poynter, head of the Bureau in Hollywood, and his superior in Washington, Lowell Mellett, initiated censorship of the film.

Speculation about the reasons for the suppression of the film have ranged from official discomfort with the film's criticism of military readiness to unease with the film's fictional dramatizations to the opinion that the film was too long and "boring." Although the correspondence among Poynter, Mellett, the Secretary of War, and the Secretary of the Navy addresses the film's use of fictional techniques and makes vague reference to political sensitivities, the problems of ethnic/cultural identity and the portrayal of Japanese Americans in particular were clearly major issues weighing on their decision.

The Office of War Information was constantly concerned with issues of race

Figure 14.21. Lt. Gregg Toland conducts a camera class at Twentieth Century–Fox.

and representation in Hollywood films.[34] A primary purpose of the agency was to promote national unity in support of the war. In July of 1942, the Bureau of Motion Pictures authored a "Government Information Manual for the Motion Picture Industry" that set out the theme of national unity as a primary concern. As Clayton Koppes and Gregory Black note:

> This was, then, "a people's war," . . . Everyone had a stake in it, regardless of class, ethnic, or religious identification: everyone contributed according to his or her ability. "Show democracy at work," the manual said, "in the community, the factory, the army." Avoid stereotypes, such as blacks in menial or comic roles. Show loyal aliens, "glad of a chance to support and help the free land of their adoption." Few aliens were fifth columnists; they should be depicted as helping the war effort of "the free land of their adoption."[35]

By the time the OWI was supervising the editing of *December 7th* the agency was well aware of the wartime politics of race and patriotism. In a 1942 OWI-sponsored survey of African Americans in New York, only one-fourth of those surveyed felt that a Japanese invasion would be injurious to their personal well being or social position. Much of the correspondence in the OWI files during its first year of existence in 1942 pertains to conflicts over representations of race and ethnicity. For example, in October 1942, just one month before the recommendation to cancel release of the long version of *December 7th*, the agency noted strong objections to the film *Air Force*—a Hollywood film made in cooperation with the U.S. Air Force—because of its racist depictions of Japanese Americans committing sabotage at Pearl Harbor and even shooting on the crew of a downed U.S. plane. The issues associated with the *Air Force* controversy closely resembled those represented in *December 7th*. Based on a review of the *Air Force* script (the film was then in production), Nelson Poynter wrote a lengthy letter to the OWI's Bureau of Motion Pictures head, Lowell Mellett, complaining that

> I believe there is a studied effort to make Japanese Fifth Columnists the alibi for our early defeats in the Pacific. Such a picture can certainly be damaging to us abroad and at home. My understanding is that the facts as gathered by Army Intelligence do not support such a thesis. . . .
>
> I believe this is an opportune case for OWI to make an issue of the handling of Army and Navy movie relations with Hollywood.[36]

BLURRED GENRES: CINEMATIC CONSTRUCTIONS OF NATIONAL AUTHORITY

In addition to differences in their depictions of race, the two *December 7th* films differ considerably in their adherence to documentary format. In November 1942, the Secretary of the Navy asked Lowell Mellett in Washington, D.C. to review the rough-cut of the film as it was being completed. Mellett responded that, "this project, as a picture for public exhibition should be stopped. . . . It is a fictional treatment of a very real fact, the tragic disaster of Pearl Harbor, and I do not believe the government should engage in fiction."[37] Again in April 1943, when the film had been completed, he reaffirmed this view in another letter, adding, "Presentation of fictional propaganda on the subject would seem to be an improper activity for the U.S. Government."[38]

In the end, the cancellation and reissue of a shortened film shifted the context and audience for film viewing. While the long version was initially intended for general release as a documentary feature film, the short version was produced solely for circulation in a military "morale" program. When the project was originally conceived, the intention was to produce a "factual motion picture" about the attack on Pearl Harbor that would play to a larger mass audience. It was only after the film had been locked away that John Ford was asked to salvage a shorter version for use in the navy's Industrial Incentive Program. In other words, this shorter version was never intended to play to a larger American audience.

Since the time of production, both versions of *December 7th* have resisted easy categorization within a single film genre. What kind of film is it? For the short film, the fact that it received a 1943 Academy Award for best documentary might seem to settle the argument. It is clearly intended to be nonfiction, as certified by the military memoranda shown at the outset.[39] However, one scholar writes that "*December 7th* is hardly a documentary at all. It is more of a short narrative film, anything but a dispassionate presentation of facts."[40] Other writers have indicated their discomfort by labeling it as "semi-documentary."[41] One of the great ironies in the body of film about Pearl Harbor is that the most widely seen feature film on the subject, *Tora! Tora! Tora!* (1970), is in fact more "historical"—that is, more concerned with a detailed recitation of documented actions and events—than *December 7th*.[42] In part this is because *Tora! Tora! Tora!* focuses primarily on the attack with virtually no overt concern for sociocultural context or matters of race, ethnicity, or national sentiment.[43]

Film scholars concerned with preserving the term "documentary" from the encroachments of re-creations, reenactments, and fictionalized characters have been quick to criticize the documentary claims of *December 7th*.[44] These critics include the obvious point that the film, in fact, was made as "propaganda," as well as extensive discussions about the mixture of recreated scenes with *actual* footage of the events of Pearl Harbor. Numerous writers have noted that the recreations of *December 7th* have been incorporated as historical footage in many postwar films, both documentary and feature, including the Disney film, *Pearl Harbor* (2001), that recreated scenes on the basis of Gregg Toland's 1942 recreated scenes.

The longer film's opening—a 40-minute dialogue between two fictional characters the day *before* the bombing—made it clear that it would not speak only in the register of documentary narration. The dissonance of actors' voices in fictional dialogue combined with that of an omniscient narrator unsettles the historical authority of the film. However, with the opening sequence eliminated, along with the fictionalized conversation that concluded the original film, the short version of *December 7th* took on much more of the look and sound of a documentary.

Yet, while reshaped into a documentary-like format, the fictionalized elements of the original version remain clearly evident in the final version. The filmmakers were as much concerned with fashioning a vision of a unified, multicultural America as with presenting a news-like account of the bombing. This is most evident in the memorial sequence (see Figures 14.5–14.18) positioned at the core of the short film. Although these men and their families were real people, the filmmakers scripted all of the dialogue for this sequence, and the voices, obviously, were also fictionalized. In addition, the parents and spouses remained silent, present only as visual authentication for the voices of the deceased. Given that much of the fictionalized dialogue (including a similar cemetery conversation between two dead veterans) in the original *December 7th* was edited for the short film, this would seem to be an unusual sequence to retain. In our analysis, however, this passage is crucial to the film's attempt to personify national subjectivity. If the reaction of audience and critics is any guide, this sequence blended easily into the narrative of the short film. This more radical departure from documentary format seemingly went unnoticed by one writer, who characterized the shorter version of *December 7th* as "shorn of all but the raids and salvage footage."[45]

The puzzle of *December 7th* provided the subject for a documentary film, *Eye of the Eagle*, made in 1984 by Britannica. The documentary, hosted by Hollywood critic, Richard Schickel, included an interview with Robert Parrish, who edited the long film into its short form. Remarkably, this documentary, like other commentaries on these films, has very little to say about the film's representation of race. Commenting on neither racist attitudes and images of the day nor the plight of Japanese Americans caught in 1941 war hysteria, the narrator simply notes that "No evidence had been found to prove any Japanese American disloyal. And who to blame for Pearl Harbor was no longer important." Instead, the Britannica documentary leaves the impression that the problems were more a matter of Gregg Toland's personal political views. Narrator Schickel states:

> *December 7th* was a film of half truths, or reenactments, of wishful thinking, of conjecture. To be sure, there were scenes of documentation— the memorial service, the salvage operation, even six minutes of the actual Japanese attack. But it was mostly Gregg Toland's personal editorial on the failure of the American foreign policy to prevent a Second World War, and the failure of the American people to be ready for that war when it came to America.

The documentary then constructs a redemptive narrative that preserves World War II as the "good war." It concludes:

> Despite its failing, Gregg Toland's *December 7th* remains a legacy for this and future generations of Americans. In his heroic images of battle, in his patriotic and heartfelt sentiment, Toland captured for us the devotion to country and duty, the unselfish sacrifice of the men who fought and died at Pearl Harbor. For them, *December 7th* is a fitting tribute and worthy memorial.

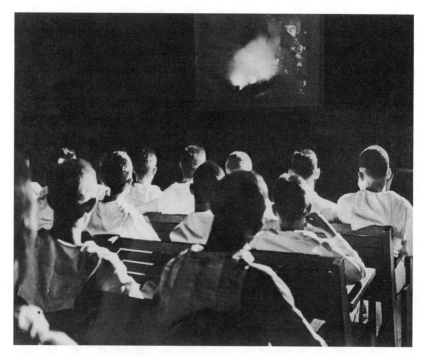

Figure 14.22. American military recruits receive training through documentary film.

The ideological messiness of the original film and its problematics of race, place, and nation are again reshaped into a recuperative narrative of war and heroic national memory. This narrative, however, remains silent about the more obvious contradictions associated with Japanese American identity and internment. Moreover, still missing entirely from this 1984 commentary, as it has been from all cinematic representations of Pearl Harbor, is the longer view that might include colonization of the islands and their incorporation into the U.S. military sphere.

The commentary of the Britannica film reminds us that Pearl Harbor remains a potent symbol of and for national consciousness. Although today one may view the two versions of *December 7th* as history, they were not about history at the time of production. They were about the formation of national sentiment in the context of a war strongly inflected with race ideology, in a nation characterized by ongoing race conflicts and struggles. As a culturally constructed event, Pearl Harbor was not just a military action that triggered a declaration of war; it was also an occasion for collective (and, in this case, official) self-fashioning, for using cinematic means to see the national community refracted through its colonial "frontier." In producing a film about an event that had already captured the national imagination, Hollywood film-makers and their military overseers could use the storytelling devices of film to renarrate long-standing tensions and contradictions in popular conceptions of race and nation. Whereas the long film represents a moment of ambiguity with regard to which racial ideology (assimilationist or exclusionist) would dominate at the outset of the war, the short film moved to resolve that tension with a more resolutely triumphant narrative of Americanization.

NOTES

We would like to thank a number of people who have contributed to the research and (re)writing of this paper. Les Waffen at the National Archives, Motion Picture Branch, assisted with the identification of relevant sources and documents, as did Daniel Martinez, historian at the Pearl Harbor memorial in Honolulu. Michael Ogden provided invaluable assistance in capturing video images from the Pearl Harbor films. We are grateful to Noel Kent for archival documents pertaining to wartime attitudes toward Japanese Americans, and to Carolyn Anderson, Daniel Bernardi, Marsha Kinder, and Jonathan Okamura for insightful comments on an earlier draft of this paper.

1. From Good Times Home Video Corporation, 1986. In fact, John Ford only supervised the production of *December 7th*. The film was mostly directed by cinematographer Gregg Toland, whose credits included camera work for *Grapes of Wrath* (1940) and *Citizen Kane* (1941). Toland traveled to Hawai'i in February 1942 for location sequences and shot the remainder in Twentieth Century-Fox studio space, completing his work in December 1942 before being assigned to another project in South America (James M. Skinner, "*December 7*: Filmic Myth Masquerading as Historical Fact," *The Journal of Military History* 55, October 1991: 510). When Ford was notified in March 1944 that the film received an Academy Award, he sent Toland a telegram of congratulations.

2. This was the first year an award was given in the newly created category of "short documentary."

3. In Stuart Hall's words, "Even the 'hegemonic' moment is no longer conceptualized as a moment of *simple* unity, but as a process of unification (never totally achieved), founded on strategic alliances between different sectors, not on their pre-given identity." (Stuart Hall, "Gramsci's Relevance for the Study of Race and Ethnicity," in *Stuart Hall: Critical Dialogues in the U.S.*, ed. David Morley and Kuan Hsing-Chen (London: Routledge 1996), 437.

4. Bill Nichols, *Blurred Boundaries: Questions of Meaning in Contemporary Culture* (Bloomington: Indiana University Press, 1994).

5. Geoffrey M. White, "Moving History: The Pearl Harbor Film(s)," *Positions: East-Asia Cultural Critique* 5, no. 3 (1998): 709–44.

6. Biographers of John Ford and other film commentators have emphasized the film's presentation of military unpreparedness as the primary reason for its suppression. See William T. Murphy, "John Ford and the Wartime Documentary," *Film and History* (February 1976): 7; Peter Stowell, *John Ford* (Boston: Twayne Publishers, 1986) 77; Tag Gallagher, *John Ford: The Man and His Films* (Berkeley: University of California Press, 1986); Skinner, "*December 7th*," 507–16, 514; Abé Mark Nornes, "December 7th" in *The Japan/America Film Wars: World War II Propaganda and Its Cultural Contexts*, ed. Abé Mark Nornes and Fukushima Yukio (Langhorne, PA: Harwood Academic Publishers, 1994), 189–91.

7. The issue of race looms much larger for contemporary viewers. For example, in his review of the video released in 1991, Richard Schickel asserted, "When the picture was first screened in Washington . . . the response was chilling. It was not its racism that offended its sponsors so much as its criticism of the Armed Forces' lack of preparedness—and perhaps the sheer boredom of the Uncle Sam sequence." Richard Schickel, "*December 7th*: The Movie," *Video Review*, 1991:80.

8. Thomas Patrick Doherty, *Projections of War: Hollywood, American Culture, and World War II* (New York: Columbia University Press, 1993). Clayton R. Koppes and Gregory D. Black, *Hollywood Goes to War: How Politics, Profits, and Propaganda Shaped World War II Movies* (Berkeley: University of California Press, 1987), 67.

9. The most notorious example of support for the Japanese military occurred on the isolated island of Niihau when Yoshio Harada, a California Japanese American, attempted to aid the escape of a downed Japanese aviator. Allan Beekman, *The Niihau Incident* (Honolulu: Heritage Press of the Pacific, 1982). The only documented case of a Japanese American assisting Japanese spying on Pearl Harbor is that of John Mikuma, who regularly acted as a taxi driver for military attachés gathering intelligence. See Burl Burlingame, *Remembrance 1941–1991* (Honolulu: Honolulu Star-Bulletin, 1991), 18.

Because local Japanese residents were an important and necessary labor source in Hawai'i's wartime economy, including its military installations, they were spared the kind of wholesale internment that occurred on the West Coast. By January 1943, just as *December 7th* was completed, suspicions and rumors had subsided enough that men of Japanese ancestry were allowed to enter military service. They turned out in record numbers, with 9,500 volunteering and 2,700 accepted for service, ultimately forming one of the most decorated units in the European campaign. Desoto Brown, *Hawaii Goes to War* (Honolulu: Editions Limited, 1989), 114.

For Americans of Japanese Ancestry (AJA), it is not stories of Pearl Harbor, but of the subsequent service of large numbers of young men in military units fighting in Europe and the Pacific that provided the public validation of their loyalty and identity as Americans. With the rise of normative multiculturalism in postwar America, stories of AJA war experiences, such as those of the famed 442 Regimental Combat Team, became the dominant trope for Japanese American wartime identity, chronicled in newspaper articles, books, films, and plays, especially during the period of fiftieth anniversary observances of the war. (See T. Fujitani, " 'Go For Broke,' the Movie: Nisei Soldiers in U.S. National, Military and Racial Discourses," in *Perilous Memories:*

The Asia-Pacific War(s), ed. T. Fujitani, G. M. White, and L. Yoneyama (Durham: Duke University Press, 2001).

10. The history of the U.S. internment policy that forcibly evicted people of Japanese ancestry from their homes, confiscated property, and relocated whole families to internment camps is documented in a large body of writings and films. See United States Commission on Wartime Relocation and Internment of Civilians, "Personal Justice Denied: Report of the Commission on Wartime Relocation and Internment of Civilians: Committee on Interior and Insular Affairs" (Washington, D.C.: U.S. Government Printing Office, 1992); Ann Koto Hayashi, *Face of the Enemy, Heart of a Patriot: Japanese-American Internment Narratives* (New York: Garland, 1995); Yamato Ichihashi, *Morning Glory, Evening Shadow: Yamato Ichihashi and His Internment Writings, 1942–1945* (Stanford: Stanford University Press, 1997); and Sandra C. Taylor, *Jewel of the Desert: Japanese American Internment at Topaz* (Berkeley: University of California Press, 1993).

11. One of the scenes of spying shows an ordinary cane cutter working on the banks of Pearl Harbor, glancing up as a destroyer glides by just a few hundred yards away (see Figure 14.1). This scene—just a few seconds long—is the only posed scene from the Ford/Toland film to have been incorporated in the Pearl Harbor documentary that shows today at the USS *Arizona* Memorial in Honolulu (see White, "Moving History," 709–44). Interestingly, this very scene recently came under attack by the Japanese American Citizens' League as perpetuating the same false stereotypes that supported internment of Japanese American citizens during the war years. As a result of their complaints, the image of the cane cutter was digitally removed from the film.

12. We hasten to add that the very same Dr. Sakamaki was founding chair of the Department of History at the University of Hawai'i, where a building is named in his honor.

13. Skinner, "*December 7th*," 507–16, 511.

14. President Roosevelt signed "Executive Order 9066" on February 12, 1942, at the very moment that Gregg Toland was traveling to Hawai'i to begin filming. With that order, the Secretary of War gained authority to remove Japanese forcibly from their homes and confiscate their property.

15. In this part of the film, the topic is Japanese American "unwillingness" to give up Japanese citizenship to become American citizens, implying national disloyalty. Interestingly, neither *December 7th* nor any of the commentary about the documentary mentions the fact that immigrants of Japanese descent were legally prohibited from obtaining American citizenship until 1952 with the passage of the *McCarran-Walter Act*. See Michael Omi and Howard Winant, *Racial Formation in the United States: From the 1960s to the 1990s* (New York: Routledge, 1994), 81.

16. In *Air Force* an American B-17 crew makes an emergency landing on a neighbor island, where "locals" shoot at them. When they finally make it to Honolulu, they find that airplanes on the runway have had their tails knocked off by a local Japanese delivery truck.

17. Doherty, *Projections of War,* 259.

18. Gregg Toland, Lieut. USNR, to Bert Cunningham, Capt. USMCR, OSS, October 23, 1942, National Archives, RG 226, OSS, entry 90, folder 382.

19. Although more than sixty civilian residents of Honolulu died in the December 7th attack (most from the "friendly" fire of poorly fused munitions fired off the ships), they were entirely invisible in the scripting of *December 7th* and, until recently, in all of the official national memory-making at the Pearl Harbor Memorial. An added irony is that the majority of these casualties were members of Hawai'i's Japanese community.

20. Cunningham to Toland, October 28, 1942, National Archives, RG 226, OSS, entry 90, folder 382.

21. "Preliminary Scenario for Motion Picture, *December the 7th,*" 9. National Archives, RG 226, entry 133, box 153, folder 1280.

22. It is ironic that the first version of *December 7th,* with all its racial paranoia, would include such a clear statement about the demonstrated loyalty of Japanese Americans during the war years. In fact, it is precisely the absence of such a direct statement in the Pearl Harbor documentary currently showing at the USS *Arizona* Memorial that evoked the formal complaint from the Japanese American Citizens League. (See note 11.)

23. See Kathy Ferguson and Phyllis Turnbull, *Oh Say, Can You See?: The Semiotics of the Military in Hawai'i* (Minneapolis: University of Minnesota Press, 1999).

24. See R. Brown and J. Kulik, "Flashbulb Memories," in *Memory Observed,* ed. U. Neisser (San Francisco: W. H. Freeman, 1982). By the end of the war, Pearl Harbor had become so well established in collective understandings of motivations for the war that President Truman invoked it in his announcement of the atomic bombings of Hiroshima and Nagasaki. See Robert Jay Lifton and Greg Mitchell, *Hiroshima in America: Fifty Years of Denial* (New York: G. P. Putnam's Sons, 1995); Ronald Takaki, *Hiroshima: Why America Dropped the Atomic Bomb* (Boston: Little, Brown, and Company, 1995), 70.

25. Donald J. Young, *December 1941: America's First 25 Days at War* (Missoula, MT: Pictorial Histories Publishing Co., Inc., 1992).

26. George H. Roeder Jr., *The Censored War: American Visual Experience During World War II* (New Haven: Yale University Press, 1993), 4–5.

27. "Lest We Forget!" Hearst Newsreel HNR 2054, 13.242, February 4, 1942, Los Angeles: UCLA Film and Television Archive Commercial Services.

28. As the final shooting was being completed for *December 7th,* Toland wrote to the head of the Office of Strategic Services that "in view of the fact that all existing footage [of the actual attack] has been publicly shown, it is necessary that we build up the attack itself and use very little of the newsreel footage." Toland to Cunningham, OSS, December 24, 1942, National Archives RG 208.

29. Susan D. Moeller, *Shooting War: Photography and the American Experience of Combat* (New York: Basic Books, 1989), 234–35.

30. Roeder, *The Censored War,* 4.

31. Correspondence associated with the film's distribution contains numerous comments such as those included in a memo from Melvin Lanphar writing from the

Navy Department's Inspector of Naval Material: "This officer just showed subject film to the officers of the INM. It is terrific. If this does not make everybody's blood boil, nothing will." District Industrial Incentive Officer, Chicago, to Chief of the Industrial Incentive Division, October 23, 1943, National Archives, RG 226, OSS, entry 90, folder 382). In a memo, Jesse French III describes reactions to the film when it was shown seven times to an estimated audience of 4,500 employees of the War Production Board: "The unanimous opinion of those attending . . . is that a major contribution has been made to the morale of our people." Here the context of film viewing was structured by the presence of a speaker supplied by the War Department and the distribution of a pamphlet titled "Lest We Forget" handed out at the door. (Jesse French, Assistant to Deputy Vice Chairman for Operations, War Production Board, to Commander S. J. Singer, Executive Officer, Industrial Incentive Division, September 27, 1943, National Archives, RG 226, OSS, entry 90, folder 382).

32. See Koppes and Black, *Hollywood Goes to War,* for a discussion of the various propaganda ("information") agencies and their functions.

33. The War Department statement reads, "The War Department will be very glad to obtain a motion picture which will present factually the conditions existing in Hawaii prior to December 7 and the story of the Japanese attack there on December 7 and the present conditions in Hawaii as they pertain to preparations for future action." The screen then fills with a note from the Secretary of the Navy saying, "I am very desirous of obtaining for the Navy Department a complete motion picture factual presentation of the attack on Pearl Harbor on December 7. As you well know, the president has stressed the highly historical import of this date."

34. The OWI censoring mechanisms took into account international, as well as domestic, race politics. Negative Asian stereotypes ran the risk of alienating Asian allies such as China, India, and the Middle East. Although the OWI did not have the right to censor film for domestic viewing, it could ban a film for international export, thus creating a financial incentive for Hollywood to conform. For instance, in reference to *Charlie Chan in the Secret Service* (1944), the OWI felt that the presentation of the lead character "would prove offensive to our Chinese allies." While these derogatory racial images were allowed in the United States, the OWI deemed it proper to ban export of the film to Europe and Asia.

35. Koppes and Black, *Hollywood Goes to War,* 67.

36. Nelson Poynter, Chief, Bureau of Motion Pictures, Hollywood Branch, to Lowell Mellett, Chief, Bureau of Motion Pictures, Office of War Information, October 19, 1942, National Archives, RG 208.

37. Lowell Mellett, Chief, Bureau of Motion Pictures, to James Forrestal, Undersecretary of the Navy, December 1, 1942, National Archives, RG 208, entry 64, box 1433.

38. Lowell Mellett, Chief, Bureau of Motion Pictures, to Secretary of War and Secretary of the Navy, April 29, 1943, National Archives, RG 208, entry 64, box 1433.

39. In doing so, it combines elements of both "ethnographic" and "historiographic" film described by Nichols in *Blurred Boundaries.*

40. Jeanine Basinger, *The World War II Combat Film* (New York: Columbia University Press, 1986), 128.

41. Skinner, "*December 7th*," 507–16, 510; Jeffrey A. Smith, *War and Press Freedom: The Problem of Prerogative Power* (Oxford: Oxford University Press, 1999), 30.

42. *Tora! Tora! Tora!* "treats its material as historical event . . . with meticulous attention to detail, to timings and characterizations that are not controversial. Watching it, it is as if one has picked up a history book and the words one reads become images. It is a docudrama of the sort that is now done regularly on PBS—a 're-enactment' of historical event in a sober manner, as factual as possible, following actual newsreels and photographs." (Basinger, *The World War II Combat Film*, 194–95)

43. In addition to the fact that the producers of *Tora! Tora! Tora!* primarily sought to create a big-screen, special effects spectacle, the absence of social history or cultural narrative from that film is probably related to the fact that it was a *bi*national production, released in two languages in the United States and Japan.

44. This, more than its content, accounts for much of the criticism of the film. Murphy ("John Ford and the Wartime Documentary," 1) calls the film a "dismal failure" as documentary. In Skinner's view, *December 7th* was "a fiasco of World War II film propaganda" (Skinner, "December 7th," 508). Doherty uses terms such as "duplicitous," "subterfuge" and "forgery" to describe the blending of "newsreel footage, staged reenactments, and special-effects work" (Doherty, *Projections of War*, 258–59; cf. Basinger, *The World War II Combat Film*, 128).

45. Skinner, "*December 7th*," 507–16, 515.

15

"COWARD, TAKE MY COWARD'S HAND"

Racism, Ableism, and the Veteran Problem in *Home of the Brave* and *Bright Victory*

Martin F. Norden

Before their eventual demise in the Red Scare era, liberal sentiments found expression in numerous Hollywood movies during the years following World War II. Their political views tempered with a heavy dose of profit-mindedness, these films focused on individuals struggling against a variety of social ills such as racism, anti-Semitism, alcohol abuse, malignant social institutions—hot box office topics, all. Undoubtedly, the person misunderstood and victimized by society had become a highly marketable Hollywood commodity during the immediate postwar period.

Within this cycle of so-termed "problem pictures," two movies managed to explore the postwar concerns of *three* disadvantaged social subgroups: African-Americans, people with physical disabilities, and veterans. In terms of simple categorization, *Home of the Brave* (1949) and *Bright Victory* (1951) fit within the mini-genre of postwar films that examine the physical, psychological, and social adjustments that veterans eventually had to make before leading productive lives as civilians. What sets *Home of the Brave* and *Bright Victory* apart from the more familiar members of this group, such as *The Best Years of Our Lives* (1946) and *The Men* (1950), is the relationship they attempt to establish between two forms of discrimination in

American society—racism and ableism—with the military as their micro-cosmic setting. It is my hope that a comparison of these two films' production history, narrative strategies, and reception will shed more light on the evolving concerns of the movie industry and U.S. society as a whole during those times. Although *Home of the Brave* and *Bright Victory* were directed by the same person (Mark Robson), featured the same actor in a prominent role (James Edwards), and conclude with the image of an African-American man and a disabled white man befriending each other, they represent notably different perspectives on racism, ableism, and veterans. In particular, the earlier film essentially engages in the more primitive strategy of simply equating various "isms" (and reducing its characters to the level of stick figures in the process). The later film, in contrast, presents a more complex treatment but couches it within a more predictable and conventional narrative framework. As I hope to show, the changes in the vision are related in large measure to the shifting contours of the American sociopolitical landscape.

A CONFLATION OF "ISMS": *HOME OF THE BRAVE*

"[Stanley] Kramer and I met in the Army, in the Signal Corps," remembered screenwriter Carl Foreman, "and we hit it off and found that we both had the same reservations about Hollywood now and the same frustrations about Hollywood, so he staggered me by telling me that he was thinking about going into independent production. I didn't even know what that meant, actually, but he explained to me it meant getting money from somebody and making your own films, and then you could get a release from somewhere. I thought that was pretty good."[1]

After producing several movies in such a fashion immediately after World War II, Stanley Kramer collaborated with writer Carl Foreman and director Mark Robson on a production that would best be remembered as Hollywood's breakthrough film on postwar race relations: *Home of the Brave*. In this film, an emotionally unstable African-American soldier and a physically disabled white soldier endure racist and ableist slurs while on duty in the South Pacific. Kramer, head of the upstart Screen Plays Corp., and financier Robert Stillman launched the project in mid-January 1949 by spending $50,000 to acquire the screen rights to Arthur Laurents's play *Home of the Brave*, which ran on Broadway during the 1945–46 season.[2]

The Laurents drama featured a white Jew in the pivotal role of the soldier who suffers the brunt of the discrimination, but Kramer was unwilling to make a film on a topic so recently explored in other films (anti-Semitism had been the main subject of, for example, the 1947 films, *Crossfire* and *Gentleman's*

Agreement). Anxious to produce the first film on postwar racism and perhaps encouraged by the timeliness of Harry Truman's 1948 executive order to desegregate the military,[3] Kramer instructed his screenwriter Carl Foreman to transform the Jewish character into one whose difference would be immediately apparent to viewers: an African-American. "It would be three times as dynamic because if the story of a Jew forced to feel different was gripping on stage, then in motion pictures, the story of a Negro would be much more so," argued Kramer. "An audience could see the difference in terms of color rather than seeing one white man saying he was Jewish, another saying he was Christian."[4]

The secrecy and speed with which Kramer and his crew created *Home of the Brave* and placed it into theaters suggest his eagerness to be the first with such a film. Code-naming the project "High Noon" in its early stages as a subterfuge, Kramer desperately wanted to conceal the project from Hollywood competitors and reporters. Indeed, he sounded rather ingenuous when pressed on the point, saying, "It was our intention to make an important entertainment feature without the usual attendant publicity, so that we could be free of pressure, suggestions and the advice of those not connected with its making. And we felt it unnecessary to exploit the fact that we were making a picture of complete reality."[5] Foreman completed the screenplay by early February 1949, and Robson began filming later that month. (Forty-eight hours before Robson commenced shooting, Kramer announced the true subject of the "High Noon" project.) The director completed the actual filming in eighteen days at a cost of well under $500,000. Dmitri Tiomkin's musical score was recorded in late March, and the first composite print of the film was ready in early April. All told, the film was completed in twenty-four days for $525,000. With United Artists handling the film's distribution, *Home of the Brave* began playing in movie theaters in mid-May, a mere four months after Kramer and Stillman purchased the screen rights and well ahead of other projects on racism announced by other studios: principally, Metro-Goldwyn-Mayer's *Intruder in the Dust* (1949), Twentieth Century-Fox's *Pinky* (1949), and Louis de Rochemont's Film Classics production of *Lost Boundaries* (1949).[6]

Home of the Brave tells the story of Peter Moss (James Edwards), a black Private First Class who serves as a member of an Army mapping unit in the South Pacific during World War II. Others in the unit include Moss's boyhood friend Finch (Lloyd Bridges), hard-boiled Sergeant Mingo (Frank Lovejoy), and T. J. (Steve Brodie), a so-labeled "blue-plate special" who resents serving as a corporal in the low-paying Army and directs his anger primarily at Moss, the only black in the unit. While surveying a Japanese-held island, the team is attacked. The assault leaves Finch dead, Mingo with a severely injured right arm, and Moss inexplicably paralyzed from the waist down. Believing Moss's disability psychosomatic, an Army psychiatrist (Jeff Corey) uses confrontational techniques to induce him to talk about both the racial prejudice directed against him and the events on the mapping mission that led to his paralysis. We eventually learn that Moss's problems stem largely from guilt over the good feelings he had when Finch, who in a panicky moment had started to call his boyhood friend a "yellow-bellied nigger," was killed by the Japanese. With the help from the medico and Mingo, Moss overcomes his psychological problems, regains the use of his legs, and makes plans for a productive life back home in the states.

Critics writing for the mainstream and trade presses were quite divided on the significance of the film. *Commonweal*'s Philip Hartung offered an enthusiastic and unqualified endorsement, as did *Variety*'s "Kahn," who suggested that "the comparatively inexpensive picture hits hard and with utter credibility. It hasn't a name that will draw at the [box office]—but when once the customers are inside the theatre, *Home* will have started a progression of comment that should win an accolade for the producer for having the courage to produce such a pic. And for having done it so well." The *Time* critic gave it a mixed review, suggesting that it treats "human beings as if they were clearly defined symbols in a propaganda tract" and that its "arguments against discrimination get badly mixed up with the abracadabra of psychiatry" but concluding that it has "novelty, emotional wallop and the excitement that comes from wrestling with a real problem." Other reviews were less charitable; Manny Farber wrote a no less than vitriolic assault on virtually every aspect of the film. Farber concluded his systematic shredding of *Home of the Brave* by noting that the film "is not quite clever or ingenious enough to conceal its profit-minded, inept treatment of important social issues." [7]

Members of the African-American press, however, offered a united front on the film during its initial run. *Chicago Defender* movie critic Lillian Scott called *Home of the Brave* "the most outstanding and honest motion picture on Negro-white relations in history," while fellow *Defender* critic Meredith Johns stated that it "comes closer to the true story of the Negro-white problem as developed in this country than anything yet made in Hollywood. It is simultaneously a stark drama of war and a powerfully presented smash at prejudice against the American Negro. . . . *Home of the Brave* far surpasses [*Crossfire* and *Gentleman's Agreement*] in boldness of script and action." *Defender* publisher John H. Sengstacke voiced his opinion as well: "No picture that Hollywood has ever released faces the problem of racial prejudice more honestly or more sympathetically, and without objectionable propaganda. I won't rest until all my friends see this unusual and gripping drama." *Ebony* ran an adulatory photo-laden essay on the making of the film, while Duane Valentry, writing for *The Crisis*, suggested that *Home of the Brave* "is hitting all America between the eyes. . . . This is a great and wonderful picture. It is far more than entertainment. It has truth and sensitivity. It will get people where a punch hurts most—around the heart." [8]

Though presumably well-intentioned, *Home of the Brave* is fraught with problematic aspects difficult to ignore. It presents Moss as more symbol than human, a sponge-like entity all too willing to accept whatever the whites tell him. In addition, he is cured in an overly rapid and facile way by the psycho-babble-spouting doctor. Most disturbing of all is the psychiatrist's curious finding that results from his "narcosynthesis" techniques: Moss suffers from discrimination mainly because he is too sensitive to others. This "blame the victim" stance is unsettling, to say the least, and undermines whatever good intentions the filmmakers had in attempting to deal with racial prejudice.

Another problem, and one more to the point of this essay, emerges during the film's last scene, as Mingo and Moss prepare to return to the United States (Mingo because of the loss of his arm, Moss because of his mental health). In an attempt to draw a parallel between racism and ableism, the filmmakers had T. J., the same soldier who has baited Moss throughout the movie, verbally abuse Mingo as well. Afterward, while waiting for a jeep to take them to the airfield, Mingo and Moss discuss T. J.'s prejudice:

MINGO: Sure, he makes cracks about you. Forget it.

MOSS: I'd like to see *you* forget it.

MINGO: What do you think I'm trying to do?

MOSS: What?

MINGO: He makes cracks about me, too.

MOSS: Yeah, but those cracks. . . . It's not the same, Mingo.

MINGO: To *him* it's the same. To that crud and all cruds like him, it's the same thing. We're easy targets for him to take potshots at.

As Mingo discusses his reactions to his injury, Moss comes to realize that the good feelings he experienced after Finch's death were not due to hatred of his friend for succumbing to racism, but to the fact that he was not the one who got shot. Mingo undergoes a learning experience, too; he emphasizes his newly acquired difference from other people until Moss notes the similarity of people beneath the surface. Drawn together by mutual understanding and buoyed by their new outlooks on life, Mingo and Moss discuss the possibility of opening a restaurant together after returning stateside. Moss is interested but initially reluctant. "Look, Mingo," he says. "A lot of people wouldn't like it, a white man and a . . . ." Mingo interrupts and seals the deal with "A lot of people wouldn't like a one-armed bartender."

As Moss and Mingo prepare to leave for the airfield, they complete their bonding ritual. Moss, seeing that Mingo is having difficulty pulling his duffel bag over his shoulder, cites the concluding line of poetry written by Mingo's wife—"Coward, take my coward's hand"—and helps him with his bag. The line refers to the entire poem, which Mingo, then newly wounded, had read to Moss to calm him while out in the jungle: "We are only two, yet our howling can encircle the world's end. Frightened, you are my only friend. And frightened, we are everyone. Someone must take a stand. Coward, take my coward's hand."

The dialogue is only one of several elements within this scene that suggest a connection between Moss and Mingo that overshadows differences in race, ability, age, and temperament. The men are to be shipped back to the United States on the same day, and Robson employed several visual strategies to strengthen the men's bond in preparation for that development. In particular, he photographed them from identical angles as they wear matching dress uniforms that contrast strongly with everyone else's fatigues and carry identically shaped duffel bags. In addition, he represented Moss as a newly left-handed person to match Mingo, whose disability has forced him to become left-handed. As the men sit side-by-side on a small bench and listen as T. J. berates them, they hold cigarettes in their left hands and make nearly identical arm movements as they smoke. In so doing, they look like virtual twins.

In brief, *Home of the Brave* attempts by verbal and visual means to link Mingo and Moss as minority group members who have suffered discrimination. In doing so, however, it sends out a decidedly mixed message about prejudice and tolerance. The film implies that a disabled white man and an able-bodied African-American man are on the same social footing (in other words, that a disabling injury to a white man abruptly "reduces" him to the status of an African-American man).[9] The situation, however, is not as simple as the film would have us believe. Moss has been the victim of discrimination all his life, while Mingo has suffered it for only a few days. In addition, the prejudice he encounters from T. J. is limited to a few random remarks, the most vicious of which is "Okay, I won't fight with a cripple." Insulting as they are, these ableist opinions of Mingo are considerably milder than T. J.'s constant, outright baiting of Moss.

In addition, the film seems to suggest that Moss and Mingo are doing the right thing by forming their own little society of two. By having them adopt an "us against the rest of the world" stance at the end of the film, *Home of the*

Brave appears to work against the liberal attitude that, along with more mammonish concerns, prompted the production in the first place: the tolerance of difference.

It is certainly arguable that economic concerns were the main force behind the Kramer/Foreman/Robson team's simple conflation of "isms." Although Kramer and Foreman had witnessed the effects of segregation first-hand while serving in the military ("as soldiers [we] had been very much impressed by Jim Crow in the Army . . . by the segregation within an army that was out there to destroy segregation, as it were," said Foreman), Kramer initially had no vested interest in exploring racism in *Home of the Brave*; in fact, he first picked up the rights to the Laurents play in 1946 with the intent of maintaining the anti-Semitism angle. (He dropped the option after executives at United Artists told him that "audiences would rip up the seats," throw "stink bombs" into theaters, and "riot in front of box offices" in response to such a film, in his words.) After watching *Crossfire* and *Gentleman's Agreement* triumph at the box office, he reacquired the rights to the play in early 1949 with the idea of transforming the Jew into an African-American. In his haste to get his movie into theaters, however, he apparently gave little thought to the implications of his decision. "Actually, the theme of *Home of the Brave* remained unchanged, for the basic conflict was the same," he stated. The *Variety* reviewer "Kahn" underscored this point by suggesting that the film "could have been the story of any victim of bigotry in the fight against the man-made hates." Years later, Kramer continued to take pride in his rather simplistic concept. "We had the idea of switching *Home of the Brave* from a Jewish problem story into the Negro vernacular," he said in the mid-1960s. "It took only three weeks to write the whole picture because we simply took the entire play, added one sequence, and kept our switch consistent. It turned out magnificently, and did very well at the box office." This "switch" also unfortunately elided some important distinctions among the "isms": following Laurents's lead, Kramer and his associates simply turned T. J., the anti-Semite/ableist, into T. J., the racist/ableist, with the differences and the ramifications arising therefrom getting lost in the shuffle.[10]

REHABILITATION AND ROMANCE: BRIGHT VICTORY

The Kramer/Foreman/Robson team split up with the director's departure from the Screen Plays Corp. shortly after *Home of the Brave*, but it did not take long for the three to conclude that a movie focusing on disabled veterans would be a worthy follow-up to their famous 1949 film. For Kramer and Foreman, it would be *The Men*, starring newcomer Marlon Brando as a troubled wheelchair-using vet. Robson, still interested in mingling racism, ableism, and the "veteran problem," would place a blinded racist veteran at center stage in *Bright Victory*.

Bright Victory carries the symbolic dimension of a disability even further than *Home of the Brave*; the blinded vet is unable to "see" beyond a fellow blinded vet's skin color, or the folly of his own racial intolerance, until the end of the movie. Like the earlier film, *Bright Victory* contains a problematic mix of concerns related to racism, ableism, and veterans, but, as I hope to show, it lays out that mixture in a markedly different way.

The vehicle that served as the basis for *Bright Victory* materialized on the cultural scene at almost exactly the same moment as the Laurents play, *Home of the Brave*. In 1945, novelist Baynard Kendrick published *Lights Out*, a book commissioned by the U.S. War Department about a blinded World War II veteran and his eventual readjustment to civilian life. Having achieved some success with *Eyes in the Night* (1942) and *The Hidden Eye* (1945), two "B" movies based on a series of earlier Kendrick novels about a blind detective,[11] Metro-Goldwyn-Mayer authorized director Clarence Brown to buy the screen rights to *Lights Out* for $10,000 shortly after the book's publication. Brown, perhaps believing the book's handling of racism was too controversial for the time, shelved the project before selling the rights in 1947 to Robert Montgomery at Universal-International for five times that amount.[12] Montgomery was slated to direct and star in this film as well, with Joan Harrison to write and produce. Harrison noted at the time that the projected film would focus primarily on the novel's love story but would also face the "Negro question" raised in the book, in the words of *New York Times* reporter Thomas Brady. The project stalled at U-I as well, however. The novel may have proven too liberal-minded for Montgomery, a Hollywood conservative activist and "friendly witness" during the infamous House Committee on Un-American Activities (HUAC) hearings in 1947. It remained on the studio's backburner until 1951 when the new team of writer-producer Robert Buckner and director Mark Robson finally brought it to the screen.[13]

Buckner and Robson decided to add a greater note of veracity to their movie by filming it on location at the U.S. Army hospital in Valley Forge, Pennsylvania. As noted by Harry Niemeyer, a *New York Times* reporter who observed the production firsthand, the filmmakers "were convinced that they could turn out a more authentic job on the grounds of the institution where all the sections devoted to the rehabilitation of the blind were ready and waiting and furnished with the necessary and authentic 'props.'" Arthur Kennedy, the stage-trained actor chosen by Buckner and Robson to play the central character, contributed further to the film's realistic veneer by receiving instruction from blinded veterans and wearing opaque contact lenses that effectively rendered him sightless during the filming. Despite mishaps such as walking off a four-foot platform into thin air, Kennedy added a considerable degree of authenticity to his performance by wearing the lenses.[14]

For the role of the blinded African-American veteran, Robson and Buckner had, in Robson's words, "long since settled on James Edwards whom we knew from *Home of the Brave.*" Executives at Universal had originally wanted an unknown in the role, but Robson intervened. "You ought to use Jim Edwards," he told them. "His *Home of the Brave* performance rated with the greatest of 1949." (Edwards eventually returned the compliment by suggesting that *Bright Victory* "is one of the best stories of the year and is perfectly directed.") With supporting players drawn from Hollywood and bit players cast locally at Phoenixville and Valley Forge, Pennsylvania, Robson and Buckner began filming in August 1950 on location at the Valley Forge General Hospital.[15]

The resulting film, *Bright Victory,* shows its lead character's disablement in a matter of minutes: Sergeant Larry Nevins (Kennedy) is serving on a three-man "wire team" in North Africa in 1943 when a Nazi bullet grazes his head by his right eye, rendering him blind. Inside an airborne troop carrier en route to a Long Island hospital, an unidentified African-American soldier wearing a neck brace sits next to the heavily bandaged Nevins and they begin chatting. The audience learns by way of their expository dialogue that Nevins is from a little upstate Florida town, while the other soldier hails from Atlanta. When Nevins asks his companion if he knows a place called the Fairview Club, the fellow replies that he once waited on tables there. Nevins immediately becomes sullen, and it is clear from his reaction that the other soldier's statement is tantamount to "I'm black." The camera holds on Nevins's silent visage for a few seconds before he asks for a nurse to sit next to him, replacing the African-American soldier.

Racial issues do not reappear in the film until well after Nevins has discovered that his blindness is permanent and has begun to adjust to a new life without sight. His life changes once again when he collides with a blinded black GI named Joe Morgan (James Edwards) in a hospital corridor. He apologizes profusely, and after the vets become acquainted—and somehow remain unaware of each other's race—they develop a strong friendship. The filmmakers visualize this relationship in various scenes: the vets playfully dunk one another while swimming, outperform everyone in a blind bowling league, and play pinball before going to a dance, where Nevins begins a close relationship with a USO volunteer, Judy Greene (Peggy Dow).

Back at the hospital after the dance, best buddies Nevins and Morgan walk arm-in-arm and talk cheerfully until Nevins notes that he has heard a rumor that several "niggers" will soon be admitted to the hospital. He continues his rather matter-of-fact observation by saying he did not know "niggers" were allowed in that hospital. On hearing the first utterance of "niggers," Morgan stops walking while Nevins continues on, as if nothing had happened. He asks, "Did you, Joe?" to which the latter solemnly notes, "Yeah, I've been here nearly seven months now." As Morgan walks past Nevins to get to his bunk, another blinded soldier remarks to Nevins, "Maybe he thought you were colored, too."

Disturbed by his own lack of sensitivity toward a close friend of several months, Nevins further alters his attitudes toward blacks after encountering discrimination while on a month-long furlough in his Florida hometown. Nevins's parents meet him at the train station and, during the car trip back home, his mother tells him about their "nigrah" maid who just left them after nine years to work in a war plant up north. She says that her son does not know "what the war has done to our nigrahs," whereupon Nevins interrupts by saying that he knows what it did to one of them and berates her talking about "our nigrahs" as if the Civil War had never ended.

Nevins's attitudes toward African-Americans continue to evolve as he personally encounters discrimination while away from the supportive environment of the hospital. He learns that his fiancée, Chris Paterson (Julia Adams), has asked her wealthy father to give him a job at his barrel factory—a hiring decision that the father would never have made otherwise, as his ableist opinions suggest: "Well, let's face it, Larry. You're no longer an able-bodied man. It's very pitiable, but it's true." The film thus implies a similarity between racism and ableism, although, significantly, Nevins would not have been denied a job because of his visual impairment. The fiancée harbors ableist views as well. She too considers Nevins helpless and so informs him, even after he tells her that he does not want charity and needs to find a job on his own. She soon breaks off their engagement, thereby allowing Nevins's long-simmering relationship with Judy Greene to turn expressly romantic. After Nevins sorts out this and other aspects of his life (he has also decided to go to law school), *Bright Victory* concludes by showing him eagerly making amends with Morgan as the vets return from their separate furloughs.

Most critics praised both *Bright Victory*'s handling of the readjustment issues faced by blinded veterans and, in particular, Arthur Kennedy's Oscar-nominated portrayal of Larry Nevins.[16] For example, Manny Farber wrote in *The Nation* that "Kennedy contributes a solid, feverish, consistent characterization full of incredibly shrewd perceptions about both Southerners and the sightless." Robert Hatch of *The New Republic*, despite ableist slurs, urged "every man, woman and child who habitually patronizes the blind, treating them like helpless cripples or mental defectives" to see the film. "Brog," who reviewed the film for *Variety*, suggested that "Robert Buckner scores both for his production conception and the intelligent scripting he gave Baynard Kendrick's novel, *Lights Out*, on which the film is based. He brings the story to the screen with a compassion and understanding that carefully sidesteps any dips into the maudlin aspects such a theme provides. The dialog is honest, as are the characters, and there is a feeling of integrity throughout the film." [17]

The African-American press also supported the film, but its rhetoric was more subdued than its coverage of *Home of the Brave*. An *Ebony* reviewer stated that *Bright Victory* "whacks solidly at intolerance in a new and moving way" and that "the picture makes its anti-bias theme a part of a conventional love-story plot. Its casual approach is significant in demonstrating Hollywood's acceptance of the Negro angle as part of a routine film." *Chicago Defender* movie critic Arnold de Mille lauded *Bright Victory* as "a motion picture that is destined to be one of the best of the year, if not the Oscar winner for 1951" and "one of the few films which deal with both the race and readjustment problems, and which handle both very cleverly and understandingly." He also suggested that the character played by James Edwards "is not superficial; it is real and very well done." He concluded his review by stating that "*Bright Victory* is without a doubt a picture well worth seeing. It will live with you a long time." [18]

The film also drew praise from other sources. "*Bright Victory* is real and true," proclaimed Lloyd Greenwood, the executive director of the Blinded Veterans Association. "It is also one of the most authentic portrayals of blindness I have yet encountered." Greenwood also noted that *Bright Victory*'s treatment of race relations made it an especially significant film, although he offered no details.[19]

Despite the accolades, *Bright Victory* falters in its treatment of racism. Indeed, its awkward and contrived handling of the issue led one critic (Robert Hatch, who otherwise praised the film) to view the subplot involving racism "as a tasteless and superficial effort to be progressive." [20] For starters, it is odd that the sightless Nevins needs only a few seconds to ascertain a GI's race on board the airborne troop carrier early in the field but does not discover Morgan's race until after several months of relatively close contact. Surely, something akin to the "Fairview Club" comment would have surfaced during that period. In addition, the filmmakers naïvely assumed that all Southern dialects sound the same, even to native speakers—a perspective that most Southerners would find laughable. (As a point of comparison, Mark Twain experimented with no fewer than seven Southern dialect variations in *The Adventures of Huckleberry Finn*, and that tale was set in only one part of the South.) I daresay Nevins and Morgan would have been savvy enough to detect the subtle differences in their speech—especially inasmuch as they were relying more heavily on their hearing, as the film suggests several times—and make educated guesses about each other's race and ethnic background in rather short order. In brief, the film is right on course in its rendering of the lifestyles of newly blinded people, but it stumbles badly through a series of plot potholes in its attempt to present an idealized world where people can be truly "blind" to skin color.[21]

What are we to make of the evolving perspectives on racism, ableism, and veterans as suggested in *Home of the Brave* and *Bright Victory?* The times had changed notably during the two years that separated the films, and I would argue that these movies, their marketing strategies, and their reception correspond rather closely to these shifts. A closer look at the sociocultural environment may reveal additional insights into the films and their concerns.

SHIFTING CONTEXTS, CHANGING INTERESTS

In a number of respects, 1949 was a peak year for Hollywood's "problem pictures." Audiences were enormously interested in them; in Chicago, for example, more than 2,000 people were turned away from the Windy City premiere of *Home of the Brave.*[22] Films that examined racism in particular—*Home of the Brave, Pinky,* and *Lost Boundaries*—proved so popular that a *Variety* reporter was moved to remark that "films' leading [box-office] star for 1949 wasn't a personality, but . . . a subject—racial prejudice."[23] Movies focusing on problems of disability were also receiving attention. For instance, Lucy Freeman reported in the *New York Times* that, in November 1949, the National Society for Crippled Children and Adults awarded the movie industry a special citation "for outstanding service on behalf of the handicapped" for recent films such as *Best Years of Our Lives, Johnny Belinda* (1948), and *The Stratton Story* (1949). In Freeman's words, "the society feels [these films] have helped to bring about a greater public understanding of the problems facing the handicapped."[24]

By the beginning of 1950, however, audience interest in racial themes and other "problem" topics began to wane and a number of follow-up films—including *Intruder in the Dust* and *No Way Out*—did not perform nearly as well at the box office.[25] In addition, a number of African-Americans were questioning the qualities of the key figure presented in *Home of the Brave. Chicago Defender* movie critic Rob Roy revealed himself as "one of those souls who think [the Peter Moss character] failed somewhat to portray what the Negro actually meant to the past world's war." Roy went on to suggest that Moss was "somewhat of a coward" and more concerned about "the color of his skin

than about the shells that were falling about." Writing in the scholarly journal *Phylon*, William Couch offered a stronger indictment of *Home of the Brave*,
placing it within a new tradition of dramas, movies, and literary works about
blacks that, while exuding goodwill, "may promote more social and artistic
confusion than previously existed." In these works, Couch argued, "the Negro
is completely stripped of effective purpose or self-will and must expect his salvation in the slow awakening of white conscience, during which time there
can be neither real success for him nor the 'success' of tragic failure, except,
insofar as his pathetic presence is accessory to that awakening." Couch characterized Moss as one of a number of African-American characters "who
succeed in completely annihilating themselves through their violation of the
most vital principles of American belief: manliness in love and in self-defense."
Calling Moss's position an "unendurable one," he noted that "it is beyond our
power to accept—it is no longer a matter of sympathetic understanding—
such deficiencies in our hero. Notwithstanding that we are disposed to react
favorably, the result is so serious a miscarriage of proper dramatic effect that
there develops instead a strong feeling of self-righteous pity, not altogether
unlike contempt, for him." Even James Edwards repudiated the character, if
only indirectly and in a moment of public relations hyperbole, when he suggested that his role in *The Steel Helmet* (1951), a movie released several months
before *Bright Victory*, was "by far the best thing I've had" since arriving in
Hollywood.[26]

By the time the long-delayed *Bright Victory* appeared in the summer of 1951,
audience interest in controversial racial topics had died down considerably.
Most critics compared the production not to *Home of the Brave* but to *The Men*,
a hard-hitting film from the year before that dwelled on the anguish and rehabilitation of disabled veterans. Indeed, *Variety*'s "Brog" devoted a mere sentence to racial issues in a nine-paragraph review of *Bright Victory*, and an
Ebony reviewer stated flatly that the film "basically is not concerned with racial prejudice, but rather makes this theme supplementary to its main plot
which concerns the troubles of a blinded vet trying to adjust to the world
around him."[27]

The Korean War had been underway for more than a year at the time of
Bright Victory's release, and the filmmakers were becoming increasingly nervous about the ways that the new wartime context might affect the general
reception of their film. (Buckner and Robson, who had begun shooting the
movie shortly after the start of the Korean conflict with the intention of re-
leasing it in January 1951 as *Lights Out*, delayed its premiere to reassess the
situation. The film finally opened more than six months later under the more
upbeat title of *Bright Victory*.) They were doubtless aware that the critically

acclaimed *The Men,* which debuted two weeks after the outbreak of the Korean War, had collapsed at the box office. "Designed as a post-war picture it was suddenly facing a pre-war mentality," *The Men's* director, Fred Zinnemann, wrote of his film. "No wonder that people whose sons, husbands and fathers were going to fight could not bear to watch a movie such as ours. It folded in two weeks." [28]

Fearful that audiences would reject *Bright Victory* as yet another film that dwelled on the lingering consequences of war, the moviemakers tried to position the film primarily as mainstream entertainment. Robson pointedly refused to call *Bright Victory* a "problem picture," even though, months earlier, he had insisted on making the film's treatment of rehabilitation issues as authentic as possible. [29] In addition, novelist Baynard Kendrick anxiously stressed the film's more conventional elements while deemphasizing its problem picture qualities. "Don't use the word rehabilitation," he told a *New York Times* reporter. "That word might frighten people away from seeing the picture. *[Bright Victory]* is not a story of the rehabilitation of the blinded war casualty in a clinical sense. It is a great emotional drama of how a man discovers a whole new life. It's a love story. . . . A very human drama. . . . Once people see the film they will enjoy a tremendous emotional experience" [30] [ellipses in original text].

The general narrative structures of *Bright Victory* and *Home of the Brave* reflect their times to an important extent. *Home of the Brave* unfolds entirely within an overseas war zone, while the bulk of *Bright Victory* occurs after its main character has been shipped stateside for rehabilitation. *Bright Victory's* emphasis on civilian life represents an obvious shift away from immediate wartime concerns to the issues facing Americans after the war. (Strictly speaking, the war is still on during Nevins's rehabilitation, but the image presented by the film is far more reflective of the postwar years than of the war years proper.)

With its smooth and sentimental predictability, *Bright Victory* represents a clear departure from the boldness and "rough-edgedness" of *Home of the Brave,* which had played in theaters only two years earlier. *Bright Victory* embodies a conformist sensibility by stressing such traditional values as romance (with "someone to love," a blind colleague informs Nevins, "there's nothing you can't do"); the primacy of domestic life; the value of adjusting one's outlook on life for the greater good; and the importance of fitting into society. These values found little expression in *Home of the Brave* (*Home* does acknowledge the latter issue, but only in its concluding moments and with the suggestion that · it would occur in an adversarial way). Unlike the bigoted but ultimately reformable Nevins whose enlightenment serves as a prelude to domestic tranquility and a full reintegration into society, T. J., *Home's* racist/ableist remains a racist/ableist at the end of the film, and Moss and Mingo still see themselves as "others": a minority of two caught up in a struggle against the rest of society with no romantic/domestic relationships to support them.[31]

The films further suggest a tilt toward a new conservatism in their positioning of the principal African-American character played by James Edwards. He is at the center of *Home of the Brave*; indeed, his memories, rendered in several lengthy flashbacks, motivate the film's main story. In *Bright Victory*, however, he is displaced by a white who endures one form of bigotry while perpetrating another, only to resolve his internal conflicts in a rather facile way with the help of his friends. In an *Ebony* interview, Robson tried none-too-convincingly to deflect attention away from his decentering of the African-American in *Bright Victory* by declaring that "Edwards has the key role in the film, for it is through him that the white soldier grows to understand himself. And the picture's comment and meaning [are] made through the character portrayed by Edwards."[32] James Edwards's Joe Morgan is an important figure, but ultimately, his role is subordinate to that of Arthur Kennedy's Larry Nevins, the locus of the conflicting forces that drive the film's narrative.

As I hope this essay has shown, *Home of the Brave* and *Bright Victory* demonstrate notably different constructions of racism and ableism within a wartime context, with the shifts in their perspectives traceable largely to concerns in the Hollywood industry and mainstream U.S. society as a whole. The combination of "problems" in both films is in itself highly problematic, leading one to question the propriety of combining them in the first place. In both movies, particularly *Home of the Brave*, the ableism issue has the appearance of being tacked onto the subject of racism, as if the filmmakers wanted to show their predominantly white audience members what it would be like to join a minority group and experience discrimination. As for *Bright Victory*, its ill-considered racial dimension vitiates its otherwise authentic representation of the readjustment issues facing blinded veterans. Although the makers of both films rightly assumed that movies with wartime settings often (and with no small irony) make the best vehicles for fostering a climate of tolerance and understanding,[33] they also found themselves relying on patently fabricated situations and easy solutions to pull together the various storylines. By dividing their attention between issues of race and ability, they unfortunately succeeded in simplifying these concerns to an untenable degree.

NOTES

1. Carl Foreman, transcript of 1981 interview, 17–18, American Film Foundation archives, Santa Monica, Calif.

2. Random House first published the theatrical script for *Home of the Brave* in 1946. The script has since been reprinted in at least two anthologies: *Best Plays of the Modern American Theatre, 2nd Series*, ed. John Gassner (New York: Crown, 1947), and *Awake and Singing: 7 Classic Plays from the American Jewish Repertoire*, ed. Ellen Schiff (New York: Mentor, 1995).

3. Following Truman's Executive Order #9981 of July 26, 1948, Defense Secretary Louis A. Johnson officially ended the armed forces segregation policy in April 1949. As the black press noted, however, the actual practice of segregation lingered beyond that date, particularly in the army. See "Armed Service Jim Crow Policy Ends," *Crisis*, May 1949, 137; "All in Step Except the Army," *Crisis*, July 1949, 201; and "Army Still Out of Step," *Crisis*, August–September 1949, 233.

4. Kramer, quoted in "*Home of the Brave*: Film About Anti-Negro Bias Made in Secret by Hollywood Ex-GIs," *Ebony*, June 1949, 60.

5. Kramer, quoted in Duane Valentry, "Local Boy Makes History," *Crisis*, November 1949, 354.

6. The film's production and distribution details may be found in Thomas F. Brady, "Crusade in Hollywood," *New York Times*, March 6, 1949; Thomas F. Brady, "Hollywood Survey," *New York Times*, March 20, 1949; and Ezra Goodman, "'Champion' Producer," *New York Times*, April 10, 1949. George Glass, Kramer's vice president and publicity director, remembered the *Home of the Brave* price tag as $370,000. See Roy Newquist, *A Special Kind of Magic* (New York: Rand McNally, 1967), 52.

7. Reviews of *Home of the Brave*, Philip T. Hartung, *Commonweal*, May 20, 1949, 149–50; "Kahn," *Variety*, May 4, 1949, 11; *Time*, May 9, 1949, 100; and Manny Farber, *Nation*, May 21, 1949, 590–91.

8. Lillian Scott, "Hollywood Independent Shows Big Studios How It's Done," *Chicago Defender*, May 14, 1949; Meredith Johns, "*Home of the Brave* Is Brave Venture for Movie Makers," *Chicago Defender*, April 23, 1949; John H. Sengstacke, quoted in "*Home of Brave* Premiere Draws Overflow Audience," *Chicago Defender*, May 28, 1949; *Ebony*, "*Home of the Brave*," 59–62; Valentry, "Local Boy," 314.

9. Interestingly, the filmmakers did not attempt to suggest a similarity between Moss and Mingo until *after* Moss has been cured of his paralysis. In so doing, they avoided what may have been an uneasy prospect for Hollywood filmmakers in the 1940s: equating a disabled African-American man with a disabled white man.

10. Foreman, interview, 27; Kramer, quoted in "*Home of the Brave*," *Ebony*, 60; Kramer, quoted in Johns, "*Home of the Brave* is Brave Venture"; "Kahn," 11; Kramer, quoted in Newquist, *A Special Kind of Magic*, 26.

11. For a close analysis of one such film, see Martin F. Norden, "The Eyes Have It: Dimensions of Blindness in *Eyes in the Night*," in *The Films of Fred Zinnemann: Critical Perspectives*, ed. Arthur Nolletti Jr. (Albany: State University of New York Press, 1999), 55–68.

12. Brown did go on to produce and direct *Intruder in the Dust*, released in late 1949.

13. Thomas F. Brady, "Hollywood Tackles the Facts of Life," *New York Times*,

March 16, 1947; Larry Ceplair and Steven Englund, *The Inquisition in Hollywood: Politics in the Film Community 1930–1960* (Garden City, NY: Anchor, 1980), 210.

14. Harry Niemeyer, "Hospital as Film Set," *New York Times*, September 3, 1950; Mark Robson, "Plea for a Flock of Film Fledglings," *New York Times*, July 22, 1951.

15. Robson, "Plea," and quoted in "*Lights Out*: Story of Blind GIs Blasts Racial Bias in Moving Way," *Ebony*, December 1950, 90; Edwards, quoted in Rob Roy, "Says James Edwards Isn't Bitter Toward Hollywood, Just Playing His Cards Better," *Chicago Defender*, July 28, 1951.

16. Humphrey Bogart won the 1951 Best Actor Oscar for his performance in *The African Queen*, but Kennedy won the New York Critics Award for Best Actor. In addition, Robert Buckner's adapted script earned him a Golden Globe for Best Screenplay.

17. Reviews of *Bright Victory*, Manny Farber, *Nation*, August 11, 1951, 118; Robert Hatch, *New Republic*, August 27, 1951, 22; "Brog," *Variety*, July 25, 1951, 6.

18. "*Lights Out*," 87; Arnold de Mille, "See *Bright Victory* as 'Oscar' Candidate," *Chicago Defender*, August 11, 1951.

19. Greenwood, quoted in "*Bright Victory* Wins Praise," *Chicago Defender*, August 4, 1951.

20. Hatch, 22.

21. On this latter point, *Bright Victory* mirrors a rather ingenuous 1949 *Ebony* essay on blindness, race, and discrimination that claims that "in the world of the blind, there are no colors—and consequently, no racial discrimination" and underscores "the obvious fact that the blind cannot distinguish between the races." See "Blindness: Visionless Americans Ignore Racial Lines, Face Unfair Job Prejudice from Seeing World," *Ebony*, June 1949, 25–29.

22. "*Home of Brave* Premiere."

23. "$20,000,000 Boxoffice Payoff for H'wood Negro-Tolerance Pix," *Variety*, November 30, 1949, 1.

24. Lucy Freeman, "War Weapons Set to Medical Tasks," *New York Times*, November 9, 1949.

25. For an assessment, see Daniel J. Leab, *From Sambo to Superspade: The Black Experience in Motion Pictures* (Boston: Houghton Mifflin, 1976), 156–57.

26. Roy, "Says James Edwards"; William Couch, Jr., "The Problem of Negro Character and Dramatic Incident," *Phylon: Atlanta University Review of Race & Culture* 11, no. 2 (1950): 127, 129, 132–33; Edwards, quoted in "*Steel Helmet*: First Movie About Korea War Has Excellent Role of Negro Medical Corpsman," *Ebony*, March 1951, 79.

27. "Brog," 6; "*Lights Out*," 88.

28. Fred Zinnemann, *A Life in the Movies: An Autobiography* (New York: Charles Scribner's Sons, 1992), 85.

29. Robson, quoted in Arnold de Mille, "Movieland's Sepia Artists Expect a Great Film Year in '51," *Chicago Defender*, December 9, 1950.

30. Kendrick, quoted in Thomas F. Pryor, "Happy, Happy Author," *New York Times*, January 28, 1951.

31. *Home* is ambiguous on any romantic relationship awaiting Moss and implies

that Mingo's wife has dumped him. "I remember her last letter," he tells the Major. "It began, 'My darling. This is the hardest letter I've ever had to write.'" A queer reading of *Home*'s final scene would doubtless shed further light on the dynamics of Moss and Mingo's new relationship. Such a reading is, alas, beyond the scope of this essay.

32. Robson, quoted in *"Lights Out,"* 90.

33. For more on this issue, see Mark A. Reid, *"Home of the Brave* (1949): The Black Soldier as the Heroic Victim" (paper presented at the Conference on the War Film: Contexts and Images, Boston, Mass., March 1988), 11.

PART IV

INDUSTRY

THE DEMANDS OF AUTHENTICITY

Addison Durland and Hollywood's Latin Images during World War II

Brian O'Neil

Will Hays, "film czar" of the Motion Picture Producers and Distributors of America, announced at a New York press conference on March 26, 1941, that Addison Durland would join Joseph Breen's staff at the Production Code Administration (PCA) in Hollywood. Hays hailed the new appointment as "another step in the industry's co-operation in the current efforts to promote hemispheric solidarity." Durland's mandate was seemingly straightforward and simple: to ensure that all Hollywood films be free from anything potentially offensive to "Latin sensibilities." Or, as the characteristically succinct and colloquial headlines of the *Film Daily* put it the following day, "Durland Will Eye Scripts for Latin-American Boners." [1]

Durland's appointment was a key element of a collaborative effort between the United States government and the American film industry, which came to be known unofficially as Hollywood's Good Neighbor policy. [2] This policy grew out of the overlapping economic interests of the studios and the current geopolitical imperatives of the U.S. government. Throughout the 1930s, 35 percent of the motion picture industry's gross revenue came from export earnings, 60 percent of which was derived from European distribution. [3] By mid-1938, with the specter of war in

Europe becoming ever greater, the studio strategists began to search frantically for untapped or undertapped foreign markets. They deemed the Latin American market a potentially lucrative safeguard against the vicissitudes of the European situation. In early 1939, all the major studios began actively producing Latin-themed "good neighborly" films aimed at pleasing Latin American audiences.[4]

At the same time that Hollywood began to devote unprecedented energy to boosting sales in Latin America, the U.S. government became increasingly concerned with the growing Nazi presence in the region, especially in Brazil and Argentina. After German forces rolled through France in mid-1940, Nelson Rockefeller urged President Franklin D. Roosevelt to align the United States more closely with the countries of the Western Hemisphere. Roosevelt responded quickly. By executive order, he created the Office of the Coordinator of Inter-American Affairs (CIAA) and appointed Rockefeller as coordinator. The office's mission was to harmonize all official relations with Latin America in order to shore up economic ties and thwart Nazi influence throughout the region. It essentially specialized in propaganda on all fronts: the press, radio broadcasts, cultural exchanges, and the film industry. Rockefeller considered the medium of film so important that he created a special Motion Picture Division and selected his old friend John Hay ("Jock") Whitney to direct it.

Whitney was fully convinced of the power that Hollywood films could exert in the two-pronged campaign of winning the hearts and minds of Latin Americans and of convincing Americans of the benefits of Pan-American friendship. To be truly effective in achieving these goals, Whitney reasoned, Hollywood would have to begin to incorporate more Latin American talent into its movies. Furthermore, the film industry must be "induced to voluntarily refrain from producing and/or distributing in the other Americas pictures that are objectionable or create a bad impression of America or Latin Americans."[5] On this second count, Whitney left nothing to chance. In order to help "induce" the film industry to refrain "voluntarily" from producing objectionable images of Latin Americans, he "strongly advised" Hays to place a Latin American specialist on the staff of the Production Code Administration, the industry's self-imposed censorship board. Hays needed little coaxing. Throughout Latin America, Hollywood's initial good neighborly efforts routinely met with protests and boycotts, and even a riot in the case of Universal's *Argentine Nights* (1940). Responding to the commotion caused by the film, *La Nación* editorialized that "as long as Hollywood insists on seeing Argentina as an incredibly ridiculous tropical country, no Pan-American understanding is possible, no matter how many 'goodwill' films or visitors are sent here."[6] Given such difficulties, Hays eagerly consented to Whitney's suggestion and hired Addison Durland.[7]

CIAA and Production Code officials viewed Durland as eminently qualified to advise the film industry on its Good Neighbor productions from a "Latin American point of view." Born in Cuba in 1903 to John Durland, a New York banker, and Carmela Nieto, a Cuban journalist, Durland lived his formative years in Havana and developed a bicultural sensibility. Given such a background, industry executives considered him a type of native informant. After completing secondary school in Cuba, he spent two years at the Peekskill Military Academy in Pomona, California, before returning to Havana for undergraduate studies at the National University of Cuba. He later worked as the head of the Cuban Tourist Commission in New York from 1935–1937. A series of newspaper and radio jobs followed, including editorships of *Revista de la Habana* and the *New York Herald-Tribune*'s Latin American wireless service. His reputation as a knowledgeable purveyor of Latin American news and culture secure, NBC named him chief of its Spanish-language division in 1940. The following year, Hays hired Durland away from NBC and assigned him to the Production Code Administration, where he stayed as the resident Latin American expert into the mid-1950s.[8]

This chapter surveys Durland's impact on Hollywood's cinematic representation of Latin Americans between 1941 and 1945, the height of the industry's Pan-American drive.[9] During this period, the studios produced an unprecedented number of Latin-themed films, often featuring imported Latin American stars. I am not interested in simply pointing out the "errors," "distortions," and "stereotypes" within these pictures. Rather, I suggest that Hollywood's Latin images, and Durland's censorship of them, reflect two socially powerful discourses. First, to a large degree, these representations mirror the imagined national identities of Latin American elites. Durland's primary function was to prevent Hollywood's Latin-themed films from offending the Latin American censor boards, whose members held the keys to film distribution in their respective countries. The criteria he used to shape these films tended to conform to the image that Latin American elites liked to convey of the region: light-skinned, modern, and civilized. Second, an examination of Durland's censorial efforts points to the resilience of Hollywood's (and, more broadly, Euro-America's) attitudes toward Latin Americans. Film scholar Ana López has argued that Hollywood films are ethnographic in their own terms, producing their own constructs of ethnicity and national identity.[10] Not surprisingly, the steadfastness of the industry's previously developed ethnography on the region limited Hollywood's effort to suddenly refigure Latin American representations. In the end, a compromise prevailed: the Latin America imagined by Hollywood became more prosperous and modern than ever before, but its inhabitants—symbolized in the roles of Lupe Vélez, Carmen Miranda, and Cesar Romero—still functioned as subordinate entertainers. Significantly,

Hollywood's constructions of an ostensibly transnational Pan-America consistently reified nationalism by implicitly putting forth notions of U.S. national identity in opposition to the Latin Good Neighbors.

CENSORSHIP AND HOLLYWOOD'S REPRESENTATIONAL APPARATUS

To properly interpret Durland's role and impact as the Production Code Administration's Latin American expert requires an understanding of his new employer. The Motion Picture Producers and Distributors of America (MPPDA), the industry trade organization established in 1922, had long been concerned with promoting self-censorship among producers in order to stave off calls for state regulation. The Association, as the MPPDA was also known, regularly issued general guidelines for producers to follow. Two Catholic activists, Martin Quigley and Daniel Lord, drafted a more systematic inventory of "Do's and Don'ts" in 1930; a document the Association adopted as its new Production Code in February 1931.[11] Still, no enforcement mechanism existed. Aware of this loophole, motion picture producers, in an effort to combat falling ticket sales in the early years of the 1930s, began to depict especially titillating scenes of sex. As historians Leonard Leff and Jerald Simmons have argued, the devastating effects of the Depression on Hollywood's financial fortunes caused desperate company presidents to allow producers to "call for the kimonos"—the preferred leisure attire of Hollywood's most popular starlets of the period—and produce stories of prostitutes, concubines, and myriad other forms of sexual sin and excess.[12]

Not surprisingly, in response to Hollywood's new emphasis on provocatively sexy scenes and themes, the Catholic Legion of Decency and other right-wing self-appointed moral guardians initiated a wave of protests and threats of boycotts. If something was not done to "clean up the movies," warned the protesters, the federal government would be asked to regulate the industry. Fearful of such government intervention, and already upset by the Legion's growing influence over the municipal censorship boards that delimited the bounds of acceptability for motion picture exhibition in nearly every major American city, the studios agreed in 1934 to establish a censorship apparatus of their own, the Production Code Administration. Through strict self-enforcement of the Code, the studios hoped that any film given the PCA seal would have little difficulty getting by the municipal boards. From the beginning, the PCA was primarily concerned with the so-called "moral issues" that had angered the Legion of Decency and civic leaders: the depictions of sex, crime, and vulgarity.

The PCA wielded ample power. Although adherence to the Code was not legally enforceable, the agreement among the Hollywood majors, whose vertically-integrated oligopoly the MPPDA represented, meant that in practice no film could be widely distributed in the United States without the PCA's seal of approval. If PCA director Joseph Breen determined that a film violated the Code, he would withhold approval until the "recommended" changes were made. Such authority meant that Breen could significantly influence movie content.[13] This influence extended not only to sex and violence, but also, under section X of the Code, to representations of foreign nationals: "The history, institutions, prominent people and citizenry of other nations shall be fairly represented." In this way, Hollywood protected the increasing profits coming from its foreign film markets. Thus, whereas Breen and his team of censors aimed to satisfy municipal censor boards domestically, they simultaneously sought to avoid irritating the various national censorship agencies within the international market. As a consequence, the PCA screened each film for possible foreign offense during its regular reviewing of storylines, shooting scripts, and finished films.[14]

As Joanne Hershfield's chapter on Dolores del Río demonstrates, Hollywood's concern over Latin American imagery and reception did not appear suddenly with the PCA's hiring of Durland. A number of Hollywood films were banned in Latin America during the 1920s and early 1930s, prompting the industry to look for new methods to help mitigate future possible blunders. During the late 1930s, Breen regularly urged producers of Latin-themed films to hire a "technical expert" or to check with their foreign departments in order to avoid a problem "from the Latin American point of view."[15] In most instances, when the studios heeded Breen's advice, they turned to the diplomatic corps of the country being depicted, either sending a copy of the shooting script to that nation's ambassador in Washington, D.C. or consulting the various consul offices located in Los Angeles. For its big-budget Good Neighbor epic *Juarez* (1939), for example, Warner Bros. hired Ernesto Romero, a reserve vice-consul of Mexico, who had served for fourteen years in the Los Angeles consular branch, as a full-time "technical advisor."[16]

In addition to contracting technical advisors, the Hollywood majors also counted on their own in-house research departments to help lend authenticity to films set in foreign lands. Studio research departments acted as ethnographic resource centers for scriptwriters and producers attempting to represent other peoples and cultures. On occasion, studio researchers played an integral role in shaping movie imagery. Again, the case of *Juarez* proves typical. Touting its upcoming saga of Mexico's only indigenous president as "a historical drama that would adhere to historical fact and atmosphere," Warner Bros. spent unprecedented amounts of time and money on preproduction research. Herman Lissauer, the studio's research department head, claimed to have consulted more than five hundred books, including many

Mexican publications in Spanish, as well as hundreds of archival documents and photographs. In the fall of 1938, the studio sent producers Hal Wallis and Henry Blanke, director William Dieterle, and star Paul Muni on a six-week tour of Mexico to "walk in the steps and breathe the same air of Benito Juarez." Muni, notorious for thoroughly immersing himself in a character, had earlier devised a special preparation technique for Latin roles. To play Mexican-American Johnny Ramirez in *Bordertown* (1935), he went "swimming in tequila" in Mexicali for two weeks. For *Juarez*, the actor spent his time in Mexico intoxicated by a mixture of cactus spirits and Juarez's native Oaxacan landscapes.[17] During the filming of *Juarez*, director Dieterle's concern for authenticity reached an ironic peak with the prison scene in which John Garfield, as Porfirio Díaz, simultaneously speaks and eats corn. The director insisted that real Mexican corn be used. With the onset of winter, the only Mexican corn available had to be ordered at a cost of more than five dollars per ear from a University of California experimental farming unit. Garfield later claimed to have eaten more than a hundred dollars of Mexican corn during the three-day shoot.[18]

While the massive quantity of research undertaken by Warner Bros. for *Juarez* was exceptional, the method and underlying cultural assumptions of the *Juarez* cast and crew fit well within the industry norm. During the 1930s–1940s, Hollywood motion pictures, as well as public discourse in the United States generally, traded on a very narrow conception of culture. American filmmakers viewed culture as transparent, unproblematic, and easily accessible through tourism and the popular press. Research departments acted as internal libraries, specializing in travel guides, picture books, and periodical coverage of foreign lands. These sources both shaped and reflected Hollywood's representations of Latin America (as well as other foreign regions). In depicting Brazilian rubber workers in *Law of the Tropics* (1941), for example, Warner Bros. relied on a 1936 *Collier's* article steeped in the socio-Darwinian racial attitudes of the period.[19] Interpreting the difficulties that Henry Ford encountered in his attempt to bring Taylorized discipline to Fordlandia, his million hectare rubber plantation and processing plant in Amazonia, the *Collier's* reporter described the workers in the following terms: "The *caboclos* [Portuguese-Indian mestizos]: What a strange and contradictory nature! What simple-minded, easygoing, kindly, superstitious, volatile and cruel creatures!"[20] While it would be simplistic to claim a deterministic relationship between Hollywood's ethnic characterizations and the sources used to construct those images, the Brazilian rubber workers depicted in *Law of the Tropics* tend to conform to the descriptions of the *caboclos* painted by *Collier's*.

By far the film industry's favorite source of visual and cultural information on remote and exotic locales was *National Geographic* magazine. First published in 1888, the monthly illustrated journal by the 1910s was the most popular authority on "the story of the world around us," as its editors marketed the magazine. Catherine Lutz and Jane Collins have argued that *National Geographic* specialized in placing images of "primitive," "non-Western" cultures in implicit contradistinction to a "modern," "Western" one.[21] The magazine's treatment of Latin America during the 1910s–1930s alternately stressed what it viewed as "modern" and "primitive" aspects of the region. The periodical ceaselessly celebrated the modern architecture and urban infrastructure of Latin America's major cities. Indeed, the two articles used as a guide for the urban street scenes in *Law of the Tropics* highlight the "Fifth-Avenue-like boulevards" of Rio de Janeiro and the explosive industrial growth of São Paulo, the "Los Angeles of Brazil."[22]

National Geographic articles focusing on the provincial and indigenous communities of Latin America, on the other hand, traded heavily on a discourse of the "primitive." The essays that Warner Bros. used to help turn Paul Muni into Benito Juarez exemplify this.[23] In a story entitled "Among the Zapotecs of Mexico," the *National Geographic* author, Herbert Corey, exposes his neocolonial assumptions in the first three paragraphs. Giving a brief schematic history lesson, Corey states that "there have been but two ages of progress in Mexico . . . the 300 years of Spanish colonial rule" and the Porfirio Díaz regime (1876–1910), which brought "peace, railroads . . . [and] opened the land to foreign capital."[24] As for the Zapotecs and other indigenous communities in Mexico, the journalist declares: "The one aim in which all Indians are united . . . is to be as nearly the Indian of prehistoric times as possible."[25] For Corey, then, Indians are an ahistorical people, inherently immune to "progress." Jeremiah Zimmerman echoes this perspective in his piece on the "Hewers of Stone," the other *National Geographic* article used by Warner Bros. for *Juarez*. While admiring the mosaic fretwork of the stone architecture at Mitla, Zimmerman found little to admire in the descendants of Mitla's builders. "The Zapotecans are," he opined, "in many respects no improvement from their remote Stone Age ancestors, and have even retrograded, so far as personal ambition, enterprise and achievement are concerned."[26] In choosing these articles, published in 1927 and 1910, respectively, as a model for depicting Zapotec Indians of the mid-nineteenth century, the makers of *Juarez* implicitly concurred with *National Geographic*'s characterization of indigenous peoples as fundamentally primitive and static.

In retrospect, it would be easy to interpret Hollywood's use of elite male diplomats as technical advisors and its reliance on secondary sources, such as *National Geographic*, as reflecting a neocolonial project. At the time, the studios adopted these measures in a genuine effort to make their Latin images more "positive" and less offensive—the very actions, of course, that Joseph Breen and the PCA urged producers to take. On occasion, Breen took a more direct stance in his attempt to expunge potentially negative Latin imagery. Reviewing the shooting script for Gene Autry's romp *South of the Border* (1939), for example, he ordered that "the bandit gang of Ramon Mendoza be composed largely of renegade Americans and other non-Mexican nationalities [and that] Mexican officials and police not be played for comedy but be shown as high-grade, intelligent men." [27] In view of the angry reception given many Hollywood films in Latin America during the pre-Durland years, however, PCA censorship of Latin characterizations proved generally inadequate.

THE EXPANDING DEMANDS OF AUTHENTICITY

The practice of obscuring national identities in films featuring foreign settings or characters partially mitigated the PCA's ineffectiveness. After the turn toward the Latin American market in 1939, however, Hollywood's Good Neighbor agenda demanded a new approach, one that emphasized "authenticity" and "realism." The assumption was that accurate representations of Latin America and its residents would translate into less insulting imagery, greater mutual understanding between Americans and Latin Americans, and, most importantly, greater box office receipts for the studios. The newer films largely replaced Latin stereotypes of alternately docile, stupid, and villainous "greasers" with new, supposedly more "positive," images of Latins as fun-seekers, flirts, and flamboyant dancers. After decades of portraying Latin America as a dangerous cultural monolith, Hollywood became sensitive to national and geographic distinctions and now invited audiences to sing and dance *Down Argentine Way* (1940), to spend *That Night in Rio* (1941), and to book a *Week-End in Havana* (1941).

The PCA expressly hired Durland to make sure that Hollywood produced "authentic," and thereby less offensive, representations of Latin America. He was well aware of the challenges that he faced in carrying out this mandate. Shortly after taking his post at the PCA, he received a request from the Motion Picture Division of the CIAA to advise MGM about the wisdom of producing a film on the Mexican revolutionary leader, Emiliano Zapata. Durland cautioned against making the film because of "the practical problems created by the demands of authenticity of characters, historical facts, and all other Mexican elements." [28]

Durland campaigned relentlessly to make Hollywood's Latin images conform to what he labeled the "demands of authenticity." In nearly every script that he reviewed, he found errors in the depictions of local and national customs and cultural practices. For years, Hollywood producers had been conflating all of Latin America with Mexico, so it was inevitable that mistakes occurred in representations of non-Mexican locales and peoples. In 1941, for example, after reading the script for Warner Bros.' Brazilian jungle drama *Law of the Tropics*, Durland lectured Jack Warner: "I note that directions call for lines to be read in Spanish. I call your attention to the fact that Portuguese is the mother tongue of Brazil." He also told Warner that "the 'milreis,' not the peso, is the Brazilian currency." [29] Durland scrupulously reviewed scripts for the authenticity of costumes, dances, and music, eliminating, for example, the Cuban congas intended for *Brazil* (1944) and the Cuban rhumbas planned for United Artists' Mexican musical *Fiesta* (1941). [30]

As a fluent speaker of both Spanish and Portuguese, Durland paid close attention to language and how Latin American audiences might possibly react to insertions of non-English dialogue, either as background or character lines. He regularly insisted to producers that all Spanish or Portuguese lines be spoken "correctly" and in the appropriate regional dialect or accent. Dialogue in a film set in Mexico, for instance, had to be spoken with a Mexican accent. If a well-known Latin American actor was cast as a nationality other than his or her own, the script had to be modified to explain any inauthenticity that might result. When the Mexican star Tito Guízar played a young Brazilian singer in *Brazil*, for example, Durland insisted that the producers "establish clearly in the story that the hero is the son of a Brazilian father and a Mexican mother. This will give ample justification to any Mexican flavor that might appear in Mr. Guizar's impersonation or use of the Portuguese language." [31] Durland's contributions to Hollywood's Good Neighbor policy also included numerous deletions of potentially embarrassing double entendres in Spanish or Portuguese. Commenting on a revised script for *Law of the Tropics*, Durland told Jack Warner: "Regarding scene 110, where the merchant shouts 'Nice *papaya*—tomatoes,' etc. Although the use of the word 'papaya' to designate the fruit of the 'Carica Papaya' is technically correct, this word should be deleted. It has become in Cuba, and elsewhere in Latin America, a common and most offensive vernacular expression for the female sex organs." [32]

Although the range of his censorial handiwork was quite wide, Durland's actions tended to assume the narrow conception of culture of his times. Acting as a one-man research department, Durland often visited the sets of particularly troublesome films and supplied the producers and directors with books and pictures (including *National Geographic*) depicting "proper authenticity." [33] Given his bicultural background and the myriad elemental errors he routinely corrected from Latin-themed scripts, Durland probably doubted

Hollywood's capability to rise to the "demands of authenticity." Still, in what amounted to incessant acts of damage control, he engaged in a sincere crusade to make Hollywood's imagined Latin America appear as authentic as possible.

As great as Durland's quest for authenticity may have been, his larger mission fell subservient to a much more practical demand: that Hollywood's Latin content be free of offensive imagery. While Durland assumed that more realistic and accurate depictions of Latin America would generally translate into less displeasing images, he also realized that too faithful an adherence to certain Latin American realities might prove irritating to his number one audience. As noted earlier, Durland was particularly determined to expurgate images potentially disagreeable to Latin American elites. He derived his estimation of elite *mentalité* from his previous experience in the region, as well as from guidelines sent directly to the studios. Once word got out that Hollywood was planning a serious Pan-American drive, diplomatic and cultural elites, no doubt reflecting on earlier cinematic insults, crafted numerous unsolicited letters to Hollywood officials indicating how their respective countries should be portrayed on screen. The racial, class, and gender biases of these elite males (all the letters were written by men) conditioned Durland's censorship policy, prompting him to reconfigure Latin America as modern, clean, and especially in the cases of Brazil and Argentina, European in complexion.[34]

The racial politics of Hollywood's Good Neighbor productions differed little from most other movies produced during the period. At this time, the only thing noticeable about African-Americans in Hollywood cinema was their virtual absence. True, in response to pressure that the National Association for the Advancement of Colored People (NAACP) placed on industry moguls at a July 1942 meeting, black images did become slightly more visible on American screens during the war years. Two all-black musicals were produced, *Stormy Weather* (1943) by Twentieth Century-Fox and *Cabin in the Sky* (1943) by MGM, and a few war movies, such as *Bataan* (1943) and *Sahara* (1943), depicted black soldiers as integral Allied fighters.[35] Still, as far as the vast majority of Hollywood's wartime films were concerned, African-Americans simply did not exist, and when they did, it was almost always in short musical numbers ("specialty acts") that could be excised for distribution in the American South.

A similar process of whitening took place in the production of Hollywood's Latin-themed films. The adverse reaction in Argentina to Fox's *Down Argentine Way*, the studio's first Good Neighbor musical featuring Carmen Miranda, set the tone for what was to follow. According to a report from the Assistant Commercial Attaché to the American Embassy in Buenos Aires, Argentinians

Figure 16.1. Nicholas Brothers in *Down Argentine Way* (1940). (Image courtesy of the Museum of Modern Art Film Stills Archive.)

were upset with, among other things, the inclusion of two dance performances by the Nicholas Brothers during the nightclub sequences. Argentine cultural overseers feared that the scenes featuring black dancers would "add to the Yankee impression" that the people of Argentina were "Indians or Africans." [36] For Miranda's second feature, *That Night in Rio*, the studio attempted to stave off such negative reception by sending the script to the Brazilian ambassador to review. Conforming to elite attitudes on race, he urged the elimination of the one scene of African-Brazilians in the film, that of two "Negro girls" singing in a cafe. The PCA concurred, and the scene was dropped. [37]

Comparable elision occurred with *Carnival in Rhythm* (1941), a Warner Bros. Technicolor short that featured African-American dancer Katherine Dunham and her troupe celebrating samba music and dance. While touring the United States as a guest of the State Department, Dr. Pedro Calmon, a prominent Brazilian historian, happened to be in Hollywood during a preview of *Carnival in Rhythm*. After the screening, Calmon expressed concern that because "all the participants are negroes" the film might lead to "misapprehension" throughout the world that "all or most Brazilians are negroes, and that all or most of their dances and music are predominantly African." To avoid such an image, he "unofficially and confidentially" recommended that all specific references to Brazil be omitted from the narration of the film. Durland saw to it that the studio carried out the professor's recommendation.[38] Hearing rumors of this and similar incidents, Claude Barnett, the executive director of the Associated Negro Press, wrote directly to Will Hays inquiring as to whether the MPPDA had sent instructions to the studios "not to use Negroes in parts portraying South Americans" and whether the industry had been urged to do so by any South American representatives. Taking a duplicitous yet "officially" accurate stance, the Hays office assured Barnett that "no feeling of racial prejudice" existed in the studios or among Brazil's diplomatic corps.[39] By such "unofficial" measures, then, Latin Americans of African descent remained invisible in Hollywood's imagined Latin America.

Durland's racial censorship targeted depictions not only of blacks, but also of all darker-skinned Latin Americans. He routinely commented on skin color, as he did, for example, to Columbia president Harry Cohn regarding the shooting script for *Canal Zone* (1941): "Scene 331: The grave diggers at the ceremony will be properly costumed, and care will be taken to avoid making them appear too shabby or *swarthy*."[40] His instructions to Louis B. Mayer concerning the MGM musical *Panama Hattie* (1942) sum up his agenda with regard to race: "Scene 18: Please take great care in the characterization, clothing, and casting of the stevedores, taxi-drivers, and other bit actors in this scene. As you know, the Latin American, in general, resents being presented as swarthy or negroid in color."[41]

In carrying out such an agenda, the need to visually maintain racial hierarchies superseded Durland's concern over "authenticity." As Durland well knew, many Latin American cities, such as Rio de Janeiro and Havana, had (and have) large African, mulatto, and mestizo populations. In Hollywood's versions of *That Night in Rio* and *Week-End in Havana*, however, everyone, including the background extras, appears white. In the foreground of Hollywood's Pan-American productions, only light-skinned Good Neighbors—like Carmen Miranda, Cesar Romero, Lupe Vélez, and Desi Arnaz—could represent the region. The whitewashing of Latin America was so complete that even the overtly racist censor board in Atlanta was impressed. Commenting on *The Gang's All Here* (1943), Busby Berkeley's hit that featured various Pan-American numbers including Carmen Miranda as the "Lady in the Tutti-Frutti Hat," the municipal censor, no doubt responding to the increased presence of African-American song and dance routines in U.S. cinema after the NAACP conference, exclaimed "At last the Producers have realized that white people CAN be entertaining without having to inject Negroes."[42]

Figure 16.2. Carmen Miranda in *The Gang's All Here* (1943). (Image courtesy of the Museum of Modern Art Film Stills Archive.)

In addition to lightening the racial hue of the region, Durland helped enforce elite conventions about gender and class relations in Latin America. In the 1942 western *Below the Border,* for example, he warned the producer:

> in scene 38, where Rosita tries to protect the jewel box from the bandit, great care should be taken in the handling of this scene where the script indicates that she will be kicking and clawing the bandit. Care should be exercised to avoid presenting Rosita behaving in an offensive manner, since she is a person of "high caste." [43]

"High caste" people, cinematic symbols of the officials Durland hoped to appease, were not to be presented as acting in an offensive manner (even while being assaulted by a thief). This elitist assumption also includes gender, as it exemplifies Durland's effort to make sure that all Latin American women portrayed on screen exhibited respectable "ladylike" qualities. Implicitly acknowledging the type of bars that U.S. servicemen frequented while stationed in Panama, Durland told Louis B. Mayer that "the girls" in *Panama Hattie,* the ones "embroiled with the soldiers and sailors in their brawl should not be characterized as Latin American, where, as you know, there is a clear division between the 'nice girl' and the prostitute. No nice girls would go around with foreign sailors."[44] While Durland efficiently removed depictions of Latin women of ill repute, he saw no problem with Hollywood's already well-entrenched stereotype of fiery and tempestuous Latin women, represented by the roles of Lupe Vélez and Carmen Miranda.

Perhaps Durland's greatest censorial objective was to pressure producers to "clean up" Latin American locales and make both the settings and people appear prosperous and modernized. Whenever a scene called for an urban setting in Latin America, Durland regularly cautioned the filmmakers "not [to] make the streets look too much like a slum." While "cleaning up" the *mise-en-scène*, Durland also sought to cleanse scripts of "broken English," again demonstrating the flexibility of his demands for authenticity. As Durland was well aware, broken English, as well as broken Spanish and Portuguese, was an unavoidable fact in the everyday exchanges between Latin Americans and North Americans. He also knew, however, that many upper-class Latins, who prided themselves on their language skills and viewed English fluency as a sign of being cosmopolitan, resented how Hollywood producers routinely had Latin characters use exaggerated and comical broken English. As a result, Durland tried to outlaw faulty English entirely, requiring that all Latin Americans who spoke English on screen to do so fluently and eloquently. An illustration of his views appears in comments regarding a treatment for Republic's *The Cowboy and the Señorita* (1944):

> I should say "Cafe Pancho" is not a happy choice. Why not change it to something more credible? As to its proprietor, I gather that he is a Mexican, and recommend that he be presented as a clean, capable, and presentable fellow, avoiding anything that might resemble that irksome Mexican comedy type, that you and I know has been the cause of much ill feeling. I happily notice that Pancho seems to have complete command of English and hope that this happy fact will prevail in the future script.[45]

Another "happy fact" was the depiction of Latin America as modern and prosperous. Durland's didactic recommendations, in harmony with the "suggestions" sent to Hollywood by Latin American elites, constantly emphasized how Latin American cities were as industrialized and advanced as any in the world and should therefore be represented as such. His comments on the Brazilian sequence in Irving Rapper's classic *Now, Voyager* (1942) are typical:

> We assume that the atmospheric shots of Rio will show, as the script indicates, the magnificence and the beauty of this great metropolis. . . . [T]he ramshackled car in which your leading characters make the trip

should be eliminated. Rio is justly proud of its modern system of transportation. Brazilians would naturally expect to see a modern taxi-cab. Its driver should not be this very ignorant, dim-witted and hysterical comic person, unable to cope with his machine. We feel sure that he will be considered a grotesque travesty. Besides, like all taxi drivers in all great cities of the world, he should know enough English to understand his passengers. Instead, Jerry after many futile attempts to give directions is compelled to resort to drawing sketches. The laughter and merriment that this character provokes in Jerry and Charlotte, and later from the [American] audiences, will be obtained at the expense of the only Brazilian character of any importance in the script.[46]

Comparing these instructions with the finished scene provides a vivid visual barometer of Durland's impact on Hollywood's representation of Latin America during World War II. In the film, a cruise ship carrying the budding lovers Jerry (Paul Henreid) and Charlotte (Bette Davis) sails into Rio harbor. "There's Sugar Loaf!" exclaims Charlotte. The scene cuts away to stock exteriors of Rio's distinctive landscape while Charlotte continues as tour guide: "And that stretch on the left is Copacabana beach." "Copacabana," Jerry replies wistfully, "there's music in the word." More atmospheric shots showcase Rio's majestic skyline, including, of course, the Christ statue atop Corcovado, before we see a vehicle driving up a winding road.[47] The "ramshackled" car originally called for in the script has indeed been upgraded to a new, luxurious cab, and the highway looks as smooth and modern as any that might be found in the hills of Hollywood (where the "on location" road shots were actually filmed). The producers, heeding the advice of Durland and CIAA advisors, also changed the driver's ethnic characterization from "Manoel, a swarthy-skinned Portuguese," as originally called for in the script, to "Giuseppe, an Italian immigrant."[48]

Yet the cabbie, played by Frank Puglia, an Italian comic actor regularly featured in Hollywood's Latin pictures, has not been taught English, nor has he been made any smarter. In an obvious attempt to thwart possible negative reactions in Brazil, Jerry tells the audience that Giuseppe does not represent an official Brazilian tourist driver. "Serves me right for picking up a car just because I liked the face of the driver instead of getting one from the regular tourist agent," he tells Charlotte. Struggling to communicate in English and broken Portuguese, Jerry asks "How much farther, Giuseppe? *Distancio, combien?*" To which Giuseppe responds with a random list of tourist trivia, "Corcovado, *Pão de Açúcar,* parakeets, birds, parrots, rubber." This provokes Charlotte, "I thought the sign on the car said English spoken driver." Implying that the communication breakdown should not be blamed entirely on Giuseppe, Jerry

Figure 16.3. In *Now, Voyager* (1942), Giuseppe (Frank Puglia) provides comic relief as an "Italian" cabbie in Rio who drives Jerry (Paul Henreid) and Charlotte (Bette Davis) backward over a cliff. (Image courtesy of the Academy of Motion Picture Arts and Sciences.)

retorts, "What he needs is a couple of Portuguese spoken passengers." Despite these disclaimers, the viewer is undoubtedly meant to identify with Jerry and Charlotte, who grow ever exasperated with Giuseppe's incompetence. When Giuseppe suddenly turns off the main highway, Jerry resorts to hand signals and tone of voice to get the driver to go back. While in the middle of a three-point turn around, Giuseppe mistakenly puts the car into reverse gear and drives it over the cliff, where it crashes into a ditch. Getting out of the vehicle, the cabbie immediately falls to his knees and begins to whimper incessantly, "*Deus Meu, Deus Meu! Que Desgraça, Que Desgraça!*" Charlotte tries to calm him the way a parent would soothe a child before he runs off hysterically to look for another car.

DURLAND'S COMPROMISING CENSORSHIP

The above scene symbolizes Addison Durland's untenable mission. The PCA's Latin American expert could hardly have met the multiple, and often countervailing, "demands of authenticity" placed upon him. As Hollywood attempted to appropriate and reconfigure Latin America to the satisfaction of audiences on both sides of the Río Bravo, the customary "Hollywood Latin" (the dumb, emotional comic) had to be reconciled, or at least merged, with the demands of Latin American elites. Or, to use the case of *Now, Voyager,* the modern architecture, roads, and automobiles of Latin America became juxtaposed with stereotypically excitable characters like Giuseppe who provided comic relief.

The above compromise—in which Latin America is urban and clean, while the "Hollywood Latin" retains one-dimensional entertainment value— symbolizes the results of Durland's censorship. As they would with Breen over moral issues, producers constantly pushed the envelope when it came to complying with Durland's recommendations. Yet, a hierarchy of obedience reigned in the industry and the studios were much more likely to challenge Durland than Breen. Constant negotiation characterized the relationship between Durland and the filmmakers. The final version of Hollywood's Latin images usually fell somewhere between Durland's orders and the producers' desire to have Latin characters retain their traditional comic or exotic function.

On a certain level, the compromises Durland struck with the studios mirrored the PCA's general policy. Whereas Breen would allow producers to treat suspect subjects like murder and adultery as long as the story contained "compensating moral values" (i.e., the guilty party paid for his or her sins and the act was duly condemned), Durland was much more likely to turn a blind eye to problematic representations if the film also featured what could be called "compensating ethnic imagery." In his correspondence concerning Universal's *Moonlight in Havana* (1942), he requested that the character of the dim-witted nightclub proprietor José Martínez be changed to another nationality "because the absence in the story of a flattering Cuban character offers no compensation."[49] *The Ox-Bow Incident* (1943), on the other hand, presented the requisite visual recompense. After screening the potentially troublesome film with the MPSA foreign committee, the censor praised Anthony Quinn for bringing dignity to his role as the Mexican among the three innocent homesteaders who are unjustly lynched by a frontier mob. In an apparent trade-off, the censor made no mention of Chris-Pin Martin's exaggerated broken English (although he did have the name of Martin's character changed from "Amigo" to "Pancho").[50] Martin, a Mexican-American actor born in Tucson, made a career in the late 1930s–early 1940s playing the dumb and fat Mexican sidekick in the *Cisco Kid* series and other westerns. His portrayal of the assistant for the mob leader in *The Ox-Bow Incident* was typical. Asked if he saw the suspect, he responds: "Sí, he not see me, I teenk. He was coming down the hill, and, and I drive my horse out of the way. So when, first, I teenk, I say hello, then, I teenk, he's pointing, I teenk, to drive the cattle."

Durland was above all a pragmatist who undoubtedly recognized the limits of his ability to reshape completely Hollywood's Latin characterizations. As per his job description, he did his utmost to mitigate the possibility of official protest. To accomplish this, he insisted that producers of questionable characterizations make whatever geographic or ethnic shifts might be necessary to preempt potentially offending a particular Latin American nation. Unconcerned with reaction from U.S. Latinos, for example, Durland made sure that the two principal characters in *Honolulu Lu* (1941), Don Esteban (Leo Carrillo) and his niece (Lupe Vélez), be portrayed as "natives of California" and that Abbott and Costello clearly establish that their high jinks in *Rio Rita* (1942) take place in Texas and not Mexico.[51] Similarly, and to the possible chagrin of Portugal, Durland had the nationality of the flirtatious navy cadets in *My Sister Eileen* (1942) and the playwrights in *Two Senoritas From Chicago* (1943) changed from Brazilian to Portuguese.[52]

Durland's pragmatism, however, took a curious turn when dealing with films that featured prominent Latin stars. He seems to have held the essentialist position that any film that featured a major Latin American star was somehow automatically immune from offensive or problematic representations. Or, perhaps he strategized, not without reason, that the use of Latin players would provide a buffer against criticism. If Latin American officials took offense at the representations in these pictures, his reasoning may have gone, they would direct their resentment toward the stars rather than the studios. Whatever his motivations, Durland consistently made little or no censorial interventions in films with major Latin performers such as Lupe Vélez, Carmen Miranda, and Cesar Romero. He often quickly determined that they would "present no problem from the Latin American point of view."

Given that Mexican officials had regularly derided Lupe Vélez's screen portrayals, Durland's lack of critical intercession concerning her films is bewildering. Since the late 1920s, Vélez's star image, both onscreen and off (she was married to Johnny Weissmuller, Hollywood's "Tarzan," between 1933–1939) was that of a "Mexican wildcat." In 1939, RKO reinforced and synthesized her celluloid image when it launched the *Mexican Spitfire* series. In the eight-film comedy cycle, produced from 1939 to 1943, Vélez plays Carmelita, a Mexican entertainer married to Dennis Lindsay (Donald Woods), an Anglo advertising executive.[53] The plots invariably revolve around the myriad ways in which Carmelita can chase away, and then ultimately win back, key business clients for Dennis, who, despite having had his patience tried, ends up reaffirming his love for Carmelita. The *Mexican Spitfire* series broke new ground in depicting a Latina not just hopelessly in love with an Anglo male, but actually married to one. Still, the stereotypes in Vélez's performances, encapsulated in the titles of the films, abound. Throughout, she displays her trademark characteristics: lots of eye-rolling, body movement, double entendres, frantic bursts of Spanish dialogue, and fractured English marked by malapropisms— the types of behavior Durland routinely tried to screen out from Hollywood's Latin characterizations.

Durland's apparent lack of concern with films featuring major Latin stars is even more striking with respect to Carmen Miranda's musical comedy cycle at Twentieth Century-Fox.[54] Owing to the popularity of new Latin rhythms like the conga and the rhumba, Latin musicals became the mainstay of the studios' Pan-American drive. Miranda was undoubtedly the genre's biggest star and, of the dozens of wartime musicals produced, her films traded to an unprecedented extent on the Good Neighbor policy. Nearly every one begins or ends with a bilingual paean to the blessings of Pan-Americanism. *Springtime in the Rockies* (1942), for example, ends with the stars Betty Grable, John Payne, Cesar Romero, and Miranda joyfully executing a rhumba-samba-conga number called "The Panamericana Jubilee." Perhaps the most excessive example of Fox's Good Neighbor messages occurs in the opening shots of Busby Berkeley's hit *The Gang's All Here* (1943). On a huge nightclub stage, a model of the SS *Brazil* is docking. Quickly, workers begin unloading the ship's cargo, which consists of a veritable inventory of Latin America's major goods for export: coffee, bananas, sugar, and, finally, Miranda herself. As Miranda enters center stage the nightclub host proclaims: "Well, there's your Good Neighbor policy! Come on honey, let's Good Neighbor it!" Miranda then proceeds to teach the audience the "Uncle Sam-ba."[55]

Miranda's musical numbers regularly stressed that cultural differences between North Americans and Latin Americans could be transcended through the international languages of music and dance. Yet, the narrative structures of her films nearly always reaffirmed the supposed superiority of American ways. In *Down Argentine Way*, for example, the American Betty Grable interferes with an Argentine horse breeder's business "for his own good." Although the breeder's son admonishes her not to intervene, she persists, and ultimately, her intervention resolves all the problems that have erupted in the film. The sexual politics of the films further represent asymmetries of power. Rarely is a Latin American "neighbor" (usually Miranda and Romero) permanently mated with the narrative's Anglo protagonists (such as Grable, Payne, Don Ameche, or Alice Faye). The characters portrayed by Miranda, in particular, remain either contentedly and coquettishly single or hopelessly attached to a Latino playboy. In short, the underlying ideological message of these films is that they (the Latin Americans) are our (white America's) good neighbors, but we are not the same. It is fine to sing, dance, and flirt together, but it is not fine to become seriously involved with each other. Indeed, despite all supposed openness and good will, these films ultimately foreclose the possibility of real understanding of the Latin "good neighbor." Instead, turning on supra-local settings and behavioral stereotypes, the Miranda films reinforce the notion that Latin America is everywhere and nowhere, and that the "Latins" are available for the colonialist pleasures of the United States.

Thus, despite Durland's call for greater regional and national specificity, Miranda's onscreen character and function are remarkably consistent. Regardless of the narrative or the locale, she remains the same from film to film. Alternately named Carmen, Rosita, Querida, Dorita, or Chiquita, she always plays an exaggerated, homogenized Latin Other. Never playing the principal lead, she functions as an exotic and spectacular fetish (filmed in state-of-the-art Technicolor) whose sources of entertainment are myriad: her garishly colorful and frequently fruit-adorned outfits, her rhythmic body gestures and dancing style, her incessantly expressive eye manipulations, and the inherent "foreignness" of her fluent Portuguese combined with the inflated accent and linguistic malaprops of her spoken English.

From today's vantage point, the screen images of Carmen Miranda and Lupe Vélez seem outrageously typecast. Clearly, for Durland, the stereotype of easily excitable Latinas conveyed little that he viewed as potentially offensive. With respect to the films of Miranda and Vélez, he once again seemed more concerned with censoring depictions of Latin America as place than Latin Americans as people. These pictures conform to one of Durland's primary objectives in that they are set entirely in urban, cosmopolitan milieus. The box office, no doubt, also buoyed Durland's lack of censorial interventions. American audiences flocked to the wartime films featuring Miranda and Vélez, and, despite rumblings among some critics and officials, so did Latin Americans.

Given the multiple demands placed upon him, Addison Durland's impact on Hollywood's Latin images during World War II ultimately amounted to a series of compromises. Undoubtedly, his actions helped to eliminate many of the more egregious representations that had regularly angered Latin American elites in the 1920s–1930s. Moreover, if a finished film still contained many questionable characterizations, Durland used his authority to block the picture's distribution in Latin America, as he did with Hal Roach's *Fiesta*. Still, the industry's need for Latins to provide comic relief and musical numbers proved unrestrainable. As illustrated in the taxi scene of *Now, Voyager,* and the screen images of Carmen Miranda and Lupe Vélez, Hollywood's Good Neighbor films blended a more modern looking Latin America with Latin Americans who, while not the villainous brutes of old, nonetheless would remain props of light entertainment, intellectually and romantically inferior. These fictional neighbors were perfectly suited to the imperialist, yet war-weary heart of the early 1940s United States. Although lively, vivid, and infinitely entertaining, Hollywood's Good Neighbor is ultimately nonthreatening and compliant under America's tutelage.

NOTES

I would like to thank my dissertation adviser, Norris Hundley, as well as George Lipsitz, Vicki Ruíz, Andrew B. Smith, Lorena Chambers, and Mark T. Gilderhus for their perspicacious comments on earlier drafts of this essay.

1. *Film Daily*, March 27, 1941. For news of Durland's appointment, see also the coverage in the *New York Times*, March 30, 1941.

2. For a more detailed study of Hollywood's Good Neighbor policy, see my dissertation, "Pan-American Visions: Hollywood's Good Neighbor Policy and U.S.-Latin American Relations, 1938–1946" (UCLA, 2000). For other general overviews of the cinematic representation of Latin Americans during World War II, see Allen Woll, *The Latin Image in American Film* (Los Angeles: UCLA Latin American Center, 1980); Emilio García Riera, *México visto por el cine extranjero, 1894–1969* 4 vols. (Mexico City: Editorial Era, 1987–1988); Gary D. Keller, *Hispanics and United States Film: An Overview and Handbook* (Tempe: Bilingual Press, 1994); Ana M. López, "Are All Latins From Manhattan? Hollywood, Ethnography, and Cultural Colonialism," in *Unspeakable Images: Ethnicity and the American Cinema*, ed. Lester Friedman (Urbana: University of Illinois Press, 1991), 404–24; Alfred Charles Richard, Jr., *Censorship and Hollywood's Hispanic Image: An Interpretive Filmography, 1936–1955* (Westport, CT: Greenwood Press, 1993); and Julianne Burton, "Don (Juanito) Duck and the Imperial-Patriarchal Unconscious: Disney Studios, the Good Neighbor Policy, and the Packaging of Latin America," in *Nationalities & Sexualities*, ed. Andrew Parker, et al. (New York: Routledge, 1992), 21–41.

3. Ruth Vasey, "Foreign Parts: Hollywood's Global Distribution and the Representation of Ethnicity," *American Quarterly* 44, no. 4 (December 1992): 618, 627.

4. These Good Neighbor productions, as they would come to be called, were essentially of three types: (1) standard Hollywood genre films with Anglo stars that were set at least partially in Latin America and featured some on-location exterior shots, such as Irving Rapper's *Now, Voyager* (1942); (2) B-grade pictures set and often partly shot in Latin America that featured mid-rung Anglo actors usually paired with aspiring Latin entertainers in romantic comedies or quasi-musicals. Most of Tito Guízar's English-language features, such as *Brazil* (Republic, 1944) and *Mexicana* (Republic, 1945), fell into this category; and (3) the big budget, self-consciously "good neighborly" Latin musicals set either in the United States or in Latin America

that featured American Anglo stars and fairly well-known Latin American personalities. Examples of these films include all of Carmen Miranda's wartime productions for Twentieth Century-Fox, such as *That Night in Rio* (1941) and *Weekend in Havana* (1941). In 1938–1939, Hollywood also briefly renewed regular production of Spanish-language features designed for Latin American release. For more on this topic, see Brian O'Neil, "Yankee Invasion of Mexico, or Mexican Invasion of Hollywood? Hollywood's Renewed Spanish-Language Production of 1938–1939," in *Studies in Latin American Popular Culture* 17 (1998): 79–104.

5. Donald W. Roland, comp., *History of the Office of the Coordinator of Inter-American Affairs* (Washington, D.C., 1947), 71.

6. *La Nación* (Buenos Aires), May 3, 1941, 10. See also, *Variety*, June 4, 1941, 3, and *New York Times*, May 8, 1941. Besides encouraging the production of Good Neighbor films, the CIAA also financed "goodwill" tours of Latin America by top Hollywood talent. Douglas Fairbanks, Jr., for example, traveled throughout South America in May 1941 and Walt Disney conducted a three-month "research trip" to Latin America in the fall of that same year.

7. *Film Daily*, January 15, 1941. While Whitney's meeting with Hays proved to be the ultimate agent of action, there was already sentiment developing within the industry for the Hays Office to hire a Latin American specialist. The actor-singer John Boles, for example, after a two-month tour of Latin America, told the Hollywood press in December 1940, that the only way American producers would stop sending "cinemagraphic insults" to Latin America would be to install a Latin Americanist in the Code office who would have complete authority to judge the authenticity of Hollywood's Good Neighbor pictures. *La Opinión* (Los Angeles), December 8, 1940.

8. On Durland's background see, *Variety*, April 2, 1941; *Film Daily*, March 27, 1941; *New York Times*, March 30, 1941 and May 8, 1941; and the *1941–1942 International Motion Picture Almanac*, ed. Terry Ramsaye (New York: Quigley Publishing Company, 1942). Durland's appointment provoked grumblings among most of the studios' foreign managers, who complained that Hays gave them no prior consultation on the matter and that the appointee came from outside the film business. Only RKO's Phil Reisman defended Durland as an expert on Latin American customs and habits and someone the industry should be proud to welcome (*Variety*, April 9, 1941). In time, the other foreign sales chiefs concurred with Reisman's assessment and saw Durland as an asset.

9. This chapter is based primarily on archival research of more than 130 Production Code files of films reviewed by Durland during this period. These records are located in the MPAA Production Code Administration files, Margaret Herrick Library, Academy of Motion Picture Arts and Sciences, Beverly Hills, CA (hereafter cited as PCA files).

10. López, "Are All Latins From Manhattan?" 404–24.

11. The best and most concise history to date on the origins of the Production Code and the PCA is Richard Maltby, "The Production Code and the Hays Office," in *Grand Design: Hollywood as a Modern Business Enterprise, 1930–1939*, ed. Tino Balio (Berkeley: University of California Press, 1993), 37–72. See also Leonard Leff and

Jerald Simmons, *The Dame in the Kimono: Hollywood, Censorship, and the Production Code From the 1920s to the 1960s* (New York: Doubleday, 1990); Gregory D. Black, *Hollywood Censored: Morality Codes, Catholics, and the Movies* (Cambridge: Cambridge University Press, 1994); Frank Walsh, *Sin and Censorship: The Catholic Church and the Motion Picture Industry* (New Haven: Yale University Press, 1996); Lea Jacobs, *The Wages of Sin: Censorship and the Fallen Woman Film, 1928–1942* (Madison: University of Wisconsin Press, 1991); and the *American Quarterly* 44, no. 4 (December 1992), a special issue devoted to "Hollywood, Censorship, and American Culture."

12. Leff and Simmons, *The Dame in the Kimono*, 8–16.

13. If by today's standards Hollywood's Classical cinema comes across as maudlin and hokey, it is due to the immense power the PCA censors had to influence screen content. To offer a quick illustrative digression on the Code's priggish dictates—one that may be increasingly difficult for us to imagine now that the "A-word" is in regular use on broadcast radio and television—in 1938, Breen cut the seemingly innocent line "and that's the first time you ever sounded like the front end of a horse" from the production script of *St. Louis Blues*. Breen to Luraschi, July 8, 1938, PCA files, *St. Louis Blues* (Paramount, 1938).

14. It should be noted that concern over foreign reception of Hollywood cinema predates the arrival of Joseph Breen or the creation of the Production Code Administration. From the beginning of the studio system in the 1910s, Hollywood producers recognized the value of making films acceptable to a mass international audience. For a rich analysis of how foreign market considerations helped shape Hollywood representations during the pre–World War II era, see Ruth Vasey, *The World According to Hollywood, 1918–1939* (Madison: University of Wisconsin Press, 1997) and Helen Delpar, " 'Goodbye to the Greaser': Mexico, the MPPDA, and Derogatory Films, 1922–1926," *Journal of Popular Film and Television* 12, no. 1 (1984): 34–41. Of course, as Vasey points out, the degree of thoroughness used to scrutinize a particular film's possible negative "foreign angle" depended largely on the economic importance of the nationality involved. As a general rule, Hollywood producers, urged on by the PCA staff, used two general strategies during the 1930s to evade possible negative foreign repercussions. The first was to cloud the national origins of its characters by minimizing direct references to nationality. The second, employed particularly in crime pictures, was to restrict villainy disproportionately to all-American Anglo types, or at least to create a relative balance between American and non-American "heavies." Vasey has pointed out how the potential market risks involved in casting ethnic villains led the studios to reduce the casting of ethnics generally. Or, put differently, the heterogeneity of Hollywood's audience, both at home and abroad, encouraged the increasing homogeneity of the screen's cast of characters. Vasey, "Foreign Parts," 624.

15. For typical examples of how the Production Code Administration censored the Latin content of feature films before Durland arrived, see the PCA files for *Tropic Holiday* (Paramount, 1938), *The Girl From Mexico* (RKO, 1939) and *La Conga Nights* (Universal, 1940).

16. Romero was paid $2,000 for his services. "Budget-Juarez," October 11, 1938;

"Vital Statistics—Juarez—From Robert Taplinger, Publicity Director," not dated; Eduardo Zambrano, Mexican Vice-Consul in Charge, to Warner Bros. Studio, May 11, 1938, Warner Bros. Archives, Special Collections, Doheny Library, University of Southern California, Los Angeles, (hereafter cited as Warner Bros. Archives), box 2, *Juarez* (1939). Unfortunately for researchers studying Hollywood's studio era, most of the production files for films made during the 1930s–1940s have been lost or remain unavailable. The Warner Bros. Archives, however, remain an exception in terms of both completeness and accessibility.

17. "Vital Statistics—Juarez—From Robert Taplinger, Publicity Director," not dated, Warner Bros. Archives, box 2, *Juarez* (1939); Woll, *Latin Image,* 38. Historical accuracy in the film, however, fell subservient to politics and the storyline, which created a personal friendship between Juarez and Lincoln and exaggerated the Mexican's feelings toward his American counterpart to the point of absolute veneration. See, *Juárez,* edited screenplay with an introduction by Paul Vanderwood (Madison: University of Wisconsin Press, 1983), 31–33.

18. Larry Swindell, *Body and Soul: The Story of John Garfield* (New York: William Morrow and Company, 1975), 142.

19. "General Research Record," May 14, 1941, Warner Bros. Archives, box 1, *Law of the Tropics* (1941).

20. Edward Tomlinson, "Jungle Gold," *Collier's* (December 12, 1936), 54. In what was known in the U.S. Press as the "Spinach Rebellion," rubber workers at Fordlandia rioted the night that the company mess hall opened in protest of the strictly American fare of corn flakes and green salads.

21. Catherine A. Lutz and Jane L. Collins, *Reading National Geographic* (Chicago: University of Chicago Press, 1993).

22. "General Research Record," May 14, 1941, Warner Bros. Archives, box 1, *Law of the Tropics* (1941). The two articles used for research on Brazilian street life were: Frederick Simpich, "Gigantic Brazil and its Glittering Capital," *National Geographic,* December 1930, 732–78, and W. Robert Moore, "As São Paulo Grows," *National Geographic,* May 1939, 657–88.

23. Research Department to Henry Blanke, Inter-Office Memo, September 8, 1938, Warner Bros. Archives, box 2, *Juarez* (1939).

24. Herbert Corey, "Among the Zapotecs of Mexico," *National Geographic,* May 1927, 501.

25. Ibid., 531.

26. Jeremiah Zimmerman, "Hewers of Stone," *National Geographic,* December 1910, 1007–09.

27. Joseph Breen to M. J. Siegel, 18 October 1939, PCA files, *South of the Border* (Republic, 1939).

28. Addison Durland Memorandum, June 1, 1948, Motion Pictures Producers Association, Washington, D.C., *Viva Zapata!*; quoted in Paul J. Vanderwood, "An American Cold Warrior: *Viva Zapata!* (1952)" and in *American History/American Film: Interpreting the Hollywood Image,* ed. John E. O'Connor and Martin A. Jackson (New

York: Frederick Ungar, 1979), 186. In addition to the demands of authenticity, Durland also expressed concern over the controversial political nature of the film. This latter issue kept the film shelved for more than ten years until Darryl Zanuck recast the Mexican revolutionary (with Marlon Brando in the lead role) as an American "cold warrior" in Twentieth Century-Fox's *Viva Zapata!* (1952). For the full history of the making of this film, see Vanderwood's article cited above.

29. Durland to Jack Warner, April 25, 1941, PCA files, *Law of the Tropics* (Warner Bros., 1941).

30. Durland to Siegel, January 5, 1944, PCA files, *Brazil* (Republic, 1944); Durland to Hal Roach, August 13, 1941, PCA files, *Fiesta* (UA, 1941).

31. Durland to Robert North, May 20, 1944, PCA files, *Brazil* (Republic, 1944).

32. Durland to Warner, May 26, 1941, PCA files, *Law of the Tropics* (Warner Brothers, 1941). Another example of this type of censorship occurred in Durland's review of the script for *Brazil* (1944) where he advised that "Mike's last name be changed. Carvalho is bound to sound too close to a similar, and very offensive Portuguese word." Durland to Siegel, January 5, 1944, PCA files, *Brazil* (Republic, 1944).

33. He did this, for example, for Gene Autry's second excursion *Down Mexico Way* (1941). See, Addison Durland, Memo for the Files, July 16, 1941, PCA files, *Down Mexico Way* (Republic, 1941).

34. For a typical letter, see Rone Amorim (General Secretary, Unió Cultural Brasil–Estados Unidos) to Will Hays, January 2, 1942, PCA files, *That Night in Rio* (20th-Fox, 1941). It should be noted that the CIAA also established a Hollywood liaison office, the Motion Picture Society for the Americas (MPSA), which doled out free advice and story ideas to the studios. The MPSA, working closely with the PCA, compiled a guide of "dos and don'ts" for Latin American representation that mirrored Durland's censorship. See Memorandum, "Taboos for Latin American Pictures," August 19, 1941, MPSA Collection, box 5, Margaret Herrick Library, Academy of Motion Picture Arts and Sciences, Beverly Hills, CA.

35. For more on the black image during World War II see, Thomas Cripps, *Slow Fade to Black: The Negro in American Film, 1900–1942* (New York: Oxford University Press, 1977), 349–89, and Thomas Doherty, *Projections of War: Hollywood, American Culture, and World War II* (New York: Columbia University Press, 1993), 205–26.

36. Motion Picture Notes by Joe D. Walstrom, U.S. Embassy, Buenos Aires, September 26, 1941, National Archives and Records Administration, Record Group 229, entry 1, box 214, Washington, D.C.

37. Darryl Zanuck to Breen, November 12, 1940, PCA files, *That Night in Rio* (20th-Fox, 1941).

38. Durland to Francis Harmon, Inter-Office Memo, December 10, 1941, MPPDA Collection, microfilm reel 6, Margaret Herrick Library, Academy of Motion Picture Arts and Sciences, Beverly Hills, CA (hereafter cited as MPPDA). This sort of anti-black racism on the part of Brazilian elites (and echoed by RKO and CIAA officials, co-producers of the film) later led to the shelving of Orson Welles's 1942 Pan-American docudrama *It's All True*. When it was learned that Welles was going to focus on the

history of samba and black contributions to Brazilian culture, the project was cut in mid-stride. See Robert Stam, "Orson Welles, Brazil, and the Power of Blackness," *Persistence of Vision* 7 (1989): 93–112.

39. Claude Barnett to Will Hays, December 17, 1941; Carl E. Milliken to Barnett, December 24, 1941; Barnett to Milliken, December 27, 1941; Durland to Milliken, January 5, 1942, MPPDA, microfilm reel 6.

40. (Emphasis added). Durland to Harry Cohn, November 28, 1941, PCA files, *Canal Zone* (Columbia, 1941). On this script, Durland also advised: "Re page 1, the line: 'Its inhabitants are a mixed race comprising Spaniards, Indians, Whites, and Negroes.' It was agreed that this dangerous racial description be omitted." Durland to Cohn, July 22, 1941.

41. Durland to Louis B. Mayer, July 3, 1941, PCA Files, *Panama Hattie* (MGM, 1942).

42. Zella Richardson to E. J. Mannix, January 8, 1944, PCA files, *The Gang's All Here* (20th-Fox, 1943). Although light-skinned, Carmen Miranda was clearly marked as "Latin" by mainstream U.S. audiences. It is not surprising, however, that within the highly polarized black-white dichotomy of the American South she could easily fit in among entertaining "white people."

43. Durland to R. E. Pirschel, December 11, 1941, PCA files, *Below the Border* (Great Western Productions, 1942).

44. Durland to Mayer, July 3, 1941, PCA files, *Panama Hattie* (MGM, 1942).

45. Durland to Walter Goetz, September 22, 1943, PCA files, *The Cowboy and the Senorita* (Republic, 1944).

46. Durland to Warner, April 6, 1942, PCA files, *Now, Voyager* (Warner Brothers, 1942).

47. The use of panoramic exteriors to enhance authenticity and establish setting was *de rigueur* for the industry's Good Neighbor productions, which were all filmed inside Hollywood studios.

48. Walter Wanger, President, Motion Picture Society for the Americas, to Nelson A. Rockefeller, CIAA, "Monthly Reports," July 1942 and August 1942, National Archives and Records Administration, Record Group 229, entry 78, box 961, Washington, D.C. Probably due to this ethnic shift, the Brazilian officials who screened *Now, Voyager,* Dr. Raul Bopp, Consul, and Jorge Guinle of the CIAA, both reported that the Brazilian sequence presented no objectionable material. The shooting scripts for the film are housed at the United Artists Collection, State Historical Society of Wisconsin, Series 1.2, box 290, Madison, Wisconsin.

49. (Emphasis in original.) Durland to Maurice Pivar, Universal, June 2, 1942 and July 28, 1942, PCA files, *Moonlight in Havana* (Universal, 1942). Durland passed on the Martínez character only after Universal hired Cuban actor Segio Orta for the role, thus "giving this part the proper flavor."

50. Durland to Jason Joy, May 12, 1942, PCA files, *The Ox-Bow Incident* (20th-Fox, 1943).

51. Durland to Cohn, September 18, 1941, PCA files, *Honolulu Lu* (Columbia, 1941); Durland to Mayer, February 6, 1942, PCA files, *Rio Rita* (MGM, 1942). In a

similar vein, for MGM's filmed version of John Steinbeck's *Tortilla Flat*, Durland declared that it was imperative that the "Americanism of the characters (paisanos, or native-born Latins) is established beyond doubt." Durland Memorandum, July 31, 1941, PCA files, *Tortilla Flat* (MGM, 1942).

52. Durland to Cohn, May 29, 1942, PCA files, *My Sister Eileen* (Columbia, 1942); Durland to Cohn, October 14, 1942, PCA files, *Two Señoritas From Chicago* (Columbia, 1943).

53. The eight films were: *The Girl From Mexico* (1939), *Mexican Spitfire* (1940), *Mexican Spitfire Out West* (1940), *Mexican Spitfire's Baby* (1941), *Mexican Spitfire at Sea* (1942), *Mexican Spitfire Sees a Ghost* (1942), *Mexican Spitfire's Elephant* (1942), and *Mexican Spitfire's Blessed Event* (1943). During this period, Vélez also appeared as essentially her Mexican Spitfire characterization under different guises in *Six Lessons From Madame La Zonga* (1941), *Playmates* (1941), *Honolulu Lu* (1941), *Ladies' Day* (1943), and *Redhead From Manhattan* (1943).

54. Fox featured Miranda in the following World War II musical comedies: *Down Argentine Way* (1940), *That Night in Rio* (1941), *Week-End in Havana* (1941), *Springtime in the Rockies* (1942), *The Gang's All Here* (1943), *Four Jills in a Jeep* (1944), *Greenwich Village* (1944), *Something For the Boys* (1944). For an insightful reading of Carmen Miranda's screen image see, Shari Roberts, "'The Lady in the Tutti-Frutti Hat': Carmen Miranda, a Spectacle of Ethnicity," *Cinema Journal* 32, no. 3 (spring 1993): 3–23.

55. As with Berkeley's other musicals of the 1930s–1940s, *The Gang's All Here* was conceived and executed as pure spectacle. In the film's most notorious number, "The Lady in the Tutti-Frutti Hat," Miranda is wheeled out to a staged desert island that is inhabited by a whirlwind of female dancers disguised as enormous bananas and strawberries. Miranda's participation in Berkeley's extravaganza raises the question as to what extent her representation was simply *participatory*, as opposed to *ethnic*, spectacle. Clearly, all of Berkeley's representations were spectacular. Yet, given her intertextual image as the embodiment of "Latin-ness," I would maintain that even within Berkeley's sea of seemingly generic spectacle, Miranda's representation sailed on a distinctly and identifiably ethnic craft.

17

STAR DANCES

African-American
Constructions
of Stardom,
1925–1960

Arthur Knight

Stars in de elements,
Shine, shine, shine.
Stars in de elements,
Shine, shine, shine.
Stars in de elements,
Shine, I want to shine,
To shine like a star
Dat's away in Glory;
Good Lord, let me shine.

—"Stars in de Elements" (chorus), traditional song,
   transcribed in Willis Lawrence James, *Stars in de
   Elements: A Study of Negro Folk Music* (1945)

Is not the world wide enough for two colors, for many little
shinings of the sun?

—W. E. B. Du Bois, "The Souls of White Folk" (1920)

There are NO negro motion picture stars.

—Fay Jackson, Hollywood correspondent for the Associated
   Negro Press Syndicate, in a letter to the ANP (1935)

PROLOGUE

Let two images, along with some of the questions—and problems—they raise, both hover over and serve as touchstones for this essay:

First, a still from the finale of the 1938 race film musical *The Duke Is Tops.* What relations do these performers have to stars and ideas of stardom? Are they—or which of them are—stars?

Second, a photograph taken by photographer Aaron Siskind in 1940 as part of a project documenting life in Harlem. Sometimes it goes by the title "Sleeping with White Pinups." What is this man's relation to stars, especially movie stars?

INTRODUCTION

At the core of questions about African Americans and stardom—the problems and possibilities of stars for African Americans *and* the problems and possibilities of the Black star—are more questions of audiences and institutions, entities between which stars emerge and between which they communicate.[1] Richard Dyer, who pioneered the study of film stars, argues, "Stars matter because they act out aspects of life that matter to us; and performers get to be stars when what they act out matters to enough people."[2] This elegant and concise formulation begs several more questions, all of which Dyer and others have been grappling with for the past fifteen years. First, questions of audience: Who is "us"? How many people is "enough people"? What do "enough" of "us" mean by "matter"? Second, institution questions: Who controls which "performers get to . . . act out" and "what they act out"? If Christine Gledhill is correct, as I believe she is, that cinema "provides the ultimate confirmation of stardom,"[3] then what happens when whole classes of performers are, for a variety of "reasons," effectively barred from the confirmation proceedings?

In working to answer these questions and then to apply the answers to an analysis of African-American stars and stardom, I focus on the period from the late 1920s to the early 1960s. This period is delimited by African-American migration to cities and the North, by consequent encounter (not so much new as on changed terms) with mass cultural forms, and by steadily rising African-American civil rights activism. Amiri Baraka summarizes the period as "a reinterpretation by the Negro of his role in this country."[4] In terms of "stars" and strictly in terms of Hollywood film stardom, the period starts in the late 1920s with the brief efflorescence of all-Black cast musicals and musical shorts, which gave rise to problematic "stars" like Stepin Fetchit, and comes to

Figure 17.1. *The Duke Is Tops* (1938).

its diffuse end between Dorothy Dandridge's Academy Award nomination for best actress in 1955 and Sidney Poitier's 1963 Academy Award for best actor.

Returning to questions about the audiences and institutions affecting the relations of Blacks and stars, it will pay to be, for a moment, firmly empirical and perhaps a bit pedantic. Who is "us"? Blacks, African Americans—in the period under consideration, colored people or negroes or Negroes—who were a *de jure* and *de facto* racially essentialized, segregated, and discriminated against people throughout the nation. African Americans were at the very least strongly encouraged to reside within a Black community and culture. Voluntary and welcomed passage of people between the Black and white worlds, especially in leisure time and especially if the Black people were not employees, predominantly moved one way—white into Black. This flow was more complex, but still intensely unequal, when we consider labor or products and material objects. Throughout this period, African Americans never earned even two-thirds of the average white income, and they always had a considerably higher—sometimes doubled—rate of unemployment. Blacks were, in the words of a Federal Theater Project living newspaper, "one tenth of the nation." However, as the above suggests, they were neither seen as nor permitted to be fully "of the nation."

All the conditions that these statements try to represent influenced the ways African Americans could see the stars—and the ways Hollywood saw

Figure 17.2. "Sleeping with White Pinups" by Aaron Siskind (1940).

(or did not see) African Americans. Returning to Dyer's formulation: How many of "us" is "enough people" to make a star? This question does not allow any precise numerical answer, but if *every* Black in the United States had gone to the movies once a week in 1946, Hollywood's peak year for attendance, African Americans would have accounted for 15 percent of the total film audience.[5] Assuming a strict coherence of taste and behavior among all African Americans—a deeply problematic assumption—perhaps this 15 percent would have been enough of the "us" of the total movie audience to ensure the creation of a star. Of course, facts suggest that anything approaching such a coherence would have been impossible. In 1920, despite the Great Migrations to many Northern cities, where movies were more widely available, 85 percent of Blacks still lived in the South; in 1940, 77 percent. Not until 1960 did 50 percent of African Americans live in the more movie-intensive North. Simply put, whether or not components of the Hollywood film industry knew how to, or could have learned how to, pay attention to African-American audiences, Hollywood did not think much could be gained by doing so. A white performer could "get to . . . matter . . . to enough people," and hence be a Hollywood star, without ever bringing a single Black patron into a theater. In contrast, a Black performer could never hope to be a Hollywood star without appealing to a vast, white-dominated mass audience. For most of the period focussed on by this essay, Hollywood studios remained skeptical of that possibility—though this skepticism possessed a strong tinge of the self-fulfilling prophecy about it.[6]

Despite all this, stars and the idea of stardom have mattered to at least some African Americans. But how? How have (some) African Americans developed meanings around stars? How have those meanings been used and changed? What cultural frames—from outside or adjacent to the movies and to mass, mainstream culture—might inflect these processes? Richard Dyer believes that audience members' senses of lived contradictions are central to "the star phenomenon" and that the multiple meanings of stars work to help smooth these contradictions. This explains, he believes, why "particularly intense star-audience relationships occur amongst adolescents and women" and might also account for "the absolutely central importance of stars in gay ghetto culture." Dyer continues:

> These groups all share a peculiarly intense degree of role/identity conflict and pressure, and an (albeit partial) exclusion from the dominant articulacy [sic] of, respectively, adult, male, heterosexual culture.[7]

Much of the above would seem to apply for African Americans—perhaps trebly so in the period of extreme transformation outlined above.

While my extension of Dyer helped provoke this essay, I can offer no "hard" data to suggest that African Americans experience "particularly intense star-audience relationships." Ideally, to take up the questions posed above, we would draw from (among other resources) a pool of oral history and recorded popular memory, combined with ethnographic participant observation. We do not have that (yet).[8] Instead, to uncover and analyze African-American constructions of stars and stardom, I draw from memoirs, the Black press, some fiction, and, more generally, Black expressive culture.

The evidence from this period will show that the social and economic circumstances of the Black audience for mass and popular culture, in concert with traditions of African-American culture(s),[9] require both broadening and specializing the meanings of "star" and "stardom." Black audiences' relationships with stars overlapped with (most) white audiences' relationships with stars. At the same time, however, Blacks' relationships with stars were voluntarily *and* necessarily more multivalent than and differently conceived from those of whites. More specifically, I argue that, while for Hollywood and its white audience there were no Black equivalents to Garbo or Gable or Garland, African Americans never lacked stars—defined from within a different set of values and constraints.

"SLEEPING WITH WHITE PINUPS"?

> But movie-time approaches, time to boo
> The hero's kiss, and boo the heroine
> Whose ivory and yellow it is a sin
> For his eye to eat of. The Mickey Mouse,
> However, is for everyone in the house.
>
> —Gwendolyn Brooks, from "The Sundays of Satin-Legs
>   Smith," *A Street on Bronzeville* (1944)

"Hollywood has established the dominant paradigm of mainstream cinema and stardom," claims Christine Gledhill.[10] Certainly, most of the movies that Black moviegoers saw from the 1920s to the 1960s (and still see today) were Hollywood films, and white stars filled those movies and the discourses around them. Granting Gledhill's claim, we still must ask, how dominant was dominant and in what ways could this dominance function for African-American filmgoers? What were Black movie-goers' relationships with Hollywood stars and their films, and how did these relationships affect African-American understandings of the star? What was the man in the second touchstone image, "Sleeping with White Pinups," doing?

The possibility emphasized by the sometime title of the photograph is that he was relating to Hollywood stars via identification with and desire for them—one of the scenarios of Black response to the movies and their stars noted with dismay by many African-American writers. In 1934, writing for the NAACP journal *The Crisis*, critic Loren Miller described one of his experiences at the movies:

> A few years ago I attended a showing of *Trader Horn*, a[n] [MGM] film, at a Negro theater. One scene depicts the "beautiful"—of course, blond—heroine in the clutches of "savage" Africans. In typical Hollywood thriller style the girl is saved just as all hope is ebbing away. . . . [T]he audience burst into wild applause. . . . I looked around. Those who were clapping were ordinary Negro working people and middle class folk. Hollywood's movie makers had made the theme so commonplace and glorious that it seemed quite natural white virtue should triumph over black vice. . . .[11]

Miller clearly believes his fellow Negro filmgoers are in danger of a sort of racial-cultural death at the hands of the movies and their unnamed, "'beautiful'—of course, blond"—stars.

A few years later, Richard Wright rewrote and further radicalized Miller's scene for Bigger Thomas's trip to the movies in *Native Son* (1940). Bigger sees first *The Gay Woman* (Wright's invention) and then *Trader Horn*. He believes the white stars accurately represent rich white people, and he tries to imagine himself in their world. Between these cosmopolitan and imperialist fantasies, however, he finds neither a vision of nor a tenable position of identification for himself.[12] In the unexpurgated version of the novel, Bigger masturbates before the start of the films, making his desire for the white pinup explicit. Moreover, the unexpurgated novel also carefully breaks down Bigger's mediated experience in order to extrapolate the consequences of transracial immediacy in collision with extreme racist, classist, and sexist hierarchies. Here, *The Gay Woman* is instead a newsreel about Mary Dalton, a "real" rich white person, who is a star of the social, economic, and cultural hierarchies that dominate Bigger, and consequently, an attraction at the movies.[13] Mary Dalton stands in for the unnamed, and thereby generalized, stars of *Trader Horn* (Edwina Booth, Harry Carey) and of the movies as a whole. Later, when the Dalton family employs Bigger, the "pinup" comes to life. Helping a drunken Mary to bed, Bigger becomes confused by the feelings aroused in the process. Terrified at the prospect of being discovered, Bigger kills Mary and sets in rapid motion the white state apparatus that will engulf and sentence him to death. First and implicitly subjugated by whiteness at the movies, Bigger will finally be explicitly subjugated by whiteness in the death chamber. It would be an exaggeration to say that Bigger Thomas is sentenced to death in *Native Son* because of his relation to Hollywood movies and their stars—but not much of one.

The signifying chain does not stop with Bigger. In the early 1960s, Malcolm X (with Alex Haley) rewrote Wright. Yet X's examples make the construction of racialized identity between the Hollywood screen and its (Black) viewer even more complicated by discarding the explicit, imperialist racism of *Trader Horn* and replacing it with liberal rac(ial)ism. Narrating Malcolm Little's transformation into Detroit Red of the Harlem underworld, X writes:

> I discovered the movies. Sometimes I made as many as five a day, both downtown and in Harlem. I loved the tough guys, the action, Humphrey Bogart in *Casablanca*, and I loved all that dancing and carrying on in such films as *Stormy Weather* and *Cabin in the Sky*.[14]

Without breaking for a new paragraph, Malcolm X continues and tells us, perhaps, what he now thinks of his "love":

> After leaving the movies, I'd make my connections for supplies, then roll my sticks, and, about dark, I'd start my rounds. I'd give a couple of ex-

tra sticks when someone bought ten, which was five dollars' worth. And I didn't sell and run, because my customers were my friends. Often I'd smoke along with them. None of them stayed any more high than I did.[15]

For Malcolm X, movies and their (now named) white stars were the narcotic that marked time until the other, "real" narcotic could be indulged.

Toni Morrison's historical novel *The Bluest Eye* (1970), set in the 1930s and 1940s, continues and further revises this critical strand. However, by shifting attention from the obvious (and individual) high stakes of Wright and X, Morrison moves her critique back toward Loren Miller's vision of movies and stars as *ordinarily* damaging, especially to young Black women. This theme works its way ambiguously through several female characters' relations to Shirley Temple (and Bill Robinson), *Imitation of Life*, Betty Grable, Claudette Colbert, and Hedy Lamarr before resolving in this passage:

[Pauline] was never able, after her education in the movies, to look at a face and not assign it some category in the scale of absolute beauty, and the scale was one she absorbed in full from the silver screen. . . . There the flawed became whole, the blind sighted, and the lame and halt threw away their crutches. There death was dead, and people made every gesture in a cloud of music. There the black-and-white images came together, making a magnificent whole—all projected through the ray of light from above and behind.

It was really a simple pleasure, but she learned all there was to love and all there was to hate.[16]

What Pauline learns from trying and failing to be Jean Harlow is that her romance is inadequate and, perhaps more damning, that she and her child are ugly. *"Everything went then,"* Pauline says. *"Look like I just didn't care no more after that."* [17]

Of course, African Americans did not experience Hollywood film only in the ways Pauline, Detroit Red, Bigger Thomas, or Miller's "ordinary Negro working people and middle class folk" did. With their decisions to leave (mostly) unnamed the Black "stars" of the movies they cite, X and Morrison point toward other possibilities not characterized wholly by domination. Considerable evidence—much of it in the form of disapproving reports from Black newspapers—suggests that African-American audiences were distracted rather than absorbed viewers. Moreover, inasmuch as this distraction was frequently characterized by critics as inappropriate laughter and commentary, it could be taken as critical.[18] Some Black writers, starting (I believe) with Ralph Ellison in the late 1940s and running through James Baldwin to bell hooks, have come to see Black audience distraction positively as, in Ellison's words, "an antidote to . . . sentimentality." "[W]hen the action goes phoney," he writes, "one will hear derisive laughter, not sobs." [19] Under such circumstances, stars would seem to cease to work.

Or do they? After all, Ellison, Baldwin, and hooks are, whether critically distracted or fully absorbed, still in the cinema. In Baldwin's famous phrase, they paid "the price of the ticket," which is Hollywood's key measure of the star's attraction. They all recognize this, yet all three cultivate a position of critical, potentially optimistic, ambivalence. With work, they suggest, stars and movies can be made to work—at least sometimes—differently.

Ellison's Invisible Man begins his famous story by disavowing the movies. These are his first two sentences: "I am an invisible man. No, I am not a spook like those who haunted Edgar Allan Poe; nor am I one of your Hollywood-movie ectoplasms." [20] Later in the novel, alone and lonely in Harlem, the southern Invisible Man goes to a western and, like Bigger Thomas, "forgets" himself, though at the same time he recognizes that "there was no one like me taking part in the adventures." [21] Still later, cold, homeless, and homesick, but diverted from another trip to the movies (where he planned to sleep), Invisible Man encounters the eviction of an elderly couple and inventories what he sees. Along with minstrel bones and freedman's papers, cracked china and houseplants, he finds "a whisky bottle filled with rock candy and camphor, a small Ethiopian flag, a faded tintype of Abraham Lincoln, and the smiling im- age of a Hollywood star torn from a magazine"—and this experience politi- cizes him. [22] Nearing the novel's climax, eulogizing a fallen comrade, Invisible Man repudiates his politics and turns the movies into a nihilistic whip, not separate in any way from visions of a "purer" Black culture:

> Aren't you tired of such stories [i.e., the eulogy]? Aren't you sick of the blood? Then why listen, why don't you go? It's hot out here. There's the odor of embalming fluid. The beer is cold in the taverns, the saxophones will be mellow at the Savoy; plenty good-laughing-lies will be told in the barber shops and beauty parlors; and there'll be sermons in two hun- dred churches in the cool of the evening, and plenty of laughs at the movies. [23]

At the novel's climax, however, set in the Harlem riots of 1935, Invisible Man is "moving past a movie house when they [his political enemies] grabbed me and started punching. But this time they'd picked the wrong spot, and the movie doorman intervened." [24] For Ellison and his Invisible Man, movies and their stars can be dangerous, but even the most "country" of Black people can reflect on, deflect, critique, enjoy, and be goaded into action by this "danger."

Baldwin and hooks are less sanguine than Ellison in their critical ambivalence. More clearly critical and less ambivalent, they see less of fate and irony in the movies and their stars and demand more individual spectatorial agency. hooks argues that (at least some) Black (usually male) viewers paid the price of the ticket to the movies and stayed, believing that merely to look too long and hard at whites was an act of resistance—even if it was mediated and displaced (and, therefore, safe). She also suggests that, especially in the segregated South, African-American viewers learned things about both white behaviors and the Black image in the white mind through the safe media of movies and television.[25]

Other Black viewers, according to hooks, go farther. They resist but also "contest, . . . revise, interrogate, and invent" as they view.[26] For hooks, these viewers are mostly contemporary women. James Baldwin stands as an example of an earlier, gay male interrogative-revisionist consumer of the movies, and especially of their stars. Baldwin's *The Devil Finds Work*, a critical memoir of his moviegoing, places the author in the position of Bigger Thomas (although Baldwin is even younger when the book begins) and shows how it is possible *not* to become Bigger. Although Baldwin certainly recognized the horrors of Hollywood, he also believed, especially when he was young, that Hollywood stars helped him see the structured inequities of race and gender. For instance, the movies gave him the ability to see that there was a "star" in his neighborhood, "a colored woman, who, to me, looked exactly like Joan Crawford." As Baldwin describes her, "[s]he seemed to be wearing the sunlight, rearranging it around her from time to time" and "was so incredibly beautiful . . . that, when she . . . started out of the store, I started out behind her." This woman was not a Hollywood star, but for his misrecognition— which Baldwin came to see was a *recognition* of beauty—young James received "so beautiful a smile that I was not even embarrassed. Which was rare for me."[27]

Perhaps more important than finding his local Joan, Baldwin found Bette Davis, who had "*my* frog eyes" and was, he thought, as "ugly" as he was and who, despite being a movie star—i.e., white and rich—"moved just like a nigger." Baldwin writes, "My first conscious calculation as to how to go about defeating the world's intentions for me and mine began that Saturday afternoon in what we called *the movies,* but which was actually my first entrance into the cinema of my mind."[28] Joan Crawford showed him beauty and its racialized unfairnesses. When he spotted his local Joan, Baldwin saw that beauty was not only white, and he also understood that few white people would ever acknowledge that. In Bette Davis, Baldwin recognized black-in-white and saw the structures meant to keep such a cultural combination unseen, unbelievable. With this critical vision, Baldwin realized that his "in-firmities"—his Blackness and ugliness—"might be forged into weapons."[29] Clearly, Hollywood stars could have their uses.

So, can we be sure that the man "sleeping with white pinups" is more like Bigger Thomas than James Baldwin? We cannot know. The picture will not tell. Looked at carefully, however, it begins to yield various possibilities, or at least more questions than a quick glance might spur. The man sleeps with his back to the pinups. Is he refusing them? They are arrayed around his dressing table mirror. Do they provide him models for his self image(s) and ideals of de-sire? Or do they serve to remind him of the dominance of white supremacy, to remind him not to feel too safe even in his "own" room? What difference does the not-exactly-white Dolores del Río up on the left make? And is that Lena Horne at the far right on the back wall? If we discovered that this man never went to the movies but, rather, in his job as a janitor of this Harlem building, that he scavenged these pictures, how might our sense of him—or of the cir-culation of white stars in Black locales—change? The picture will not answer, but I hope I have convinced you that any answers to such questions must be complex—at least as complex as Gwendolyn Brooks's Satin-Legs Smith "boo-ing" and "sinning" simultaneously.

BLACK STARS: CROSSING OVER, CROSSING BACK, AND MASS MEDIATION

> People like [Black singer and dancer] Florence Mills make this world a better place to live in. She did a helluva lot to wipe out race prejudice. If all they say about the Hereafter is true, then the Heavenly Gates must a swung ajar for Florence Mills to enter an Shine in Heaven, cause she sure did shine down here. That was some year and month of disappointments in Harlem, November 1927. The Republicans swept Harlem, Marcus Garvey was bein deported an our Queen a Happiness died.
>
> —"Harlem Show Girl" to Federal Writers Project interviewer, Vivian Morris (1939)

Consider the word "star" in a few African-American contexts. Frederick Doug-lass entitled his foundational Black periodical the *North Star* (started in 1847), referring, of course, to the beacon of freedom for slaves. W. E. B. Du Bois's uplift pageant was "The Star of Ethiopia" (1913, performed at least into the 1920s). Marcus Garvey's shipping line was the Black Star (1920). Figural uses of the star also abound in African-American cultural practices. Stars proliferate on Harriet Powers's famed Bible Quilts made in the late 1800s and on memorial quilts, like Alice Neal's "Mary Bright Memorial Quilt" made in 1956. They feature in church names and church signs (e.g., Morning Star Baptist Church) and the names and symbols of secular institutions (e.g., the Detroit Stars Negro League baseball team [1919–1933]) and secret societies like the Eastern Star order. Stars adorn many sorts of African-American costumes, ranging from the occasional and nonprofessional (outfits for Mardi Gras, in which one of the Black lodges is the Golden Star Hunters, and for carnival-goers, civil rights marchers, and Emancipation Day celebrators) to the formalized and professional (the star headdresses worn by the likes of Bessie Smith and Florence Mills and the sheriff-like stars favored by bluesmen). From at least the early twentieth century, the star figured in advertisements meant to sell commodities—often themselves emblazoned with stars—to African-American consumers. Lithographs and printed pillow tops honoring W. E. B. Du Bois, Booker T. Washington, and Frederick Douglass, among others, are advertised with the headline "our Beacon Lights," and the illustration—an example of the product—shows small oval portraits of the luminaries guarded by a Black angel and lit from above by a radiant star. Similarly, no matter which corporation manufactured them, race records frequently used figures of stars—often as frames for photographs of the recording stars, who themselves might be wearing stars—in their ads and on their record sleeves.[30]

This list could be expanded many fold, but the main point would not change: in African-American culture(s) the star is, historically, a dense, syncretic bundle of concepts, figurations, and processes. Alone this does not distinguish the ubiquity of the star in Afro-America from its frequent use in mainstream America; after all, Garvey's Black Star line was signifying on the White Star line of *Titanic* fame. However, the possibility and logic of such a revision—that the Black Star was conceived as a mode of connection for a diasporic community, while the White Star was a luxury—points toward the common foundation shared by disparate African-American notions of the star. This foundation—in cycles of turn and re-turn, in circles of culture and community, in principles of shared vision and guidance—inflects, for many African Americans, the possibilities, meanings, and expectations of Black movie stars. A good metaphor for this common foundation is a West African–derived African-American dance form sometimes called the "star dance."

The star dance described the dances performed by individuals inside the dancing circles of the ring shouts of slave culture(s). A break dancing circle represents a contemporary urban extension of the star dance, although similar circles can be seen in photographs of the Big Apple, Lindy hop, and jitterbug from the 1920s through the 1940s. In all these dances, performers emerge—or break—into the center of the circle, perform their "star" turn, and then return to the circle to support the next star. Star dancing seems to have had two key qualities: it provided a secular(izing) extension and elaboration of the ring shout's ritual, religious form, and it existed as a structure, a relation of individual and group, rather than as a content or a specific series of moves with a fixed meaning. More accurately, star dancing structure was its content, and in that content—the relation of "star" and group—the dance reinforced and represented, but also modified, other African-American cultural patterns of religion and community, e.g., call and response.[31]

In the dominant paradigm of mainstream stardom, a star is to ascend, never to return. In Richard Dyer's phrase, the performer becomes a star by becoming a "star text," a "person" available wholly through mediated forms. The meaning of the star depends on a distance and a hierarchy that is held so constant as to become familiar, a distance that is far enough to create the illusion of uniqueness, if not perfection. This view of the star requires a tremendous institutional structure—like Hollywood—that does not challenge the fundamental precepts of dominant society. Maintaining the simultaneous presence and absence of the Hollywood star requires extraordinary economic resources, which the "star text" cannot avoid representing.

In African-American culture(s), as the star dance suggests, a star can emerge (from) within a community, perform a turn, and then return, at which time a new star, called by and responding to the previous star, takes a turn. The turn is simultaneously a horizontal trip into the center of the circle of culture and community *and,* in terms of the quality and merit of the individual's performance, a break, an ascension. As a consequence, the individual turn is both profoundly different from and potentially cognate with the mainstream model of stardom. The star dance is an African-American form that asserts a Black community identity and, at the same time, opens an important space for Black assimilation and white acceptance.

Here resides the primary productive tension—the "matter" or meaning—of the Black star and Black stardom for African-American audiences. Will (or should) the Black star remain within the circle? Will (or should) the star continue to ascend completely out of the circle and into mainstream stardom? Or, more likely given white prejudice, will such an ascent end up stuck somewhere between realms, a star in neither sphere?

As early as 1857, slave narrative hints at the complex position and meaning of the Black star as confluence of Black and white values and of (potential)

Black assimilation and (potential) white acceptance. According to Austin Steward's account:

> House servants were . . . "the stars" of the [slave quarter] party: all eyes turned to them to see how they conducted [themselves]. . . . The field hands . . . look to the house servants as a pattern of politeness and gentility. And indeed, it [their dance] is often the only method of obtaining any knowledge of the manners of what is called "genteel society. . . ." [32]

In this account, the house slaves—placed higher in the plantation hierarchy by the master, making them the very vulnerable beneficiaries of subclass and caste—"star" at the slave party, which would have almost certainly included a star dance. They bring, in dance historian Katrina Hazzard-Donald's estimation, European dance forms into the circle,[33] and in doing so, they bring new knowledge, reveal expanded horizons of opportunity, and raise questions of status of all kinds (e.g., house v field, servant v hand v slave). These questions in turn require relativizing quotation marks around terms of value like "star" and "genteel society." Other analysts have shown how African-American models of star dancing intersected with and influenced white plantation culture.[34] Such intersections, however, almost always took place at the location of the individual performer, *the* star, rather than at the group or circle and its relations with its stars. Whites might imitate individual African-American performers or pluck individual performers from the collective for display, but they apparently never imitated the circle or chose to promote *it* for display. Because the star dance neither reinforced nor represented the rising values of modern American capitalism, its structure and the values it embodied were opaque—interesting and exotic, but also primitive, weird, savage, and, especially in their collective aspect, dangerous—to white audiences.[35]

By the period this essay examines, the problem of the Black star (and his or her Black audience) would be distilled in the manner described by Ralph Matthews, theatrical editor of the *Baltimore Afro-American*:

> The big names among Negro performers are only those who have appealed to the whimsicalities of the white race and conformed to their idea of what a Negro should be.
>
> Those who have confined their activities exclusively to what we might term the Negro theatre, have either vanished completely from the arena or are wallowing in mediocracy [sic]. The American black man honors only those whom the gods have chosen.
>
> [T]he hothouse of Negro theatricals, . . . in the path of the vitaphone, the radio and other mechanized forms of entertainment, . . . has almost

moldered into decay with a few outposts still remaining. Harlem is now the mecca of the Negro theatre and Broadway is the goal. This means assimilation.[36]

Matthews seems to want to believe that this Black assimilation—with the performers apparently only following their Black audience—will be met with an equal measure of white acceptance. Given the obvious imbalances of social, economic, and cultural power in the "mechanized" U.S. entertainment industry, he cannot be optimistic. Emphasizing his point, Matthews does not name a single, contemporary "big name . . . Negro performer."

In the same 1934 volume in which Matthews's critical essay appears, Floyd Snelson of the *Pittsburgh Courier* provides an implicit counterpoint in "Some Notes on the Musical and Theatrical Negro Stars of America," a list of forty-seven performers or performing ensembles.[37] Snelson lists the "big names," Paul Robeson and Stepin Fetchit, for example, who fit Matthews's point about white approbation. However, his list also incorporates many performers whose exposure to and success with white audiences was much more limited. Snelson's inventory also suggests that Matthews's point could be given another valence.

Within the star dance model of stardom, with luck, grace, and skill, each star may travel/rise again. The stars do not (just) "vanish" or "wallow in mediocrity"; rather, they take turns at starring. Moreover, the community circle has words, such as "crossing over" or "getting over," to name the phenomenon of the star who rises out of the circle.[38] I argue below that African-American audiences view this phenomenon as disappointing only *if* the star refuses to travel back. Black audiences certainly saw, understood, and partook of the Hollywood stars and Hollywood's model for stardom. However, in the many variations and extensions of the star dance that resonated through African-American culture(s), they also had an alternative model for stardom, which was an implicit, and occasionally an explicit, critique of the mainstream Hollywood model of stardom and the structures that support it.[39]

The industrialization, mechanization, and mediation upon which Hollywood and its star system were built made (and make) more difficult the crossover star's trip back to the circle. Certainly, such mechanisms could not incorporate patterns of star turn-taking, and the rationalized Hollywood system had no incentive and no stake in representing or creating community circles. Nonetheless, in this period of swift and vast change for so many, African Americans did not abandon the movies. Rather, many worked to make and control a place for Black cultural practices *in,* instead of just at, the movies.

One mechanism for doing this, beginning as early as the 1910s, was making race films and race film "stars," thereby trying to translate directly into the industrialized mechanisms of filmmaking something like the community circle of the star dance. Here, from 1924, as the first wave of race filmmaking had crested and was falling, is a Black occasional critic, Billy Booster, proposing to stem the tide: "[I]f [race film] producers would get recognized stars to star in their pictures, I think their pictures would draw; and if they draw, it is a cinch that the managers of the Colored theaters will book them." [40] Who were these "recognized stars"? Booster mentions Charles Gilpin (the first Emperor Jones), Flournoy Miller and Aubrey Lyles (of the Harlem-to-Broadway musical hit, *Shuffle Along*), Harry Fiddler, Sam Langford, Evelyn Preer, and S. H. Dudley—all performers who were familiar primarily to African-American audiences. These, Booster claims, are the stars who could draw Black audiences to race films. Building from this, he goes on to make two interrelated assertions about the possibilities of race film and race film stardom:

> Each of these stars, surrounded properly, would make other stars, for each picture would show someone who possessed personality and ability and who soon could be starred. . . . What we really need is stars to star the picture, and not pictures to star the stars, as the day is gone when people will pay to see a Colored picture simply because it is a Colored picture. [41]

Booster calls for race film to draw on the traditional forms of the star dance—the arts of live performance—*and* to adopt the semi-assimilated standards he deems necessary to an era of community-verging-on-mass rather than folk (re)production. All of this, however, was to be done for the purpose of extending a renewed star dance into film.

Perhaps the race film producer that came closest to Booster's goal was Million Dollar Productions, which in the late 1930s released a series of films, including *The Duke Is Tops* (1938), the film that provides my first touchstone image. This and three other Million Dollar films starred *not* Lena Horne, who is in the center of the starring row shown in Figure 17.1 and was appearing in her first film, but Ralph Cooper, who is to the left of Horne in the compositional center of the still.

Cooper's race film stardom was built on a long career as a dancer, bandleader, and host of the amateur night at Harlem's Apollo Theater, which was also broadcast on the radio. [42] He was precisely the kind of Black star Billy Booster had had in mind. Indeed, Cooper's Black stardom was enough to support a steady stream of Black press publicity before it worked to drive his six films (one before and one after his Million Dollar series) and to give rise to at least one fan club. However, Cooper's stardom was also short lived, contradictory, and frustrating. He made his way into race films only after being called and rebuffed by Hollywood, and like the studios (and virtually all the sound-era independents), Million Dollar was a white-owned, -financed, and -run company. Nevertheless, and in spite of its auspicious name, Million Dollar could not penetrate the tight oligopoly of the American movie business, and Cooper's film career was over in three years.

In the light of these circumstances, Cooper's starring roles become especially telling. In three of his films—*Dark Manhattan* (Renaldo Films 1937), *Bargain With Bullets* (Million Dollar 1937), and *Gang War* (Million Dollar 1939)—he plays a gangster, akin to Scarface and Little Caesar, whose criminal path to individual success ends in death. The fact that everyone in the world of Cooper's gangsters is Black, including the police, is at once absorbing and ironic. The all-Black world exists in these films as a sort of utopia—a white-free zone—where African Americans easily occupy every conceivable social position. This utopia, however, makes the gangster's criminality seem purely pernicious (his crimes are always, necessarily Black on Black) and unfathomable. A second irony comes from the recognition that the real, racist world, which (over)determines the conditions of film production, is so constraining that not even a glimmer of white can be permitted in a "race" film's world because such a glimmer might make the gangster's behavior all too understandable. Cooper's last film, *Am I Guilty?* (Supreme Pictures, 1940), turns this circumstance on its head by making the actor an idealistic doctor who is "bought" by a charitable donation given by some gangsters, forced to aid them, and then nearly convicted as one of them. Though *Am I Guilty?* also uses an all-Black milieu, it at least hints at the material and economic complexities that partially determine how people behave.

The Duke Is Tops, however, is Cooper's most interesting film for pondering his stardom, and Black stardom more generally. It features Cooper as a bandleader and producer, a role built directly on his career before film, and tells a backstage story that reflects directly on issues of success and stardom. *The Duke Is Tops* starts with the failure of Duke's latest touring show and the simultaneous "discovery" by big city agents of the talents of his fiancée, Ethel (Lena Horne). Duke forces Ethel to take the opportunity. She goes to the city, and Duke joins an old friend, Dr. Durando (Lawrence Criner), on the medicine show circuit. The trade press and radio broadcasts alert Duke that Ethel is not sparking in the city, so Duke and his medicine show track her down and join her show; together, they have a huge hit. As with the other Cooper films, *The Duke Is Tops* depicts an all-Black world, but here its implications—in keeping with the musical genre—are more clearly utopian. In *The Duke Is Tops*, individual but lawful initiative of Black individuals in concert with Black audiences makes Black stars, but only when the individuals have a group with and against which to perform and from which other stars may emerge. *And* these audiences and their stars possess a web of mass communications media, periodicals, and radio that extends and maintains their shared connective circle(s).

The Duke Is Tops labors to instantiate this network—this Black mass media circle—by representing it in the story and by being its vehicle in the real world of mass media in the late 1930s. However, the film's project is tremendously fragile, if not utterly contradictory. The delicate nature of the mass mediation of the circle is made clearest by the fact that none of the big production numbers has a diegetic audience. Duke's medicine show has a participatory Black audience. However, because the audience for the big show must be not only the stand-in for the film's audience, but also one that, in the star-making rhetoric of the film, must transcend—be bigger and therefore more multiracial than—the film audience, the finale's audience is unrepresentable, and so a gap opens in the utopian circle. Ralph Cooper fell out of public sight through that gap between Black and white, while Lena Horne would travel and rise—in a qualified way—through it.

The other, and ultimately more favored mechanism, for making a Black space in the movies was to work through Hollywood; to place a performer inside the Hollywood mechanism and, then, drawing on previous Black star quality (when it existed), to open and expand the circle to create (or keep) the performer before the Black audience as a Black star, overlaid now with his or her position as a Hollywood performer. Initially, many Black critics found this mechanism offensive. In 1934, Fay Jackson inveighed against this when she wrote to the American Negro Press (ANP) that "There are NO negro motion picture stars." [43] Loren Miller was more vitriolic:

> What space [in the Black press] . . . not given over to the publicity men is reserved for pumping some Negro bit actor up to the dimensions of a star! One not acquainted with American life and reading only a Negro newspaper theatrical page could believe easily enough that some 45-second Negro bit player, depicting a servant, was the star of the film being reviewed! [This] . . . is the abjectness of a beggar fawning over a penny tossed him by his lord. It is an acceptance of our "place." [44]

Yet, here is I. Roland, secretary of the ANP (whose boss, Claude Barnett, claimed to agree with Jackson and Miller), writing to Warner Bros. two years later:

> One [promotional] picture of *The Singing Kid* [an Al Jolson film that was advertised as a Cab Calloway film in many Black neighborhoods] shows four girls dancing on the steps. The other shows chorus girls

dancing in the foreground and Cab Calloway and his orchestra in the background. . . .

Would it be possible for you to send us the names of the persons in these pictures, reading from left to right?[45]

The response from the New York publicity office of Warner Bros. makes clear how patently absurd this request was in Hollywood terms: "We are unable to supply the names of the dancing girls because the names of incidental members of a cast are never kept on record."[46]

To treat non-stars as stars is ridiculous. But the counterargument is that these dancers and Calloway orchestra members *are* (or may become) stars in a different, Black universe—and to be a star there, one must be connected, known, named.[47]

What concerned critics like Jackson and Miller, however, was not unnamed chorines but, rather, the regular Hollywood Black supernumeraries of the 1930s and 1940s. From a Black critical perspective, the problem, which came to crisis in the mid-1930s and early 1940s around figures like Louise Beavers and Stepin Fetchit and gained focus with Hattie McDaniel's Oscar for *Gone With the Wind*, was this: the Hollywood Black supernumeraries were stable enough onscreen figures that they verged on being minor Hollywood stars—certainly regular, recognizable, credit line-worthy character actors.[48] The Hollywood Blacks, however, were not moving. They were neither true "motion picture stars" nor, more importantly, circulating Black stars who kept in touch with their Black audience through live performance and touring.[49] They had not quite crossed over—passed into white culture—*and* they would not come back, and this made an increasing number of Black viewers feel vulnerable. Roles that, ten years earlier, had seemed like opportunities and then types and then stereotypes were now becoming laminated to a limited number of ossified Black performers.

Lena Horne's NAACP-supported move into an MGM contract and the NAACP's other interventions in Hollywood were meant to change this situation.[50] To a certain extent, they did: Lena Horne never played a maid and she never had to clown, but she also never played a dramatic, nonmusical role, and most often she played "herself," a singer. This type-casting frustrated some Black critics, and it certainly frustrated—enraged, even—Horne. However, it also ensured her Black stardom.

The racist obstruction of Horne's career as a movie star, combined with her ambitions and politics, caused her to continue her career as a musician and touring live performer, which, in turn, caused her to continue to have, and further develop, direct, interactive contact with Black (as well, of course, as white) audiences. Paradoxically, the isolated quality of most of Horne's film appearances, the very quality that forced her departure(s) from Hollywood, also supported her as a Black star. Her structurally isolated numbers signaled Hollywood's racism, and, as a consequence, served as prompts to Black solidarity, expressed via the Black press, which never missed an opportunity to report the excision of Horne's numbers by Southern censors.[51] At the same time, through their isolation, Horne's numbers permitted her to avoid a different level of racism—namely, the entrapment in confined roles and the conventional narratives that "explain" such roles. Such entrapments worked against the Hollywood Blacks but also against a more activist figure like Paul Robeson.[52] By allowing (or demanding) from interested viewers a degree of spectator participation that a larger "role" would not permit, Horne's isolated numbers also allowed an oddly, complexly pleasurable sign of, response to, and prompt to resistance of racism. If a fan wanted Horne's "character's" story, she or he had to make it up, or go looking for it in the other components of her "star text," because, unlike with the stories of white stars, such a story was not even vestigially present in most of her films. If a fan went looking, or likely even thought for long about Horne's story, she or he quickly came up against problems of racism and cultural difference in the United States— problems that were not at all "the larger than life" stuff of mainstream stars.

Significantly, many of the Black periodicals that contributed to Horne's star text also worked to ensure that the role of "singer" remained the dominant component of her stardom. In January 1943, after she had signed a contract with MGM and completed one Hollywood film and just as *Cabin in the Sky* was about to start production, she appeared for a second time on the cover of *The Crisis,* identified as "Songstress Lena Horne"—hardly a variation from her first cover (in February 1941) as "Lena Horne: Featured Vocalist with Charlie Barnet Band." In late 1945 and early 1946, when a photo service ran an ad for pinups of Horne in *The Crisis,* she continued to be labeled a singer, not a movie actress or a star.[53] Why? Of course, Lena Horne *was* (and is) a singer, and that is what permitted her to "cross over" into the Hollywood machine *and* come back to the circle, to approach Hollywood stardom *and* be a Black star.

Remaining a singer, a principally live, nonnarrative, nonnarrativized performer, allowed Horne to maintain continuity with the other Black stars— athletes, musicians, dancers, and theater performers—that *The Crisis* favored for its covers.[54] Unlike the Black Hollywood players who so frustrated the NAACP, Black critics, and increasing numbers of ordinary Black viewers around 1940, these Black stars remained collaboratively connected with their audience(s). They lived and worked directly under the racist conditions their audiences also experienced. Moreover, their performances illuminated those conditions—often intentionally, as when Horne protested Jim Crow seating arrangements during USO tours, and sometimes not, as when any number of performers dealt with racist heckling, harassment, or even physical assault. Black performers of all sorts, including performers in the movies, embodied Black aspiration, ability, and freedom. However, when they *traveled* the country and world pursuing their livelihoods—as the dancers in the star dance were said to "travel" the circle—Black stars also embodied African-American social and cultural history, connectedness, courage, and the expressive freedom possible within the racialized limits of sociopolitical freedom in the United States.

In her analysis of Black women in Hollywood, Karen Alexander argues that Lena Horne "fell back on singing and personal appearances to sustain her public persona." [55] I maintain that "falling back" does not capture what a performer, like Horne, working through ideas of Black stardom in the period examined, could—and, perhaps, still can—do with such a return. No doubt Hollywood used and abused Black stars like Horne, Louis Armstrong, Duke Ellington, and many others. We should not underplay African-American performers' (or audience's) frustrations with Hollywood and the limits imposed on Black movie "stars" by Hollywood. Neither should we romanticize the rigors of traveling the circle—touring—in an era of increasingly commodified expressive culture, when performers must always both collaborate and compete with circulating, recorded versions of their own and others' performances. Nor, given this, should we minimize the practical appeal a relatively stable movie career must have offered Black movie "stars" from Hattie McDaniel and Stepin Fetchit to Dorothy Dandridge and Sidney Poitier (and to Whitney Houston and Denzel Washington). [56]

Nonetheless, there were Black stars without—or beyond—the movies. These performers were used by Hollywood, but they also used Hollywood for money, advertising, "confirmation" of an aspect of their stardom, and as an adjunct to and respite from travel. Then they left, illuminating with their motion the limitations (some of the poverty) of Classical Hollywood stardom, and the possibilities (and some of the riches) of Black stardom.

CODA

This essay originated in a single image (attached to—but in advance of—a sound):

Figure 17.3. William "Bootsy" Collins.

The person in this picture is William "Bootsy" Collins, bass player extraordinaire and, quite clearly, a star. Right?

As I hope the foregoing has made clear, my question is not—cannot be—a rhetorical one. Its answer is not easy, being both obvious and obscure. What is obvious is that in a nearly literal, almost embodied way, Bootsy *is* a star. What is obscure is the status or function of the assertion Bootsy's costume—his mise-en-scène, really—seems to make. Despite a long (and continuing), productive, influential, and, in some sense, "high profile" career of performing and recording music, Bootsy is known to comparatively few people. That few have ever seen or heard of Bootsy makes his star(dom) seem suspect—ironic, campy, pathetic, egotistical, or inaccurate. More important, though, is that most of those who know of Bootsy probably first encountered him in this guise and would not recognize him out of it. Hence, those people were not given a choice of whether or not to consider him a star. Whereas we (are supposed to) believe stardom is a rigorous, but also mysterious and "natural," almost Darwinian, process, Bootsy allows no such neat fiction(s). But is this wonderfully silly costume really so meaningful?

One of the things we check when we search for meaning is consistency (a mark of individual and cultural "intention"), and Bootsy's costume is certainly consistent with African-American performers' use of the star, and it is also consistent with itself.[57] It is also the costume he continues to wear; you can check for yourself at your local record store or on the World Wide Web. Bootsy is still a star.

What does Bootsy's consistent choice of costume mean, then? Because it is both constant *and* excessive, I think it means: Have serious fun. I'm getting paid—and I should, because you are getting your money's worth! I *am* a star—get used to it—and enjoy it—or ignore it, if you can. And, finally: I *am* emphatically here, and I belong here, but I am not from here. I am an alien in this land—at least as "this land," where to be a "true" star I cannot be a Black star, is currently constituted. What are you going to do about it?

While I was making a slide of Bootsy for the presentation of this essay, David Knight (no relation), who works at my local record store and was kind enough to let me manipulate his stock, asked what I was doing. After I explained, he said, "Well, Bootsy's definitely a star." Then, after a moment's reflection, he said, "Bootsy was a star *before* he was a star." Exactly. And it is a terrible shame—though it also does not matter much for Bootsy's variety of stardom—that he will probably never make it in the movies.

NOTES

Thanks to my cousin David LaRussa, who gave me *Stretchin' Out with Bootsy's Rubber Band* in 1977, which led down a long road to this essay; Grey Gundaker, without whose inspiration, ideas, and aid, this paper simply would not have happened; Mark Tucker and Kimberly Phillips, who provided stimulating conversation and useful information during the revision process; audiences at the 1996 Society for Cinema Studies Conference and at the American Studies Brown Bag Seminar and the English Club Lecture Series, both at The College of William & Mary, who listened patiently and gave me valuable comments; and Martha Howard, David Thompson, Pam Robertson, and Rick Wojcik, who read drafts, gave great advice, and, along with other friends too numerous to list here, provided much needed moral support. Even with all this help, "Star Dances" is entirely my fault.

1. I mean "communicate" at a literal level. Researching British female audiences of the 1940s and 1950s, Jackie Stacey found that in 1940, more than 40 percent of the letters to the editor of *Picturegoer*, a British fan magazine, concerned stars. *Stargazing: Hollywood Cinema and Female Spectatorship* (New York: Routledge, 1994), 54. The image (visual or verbal) of a star inundated with fan mail is also a common and compelling one, supporting the anecdotal sense that audiences communicated *to* film studios *about* and *through* stars. For more on this aspect of Hollywood stardom, see volumes 2, 3, and 5 of *The History of American Cinema*, ed. Charles Harpole (Berkeley: University of California Press), and John Belton, *American Cinema/American Culture* (New York: McGraw-Hill, 1994), 83–114.

2. Richard Dyer, *Heavenly Bodies: Film Stars and Society* (New York: St Martin's Press, 1986), 19.

3. Christine Gledhill, "Introduction," in *Stardom: Industry of Desire*, ed. Christine Gledhill (New York; Routledge, 1991), xiii.

4. LeRoi Jones (Amiri Baraka), *Blues People: Negro Music in White America* (New York: Morrow Quill, 1963), 96.

5. Denzel Washington applies a similar version of this logic to evaluating his own tenuous, contemporary Hollywood stardom in Lloyd Grove, "A League of His Own," *Vanity Fair*, October 1995, 242–47.

6. We have no way of knowing, definitively, African-American (or any) patterns of moviegoing from this period. The only data I have found are specific to Chicago high school students (a sample of 1,687: 335 white boys, 366 white girls, 405 Black boys, 581 Black girls) in 1941. "Two-thirds of the white and nearly three-fourths of the Negro pupils stated that they attended movies at least once a week. Furthermore, thirty-three per cent of the Negro and twenty-nine per cent of the white pupils indicated that they patronized the movies twice a week; and twelve per cent of the Negro and three per cent of the white pupils divulged an average movie attendance of three times each week." Paul Witty, Sol Garfield, and William Brink, "Interests of High-School Students in Motion Pictures and the Radio," *Journal of Educational Psychology* 32, no. 3 (March 1941): 179–80.

7. Richard Dyer, *Stars* (London: British Film Institute, 1979), 37.

8. See Dyer, *Heavenly Bodies*, and Stacey, *Stargazing*. For a critique of Dyer, see Janet Staiger, *Interpreting Films: Studies in the Historical Reception of American Cinema* (Princeton, NJ: Princeton University Press, 1992), 154–77. For another model of *historical* reception studies, see Miriam Hansen, *Babel and Babylon: Spectatorship in American Silent Film* (Cambridge: Harvard University Press, 1991). There have been many other studies of reception in the last ten years (many analyzing television rather than film), but most of these concentrate on the present. I am aware of only two studies—one historical, one contemporary—that specifically take up African-American reception: Mary Carbine, "'The Finest Outside the Loop': Motion Picture Exhibition in Chicago's Black Metropolis, 1905–1928," *Camera Obscura* 23 (May 1990): 9–42, and Jacqueline Bobo, *Black Women as Cultural Readers* (New York: Columbia University Press, 1995).

9. I use this convention to suggest that Black culture in America is an identifiable set of traditions and practices while being, at the same time, resolutely multiple and fluid.

10. Gledhill, "Introduction," *Stardom*, xiii.

11. Loren Miller, "Uncle Tom in Hollywood," *The Crisis* 41, no. 11 (November 1934): 329.

12. Richard Wright, *Native Son* (New York: Perennial, 1989 [1940]), 32–37.

13. Wright made the changes in *Native Son* at the behest of the editors of the Book of the Month Club. Wright's unexpurgated final draft of the novel is published (along with correspondence relating to the changes he made for the BOMC) in Richard Wright, *Early Works* (New York: Library of America, 1991). Some of my insights into this passage from Wright were inspired by Christopher Looby, "Bigger Thomas at the Movies" (unpublished manuscript).

14. Malcolm X and Alex Haley, *The Autobiography of Malcolm X* (New York: Ballantine, 1992 [1965]), 99. The movies make another, and earlier, appearance in *The Autobiography*, when X narrates his mortification at watching Butterfly McQueen in *Gone With the Wind* (32).

15. Ibid., 99.

16. Toni Morrison, *The Bluest Eye* (New York: Washington Square Press, 1970), 19–20, 57–58, 97.

17. Ibid., 98–100.

18. Mary Carbine makes this argument for Black Chicago audiences during the silent era in "'The Finest Outside the Loop,'" and two important Harlem Renaissance authors—Wallace Thurman in "Cordelia the Crude," *Fire!!* 1 no. 1 (1926): 5–6 and Claude McKay, *Home to Harlem* (Boston: Northeastern University Press, 1987 [1928]), 314–15—describe distracted Black film audiences.

For a particularly pointed post-sound Black diatribe against Black audiences, see Charles Stewart, "Many Can't Appreciate Finer Types of Entertainment, Stewart Finds: Scores Those Who Guffaw During Most Tragic Moment of Picture; Peculiar Sense of Humor," *Norfolk Journal and Guide*, January 8, 1938, 16.

19. Ralph Ellison, "The Shadow and the Act," in *Shadow and Act* (New York: Vantage, 1972 [1964]), 280. Baldwin, analyzing *The Defiant Ones* (1959), makes a similar claim in *The Devil Finds Work* (New York: Laurel, 1976), 77–78.

20. Ralph Ellison, *Invisible Man* (New York: Vantage, 1989 [1952]), 1.

21. Ibid., 170.

22. Ibid., 271.

23. Ibid., 456–57.

24. Ibid., 482.

25. bell hooks, "The Oppositional Gaze," *Black Looks: Race and Representation* (Boston: South End Press, 1992), 117–18. hooks is responding to, and attempting to complicate, Manthia Diawara's "Black Spectatorship: Problems of Identification and Resistance" in *Black American Cinema*, ed. Manthia Diawara (New York: Routledge, 1993), 211–20.

26. hooks, 128.

27. Baldwin, *The Devil Finds Work*, 4.

28. Ibid., 7–10. Baldwin's sexuality—his gayness—seems crucial to his use of the movies; certainly, the stars he most identified with were (or became) gay, camp icons. As far as I know, no work has been done on African Americans and "camp" aesthetics, but Pamela Robertson's work, *Guilty Pleasures: Feminist Camp from Mae West to Madonna* (Durham: Duke University Press, 1996), provides a model for broadening the purview of camp.

29. Baldwin, *The Devil*, 9–10.

30. The "Beacon Lights" ad can be found in *The Crisis*, July 1913, 150. For an example of a race records ad that shows Bessie Smith wearing a star headdress, framed inside a star, and referred to as a star (along with others), see Columbia records ad, *Chicago Defender*, December 20, 1924; for two instances of race record envelopes—one from Brunswick, the other Vocalion—featuring stars (as well as comparison examples of other genres of recordings from the early 1930s, none using star figures), see Harry Smith, ed., "American Folk Music " (Washington, D.C.: Smithsonian Folkways Records, 1997 [1952]).

The association of the star with Afro-America in the United States is by now so complete that, when the *New Yorker* published a "Black" issue (April 29/May 6, 1996), its cover featured a silhouetted profile of a Black head crowned with white stars, with the issue theme—"Black in America"—printed in an upside-down blue star over the "N" of the magazine's title.

31. See Katrina Hazzard-Donald, "The Circle and the Line: Speculations of the Development of African American Vernacular Dancing," *Western Journal of Black Studies* 20, no. 1 (spring 1996): 28–38. The sources for information on the shout, the circle, and the ring in African and African-American culture(s) are many, various, and sometimes contentious. See, for example, Robert Ferris Thompson, *African Art in Motion* (Berkeley: University of California, 1974); Eileen Southern, *The Music of Black Americans: A History*, 2d ed. (New York: Norton, 1983); and Sterling Stuckey, *Slave Culture: Nationalist Theory and the Foundations of Black America* (New York: Oxford

University Press, 1987). For examinations of contemporary continuations of the circle, see Tricia Rose, *Black Noise: Rap Music and Black Culture in Contemporary America* (Hanover, NH: Wesleyan University Press, 1994); Sally Baines, *Writing Dancing in the Age of Postmodernism* (Hanover, NH: Wesleyan University Press, 1994); and Nelson George, *Buppies, B-Boys, Baps, and Bohoes: Notes on Post-Soul Black Culture* (New York: HarperPerennial, 1994).

32. Austin Steward, *Twenty-Two Years a Slave, and Forty Years a Freeman: Embracing the Correspondence of Several Years While President of Wilberforce Colony, London, Canada West* (Rochester, NY: William Alling, 1857), 20–21, quoted in Hazzard-Donald, "The Circle and the Line," 34.

33. Hazzard-Donald, "The Circle and the Line," 34.

34. See, for example, Roger D. Abrahams, *Singing the Master: The Emergence of African-American Culture in the Plantation South* (New York: Pantheon, 1992).

35. For a telling example of a metaphoric use of the star as a marker of stasis by white (imperial) culture, see Alan Trachtenberg, *The Incorporation of America: Culture and Society in the Gilded Age* (New York: Hill & Wang, 1982), 12.

36. Ralph Matthews, "The Negro Theatre—A Dodo Bird," in *Negro: An Anthology*, ed. Nancy Cunard, ed. and abridged by Hugh Ford (New York: Frederick Ungar, 1970 [1934]), 196.

37. Floyd Snelson, "Some Notes on the Musical and Theatrical Negro Stars of America," Cunard, ed., *Negro*, 187–91. Among the stars named by Snelson, only five are noted for any work in film.

38. For a brief analysis of the history of the phrase "cross over," see Gerald Early, *Tuxedo Junction* (New York: Ecco, 1989), xiii–xiv. For a much fuller analysis of the idea of cross over, see his *One Nation Under a Groove: Motown and American Culture* (New York: Ecco, 1995).

39. To keep things from sounding too cozy, I should point out that some performers come to feel the star dance circle—the community—is a constraint and actively work to escape; that a call or a response to a star turn can be "cool" as well as "warm"; and that star dance processes are not without rules and standards. These processes often take place in the framework of what Ralph Ellison, describing jazz improvisation, has called cooperative competition. Stars can be "cut" and crash to earth, but if they are in the circle, they do not have too far to fall, and there is the expectation of other opportunities for other trips, other flights. All of Ellison's essays on music in *Shadow and Act* make this claim, though in a variety of forms. For more on the rules, standards, and ways of learning in one such process, i.e., jazz, see Paul F. Berliner, *Thinking in Jazz: The Infinite Art of Improvisation* (Chicago: University of Chicago, 1994).

40. Billy Booster, "Are Race Pictures a Failure?" *Chicago Defender*, December 27, 1924.

41. Ibid.

42. See Ralph Cooper, with Steve Dougherty, *Amateur Night at the Apollo: Ralph Cooper Presents Five Decades of Great Entertainment* (New York: HarperCollins, 1990). For another analysis of Cooper (and late 1930s "race" films more generally), see

Clyde Taylor, "Crossed Over and Can't Get Black," *Black Film Review* 7, no. 4 (1993): 22–27. For more on Million Dollar Productions, see Brian Taves, "The B Film: Hollywood's Other Half" in *Grand Design: Hollywood as a Modern Business Enterprise 1930–1939*, History of American Cinema, vol. 5 (Berkeley: University of California Press, 1993), 313–50.

43. Faye Jackson to Claude Barnett, January 31, 1934, Claude A. Barnett papers (microfilm), part 3, series D (Frederick, MD: University Publications of America).

44. Miller, "Uncle Tom in Hollywood," 336.

45. I. Roland to Herbert Crooker, Warner Bros., New York Office, March 28, 1936, Barnett papers.

46. Crooker to Roland, March 30, 1936, Barnett papers. In "I Tried to Crash the Movies," the (fascinating) cover story for the August 1946 *Ebony*, frustrated actress Avanelle Harris revealed that she was one of those unnamed chorines in *The Singing Kid*—her first of many similar and unrewarding roles.

47. For one piece of evidence showing—and reflecting on—what seems to be an extraordinary Black response to a minor role in a film, see Tommye Berry, "Kansas City Likes Film *Hooray For Love*," *Chicago Defender*, August 17, 1935.

48. Theodore Miles and Leon H. Hardwick in their article, "Negroes in White Pictures: 1940–41," in *The Negro Handbook*, ed. Florence Murray (New York: Wendell Malliet, 1942) note: "Hattie McDaniel, Ben Carter, Mantan Moreland, Eddie Anderson (Rochester), and Jack Randall were included in Hollywood's semi-official roster of rated motion picture stars and featured players for 1940. The ratings, compiled annually for the industry by *Variety*. . . , is [sic] based on box-office drawing power. . . . No colored player was listed as a 'star.' . . ." (226) Members of the lists were selected for inclusion and ranking by the studios that had them under (short-term) contract. While negotiating with MGM's publicity department about how McDaniel should appear on *Gone With the Wind* souvenir programs and whether she should appear at the film's premiere (she did not attend), David O. Selznick may have best captured McDaniel's status, as well as Hollywood's complex sense of the gradations and ideology of stardom: "she really gives a performance that if merit alone ruled, would entitle her practically to co-starring." Selznick to Howard Dietz (MGM), November 30, 1939, quoted in Carlton Jackson, *Hattie: The Life of Hattie McDaniel* (Lanham, MD: Madison Books, 1990), 47. Avanelle Harris is also illuminating on the race politics of billing in "I Tried to Crash the Movies."

49. Louise Beavers did make two "race" films in the late 1930s and made a personal appearance tour to support at least one of them. The Black newspapers reported this tour with some excitement. Hattie McDaniel never appeared in "race" films and her appearance tour in support of *Gone With the Wind* proved to be disappointing. See Jackson, *Hattie*, 55–72. Jackson quotes extensively from critical mail that McDaniel received from African-Americans later in her career.

50. For more on these events, see Thomas Cripps, *Slow Fade to Black: The Negro in American Film, 1900–1942* (New York: Oxford University Press, 1977), as well as his *Making Movies Black: The Hollywood Message Movie from World War II to the Civil Rights Era* (New York: Oxford University Press, 1993). See also Lena Horne with Richard

Schickel, *Lena* (New York: Limelight, 1986 [1965]) and Shari Roberts, "'Stormy Weather': Lena Horne and the Erotics of Miscegenation," in *Seeing Stars: Feminine Spectacle, Female Spectators, and World War II Hollywood* (Ph.D. diss., University of Chicago, 1993).

51. Reports of this (for Horne especially, but involving other performers as well) are ubiquitous in the Black press; see, for example, "Dixie Censors at Work," *Negro Digest* 2 no. 11 (September 1944): 30 (reprinted from *Variety*, July 12, 1944).

52. For an examination of Robeson in terms of stardom, see Ed Guerrero, "Black Stars in Exile: Paul Robeson, O. J. Simpson, and Othello" in *Paul Robeson: Artist and Citizen*, ed. Jeffrey C. Stewart (New Brunswick, NJ: Rutgers University Press/Paul Robeson Cultural Center, 1998).

53. Alpha Photo Service, "Glamour Queens of Song and Swing," advertisement, *The Crisis*, July 1945, 203.

54. In fact, the people most favored for *The Crisis* covers—school teachers, activists, representative figures (e.g., voters, children, high school and college graduates)—might be the best examples of the "ordinary" Black star.

55. Karen Alexander, "Fatal Beauties: Black Women in Hollywood," in Gledhill, *Stardom*, 51.

56. In the 1950s, following belatedly in Horne's wake, Dorothy Dandridge and Sidney Poitier made the idea of the Black *movie* star, a performer known and circulated primarily through movies and one recognized as a star by producers and audiences alike, no longer (entirely) oxymoronic. However, in what would have to be another essay, I would argue that general movie stardom was gained at considerable cost to Black stardom.

57. For a detailed analysis (fully and illuminatingly illustrated) of a (perhaps *the*) quintessential non-star/Black star, see John Szwed, *Space Is the Place: The Lives and Times of Sun Ra* (New York: Pantheon, 1997).

18

LISTENING TO RACE

Voice, Mixing, and Technological "Miscegenation" in Early Sound Film

Sarah Madsen Hardy and Kelly Thomas

Sound has made the negro the "big thing" of the film-moment.

—Harry Potamkin, "The Aframerican Cinema"

In a 1929 issue of the film journal *Close Up* devoted to the topic of "Negro art for the cinema," African-American writer Geraldyn Dismond attributes the relatively large influx of black actors in Hollywood film to the advent of sound: "It is significant that with the coming of talkies, the first all-Negro feature pictures were attempted by the big companies."[1] Dismond refers specifically to King Vidor's *Hallelujah* (1929), the first post-synchronized sound film, and Paul Sloane's *Hearts of Dixie* (1929), which soon followed. Her comment underscores a fundamental shift in Hollywood's treatment of race, especially blackness, that has yet to be explored fully in contemporary film criticism.[2] Until the late 1920s, black actors rarely appeared in Hollywood productions and then only in minor roles or as extras. During the silent era, primary or supporting roles depicting black characters were usually performed by white actors in blackface, as seen most memorably in *Birth of a Nation* (1915) and film versions of *Uncle Tom's Cabin*.[3] Despite a clear trend toward naturalistic performance style and scenic verisimilitude over the course of the silent era, white actors continued to be cast for black parts, sometimes performing not only with darkened skin but also with the white lips and other exaggerated racial markings conventional to minstrelsy.[4] While such casting can be seen as a continuation of a familiar theatrical convention for representing blackness, it also accomplished the task of segregating casts, an arrangement that directors like Griffith considered essential for upholding the virtue of white female stars. Moreover, most producers would not consider casting African Americans because so few had formal training as actors, and predominant racist sentiment held that neither blacks nor their narratives were suited for the type of art represented by the cinema.[5]

With the advent of synchronized sound in 1927, however, Hollywood's attitudes toward African-American actors and characters began to change. While silent features tended to pair blackface actors with intertitles written in "dialect," the added dimension of sound was seen as allowing for a more authentic depiction of black otherness through synchronized dialogue. Not only would predominantly European-American audiences behold racial difference in the silver screen's highly contrasted images, but also, with the talkies, they could hear the distinctive enunciation and tonality ascribed to black speech. The dramatization of black voice, however, relied both on authenticity (bona fide black players) and on a representation of dialect that confirmed stereotypes of blacks as always Southern, rural, and uneducated. Consequently, the convention of blacked-up whites mimicking dialect did not meet the expectations of authenticity brought about by synchronized dialogue. Therefore, as the Hollywood filmmaking apparatus incorporated sound, demand for black actors increased. In fact, white and black critics alike proclaimed that the talkie was particularly well suited for the reproduction of the distinctive qualities of the black voice. Nonetheless, the range of black characters that Hollywood films depicted remained insultingly narrow; as Michael Rogin suggests, this change in casting simply installed blacks in roles previously performed in blackface.[6] The early political efforts of W. E. B. Du Bois and Booker T. Washington and later efforts of the Harlem Renaissance began to have widespread effects during the 1920s, prompting an increasing consciousness on the part of contemporary African Americans regarding their collective reputation and image. As a result, the predominance of caricatured renderings of blacks and their ensuing influence on European Americans' attitudes toward African Americans provoked passionate debate over the role of film in the representation of blackness.

Even at its height during the incorporation of sound, this debate was nonetheless overshadowed by a larger, but decidedly less inflammatory, controversy over the aesthetics of sound film. Although live sound effects and musical accompaniment had constituted an integral component in the exhibition of silent film from its inception, the advent of synchronized sound made simultaneous and standardized dialogue and other sound effects practicable. The increasing technological and economic feasibility of sound prompted international debates internationally about its impact on film aesthetics and the medium's social import. Proponents of synchronized sound saw it as a tool for enhancing film's realism, allowing spectators to become immersed in a near seamless representation of reality. While few filmmakers actually condemned sound as a whole, opponents such as Soviet filmmakers Sergei Eisenstein and Vsevolod Pudovkin and silent film comedian Charlie Chaplin objected to synchronous dialogue on the grounds that, as a competing element, speech disrupted the visual coherence and unique expressiveness of the screen's images. Relying on a rhetoric of technological purity, opponents saw the era of sound-on-film as an incendiary experiment that mixed components—sound and image—better left separate. Translating this anxiety into racial discourse, Rebecca Egger suggests that sound film, in fact, was being critiqued as a "technology of miscegenation." [7]

Returning to Dismond's discerning comment, then, we would like to emphasize that one of the least explored discourses surrounding the advent of sound is that of race. With film, the historically unequal power relations between African Americans and European Americans becomes transformed into the binaries of silence/speech and silent/talkie, terms integral to discussions about the advent of sound and to the history of film itself. By investigating why the sound/silence dichotomy is so potent a racial metaphor, we address how technology and ideology work together to negotiate tensions surrounding the shifting meanings of race in the popular American imagination during the early sound period of U.S. cinema. Moreover, we look at how discursive anxieties about racial identity and difference are mapped onto the theoretical debate about this revolutionary film technology, both within the newly codified classicism of Hollywood and in the alternative arena of independent race films made for segregated black audiences.

We examine John M. Stahl's 1934 *Imitation of Life*—a state-of-the-art sound production and one of the first Hollywood melodramas to depict interracial relations and cast blacks in prominent roles—as well as a roughly contemporaneous low-budget race film, Oscar Micheaux's 1932 *Ten Minutes to Live*. The films are different in many and obvious ways: one is a classic woman's melodrama; the other, an impenetrable musical thriller. However, they share a preoccupation with mapping cultural issues of racial definition and difference onto aesthetic issues presented by cinema's rapidly changing capacity to incorporate sound.

THE RACIAL POLITICS OF PANCAKES

Predominantly white publications such as the *New York Times*, *Variety*, and *Amsterdam News* gave generally positive reviews to Stahl's adaptation of Fannie Hurst's 1932 best-selling novel *Imitation of Life*, a bittersweet American success story about a widowed white woman, Bea, and her black housekeeper and business partner, Delilah. The prosperity of the women's restaurant and line of ready-made pancake mix is somewhat diminished by troubled relationships with their teenage daughters: Jessie pines for her mother's boyfriend, and fair-skinned Peola, attempting to pass as white, forsakes her mother. At a time when very few black actors played substantial roles in Hollywood films, much less roles that deviated from minstrel stereotypes, moviegoers and critics were engrossed by the poignant rendering of Peola's (Fredi Washington) dilemma of looking white but being black. In fact, in its weekly synopsis of current films for theater exhibitors, *Variety* largely ignored the romantic plot involving Bea (Claudette Colbert), arguing instead that *Imitation* "may make some slight contribution to the cause of greater tolerance and humanity in the racial question." [8] *The Literary Digest*, however, was less forgiving of the film's half-hearted treatment of racial relations, awarding *Imitation* a lukewarm "AA" (out of four) rating and noting that "the screen is extremely careful to avoid its most dramatic theme, obviously because it fears its social implications." [9] In the *Journal of Negro Life*, Sterling A. Brown addresses these implications more directly. Instead of dwelling on the issues of passing and miscegenation that concerned most white reviewers, he focuses on the film's insidious perpetuation of well-worn stereotypes of the "tragic mulatto" and the "contented Mammy." Brown describes the passing episodes as "unbelievable" and Delilah's (Louise Beavers) exaggerated dialect and naive comments about "colored folks" as "straight out of Southern fiction." [10] Beavers's and Washington's characters were, comparatively, some of the best roles Hollywood had offered black actors to that point. Nonetheless, Delilah and Peola, as Brown's disapproving criticism elucidates, work to assuage white guilt while reinscribing the privilege of whiteness and solidifying the cultural boundaries that distinguished black from white. Brown's indignation sparked debates within the black community about the media's representation of African Americans. While some blacks viewed Beavers's and Washington's presence in the film as evidence of progress, Los Angeles black radicals like Leon Washington, editor of Los Angeles's *Sentinel*, insisted that roles based on stereotypes were both offensive and deleterious to the race. (The radicals were famous for vocally challenging overly optimistic sentiments, held both by whites and conservative blacks, that African Americans were making tremendous progress in the Hollywood film industry.) [11]

Brown's "sensitivity" toward the issue of stereotypes also drew, in part, upon the long-standing indignation in black communities surrounding the revitalization of the mammy image in popular culture. Writing about the glorification of mammy in New South ideology from 1906 to the mid-1920s, historian Cheryl Thurber suggests that the mammy was less a real social role in the antebellum South than a "character probably created by nostalgic southern whites to ease their troubled racial consciousness." [12] Perhaps more importantly, the invention of the mammy functioned as a kind of cultural solution to the question of social change and reform during the Progressive era. Rather than simply easing the conscience of "enlightened" whites, the mammy symbolized the New South's commitment toward economic and social transformation. Including the development of infrastructure, enforcement of child labor and temperance laws, and the democratization (at least among European Americans) of social services, these changes went hand-in-hand with large-scale industrialization and urbanization. [13] Although it ultimately worked to reinforce racist ideologies, this economic transformation is often heralded as having ushered the South into the modern era and assimilating the region to the cultural ethos of the nation as a whole. Signifying the South's renunciation of an older, more explicitly discriminatory system of race relations, the mammy was, in a sense, part of a nationalist mythology representing the growing cultural unity in the United States and, by extension, its position as a rising world economic power. Thus, the racist nostalgia and oversimplification of the lives of African-American women under slavery that the mammy embodied was tied discursively to the economic future of the United States in an industrialized modernity.

Perhaps the most familiar example of the connection between mammy figures and the fruits of industrialization is Aunt Jemima, the trademark image dominating the sales of pancakes, waffles, and syrup for more than one hundred years. With a beaming smile and wide-open eyes, Aunt Jemima first appeared at the Chicago World's Fair of 1893. [14] The Aunt Jemima Corporation began as the capitalist venture of two white men who saw a future in self-rising pancake flour that only required the addition of water. In marketing the ready-mix, the entrepreneurs decided that their pancake flour should be identified with the tradition of Southern cooking. They found their symbol in the likeness of a stereotypical Southern mammy on a poster advertising a pair of blackface minstrels. The name "Aunt Jemima" comes from a tune played while the minstrels performed wearing a costume of aprons and bandannas. The source of the product's benevolence and appeal lay in the logo's blank blackness, a screen on which consumers projected fantasies of both black femininity and the history of U.S. race relations. Whitewashing the violent history of the South in order to promote a national economy and culture, the mammy's face rewrote the memory of slavery and the effects of Jim Crow. In an effort to create a truly national distribution and combat the effects of the Depression years of the 1930s, Quaker proposed a revitalization of the Aunt Jemima image, making it ubiquitous through promotions of Aunt Jemima rag dolls available with product coupons. When *Imitation of Life* was released in November 1934, it would have been quite common for contemporary audiences to associate Beavers's Delilah with Quaker's omnipresent trademark.[15]

Explicitly identifying images of the mammy with technologies of mass production, Stahl's film forges the connection among increased industrial production, the development of a national popular culture, and white liberalism's attempts to ameliorate race relations. Recalling the manner in which the mammy figure has historically signaled economic shifts and technological development, *Imitation of Life* explores this much neglected and, admittedly, often obscure array of associations through cinema sound technology. Exemplifying Hollywood's successful incorporation of new technology, the film's self-conscious and stylized use of sound functions as the film industry's analogue to the New South's industrialization. Moreover, as a figure of the past and tradition, the mammy, and hence Delilah, represents that from which technology can break and escape as much as she stands for social reform and progress. Delilah symbolizes the silent era, an idealized period in the development of film made obsolete by the new technology of sound.

The mammy, then, came to serve as modern America's simulation of its own past, justifying not only its present social and economic conditions but the maintenance of a racially divided future. Showcasing Hollywood's innovations, *Imitation of Life* demonstrates that one of the most spectacular and easily recognized results of the increased industrialization in the late 1920s lay in the film industry's incorporation of sound recording technology. Significantly, like its groundbreaking predecessors, *The Jazz Singer* (1927) and *Hallelujah*, the film's narrative conjoins the development of sound with the history of racist stereotypes and contemporary conversations about race relations.

By 1934, Hollywood was already beginning to solidify a classical film sound aesthetic based on synchronized dialogue that heightened the sense of realism and on non-diegetic music that bolstered the cinema's emotional impact. Although Stahl adhered to Hollywood's prevailing attitudes toward sound as a means of reproducing reality, his idiosyncratic manipulation and modulation of sound, silence, music, and dialogue afforded him an active role in Hollywood's new regime while he was still ideologically invested in the silent era. In emphasizing the verisimilitude of small, localized sounds, Stahl approached synchronized sound with a commitment to record reality. However, the soundtrack's clearly defined sounds, especially those supposedly relegated to the background, are often "discrete"; that is, they are selective and distinct to the extent that they often become separate from each other and, as Martin Rubin argues, "to a certain extent, from the images that contain them."[16] Stahl's film reproduces realistic sound, but some sounds are *too distinct* to be realistic.[17] Similarly, the soundtrack's silences are pronounced and often self-consciously protracted; at times, Stahl's instances of silence come across as the jarring, unnatural sound of a blank tape instead of the conventional room tone used for portraying silence. Rubin explains that although Stahl's method is determined, in part, by the simplified mixing technology and prevailing recording practices that privileged mimetic sound, "Stahl takes the convention and pushes it, determines it excessively, and so forges it into a style."[18]

Working within Hollywood conventions, Stahl visually and narratively constructed a dichotomy of black/white that corresponds in striking ways to the dichotomy of image/sound circulating in early debates over the use of sound. This explicitly racialized relationship between sound and image reveals Stahl's anxiety about the "technology of miscegenation," to use Egger's term. Examining the way in which the development of new technology coded for racial mixing, Egger suggests that, "Posited as the fantasized product of a prelapsarian era in which film declined to engage in the messy intermixing of categories, the silent film becomes the marker of its proponent's attachment to notions of purity and separation that are, it would seem, as threatened as the silent film itself."[19] Stahl, who was almost a victim of the faltering economy and technological obsolescence, exhibited personal anxiety over the mixing of categories, specifically the collapse of image/sound and black/white binaries.[20] Revealing his ambivalence about the talkies and his nostalgia for the silent era, Stahl writes:

> Anyone who doesn't think this business is getting tougher and tougher for the director, as well as a lot of other people . . . simply doesn't know his footage. . . . In the dear, dead days of silent pictures we could fix up anything with a printed title. . . . The advent of the talking picture within the past four years has ushered in an entirely new phase of this bewildering and fast-growing industry, and what the future may bring forth no man can tell.[21]

Stahl's irritation with the resulting difficulties of converting to sound is reflected in *Imitation*'s perceptible investment in nostalgic images of subservient blacks. Upon the film's release, *Literary Digest* criticized Stahl's rendering of Hurst's novel for "appear[ing] to regard [Peola's character] with a bit of distaste" and for preferring Delilah "because she is of the meek type of old-fashioned Negro that, as they say, 'knows his place.'"[22]

Imitation of Life remains deeply ambivalent about its representation and treatment of blackness: ostensibly, the film exhibits a liberal sensibility in its portrayal of an interracial partnership, but it ultimately enacts a conservative reinscription and normalization of racial divisions.[23] Although Bea and Delilah are both single mothers struggling to raise their daughters with dignity, neither the film's narrative nor its technical components let us forget that the women's "quasi-companionate" relationship is hierarchized along lines of race.[24] In fact, their business relationship relies on racialized and gendered divisions of labor: Bea's business acumen and salesmanship parlay Delilah's family pancake recipe into the multimillion-dollar Aunt Delilah Corporation, which manufactures ready-mix batter. Despite their mutual change in fortune, Delilah wants nothing more than to remain Bea's housekeeper. While Bea's verbal agility and white skin transform her into an elegant Manhattan socialite and powerful female CEO, Delilah's silent, beaming face, the synecdoche for African-American folk culture, becomes frozen into the trademark image for the product. Despite its sympathetic portrayal of interracial friendship and enterprise, the narrative disciplines black as well as white women who attempt to leave or transcend their traditional position in a racist and anti-feminist social hierarchy.

Not surprisingly, however, the black women suffer most. The film closes having resolved the plot's racial tension—namely, the dual threat of passing and miscegenation—by killing off the long-suffering Delilah and shipping Peola off to a "high-toned" college, supposedly evidence of her newfound maturity and acceptance of her blackness. The narrative, however, also berates white women for jeopardizing the sanctity of the mother-daughter bond. Chastised for representing herself as "B. Pullman," CEO of a national corporation, Bea is forced to choose between her daughter and her lover. Although she reclaims her maternal role and resigns from the company, complaining that she has "never known silence," Bea nonetheless maintains her wealth and social standing. Significantly, in the final scene, Bea regains her daughter's love; as Bea and Jessie embrace, they are illuminated by Delilah's neon image flashing overhead, an electric yet ghostly reminder of her sacrifice for their benefit. The shot establishes a correlation between the social and economic progress of white women and the servitude of blacks while simultaneously spinning a cautionary tale about the dangers of crossing gender and racial boundaries.

The narrative's conservatism is further reinforced by the director's stylized

Figure 18.1. Delilah (Louise Beavers) and Bea (Claudette Colbert) in *Imitation of Life* (1934).

use of sound and music that reveals anxieties about the mixing of distinct realms epitomized by an interracial enterprise and nontraditional family. As the film opens, two distinct musical themes signal the cultural and racial divisions in the narrative. Although the significance of this difference is ambiguous at first, as the film progresses it becomes clear that the themes correspond to Bea and Delilah respectively as musical leitmotifs. Accompanying the film's opening titles, this non-diegetic music fluctuates between a chorus gravely singing "Nobody Knows the Trouble I've Seen," a recognizable African-American spiritual of the period, and the film's orchestral theme music. Compared to the rich but somber spiritual, the orchestral melody is pleasantly buoyant. The merging of the sound of the gospel choir into the orchestral film score illustrates how a type of music affiliated with industry and technology supersedes gospel music and the black culture it signifies in much the same way that Bea appropriates Delilah's family recipe. In this way, the film aligns gospel music with primitive and non-technologized culture that Delilah embodies. For Stahl, then, African-American spiritual singing seemed representative of a more "natural" style of life because of its origins in black folk culture. The transformation in modes of production signaled by the supersession of a signifier of racial otherness, in this case blackness, by a Hollywood score foregrounds not only the racial divisions in the narrative but also their absorption into the very apparatus of filmic production.

While the music playing over the main titles constructs a hierarchical relationship between speech and silence, the opening scene emphasizes the selectively modulated soundtrack by using sound both to motivate Bea's movement through space and to construct the spectator's understanding of the narrative. In this scene, baby Jessie's cries force Bea to end a telephone conversation. Before she hangs up, however, the camera cuts to a static image of Delilah framed behind the screen door. Thus, our introduction to Delilah consists of a silent, framed image accompanied by the offscreen sound of Bea's high-pitched, mellifluous voice. We *see* Delilah, but we *hear* Bea. The film maintains this association throughout: Delilah remains aligned with silence while Bea is connected to sound, specifically speech. Even when Delilah reaches forward to press the buzzer, the camera lets the sound correspond with her image only for a fraction of a second before it cuts to Bea climbing the stairs. As a result, the sound of the buzzer extends over the cut and to the reaction shot of Bea. Herein, the divisions between sound and silence become material and work to construct the viewers' sense of diegetic space. Moreover, the spatial dislocation suggested by the soundtrack's discrete components epitomizes the aural-spatial dyslexia that serendipitously led Delilah to Bea's chaotic residence in the first place. With a deep, placid voice, Delilah explains, "Ise come in answer to your advertisement for a girl." Obviously, Bea is not in a financial position to solicit domestic help. She replies that Delilah is at the wrong place: "This is Astor *Street*. Astor *Avenue* is way the other side of town." Although innocent enough, Delilah's mistake epitomizes her lack of understanding of the linguistic designations indicating geographic as well as socioeconomic stratification in Atlantic City's white community. Her error reveals the discrepancies between black and white cultural knowledge of the city and the spatial restriction of movement enforced upon African Americans by racist ideology. The audible differences in voice and diction underscore these discrepancies.

The disjointedness of image and soundtrack counters contemporary notions that hailed the seamless integration of sound and image as a great tool for the representation and advancement of African-American people and culture. Although Delilah's dialect and speech were understood as enriching the industry's portrayal of African Americans, the film's narrative, cutting, and sound mixing effectively work to silence her. The film develops this correlation between blackness and silence during the scene in which Bea devises the name and logo for their restaurant. While consulting with the painter who will renovate their restaurant space, Bea is struck with inspiration by seeing

Delilah's face and beseeches the workman to use it as a model for the business sign. Reminiscent of the scene during which Bea and Delilah meet, this scene offers another close-up, static image of Delilah, and again, we *see* her while we *hear* Bea's verbal machinations. However, Delilah's friendly smile is clearly not what Bea had in mind. "No! A great big one!" she directs, throwing out her arms in exaggeration. Delilah responds by transforming herself into a stereotypical smiling mammy: "*Oh, yes'm,*" she replies in an exaggerated African-American dialect, freezing her large, round face in a buffoonish blackface pose with wide eyes and a huge grin. Stahl's cutting of the close-up shot/reverse-shot further emphasizes the static nature of the pose that Delilah naively maintains longer than necessary and implies that in holding the pose, Delilah not only projects the image of a mammy, but also plays the part. The soundless, static close-up of Delilah's caricatured smile becomes the reified image of black culture commodified as the logo for Aunt Delilah's Pancakes. While Bea's clear, high-pitched voice demands attention, dominating the realm of sound, Delilah functions as a metaphor for the silent image and silent film itself. Even as the African-American woman becomes a spectacular silent image, she is objectified as happily disempowered and devoid of agency.

Bea's commodification of Delilah's visage begins as a simple hand-painted restaurant sign that later becomes reproduced on millions of pancake ready-mix boxes and, ultimately, as a towering neon sign on the banks of the Hudson River. This transformation of Bea and Delilah's business from a petty bourgeois enterprise to a national corporation exemplifies the mammy's historical connection to industrial production. This relationship becomes clear in an important montage scene marking the narrative's midpoint. A common filmic convention for indicating the passage of time, the montage stands in for ten years in the narrative, spanning from America's boom years of the early 1920s to the film's present time of the early 1930s and economic depression. The montage blends dates and newspaper headlines with brief scenes featuring factory machinery in motion and close-ups of dark-skinned hands packing Aunt Delilah Pancake Flour mix into boxes emblazoned with Delilah's mammy image. As a bridge between the last Atlantic City scene and the first New York City scene, the montage sequence denotes Bea and Delilah's geographical and spatial progression from their cramped living quarters behind the restaurant along the boardwalk to a bi-level mansion ensconced in an elite Manhattan cul-de-sac. The sequence concludes with a full shot of the enormous neon sign flashing with Delilah's image and the slogan "OVER 32 MILLION BOXES SOLD." With its fast-paced soundtrack of non-diegetic music and layered images of industrial machinery packing and moving countless pancake flour boxes, the sequence alludes to newsreels that celebrated America's boom in industrial activity in the 1920s, a time when Fordist narratives of efficiency were applied to numerous aspects of life. However, the montage also recalls an earlier era of the experimental silent films of Eisenstein and Pudovkin, the demise of which many contemporary critics attributed to the advent of synchronized sound. Thus, while the montage sequence celebrates the technological wonder of sound film as a mass-produced art, it employs techniques exemplifying the purity of sound and image and their complementary yet nonsynchronized (segregated) relationship. Technological and social progress, the film admonishes, should develop unevenly, reinforcing traditional racial hierarchies.

Although the film seems invested in constructing and maintaining racial distinctions on local and national levels, Peola's character continually frustrates these efforts by refusing to correspond visually to her racial designation. While Peola's skin is very fair, her desire to be white is forever denied by the fact of her mother's dark complexion, which marks Peola as black. When associated with Delilah, Peola must submit to the binary racial discourse that defines her as black and endure the ensuing racism. Although Peola can easily, almost effortlessly, pass for white, her light complexion presents a double threat to categories of identity and their corresponding social privilege: presumably the product of miscegenation, Peola, through passing, also threatens to further the mixing of the races. As a biracial figure in the racist and segregated United States, Peola presents the audience with the problem of passing, "of [racial] identity being predicated on the false promise of the visible as an epistemological guarantee."[25] Peola's ability to pass, then, undercuts the audience's ability to determine race visually and, in turn, questions the very sense—sight—upon which the filmic experience had been predicated. Challenging sight as a mode of knowledge, as a means of understanding reality, Peola's passing, which is ultimately exposed *as* passing—as artifice—both reveals the constructed quality of whiteness and undermines the reality effect of film itself. Because early sound film aspired to an ideal of realism based on merging image and sound, the "deceit" represented by racial passing impairs Hollywood's claims to truth. Moreover, passing makes plain the industry's inability to understand otherness in anything other than dichotomies of black/white and silence/sound.

Ultimately, the film forces Peola to accept her blackness and attributes Delilah's death to her heartbreaking sadness after Peola leaves home. At Delilah's lavish funeral, Peola both recognizes the extent to which her mother identified as black and submits to the overwhelming pressure of the mainstream ideology of racial binarism. Although Peola blends into the white crowd curiously watching Delilah's elaborate funeral procession, the guilt is too much for her, and she runs to the hearse, breaking from the crowd and its privilege of obscurity. Immediately, she "becomes" black, identified with the African-American musicians and their somber dirge. Embraced and consoled by Bea, Peola's racial status is confirmed when she takes her place in the front of the limousine beside the chauffeur, a servant. The narrative resolves the racial tension by having Peola attend a southern, black college, erasing all traces of blackness in Bea's life save for the giant neon sign that constantly flashes Delilah's approving smile. The complexity of Peola's indeterminate racial status is replaced by the cartoonish simplification of race that the mammy represents. Choosing simulation over reality, the film reveals its own nostalgia for social and representational purity—for silent film's separation of sound and image and black and white. In spite of the film's apparent desire for purity, however, the tension between the narrative and the soundtrack illustrates how these filmic binaries, in the end, ultimately deconstruct themselves and undermine Stahl's nostalgia, denying him a return to the "good old days" of silent film.

THE PRODUCER'S MISTAKE

While Classical Hollywood cinema occupied a privileged position with regard to formulating and advancing a particular relationship between sound and race in film, a look at a contemporaneous race film provides a vital counterpoint for understanding Hollywood's construction of the relationship between sound and blackness and hence, the assumed hegemony of the white speaking subject. Independent African-American filmmaker Oscar Micheaux strove throughout his career to produce realistic images of black life for black consumption, remaining both peripheral and subject to the racialized aesthetics of popular visual culture that dominated Hollywood's conventions of realism. His 1932 part-sound, part-silent *Ten Minutes to Live* is ostensibly a mystery about Harlem nightlife. It opens with a race film producer asking a middle-aged woman to recommend an actress for him to cast, one who sings and dances. The woman suggests in polite, stilted dialogue—distorted by the same low quality sound that runs through the film—that he go to see Ida Groves at the Libya nightclub, the setting where the several subplots unwind. The movement from parlor to nightclub speaks to Micheaux's larger dilemmas, both as a black independent filmmaker making the transition to sound and as a self-fashioned "great man" and leader of his race. The contrast between the polite speech of the parlor and the popular music of the nightclub emblematizes the contrast between respectability and primitivism, two dominant paths toward African-American identity in modern culture.

Micheaux began his career with a strong belief that American dreams of economic self-determination and cultural progress could include African Americans. He admired Booker T. Washington and shared his turn-of-the-century ethos of self-regeneration and racial progress. With entrepreneurial gusto, Micheaux began to write novels and then make films, often based on his own heroic bootstrapping.[26] In his first film, *The Homesteader* (1919), the upstanding, enterprising hero's integration amongst whites on the western plains is set against the corruption of big city nightlife, posited as a separate African-American cultural milieu. Within the visual economy of his early films, Micheaux creates exemplars of ideologically assimilative racial progress, as well as contrasting negative, even stereotypical, representations of black characters. The inception of race films was motivated through the need to answer overtly defamatory images of blacks in mainstream culture, most notably *Birth of a Nation.*[27] However, critics, including some of the pioneers of black film history, have often accused Micheaux of using stereotypes and reproducing racial hierarchies through casting by color.[28] It is undeniable that he helped create an African-American star system that was distinctly light-skinned. Micheaux's intention seems less to refute the degrading stereotypes of blacks particularly virulent in visual culture than to distinguish them from a model of black American identity that was both dignified and sensible. Writing about the trope of the "New Negro," Henry Louis Gates, Jr. argues that the term itself is paradoxical, implying on the one hand a "concern with time, antecedents, and heritage," and a shared racial past, and on the other, "the cleared space" of a free and individuated subjectivity.[29] Gates explains: "A paradox of this sort of self-willed beginning is that its 'success' depends fundamentally on self-negation, a turning away from the 'old Negro' and the labyrinthine memory of black enslavement and toward the register of the 'New Negro,' an irresistible, spontaneously generated black and sufficient self."[30] Thus, while in mainstream culture, minstrelized caricatures such as the mammy may serve as a romanticized and reassuring icon of the past and tradition for whites, as in the case of Stahl's Delilah, when Micheaux recirculated minstrelized representations before black audiences, he did so to offer counterexamples that index racial progress *beyond* the traumatic legacy of enslavement. Film was the "new art" and race films provided an ideal site for reconstructing the public image of African Americans within the relative cultural privacy of all-black theaters.

Having begun in the early 1910s, race film production reached an all-time high in 1921. Historian Henry T. Sampson attributes this development to the investment in black theaters by African-American businessmen across the country as well as a strong black press and a surplus of talent from the stage.

In the late 1920s, however, the race film industry went into a sudden slump, due in part to the fact that more and more of the theaters catering to black audiences were bought out by whites, some of whom refused to book African-American productions. Also significant was the fact that both the quality and cost of mainstream cinema, now centralized in Hollywood, were rising steeply. Despite, or perhaps because of, the success of all-black cast Hollywood talkies, most of the independent race film companies had gone under by 1934.[31]

When Micheaux made *Ten Minutes* in 1932, the economics of filmmaking shifted and so had the cultural ethos around race. It did not escape Micheaux's attention that Harlem was in vogue, with black entertainers drawing white crowds in record numbers. So he began to incorporate musical and comedy routines in all of his films, a convention shared by virtually all films featuring black casts in this period. Marketing his films to white theaters, he touted his company as "the only consistent producers of All-Talking Negro Photoplays" and promised a product that was "modern in theme, which pleases your flapper patrons—each picture has a bevy of Creole beauties—with bits of the floor shows from the great night clubs of New York, with singing and dancing as only Broadway Negro entertainers know how to deliver."[32] Micheaux also tried to penetrate the white market with musical shorts, but this plan failed in the face of Hollywood's preemptive success in creating shorts featuring the biggest black stars.[33]

Mainstream popular culture had come to appreciate and appropriate much of traditional black culture and transform it into the newest trend in mass entertainment, especially in the arenas of music and performance. This mixing of cultural traditions and economic resources that Ann Douglas has called "black-and-white art" had particular implications for the Hollywood film industry, poised on the verge of international dominance. As Douglas notes, "One of America's strongest—if seldom acknowledged—incentives in taking the lead in post-print media development was that much of its most important, most marketable cultural legacy was fully susceptible to no other means of transmission and commodification; the conjunction of black performance tradition and white media was crucial to its bid for cultural hegemony."[34]

The mass media's growing interest in the often primitivized, hybrid culture of Harlem—which Douglas describes as "mongrel"—changed the terms of Micheaux's struggle, jeopardizing his racial philosophy as well as his livelihood. Whereas early in his career Micheaux deployed negative tropes of the primitive to represent a past of racial subjugation, a younger generation of black artists was now gaining visibility—and audibility—in mainstream popular culture through aesthetics that re-valued black folk culture as modern, not least because of its technological reproducibility through the new mass media. With black talent sold by white business, the primitive had become technological.

In light of this cultural shift, Micheaux's ambivalence regarding how best to represent the image of blackness in a popular medium appears to have grown, an issue that is amplified as the plot of *Ten Minutes* unfolds. Two women named Ida sing and dance at the Libya: the recommended Ida Groves, who is subdued and sweet, and the wilder, more sexualized Ida Morgan. Ida Groves wears a dress with long, flowing sleeves and a skirt that falls below her knees, although she does lift it high when she finishes her song and does a tap number. Ida Morgan wears a glittery bikini top, fringed tap pants, and a giant peacock headpiece, and she dances with greater abandon. When the demure Ida Groves approaches the film producer's table, he intentionally "mistakes" the name he was referred, asking instead to speak to the more exotic performer. It is Ida Morgan he offers a shot at mini-stardom. The producer, a stand-in for Micheaux, teeters between the particular lures of respectability and primitivism, but in the end, he chooses the image of blackness that sells.[35] Ironically, then, the "primitive" dancer (calling up associations of exoticism associated with Africa, flagrant self-display, and animality) is also the modern choice, emblematic of the technological progress of sound film and the lucrative commodification of black artists in the mass media.

Ten Minutes stands at the crossroads between sound and silence, critically but helplessly entangled in the dominance of Hollywood's style and its constructions of race. On the one hand, it has been normalized as a "crime melodrama" and on the other, deemed "unintentionally surreal" if "formally adventurous."[36] Neither of these descriptions gives credence to the complex manipulation of sound and image that Micheaux displays in this film. Not despite but because of its substandard technical and production qualities, *Ten Minutes* serves as a rich aesthetic document of the dilemmas of independent African-American cinema. Despite his desire to do things the way "the boys on the Coast"[37] did, Micheaux constantly confronted the roadblocks epitomized by the twin meanings of Jim Crow: the overt financial and political limitations caused by racial prejudice and segregation and the more subtle and internalized identity constructions of racist culture signaled by minstrelsy. Micheaux never ceased to struggle against these limitations.

Nevertheless, the compromised conditions of production—conditions always key to the development of different aesthetics—are central to his artistry. The great success of Hollywood sound ended the heyday of the race film, putting most of Micheaux's fellow pioneers out of business. While Micheaux expressed a desire to operate like a Hollywood producer, he was increasingly aware that he could not. What Micheaux created—not in spite of, but *through* his limitations—is an aesthetic statement: inelegant but strange and compelling. The two Idas and the split they represent express an ambivalence that runs through the film about how blacks get to "be somebody" in the United States. The representations of respectable progress and ironic primitivism interrupt each other throughout the baroque and obscure narrative but nowhere more clearly than in Micheaux's self-conscious deployment of intentional mistakes in sound. His film's technically inferior sound reflects upon the difficulty of representing black subjectivity through speech, making a critical intervention in debates over Hollywood's codification of realism, its often conflated ideologies of racial and technological progress, and its appropriation and commodification of primitivized blackness.[38]

The narrative structure of *Ten Minutes* is almost incomprehensible. It makes sense to assume that the two parts of the film, "The Faker" (a talkie) and "The Killer" (predominantly silent), were at least at some point conceived of as two separate movies since they are so different aesthetically, and their only connection in terms of plot is the nightclub location.[39] The Libya nightclub is the setting for the overlapping anecdotes and musical routines of Part One, "The Faker," and the club frames Part Two, "The Killer," which is told primarily in flashback. Even when considered separately, the two stories are highly fragmented, ambiguous, and largely drained of the suspense implied by the title. Furthermore, the sound is edited to emphasize the many breaks in plot, technique, and generic expectation. Against the logic of continuity, *Ten Minutes* destabilizes a unified viewing position and moves against the increasingly homogenizing force of the dominant aesthetic. Because Micheaux could neither circumvent political and cultural segregation nor afford to mix his soundtrack according to the most recent developments in technology, he was left with an aesthetics of interruption and contrast.

The separation and reintegration of several tracks greatly enhanced the ability of editors to guarantee flow in a way that Mary Ann Doane has claimed is parallel to continuity editing in its power to homogenize the experience of the spectator and conceal the "highly specialized and fragmented process, the bulk and expense of the machinery essential to the production of a sound track which meets industry standards."[40] Micheaux could hardly produce a film with the aural flow of state-of-the-art sound. In his earlier *Within Our Gates*, he used parallel editing to rupture time and interrupt the assumption of its natural, progressive flow. This interruption underscores parallel editing as a filmic technique and creates critical distance. In *Ten Minutes*, Micheaux incorporated sound in a similar way, using new technology to enhance the "reality" of the movie-viewing experience against itself. In doing so, he called attention to how blackness was spoken and heard within popular culture's racialized dichotomy of black/white.

These aural "mistakes" are evidence of Houston Baker's suggestion that through the dominant culture's expectation of verbal meaninglessness rises an African-American aesthetic of making sense out of nonsense. Despite the seeming chaos of the film's plot, a cultural logic of sound can be discerned. Micheaux juxtaposed music, speech, and silence—the three main elements of sound at play in the film—to provide vivid contrast. "The Faker" explores the representational relationship between music and speech as signs of respectability and primitivism, a relationship very much entwined in questions of fakeness and authenticity. The African-American cultural site of the nightclub provides the location for this drama; the club's name, "The Libya," underscores the imaginary, originary "Africanness" of this context. This section of the film is structured by an ironic contrast between "unnatural"-sounding speech and "natural" musical expression within a racialized sound aesthetic. The film's visual aesthetics reinforce the mysteries of racial definition as the convoluted plot and use of double casting play on the viewer's and the characters' inability to recognize what is genuine and what is fake.

"The Killer" explores the relationship between speech and silence as a more basic, deadly threat to black identity, one that plagues Micheaux as he struggles to keep race films viable despite the new difficulties of sound. This section is mostly silent, with melodramatic background orchestration, a shift underlined by the device of a mute and deaf villain, and interrupted occasionally by the two protagonists' scratchy recorded speech. As opposed to the in-between, culturally specific scene of the club, the location for the struggle between speech and silence is signaled by an emphasis on the contrast between public and private spaces. The silence of "The Killer" provides a counterpoint to the highly stylized and systematic exploration of sound in the structure of "The Faker." Their conjunction highlights the contrast between silent film and talkie, and because the sound sequence precedes the silent, the possibility of representational fullness within the silent section is excluded. After characters speak and sing in "The Faker," the audience can't help but "hear" the silence in "The Killer" as a lack. Like the villain, the viewers are deafened.

Doane has described sound as "the bearer of meaning which is communicable and valid but unanalyzable. Its realm is that of mystery."[41] Baker defines sound as the key to modern African-American discursive practices, arguing that "a nation's emergence is always predicated on the construction of a field of meaningful sounds."[42] We would like to suggest that the true mystery of *Ten Minutes* lies not in the ultimately undramatic plot but in the enigma and meaning of sound. The film's metadiscourse of sound makes meaning out of seeming narrative nonsense. Decoding such meaning is important because out of it emerges clues of an alternative consciousness opposed to the systematically racist sounds of Hollywood, those sounds—to borrow from Eric Lott—of minstrel "love and theft."[43]

Most of Micheaux's early talkies showcased synchronized music rather than speech, an emphasis typical for sound films featuring all-black casts, whether produced by Hollywood studios or independent companies. No exception, *Ten Minutes* includes a half-dozen musical numbers. Doane cites Jean Comolli's argument that Classical Hollywood sound is organized around the notion of the "individual as master of speech." [44] Micheaux's sound is, once again, a destabilizing force, decentering speech and emphasizing its unnatural qualities in comparison to music through both technology and performance style. Doane claims that any indication of "unnatural" speech is condemned as a way to preserve the status of speech as an "individual property right." [45] From the other side of the color line, Micheaux reflects the troubled relation of speech to subjectivity for African Americans, one that echoes the producer's choice of a primitivized performer and the logic of intentional mistake.

We understand this choice as bound by the figure of the minstrel. Micheaux adopts and adapts the place of minstrelsy in U.S. national culture and, more particularly, its place in the rise of sound. Baker identifies minstrelsy as a central paradigm through which the modern African-American subject must negotiate speech. Minstrelsy, he notes, is "a mnemonic ritual object that constituted the form that any African American who desired to be articulate—to speak at all—had to master." [46] The way blacks sound is always filtered through the mask of the minstrel, he argues, "a device designed to remind white consciousness that black men and women are mis-speakers bereft of humanity." [47] Baker claims that "it is first and foremost the mastery of the minstrel mask by blacks that constitutes a primary move in African-American discursive modernism." [48] Constantly distorted and coopted through minstrelsy, black speech had never been an "individual property right," neither had it been representable in popular culture as "natural." In this way, the logic of sound's speech-centered progress fails to encompass the minstrelized and denaturalized conditions of possibility for black speech.

The act of black minstrel teams, like those whose sketch is the centerpiece of "The Faker," were advertised in the press with the slogan "two *real* coons." [49] Their performance plays on ideas of what real and natural blackness sounds like, or more appropriately, what blacks sound like when they speak *through* the voice of "coons." The sketch's very placement in the drama reflects Micheaux's negotiation of minstrelized identity. The sketch is preceded by a scene with a young man and woman who are the protagonists of one of the film's many attenuated story lines. They talk earnestly of a future—he is a "man of means" and she wants to "be somebody." Although the narrative implies that he is a "faker" out to deceive her, these characters at first seem typical of the bourgeois view of black life that Micheaux had been criticized for snobbishly promoting, and perhaps even of an idealistic view of racial progress of which Micheaux himself was a shining example. The couple's vocal performances are clipped and stilted, with each word carefully pronounced and stressed, lacking the rhythm and inflection of spontaneous speech. In the following scene, a black minstrels' sketch undermines—in both sound and sense—all the couple represents by mocking racial progress through a performance whose humor is derived from error and inversion or, in other words, meaningful nonsense.

1: I'm trying to get you to keep up with me all the time. You gotta stop talking about going to jail—uplift yourself! Elevate! Be somebody! Follow in the footsteps of great men!

2: Now what's the use of bein' somebody and elevatin' if I don't have anything to eat?

1: That's all right—you elevate and then you can eat!

2: Out there enjoyin' the fresh air. Fresh air don't mean nothin' to me. I need less livin' and more food than a whole lot of freedom and starvin' to death.

1: Sure—you oughta be satisfied.

2: I—I never forget the words my grandma used to tell me. . . .

1: What was that?

2: When I was a little boy she used to hold me on her lap, look into my big blue eyes, and push my golden locks back from my forehead, say, "Son, my dear son, where there's a will there's a way."

1: She was right.

2: I gotta will to eat but I can't find a way!

The sketch goes on to mis-speak a narrative of black and white national heroes from Lincoln to Garvey and ends with the team breaking into a duet, with one pseudo-improvisationally finishing the other's lines with nonsense lyrics.

1: Me and you can be just as great as [Lindenberg]. All you gotta do is to help me out. Right here and now in my pocket I gotta song that I wrote no more no long. There ain't nothin' to do but for you to help me. I got the song but I ain't got the finish.

2: Oh you want me to help you?

1: You rhyme it with me.

The sketch is characterized by a kind of stylized "badness," emphasizing intentional mistakes based on minstrelized African-American speech. The black blackface artists doubly invert the sound, as well as the image, of the degraded minstrels, mocking the misunderstanding of the black experience within a progress-driven paradigm of self-made manhood that is itself blissfully ignorant. While the minstrels discuss the same subjects as the couple, they intentionally flaunt their nonsensical phrases and poor grammar in order to demonstrate how "unnatural" it is for African Americans to speak of upward mobility. In this way, the minstrel sketch reinforces Micheaux's ambivalence about racial progress. The pair play on the contradictions of being both black and getting to "be somebody" in the national mythology (a mythology to which Micheaux seemed to ascribe a decade earlier), as evidenced in the attribution of Patrick Henry's "Give me liberty or give me death" to Frederick Douglass—"and they shot him."

The textual discourse parodying the meaning of progress toward "being somebody" echoes the subtextual question of the technological progress represented by sound. The self-conscious mistakes in the characters' speech are echoed in Micheaux's poor production values even though in the sketch the question of sound quality is not an issue. The young couple's over-enunciated diction may be a response to the poor sound equipment, but that cannot be the whole story. In refuting the stereotype of blacks as mis-speakers, they sound *over*-educated, unnatural. The comedians, who as stage performers and satirists should come across as *less* natural, sound much less stilted, even as they reinforce racist stereotypes about black speech. Set against the melodrama of the upwardly striving couple, the sketch ironically inverts natural and unnatural through the vocal performance as much as it does by the more obvious deployment of image: the double fakery of blacks in blackface. By the end of the sketch, the possibilities for "being somebody"—or, by analogy, for the "property right" of the individual identity of a speaking subject—are to be found in music, not speech. The closest the black performers can get to elevating themselves to the status of national heroes—"boys" like Lincoln and "Lindenberg" (Charles Lindbergh) who are symbols of national unity and technological progress, respectively—is to speak through the minstrel mask. Likewise, Micheaux self-consciously fashioned himself as a great man, but found himself driven to choose a discourse of subjectivity based on music, mistake, and seeming nonsense.

Micheaux ensures that the upwardly mobile couple be viewed ironically and that their performances are read as an even more stylized representation than the sensationalized blackness of the minstrel duo. The latter's parodic and disorderly rendition of national and personal progress inverts the standards of truthful fact and realistic representation. The minstrels' performance primes the audience to read cinematic representations against the grain of traditional understandings of technological progress that work toward producing a hegemonic realism that excludes and silences African Americans. This sense of critical detachment pulls against the forward-looking ideology of Hollywood conventions. Intentional mistakes in sound reflect on the minstrelized and denaturalized conditions of possibility for black speech, expressing how the logic of sound film's "progress" fails to encompass the difficulty of representing black subjectivity. If Classical Hollywood cinema seems concerned on some level that sound film is a miscegenated technology, Micheaux's deployment of unmixed sound ironically suggests how sound technology underlines the segregation endured by the independent black voice within modern mass culture and reveals his skepticism about both the possibility and desirability of assimilation.

LISTENING TO RACE

Musicologist and film historian Kathryn Kalinak observes that the advent of sound on film "ignited a revolution in cinematic practice whose battleground was the soundtrack." [50] In addition to those struggles over the film industry's technical, aesthetic, and economic interests to which Kalinak refers, we have shown that in Classic studio productions and independent features alike the battleground of the soundtrack may be understood as a site of ideological struggles over the meanings of racial difference and the tensions of race relations. The aesthetic options opened up by sound generated new strategies in a discursive battle that was already underway over the place of race, particularly blackness, in modern U.S. culture.

As silent directors who made the difficult transition into sound, Stahl and Micheaux established their reputations by making films that, to varying degrees and in varying ways, are preoccupied with race. Although *Imitation of Life* and *Ten Minutes to Live* ostensibly have little in common, we have argued that, if one listens carefully, both of their soundtracks address a larger national racial problematic. As texts representative of different sides of the color line and all that division signifies, these films illustrate the various and far-reaching effects of synchronized sound, both as a discourse and a technological reality.

NOTES

We would like to thank Bill Paul for his helpful criticism of an earlier version of the Stahl reading.

1. Geraldyn Dismond, "The Negro Actor and the American Movies," *Close Up* 2 (Aug. 1929): 93–94.

2. From the outset, let us clarify that our use of the words *race*, *black*, and *white* in this essay is based on an understanding of race as socially constructed. Indeed, it is our project to discuss early sound cinema's engagement with the discursive construction of racial meanings and metaphors. Due to the scope of the essay and the nature of our material, we do not address the complex range of modern American racial categories, but focus on the dominant black/white binary. As the terms *race film* and *Hollywood film* indicate, within this binary only the term of difference, of blackness, is marked as "race." While we are, to a certain extent, subject to this language, we use it self-consciously, and the very basis of our interpretive approach assumes that the marked and the unmarked terms of this binary are mutually constitutive.

3. There were at least ten silent versions of *Uncle Tom's Cabin*, ranging from Edwin Porter's 1903 landmark to the elaborate and popular Universal production in 1927, as well as numerous variations on the theme, such as *Uncle Tom's Gal* (1925) and *Topsy and Eva* (1927). Sam Lucas was the first black man to play Uncle Tom on film in a 1914 World production. Other parts in the film were played by white actors in blackface.

4. Richard Dyer comments on the inconsistent casting of black characters in *Birth of a Nation*, which relies on black actors for bit parts and uses white actors—some simply with darkened skin and some with the outright theatrical make-up of minstrelsy—in other black roles. See Dyer, "Into the Light: The Whiteness of the South in *The Birth of a Nation*," in *Dixie Debates: Perspectives on Southern Culture*, ed. Richard H. King and Helen Taylor (London: Pluto Press, 1996), esp. 167–68.

5. Henry Sampson offers a detailed history of black characters in American films during the silent era, exploring the use of white characters in blackface, as well as cases where black actors performed alongside blacked-up whites. See Sampson, *Blacks in Black and White: A Source Book on Black Films* (Metuchen, NJ: Scarecrow Books, 1995).

6. Michael Rogin, *Blackface/White Noise: Jewish Immigrants in the Hollywood Melting Pot* (Berkeley: University of California Press, 1996), 119.

7. Rebecca Egger, "Deaf Ears and Dark Continents: Dorothy Richardson's Cinematic Epistemology," *Camera Obscura* 30 (May 1992): 17. The connection that Egger forges among racial discourses and film technology and aesthetics suggests that multiple discourses were at work in shaping the integration and reception of sound technology. Alan Williams touches on this when he suggests that the transition to sound has a much more complex and multifaceted history than is evident in most historical and critical accounts. Traditional accounts of the transition were based on assumptions that cinema was characterized by a drive toward realism and that film

would naturally evolve technically to include speech. In opposition to these accounts, Williams argues that the timing of sound's incorporation depended more on U.S. and international disputes over patents and a lack of mechanical standardization in the industry than on public expectations of realism or a deficiency in synchronized sound technology, which was available as early as 1900. See Williams, "Historical and Theoretical Issues in the Coming of Recorded Sound to the Cinema," in *Sound Theory/Sound Practice*, ed. Rick Altman (New York: Routledge, 1992), 127.

8. Review of *Imitation of Life*, *Variety*, November 27, 1934, 15.

9. "On the Current Scene," *Literary Digest*, December 8, 1934, 31.

10. Sterling A. Brown, "Imitation of Life: Once a Pancake," *Opportunity: A Journal of Negro Life* (March 1935), 88. Ironically, Beavers allegedly force-fed herself to increase her size and struggled to develop a Southern accent so that she could play mammy roles. See Donald Bogle, *Toms, Coons, Mulattos, Mammies, and Bucks: An Interpretive History of Blacks in American Film*, 2d ed. (New York: Continuum, 1989), 63. Even after she established herself in the part, Beavers was snubbed while auditioning for the mammy in *Gone with the Wind* (1939)—surely one of the most coveted black film roles of the time—because she showed up for her screen test in furs; see Carlton Jackson, *Hattie: The Life of Hattie McDaniel* (Lanham, MD: Madison Books, 1990), 46–48.

11. For a discussion of the Los Angeles black radicals and the earlier Ink Slingers who followed W. E. B. Du Bois, see Bruce Tyler, *From Harlem to Hollywood: The Struggle for Racial and Cultural Democracy 1920–1943* (New York: Garland Publishing, Inc., 1992), esp. chap. 2: "From Harlem to Hollywood." Du Bois's censure against Hollywood's depictions of blacks crystallized around D. W. Griffith's *The Birth of a Nation*; see Tyler, 4–6.

12. Cheryl Thurber, "The Development of the Mammy Image and Mythology" in *Southern Women: Histories and Identities*, ed. Virginia Bernhard (Columbia: University of Missouri Press, 1992), 87.

13. For the correlation between the New South and progressivism, see Edward Larson, *Sex, Race, and Science: Eugenics in the Deep South* (Baltimore: Johns Hopkins University Press, 1995), 14–17.

14. For a rather one-sided history of the Aunt Jemima advertising campaign, see Arthur Marquette, *Brands, Trademarks, and Good Will: The Story of the Quaker Oats Company* (New York: McGraw-Hill, 1967), 137–58.

15. Aside from the notable exception of Lauren Berlant, most critics of the film, however, do not explore Delilah's association with Aunt Jemima or the mammy's relationship to twentieth-century industrialization and the commodification of blackness. Berlant suggests that by responding to Delilah as a preconceived cultural commodity image, members of the audience are ironically exploited by the logic of commodity fetishization and consumer capitalism by having a "collective identity" based on a trademark. Moreover, through such a collective identity, the audience has both a share and a stake in maintaining the exploitation of Delilah. See Berlant, "National Brands/National Body: *Imitation of Life*, " in *Comparative American Identities*, ed. Hortense Spillers (New York: Routledge, 1991), 125.

16. Martin Rubin, "The Voice of Silence: Sound Style in John Stahl's *Back Street*," in *Film Sound*, ed. Elizabeth Weis and John Belton (New York: Columbia University Press, 1985), 278.

17. French film theorist Michel Chion calls this practice of making a sound appear more "real" than reality *rendered sound*. See *Audio-Vision: Sound on Screen*, trans. and ed. Claudia Gorbman (New York: Columbia University Press, 1994), esp. chap. 5: "The Real and the Rendered," 95–122.

18. Rubin, "Voice of Silence," 277.

19. Egger, "Deaf Ears," 20.

20. Stahl established himself as a director of silent films with his first feature film in 1918. During this era, he also had a hand in promoting minstrel stereotypes by directing Stepin Fetchit's first film, *In Old Kentucky* (1927). However, after this film until 1930—a key period in the integration of sound technology—Stahl did not have a directorial credit and found himself unemployed after selling his part of production company Tiffany-Stahl (Rubin, "Voice of Silence," 284). Stahl signed with Universal, a minor studio, in 1930.

21. John M. Stahl, "Oh, the Good Old Days: Gone Are the Days When Directing Was a Cinch," *The Hollywood Reporter*, May 16, 1932, 23. Stahl's sentiments are evident in *Back Street*, the film he was directing at the time. Rubin argues that *Back Street* "stigmatizes the apparatus of technological progress (not only the automobile but also the telephone, thereby evoking another form of mechanical voice transmission: the microphone) and it valorizes an idealized romantic past represented by image and music" (Rubin, "Voice of Silence," 284).

22. "On the Current Scene," *Literary Digest*, December 8, 1934, 31.

23. Because the film's plot, which features two single mothers, one white, the other black, ostensibly concerns the maternal and familial, critics often limit their analysis of the film to questions of genre and are reluctant to consider the film's formal composition or to contextualize it in terms of some of the era's defining cultural factors. Likewise, most readings of the film inevitably position it in relation to Douglas Sirk's 1954 version, as in Lucy Fischer's collection of essays devoted to the two films, *Imitation of Life* (New Brunswick, NJ: Rutgers University Press, 1991).

24. Berlant, "National Brands, National Body," 114, suggests that Bea and Delilah's relationship is strongly homosocial if not homosexual. Fischer speculates that Fannie Hurst's unconventional friendship with Zora Neale Hurston may have influenced Hurst's conception of the novel. Hurst employed Hurston as a secretary, but she was not suited for secretarial duties. Hurst kept her on as a chauffeur and companion. For Fischer's interpretation of their relationship, see *Imitation of Life*, 12–14. The Fischer anthology also includes excerpts from tributes the women wrote for each other, 173–79.

25. Amy Robinson, "It Takes One to Know One: Passing and Communities of Common Interest," *Critical Inquiry* 20 (1994): 716.

26. For biographical information about Micheaux, as well as an exploration of his use of autobiographical characters, see Pearl Bowser and Louise Spence, "Identity and Betrayal: *The Symbol of the Unconquered* and Oscar Micheaux's 'Biographical

Legend,'" in *The Birth of Whiteness: Race and the Emergence of U.S. Cinema*, ed. Daniel Bernardi (New Brunswick, NJ: Rutgers University Press, 1996).

27. Sampson identifies the Lincoln Motion Picture as the first race film company, established in 1916, though some films may have been made by blacks earlier (see Sampson, *Blacks in Black and White*). In addition to other factors, the large public protest over *Birth of a Nation* gathered cultural activists around the question of black self-representation on film and inspired a number of race filmmakers, most notably in the case of *The Birth of a Race*, a race film answering *Birth of a Nation* directly. For an account of this film's context and production, see Thomas Cripps, "The Making of *The Birth of a Race*: The Emerging Politics of Identity in Silent Movies," in Bernardi, *The Birth of Whiteness*.

28. The debate about Micheaux's use and misuse of racial stereotypes has been one of the central issues in Micheaux criticism. For a sample of this debate, see Joseph A. Young, *Black Novelist as White Racist: The Myth of Black Inferiority in the Novels of Oscar Micheaux* (New York: Greenwood Press, 1989); J. Ronald Green and Horace Neal, Jr., "Oscar Micheaux and the Racial Slur," *Journal of Film and Video* 40 (1989); and Clyde Taylor, "Crossed Over and Can't Get Black," *Black Film Review* 7 (1993). bell hooks comes to Micheaux's defense in "Micheaux: Celebrating Blackness," *Black American Literature Forum* 25, no. 2 (summer 1991). Clearly, Micheaux's deployment of racialized images is highly charged and uneven. Criticism has turned away from assessments of positive and negative images and toward questions of aesthetics and ideology, including reassessments of Micheaux as new material is discovered. Decisive in this turn was the rediscovery of a version of Micheaux's daring and controversial lynching melodrama, the 1920 *Within Our Gates*, at the Cineteca España in Madrid. The film became available for screening in the United States in 1990.

29. Henry Louis Gates, Jr., "The Trope of the New Negro and the Reconstruction of the Image of the Black," *Representations* 24 (fall 1988): p. 132. Although the term "New Negro" is most strongly associated with Alain Locke's 1920 anthology of the same name, Gates dates the use of this term in popular discourse from 1895. The concept of the New Negro identity was first associated with the end of Reconstruction and the beginning of a new century, anticipating the force and coherence that this title took on in the Harlem Renaissance.

30. Ibid., 132.

31. Sampson, *Blacks in Black and White*, 9, 18.

32. Quoted in ibid., 163.

33. Ibid., 163–64.

34. Ann Douglas, *Terrible Honesty: Mongrel Manhattan in the 1920s* (New York: Noonday Press, 1995), p. 426. Douglas focuses exclusively on a single decade and specific location. However, in keeping with what she argues, the trends that began there had a huge cultural impact, comprising an important chapter in the development of mass culture.

35. Indeed, it did sell; a reviewer for the *Kansas City Call* writes that "a bit of torrid dancing of a chorus of beauties is one of the highlights of the production" (Sampson, *Blacks in Black and White*, 432).

36. As the American Museum of the Moving Image's Micheaux film series program describes it, *Ten Minutes*, "Micheaux's most unintentionally surreal, formally adventurous film, is filled with strange prophecies, elaborate devices, and bizarre editing as the action unfolds against a succession of nightclub acts at the Club Libya." Until recently, Micheaux's work has been treated mostly in terms of its historical and sociological significance. Critical attention has now, however, turned to Micheaux's aesthetic vision and his unique style, with scholars like Pearl Bowser, Louise Spence, J. Ronald Green, and Jane Gaines analyzing Micheaux's nuanced responses to the racial unconscious of early film and the incipient classicism of Hollywood. In particular, see J. Ronald Green, "Twoness in the Style of Oscar Micheaux," and Jane Gaines, "Fire and Desire: Race, Melodrama, and Oscar Micheaux" both in *Black American Cinema*, ed. Manthia Diawara (New York: Routledge, 1993).

37. Richard Gehr, "One Man Show," *American Film*, May 1991, 39.

38. Green is one of the few critics to address Micheaux's sound aesthetics. His argument in "Twoness" also engages Micheaux's aesthetics of "mistake," including its relationship to the blues. He frames Micheaux's style as more "a retention of early film traits, from before the advent of glossy illusionism, than as a failed imitation of White movies" (40). Although we find Green's formulation illuminating, we understand Micheaux to be more actively engaged in answering Hollywood aesthetics.

39. The film is based on a collection of short stories by Micheaux, *Harlem after Dark*.

40. Mary Ann Doane, "Ideology and the Practice of Sound Editing and Mixing," in *Film Sound*, ed. Elisabeth Weis and John Belton (New York: Columbia University Press, 1985), 57–58.

41. Ibid., 56.

42. Houston Baker, Jr., *Modernism and the Harlem Renaissance* (Chicago: University of Chicago Press, 1987), 71.

43. See Eric Lott's *Love and Theft: Blackface Minstrelsy and the American Working Class* (New York: Oxford University Press, 1993) for an examination of the minstrel stage in the nineteenth century, another—in some ways parallel—instance of white appropriation of black culture.

44. Doane, "Ideology," 58.

45. Ibid.

46. Baker, *Modernism*, 21.

47. Ibid.

48. Ibid., 17.

49. Ibid., 20.

50. Kathryn Kalinak, *Settling the Score: Music and the Classical Hollywood Film* (Madison: University of Wisconsin Press, 1992), 60.

19

"EXTREMELY DANGEROUS MATERIAL"

Hollywood and the "Ballad of Frankie and Johnnie"

Peter Stanfield

If America has a classical gutter song, it is the one that tells of Frankie and her man.

—Carl Sandburg, *American Songbag,* 1927

Dear Mr. Mayer

We have read the Frankie and Johnnie number for your proposed picture "Ziegfeld Follies." We regret to report that we feel this subject matter would be unacceptable from the standpoint of the Production Code, on account of its flavor of prostitution and excessive sex suggestiveness.

Furthermore, it has been the practice of censor boards generally to delete even the mention of this song, whenever any attempt has been made to inject it into pictures.

We strongly urge, therefore, that you steer away entirely from this extremely dangerous material and substitute something else.

Cordially yours,

Joseph I. Breen, Director, Production Code Administration, 1944.[1]

Figure 19.1. Frankie (Helen Morgan) and Johnnie (Chester Morris). (Image courtesy of British Film Institute Stills, Posters, and Designs.)

During the late 1920s to mid-1930s the ballad of "Frankie and Johnnie," which recites that tale of a betrayed lover who exacts violent revenge on the "man who done her wrong," sustained remarkable popularity. It was bolstered through commercial recordings by popular and vernacular artists, reproduced in folk song collections, adapted as stage and puppet plays, represented in poetry and fine art, used as the basis for two Hollywood screenplays, and appeared either as a discrete performance or as part of the soundtrack in a number of other films. Even bars and drinks were named after the couple.

The story of Frankie and Johnnie speaks to a diverse set of contradictory contemporary cultural desires and fears, resulting in a series of ambiguities that color the song's reception. Depending on its context, the song could invoke either a rural or urban setting, either past or present; it could be romantic or sordid; the protagonists could be either black or white or a mixed couple; Frankie could be male or female; she or he could be either tragic victim or a triumphant avenger; the song can assume a decidedly moral overtone or it can refuse to judge the characters. Regardless, the song maintained a decidedly déclassé outlook on life, and it told a definitively American tale.

This chapter seeks to understand the popularity of the song and how and why Hollywood made use of it. I argue that the specific appeal of the song was its ability to invoke a lewd, violent, vital, and racially confused vision of American life—Carl Sandburg's "gutter"—which in turn brought the song, when used by Hollywood, within the domain of the Production Code Administration (PCA)—Joe Breen's "extremely dangerous material"—where it was deemed to be censurable. Using the critical and historical work on the Production Code Administration by Richard Maltby, Lea Jacobs, and Ruth Vasey, I show how and why the song was censored.[2] The instantly recognizable melody enabled filmmakers to use the song to signify desires, impulses, and moral values that could not be relayed to an audience in an unadulterated and unambivalent manner for fear of the censor's scissors. However, as the song became overworked as a motif, the set of concerns it was meant to suggest to an audience became ever more fixed and direct—ambiguity dissolved. Used originally to mask offensive material, the song became censurable.

I further argue that what made the song "American" was the central ambiguity around the characters' racial status. When this is compounded by either overt or covert references to illicit lifestyles—prostitution, excessive drinking, drugs, gambling, and violence: the very things that made the story so enticing to filmmakers—it becomes censurable. Specifically, however, it is the instability of racial boundaries that makes the song "extremely dangerous material." *Her Man* (1930) and *Frankie and Johnny* (1936), the two films based on the song, are contextualized by an intertextual history of "Frankie and Johnnie," which explains how and why the ballad became America's quintessential "gutter" song. Hollywood in these two films, and in its use of the song elsewhere, attempted to exploit and contain the story's lascivious content by positioning it as a cautionary tale where what is most at stake is the characters' whiteness. Unable to dramatize overtly the full effect of the couple's desires and actions, the filmmakers rely on audience recognition of an equation between moral values and racial characteristics. The more abject the couple or individual becomes, the more closely he/she is aligned with images of blackness.

ORIGINS AND INTERTEXTS

Shapiro & Bernstein copyrighted "Frankie and Johnnie" in 1912. The words and music were credited to Ren Shields and the Leighton Brothers, a popular blackface vaudeville team, but they were no more the song's authors than Hughie Cannon, the writer of the "coon" song "Bill Bailey, Won't You Please Come Home," who published the first commercial version of the ballad in 1904 under the title, "He Done Me Wrong." Neither was Frank Crumit its proprietor, despite his claim of "complete authorship." A singer of novelty numbers ("Abdul Abulbul Amir"), Crumit had the biggest "hit" recording of the song in 1927. In fact, the song has no one author or any certain origin.[3]

The most often repeated origin, and the one with the most substantial empirical data to back up its claims, is the 1899 killing in St. Louis of Allen Britt by Frankie Baker (the two were a black couple). A contemporary newspaper account of the slaying described her as "an ebony hued cake-walker."[4] The commonly recognized racial roots of the ballad through the stories of its origin, its early dissemination as part of blackface routines,[5] its emergence into a popular public arena during the widespread ragtime and "coon" songs fad, and the continued mimicry, through jazz, of black culture by white performers consolidated the connotation that the ballad offered a privileged view of the new urban black population.[6] John Huston, writing in 1930 about the social world of turn-of-the-century St. Louis, the setting in which the ballad was formed and depicted, noted that:

> St. Louis became known as the toughest town in the west. Boogie-joints and bucket-shops opened on Twelfth, Carr, Targee, and Pine Streets. The fast colored men and women lived up to their necks. Stack-o-lee stepped out and made a legend of his Stetson hat. The girls wore red for Billy Lyons. Duncan killed Brady. The ten pimps that bore the dead were kept on parade between the infirmary and the graveyard.[7]

Certainly, the ballad was already well known across the continent in 1912 when the Leighton Brothers changed the male protagonist's name from Albert to Johnnie in their bid to secure copyright. The popularity of this version ensured that the man who did Frankie wrong would be henceforth known as Johnnie, although Albert would never entirely disappear from recorded versions.

The song's malleability and adaptability to a number of performance styles partly explains its wide appeal. Recordings by jazzmen, such as King Oliver (1929 and 1930), and blues queens Mamie Smith (1923) and Bessie Smith (1924) continued to confirm the image of Frankie and Johnnie as black. While at the more pop end of the market, best personified by Frank Crumit's version, jazz inflections usually stud the instrumentation and arrangement to help emphasize the illicit nature of love and murder in the underworld. Commercial recordings of the ballad must rely on innuendo, suggestion, and prior knowledge of more "authentic" versions if the vulgar and lewd subject is to be acknowledged. The details of Frankie's relationship to Johnnie tend to be carried by the lines: "Frankie and Johnnie were lovers / Lawdy, how they did love /

Swore to be true to each other/True as the stars above/ . . . /Frankie was a good girl everybody knows/Paid about a hundred dollars for Johnnie's suit of clothes." The couple appears to be in love, but Frankie is doing all the giving and Johnnie all the taking. More explicit published versions reveal that Johnnie is using Frankie so he can take her money and give it to his other lover, Nelly Bly (or some other woman with a similar name): "Frankie she shot Albert/And I'll tell you the reason why/Ever' dollar bill she gave Albert/he'd give to Alice Blye." While their occupations—as a prostitute and her pimp—are easily "read" into these versions, the explicit versions dissolve all ambiguity: "Frankie goes down to the whore house/Peeks in at the window so high/There she sees her lover, Johnnie/Finger fuckin' Nellie Bly."

The ballad was also performed in vernacular recordings by both black and white musicians. Jimmie Rodgers, "the father of country music," produced the best-known "white" version of the song in 1929. In the same year, the black Dallas songster Nick Nichols recorded a two-part version. There is little discernible difference in the storylines between the black and white vernacular recordings. In all, Frankie and Johnnie profess their love for one another, but fickle Johnnie finds comfort in another woman's arms. Frankie discovers his betrayal and guns him down. Arrested by the police, she is taken before the judge. Whether Frankie is exonerated or executed depends upon the whims of the singer, rather than on any particular racial construction. However, the "tongue-in-cheek amorality" of Nichols's version, as blues historian Paul Oliver has noted, "would have appealed at a time when blacks believed that they had little justice in the courts and had often found that pretending naiveté, or repentance . . . was as likely to turn the case in their favor, as any attorney's pleading." [8] Frankie, drunk on gin and celebrating Johnnie's murder, seduces the judge by dancing the "shim-shim" in the courtroom: "Frankie she start to shimmy, and the judge begin to smile/Says. My golly, she's a pippin, oh, she's my angel chile, I'll be her man and I won't do her wrong."

Published versions do exist that allude to the characters' race—"Listen here, Mr. Bartender, don't tell me no lies. /Have you seen that Nigger Albert? With the girl they call Katy Fly?" [9] Commercial recordings, however, tend to forsake any direct references to race. The presumption is that the characters belong to the same race as the singer. In a version of the ballad published in 1932, this racial ambiguity is played upon by the African-American poet and Howard University professor, Sterling A. Brown, who also produced other reworkings of black folklore. Frankie is the white "halfwit" daughter of a "red-faced cracker, with a cracker's thirst," and Johnnie is a black field hand. Frankie flirts, teases, and tempts Johnnie, giving no more thought to her actions than she does when pulling "wings off of living butterflies," whipping dogs, and throwing "stones at the brindle calf." Johnnie eventually succumbs to her temptations, but before long Frankie's father discovers the "lovers" and Johnnie is lynched: "Frankie, she was spindly limbed with corn silk on her head, Johnnie was a nigger, who never had much fun—They swung up Johnnie on a tree, and filled his swinging hide with lead, And Frankie yowled hilariously when the thing was done."[10]

Brown overtly politicizes the ballad. He takes it out of the city and into the countryside, a unique setting among African-American versions of the tale. The transplantation denies the characters' attempts to assert their individuality against the claims of the city and modernity. Brown moves the characters back to the root of American racism—the rural South—making the relationship between blacks and whites recognizable. What, in part, gives urban versions of the tale power is that the racial world of the turn-of-the-century American city is in some ways unknown and unrecognizable; where are the borders and boundaries in a city defined by a polyglot citizenship? Nevertheless, Brown saw in the song's dual appeal to black and white audiences a politics of race that otherwise remains at best, as in Nick Nichols's version, latent.

When Thomas Hart Benton included a scene from "Frankie and Johnnie" in his public mural celebrating "Typical Scenes of Missouri" (1936), including portraits of slave blocks and Jesse James, he "produced an immediate uproar" in the media. The press deemed his image of a black Frankie shooting a black Johnnie in the backside "offensive" and an affront to Missouri's "growing refinement and nobility." Benton chose to use Frankie and Johnnie because he understood them to be quintessentially American, and therefore an aid in his confrontation with European artistic and "aesthetic colonialism" in America.[11] Regardless of whether the ballad makes specific references to American locales or not, it is the racial complexities that make the story definitively American. In the tale of "Frankie and Johnnie," America's indigenous vulgarity is signified by its black parentage, which is compounded by the underworld saloon setting; images of alcohol, gambling, pimps and prostitutes, violence, and murder; and occasional references to drugs ("An there sat Albert a-hittin' the pipe to beat hell").[12]

John (Jack) M. Kirkland's play *Frankie and Johnnie* opened at New York's Republic Theater in September 1930. The police, who raided the play during its try-out, were "offended," according to theater historian Gerald Bordman, "by its story, its characters, and lines such as the one defending prostitution as 'the only profession for which women are exclusively equipped.'"[13] Reviewing the play for the Studio Relations Committee (the precursor to the Production Code Administration), Lamar Trotti wrote: "This is unbelievable cheap melodrama and I can't conceive of any company being interested in it. It is of course entirely out so far as the Code is concerned as is censurable from beginning to end." [14] On reading Trotti's comments, another staff member wrote back to him noting "that Pathé has already produced a picture based on this property. When you see *Her Man* you will hardly recognize it as the child of such a parent." In fact, *Her Man,* which had begun life as *Frankie and Johnnie,* was not based on this property but on an original screenplay by Tay Garnett and Howard Higgin. Nevertheless, the proximity of play dates between the drama and the film caused *Variety* to note, "Plenty of "Frankie and Johnnie" publicity around New York of late with the dirty play of that title pinched. The picture here merely basing [sic] that verse is not dirty." [15] In the same year, a young John Huston gained some success with a puppet show, *Frankie and Johnnie,* that also played New York. Huston published the play alongside thirteen versions of the ballad and some beautifully evocative illustrations by Miguel Covarrubias. Frankie's execution bookends the play, a tragic version. In between, Huston revels in a highly stylized vulgarity.

Other ballads of the period that emerged from the same locale and culture, such as "Staggerlee," feature a male protagonist as the central point of identification. In contrast, "Frankie and Johnnie" focuses on an active female sexuality that operates outside of the domestic sphere. While in some versions, Frankie is punished for her misdeeds, the audience's sympathies are exclusively with her (excepting in Sterling A. Brown's version, which places Johnnie as the victim). Jimmie Rodgers completes his telling of the tale by taking an amoral stance: "This story has no moral/This story has no end/The only thing it goes to show/Is there ain't no good in men." The tragic figure is the woman and, with only one or two exceptions, Hollywood's use of the ballad would be to foster identification with and/or the character development of the female principal.

In the first part of the following section, I examine how and why "Frankie and Johnnie" is used as a musical motif in a number of Hollywood productions from the early to mid-1930s. Particularly, I consider its use as a signifier of specific character types and locales: abject women and déclassé settings. The characters are identified as abject by images and dialogue that work in coordination with the ballad to suggest their whiteness is in the process of dissolution. Existing in the realm of the vulgate, "Frankie and Johnnie" uses common speech that is racially coded as black, which in the context of an urban milieu represents illicit desires that transgress moral and sexual values that are normatively coded as white.

FRANKIE AND JOHNNIE GO TO THE MOVIES

In a memorable and early scene from MGM's *Three Godfathers* (1936), Bob (Chester Morris), a cowboy Johnnie in search of his Frankie, fails to seduce

Molly, a blonde paragon of virginal purity. Bob revives his spirits in the saloon and turns his attention to Blackie, the town's resident chippy (prostitute). To the piano accompaniment of "Frankie and Johnnie," Bob and Blackie dance into the fade-out as Bob tells her, "I danced at the social, but it didn't get me anywhere." The PCA demanded that the fade-out eliminate the tag line, "wonder how I'll do with you." However, the instantly recognizable refrain from "Frankie and Johnnie" carries enough lustful significance to compensate for the lost dialogue. Bob's motives are overt. Having failed with the good girl, he seeks comfort with someone from his own moral level. Though Blackie's occupation is not overtly announced, she is the only female in the saloon and her dress, hairstyle, makeup, and body posture strongly contrast the good girl. Blackie's name, dark hair, sexually revealing black dress, heavy makeup, and slovenly physicality imply an almost explicit racial distinction between her and Molly (a Protestant Mary).

The ballad of "Frankie and Johnnie" signifies a world defined by the promises and limits of the saloon, whether it is located on the Western frontier or on the frontier between urban black and white neighborhoods. The song plays out a series of conflicts that are posed as operating on the frontiers of modernity. For white characters, this is most ably signified through the shift from rural to urban lifestyles; for black characters, through defining individual agency within an urban space. Either way, the saloon is where these conflicts are most profoundly located and realized. Specifically, the conflicts are between the opposing calls of the homosocial space of the public house and the heterosocial space of the domestic home. In the saloon, progressive civilizing impulses clash with the primitive instincts of its habitués.

The saloon holds out not only the promise of liquor but also of illicit sexual pleasures, either figured in the songs and dances performed by women or through the company of prostitutes and their pimps. This is the world portrayed in Mae West's first major film, *She Done Him Wrong* (1933). The title is drawn from the refrain of "Frankie and Johnnie," which West performs in the film. The film was an adaptation of West's stage play, *Diamond Lil* (1927), which she also turned into a novel. The setting is a concert saloon in the Bowery in the 1890s. Lou (West) is the saloon's hostess and main attraction. The plot revolves around the traffic of white girls, who are procured in the saloon and shipped to Latin America. The naïve young white girls, valued for their whiteness, are contrasted with the exotic otherness of the characters who threaten their sanctity and with Lou's weary worldliness, which is reinforced through her performance of blues songs that diminish her whiteness.

The performance of "Frankie and Johnnie" is one of the film's big numbers. West had sung the song in the stage play. Robert Garland in the *New York Evening Telegram* wrote: "It is worth swimming to Brooklyn to see her descend

Figure 19.2. Bob (Chester Morris): a cowboy searching for his Frankie (*Three Godfathers*, 1936). (Image courtesy of British Film Institute Stills, Posters, and Designs.)

those dance hall stairs, to be present when she lolls in a golden bed reading the *Police Gazette*, murders her girlfriend, wrecks the Salvation Army, and sings as much of 'Frankie and Johnnie' as the mean old laws allow."[16] Obviously aware of more salacious versions of the song, Garland confirms the idea of the real and/or imaginary excessive signification that the song could carry, particularly when contextualized by the appropriate racial, sexual, and social setting.

If *She Done Him Wrong* represents the urban frontier of the later part of the nineteenth century, when physical pleasures appeared less heavily policed— the film's source play was written during, and as a reaction to, Prohibition— then *Barbary Coast* (1935), which transposes the gangster genre to California at the height of the Gold Rush, represents a more familiar frontier milieu, where the racial identity of Americans is more clearly an issue. Louis Chamalis (Edward G. Robinson) controls San Francisco and owns the Bella Donna saloon, where he tricks miners out of their booty. Penniless Mary Rutledge (Miriam Hopkins) has traveled by ship from New York to marry a man she has never met. On her arrival, she discovers he has been killed after losing his money to Chamalis. The only thing of value that she possesses is her whiteness. Disembarking from the ship, Mary is met by gasps of surprise and desire. "Suffering snakes, a white woman," says Old Atrocity (Walter Brennan), who ferries her from ship to shore. His observation is repeated and then reinforced by a call from a group of men waiting at the quay-side. "What you got there?" they shout to him. "A white woman," he answers. "You're lying!" they respond. "No I'm not. A New York, white woman—whiter than a hen's egg." The scene introduces the main musical themes, a medley of Stephen Foster's minstrel tunes, interspersed with other nineteenth-century signature tunes, such as "Molly Malone." The men, making a great fuss, carry Mary across the muddy streets and walk her past a line of bars from which piano renditions of more minstrel tunes are heard. The music changes to an Oriental theme as they pass a group of Chinese men. "Opium, miss," says one of her chaperones, "opium and Chinamen sure perfume up a stink." This image of a godless alien hellhole regains its American specificity when an offscreen female sings a few lines of "Frankie and Johnnie." In the Bella Donna, a trio on stage are stopped midway through a performance of "Camptown Races" by the sight of the white woman now in their midst. Louis Chamalis, like all the men, is instantly smitten with Mary. He renames her Swan, and she starts work at the crooked roulette wheel.

Though the dialogue denies any physical relationship between Chamalis and Mary, her sense of self-loathing and her easy manner when knocking back hard liquor suggest a kept woman. When Chamalis demands that she love him, her reply is that he should be content with what he has: "Do you still think I'm Mary Rutledge?" she asks him. "Do you think I'm still a white woman?" Progress, both moral and material, is measured by the characters' distance from the image of blackness that so thoroughly marks the patrons of the saloon. In the *Barbary Coast*, blackness is equated with the deep mud

Figure 19.3. Mary (Miriam Hopkins) and Chamalis (Edward G. Robinson): "Do you still think I'm a white woman?" (*Barbary Coast,* 1935). (Image courtesy of British Film Institute Stills, Posters, and Designs.)

through which the characters endlessly trudge: it is the primal element out of which America is formed, but, like the mud, it is destined to be cleaned away. "Rome wasn't built in a day," says the town's first newspaperman. "The paths of empire have always started in mud and ended in glory." If America is to "grow up" then it needs to leave the saloons and songs like "Frankie and John-nie" to slip back into the primordial murk out of which they emerged.

Outside the saloon, but linked to it through drink, the song is used as a signifier of abject femininity. Wrapped around the central story of a pregnant female murderer, who is transferred from prison to a maternity hospital in *Life Begins* (1932), are a number of vignettes that depict a "variety of maternal re-actions." Florette (Glenda Farrell) is a "good-time girl" who has given birth to twins. She rejects motherhood and takes comfort in the gin she hides in her hot water bottle. Her babies are put up for adoption, but when she hears a pro-spective foster parent discussing the separation of the twins she becomes pos-sessive and discovers her maternal instincts. However, the fact that she is a

Figure 19.4. Lillian (Jean Harlow) and her boss (Chester Morris) in *Red-Headed Woman* (1932). (Image courtesy of British Film Institute Stills, Posters, and Designs.)

potentially unsuitable mother is underscored when she sings "Frankie and Johnnie" as a lullaby to one of her babies.[17]

Red-Headed Woman (1932), one of Hollywood's fallen women cycle documented by Lea Jacobs, caused considerable controversy because of its story of a working-class gold digger who uses sex to get what she wants. When her boss (Chester Morris) stays home with his wife rather than making love to her, the heroine Lillian (Jean Harlow) consoles herself by drinking cheap alcohol and getting sloppy drunk as "Frankie and Johnnie" plays on her phonograph. The song functions to confirm her illicit desires and debased and corrupt femininity. As the PCA became more effective in predicting censors' prejudices, the image of the drunken woman, brilliantly portrayed here by Harlow, disappeared from Hollywood's productions and so did songs like "Frankie and Johnnie" that too overtly signified "obscenities."

The public notoriety of "Frankie and Johnnie" meant that by 1936, when Twentieth Century-Fox wanted to use the song in *Banjo On My Knee*, Joe Breen at the PCA strongly advised against its inclusion: "use of the song Frankie and Johnnie is generally deleted by political censor boards. The music alone may be acceptable. We suggest, however, that this be changed." [18] The producers replaced "Frankie and Johnnie" with "St. Louis Blues." The change made no discernible difference to the film inasmuch as both songs carry the same basic images of wanton women and irresponsible men. The usefulness of "Frankie and Johnnie" to producers was the fact that it was instantly recognizable, but the notoriety that helped produce this public recognition was increasingly problematic as it was clearly used to signify a set of desires and values inimical to censor boards.

"THE WHORE & GAMBLER, BY THE STATE LICENC'D, BUILD THAT NATION'S FATE."

—William Blake, *Auguries of Innocence*

Lea Jacobs argues that self-regulation in the 1930s, rather than quasi-legally enforcing producers to cower before its demands, was "above all a way of figuring out how stories deemed potentially offensive could be rewritten to make them acceptable." Controversial subject matter was not outlawed by the industry and its censors but "treated as problems of narrative and form." [19] Filmmakers intentionally sought to construct key dramatic moments that potentially violated the Production Code with what Jacobs calls an "instability of meaning," [20] the intentional creation of ambivalence. However, this needed to be set against an equal need on the part of the filmmakers to reduce ambiguity, so that the film remained both accessible and comprehensible to as wide an audience as possible.

This, as Richard Maltby argues, meant the studios had to develop a system of representational conventions that allowed films to play to a heterogeneous audience without alienating any particular segment. Quoting Colonel Jason

S. Joy (the director of the Studio Relations Committee), Maltby suggests these representational conventions enabled conclusions to be "drawn by the sophisticated mind, but [which] would mean nothing to the unsophisticated and inexperienced." [21] Initially, "Frankie and Johnnie" was used as a sign, for example, of the abject woman (specifically, of prostitution), with no direct reference to the character's profession. The musical refrain reveals the character's trade to the "sophisticated mind" while remaining indistinct, or unproblematic, to the "unsophisticated or inexperienced." While this enabled Hollywood to deal with all sorts of potentially controversial material, films based on or that used the ballad of "Frankie and Johnnie" proved to be less than amenable to the process of what Jacobs calls the industry's "indirect modes of representation." [22]

Her Man, the first film produced that was based on the ballad, secured very positive reviews and box office when it played the large first-run metropolitan theaters.[23] In its review, Variety deemed the film to be free of the ballad's "dirty" elements and a cautionary and salutary tale for innocent girls.[24] However, when the picture moved to small-town, rural, and neighborhood cinemas, it attracted damaging criticism from newspaper editors and concerned citizens. For example, the chair of the "Motion Pictures Advisors in the Massachusetts State Federation of Women's Clubs" wrote to the Motion Picture Producers and Distributors of America (MPPDA) complaining that Her Man had been screened to a Saturday afternoon matinee audience of 500 children on a double bill with Santa Fe Trail. She denounced the film as "a degrading picture from every standpoint and the most drinking picture we have ever seen." [25] In other circumstances, the industry could have evoked what Ruth Vasey labels the "transparent principle of 'deniability,'" [26] but the equally transparent premises on which the story of Frankie and Johnnie is based would have made any denial of the low moral gravity of the characters a clear act of sophistry. The popularity of Frankie and Johnnie, in all it various forms, meant that it was always likely that Hollywood would continue to exploit the story. In so doing, however, it had to attempt to contain the more risqué elements that made the story so attractive. This is what Maltby calls a "strategy of representation, by which a transgressive spectacle could be contained within a repressive narrative structure." [27] How Hollywood negotiated among the material, the censors, and its audiences is part of the story told here.

In order to establish the underworld of Frankie and Johnnie, the filmmakers used racial signifiers that announced the characters' debased state. A Studio Relations Committee (SRC) employee, reviewing the first complete script of Her Man, asked the filmmakers to be "careful" with the "atmospheric shots of the Barbary Coast showing whites, blacks and yellows, houses of prostitution . . . pimps in the crowd, [and] the "mad music and madder dancing." The more fixed a character's "whiteness," the higher standing in which their moral value is held. The drive of the story of *Her Man* is to move Frankie out of the "darkness" of saloon culture and into the light and whiteness of the world outside.

The SRC reviewer found the whole project objectionable: "the story in its self is pretty bad, with no apparent reason for making it. There is no moral in it . . . in short it is a bunch of apple strudel with a lot of hooey poured over it." Without major changes the only way it can be saved, he writes, is to make a burlesque of it. "It would be great in the way 'Ten Nights in a Barroom' (a classic nineteenth-century temperance novel) would be and they would have good comedy." Jacobs notes the producers' use, with some regularity, of comedy as a ploy to get around censors' prohibitions.[28] Writer and director Tay Garnett would keep the central romance between Frankie (Helen Twelvetrees) and Dan (Phillips Holmes), the man who saves her from Johnnie, relatively straight-faced, but he did introduce a series of running gags performed by Dan's drunken sailor friends (played by James Gleason and Harry Sweet) to offer respite from the intensity of Frankie's and Dan's relationship. This idea is supported in the *Exhibitors Herald World*'s review of the film: "Even in the climax, when a life or two is in danger, the [comedy] stops the tears, and the belly laughs reissue."[29]

The biggest problem in producing a script that would satisfy the SRC was how to maintain the story of Frankie and Johnnie without making it obvious that he is her pimp and she his prostitute. As the SRC reviewer concluded, "to treat this story, which has to do with a kept man and his ladylove, with anything but levity seems out of the question." It was a problem that remained unsolved in the second draft of the script.

> Johnnie is one of the most despicable types of men. He is nothing less than a worm. . . . There is as much moral value in this picture as there is in a five week old kippered herring. . . . There is so much drinking, carousing and scenes of bawdy houses that I do not see how this picture can get by as it is now. You are simply dragged through six or eight reels of filth; you wallow in it neck-high, and scream for the whole business to end. All this babble about reformed prostitutes and the creating of sympathy for harlots in general is a lot of tripe, made worse by the inclusion of songs about a vine-covered cottage.

The following month's rewrites offered little improvement: "we look upon the present story as comparatively unattractive, sordid and weak." Most significantly, Frankie could not just be saved; the filmmakers had to establish that she had been a "good girl" from "the beginning." This meant downplaying Frankie's relationship with Johnnie and emphasizing the love story between her and Dan. However, Frankie, in some respect, had to be shown living an illicit life that was tied to her relationship with Johnnie, so that Dan could rescue and redeem her.

The SRC was unhappy with Johnnie's relationship with Frankie because it was based on exploitation, and he was shown to be unfaithful to her. However, as Tay Garnett pointed out, to "make the relationship between Frankie and Johnnie one of sincere attachment, and to eliminate any indication that Johnnie was unfaithful to Frankie, would cause Frankie and Dan to lose sympathy the instant they planned for Frankie to leave Johnnie." Frankie's illicit acts would be limited to getting customers to buy her drinks and the suggestion of pickpocketing. Eventually, the script passed the censors; the finished film, given a certificate. It then immediately ran into controversy.

The original script set the story on the Barbary Coast at the turn of the century to circumvent Prohibition and give the producers a historical angle to exploit. However, during rewrites, the story became set in the present and the locale became Havana, before becoming an unidentified island off the coast of America and, finally, in post-release publicity, a Parisian dive. Unfortunately for the producers, stock footage of Cuba's best-known landmark, Morro Castle, was left in the release prints, and the image of the castle was used in posters and other publicity material. The copy to the Morro Castle poster read: "scarlet streets of the wickedest pleasure mad city of the Universe." The Cuban embassy protested, prompting concern that other Latin American countries would close their markets to the film.[30]

The shifting of the story's location from the United States to a "mythical island" off its coast allowed *Her Man* to present the United States as a moral alternative to the island city's dens of iniquities. The island inhabitants are represented as low class, itinerant, lawless, polyglot in character, and racially diverse. The United States, on the other hand, is represented as classless, domesticated, policed, and white. The film opens with Annie, a worn-out chippy, trying to disembark from a ship. Recognized by the American police, she is sent back to the island. As she tried to gain entry, "No Place Like Home" plays quietly in the background.

On her return to the island, Annie enters the Thalia (the Greek muse of comedy) bar, the setting for most of the action. Later, when Dan makes his play for the attentions of Frankie, this déclassé environment will be contrasted with the sentiments expressed in the song Dan sings to Frankie, "Somehow I Know," which calls up the image of the "vine-covered cottage" that the SRC reviewer found so unappealing. The idyll to which the song alludes is to be read as

America, and the miseries and travails of the two lovers will not be over until they have successfully made their way back "home." Annie's failure to gain entry into the States will be Frankie's fate unless she can leave this polyglot world behind.

In *Frankie and Johnny*, the imminent threat to the characters' whiteness is revealed by contrasting them directly with black characters. Invited to a "colored wedding," Frankie (Helen Morgan) and Johnny (Chester Morris) position themselves as spectators: "They're so simple and sincere. So carefree and happy. They're not afraid of themselves," says Frankie. "What do you mean by that, Frankie?" replies Johnny. "I mean you, Johnny." But Johnny is none of these things.

Variety speculated that the "colored" wedding scene was "dragged in bodily presumably to introduce a song number." The scene begins with a close-up on the grinning mouth of the bridegroom. The preacher declares the couple man and wife and then the outdoor congregation makes a break for the food. Close-ups of black faces pulling the cooked flesh off chicken legs follows. Then the congregation bursts into a song and dance, "Get Rhythm in Your Feet." Beyond its use to introduce a song-and-dance number, the colored wedding exists to distance Frankie and Johnny from the image of blackness that has begun to accrue around their personae. Theirs is a barely legitimate existence, operating far outside the white middle-class ideal.

Frankie and Johnny was conceived as an American version of Shakespeare's romantic tragedy, *Romeo and Juliet*. Toward the end of the story, Frankie takes Johnny to a performance of the play. "They're kind of like us," she tells Johnny. Frankie is overromanticizing their situation, however, and imaginatively trying to escape the vulgar world she is made to inhabit. The setting is St. Louis in the 1870s. Frankie is a singer at the Mansion House, a saloon, concert hall, and, presumably, a brothel. However, through costume, dialogue, deportment, composition within the frame, and contrast with her fellow performers and the habitués of her place of employment, she acquires a cultural refinement at odds with her situation. Her act follows a male performer who is dressed in a jockey's outfit and sings "De Camptown Races." This Stephen Foster blackface minstrel tune plays against Frankie's sentimental rendition of "Give Me a Heart to Sing To." This is to be Frankie's last performance at the Mansion House. She intends to marry Curly, a good man who wants to take her West to new beginnings. As the song moves toward its climax, Nelly Bly wakes her drunken companion and he interrupts the performance. Nelly, who smokes cheroots, is Frankie's nemesis. It is she who makes it impossible for Frankie to leave the vulgar culture of the saloon behind, and this entrapment is Frankie's tragedy.

Toward the end of the wedding scene, Frankie sings a romantic song to Johnny. At first, the black voices from the wedding conflict with the melody she carries, but soon the voices fall into line and offer support and depth to her performance. This is part of a conflict, waged throughout the film, between vulgarity and refinement with the former defined as black; the latter, white. This time Frankie suppresses the vulgar and her refined sensibility wins out. In the following scene, Frankie and Johnny marry, but this image of romance does not last and Frankie's dominion over the vulgar proves illusory: she and Johnny slip back into an underworld.

In the script rewrites of *Her Man*, the character of Johnnie all but fades out of the scenario. The fundamental events in the ballad—Frankie's love for Johnnie, his betrayal, and death—no longer structure the narrative. Johnnie now exists as a foil and a contrast to Frankie's first true love, Dan. Dan, as played by Phillips Holmes, is a tall, muscular man with curly blonde hair, a soft voice, and a winning smile. His height, physique, and hair make him stand out from the crowd. He wears a sailor's jacket, bellbottom trousers, and a heavily worn striped T-shirt. The holes in his shirt grow larger through the course of the film, offering ever more revealing glimpses of his body. In contrast, Johnnie, as played by Ricardo Cortez, is marked as being abnormally narcissistic. He is small, dark, and snappily dressed. His hair is neat and oiled, and he wears tailored clothes. Key scenes show him preening in the mirror, and at the point of his death, his last action is to adjust his tie. His continual play with a little phallic penknife finally confirms the suggestion of his moral degradation and gender deviance.

Johnnie's Latin appearance, dandy persona, and immoral actions—in his first act in the film, he throws a knife in the back of a rival for Frankie's services—effeminizes this archetypal badman. Cortez's Johnnie, like Morris's Bob in *Three Godfathers*, personifies the figure of the "bad man": Bob, it is said, will "kill anything from a baby to an old woman," but, unlike the figure of Staggerlee, he is also a lady's man, someone of suspect masculine traits. In Hollywood's portrayal of the character of Johnnie, this means he will be visually located as being nonwhite, an effect achieved by contrasting him with a paragon of white masculinity. In *Her Man*, the character of Dan performs this task. This is signaled not only in terms of physical differences, but also through the soundtrack. Dan sings a sickly sweet sentimental parlor song. In contrast, Johnnie and his band play hot jazz, and it is Johnnie's presence, rather than that of Frankie, that keys in the refrain from the ballad.

The growth in the popularity of the ballad parallels the rise in interest not only in indigenous black culture, expressed most profoundly in the performance of jazz, but also in the fad for explicitly sexualized and "foreign" dances

Figure 19.5. Dan and Frankie. (Image courtesy of British Film Institute Stills, Posters, and Designs.)

such as the tango. Gaylyn Studlar, in her study of stardom and masculinity in the Jazz Age, notes how the figure of Rudolph Valentino complemented and developed a masculinity that "defied normative standards of robust, ebulliently childish American masculinity," and how this "deviant" form was commonly coded as "darkly foreign" and therefore "dangerous." [31] In these two films, the figure of Johnnie conforms to this type, but is given a new twist because he is so clearly defined as the villain. [32] In *Frankie and Johnny*, the character begins the film masquerading as a country boy, a feigned image of innocence, but as he spends more time in the city, he becomes increasingly effeminate: Johnny is now a man-about-town. A flaneur dressed to the nines, he lounges around in silk dressing gowns, his suits are cut tightly into the waist, his sideburns are as fanciful as those of a Latin lover, and he no longer supports himself but relies on Frankie. In the final scenes, he is made to look pathetic and inadequate as he attempts to seduce Nelly Bly. As his potency diminishes, so does his whiteness.

Frankie's first and still true love is Curly, whose masculinity and race are never questioned. He wanted to take Frankie to California. On the other hand,

Figure 19.6. Johnny as narcissist. (Image courtesy of British Film Institute Stills, Posters, and Designs.)

Johnny does not look to the West as a way to improve his fortune but to the South, to New Orleans. There he believes he can change his streak of bad luck. Johnny's counter to the American image of progress (going South instead of West) is echoed by the incremental dissolution in his whiteness.

On the other hand, Frankie, in *Her Man*, is blonde, her female opponent, Nelly Bly, is dark. Frankie sheds her barroom gladrags as the film progresses. She visits church for the first time and is figuratively reborn through the agency of Dan (she does not know her birth date and he gives her one). The shoes that signified her and Annie's life on the streets are symbolically washed away into the gutter, and her selfless actions to protect her first true love from Johnnie's murderous plans enable her final redemption. This brings the formation of the couple and a home in the United States, which is the given reward for a life cleanly lived.

In contrast, Frankie, in *Frankie and Johnny*, is finally too corrupted by her relationship with Johnny to be redeemed. The screenplay attempts to "rescue" Frankie from the corrupting influence of the habitués of the Mansion House and her implied trade by constructing around her a facade of refined culture by which it is hoped she will be defined. Frankie's transgression is that she has fallen for a no-account scoundrel of a man who lives off women. The film-makers hoped to exploit and contain this potentially censurable scenario by suggesting that Frankie was not fully of this diseased world, that her fall from the white world of high culture comes to mark her as a tragic figure, and that the Code's prohibition against rewarding her through the formation of the couple compounds the tragedy.

All Star and Select Productions' picture *Frankie and Johnny* was released at the beginning of May 1936. The production had begun more than two years earlier. What had at first seemed a novel idea that would exploit the image of the Gay Nineties made popular in *She Done Him Wrong* and *The Bowery* (1933) now seemed hackneyed and rather tired.[33] A script was sent to the PCA in February 1934. The response noted the "questionable nature" of the material and that the story was "most certainly open to serious question, both from the standpoint of the industry standards contained in the Production Code and from the standpoint of official censorship." By then, however, production was already underway. Filming was completed in September, but the PCA with-held a certificate on the grounds that the film was little more than "a sordid sex drama." In October, the PCA asked the producers to remove all uses of the song "Frankie and Johnnie" from the film. It remained in the release print as an occasional instrumental piece. Before granting a certificate, the PCA asked that the producers clearly show that Frankie's relationship with Johnny is "wrong and sinful" and that the film would not allow her to escape the con-sequences of her actions by offering her the promise of future happiness with the man she had earlier jilted for Johnny.[34]

Her Man rode the wave of popularity for versions of the song that appeared at the tail end of the 1920s and the beginning of the 1930s. By the time *Frankie and Johnny* played in theaters, however, the fad had waned, and the song's use-fulness as a signifier of wanton men and women of dubious moral standing and racial status was played out. Nevertheless, by 1945 (and despite Joe Breen proscribing its use a year earlier to the producers of *Ziegfeld Follies*), the song was back again as a piano instrumental in a gold rush barroom scene in the Droopy cartoon, *The Shooting of Dan McGoo* (MGM, 1945); four years later in the comedy Westerns, *The Beautiful Blonde from Bashful Bend* (Twentieth Century-Fox, 1949) and *The Gal Who Took the West* (Universal, 1949); and again in cartoon form in *Rooty Toot Toot* (Columbia, 1952).

The song in these films no longer signifies an abject world but now oper-ates as a nostalgic motif of frontier America, its once racialized, lewd, and salacious subject matter contained within these films' comic field. The inoc-ulization of the ballad would come to some sort of fruition with the folk song revival of the late 1950s and early 1960s.[35] The 1960s folk singers would reclaim an authenticity for the ballad that would help mitigate its nostalgic use by Hollywood in the late 1940s and early 1950s. These late twentieth-century troubadours and minstrels, however, could not retrieve the sense of frisson the song once carried for its audience in the late 1920s and early 1930s, so much of which depended on their proximity to the turn-of-the-century polyglot urban environment with its concomitant fears of miscegenation that the ballad so successfully exploited.

NOTES

1. Quoted in Hugh Fordin, *The World of Entertainment! Hollywood's Greatest Musicals* (New York: Doubleday, 1975), 121–22.

2. Lea Jacobs, *The Wages of Sin: Censorship and the Fallen Woman Film, 1928–1942* (Berkeley: University of California Press, 1997); Richard Maltby, "The Production Code and the Hays Office" in *Grand Design: Hollywood as a Modern Business Enterprise, 1930–1939*, ed. Tino Balio (Berkeley: University of California Press, 1995), 37–72; Ruth Vasey, *The World According to Hollywood, 1918–1939* (Exeter: University of Exeter Press, 1997).

3. The following texts helped to construct this account of the origins and intertexts of the ballad and provided most of the quoted lyrics: Peter Van Der Merwe, *Origins of the Popular Style: The Antecedents of Twentieth-Century Popular Music* (Oxford: Clarendon Press, 1992), 184–97; Vance Randolph, *Ozark Folksongs vol. 2. Songs of the South & West* (Columbia: University of Missouri Press, 1980, [1946–50]), 124–36; Peter Grammond, *The Oxford Companion to Popular Music* (Oxford: Oxford University Press), 207; John A. Lomax and Alan Lomax, *American Ballads and Folk Songs* (New York: Macmillan, 1934), 103–111; Bruce R. Buckley, *Frankie and Her Men: A Study of the Interrelationships of Popular and Folk Traditions* (Ph.D. diss., Indiana University, 1961); John Russell David, *Tragedy in Ragtime: Black Folk Tales From St. Louis* (Ph.D. diss., Saint Louis University, 1976).

4. John Huston, *Frankie and Johnnie* (New York: Albert & Charles Boni, Inc., 1930), 111. See also Paul Oliver, *Songster and Saints: Vocal Traditions on Race Records* (London: Cambridge University Press, 1984), 235.

5. One of the earliest recordings of the ballad (1922) was by the blackface minstrel Al Bernard, who billed himself as "The Boy From Dixie."

6. James H. Dormon, "Shaping the Popular Image of Post-Reconstruction American Blacks: The 'Coon Song' Phenomenon of the Gilded Age," *American Quarterly* 40, no. 4. (1988), 440–77.

7. Huston, *Frankie and Johnnie*, 106–7.

8. Oliver, *Songster and Saints*, 237–38.

9. Huston, *Frankie and Johnnie*, 150.

10. Sterling A. Brown, *The Collected Poems of Sterling A. Brown* (New York: Harper & Row, 1980), 44.

11. David, *Tragedy in Ragtime*, 204–5.

12. Huston, *Frankie and Johnnie*, 146.

13. Gerald Bordman, *American Theatre: A Chronicle of Comedy and Drama, 1930–1969* (New York: Oxford University Press, 1996), 7.

14. This and the following quotations that relate to censorship and *Her Man* are taken from the Production Code Administration file on the film stored in Margaret Herrick Library, Academy of Motion Picture Arts and Sciences (AMPAS).

15. *Variety*, September 17, 1930.

16. Quoted in Fergus Cashin, *Mae West: A Biography* (London: W. H. Allen, 1981), 80.

17. The film is discussed at some length by Nick Roddick, *A New Deal in Entertainment: Warner Bros. in the 1930s* (London: British Film Institute, 1983), 169–71.

18. PCA file, *Banjo On My Knee*, Margaret Herrick Library, AMPAS.

19. Jacobs, *Wages of Sin*, x.

20. Ibid., 35.

21. Maltby, "The Production Code," 40.

22. Jacobs, *Wages of Sin*, 35.

23. *Her Man* premiered in New York on October 3, 1930. With the odd exception—the *New York Times* claimed it was "a hodge-podge of sentimentality" (October 6, 1930)—the film was widely celebrated by the critics. *Motion Picture* magazine countered the *Times* critic: "Tay Garnett's deft hand lifts what might be a maudlin theme into a guaranteed entertainment and makes barroom sentimentality convincing, even sophisticated" (December 1930, 63). Another fan magazine, *Picture Play*, called the film a "rattling good picture," which they recommended "without reservation." Like many other reviews, this one praised the fact that "dialogue is subordinate to action," which reaches a climax in the free-for-all bar fight between Dan and Johnnie and their respective cronies: "For a more terrific fight I never have witnessed, nor one that conveys less restraint or calculated fury" (January 1931, 24–25, 65). The *Exhibitors Herald World* concurred: "To my mind Garnett's fight sequence outdoes any heretofore" (September 13, 1930). Other trade journals were also generally positive. *Film Daily* called the film the "best drama of its kind to come along in quite a while" (September 21, 1930). *Motion Picture News* (September 27, 1930) and *Variety* (September 17, 1930) noted the quality of the acting and direction and gave wholly celebratory reviews. The tabloid press, if the New York dailies are any kind of guide, were also enthralled by the picture, echoing the sentiments of the trade and fan press. Pathé reproduced eight positive film reviews from the New York press as an advertisement for the film in *Exhibitors Herald World* (October 11, 1930).

24. *Variety* (September 17, 1930).

25. John Andrew Gallagher, "Rediscovering Her Man," *Films in Review* 46, nos. 9/10 (November/December 1995), 36–45.

26. Vasey, *The World*, 107.

27. Richard Maltby, *Tragic Heroes? Al Capone and the Spectacle of Criminality, 1948–1931* (unpublished paper).

28. Jacobs, *Wages of Sin*, 66–70.

29. *Exhibitors Herald World*, September 13, 1930, 38.

30. See Vasey, *The World*, 118, 123, 211.

31. Gaylyn Studlar, *This Mad Masquerade: Stardom and Masculinity in the Jazz Age* (New York: Columbia University Press, 1997), 151–52.

32. Pathé's attempts to protect the film from being censured or banned by Latin American governments led to reviews that attempted to resituate the film in France and to cast Johnnie more overtly as a Latin dancer: "*Her Man* carries a new angle for an underworld, that of a French knife throwing Apache in modern dress, with girls under his control. Nearly the entire picture is localed in a Paris dive." *Variety* (September 17, 1930).

33. The *Motion Picture Herald* critic reviewed the film "with an audience composed of newspapermen and fluffy dowagers, all of whom remained silent throughout the entire film and continually fidgeted in their seats, perhaps from the heat" (May 23, 1936, 45). The reviewer cites two extremes of gendered audiences to suggest that the film would not find a specific audience, never mind a heterogeneous one. Frank S. Nugent in the *New York Times* thought the film "slightly more lachrymose and off-key than a whiskey tenor" (May 25, 1936). *Variety* considered it to be "unusually slovenly entertainment" (May 27, 1936). The film's distributor tried to boost interest through the occasional publicity stunt, such as organizing a "cycle excursion" from New York, on which "prizes for the most original gay-nineties costumes were given to members of the bicycling party" (*Motion Picture Herald*, May 30, 1936). It was to little effect, however, and the film appears to have fulfilled *Variety*'s prediction that it would be "lucky to make dual bookings in most localities." Both the *New York Times* and *Variety* noted the difficulties the filmmakers experienced with the "Hays code office," speculating on whether this "dehydrating" process ruined a good film or whether it was "pretty bad" from the beginning.

34. Quotations from the Production Code Administration files and some details of the film's production are drawn from the entry on *Frankie and Johnny* in *American Film Institute Catalog—Feature Films 1931–1940*, 699–700.

35. For example, its inclusion in Tom Glazer, *A New Treasury of Folk Songs* (New York: Bantam, 1961). For an exemplary history of the folk revival, see Robert Cantwell, *When We Were Good: The Folk Revival* (Cambridge: Harvard University Press, 1996).

SELECT BIBLIOGRAPHY

Beretta E. Smith-Shomade

WHITENESS STUDIES AND CRITICAL RACE THEORY

Allen, Theodore. *The Invention of the White Race.* New York: Verso, 1994.

Babb, Valerie. *Whiteness Visible: The Meaning of Whiteness in American Literature and Culture.* New York: New York University Press, 1998.

Berger, Maurice. *White Lies: Race and the Myths of Whiteness.* New York: Farrar, Strauss, Giroux, 1999.

Bernardi, Daniel, ed. *The Birth of Whiteness: Race and the Emergence of United States Cinema.* New Brunswick: Rutgers University Press, 1996.

———. *Star Trek and History: Race-ing Toward a White Future.* New Brunswick: Rutgers University Press, 1998.

Bhabha, Homi K. "The White Stuff." *Artforum* 36.9 (May 1998): 21–24.

Bonnett, Alastair. "'White Studies': The Problems and Projects of a New Research Agenda." *Theory, Culture, and Society.* 13.2 (1996): 145–55.

Clark, Christine and James O'Donnell, eds. *Becoming and Unbecoming White: Owning and Disowning a Racial Identity.* Westport, CT: Bergin & Garvey, 1999.

Crenshaw, Carrie. "'Resisting Whiteness': Rhetorical Silence." *Western Journal of Communication.* 61.3 (summer 1997): 253–279.

Cuomo, Chris and Kim Hall. *Whiteness: Feminist Philosophical Reflections.* Lanham, MD: Rowman & Littlefield, 1999.

Delgado, Richard and Jean Stefancic, eds. *Critical Race Theory: The Cutting Edge.* Philadelphia: Temple University Press, 2000.

———, eds. *Critical White Studies: Looking Behind the Mirror.* Philadelphia: Temple University Press, 1997.

Dominguez, Virginia. *White By Definition: Social Classification in Creole Louisiana.* New Brunswick: Rutgers University Press, 1994.

Dyer, Richard. "The Colour of Virtue: Lillian Gish, Whiteness and Femininity." In *Women and Film: A Sight and Sound Reader,* edited by Pam Cook and Philip Dodd. Philadelphia: Temple University Press, 1993.

———. "Into the Light: The Whiteness of the South in *The Birth of a Nation.*" In *Dixie Debates: Perspectives on Southern Culture,* edited by Richard H. King and Helen Taylor. London: Pluto, 1996.

———. "There's Nothing I Can't Do! Nothing! Femininity, Seriality, and Whiteness in *The Jewel in the Crown.*" *Screen.* 37.3 (1996).

———. "White." *Screen.* 29.4 (autumn, 1988): 44–64.

———. *White.* New York: Routledge, 1997.

Dyson, Lynda. "The Return of the Repressed? Whiteness, Femininity, and Colonialism in *The Piano.*" *Screen.* 35 (1995).

Entman, Robert. *The Black Image in the White Mind: Media and Race in America.* Chicago: University of Chicago Press, 2000.

Fanon, Frantz. *Black Skin, White Masks.* New York: Grove Press, 1967.

Favor, J. Martin. *Authentic Blackness: The Folk in New Negro Renaissance.* Durham, NC: Duke University Press, 1999.

Feagin, Joe R. and Hernan Vera. *White Racism: The Basics.* New York: Routledge, 1995.

Fine, Michelle et al., eds. *Off White: Readings On Race, Power, and Society.* New York: Routledge, 1997.

Fishkin, Shelley Fisher. "Interrogating Whiteness, Complicating Blackness: Remapping American Culture." *American Quarterly.* 47.3 (September 1995): 428–66.

Frankenberg, Ruth, ed. *Displacing Whiteness: Essays in Social and Cultural Criticism.* Durham, NC: Duke University Press, 1997.

———. *Local Whiteness, Localizing Whiteness.* Durham, NC: Duke University Press, 1996.

———. *White Women, Race Matters: The Social Construction of Whiteness.* Minneapolis: University of Minnesota Press, 1993.

Frye, Marilyn. "On Being White: Thinking Toward a Feminist Understanding of Race and Race Supremacy." In *The Politics of Reality: Essays in Feminist Theory,* edited by Marilyn Frye. Trumansburg, NY: Crossing Press, 1983, 110–27.

Gabriel, John. *Whitewash: Racialized Politics and the Media.* New York: Routledge, 1998.

Gallagher, Charles. "White Reconstruction in the University." *Socialist Review.* 24 (1995).

Gates, Henry Louis, K. A. Appiah, and Michael Vasquez. *The White Issue: A Special Issue of Transition.* Durham, NC: Duke University Press, 1998.

Gilman, Sander L. "Black Bodies, White Bodies: Toward an Iconography of Female Sexuality in Late Nineteenth-Century Art, Medicine, and Literature." In *Race, Writing and Difference,* edited by Henry Louis Gates, Jr. Chicago: University of Chicago Press, 1985.

Giroux, Henry A. "Rewriting the Discourse of Racial Identity: Toward a Pedagogy and Politics of Whiteness." *Harvard Educational Review.* 67.2 (summer 1997): 285–320.

Gutierrez, Gabriel. "Deconstructing Disney: Chicano/a Children and Critical Race Theory." *Aztlan.* 25.1 (spring 2000): 7–47.

Hale, Grace Elizabeth. *Making Whiteness: The Culture of Segregation in the South, 1890–1940.* New York: Pantheon Books, 1998.

Haney-Lopez, Ian. *White by Law: The Legal Construction of Race.* New York: New York University Press, 1996.

Harris, Cheryl I. "Whiteness as Property." *Harvard Law Review.* 106.8 (June 1993): 1707–91.

Hartigan, John Jr. "Establishing the Fact of Whiteness." *American Anthropologist.* 99.3 (September 1997): 495–505.

Hatt, Michael. "Ghost Dancing in the Salon: The Red Indian as a Sign of White Identity." *Diogenes.* 45.1 (spring 1997): 93–110.

Hill, Mike. *Whiteness: A Critical Reader.* New York: New York University Press, 1997.

hooks, bell. "Representing Whiteness in the Black Imagination." In *Cultural Studies,* edited by Lawrence Grossberg et al. New York: Routledge, 1992.

Horsman, Reginald. *Race and Manifest Destiny: The Origins of American Racial Anglo-Saxonism.* Harvard University Press, 1986.

Hyde, C. "The Meanings of Whiteness." *Qualitative Sociology.* 18 (1995).

Ignatiev, Noel. *How the Irish Became White.* New York: Routledge, 1995.

Ignatiev, Noel and John Garvey, eds. *Race Traitor.* New York: Routledge, 1996.

Jacobson, Matthew Frye. *Whiteness of a Different Color: European Immigrants and the Alchemy of Race.* Cambridge, MA: Harvard University Press, 1998.

Jordan, Winthrop D. *The White Man's Burden: Historical Origins of Racism in the United States.* New York: Oxford University Press, 1974.

———. *White Over Black: American Attitudes Toward the Negro, 1550–1812.* Chapel Hill, NC: University of North Carolina Press, 1968.

Kaplan, Sidney. *American Studies in Black and White: Selected Essays, 1949–1989.* Amherst: University of Massachusetts Press, 1991.

Kincheloe, Joe, ed. *White Reign: Deploying Whiteness in America.* New York: St. Martin's Press, 1998.

Knadler, Stephen P. "Untragic Mulatto: Charles Chesnutt and the Discourse of Whiteness." *American Literary History.* 8.3 (fall 1996): 426–48.

Kuo Wei Tchen, John. "White Patriarchy." In *Moving the Image: Independent Asian Pacific American Media Arts,* edited by Russell Leong. Los Angeles: UCLA Asian American Studies Center, 1991.

Ledbetter, James. "The Unbearable Whiteness of Publishing." *The Village Voice.* 40.30 & 31 (July 1995 and August 1995).

Lipsitz, George. *The Possessive Investment in Whiteness: How White People Profit from Identity Politics.* Philadelphia: Temple University Press, 1998.

————et al. "The Possessive Investment in Whiteness: Racialized Social Democracy and the White Problem in American Studies." *American Quarterly.* 47.3 (September 1995): 369–427.

————. "Toxic Racism." *American Quarterly.* 47.3 (September 1995).

Lott, Eric. "The Whiteness of Film Noir." In *Whiteness: A Critical Reader,* edited by Mike Hill. New York: New York University Press, 1997, 81–101.

————. "White Like Me: Racial Cross-Dressing and the Construction of American Whiteness." In *Culture of United States Imperialism,* edited by Amy Kaplan and Donald E. Pease. Durham, NC: Duke University Press, 1993, 474–95.

————. "Whiteness: A Glossary." *Village Voice.* May 18, 1993: 38–39.

Mahoney, Martha R. "Segregation, Whiteness, and Transformation." *University of Pennsylvania Law Review.* 143 (1995).

McMillen, Liz. "Lifting the Veil from Whiteness: Growing Body of Scholarship Challenges a Racial Norm." *Chronicle of Higher Education.* (September 8, 1995): A23

Michaels, Walter Benn. "The Souls of White Folk." In *Literature and the Body: Essays on Populations and Persons,* edited by Elaine Scarry. Baltimore: John Hopkins University Press, 1988.

Morrison, Toni. *Playing in the Dark: Whiteness and the Literary Imagination.* Cambridge: Harvard University Press, 1992.

Mullen, Harryette. "Optic White: Blackness and the Production of Whiteness." *Diacritics.* 24. 2–3 (1994): 71–89.

Nakayama, Thomas K. and Robert L. Krizek. "Whiteness: A Strategic Rhetoric." *The Quarterly Journal of Speech.* 81.3 (1995): 291–309.

Nakayama, Thomas and Judith Martin, eds. *Whiteness: The Communication of Social Identity.* Thousand Oaks, CA: Sage Publications, 1999.

Nishime, Leilani Linda. "Creating Race: Genre and the Cultural Construction of Asian American Identity." *Dissertation Abstracts.* 98.5 (November 1997): 1782.

Oliver, Melvin L. and Thomas M. Shapiro. *Black Wealth/White Wealth: A New Perspective on Racial Inequality.* New York: Routledge, 1995.

Patton, Cindy. "White Racism/Black Signs: Censorship and Images of Race Relations." *Journal of Communications*. 45.2 (spring 1995): 65–77.

Penn, W. S., ed. *As We Are Now: Mixblood Essays on Race and Identity*. Berkeley: University of California Press, 1997.

Pfeil, Fred. *White Guys*. New York: Routledge, 1995.

Posnock, Ross. *Color and Culture: Black Writers and the Making of the Modern Intellectual*. Cambridge: Harvard University Press, 1998.

Puar, Jasbir K. "Resituating Discourses of Whiteness and Asianness in Northern England." *Socialist Review*. 24 (1995).

Rafael, Vicente L. "White Love: Surveillance and Nationalist Resistance in the U.S. Colonization of the Philippines." In *Cultures of United States Imperialism*, edited by Amy Kaplan and Donald E. Pease. Durham, NC: Duke University Press, 1993.

Rafter, Nicole Hahn. *White Trash: The Eugenic Family Studies, 1877–1919*. Boston: Northeastern University Press, 1988.

Rhines, Jesse Algeron. *Black Film, White Money*. New Brunswick: Rutgers University Press, 1996.

Roediger, David, ed. *Towards the Abolition of Whiteness: Essays on Race, Politics, and Working Class History*. New York: Verso, 1994.

Roediger, David. *The Wages of Whiteness: Race and the Making of the American Working Class*. London: Verso, 1991.

Rogin, Michael. *Blackface, White Noise: Jewish Immigrants in the Hollywood Melting Pot*. Berkeley: University of California Press, 1996.

Ronald, L. "White Space, White Privilege: Mapping Discursive Inquiry into the Self." *Quarterly Journal of Speech*. 85.1 (February 1999): 38–54.

Sacks, Karen B. "How Did Jews Become White Folks?" In *Race*, edited by Steven Gregory and Roger Sanjek. New Brunswick: Rutgers University Press, 1994.

Sanchez, George J. "Reading Reginald Denny: The Politics of Whiteness in the Late Twentieth Century." *American Quarterly*. 47 (1995).

Saxton, Alexander. *Rise and Fall of the White Republic: Class Politics and Mass Culture in Nineteenth-Century America*. New York: Verso, 1990.

Seshadri-Crooks, Kalpana. *Desiring Whiteness: A Lacanian Analysis of Race*. New York: Routledge, 2000.

Shome, Raka. "Race and Popular Cinema: The Rhetorical Strategies of Whiteness in *City of Joy*." *Communication Quarterly*. 44.4 (1996): 502–18.

Shohat, Ella and Robert Stam. *Unthinking Eurocentrism: Multiculturalism and the Media*. New York: Routledge, 1994.

Smith, Shawn Michelle. " 'Baby's Picture Is Always Treasured': Eugenics and the Reproduction of Whiteness in the Family Photograph Album." *Yale Journal of Criticism*. 11.1 (spring 1998): 197–220.

Stowe, David W. "Uncolored People: The Rise of Whiteness Studies." *Lingua Franca*. 6.6 (September/October 1996): 68–77.

Tardon, Raphael. "Richard Wright Tells Us: The White Problem in the United States." *Action* (October 24, 1946). Reprinted in Kenneth Kinnamon and Michel Fabre. *Conversations with Richard Wright.* Jackson: University Press of Mississippi, 1946.

Taylor, Henry Louis, Jr. "The Hidden Face of Racism." *American Quarterly.* 47.3 (September 1995).

Torres, Rodolfo, Louis Miron, and Jonathan Xavier Inda, eds. *Race, Identity, and Citizenship: A Reader.* Malden, MA: Oxford, 1999.

Ware, Vron. *Beyond the Pale: White Women, Racism, and History.* New York: Verso, 1992.

Warren, Jonathan W. and Winddance Twine. "White Americans, the New Minority? Non-Blacks and the Ever-Expanding Boundaries of Whiteness." *Journal of Black Studies.* 28.2 (November 1997): 200–18.

Wray, Matt and Annalee Newitz, eds. *White Trash: Race and Class in America.* New York: Routledge, 1997.

Young, Robert. "The Jewish Nose: Are Jews White? Or the History of the Nose Job." In *The Jew's Body*, edited by Sander Gilman. New York: Routledge, 1991.

———. *White Mythologies: Writing History and the West.* New York: Routledge, 1990.

RACE AND CLASSICAL HOLLYWOOD CINEMA

Aleiss, Angela. "Prelude to World War II: Racial Unity and the Hollywood Indian." *Journal of American Culture.* 18.2 (summer 1995): 27–36.

———. "A Race Divided: The Indian Westerns of John Ford." *American Indian Culture and Research.* 18.3 (summer 1994): 167–86.

———. "Race in Contemporary American Cinema: Part IV-Native Americans: The Surprising Silents." *Cineaste.* 27.3 (1995): 34–35.

———. "The Vanishing American: Hollywood's Compromise to Indian Reform." *Journal of American Studies.* (December 1991): 467–72.

American Film Institute, Alan Gevinson, ed. *Within Our Gates: Ethnicity in American Feature Films, 1911–1960* (Berkeley: University of California Press, 1997).

Augusto, Sérgio. "Hollywood Looks at Brazil: From Carmen Miranda to Moonraker." In *Brazilian Cinema*, expanded edition, edited by Randal Johnson and Robert Stam. New York: Columbia University Press, 1995.

Bataille, Gretchen M. and Charles L. P. Silet, eds. *The Pretend Indians: Images of Native Americans in the Movies.* Ames: Iowa State University Press, 1980.

Berg, Charles Ramirez. "Stereotyping in Films in General and of the Hispanic in Particular." *Howard Journal of Communications.* 2.3 (summer 1990): 286–300.

Berkhofer, Robert F., Jr. *The White Man's Indian: Images of the American Indian from Columbus to the Present.* New York: Vintage, 1978.

Bernstein, Matthew and Gaylyn Studlar. *Visions of the East: Orientalism in Film.* New Brunswick: Rutgers University Press, 1997.

Berumen, Frank Javier Garcia and Frank J. Garcia. *Chicano: Hispanic Image in American Film.* New York: Vantage Press, 1994.

Bird, S. Elizabeth. "Tales of Difference: Representations of American Indian Women in Popular Film and Television." In *Mediated Women: Representations in Popular Culture,* edited by Marian Meyers. Cresskill, NJ: Hampton Press, 1999.

Bogle, Donald. *Blacks in American Films and Television: An Encyclopedia.* New York: Simon & Schuster, 1989.

———. *Dorothy Dandridge: A Biography.* New York: Amistad, 1997.

———. *Toms, Coons, Mulattos, Mammies and Bucks: An Interpretive History of Blacks in American Films.* New York: Continuum, 1989.

Browne, Nick. "Race: The Political Unconscious of American Film." *East West Film Journal.* 6.1 (1992): 5–16.

Burton, Julianne. "Don (Juanito) Duck and the Imperial-Patriarchal Unconscious: Disney Studios, the Good Neighbor Policy, and the Packaging of Latin America." In *Nationalities & Sexualities,* edited by Andrew Parker, et al. New York: Routledge, 1992.

Callaghan, David Scott. "Representing the Vietnamese: Race, Culture, and the Vietnam War in American Film and Drama." *Dissertation Abstracts.* 59.4 (October 1998): 1010.

Cameron, Kenneth M. *Africa on Film: Beyond Black and White.* New York: Continuum, 1994.

Caputi, Jane and Helene Vann. "Questions of Race and Place: Comparative Racism in *Imitation of Life* and *Places in the Heart.*" *Cineaste.* 15.4 (1987): 16–21.

Carby, Hazel. *Race Men.* Cambridge: Harvard University Press, 1998.

Carroll, Noël. "King Kong: Ape and Essence." In *Planks of Reason: Essays on the Horror Film,* edited by Barry Keith Grant. Metuchen, NJ: Scarecrow, 1984.

Chandler, Karen Michele. "Wages of Innocence, Wages of Sin: Melodramatic Fictions of Love, Class, and Race in Modern America, 1890–1940." *Dissertation Abstracts.* 55.5 (1994): 1261A.

Churchill, Ward, ed. *Fantasies of the Master Race: Literature, Cinema, and the Colonization of American Indians.* San Francisco: City Lights Books, 1998.

Clark, Ginger. "Cinema of Compromise: Pinky and the Politics of Post..." *Western Journal of Black Studies.* 21.3 (fall 1997).

Couvares, Francis G. "The Good Censor: Race, Sex, and Censorship in Early Cinema." *Yale Journal of Criticism.* 7.2 (fall 1994): 233–51.

Cripps, Thomas. *Black Film as Genre.* Bloomington: Indiana University Press, 1978.

———. "Dark Spot in the Kaleidoscope: Black Image in American Film." In *The Kaleidoscopic Lens: How Hollywood Views Ethnic Groups,* edited by Randall M. Miller. Englewood, NJ: Jerome S. Ozer, 1980.

———. *Making Movies Black: The Hollywood Message Movie from World War II to the Civil Rights Era.* New York: Oxford University Press, 1993.

———. *Slow Fade to Black: The Negro in American Film, 1900–1942.* New York: Oxford University Press, 1993.

———. "Winds of Change: *Gone with the Wind* and Racism as a National Issue." In *Recasting: "Gone with the Wind" in American Culture: The Loss of American Innocence,* edited by Darden Asbury Pyron. Miami: University Press of Florida, 1983.

Cunningham, John. "A Second Look." *Cineaste.* 22.2 (1996): 40–41.

Dagle, Joan and Kathryn Kalinak. "The Representation of Race and Sexuality: Visual and Musical Construction in *Gone with the Wind.*" *Post Script.* 13.2 (winter-spring 1994): 14–27.

Dearborn, Mary V. *Pocahontas's Daughters: Gender and Ethnicity in American Culture.* New York: Oxford University Press, 1986.

DelGaudio, Sybil. "The Mammy in Hollywood Film, I'd Walk a Million Miles for One of Her Smiles." *Jump Cut.* 28 (April 1983): 23–25.

Derrick, C. "Race and *Touch of Evil.*" *Sight and Sound.* 6.11 (November 1996): 72.

Doane, Mary Ann. "Dark Continents: Epistemologies of Racial and Sexual Difference in Psychoanalysis and the Cinema." *Femmes Fatales: Feminism, Film Theory, and Psychoanalysis.* New York: Routledge, 1991.

Dunkerley, James. "All That Trouble Down There: Hollywood and Central America." In *Mediating Two Worlds,* edited by John King et al. London: British Film Institute Publishing, 1993.

Dyer, Richard. "Four Films of Lana Turner." In *Imitations of Life: A Reader on Film and Television Melodrama,* edited by Marcia Landy. Detroit: Wayne State University Press, 1991.

———. "Paul Robeson: Crossing Over." In *Heavenly Bodies: Film Stars and Society,* edited by Richard Dyer. New York: St. Martin's Press, 1986.

———. "The Colour of Entertainment." *Sight and Sound*. 5.11 (November 1995): 28–31.

Ellis, Kirk. "On the Warpath: John Ford and the Indians." *Journal of Popular Film and Television*. 8.2 (winter 1981): 34–41.

Everett, Anna. "The Other Pleasures: The Narrative Function of Race in the Cinema." *Film Criticism*. 20.1–2 (fall-winter 1995–1996): 26–38.

Feng, Peter. "In Search of Asian-American Cinema." *Cineaste*. 21.1–2 (1995): 32–36.

Fiedler, Leslie A. "The Anti-Tom Novel and the Great Depression: Margaret Mitchell's *Gone With the Wind*." In *Gone With the Wind as Book and Film*, compiled and edited by Richard Harwell. Columbia: University of South Carolina Press, 1983.

Fienup-Riordan, Ann. *Freeze Frame: Alaska Eskimos in the Movies*. Seattle: University of Washington Press, 1995.

Film & History. Vol. XXIII. Nos. 1–4 (1993). Special issue on "The Hollywood Indian."

Fischer, Lucy, ed. *Imitation of Life*. New Brunswick: Rutgers University Press, 1991.

Flitterman-Lewis, Sandy. "Imitation(s) of Life: The Black Woman's Double Determination as Troubling Other." *Literature and Psychology*. 34.4 (1988): 44–57.

French, Warren, ed. *The South and Film*. Jackson: University Press of Mississippi, 1981.

Friar, Ralph E. and Natasha A. Friar. *The Only Good Indian: The Hollywood Gospel*. New York: Drama Book Specialists, 1972.

Gabler, Neal. *An Empire of Their Own: How the Jews Invented Hollywood*. New York: Crown Publishers, 1988.

Gaines, Jane. "Fire and Desire: Race, Melodrama, and Oscar Micheaux." In *Black American Cinema*, edited by Manthia Diawara. New York: Routledge, 1993.

———. "White Privilege and Looking Relations: Race and Gender in Feminist Film Theory." *Cultural Critique*. 4 (winter 1986): 13–27.

Georgakas, Dan. "They Have Not Spoke: American Indians in Film." In *The Pretend Indians: Images of Native Americans in the Movies*, edited by Gretchen M. Bataille and Charles L. P. Silet. Ames: Iowa State University Press, 1980.

Godden, Richard and Mary A. McCay, "Say It Again, Sam(bo): Race and Speech in *Huckleberry Finn* and *Casablanca*." *Mississippi Quarterly*. 49.4 (fall 1996): 657–682.

Gosselin, Adrienne Johnson. "Racial Etiquette and the (White) Plot of Passing:

(Re)Inscribing 'Place' in John Stahl's *Imitation of Life.*" *Canadian Review of American Studies.* 28.3 (1998): 47–68.

Green, Rayna. "The Pocahontas Perplex: The Image of Indian Women in Culture." *Massachusetts Review.* 16 (1975): 698–714.

Guerrero, Edward. *Framing Blackness: The African American Image in Film.* Philadelphia: Temple University Press, 1993.

Hadley-Garcia, George. *Hispanic Hollywood: The Latins in Motion Pictures.* Secaucus, NJ: Citadel, 1991.

Ham, Debra Newmann. *The African-American Mosaic: A Library of Congress Resource Guide for the Study of Black History and Culture.* Washington, D.C.: Library of Congress, 1993.

Hannon, Charles. "Race Fantasies: The Filming of Intruder in the Dust." In *Faulkner in Cultural Context,* edited by Donald M. Kartiganer, et al. Jackson: University Press of Mississippi, 1997.

Harris, Tina M. and Deidra Donmoyer. "Is Art Imitating Life?: Communicating Gender and Racial Identity in *Imitation of Life.*" *Women's Studies in Communication.* 23.1. (winter 2000): 91–111.

Hershfield, Joanne. "Race and Romance in *Bird of Paradise.*" *Cinema Journal.* 37.3 (spring 1998): 3–15.

Heung, Marina. "What's the Matter with Sara Jane? Daughters and Mothers in Douglas Sirk's *Imitation of Life.*" *Cinema Journal.* 26.3 (spring 1987): 21–43.

Higashi, Sumiko. "Ethnicity, Class, and Gender in Film: DeMille's *The Cheat.*" In *Unspeakable Images: Ethnicity and the American Cinema,* edited by Lester D. Friedman. Urbana: University of Illinois Press, 1991.

———. "Melodrama, Realism, and Race: World War II Newsreels and Propaganda Film." *Cinema Journal.* 37.3 (spring 1998): 38–61.

Hilger, Michael. *From Savage to Nobleman: Images of Native Americans in Film.* Metuchen, NJ: Scarecrow, 1995.

———. *The American Indian in Film.* Metuchen, NJ: Scarecrow, 1986.

Hoppenstand, Gary. "Yellow Devil Doctors and Opium Dens: A Survey of the Yellow Peril Stereotypes in Mass Media Entertainment." In *The Popular Culture Reader,* 3d ed., edited by Christopher D. Geist and Jack Nachbar. Bowling Green, OH: Bowling Green University Popular Press, 1983.

Jojola, Ted. "Absurd Reality: Hollywood Goes to the Indians." *Film & History.* 23.1–4 (1993): 7–16.

Jewell, K. Sue. *From Mammy to Miss America and Beyond.* New York: Routledge, 1993.

Jones, Christopher John. "Image and Ideology in Kazan's Pinky." *Literature/Film Quarterly.* 9.2 (1981): 110–20.

Keller, Gary D., ed. *Chicano Cinema: Research, Reviews, and Resources.* Binghamton, NY: Bilingual Review/Press, 1985.

————. *Hispanics and United States Film: An Overview and Handbook.* Tempe, AZ: Bilingual Press, 1994.

Kelly, Thomas O. II. "Race and Racism in the American World War II Film: The Negro, the Nazi, and the 'Jap' in Batann and Sahara." *Michigan Academician.* 24.4 (summer 1992): 571–83.

Kennedy, Lisa. "The Body in Question." In *Black Popular Culture*, edited by Gina Dent. Seattle: Bay Press, 1992.

Kilpatrick, Jacquelyn. *Celluloid Indians: Native Americans and Film.* Lincoln: University of Nebraska Press, 1999.

King, John, Ana Lopez, Manuel Alvarado, eds. *Mediating Two Worlds: Cinematic Encounters in the Americas.* London: British Film Institute Publishing, 1993.

Kisch, John and Edward Mapp. *A Separate Cinema: Fifty Years of Black-Cast Posters.* New York: Farrar, Straus, and Giroux, 1992.

Klotman, Phyllis Rauch. *Frame by Frame: A Black Filmography.* Bloomington: Indiana University Press, 1979.

Larson, Charles R. "The Black King: Forgotten 'Black?' Classic." *Journal of Popular Film and Television.* 20.2 (summer 1992): 17–25.

Leab, Daniel J. *From Sambo to Superspade: The Black Experience in Motion Pictures.* Boston: Houghton Mifflin, 1975.

Lhamon, W. T. Jr. *Raising Cain: Blackface Performance from Jim Crow to Hip Hop.* Cambridge: Harvard University Press, 1998.

Lipsitz, George. "Genre Anxiety and Racial Representation in 1970s Cinema." In *Refiguring American Film Genres: History and Theory.* Berkeley: University of California Press, 1998.

List, Christine. *Chicano Images: Refiguring Ethnicity in Mainstream Film.* New York: Garland, 1996.

Lopez, Ana M. "Are All Latinas from Manhattan? Hollywood, Ethnography, and Cultural Colonialism." In *Unspeakable Images: Ethnicity and the American Cinema*, edited by Lester D. Friedman. Chicago: University of Illinois Press, 1991.

Luhr, William. "The Scarred Woman Behind the Gun: Gender, Race, and History in Recent Westerns." *Bilingual Review/La Revista Bilingüe.* 20.1 (1995): 37–44.

Lund, Karen C. *American Indians in Silent Film: Motion Pictures in the Library of Congress.* Washington, D.C.: Library of Congress, August 1992.

Maltby, Richard. "A Better Sense of History: John Ford and the Indians." In *The Movie Book of the Western*, edited by Ian Cameron and Douglas Pye. London: Studio Vista, 1996.

Manchel, Frank. "Cultural Confusion: A Look Back at Delmar Dave's *Broken Arrow*." *Film & History.* 23.1–4 (1993): 57–69.

Marchetti, Gina. "Contradictions and Viewing Pleasure: The Articulation of Racial, Class, and Gender Differences in *Sayonara*." In *Multiple Voices in Feminist Film Criticism*, edited by Diane Carson, et al. Minneapolis: University of Minnesota Press, 1994: 243–53.

———. *Romance and the "Yellow Peril": Race, Sex, and Discursive Strategies in Hollywood Fiction*. Berkeley: University of California Press, 1994.

———. "The Threat of Captivity: Hollywood and the Sexualization of Race Relations in *The Girls of White Orchid* and *The Bitter Tea of General Yen*." *Journal of Communication Inquiry*. 11.1 (winter 1987): 29–42.

———. "White Knights in Hong Kong: Race, Gender, and the Exotic in *Love Is a Many-Splendored Thing* and *The World of Suzy Wong*." *Post Script*. 10.2 (winter 1991): 36–49.

Miller, James A. "The Case of Early Black Cinema." *Critical Studies in Mass Communication*. 10.2 (June 1993).

Miller, Randall M. "The Entertaining Anachronism: Indians In American Film." In *The Kaleidoscopic Lens: How Hollywood Views Ethnic Groups*, edited by Randall M. Miller. Englewood, NJ: Jerome S. Ozer, 1980.

Neale, Steve. "Vanishing Americans: Racial and Ethnic Issues in the Interpretation and Context of Post-War 'Pro-Indian' Westerns." In *Back in the Saddle Again: New Essays on the Western*, edited by Edward Buscombe and Roberta Pearson. London: British Film Institute, 1998.

Nolley, Ken. "John Ford and the Hollywood Indian." *Film & History*. 23.1–4 (1993): 44–56.

Noriega, Chon. "Citizen Chicano: The Trials and Titillations of Ethnicity in the American Cinema, 1935–1962." *Social Research*. 58.2 (summer 1991): 413–38.

Noriega, Chon. "Internal Others: Hollywood Narratives about Mexican-Americans." In *Mediating Two Worlds*, edited by John King et al. London: British Film Institute Publishing, 1993.

Olsen, Vickie. "The Subordination of Gender to Race Issues in the Film Musical *South Pacific*." In *Gender, I-Deology: Essays of Theory, Fiction and Film*, edited by Chantal Cornut-Gentille D'Arcy, et al. Amsterdam, Netherlands: Rodopi, 1996, 345–57.

Omi, Michael. "In Living Color: Race and American Culture." In *Cultural Politics in Contemporary America*, edited by Ian H. Angus, et. al. New York: Routledge, 1989, 111–22.

O'Neil, Brian. "Yankee Invasion of Mexico, or Mexican Invasion of Hollywood? Hollywood's Renewed Spanish-Language Production of 1938–1939." *Studies in Latin American Popular Culture*. 17 (1998).

Owens, Louis. *Mixblood Messages: Literature, Film, Family, Place*. Norman: University of Oklahoma Press, 1998.

Parish, James Robert. *Black Action Films: Plots, Critiques, Casts, and Credits for 235 Theatrical and Made-for-Television Releases.* Jefferson, NC: McFarland, 1989.

Pines, Jim. *Blacks in Film.* London: Studio Vista, 1975.

Pyron, Darden Asbury, ed. *Recasting: Gone with the Wind in American Culture: The Loss of American Innocence.* Miami: University Press of Florida, 1983.

Quart, Leonard. "The Triumph of Assimilation: Ethnicity, Race, and the Jewish Moguls." *Cineaste.* 18.4 (1991): 8–11.

Reckley, Ralph, ed. *Images of the Black Male in Literature and Film: Essays in Criticism.* Baltimore: Middle Atlantic Writers Association Press, 1994.

Reid, Mark. *Redefining Black Film.* Berkeley: University of California Press, 1993.

Renov, Michael. "Warring Images: Stereotype and American Representations of the Japanese, 1941–1991." In *The Japan/America Film Wars: World War II Propaganda and Its Cultural Contexts,* edited by Abe Mark Nornes and Fukushima Yukio. Langhorne, PA: Harwood Academic Publishers, 1994.

Reyes, Luis and Peter Rubie. *Hispanics in Hollywood: An Encyclopedia of Film and Television.* New York: Garland, 1994.

Rhines, Jesse Algeron. "Making America Home: Racial Masquerade and Ethnic Assimilation in the Transition to Talking Pictures." *Journal of American History.* 79 (December 1992): 1050–77.

———. "Race in Contemporary American Cinema: Part IV-The Political Economy of Black Film." *Cineaste.* 21.3 (1995): 38–39.

Richard, Alfred Charles Jr. *Censorship and Hollywood Hispanic Images: An Interpretive Filmography, 1936–1955.* New York: Greenwood, 1993.

———. *Contemporary Hollywood's Negative Hispanic Image: An Interpretive Filmography, 1956–1993.* Westport, CT: Greenwood, 1994.

———. *The Hispanic on the Silver Screen: An Interpretive Filmography From the Silents into Sound, 1898–1935.* New York: Greenwood, 1992.

Rios-Bustamante, Antonio. "Latino Participation in the Hollywood Film Industry, 1911–1945." In *Chicanos and Film: Representation and Resistance,* edited by Chon A. Noriega. Minneapolis: University of Minnesota Press, 1992.

Roberts, Diane. *The Myth of Aunt Jemima: Representations of Race and Region.* New York: Routledge, 1994.

Roberts, Shari. "The Lady in the Tutti-Frutti Hat: Carmen Miranda, a Spectacle of Ethnicity." *Cinema Journal.* 32.3 (spring 1993): 3–23.

Robertson, Pamela. "Mae West's Maids: Race, 'Authenticity,' and the Discourse of Camp." In *Camp: Queer Aesthetics and the Performing Subject: A Reader,* edited by Fabio Cleto. Ann Arbor: University of Michigan Press, 1999.

Rogin, Michael. "Blackface, White Noise: The Jewish Jazz Singer Finds His Voice." *Critical Inquiry.* 18 (spring 1992): 417–453.

———. "'Democracy and Burnt Cork': The End of Blackface, the Beginning of Civil Rights." In *Refiguring American Film Genres: History and Theory*, edited by Nick Browne. Berkeley: University of California Press, 1998, 171–207.

———. "Making America Home: Racial Masquerade and Ethnic Assimilation in the Transition to Talking Pictures." *Journal of American History*. 79 (December 1992): 1050–77.

Rollins, Peter C. and John O'Connor, eds. *Hollywood's Indian: The Portrayal of the Native American in Film*. Lexington: University Press of Kentucky, 1998.

Rony, Fatimah Tobing. *The Third Eye: Race, Cinema and Ethnographic Spectacle*. Durham, NC: Duke University Press, 1996.

Sears, Cornelia. "Africa in the American Mind, 1870–1955: A Study in Mythology, Ideology, and the Reconstruction of Race." *Dissertation Abstracts*. 59.3 (1998).

Sharp, Saundra, ed. *Black History Film List: 150 Films and Where to Find Them*. Los Angeles: Poets Pay Rent, Too, 1989.

Slotkin, Richard. *Gunfighter Nation: The Myth of the Frontier in Twentieth-Century America*. New York: HarperPerennial, 1993.

Smith, Valerie. "Reading the Intersection of Race and Gender in Narrative of Passing." *Diacritics*. 24.2–3 (summer-fall 1994): 143–57.

Snead, James. *White Screens/Black Images: Hollywood from the Dark Side*, edited by Colin MacCabe and Cornel West. New York: Routledge, 1994.

Stables, Kate. "'Dark Continent' of Film Noir: Race, Displacement and Metaphor in Tourneur's *Cat People* (1942) and Welles' *The Lady from Shanghai* (1948)." In *Women in Film Noir*, edited by E. Ann Kaplan. London: British Film Institute, 1998.

Stam, Robert. "Orson Welles, Brazil, and the Power of Blackness." *Persistence of Vision*. 7 (1989): 93–112.

Stanfield, Peter. "'An Octoroon the Kindling': American Vernacular and Blackface Minstrelsy in 1930s Hollywood." *Journal of American Studies*. 31.3 (1997): 407–38.

———. "From the Vulgar to the Refined: American Vernacular and Blackface Minstrelsy in *Showboat* (1936)." In *Musicals: Hollywood and Beyond*, edited by Bill Marshall and Robynn Stillwell. Exeter: Intellect Press, 1999.

Stokes, Melvyn. "Crises in History and the Response to Them as Illustrated in *The Birth of a Nation* and *Gone with the Wind*." *La Licorne*. 36 (1996).

Taylor, Clyde R. *The Mask of Art: Breaking the Aesthetic Contract—Film and Literature*. Bloomington: Indiana University Press, 1998.

Thurber, Cheryl. "The Development of the Mammy Image and Mythology." In *Southern Women: Histories and Identities*, edited by Virginia Bernhard. Columbia: University of Missouri Press, 1992.

Tyler, Bruce. *From Harlem to Hollywood: The Struggle for Racial and Cultural Democracy 1920–1943*. New York: Garland, 1992.

Vargas, Jocelyn A. Geliga. "Who Is the Puerto Rican Woman and How Is She?: Shall Hollywood Respond?" In *Mediated Women: Representations in Popular Culture*, edited by Marian Meyers. Creskill, NJ: Hampton Press, 1999.

Walker, Jeffrey. "Deconstructing an American Myth: Hollywood and *The Last of the Mohicans*." *Film & History*. 23.1–4 (1993).

Wallace, Michelle. "Race, Gender, and Psychoanalysis in Forties Film: *Lost Boundaries, Home of the Brave*, and *The Quiet One*. In *Black American Cinema*, edited by Manthia Diawara. London: Routledge, 1993: 257–71.

White, Armond. "Stepping Forward Looking Back." *Film Comment*. 36.2 (March/April 2000): 32–39.

Willis, Sharon. *High Contrast: Race and Gender in Contemporary Hollywood Film*. Durham, NC: Duke University Press, 1997.

Winokur, Mark. *American Laughter: Immigrants, Ethnicity, and 1930s Hollywood Film Comedy*, vol. 1. Secaucus, NJ: Citadel, 1995.

Winter, Thomas. "The Training of Colored Troops: A Cinematic Effort to Promote National Cohesion." In *Hollywood's World War I: Motion Picture Images*, edited by Peter C. Rollins. Bowling Green, OH: Bowling Green State University Press, 1997.

Woll, Allen L. and Randall M. Miller. *Ethnic and Racial Images in American Film and Television*. New York: Garland, 1987.

Wong, Eugene Franklin. *On Visual Media Racism: Asians in the American Motion Pictures*. New York: Arno, 1978.

Wood, Gerald. "From The Clansman and *Birth of a Nation* to *Gone with the Wind*: The Loss of American Innocence." In *Recasting: "Gone with the Wind" in American Culture: The Loss of American Innocence*, edited by Darden Asbury Pyron. Miami: University Press of Florida, 1983.

Young, Lola. *Fear of the Dark: Race, Gender and Sexuality in the Cinema*. New York: Routledge, 1996.

CONTRIBUTORS

ERIC AVILA teaches at the Cesar Chavez Center for Interdisciplinary Instruction, Chicana and Chicano Studies, at the University of California, Los Angeles. His project "Reinventing Los Angeles: Popular Culture in the Age of White Flight, 1940–1965" is a regional study of popular culture and its significance within the racial/ethnic geography of postwar Los Angeles.

AARON BAKER is assistant professor of humanities at Arizona State University. He has published articles on Italian/American culture and sports films, and he coedited *Out of Bounds: Sports, Media, and the Politics of Identity*.

DANIEL BERNARDI is assistant professor of media arts at the University of Arizona, where he teaches courses on popular culture, new media, and science fiction. He is editor of *The Birth of Whiteness: Race and the Emergence of U.S. Cinema* and author of *Star Trek and History: Race-ing Toward a White Future*. He has also published in *Film and History, Science Fiction Studies,* and *Stanford Humanities Review*.

KARLA RAE FULLER received her M.F.A. in film from Columbia University and her Ph.D. in film studies from Northwestern University. Her dissertation discusses the construction of Asian roles through performance by Caucasian actors during the Hollywood studio era. She has published articles in *Jump Cut* and *Spectator* and is currently teaching in the Department of Film and Video at Columbia College, Chicago.

ANDREW GORDON is associate professor of English and director of the Institute for the Psychological Study of the Arts at the University of Florida, where he teaches contemporary American literature and film. He is author of *An American Dreamer: A Psychoanalytic Study of the Fiction of Norman Mailer,* and he has also written more than forty essays in journals such as *Modern Fiction Studies, Science Fiction Studies, Literature and Psychology,* and *The Psychoanalytic Review.* He has collaborated with Hernan Vera on a series of articles on "the sincere fictions of the white self," the most recent being an article in the French journal *Gradiva* on three film versions of *Mutiny on the Bounty.*

ALLISON GRAHAM is professor of communication and media studies at the University of Memphis. She is the author of numerous works on European film and American popular culture, including *Framing the South: Hollywood, Television, and Race during the Civil Rights Struggle.* She coproduced and codirected *At the River I Stand,* a documentary film on the 1968 Memphis Sanitation Workers Strike and the assassination of Martin Luther King Jr., which was nominated for an Emmy and received the Erik Barnouw Award from the Organization of American Historians.

JOANNE HERSHFIELD teaches media studies and video production in the Department of Communication Studies at the University of North Carolina–Chapel Hill. She is author of *The Invention of Dolores del Río* (Minnesota, 2000) and *Mexican Cinema, Mexican Woman, 1940–1950* and coeditor of *Mexico's Cinema: A Century of Film and Filmmakers;* she has also published in *Cinema Journal, Wide Angle,* and *Canadian Journal of Film Studies.* She produces documentaries and is currently working on a video about Hispanics in the American South.

CINDY HING-YUK WONG is assistant professor of communications at the College of Staten Island, City University of New York. Her research focuses on grassroots and community media and on visual film festivals as urban and cinematic events. She is the producer and director of the video *Leaving Home: Two Chinese Vietnamese Buddhist Lives.*

ARTHUR KNIGHT teaches American studies and English at the College of William and Mary. He is the author of *Dis-Integrating the Musical: African American Musical Performance and American Musical Film, 1927–1959.*

SARAH MADSEN HARDY is a Ph.D. candidate in English at the University of Michigan. Her dissertation, "Moving Americans: Silent Cinema and National Subjectivity," explores film's power to inscribe national history visually and viscerally.

GINA MARCHETTI is associate professor at the University of Maryland, College Park. Among her publications are *Romance and the "Yellow Peril": Race, Sex, and Discursive Strategies in Hollywood Fiction.* She is currently a visiting senior fellow at the School of Communication Studies, Nanyang Technological University, Singapore.

GARY W. McDONOGH is professor and director of the Growth and Structure of Cities Program at Bryn Mawr College. He is author of *Good Families of Barcelona: A Social History of Power in the Industrial Era* and *Black and Catholic in Savannah, Georgia*; he is coeditor of *The Cultural Meanings of Urban Space*.

CHANDRA MUKERJI is professor of communication and sociology at the University of California, San Diego. Her previous works include *Territorial Ambitions and the Gardens of Versailles*; *The Gardens of Le Notre* (with Becky Cohen); *Rethinking Popular Culture* (coedited with Michael Schudson); *A Fragile Power*; and *From Graven Images: Patterns of Modern Materialism*. She is also author of "Monsters, Muppets, and Methods," a chapter in *Cultural Studies and the Sociology of Culture*.

MARTIN F. NORDEN teaches film as a professor of communication at the University of Massachusetts–Amherst. His work has appeared in such journals as *Wide Angle*, *Film Criticism*, *Journal of Popular Film and Television*, and *Paradoxa*, as well as in many anthologies. His book *The Cinema of Isolation: A History of Physical Disability in the Movies* has been translated into Spanish. He maintains a home page at http://www-unix.oit.umass.edu/~norden.

BRIAN O'NEIL is assistant professor of history at the University of Southern Mississippi, specializing in U.S.–Latin American relations, cultural studies, and film history. His other publications include "Yankee Invasion of Mexico, or Mexican Invasion of Hollywood? Hollywood's Renewed Spanish-Language Production of 1938–1939," *Studies in Latin American Popular Culture* 17 (spring 1998) and "So Far from God, So Close to Hollywood: Dolores Del Río and Lupe Vélez in Hollywood, 1925–1944," in *Strange Pilgrimages: Travel, Exile, and Foreign Residency in the Creation of Identity in Latin America, 1800–1990* (edited by Karen Racine and Ingrid Fey).

ROBERTA E. PEARSON is senior lecturer in the School of Journalism, Media, and Cultural Studies at Cardiff University. She is author of *Eloquent Gestures: The Transformation of Performance Style in the Griffith Biograph Films*; coauthor of *Reframing Culture: The Case of the Vitagraph Quality Films*; and coeditor of *Back in the Saddle Again: New Writings on the Western*. She is also coeditor of *Critical Dictionary of Film and Television Theory* and *American Cultural Studies: A Reader*.

MARGUERITE H. RIPPY is assistant professor at Marymount University in Arlington, Virginia. She is a Ph.D. candidate at Indiana University, where she is completing her dissertation, "Visual Differences: Miscegenation and Desire in

Twentieth-Century American Film and Drama." She has published articles on the representation of women in film and drama, addressing topics ranging from the performance of sexuality and race in Hollywood cinema to representations of women in Shakespeare's drama. She has also designed educational leadership programs and remains interested in the intersection between national politics and education.

NICHOLAS SAMMOND received his Ph.D. from the Communication Department at the University of California, San Diego. He is currently revising his dissertation, "The Uses of Childhood: The Making of Walt Disney and the Generic American Child, 1930–1960," for publication.

BERETTA E. SMITH-SHOMADE is assistant professor at the University of Arizona. Her research and teaching focus on the intersections of film and television representation with people of color, gender, and identity. She is completing a book that situates African-American women's image, history, and cultural legacy within various television genres.

PETER STANFIELD is senior lecturer in the media arts faculty of Southampton Institute. He is author of *Dixie Cowboys: 1930s Series Westerns*; *A Genealogy of Cowboy Minstrels or, The Strange History of the Singing Cowboy*; and *West of the Divide: Hollywood and the 1930s Western*. His latest project is titled " 'An Octoroon in the Kindling': Hollywood and the Making of an American Vernacular."

KELLY THOMAS is a doctoral candidate of English language and literature at the University of Michigan. She is completing a dissertation on white trash in twentieth-century American culture.

HERNAN VERA is professor of sociology at the University of Florida and coauthor (with Joe Feagin) of *White Racism* and (with Joe Feagin and Nikitah Amani) of *The Agony of Education: Black Students in White Universities*. He specializes in the sociology of race relations and has published more than sixty articles in sociological journals. With Andrew Gordon, he has collaborated on a series of articles concerning "the sincere fictions of the white self," about white self-representations in Hollywood cinema over the decades.

KAREN WALLACE received an M.A. in American Indian studies and a Ph.D. in English from the University of California, Los Angeles. She is currently assistant professor of English at the University of Wisconsin, Oshkosh.

THOMAS E. WARTENBERG is professor of philosophy at Mount Holyoke College, where he also teaches in the film studies program. He is author of *Unlikely Couples: Movie Romance as Social Criticism* and *The Forms of Power: From Domination to Transformation,* and he is editor of *Rethinking Power* and coeditor of

Philosophy and Film. He is series editor of Thinking through Cinema, a book series published by Westview Press. In addition to his work on film, he has published widely in various areas of philosophy.

GEOFFREY M. WHITE is senior fellow at the East–West Center in Honolulu and a member of the graduate faculty in the Department of Anthropology, University of Hawaii. He has published on a wide range of topics in anthropology, psychology, and cultural studies. His current work focuses on war memory and historical representation, with particular interest in World War II in the Pacific.

JANE YI is a doctoral candidate of American studies, University of Hawaii, and a degree fellow at the East–West Center in Honolulu. Her research interests focus on the cultural politics of immigration and representations of Asian American identities in literature and film.

INDEX